I0885039

International Criminal Law Series

Founding Editor
M. Cherif Bassiouni †

Editor-in-Chief
William Schabas, Professor of International Law, Department of Law, Middlesex University; Professor of International Criminal Law and Human Rights, Leiden University; Honorary Chairman, Irish Centre for Human Rights, National University of Ireland, Galway; Canada/Ireland

Editorial Board

Kai Ambos, Judge at the Kosovo Specialist Chambers (KSC), The Hague; Professor of Law and Head, Department for Foreign and International Criminal Law, Georg August Universität; Gottingen, Germany

Mahnoush Arsanjani, Member, Institut de Droit International; former Director, Codification Division, United Nations Office of Legal Affairs, Iran

Mohamed Chande Othman, Chief Justice, Court of Appeal of Tanzania; Dodoma, Tanzania

Adama Dieng, Former Special Adviser on the Prevention of Genocide; former Registrar, International Criminal Tribunal for Rwanda; former Secretary General, International Commission of Jurists, Senegal

Mark Drumbl, Class of 1975 Alumni Professor of Law, Director, Transnational Law Institute, Washington and Lee University School of Law, USA

Chile Eboe-Osuji, former President, International Criminal Court and Distinguished International Jurist & Special Advisor to the President, Lincoln Alexander School of Law, Toronto Metropolitan University, Canada

Geoff Gilbert, Professor of Law and Head of the School of Law, University of Essex, Colchester UK

Philippe Kirsch, *Ad hoc* Judge, International Court of Justice; former President, International Criminal Court; Ambassador (Ret.) and former Legal Advisor, Ministry of Foreign Affairs of Canada; Sallēles d'Aude, Belgium/ Canada

André Klip, Professor of Law, Department of Criminal Law and Criminology, Faculty of Law, Maastricht University; Maastricht, The Netherlands

Errki Kourula, Former Judge and President of the Appeals Division, International Criminal Court; The Hague, Finland

Motoo Noguchi, Former Chair of the Board of Directors, ICC Trust Fund for Victims and former UN International Judge at the Khmer Rouge Trials in Cambodia; Attorney at Law at Iwatagodo in Tokyo, Japan

Diane Orentlicher, Professor of International Law, Co-Director, Center for Human Rights and Humanitarian Law, Washington College of Law, American University; Washington, USA

Fausto Pocar, Judge and former President, International Criminal Tribunal for the Former Yugoslavia; President, International Institute of Humanitarian Law; Professor of International Law Emeritus, University of Milan; Italy

Leila Nadya Sadat, Henry H. Oberschelp Professor of Law, Director, Whitney R. Harris World Law Institute, Washington University School of Law; Alexis de Tocqueville Distinguished Fulbright Chair, University of Cergy-Pontoise; St. Louis, France/ USA

Michael Scharf, Dean and John Deaver Drinko-Baker & Hostetlier Professor of Law, Director, Frederick K. Cox International Law Center, Case Western Reserve University School of Law; Cleveland, USA

Ulrich Sieber, Director emeritus at t Max Planck Institute for the Stu of Crime, Security and Law in Freiburg, Germany and honora professor and faculty member a the law faculties of the Univers of Freiburg and the University Munich, Germany

Goran Sluiter, Professor of Law, Department of Criminal Law a Criminal Procedure, Faculty of Law, University of Amsterdam; Amsterdam, The Netherlands

Françoise Tulkens, Former Vice-President, European Court of Human Rights; Strasbourg, Fra

Xuimei Wang, Professor of International Criminal Law, College for Criminal Law Scien Beijing Normal University; Executive Director, ICC Project Office; Beijing, China

Christine van den Wyngaert, Judge Kosovo Specialist Chambers; former Judge, International Criminal Court; former Judge, International Criminal Tribuna for the Former Yugoslavia; form Ad hoc Judge, International Co of Justice, Belgium

Gert Vermeulen, Professor of Crimi Law, Director, Research Group Drug Policy, Criminal Policy ar International Crime, Ghent University; Extraordinary Professor of Evidence Law, Maastricht University; Ghent, Belgium

Giuliana Ziccardi Capaldo, Profess of International Law, Faculty o Law, University of Salerno; Salerno, Italy

VOLUME 21

The titles published in this series are listed at *brill.com/icls*

Governing the International Criminal Court

Governing the International Criminal Court

The History and Practice of the Assembly of States Parties to the Rome Statute

By

Ezequiel Jiménez Martinez

BRILL | NIJHOFF

LEIDEN | BOSTON

The Library of Congress Cataloging-in-Publication Data is available online at https://catalog.loc.gov

Typeface for the Latin, Greek, and Cyrillic scripts: "Brill". See and download: brill.com/brill-typeface.

ISSN 2213-2724
ISBN 978-90-04-74996-2 (hardback)
ISBN 978-90-04-74997-9 (e-book)
DOI 10.1163/9789004749979

Copyright 2026 by Ezequiel Jiménez Martinez. Published by Koninklijke Brill BV, Plantijnstraat 2, 2321 JC Leiden, The Netherlands.
Koninklijke Brill BV incorporates the imprints Brill, Brill Nijhoff, Brill Schöningh, Brill Fink, Brill mentis, Brill Wageningen Academic, Vandenhoeck & Ruprecht, Böhlau and V&R unipress.
Koninklijke Brill BV reserves the right to protect this publication against unauthorized use. Requests for re-use and/or translations must be addressed to Koninklijke Brill BV via brill.com or copyright.com.
For more information: info@brill.com.

This book is printed on acid-free paper and produced in a sustainable manner.

For Lorenzo

Contents

Acknowledgements

This book is the result of countless moments of support and encouragement from a multitude of people in the United Kingdom, Argentina, Poland, Spain and the Netherlands. I am both relieved and thankful they will see their rally in the many words ahead. While the topic might seem a bit obscure or rather too specific, I am hopeful it managed to combine a sense of practicality with the idealism that put me in front of this challenge. One can become too distracted or disappointed by the grave injustices we witness today to remember change can happen if institutions set up to make the international justice machinery work, actually work. Thankful for the great opportunity of time, support and encouragement, I hope this study of the Assembly of States Parties to the Rome Statute can help motivate action when justice has become, at times, elusive.

I owe a debt of gratitude to Professor William Schabas for his advice, supervision and relentless encouragement to think of this book as a vehicle to contribute not in isolation, but as a scholar. More so for his guidance at each Ph. D. seminar at Middlesex University, webinars and for the time spent at the Second Doctoral Seminar at the Siracusa International Institute in 2023. I am also grateful for Dr. Giulia Pecorella's advice early on this process on how to structure my thinking and, extremely importantly, improve my writing. I am equally thankful to my former colleagues at the Middlesex School of Law and to Professor Alice Donald for her valuable support. To the librarians at the Sheppard Library, in particular Sue Joyce, my admiration and appreciation for their much-needed assistance.

To my parents, Virginia and Ricardo, from whom I have learned to care deeply about justice and the power of education. To my siblings and extended family for their constant care and for putting up with me as I explained iterations of this book. And crucially to Kasia, not only my editor-in-chief but the source of resilience, patience and love that made this possible. Finally this book is dedicated to Lorenzo, whom I hope will find this book an attempt to promote justice and peace in a tumultuous world.

Barcelona
June 2025

CHAPTER 1

Introduction

1 A Statute, a Court and an Assembly of States Parties

The Statute of the International Criminal Court was agreed in Rome by States in 1998. While the treaty entered into force on 1 July 2002, the Court only became fully operational at the end of the second resumption of the first session of the Assembly of States Parties on 12 April 2003. Indeed, only after 87 States Parties, gathered in New York, elected the first Prosecutor,[1] the Court was fully functional with, among other critical building blocks, 18 judges, an interim Registrar, a budget and guidelines to begin recruiting staff across all organs. While the literature covering the emergence and development of the Court understandably prioritized its judicial mandate in the Rome Statute, this book argues that without fully appraising the Assembly of States Parties, such analysis is limited. This is so because Article 112, in Part 11 of the Rome Statute, created a governance body assigning to the States Parties a number of critical functions impacting the life of the Court.[2] For example, as this book covers, the Assembly of States Parties retained the overall governance and management responsibility over the Court, elected and decided on the removal of the judges and the Prosecutor, set the annual budget, legislated changes to the Rules of Procedure and Evidence, dealt with non-cooperation and remained the sole authority to amend the Statute. These critical functions help the argument that without studying the history and practice of the Assembly of States Parties, a full understanding of how the International Criminal Court performed on its mandate during its first twenty years, between 2002 and 2021, might be incomplete.

By virtue of Article 112, the Assembly is made up of representatives of States Parties, each having one vote. Non-party States that signed the Final Act of the Rome Conference or the Statute may participate as observers. The Assembly must meet at least once a year. States Parties aim to make decisions by consensus across important statutory responsibilities such as elections, financial oversight, disciplinary measures and removal of elected officials, oversight of

1 Report of the First Session (First and Second Resumptions) of the Assembly of States Parties to the Rome Statute of the International Criminal Court, New York, 3–7 February and 21–23 April 2003, ICC-ASP/1/3/Add.1 (2003) 1.

2 Article 112, Rome Statute of the International Criminal Court (2002) 2187 UNTS 90.

© EZEQUIEL JIMÉNEZ MARTINEZ, 2026 | DOI:10.1163/9789004749979_002

auxiliary judicial instruments, enforcement of cooperation and the review and amendments of the Rome Statute. In sum, the Assembly is the 'management oversight and legislative body of the International Criminal Court'.[3] To aid the work of the Assembly, an elected Bureau composed of one President, two Vice-Presidents and 18 members at large, is mandated with a three year term to 'assist the Assembly in the discharge of its responsibilities'.[4] The Bureau provides ongoing and uninterrupted governance oversight to the Court. It does so assisted by a member-led Working Group in New York and another one in The Hague. These flexible groupings enable the Bureau to carry out its responsibilities in between regular annual sessions. In addition, the Rome Statute afforded the Assembly the power to create subsidiary bodies in its quest to govern the Court. As Figure 1 illustrates,[5] subsidiary bodies, such as the Committee on Budget and Finance, play a significant role in motivating policy and practical changes in the Court. The Assembly is supported by a permanent Secretariat. In essence, the Assembly is the statutory vehicle by which the drafters in Rome, and in particular States Parties, 'pursue certain goals in the particular field in which the organization is competent'.[6]

There were 123 States Parties by the end of the twentieth session of the Assembly in 2021. The Africa regional group was the largest represented with 33 States followed by 28 Latin American and Caribbean States, 25 Western European and Other States, 19 from the Asia-Pacific Group and 18 Eastern European States.[7] States Parties, as the masters of the Rome Statute, had a duty to govern the Court as they were also bound to respect its independence. This palpable tension was obvious when, for example, examining the financial oversight policy or amendments to the Rules of Procedure and Evidence that States Parties pursued in the first 20 years of the Assembly. Yet, such unease is exactly what is worth analysing as it offers a true picture of the Rome Statute system, meaning, a set of interrelated actors and policy aims directed at fighting impunity that go beyond judicial functions described in the Statute. Indeed, the Chambers, the Office of the Prosecutor, the Registry, the Assembly

3 Assembly of States Parties to the Rome Statute, About, available at: <https://asp.icc-cpi.int/assembly> accessed 4 January (2024).

4 Article 112(3)(c), Rome Statute of the International Criminal Court (2002) 2187 UNTS 90.

5 Assembly of States Parties to the Rome Statute, ASP Organigramme, available at: <https://asp.icc-cpi.int/assembly/asp_organigramme> accessed 18 December 2021.

6 Blokker, Niels, 'Constituent Instruments – Creating a Genie that May Escape From the Bottle?' in Cogan, Jacob Katz, Hurd, Ian and Johnstone, Ian (eds), The Oxford Handbook of International Organizations (Oxford University Press 2016) 950.

7 Assembly of States Parties to the Rome Statute, States Parties, available at: <https://asp.icc-cpi.int/states-parties> accessed 19 December (2021).

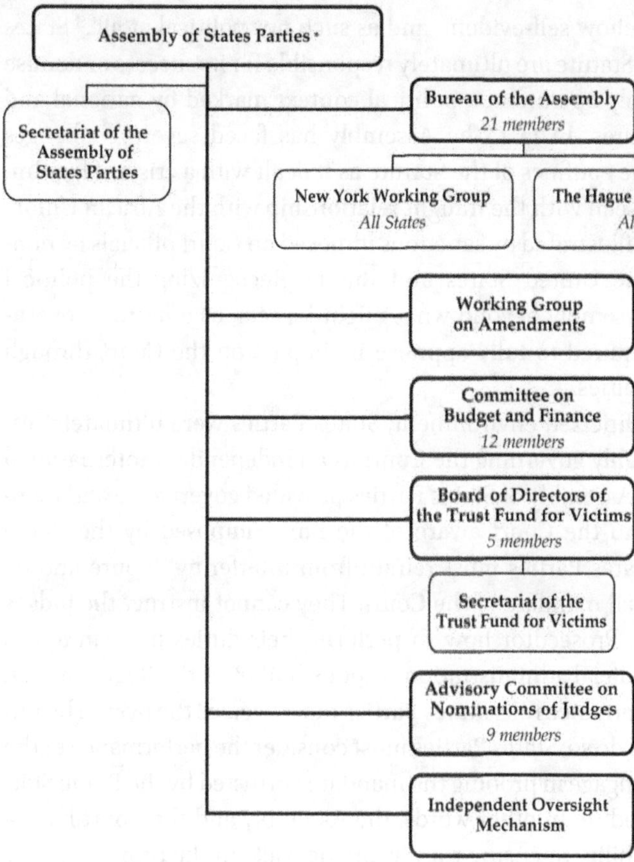

FIGURE 1.1 Assembly of States Parties to the Rome statute organigram (2021)

of States Parties and subsidiary bodies like the Trust Fund for Victims or the Independent Oversight Mechanism, and even the role of the United Nations Security Council and civil society, are part of this system. As such, the need for a governing body intrinsically responsible for the coordination of such an environment became paramount.

This is why the 2020 Independent Expert Review of the Court concluded, 'as an international organisation, States Parties reasonably expect to be able to guide and shape the institution'.[8] This is also the reason why the choices pursued by the Assembly of States Parties to shape the Court must not be simply

8 Report of the Independent Expert Review of the International Criminal Court and the Rome Statute System, ICC-ASP/19/16 (2020) 11.

understood as 'somehow self-evident, and as such not political at all'.[9] States Parties to the Rome Statute are ultimately responsible for its success or demise at the same time they operate in a political context marked by national and international pressures. In fact, the Assembly has faced severe challenges to operate within the confines of the Statute as it dealt with a crisis of legitimacy from within, as seen with the fraught relationship with the African Union, and from outside as illustrated by sanctions imposed on Court officials by non-party States like the United States and Russia. Recognizing the political dimension of the Assembly beyond what might be seen as a narrow governance function is required to fully appraise its impact on the Court through statutory responsibilities.

Yet, even in a politicized environment, States Parties were ultimately responsible for thoroughly governing the Court as an independent international organization.[10] The Assembly of States Parties provided governance and management oversight to the Court aware of the limits imposed by the Rome Statute. Notably, States Parties must refrain from interfering de jure and de facto with the judicial mandate of the Court. They cannot instruct the judges or the Office of the Prosecutor how to perform their duties nor can States Parties direct the judicial administration responsibilities of the Registrar. Yet, because of their governance role, States Parties must oversee the overall health of the institution. To do so, States Parties must consider the performance of the Court and actively engage in probing the mandate entrusted by the Rome Statute is closely adhered to. In other words, the Assembly and the Court have a duty and a responsibility to ensure they 'walk the walk on the principles they proclaim'.[11] This relationship of interdependence[12] is akin to national judicial systems whereas the judiciary can be reasonably overseen by political masters. In this context, however, the International Criminal Court has faced criticism for its inability to produce judicial results measured, for example, in the number of convictions. It has also encountered internal challenges about the qual-

9 Koskenniemi, Martti, "A Trap for the Innocent …" in Kreß, Claus and Barriga, Stefan (eds), The Crime of Aggression: A Commentary (Cambridge University Press 2016) 1379.

10 Goldstone, Richard J, 'The International Criminal Court: Origins, Challenges and Desirable Reforms to Strengthen It' in Falk, Richard and Lopez-Claros, Augusto (eds), Global Governance and International Cooperation (Routledge 2024) 378.

11 Vasiliev, Sergey, 'The Crises and Critiques of International Criminal Justice' in Heller, Kevin Jon and others (eds), The Oxford Handbook of International Criminal Law (2nd edn, Oxford University Press 2020) 650.

12 Peake, Jessica, 'Interdependence at the International Criminal Court: Reconceptualizing our Understanding of the Court and its Failures' (2022) 26 (2) UCLA Journal of International Law and Foreign Affairs 99.

ity of certain judicial decisions, lack of collegiality among judges, allegations of misconduct by members of the Prosecution and Registry, and documented bullying and harassment of staff.[13] The United Kingdom delegate to the seventeenth session of the Assembly in 2018 described the sentiment of unmet expectations set in Rome recalling that 'after 20 years, and 1.5 billion Euros spent we have only three core crime convictions'.[14] More so, Evenson,[15] Wilmshurst,[16] Trahan,[17] Vasiliev,[18] Clements[19] and Smith[20] have pointed out at failures of management, prosecutorial discretion, trial strategies, outreach, participation of victims and ways of working by judges, all affecting the performance of the Court, which is under the purview of States Parties.

Given this circumstance, in 2019, four former Presidents of the Assembly of States Parties – Prince Zeid Raíad Zeid Al-Hussein (Jordan), Bruno Stagno Ugarte (Costa Rica), Christian Wenaweser (Liechtenstein) and Tiina Intelmann (Estonia) – wrote that they were 'disappointed by the quality of some of its judicial proceedings, frustrated by some of the results, and exasperated by the management deficiencies that prevent the Court from living up to its full potential'.[21] Such criticism can only be fairly addressed by examining the strengths and weaknesses of the institution as a whole rather than a myopic

13 Report of the Independent Expert Review of the International Criminal Court and the Rome Statute System, ICC-ASP/19/16 47.

14 Statement by Andrew Murdoch, Legal Director to the International Criminal Court Assembly of States Parties, at its 17th session in The Hague, available at: <https://www.gov.uk/government/speeches/uk-statement-to-icc-assembly-of-states-parties-17th-session> (2018).

15 Evenson, Elizabeth, 'Too Few Trials, Too Many Tribulations: The ICC's Terrible Year and Where to Go from Here' (2020) 52 (1) Case Western Reserve Journal of International Law 442.

16 Wilmshurst, Elizabeth 'Strengthen the International Criminal Court' (Royal Institute of International Affairs, 2019) <https://www.chathamhouse.org/expert/comment/strengthen-international-criminal-court> accessed 12 June 2019.

17 Trahan, Jennifer, 'The Assembly of States Parties' in deGuzman, Margaret and Oosterveld, Valerie (eds), The Elgar Companion to the International Criminal Court (Edward Elgar Publishing 2020) 259.

18 Vasiliev, (2020) 632.

19 Clements, Richard, 'ReVisiting the ICC Registry's ReVision Project' (2019) 17 Journal of International Criminal Justice 272.

20 Smith, Stephen Eliot, 'Is the International Criminal Court Dying? An Examination of Symptoms' (2022) 23 Oregon Review of International Law 76.

21 Prince Zeid Raíad Zeid Al-Hussein and others, 'The International Criminal Court Needs Fixing' (Atlantic Council, 2019) <https://www.atlanticcouncil.org/blogs/new-atlanticist/the-international-criminal-court-needs-fixing> accessed 24 April (2019).

focus on the Court alone. Indeed, the 2020 Independent Expert Review identified the tension between the 'ICC and the ASP'[22] across its findings. The experts observed 'mutual distrust and suspicion' while also recognizing 'a highly complex and unusual organism where confidentiality and independence of decision-making are central to the proper functioning of the institution'.[23] Such an 'organism' is the sum of its constituent parts: a State Party–led governance body and an independent Court.[24] It is in this context that this book aims to improve the understanding of how the Assembly of States Parties performed its statutory responsibilities to govern the International Criminal Court in its first twenty sessions between 2002 and 2021.

2 The Assembly of States Parties as an International Judicial Governance Institution: A Map

To understand how the Assembly of States Parties performed its statutory responsibilities to govern the International Criminal Court, it is helpful to place the inquiry within the existing body of research examining the practice of international judicial governance institutions, also known as injugovins.[25] The Assembly of States Parties is the injugovin of the International Criminal Court as the United Nations General Assembly and the Security Council are to the International Court of Justice.[26] Blokker has led the innovative research into these governance institutions showing how their decisions 'are of fundamental importance for the way in which international courts and tribunals can carry out their judicial tasks independently'.[27] Despite the inherent impact injugovins have on their respective judicial institutions, their thorough

22 Report of the Independent Expert Review of the International Criminal Court and the Rome Statute System, ICC-ASP/19/16 11.

23 Ibid 210.

24 Mégret, Frédéric, 'Rethinking the International Criminal Court as the Court of its State Parties' in Palmer, Emma and others (eds), Futures of International Criminal Justice (Routledge 2021) 25.

25 Blokker, Niels, 'The Governance of International Courts and Tribunals' in Follesdal, Andreas and Ulfstein, Geir (eds), The Judicialization of International Law: A Mixed Blessing? (Oxford University Press 2018) 27.

26 Ibid.

27 Ibid. See also: Blokker, Niels, 'Governance of the International Tribunal of the Law of the Sea: The Role of the Meeting of States Parties to the Law of the Sea Convention' in Del Vecchio, Angela and Virzo, Roberto (eds), Interpretations of the United Nations Convention on the Law of the Sea by International Courts and Tribunals (Springer International Publishing 2019) 81.

study remains 'to some extent a terra incognita'.[28] In particular, the Assembly of States Parties has been 'often overlooked',[29] 'hardly known and rarely published on, in academia or by the media',[30] and without ample 'sociological-legal knowledge'[31] about its function. In fact, there is an active call to bring 'more minds to the table to consider governance enhancements'[32] for the Assembly. As the 'external authority',[33] understanding how the Assembly's practice affects the functioning of the Court contributes to the notion of 'guardianship'[34] advanced by Bergsmo and others. Meaning, the 'non-waivable duty of care'[35] States Parties have towards the Court. Indeed, as the injugovin of the Court, the Assembly's governance responsibility is absolute in a context of a relationship 'between the tribunals and their parent bodies'.[36]

In this sense, the Assembly exerts governance and oversight over the Court in a number of areas outlined by the Rome Statute. To aid the exploration of these areas, it is worth recalling Llewellyn's approach to these concepts within his contribution to the injugovin literature. In his study of the United Nations, Llewellyn defined governance as the 'institutional structures and processes through which the oversight functions are carried out, the two-way nature of the relationship between the tribunals and their oversight bodies'.[37] In other words, the Assembly governs the Court as it negotiates, designs and makes decisions across the assigned regulatory framework of the Statute including financial oversight, enforcement of cooperation, election of judges and the Prosecutor and other key tasks assigned to multiple subsidiary bodies. For example the choices made by the Assembly when operationalizing the Independent Oversight Mechanism had a direct impact on its ability to oversee

28 Blokker, 'The Governance of International Courts and Tribunals' (2018) 41.

29 Villacis, Renan, 'Working Methods of the Assembly of States Parties to the Rome Statute' (2018) 18 (3) International Criminal Law Review 564.

30 de Hoon, Marieke and Lohne, Kjersti, ''All the World's a Stage': Constituting International Justice at the ICC's Assembly of States' in Boer, Lianne J.M and Stolk, Sofia (eds), Backstage Practices of Transnational Law (Routledge 2019) 74.

31 Vasiliev, Sergey, 'Judicial Governance Entities as Power-Holders in International Criminal Justice: A Plea for a Socio-Legal Enquiry' in Bergsmo, Morten and others (eds), Power in International Criminal Justice (Torkel Opsahl Academic EPublisher 2020) 482–483.

32 Bergsmo, Morten and others, 'ICC State-Party Governance in Times of Disunity' (2023) Policy Brief Series No. 146 Torkel Opsahl Academic EPublisher 1.

33 Blokker, 'The Governance of International Courts and Tribunals' (2018) 38.

34 Bergsmo and others, 4.

35 Ibid.

36 Llewellyn, Huw, An Institutional Perspective on the United Nations Criminal Tribunals: Governance, Independence and Impartiality (Brill | Nijhoff 2021) 13.

37 Ibid.

and investigate the conduct of elected officials. In the same way, the examination of the annual budget by the Committee on Budget and Finance yielded significant power over the Court's capacity to fulfil its mandate. The same logic applies to States Parties' power to amend the Statute. As Vasiliev argued, the success of international judicial institutions 'to a large extent depend on how well those essential functions are carried out'.[38]

In this context, it is necessary to locate what are the statutory responsibilities of the Assembly of States Parties towards the Court. Part of the answer to this question lies in the history of international judicial governance institutions as well as the travaux préparatoires[39] of the Rome Statute in relation to the Assembly of States Parties. It was not until late in the negotiations in the Preparatory Committee for the Rome Conference that States Parties agreed to create an independent international organization and the Assembly as its injugovin.[40] At the same time, governance provisions for international judicial institutions by States Parties to a multilateral treaty did not originate solely with Article 112 in the Rome Statute. There is a rich history that can be traced to three key moments in 1937, 1943 and 1981 that offer an insight into policy options pursued by States at the Rome Conference in 1998. In both cases, as covered in this book, choices made in the past have influenced how the Assembly has performed its statutory duties between 2002 and 2021.

Acknowledging the history of the Assembly, it is also possible to map across the Rome Statute which functions are assigned to States Parties. For this rea-

38 Vasiliev, 'Judicial Governance Entities as Power-Holders in International Criminal Justice: A Plea for a Socio-Legal Enquiry' (2020) 482–483.

39 Rao, S Rama, 'Financing of the Court, Assembly of States Parties and the Preparatory Commission' in Lee, Roy S. (ed), The International Criminal Court: the Making of the Rome Statute: Issues, Negotiations and Results (Martinus Nijhoff Publishers 1999) 408; Sadat, Leila Nadya, The International Criminal Court and the Transformation of International Law: Justice for the New Millennium (Transnational Publishers 2002) 98; Gradoni, Lorenzo, 'Article 112 Assemblée Des Etats Parties' in Fernandez, Julian and others (eds), Statut de Rome de la Cour Pénale Internationale: Commentaire Article par article (Pedone 2012) 2007; Rao, S Rama and Ambach, Philipp, 'Article 112 Assembly of States Parties' in Ambos, Kai and Triffterer, Otto (eds), The Rome Statute of the International Criminal Court: A Commentary (3 edn, Beck/Hart 2016) 2217; Schabas, William A, The International Criminal Court: A Commentary on the Rome Statute (2nd edn, Oxford University Press 2017) 1434; Klamberg, Mark, 'Article 112 – Assembly of States Parties' in Klamberg, Mark (ed), Commentary on the Law of the International Criminal Court (Torkel Opsahl Academic EPublisher 2017) 726.

40 Bos, Adriaan, 'Assembly of States Parties' in Cassese, Antonio and others (eds), The Rome Statute of the International Criminal Court: A commentary (Oxford University Press 2002) 302.

son, the book pays special attention to the historical development of the Assembly. By doing so, it becomes clear that Article 112 only describes partially the full suite of responsibilities assigned to the Assembly. In fact, as covered in this book, the Assembly is called to take specific actions across governance and management, elections, financial oversight, supervision of auxiliary judicial instruments, enforcement of cooperation and the review and amendments of the Rome Statute. For each of these statutory responsibilities, the Assembly is specifically tasked to perform a critical function for the operations of the Court. To achieve this, in some cases, States Parties have created dedicated subsidiary bodies or other forms of coordination to act upon their mandate. For example to elect the second and third Prosecutor under Article 43(4), the Assembly created a time-bound and bespoke process in 2011 and 2021. Similarly, the Working Group on Amendments was created to filter proposals by States Parties affecting the subject-matter jurisdiction of the Court. Indeed, as the Assembly gained institutional maturity over 20 sessions between 2002 and 2021, their approach to governance and oversight changed and became more sophisticated. Coming back to Llewellyn, the Assembly established several 'structures and processes'[41] to govern the Court. For example, while the Advisory Committee on Nomination of judges and the Independent Oversight Mechanism were the only two subsidiary bodies mentioned in the Rome Statute, the Assembly had created seven with five in operation by the twentieth session.[42] The autopoietic characteristic of the Assembly of States Parties was not only required for the 'adaptability of the Court to forthcoming needs',[43] but to fulfil the several responsibilities assigned by the Rome Statute. In this sense, this book follows a map, as seen in Table 1.1, outlining the functions States Parties were specifically expected to fulfil.

Outside the literature stimulated by Blokker, scholars and practitioners have recognized the role of the Assembly of States Parties, albeit without a unifying characterization criteria and mostly in general terms. For example, Sadat described the Assembly as the 'Court's organe plenier',[44] but solely focused on its general powers. Gallant and Ambos have characterized the

41 Llewellyn, 13.

42 Villacis, 567.

43 Nesi, Giuseppe, 'The Organs of the International Criminal Court and their Functions in the Rome Statute: the Assembly of States Parties' in Lattanzi, Flavia and Schabas, William (eds), Essays on the Rome Statute of the International Criminal Court, vol 1 (Editrice il Sirente 1999) 248.

44 Sadat, 98.

TABLE 1.1 Statutory responsibilities of the Assembly of States Parties

Function	Rome Statute
Governance and Management Oversight	Article 2 Relationship of the Court with the United Nations Article 3(2) Seat of the Court Article 46(2) Removal from Office Article 47 Disciplinary Measures Article 112(1)–(10) Assembly of States Parties Article 119(2) Settlement of Disputes
Election of Judges	Article 36 Qualifications, Nomination and Election of Judges Article 37(1) Judicial Vacancies Article 112(2)(e) Assembly of States Parties
Election of the Prosecutor and Deputy	Article 42 (4) The Office of the Prosecutor
Election of the Registrar	Article 43 (4) The Registry
Financial Oversight	Article 49 Salaries, Allowances and Expenses Article 112(2)(d), (4) and (8) Assembly of States Parties Article 113 Financial Regulations Article 116 Voluntary Contributions
Auxiliary Judicial Instruments Oversight	Article 9(1)–(2) Element of Crimes Article 44(3)–(4) Staff Article 51(1)–(3) Rules of Procedure and Evidence Article 52(3) Regulations of the Court Article 79(1) and (3) Trust Fund for Victims
Enforcement of Cooperation	Article 87(5)(b) and (7) Requests for Cooperation: General Provisions Article 112(2)(f) Assembly of States Parties
Amendments and Review of the Statute	Article 121(1)–(6) Amendments Article 122 Amendments to Provisions of an Institutional Nature 123(1) Review of the Statute

Assembly as a 'political'[45] or 'quasi-political organ'[46] without providing a further qualification of this label beyond the decision-making powers of States Parties. Donat Cattin,[47] Rao,[48] Bos,[49] Barberini,[50] Gradoni,[51] Roberts,[52] de Gabriel,[53] Schabas,[54] Ambach[55] and Klamberg[56] have described in fuller details the responsibilities of the Assembly, though mostly from the perspective of the negotiating history and powers in the Rome Statute. Among these authors, Ambach's contribution is the most expansive, covering selected current developments of the regular sessions of the Assembly of States Parties. O'Donohue,[57] du Plessis and Grevers,[58] Vasiliev[59] and Trahan have also singled out specific

45 Ambos, Kai, Treatise on International Criminal Law 1 (Oxford University Press 2013) 31.

46 Gallant, Kenneth S, 'The International Criminal Court in the System of States and International Organizations' (2003) 16 (3) Leiden Journal of International Law 559.

47 Donat Cattin, David, 'Decision-Making in the International Criminal Court: Functions of the Assembly of States Parties and Independence of the Court's Judicial Organs' in Lattanzi, Flavia and Schabas, William (eds), Essays on the Rome Statute of the International Criminal Court, vol 2 (Editrice il Sirente 1999) 72.

48 Rao, (1999) 399.

49 Bos, (2002) 297.

50 Barberini, Roberta, 'Assemblea Degli Stati Parte' in Lattanzi, Giorgio and Monetti, Vito (eds), La Corte Penale Internazionale: Organi, Competenza, Reati, Processo (Giuffrè Editore 2006) 1561.

51 Gradoni, (2012) 2005.

52 Roberts, Geoff, 'Part 11 Assembly of States Parties' in de Hert, Paul and others (eds), Code of International Criminal Law and Procedure, Annotated (Larcier 2013) 495.

53 de Gabriel, Eulalia, 'Érase Una Vez... La Responsabilidad Penal Internacional: Del Impacto De La Primera Guerra Mundial En Su Evolución Conceptual Y Pre-Normativa' in Gamarra Chopo, Yolanda and Fernández Liesa, Carlos R (eds), Los Orígenes del Derecho Internacional Contemporáneo Estudios Conmemorativos del Centenario de la Primera Guerra Mundial (Institución Fernando El Católico 2015) 247.

54 Schabas, 1433.

55 Ambach, Philipp, 'Article 112 Assembly of States Parties' in Ambos, Kai (ed), The Rome Statute of the International Criminal Court: A Commentary (4 edn, Beck/Hart 2022) 2767.

56 Klamberg, Mark, 'Article 112 – Assembly of States Parties' in Klamberg, Mark, Nilsson, Jonas and Angotti, Antonio (eds), Commentary on the Law of the International Criminal Court: The Statute, vol 2 (Torkel Opsahl Academic EPublisher 2023) 999.

57 O'Donohue, Jonathan, 'The ICC and the ASP' in Stahn, Carsten (ed), The Law and Practice of the International Criminal Court (Oxford University Press 2015) 105.

58 du Plessis, Max and Grevers, Christopher, 'The Role of the Assembly of States Parties for the ICC' in Steinberg, Richard H (ed), Contemporary Issues Facing the International Criminal Court (Brill Nijhoff 2016) 160.

59 Vasiliev, 'Judicial Governance Entities as Power-Holders in International Criminal Justice: A Plea for a Socio-Legal Enquiry' (2020) 483.

actions by States Parties across 'administrative, legislative, and operational'[60] responsibilities. Villacis,[61] in addition, has written perhaps the only academic contribution about the working methods of the Assembly. However, while these contributions are important to understand the governance function of the Assembly, they highlight specific themes, particular sessions or only cover parts of the overall responsibilities assigned by the Statute to the Assembly. The targeted approach to the study of the Assembly of States Parties might be explained by the 'sheer number of governance functions vested in the ASP'.[62] In this sense, and in conversation with this body of work, the objective of this book is to provide a more complete overview of the governance and oversight function of the Assembly of States Parties for its 20 sessions between 2002 and 2021.

In doing so, this book intends to contribute to the emerging focus on international judicial governance institutions from the under-studied perspective of the Assembly of States Parties. It also aims to expand the focus of scholars studying the International Criminal Court beyond the judicial functions described in the Rome Statute. Finally, it hopes to be a resource to key actors in the Rome Statute system as they address the recommendation of the Independent Expert Review calling for a 'discussion among stakeholders … on the strategic vision for the Court for the next ten years, which will enable the Court and the ASP to focus their efforts of implementing the Rome Statute in the same direction'.[63]

3 The Book Outline

To provide an overview of the governance and oversight function of the Assembly of States Parties towards the Court between 2002 and 2021, the book reflects on three leading questions. First, the book tries to dispel the historical and legal process leading to the establishment of the Assembly of States Parties. Subsequently, and building from the negotiation history, the book considers the specific responsibilities assigned by the Rome Statute to the Assembly of States Parties. Finally, the book hones into the practice of

60 Trahan, (2020) 231–232.
61 Villacis, 1571.
62 Vasiliev, 'Judicial Governance Entities as Power-Holders in International Criminal Justice: A Plea for a Socio-Legal Enquiry' (2020) 559.
63 Report of the Independent Expert Review of the International Criminal Court and the Rome Statute System, ICC-ASP/19/16 211.

the Assembly by reviewing notable moments in its institutional evolution between 2002 and 2021.

To answer these questions the research process engaged with a vast archive of documents produced for virtually every area of the history and practice of the Rome Statute. In particular, this book explored relevant historical antecedents of the Assembly and traced the main actions taken by States Parties and by the Assembly's Bureau between 2002 and 2021. These actions were studied by focusing on statutory responsibilities linked to governance and management, elections, financial oversight, oversight of auxiliary judicial instruments, enforcement of cooperation and the review and amendment of the Rome Statute. For these areas, the research focused on the normative framework and the practice of the Assembly. It also reflected on the findings of the 2020 Independent Expert Review report.[64] The decision to focus on the first twenty sessions of the Assembly corresponded to two reasons. First, it enabled the author to narrow down the scope of inquiry by covering a long enough period to discern the development of the practice of the Assembly. Secondly, the twentieth session in 2021 was an important moment of leadership renewal at the Court with a new Prosecutor, two Deputy Prosecutors, six judges and a new composition of the Bureau, including a new Assembly President. The 2021 session also examined the emerging outcomes of the Independent Expert Review process. Together, these factors point to the twentieth session in 2021 as an appropriate moment to limit the temporal scope of the research. These methodological choices, however, reasonably limit the engagement of this book with deeper questions about governance models in other international organizations, a deeper theoretical examination about the legal nature of the Assembly of States Parties and a complete discussion of the Independent Expert Review. In the labouring search of balance between a primer account of the Assembly and depth of analysis, the author still hopes the forthcoming chapters are useful to appraise the under-studied subject of how States Parties have governed the International Criminal Court.

In this context, the research reviewed 154 resolutions, seven decisions, four recommendations, two declarations and selected papers of the sessions of the Assembly between 2002 and 2021, including the Kampala Review Conference in 2010.[65] In addition, given the management and oversight function of the Bureau of the Assembly, the author analysed 266 available meeting records, corresponding with 1081 agenda items. However, there was substantial dis-

---

64 Ibid.

65 Assembly of States Parties to the Rome Statute, ASP Sessions, available at: <https://asp.icc-cpi.int/sessions> accessed 4 January (2024).

crepancy between the number of meetings reported by the Bureau during its annual oral report to the Assembly and the records available online in the ICC Legal Tools Database website (see Table 1.2).[66] While the Bureau reported 255 meetings between 2002 and 2021, the official website contained records for 266 meetings. Furthermore, based on the research carried out, 31 meetings were missing from the documentation hosted online. Notably and regrettably for the aims of this book, the public record did not contain the meeting documents of the Bureau during the first to third session of the Assembly between 2002 and 2004 and during the Kampala Review Conference. In the course of the research, the author engaged with and alerted the Legal Tools Database staff regarding the missing documentation; however, their inclusion was pending at the moment of writing.[67]

To situate the overall analysis within the long history of international judicial governance institutions, Chapter 2 discusses three key moments in 1937, 1943 and 1981 that offer an insight into policy options pursued by States at the Rome Conference in 1998. Chapters 3 and 4 follow in detail the legislative history of the Assembly of States Parties during the preparatory process and at the Rome Conference to uncover the statutory responsibilities assigned to the Assembly. Chapter 4 in particular also explores the Preparatory Commission setting up the operations of the Court and the Assembly between 1999 and 2002. The following chapters review the practice of the Assembly of States Parties between 2002 and 2021 across governance and management (Chapter 5), elections, disciplinary measures and removal of officials (Chapter 6), financial oversight (Chapter 7), enforcement of cooperation (Chapter 8) and oversight of auxiliary judicial instruments, Statute amendments and review (Chapter 9).

The second chapter investigates relevant governance provisions in 1937, 1943 and 1981 within the long history of multilateral judicial institutions preceding Article 112 in the Rome Statute. The legacy of the 1937 Convention for the Creation of an International Criminal Court, the 1943 draft Convention for the Creation of an International Criminal Court and the 1981 draft Convention on the Establishment of an International Penal Tribunal in the context of the

66 ICC Legal Tools Database, available at <https://www.legal-tools.org> accessed 4 January 2024. See also: Bergsmo, Morten, Bekou, Olympia and Jones, Annika, 'Complementarity After Kampala: Capacity Building and the ICC's Legal Tools' (2010) 2 Goettingen Journal of International Law 791.

67 The author also contacted and alerted the Secretariat of the Assembly of States Parties but received no response.

TABLE 1.2 Assembly of States Parties Bureau meeting records

Presidency	Years in office / session	Missing records
H.R.H. Prince Zeid Raíad Zeid Al-Hussein (Jordan)	2002–2004 / ASP 1–3	All meetings
Mr. Bruno Stagno Ugarte (Costa Rica)	2005–2008 / ASP 4–6	17 meetings (ASP Session 4, 2005) Meeting 7 (ASP Session 6, 2008) Meeting 8 (ASP Session 7, 2008)
Mr. Christian Wenaweser (Liechtenstein)	2008–2010 / ASP 7–9	Meetings 5–6 (ASP Session 8, 2009) All meetings (Kampala Review, 2010) 5 meetings (ASP Session 9, 2010)
Ms. Tiina Intelmann (Estonia)	2011–2013 / ASP 10–12	Meeting 19 (ASP Session 10, 2011) Meetings 2–4 and 19 (ASP Session 11, 2012)
Mr. Sidiki Kaba (Senegal)	2014–2017 / ASP 13–16	–
Mr. O-Gon Kwon (Republic of Korea)	2018–2020 / ASP 17–19	–
Ms. Silvia Fernández de Gurmendi (Argentina)	2021(-2023) / ASP 19–20 (-22)	–

1976 Apartheid Convention are useful to appraise the Assembly of States Parties to the Rome Statute. This is the case as each of these instruments delineated a specific role for States Parties to enable the mandate of an international criminal court to fight impunity within each historical context. These three key moments also developed State Party responsibilities for governance and management, financial oversight, election of judges and prosecutors and enforcement of cooperation, which can now be found in the Rome Statute. By studying these three pivotal moments in the history of governance choices for multilateral judicial institutions, the chapter reveals the politics, opportunities and constraints faced by all relevant actors to creatively forge the State-led governance structures that later influenced the ink and letter of Article 112 in Rome. This chapter also offers a summary of the historical milestones leading to the 1989 United Nations General Assembly's resolution 44/39 paving the way towards the preparatory process for the 1998 Rome Conference.

The third chapter explores the Rome Conference preparatory process between 1990 and 1998. In particular it traces the negotiations between 1994 and 1998 when it was decided to establish an international criminal court as an international organization governed by its States Parties. It is in this period the Assembly of States Parties to the Rome Statute was finally proposed in the context of the last session of the 1998 Preparatory Committee. The fourth chapter, on the other hand, focuses on the outcomes of the Rome Conference in relation to Article 112 and the sessions of the Preparatory Commission in 1999–2002 as the embryonic moment for the Assembly of States Parties. Chapter 4 also traces the choices that shaped the debate during this period marking the beginning of the Assembly. The combined analysis of both chapters reveals that providing the International Criminal Court with an effective governing body was isolated to specific junctures during the negotiations, without considering the function of such body in the larger institution and effort to create a system of international justice. The work of the Preparatory Commission tried to rectify this outcome, albeit only focusing on procedural steps to the creation of the Assembly rather than its significance as the governing body of the newly operational Court.

Consequently, Chapter 5 examines the governance and management practice of the Assembly of States Parties between its first and twentieth session. In particular it locates and analyses this function across Articles 112(1)–(10) and 119(2) in terms of structure and overall powers, Articles 2 and 3(2) for the approval of the relationship agreement with the United Nations and the host country, and Articles 46(2), 47 and 112(2)(b) for the responsibility to provide management oversight to elected officials. To understand the governance and management set-up that has prevailed since 2002, this chapter also covers the main decisions taken during the foundational first session of the Assembly of States Parties in New York. This chapter elaborates on the organizational choices that have shaped the Assembly over 20 years including its Bureau, subsidiary organs, modes of decision making, annual meetings, the relationship with the United Nations and the host State as well as how States Parties have defended the Court from external political attacks.

When considering the power of the Assembly to elect, sanction and remove judges, the Prosecutor, Deputy Prosecutor, and indirectly, the Registrar, the sixth chapter uncovers institutional deficits that precluded the election of the most suitable candidates and effective oversight of their performance. This chapter describes the Assembly's slow-walk towards the establishment of the Advisory Committee on Nomination of judges, the weak procedure for the election of the Prosecutor and lack of a permanent vetting system for elected officials. In addition, it shows how the Assembly was confronted with public exposes criticizing the conduct of elected officials, for example, of the first Prosecutor, urging States Parties to take corrective action. In this sense, the chapter describes interrelated provisions located primarily across the Rome Statute,[68] Rules of Procedure of the Assembly,[69] Rules of Procedure and Evidence,[70] and the Regulations of the Court,[71] and secondarily in the Staff Regulations[72] and Rules,[73] guiding the role of the Assembly in disciplinary measures and removal of elected officials. Overall, this chapter finds the dual role of States Parties to elect and oversee the performance of senior officials has suffered from weak institutional oversight tools prone to political manoeuvres.

The seventh chapter focuses on the financial oversight power of the Assembly. Departing from Article 112(2)(d), with corresponding clauses across other parts of the Statute, notably in Part 4 and 12, States Parties approved 20 budgets between 2002 and 2021, totalling €2,22 billion. The chapter focuses on the negotiated process between the Court and States Parties to approve the annual budget, including the role of the Committee on Budget and Finance. In doing so, the analysis reveals how the Assembly has tightened its financial oversight grip over time, possibly risking judicial independence. This chapter also discusses the main challenges of States Parties' arrears and the failure of the United Nations Security Council to provide funds for the cost of referrals to the Court.

The eighth chapter explores the role and impact of the Assembly in enforcing cooperation with the Court. The lack of assistance to the Court by States Parties and other States under the obligation to do so put undue pressure on the judicial mandate between 2002 and 2021. The chapter shows that, despite receiving 11 referrals of non-cooperation from the Court between 2010 and 2021, the Assembly did not succeed in changing recalcitrant behaviour from non-compliant States. In fact, even as States Parties deployed a range of diplo-

68 Articles 46(2) and 47, Rome Statute of the International Criminal Court (2002) 2187 UNTS 90.

69 Rules 11, 81 and 82, Rules of Procedure of the Assembly of States Parties, ICC-ASP/1/3 (2002).

70 Rules 26, 29 and 30, Rules of Procedure and Evidence, ICC-PIOS-LT-03–004/19 (2002).

71 Regulations 121 and 123, Regulations of the Court, International Criminal Court, ICC-BD /01–05–16 (2022).

72 ICC-ASP/2/Res.2 Staff Regulations for the International Criminal Court (2003).

73 Staff Rules of the International Criminal Court, ICC/AI/2015/004/Cor.1 (2015).

matic measures to influence cooperation with the Court, these remained largely ineffective. In this context, the chapter offers an overview of the referrals received from the Court and the tactics developed by States Parties to address non-cooperation.

Chapter 9, the final section covering the practice of statutory responsibilities of the Assembly, considers the oversight of auxiliary judicial instruments and, given their close legal relationship, the amendments and review of the Rome Statute. In relation to States Parties' oversight of auxiliary judicial instruments, the chapter explores the actions taken by the Assembly to operationalize and amend over time the Elements of Crimes, the Rules of Procedure and Evidence, the Staff Regulations, the Regulations of the Court and the Trust Fund for Victims. Acting under Article 112(2)(g), where the Assembly performed other functions than those described in Part 11, the chapter focuses on the challenge States Parties faced to respect the independence of the Court while legislating on key legal texts like the Rules of Procedure and Evidence. In particular, this section covers the tumultuous relationship of the Assembly with the African Union as the legal situations of Sudan and Kenya progressed through the Court. The second part of Chapter 9 discusses the five amendments to the Statute between 2002 and 2021,[74] the Kampala Review Conference and the Independent Expert Review process commissioned by States Parties in 2019. In particular, this section discusses the first report of the Review Mechanism, the State-led body established by the Assembly to implement the recommendations from the Independent Expert Review.

The overall picture emerging from this research shows that across its statutory responsibilities, the Assembly of States Parties has impacted the life of the International Criminal Court in tangible ways. From the under-studied point of view of the Assembly as the injugovin of the Court, States Parties' choices and decisions between 2002 and 2021 have affected the institutional governance and judicial capabilities outlined in the Rome Statute. In particular, on the institutional governance side, this book finds that the Assembly underwent a period of maturity as States Parties recognized their role over time. In this developmental process, the Assembly faced inherent challenges to its political role as it also navigated through novel obligations imposed to the Assembly by the Statute. For example, the Assembly's approach to electing the Court's Prosecutor or the choices made for evaluating amendments during the first Review Conference in Kampala in 2010 shaped subsequent ways of working. This book also found the Assembly of States Parties had a dispropor-

74 Assembly of States Parties to the Rome Statute, Rome Statute and Other Agreements, available at: <https://asp.icc-cpi.int/assembly> accessed 5 January (2024).

tionate impact on some judicial functions led by the Court. Notably, the intricate issue of adequate financial investment on the Court severely limited the capability of the organs of the Court. In a similar way, States Parties' amendments to the Rules of Procedure and Evidence raised serious concerns about the line between oversight and encroachment upon judicial independence. The alarming inability of the Assembly of States Parties to enforce Court-mandated orders for cooperation was another notable issue disproportionately affecting the judicial mandate. In this troubling context, the study of the Independent Expert Review report and subsequent Review Mechanism began to show early signs of course correction, mostly by cementing a two-way process for the Court and States Parties to advance, jointly, the aims of international justice, as the Rome Statute entered its third decade.

CHAPTER 2

Three Key Moments in the Long History of the Assembly of States Parties to the Rome Statute

1 Introduction

Governance provisions for international judicial institutions by States Parties to a multilateral treaty did not originate solely with Article 112 in the Rome Statute of the International Criminal Court. In fact, there is a rich history that can be traced to three key moments in 1937, 1943 and 1981 that offer an insight into policy options pursued by States at the Rome Conference in 1998. While the Nuremberg and Tokyo judicial mechanisms can be added to a historical analysis, this chapter prioritizes multilateral precedents in the context of the League of Nations and the United Nations as these organs provided the space for States engagement beyond the main powers.

In this context, the legacy of the 1937 Convention for the Creation of an International Criminal Court, the 1943 draft Convention for the Creation of an International Criminal Court and the 1981 draft Convention on the Establishment of an International Penal Tribunal in the context of the 1976 Apartheid Convention is necessary to appraise the Assembly of States Parties to the Rome Statute. This is the case as each of these instruments delineated a specific role for States Parties to enable their mandate as a criminal court to fight impunity within each historical context. These three key moments have also developed State Party responsibilities for governance and management, financial oversight, election of judges and prosecutors and enforcement of cooperation, which can now be found in Article 112 in the Rome Statute. By studying these three key moments in the history of governance choices for international judicial institutions, this chapter aims to reveal the politics, opportunities and constraints faced by all relevant actors to creatively forge the State-led governance structures that later influenced the ink and letter of Article 112 in the Rome Statute. In doing so, this chapter describes the 1937, 1943 and 1981 governance instruments while also offering a summary of the milestones leading to the 1989 United Nations General Assembly's resolution 44/39 paving the path towards the preparatory process for the 1998 Rome Conference.

© EZEQUIEL JIMÉNEZ MARTINEZ, 2026 | DOI:10.1163/9789004749979_003

2 A Beginning for an Institution Judiciaire Internationale

As the seminal work produced by Cherif Bassiouni and William Schabas confirmed, from time immemorial there has been a desire across epochs to uphold 'principles of legitimacy for resorting to war and particular rules for its conduct'.[1] In this quest to create justiciable rules and organizations responsible for their governance several precedents to the Assembly of States Parties can be examined. For example Gustave Moynier's 1872 proposal to create 'une Institution Judiciaire internationale propre à prévenir et à réprimer les infractions à la Convention de Genève'.[2] Moynier's institution is recognized in the literature as a distant cousin of the International Criminal Court.[3] The Permanent Court of Arbitration created in 1899 and further developed in 1907[4] is another precedent in the development of governance provisions to international judicial institutions. For example, the Permanent Administrative Council, described in Article 28 in the 1899 Convention, and changed minimally in 1907 under Article 49,[5] gave it direct management oversight over the International Bureau, the Registry of the Court.[6] This is a familiar formulation also found in Article 112 of the Rome Statute whereas a Bureau of States Parties retained a responsibility to oversee the administration of the Court.

The 1920 Advisory Committee of Jurists' work to establish the Permanent Court of International Justice belongs to the rich history developing governance provisions to an international judicial institution. Emanating from the founding document of the League of Nations, member States agreed to submit

1 Bassiouni, M Cherif and Schabas, William A, The Legislative History of the International Criminal Court 1(2 edn, Brill | Nijhoff 2016) 10.

2 Hall, Christopher Keith, 'The First Proposal for a Permanent International Criminal Court' (1998) 38 (322) International Review of the Red Cross Archive 1.

3 Moynier, Gustave, 'Note sur la création d'une institution judiciaire internationale propre a prévenir et a réprimer les infractions a la convention de Genève' (1872) 3 (11) Bulletin International des Societes de Secours aux Militaires Blesses 124; de Gabriel, Eulalia, 'La Propuesta del Tribunal Penal Internacional de Gustave Moynier, un Proyecto Antiguo Recientemente Rescatado (1872–1998)' in Carrillo Salcedo, Juan Antonio (ed), La Criminalización de la Barbarie: la Corte Penal Internacional (Consejo General del Poder Judicial 2000) 11.

4 Caron, David D, 'War And International Adjudication: Reflections on the 1899 Peace Conference' (2000) 94 (1) American Journal of International Law 14.

5 Scott, James Brown, The Proceedings of The Hague Peace Conferences (Oxford University Press 1920) 138–139.

6 Convention for the Pacific Settlement of International Disputes (signed at The Hague 18 October 1907) 36 Stat. 2199.

to arbitration or inquiry 'any dispute likely to lead to a rupture'.[7] To this effect, meeting in the Peace Palace in June and July 1920, Baron Descamps, the chair, advocated to establish a High Court of International Justice to prosecute cases referred by the League of Nations.[8] Elihu Root, from the United States, on the other hand, voiced concerns whether States were 'prepared to modify their sovereign rights' fearing the League of Nations could be transformed into a 'super-State'.[9] Descamps' proposal would be considered as 'premature'[10] by States in the Third Committee of the Assembly of the League of Nations. Writing in 1935, Caloyanni Mégalos, one of the founders of the Association Internationale de Droit Pénal questioned: 'must we have more tragedies before the Assembly of the League of Nations abandons the word 'premature'?'.[11] Indeed, as States grappled with inaction during the interwar period, Mégalos was joined by scholars in the International Law Association, the Association Internationale de Droit Pénal and the Inter-Parliamentary Union[12] seeking to establish an international criminal court.

In these attempts the crucial question of the role of States in governing such judicial institutions was advanced by Raphael Lemkin,[13] Hugh Bellot[14] and Vespasian Pella.[15] In fact, the inaction of States to establish an international

7 Article 12, Treaty of Peace between the Allied and Associated Powers and Germany, Paris Peace Conference, XIII 55, 740, 743; Senate document 51, 66th Congress, 1st session (1919).

8 Advisory Committee of Jurists, Procès-Verbaux of the Proceedings of the Committee June 16th to July 24th 1920, with Annexes (1920) 49.

9 Ibid 505.

10 League of Nations, The Records of the First Assembly Plenary Meetings, Meetings Held from the 15th of November to the 18th of December 1920 in Geneva (1920) 280.

11 Caloyanni, Mégalos, 'The Proposals of M. Laval to the League of Nations for the Establishment of an International Permanent Tribunal in Criminal Matters' (1935) 21 Transactions of the Grotius Society 86.

12 Albers, Martin, 'Between the crisis of democracy and world parliament: the development of the Inter-Parliamentary Union in the 1920s' (2012) 7 (2) Journal of Global History 189.

13 Segesser, Daniel Marc and Gessler, Myriam, 'Raphael Lemkin and the international debate on the punishment of war crimes (1919–1948)' (2005) 7 (4) Journal of Genocide Research 456.

14 International Law Association, Obituary Hugh H. L. Bellot, D.C.L. (International Law Association Reports of Conferences, 1928) 1; Segesser, Daniel Marc, 'Hugh H. L. Bellot: A Life in the Service of the Prevention and Punishment of War Crimes and Crimes Against Humanity' in Mégret, Frédéric and Tallgren, Immi (eds), The Dawn of a Discipline: International Criminal Justice and Its Early Exponents (Cambridge University Press 2020) 14.

15 Mamolea, Andrei, 'Vespasian V. Pella: International Criminal Justice as a Safeguard of Peace, 1919–1952' in Mégret, Frédéric and Tallgren, Immi (eds), The Dawn of a Discipline:

criminal court was at the heart of the debate.[16] Yet, Moynier's initial push together with efforts in 1899 and 1920 gave way to the negotiations of the 1937 Convention for the Creation of an International Criminal Court, a first attempt at building a criminal dispute settlement scheme monitored and governed by States.

3 The 1937 Convention for the Creation of an International Criminal Court

The study of the 1937 Convention for the Prevention and Punishment of Terrorism, and the accompanying Convention for the Creation of an International Criminal Court is an important antecedent to appreciate the current role of the Assembly of States Parties to the Rome Statute. This is the case as the drafting choices in 1937 inspired the 1948 Genocide Convention and most importantly, Cherif Bassiouni and Arthur Robinson's 1988 proposal paving the path towards the 1998 Rome Conference.[17] The 1937 instrument also proposed language and governance responsibilities to States Parties that resemble current functions of the Rome Statute Assembly in the areas of management, financial oversight and election of judges to the Court (see Table 2.1). In this context, this section briefly describes the context in which the 1937 Convention emerged and key aspects inspiring Article 112 in the Rome Statute.

The assassination of Louis Barthou, the French Foreign Minister, and Prince Alexander of Yugoslavia in Marseilles in October 1934 triggered the creation of the 1937 Convention.[18] Tasked by the League of Nations to codify the crime of terrorism with a corresponding criminal court,[19] the Committee for the International Repression of Terrorism gathered in three sessions between 1935 and

International Criminal Justice and Its Early Exponents (Cambridge University Press 2020) 22.

16 de La Cuesta, José Luis and Ottenhof, Reynald, 'The Association Internationale de Droit Pénal and the Establishment of the International Criminal Court' (2015) 86 (3) Revue internationale de droit pénal 1243.

17 Bassiouni, M Cherif, 'Codification of International Criminal Law' (2016) 45 (3) Denver Journal of International Law and Policy 348.

18 Bassiouni, M Cherif, International Terrorism: Multilateral Conventions (1937–2001) (Brill Nijhoff 2001) 43.

19 Çakmak, Cenap, A Brief History of International Criminal Law and International Criminal Court (Palgrave Macmillan 2017) 46.

1937,[20] with Vespasian Pella as rapporteur. The initial proposal in 1935 envisaged an international criminal court created by a multilateral treaty with automatic jurisdiction over the crime of terrorism. In doing so it identified a role for the 'High Contracting Parties'.[21] A key responsibility was the nomination and election of judges. Closely resembling Article 36 in the Rome Statute, the Committee concurred on a formula consisting of two groups:

> (a) Criminologists possessing the qualifications required for appointment to the highest judicial offices in their own country or who are or have been members of courts of criminal law
> (b) Jurists who are acknowledged authorities on criminal law.[22]

By the second session in 1936, after States criticized the first report of the Committee,[23] the automatic premise of international criminal jurisdiction was removed. The change meant that States had the option to accede to two separate conventions: one agreeing the definition of the crime, and another creating international jurisdiction over it. Nevertheless, the separate Convention for the Creation of an International Criminal Court contained a number of provisions under the purview of the High Contracting Parties under Article 46.[24] Titled 'Meeting of High Contracting Parties', Article 46 may be considered the earliest antecedent to the Assembly of States Parties to the Rome Statute. At first sight, the governance structure contained in Article 46 reveals a role for the collective of States Parties in financial and governance questions. But a closer look to Article 46(2) granting States Parties the possibility to 'also decide what modifications are necessary in order to attain the objects of the present Convention',[25] embodies a greater desire to expand the remit of the

20 Saul, Ben, 'Attempts to Define 'Terrorism' in International Law' (2005) 52 (1) Netherlands International Law Review 62.

21 Committee for the International Repression of Terrorism, Report to the Council on the First Session of the Committee, held from April 30th to May 8th, 1935. Doc C. 184. M. 102. 1935-V. (1935) Appendix II, International Criminal Court, Article 21 and 22.

22 Committee for the International Repression of Terrorism, Report to the Council on the First Session of the Committee, held from April 30th to May 8th, 1935. Doc C. 184. M. 102. 1935-V. (1935) Appendix II, International Criminal Court, Article 19.

23 Committee for the International Repression of Terrorism, Report to the Council on the Second Session of the Committee, held from January 7th to 15th, 1936. Doc. C.36.1936.V. (1936) 2.

24 Article 46, Convention for the Creation of an International Criminal Court (16 November 1937) LoN Doc. C.547.M384.1937.V.

25 Article 46, Convention for the Creation of an International Criminal Court (16 November 1937) LoN Doc. C.547.M384.1937.V.

TABLE 2.1 Convention for the Creation of an International Criminal Court (1937)

Function		Rome Statute (1998)
Governance and Management Oversight – Financial Oversight	Article 46 (1) The representatives of the High Contracting Parties shall meet with a view to taking all necessary decisions concerning: (a) The constitution and administration of the common fund, the division among the High Contracting Parties of the sums considered necessary to create and maintain such fund and, in general, all questions bearing on the establishment and the working of the Court (b) The organisation of the meetings referred to below in paragraph 3. (2) At their first meeting, the representatives of the High Contracting Parties shall also decide what modifications are necessary in order to attain the objects of the present Convention. (3) The Registrar of the Court shall convene subsequent meetings in conformity with the rules established to that effect. (4) All questions of procedure that may arise at the meetings referred to in the present article shall be decided by a majority of two-thirds of the High Contracting Parties represented at the meeting.	Articles 112(1), 112(2)(g), 112(7)(b) and 115

court, including expanding jurisdiction into other nascent areas of international criminal law. Article 46(2) would be instrumental in motivating the choices of Cherif Bassiouni's 1981 proposal for an International Penal Tribunal in the context of the 1976 Apartheid Convention.[26] Moreover, Article 46(1)(a) also outlined the financial oversight responsibility of States Parties to cover

26 Study on Ways and Means of Insuring the Implementation of International Instruments such as the International Convention on the Suppression and Punishment of the Crime

the operational costs of the court based on scales agreed by the High Contracting Parties.[27] The intention behind this clause has survived in Part 12 in the Rome Statute.[28]

Academic commentary at the time hailed the 'boldness of the conceptions'[29] underlying the inherent role of High Contracting Parties to utilize their legislative powers to expand the Court's jurisdiction.[30] The Convention for the Prevention and Punishment of Terrorism had 19 signatures by 1938 but only one ratification from India.[31] The Convention for the Creation of an International Criminal Court fared a worse outcome with no ratification, never entering into force.[32] However, the actions by the London International Assembly calling for the creation of an international criminal court in 1943 would reinvigorate this debate.

4 The 1943 Draft Convention for the Creation of an International Criminal Court

The London International Assembly met 300 times between 1941 and 1943 under the chairmanship of Belgian judge Marcel de Baer to 'consider the principles of post-war policy'.[33] The Assembly's final 450-page report in 1943 is considered the blueprint for the United Nations War Crimes Commission.[34] The report included a draft Convention for the Creation of an International

---

of Apartheid, including the establishment of the International Jurisdiction Envisaged by the Convention, UN Doc. E/CN.4/1426 (1981) 17.

27 Committee for the International Repression of Terrorism, Report to the Council on the Second Session of the Committee, held from January 7th to 15th, 1936. Doc. C.36.1936.V. (1936) Article 40.

28 Article 115, Rome Statute of the International Criminal Court (2002) 2187 UNTS 90.

29 Hudson, Manley O, 'The Proposed International Criminal Court' (1938) 32 (3) American Journal of International Law 552.

30 Pella, Vespasian 'Towards an International Criminal Court' (1950) 44 (1) American Journal of International Law 37; Ciucă, Aurora, 'Romanian Contributions to the Codification of International Law: Vespasian V. Pella' (2018) 5 (2) European Journal of Law and Public Administration 7.

31 Çakmak, 47.

32 Bassiouni, International Terrorism: Multilateral Conventions (1937–2001) 44.

33 von Lingen, Kerstin, 'Setting the Path for the UNWCC: The Representation of European Exile Governments on the London International Assembly and the Commission for Penal Reconstruction and Development, 1941–1944' (2014) 25 (1) Criminal Law Forum 62.

34 Plesch, Dan, Human Rights After Hitler: The Lost History of Prosecuting Axis War Crimes (Georgetown University Press 2017) 54–55.

Criminal Court[35] with substantive oversight provisions in Article 55 on the 'Meeting with Representatives of High Contracting Parties'.[36] The 'meeting'[37] described in Article 55 was akin to the sessions of the Assembly of States Parties to the Rome Statute as it was tasked with core responsibilities for the election of judges (Article 10), the election of the Procurator General and deputies (Article 21), cooperation with the court (Article 52), execution of orders of arrest by local police (Article 25 (3)) and financial support (Article 53). Indeed, together with Article 46 of the 1937 Convention for the Creation of an International Criminal Court, this second instrument is a direct antecedent to the Rome Statute Assembly (See Table 2.2).

A reading of Article 55(1) makes it clear the collective of High Contracting Parties were the ultimate decision-makers for the intended functioning of the court. Provided that the Procurator General could participate in decision-making, a role not assigned to the Prosecutor in the Rome Statute, High Contracting Parties could consider 'all other questions bearing on the establishment and the working of the Court'.[38] Interestingly, in order to secure the arrest and transfer of suspected Axis criminals, the 1943 draft stipulated the creation of an international constabulary appointed and controlled by the judges.[39] As such, each High Contracting Party agreed under Article 25(3) to 'confer upon the Constabulary the necessary power to call the assistance of the local police'. To do so, and to support the jurisprudence of the court, High Contracting Parties also agreed under Article 52 to 'adjust their national legislation to meet the requirements of the present Convention'.[40] A product of its time, this provision is a distant relative of Part 9 and Article 112(2)(f) of the Rome Statute. The responsibility on election of judges in Article 10 and financial oversight in Article 53 also expected continuous governance and management oversight to the court, including electing additional judges under Article 55(1)(b). The similarities of the governance role of States Parties to the 1943 and the 1998 treaties reveals a continuum in the intention to oversee each international criminal court bearing in mind the ultimate aim of fighting impunity, 75 years later.

35 Schabas, William A, 'The United Nations War Crimes Commission's Proposal for an International Criminal Court' (2014) 25 (1) Criminal Law Forum 173.

36 Historical Survey of the Question of International Criminal Jurisdiction, UN Doc. A/CN.4/7 (1949), Appendix 9.B, Draft Convention for the Creation of an International Criminal Court (London International Assembly, 1943).

37 Ibid.

38 Ibid.

39 Ibid.

40 Ibid.

TABLE 2.2 Draft Convention for the Creation of an International Criminal Court (1943)

Function		Rome Statute (1998)
Governance and Management Oversight	Article 55 – Meeting with Representatives of High Contracting Parties (1) Representatives of the High Contracting Parties shall meet whenever necessary together with the Court and the Procurator General with a view to taking all necessary decisions concerning: (d) All other questions bearing on the establishment and the working of the Court (e) The prolongation or curtailment of the Court's existence. (3) The Registrar of the Court shall act as Secretary of those meetings; he shall convene subsequent meetings in conformity with the rules which may be established to that effect or the orders of the Court.	Articles 112(2)(a), 112(5), 112(6), 112(9) and 121(3)
Election of Judges	Article 10 – Election of Judges (3) The appointment of the original judges shall be made by a joint decision of the High Contracting Parties. Such appointment shall be made regardless of the nationality of the judge, but it shall take into account that the Court should represent the principal legal systems of the world and that it should ensure a fair representation of the countries that have been occupied by the enemy. Such appointment shall be made not more than two months after the time when the present Convention has been signed by seven High Contracting Parties. Article 55 – Meeting with Representatives of High Contracting Parties (1)(b) The appointment of additional judges	Articles 36 and 112(2)(e)
Election of the Prosecutor	Article 21 – Prosecuting Authority (1) The appointment of the original Procurator General shall be made in the way prescribed in article 10, section 3, for the judges	

TABLE 2.2 Draft Convention for the Creation of an International Criminal Court (*cont.*)

Function		Rome Statute (1998)
	Article 55 – Meetings with Representatives of High Contracting Parties (1)(c) The appointment of additional deputies-Procurator General as provided in article 21, section 2	Article 42(4)
Financial Oversight	Article 53 – Common Fund (2) The salaries of the judges, of the Procurator General and of the other officers of the Court shall be payable from this fund on a scale fixed by the High Contracting Parties, as well as any pensions which may be payable to their widows. Article 55 Meetings with Representatives of High Contracting Parties (1) (a) The constitution and administration of the common fund and the division among the High Contracting Parties of the sums considered necessary to create and to maintain such fund	Articles 49, 113 and 115

The pioneering work of the London International Assembly led to the creation of the United Nations War Crimes Committee in 1944.[41] Committee II on Enforcement, responsible for the preparations of 'trial and punishment of persons responsible for war crimes'[42] considered the 1943 draft but did not adopt it.[43] Evidently, as Schabas noted, the 'focus of discussion was not on the

41 Plesch, Dan and Sattler, Shanti, 'Changing the Paradigm of International Criminal Law: Considering the Work of the United Nations War Crimes Commission of 1943–1948' (2013) 15 (2) International Community Law Review 203; Plesch, Dan and Sattler, Shanti, 'A New Paradigm of Customary International Criminal Law: The UN War Crimes Commission of 1943–1948 and its Associated Courts and Tribunals' (2014) 25 (1) Criminal Law Forum 17.

42 United Nations War Crimes Commission, History of the United Nations War Crimes Commission and the Development of the Laws of War (1948) 124.

43 Ibid 452.

detailed provision for the structure and operations of the court but rather on the definitions of crimes and the applicable law'.[44] The focus on provisions detailing a governance role of States Parties to an international criminal court decreased over time. The fragmented drafting and political approach to describing such role would not return to specifying treaty powers for States Parties under a single provision until 1981 thanks to the work of States within the nascent United Nations.

5 The 1981 Draft Convention on the Establishment of an International Penal Tribunal for the Suppression and Punishment of the Crime of Apartheid and Other International Crimes

The United Nations became the vessel for the pursuit to establish an international criminal court after 1945. Already General Assembly resolution 95(I) on the 'Affirmation of the Principles of International Law recognized by the Charter of the Nürnberg Tribunal'[45] from 1946 spurred a debate on the development of international criminal jurisdiction, its codification and application that would last 52 years, at least, until 1998. For example, Article 6 of the Convention on the Prevention and Punishment of the Crime of Genocide included language on international criminal jurisdiction, albeit without creating a corresponding tribunal.[46] However, to uncover options to instrumentalize Article 6 of the Genocide Convention, the General Assembly invited the International Law Commission to study the matter in 1948.[47] For Rosenne, this resolution 'must be regarded as the starting point of the process that led to the Rome Statute of 1998'.[48] This process gave way to the Committee on International Criminal Jurisdiction which was tasked to prepare 'a preliminary draft convention'[49] on international criminal jurisdiction for consideration at the General Assembly.

---

44 Schabas, 'The United Nations War Crimes Commission's Proposal for an International Criminal Court' 178–179.

45 UNGA Res A/95(I) (1946).

46 Historical Survey of the Question of International Criminal Jurisdiction, UN Doc. A/CN.4/7 1949 45–46.

47 UNGA Res 3/260/B (III) (1948).

48 Rosenne, Shabtai, 'Antecedents of the Rome Statute of the International Criminal Court Revisited' (2000) 75 (1) International Law Studies 394.

49 UNGA Res A/1639 (1950).

Meeting in 1951[50] and 1953,[51] the Committee's work reflected a rigid position 'the common will of States should be maintained as the basis of the court, and States which had not expressed their will to support the court should therefore have no influence upon its composition'.[52] As such, as Bassiouni and Schabas confirmed, while the 1951 Committee created 'what it felt was the best possible structure for an international criminal court', the 1953 attempt 'had become less optimistic and bowed to political pressure'.[53] In a repeating pattern from previous attempts, like in 1937 and 1943, the General Assembly took no decisive action on the reports even as States also considered the Code of Offences Against the Peace and Security of Mankind and tried to define the crime of aggression.[54] The pursuit for an international criminal court governed by States Parties emerged again but in the context of the 1976 Convention on the Suppression and Punishment of the Crime of Apartheid.[55]

The United Nations Commission on Human Rights' Ad-Hoc Working Group on Southern Africa entrusted Cherif Bassiouni, with the assistance of Professor Daniel Derby, to prepare a draft statute to implement Article 5 of the Apartheid Convention which provided international criminal jurisdiction for such crime.[56] The herculean effort in the report to device a workable, yet future-proof, international criminal court is one of the many lasting legacies of Professor Bassiouni. In his own words, the 1981 statute 'is another link in the arduous progress of the humanitarian development of the Rule of Law'.[57] A link closely related to previous efforts in 1937 and 1943. Aware of the political constraints of the day, Bassiouni proposed the establishment of the International Penal Tribunal via a multilateral convention capable of adjudicating the crime of apartheid, but similarly able to gain jurisdiction over additional

50 Report of the Committee on International Criminal Jurisdiction, UN Doc. A/2136 (1951).

51 Report of the Committee on International Criminal Jurisdiction, UN Doc. A/2645 (1953).

52 Report of the Committee on International Criminal Jurisdiction, UN Doc. A/2136 (1951) para. 49.

53 Bassiouni and Schabas, 65.

54 Bassiouni, M Cherif, 'The History of the Draft Code of Crimes Against the Peace and Security of Mankind' (1993) 27 (1–2) Israel Law Review 253.

55 International Convention on the Suppression and Punishment of the Crime of Apartheid (adopted 30 November 1973, entered into force 18 July 1976) 1015 UNTS 243.

56 Bassiouni, M Cherif, 'Chronology of Efforts to Establish an International Criminal Court' (2015) 86 (3) Revue Internationale de Droit Pénal 1167–1168.

57 Bassiouni, M Cherif and Derby, Daniel H, 'Final Report on the Establishment of an International Criminal Court for the Implementation of the Apartheid Convention and Other Relevant International Instruments' (1981) 9 Hofstra Law Review 592.

crimes defined in other conventions.[58] Akin to the 1937 Convention on the Creation of an International Criminal Court for the crime of terrorism, Bassiouni's proposal covered the crime in question without curtailing the option to extend jurisdiction to other crimes over time by an exclusive governance decision of States Parties (see Table 2.3).

In summary, the International Penal Tribunal was a permanent court located in the Peace Palace in The Hague with an independent Prosecutor and with the competence to investigate and prosecute individuals, States and organisations. The Tribunal, manifestly, had jurisdiction over the crime of apartheid as defined by the Convention. In addition, Article 4(2) considered the option to add jurisdiction over crimes recognized in other multilateral conventions by supplemental agreements. Fundamentally, Bassiouni envisaged the International Penal Tribunal as an institutional framework applied to instruments containing an aut dedere aut judicare obligation upon States Parties, including, but beyond, the crime of apartheid.[59] A tours d'horizon over the statute reveals it was drafted by a legal expert rather than a diplomat primarily interested in reaching consensus at the expense of clarity and specificity. Such is the case that the provision outlining the role of States Parties to the Tribunal is the lengthiest and most detailed compared to the 1937 and 1943 examples covered in this chapter.

Right from the outset, a governance body, the Standing Committee of States Parties, was listed under Article 3 as one of the main organs of the International Penal Tribunal. The explanation for placing the Standing Committee of States Parties as an organ of the Tribunal resided in its legislative power to expand the jurisdiction over other crimes listed in multilateral conventions. In other words, by virtue of Article 17(5)(c), the Standing Committee of States Parties 'may propose to States Parties international instruments to enhance the functions of the Tribunal'.[60] For Bassiouni, this provision was 'one of the most significant functions of the Standing Committee' because its legislative power to propose 'new norms of international criminal law or standards'.[61] Providing this power to a corpus of States Parties was a vehicle to ensure the

58 Study on Ways and Means of Insuring the Implementation of International Instruments such as the International Convention on the Suppression and Punishment of the Crime of Apartheid, including the establishment of the International Jurisdiction Envisaged by the Convention, UN Doc. E/CN.4/1426 2.

59 Ibid 30.

60 Ibid 29.

61 Ibid 55.

progressive jurisdictional reach of the Tribunal without the need to recreate contested political spaces.

Bassiouni's 'quasi-legislative body'[62] was needed to oversee policy and administrative questions of the International Penal Tribunal. Thus, Article 17 described the role and responsibility of the Standing Committee of States Parties in seven sections. Article 17(1) to (3) described the governance structure of the Standing Committee whereas one representative from each State Party met twice a year at the seat of the Tribunal under the leadership of a presiding officer.[63] In a similar vein, Rome Statute Articles 112(1) and (6) follow a similar logic to the set-up of the Standing Committee.[64] In contrast, however, Bassiouni's Standing Committee was silent about voting procedures. Yet, membership to the Standing Committee was precluded for States Parties making any reservation to the 'Tribunal's jurisdiction, competence and the effects of its judgements'.[65] Bassiouni's commentary does not explain what the status of those States would have been, perhaps akin to observer States under Article 112(1) of the Rome Statute, but his formula did signal only States with demonstrable political support to the Tribunal could lead its governance function. Moreover, Bassiouni's proposal gave States flexibility to amend the rules of procedure of the Committee under Article 18(1).[66]

Sections (4) to (7) in Article 17 described the powers assigned to the Standing Committee. Article 17(4) served two purposes in the convention. First, it acted as an omnibus clause for the functions assigned to the Standing Committee, while protecting the independence of the Court:

> The Standing Committee shall have the power to perform the functions expressly assigned to it under this Convention, plus any other functions that it determines appropriate in furtherance of the purposes of the Tribunal that are not inconsistent with this Convention, but in no way shall those functions impair the independence and integrity of the Court as a judicial body.[67]

62 Ibid 46.

63 Ibid 29.

64 Article 112, Rome Statute of the International Criminal Court (2002) 2187 UNTS 90.

65 Study on Ways and Means of Insuring the Implementation of International Instruments such as the International Convention on the Suppression and Punishment of the Crime of Apartheid, including the establishment of the International Jurisdiction Envisaged by the Convention, UN Doc. E/CN.4/1426 44.

66 Ibid 55.

67 Ibid 29.

The second purpose of the omnibus function of 17(4) framed the duty of the Standing Committee to elect the judges and the Procurator. Bassiouni proposed a court made of twelve full-time judges elected for maximum period of eight years taking into consideration that only two judges could be of the same nationality. Judges had to be experts either in international criminal law or human rights, or qualified to serve on the highest courts of their country, and represent the major legal and cultural systems of the world. Similar provisions can be found in 1937 and in Article 36 of the Rome Statute, with additional requirements such as gender parity in the bench.[68] In this sense, while not clarifying voting requirements for electing judges, Article 14(3) mandated States Parties to meet as a corpus to elect the bench.

Article 15(2) described the election of the Procurator from a list of minimum three candidates by the Standing Committee. As with the election of judges, the voting requirement was not mentioned, however, the same section mentioned the procedure to remove the Procurator. Unlike the Rome Statute, the judges sitting en banc could remove the Procurator by two-thirds majority 'for incompetence, conflict of interest, or manifest disregard of the provisions of this Convention or material Rules of the Tribunal'.[69] That a political body decided on the appointment of the Procurator but the judges decided the merits for removal corresponded with Bassiouni's assessment that 'States are in a superior position to become aware of suitable candidates, while the Court is in a superior position to judge legal competence and estimate probable devotion to impartiality'.[70]

Moving past the omnibus clause, Bassiouni lifted three particular responsibilities for the Standing Committee under Article 17(5): mediate disputes over treaty interpretations, encourage the universality of the Tribunal, and 'propose to States Parties international instruments to enhance the functions of the Tribunal'.[71] In Bassiouni's words, of these three responsibilities, 'one of the most significant functions may be with respect to proposing action to initiate and propose new norms of international criminal law or standards for its application by the Tribunal'.[72] As explained before, by granting this power to States Parties, the Standing Committee was envisioned as the vehicle to

68 Article 36(3)(a), Rome Statute of the International Criminal Court (2002) 2187 UNTS 90.

69 Study on Ways and Means of Insuring the Implementation of International Instruments such as the International Convention on the Suppression and Punishment of the Crime of Apartheid, including the establishment of the International Jurisdiction Envisaged by the Convention, UN Doc. E/CN.4/1426 28.

70 Ibid 54.

71 Ibid 29.

72 Ibid 55.

ensure the progressive jurisdictional reach of the Tribunal without the need to recreate contested political spaces. In Bassiouni's words, 'having secured an international legislative basis, nothing precludes the States Parties to this draft Convention from enlarging upon its jurisdiction'.[73] To achieve this objective, the convention could be amended by a three-fourths vote of the Standing Committee and would enter into force when all States Parties in the Committee ratified the change.[74]

Of the remaining two specific responsibilities listed for the Standing Committee of States Parties, Article 17(5)(a) dealt with a standard provision in multilateral agreements to settle disputes. However, bearing in mind Article 17(4) enshrining the independence of the Tribunal, a key clause was missing to afford the judges with the power to determine disputes over judicial functions. Similarly, the text was silent about the length of time allocated for mediation and the consequences if the effort failed, including whether States Parties could access the International Court of Justice. This omission is curious given the Apartheid Convention of 1976, in Article 12, granted States this right.[75] In comparison, Article 119 of the Rome Statute deals with judicial and treaty interpretation disputes among States Parties, allocating to the Assembly of States Parties the primary role to reach a negotiated outcome before referring the case to the International Court of Justice.[76]

The final specific responsibility of the Standing Committee of States Parties listed in Article 17(5) was their obligation to encourage the universality of the Tribunal. One imagines the presiding officer and alternates of the Standing Committee taking a prominent and public role calling for the prompt ratification of the convention across the world. In contrast, interestingly, the Rome Statute does not explicitly assign to the Assembly of States Parties a role to ensure more States recognise the jurisdiction of the Court. While it is certainly true the Rome Statute contains several inferences about the importance that the 'most serious crimes of concern to the international community as a whole must not go unpunished',[77] the categorical responsibility to seek its universality is absent in Article 112.[78]

---

73 Ibid 46.

74 Ibid 45.

75 Article 12, International Convention on the Suppression and Punishment of the Crime of Apartheid (adopted 30 November 1973, entered into force 18 July 1976) 1015 UNTS 243.

76 Article 119(2), Rome Statute of the International Criminal Court (2002) 2187 UNTS 90.

77 Preamble, Rome Statute of the International Criminal Court (2002) 2187 UNTS 90.

78 ICC-ASP/5/Res.3 Strengthening the International Criminal Court and the Assembly of States Parties (2006).

Article 17(6) conditioned the participation of States Parties in the Standing Committee to whether they had complied with their financial contributions and fulfilled their cooperation obligations with the Tribunal. With a role to provide financial oversight to the Tribunal, Bassiouni clarified that States in arrears would be suspended from participating in the Standing Committee.[79] The duty to cooperate explicitly included financially supporting the Tribunal in accordance with the same income assessment levels as the United Nations. The Standing Committee had under Article 18(4) the responsibility to approve or reject in full the Tribunal's annual budget, which included the necessary funding for the Standing Committee.[80] The task to prepare the budget rested in the Secretariat of the Tribunal as a neutral body.[81] Up until Bassiouni's draft, only the 1937 attempt contained a financial oversight provision for an international criminal court.

The obligation to cooperate with the Tribunal was another requirement for participation in the Standing Committee under Article 17(6). The corresponding general obligation in Article 27(2) noted, 'States Parties shall provide the Court with all means of judicial assistance and cooperation'.[82] Bassiouni did not comment on the function of the Standing Committee to oversee effective cooperation with the Tribunal[83] and a mechanism to determine instances of non-cooperation. However, Article 17(6) did refer to the consequences of non-cooperation insofar 'the Standing Committee may exclude from participation representatives of States Parties…that failed to carry out their obligations under this Convention'.[84] Compared with Part 9 in the Rome Statute, Bassiouni's approach made the consequences of non-cooperation with the court tangible for recalcitrant States, including, presumably, their inability to participate in the election of judges and the Procurator.

Article 17(7) was the most distant from the Assembly of States Parties to the Rome Statute. The corresponding provision for this role appears in Article 8(6) whereas the Procurator or a member State Party to a case may ask the Standing Committee to mediate in the event there was a conflict between such State

---

79 Study on Ways and Means of Insuring the Implementation of International Instruments such as the International Convention on the Suppression and Punishment of the Crime of Apartheid, including the establishment of the International Jurisdiction Envisaged by the Convention, UN Doc. E/CN.4/1426 55.

80 Ibid 30.

81 Ibid 56.

82 Ibid 42.

83 Ibid 62.

84 Ibid 29.

and the court.[85] A possible comparable clause in the Rome Statute might be the power of the United Nations Security Council to defer a situation under Article 16.[86] It is not clear in Bassiouni's analysis the relationship between Article 17(4) and 17(7) in regard to the independence of the Tribunal and Procurator from political interference. One can imagine how the conciliation procedure could have been used by States Parties to escape prosecution. The conciliation process had one year to conclude, pending renewal with the consent from the State Party and the court. In essence, as political negotiations took place under the auspices of the Standing Committee, the case in the court was effectively deferred.

In conclusion, Bassiouni was aware of the originality of the proposal to create a quasi-legislative body to oversee the governance affairs of the Tribunal, and thus drafted Article 17 and its interrelated provisions with ample detail. As explained above, the detailed description of the role and responsibilities of Bassiouni's Standing Committee come remarkably close to those of the Assembly of States Parties to the Rome Statute, and thus, is a significant antecedent for the study of the history of Article 112.

Unanimously accepted by the Ad-Hoc Working Group,[87] the summary records of the meeting indicate little engagement with the substantive provisions of Bassiouni's work.[88] The Commission then decided to seek the views of States Parties to the Apartheid Convention.[89] The draft statute was circulated to States Parties in 1981, but in Bassiouni's words, 'the 'Western block' was not ready to establish an international criminal court only for the prosecution of the crime of apartheid'.[90] Thus, no further United Nations action ensued. Professor Bassiouni, on the other hand, would go on to publish his groundbreaking work in 1987[91] and begin a concerted effort to 'convince scholars and world leaders'[92] about his project.

85 Ibid 23.

86 Article 16, Rome Statute of the International Criminal Court (2002) 2187 UNTS 90.

87 Commission on Human Rights, Thirty-Seventh Session, Summary Record of the 1596th Meeting, 11 of February 1981, UN Doc. E/CN.4/SR.1596 (1981).

88 Ibid para. 50.

89 Commission on Human Rights, Report on the Thirty-Seventh Session (2 February–13 March 1981), UN Doc. E/1981/25 paras. 323–324.

90 Bassiouni, 'Chronology of Efforts to Establish an International Criminal Court' 1169.

91 Bassiouni, M Cherif, A Draft International Criminal Code and Draft Statute for an International Criminal Tribunal (Martinus Nijhoff Publishers 1987) 54.

92 Bassiouni, 'Chronology of Efforts to Establish an International Criminal Court' 1169.

TABLE 2.3 Draft Convention on the Establishment of an International Penal Tribunal (1981)

Functions		Rome Statute (1998)
Governance and Management Oversight	Article 17 – The Standing Committee (1) The Standing Committee shall consist of one representative appointed by each State-Party. (2) The Standing Committee shall elect by majority vote a presiding officer and alternate presiding officer and such other officers as it deems appropriate. (3) The presiding officer shall convene meetings at least twice each year of at least one-week duration each at the seat of the Tribunal and call other meetings at the request of a majority vote of the Committee. (4) The Standing Committee shall have the power to perform the functions expressly assigned to it under this Convention, plus any other functions that it determines appropriate in furtherance of the purposes of the Tribunal that are not inconsistent with this Convention, but in no way shall those functions impair the independence and integrity of the Court as a judicial body. (5) In particular, the Standing Committee may: (a) Offer to mediate disputes between States-Parties relating to the functions of the Tribunal; and(b) Encourage States to accede to the Convention; and, (c) Propose to States-Parties international instruments to enhance the functions of the Tribunal. (6) The Standing Committee may exclude from participation representatives of States-Parties that have failed to provide financial support for the Tribunal as required by this Convention or States-Parties that failed to carry out their obligations under this Convention. (7) Upon request by the Procuracy, or by a party to a case presented for adjudication to a Chamber of the Court, the Standing Committee may be seized with a mediation and conciliation petition. In that case the Standing Committee shall within 60 days decide on granting or denying the petition from which there is no appeal. In the event that the Standing Committee grants the petition, Court proceedings shall be stayed until such time as the Standing Committee concludes its mediation and conciliation efforts, but not for more than one year except by stipulation of the Parties and with the consent of the Court. Article 33 – Reservations (1) States may make any reservations to this Convention but shall not be deemed States-Parties for the purposes of representation in the Standing Committee if the reservation is as to a material aspect of the Tribunal's jurisdiction, competence, and the effects of its judgments.	Articles 112(1), 112(2)(a)–(g), 112(3)(a), 112(4), 112(6), 112(8), 119(2)

TABLE 2.3 Draft Convention on the Establishment of an International Penal Tribunal (1981) (*cont.*)

Functions		**Rome Statute (1998)**
Auxiliary Judicial Instruments Oversight	Article 18 – General Institutional Matters (1) Each of the Organs of the Tribunal shall formulate and publish its own Rules in accordance with the Standards set forth in the Fourth Part to regulate its functions under this Convention, but the Rules of the Procuracy and Secretariat shall be subject to approval by a majority of the Court en banc.	Articles 44(3), 52(3), 79(3), 112(9)
Election of Judges	Article 14 – The Court (1) The Court shall consist of twelve judges, no more than two of whom shall be of the same nationality, who shall be elected by the Standing Committee of States Parties from nominations submitted thereto. (3) Judges shall be elected by secret ballot and the Standing Committee of States Parties shall strive to elect persons representing diverse backgrounds and experience with due regard to representation of the major legal and cultural systems of the world. (4) Elections shall be coordinated by the Secretariat under the supervision of the presiding officer of the Standing Committee of States-Parties and shall be held whenever one or more vacancies exist on the Court.	Articles 36, 37 (1)
Election of the Prosecutor	Article 15 – The Procuracy (2) The Procurator shall be elected by the Standing Committee of States-Parties from a list of at least three nominations submitted by members of the Standing Committee and shall serve for a renewable term of six years, barring resignation or removal by two-thirds vote of the judges of the Court en bane for incompetence, conflict of interest, or manifest disregard of the provisions of this Convention or material Rules of the Tribunal.	Articles 42(4) and 46(2)(b)
Financial Oversight	Article 18 – General Institutional Matters (4) Each of the Organs of the Tribunal shall cooperate with the Secretariat in formulating its budget request and such budget requests shall be presented to the Court en banc for modification or approval, subject to adoption or rejection in their entirety by the Standing Committee. Article 27 – General Principles (6)(a) Provide financial support to the Tribunal in the proportion they would be assessed under contemporaneous General Assembly apportionments established in Article 17 of the Charter of the United Nations, payments being due within six months of the adoption of a budget by the Standing Committee; and (6)(b) Budgetary needs of the Tribunal shall be computed after taking into account income from voluntary contributions and fines collected by the Tribunal.	Article 112(2), 115(a) and 116

TABLE 2.3 Draft Convention on the Establishment of an International Penal Tribunal (1981) (*cont.*)

Functions		**Rome Statute (1998)**
Amendments and Review of the Statute	Article 35 – Amendments (1) This Convention may at any time be amended by a vote of three-fourths of the members of the Standing Committee, subject to ratification of such amendments by the same number of States-Parties represented in the Standing Committee. (2) Upon petition by a State-Party to the Standing Committee the jurisdiction of the Court may be expanded to include additional crimes or classes of offenders and measures in respect of guilt when this is sought by a State capable of exercising compulsory process upon the accused; and this may be on either an ad hoc or permanent basis and shall be embodied in a Supplemental Agreement between the requesting State and the presiding officers of the Standing Committee acting for and on behalf of the said Standing Committee.	Articles 121 and 123

6 1989: On the Way to Rome

As Bassiouni conducted his work, the dormant 1954 Draft Code of Offences, which contained a path for international criminal jurisdiction, was re-circulated for comments by governments in 1978.[93] In 1981, the International Law Commission began considering the matter under Special Rapporteur Doudou Thiam.[94] His 13 reports published between 1982 and 1995[95] effectively re-started the drafting of the Code.[96] However, they also provided the framing to embed the now-famous 1989 General Assembly resolution 44/39, sponsored by Trinidad and Tobago, requesting the International Law Commission to address the establishment of an international criminal court.[97] This particular moment inadvertently inaugurated the epoch of 'rapidly changing times'[98] leading to the Rome Conference in 1998.

Speaking at the fifteenth Special Session of the General Assembly in 1988 dedicated to disarmament,[99] Trinidad and Tobago Prime Minister Arthur

93 UN Doc. A/33/PV.86 (1978) para. 68.
94 UNGA Res 36/106 (1981).
95 Bassiouni, 'The History of the Draft Code of Crimes Against the Peace and Security of Mankind' 260.
96 Bassiouni and Schabas, 66–67.
97 UNGA Res 44/39 (1989).
98 Bassiouni and Schabas, 68.
99 UNGA Res 42/40 (1987).

Napoleon Raymond Robinson proposed to 'examine the existing international criminal codes and, in the long term, instituting an international criminal court'[100] for the issue of illegal drug trafficking. The idea to embed Trinidad and Tobago's request within the drafting of the Code of Crimes emerged during the negotiations at the Sixth Committee in 1989. Aware of the ongoing consideration of drug trafficking as a potential crime in the Code,[101] the delegate from Brazil, with support from France[102] and Iran,[103] urged the Committee to refer Trinidad and Tobago's request to the International Law Commission.[104] Reaching a level of consensus on the issue not seen before, the resolution was adopted without a vote and was referred to the General Assembly.[105] On 4 December 1989, weeks after the fall of the Berlin Wall, resolution 44/39 was adopted without a vote, prompting Guillaume Pambou-Tchivounda from Gabon, Rapporteur of the Sixth Committee, to acknowledge the 'result bears witness to the excellent spirit which perhaps even more than usual has prevailed in the work of the Sixth Committee this year'.[106]

Prime Minister Robinson's speech in 1988 uplifting the need to create an international criminal court was no accident. Robinson was not only a trained lawyer, and long-time member of the Association Internationale de Droit Penal[107] but a confessed supporter of the establishment of an international criminal court and friend of the titans behind the project: former Nuremberg Prosecutor Benjamin Ferencz, and Professor Cherif Bassiouni.[108] Taking inspiration from Vespasian Pella and the 1937 Convention for the Creation of an International Criminal Court, Bassiouni and Robinson thought a similar approach could be applicable to drug trafficking crimes. In developing the proposal made in 1988, both were acutely 'sceptical of the merits of having a permanent international criminal court for one category of crimes, and one

100 Verbatim Record of the Fifth Plenary Meeting of the Fifteenth Special Session of the General Assembly, UN Doc. A/S-15/PV.5 (1988) para. 51.

101 Report of the International Law Commission on the Work of its Forty-First Session, 2 May – 21 July 1989, UN Doc. A/44/10 (1989) 65–66.

102 UN Doc. A/C.6/44/SR.40 (1989) para. 6.

103 Ibid para. 22.

104 UN Doc. A/C.6/44/SR.38 (1989) para. 40.

105 UN Doc. A/C.6/44/SR.46 (1989).

106 Provisional Verbatim Record of the Seventy-Second Meeting of the Forty-Four Session of the General Assembly, UN Doc. A/44/PV.72 (1989) 20.

107 Bassiouni, M Cherif, 'A Glimpse of the Association's History and Some of the Contributions of Its Members' (2015) 86 (3) Revue internationale de droit pénal 818.

108 Schiff, Benjamin, Building the International Criminal Court (Cambridge University Press 2008) 37.

which was not amongst the most serious international crimes'.[109] Nonetheless, they believed 'it was a way of opening the door to the United Nations revisiting the question after the long history of failure'.[110] Their strategy would set in motion the once in a generation process that led to a majority of States finally reaching consensus to establish the International Criminal Court in 1998. In 2014, after the passing of Robinson, the International Criminal Court named the main courtroom in his honour.[111]

7 Conclusion

The impetus to include a specific governance provision in the Rome Statute under Article 112 benefited from a long and rich history including three key moments in 1937, 1943 and 1981. Indeed, each of these instruments creating an international criminal court grappled with the specific role for States Parties to fight impunity within their historical context. The 1937 Convention for the Creation of an International Criminal Court included a meeting of High Contracting Parties in Article 46 to oversee and fund the work of the court while also considering the progressive expansion of jurisdiction over time. Even as this effort failed, the 1943 draft Convention for the Creation of an International Criminal Court confirmed the continuous necessity to adjudicate crimes internationally and a specific role for States. Thus, High Contracting Parties in Article 55 of the 1943 draft Convention were tasked with core responsibilities for the election of judges (Article 10), the election of the Procurator General and deputies (Article 21), cooperation with the court (Article 52), execution of orders of arrest by local police (Article 25 (3)) and financial support for the court (Article 53). Indeed, together with Article 46 of the 1937 Convention for the Creation of an International Criminal Court, these are direct antecedents to the Rome Statute Assembly. Borrowing ideas from 1937, Article 17 in Bassiouni's 1981 draft Convention on the Establishment of an International Penal Tribunal in the context of the 1976 Apartheid Convention is remarkable in its proximity to the Assembly of States Parties to the Rome Statute. Article 17 on the Standing Committee of States Parties outlined key responsibilities across the election of judges and the Procurator, financial oversight, cooperation with the court, settlement of disputes and, most

109 Bassiouni, 'Codification of International Criminal Law' 348, at footnote 104.

110 Ibid.

111 Statement by the International Criminal Court on the passing of Arthur Robinson, 9 April 2014, ICC-CPI-20140409-PR992 (2014).

importantly, 'a quasi-legislative'[112] powers to endow the court with expanding jurisdiction beyond apartheid.

The three key moments described in this chapter developed specific governance responsibilities for States Parties that can now be found in Article 112 in the Rome Statute. The 1937, 1943 and 1981 precedents were important for the road to the Rome Conference as the United Nations General Assembly agreed in 1989 to pursue the project with renewed focus. Benefiting from the wisdom and expertise of Cherif Bassiouni, the period between 1990 and 1998 was plagued with legal controversies, political opposition to international criminal jurisdiction and lack of time across the preparatory process. However, seizing the historical moment, a coalition of States, civil society and academia succeeded in creating a tipping point to finally discuss and adopt a treaty creating the International Criminal Court, including affording a governance role for States Parties.

---

112 Study on Ways and Means of Insuring the Implementation of International Instruments such as the International Convention on the Suppression and Punishment of the Crime of Apartheid, including the establishment of the International Jurisdiction Envisaged by the Convention, UN Doc. E/CN.4/1426 46.

CHAPTER 3

The Emergence of the Assembly of States Parties to the Rome Statute (1990–1998)

1 Introduction

Only after a dedicated working group within the International Law Commission was formed in 1990[1] to respond to Trinidad and Tobago's sponsored resolution 44/39,[2] concerns about the institutional design of the court began to emerge.[3] Before this time, between 1983 and 1994, Thiam's reports, the International Law Commission as a whole, and governments did not place emphasis on the governance and oversight of the future court. It was only during negotiations between 1994 and 1998 that the project for the establishment of an international criminal court, and how it should be governed by States Parties, awakened in the United Nations. It is in this period the Assembly of States Parties to the Rome Statute was finally proposed in the context of the last session of the 1998 Preparatory Committee. Thus, this chapter first discusses the proposals put forward by the International Law Commission and in particular the draft statute of 1994. Secondly, the chapter describes the negotiations during the Ad Hoc and Preparatory Committee's sessions between 1995 and 1998 with an emphasis on the last meeting in March–April 1998 when the provision about the Assembly of States Parties finally emerged.

2 1990–1994: The Work of the International Law Commission

Based on Trinidad and Tobago's sponsored resolution 44/39,[4] the International Law Commission focused on the question of an international criminal court between 1990 and 1994. In particular, Doudou Thiam, the Special

1 Report of the International Law Commission on the Work of its Forty-Second Session, 1 May – 20 July 1990, UN Doc. A/45/10 (1990) 8.

2 UNGA Res 44/39.

3 Report of the International Law Commission on the Work of its Forty-Second Session, 1 May – 20 July 1990, UN Doc. A/45/10 23.

4 UNGA Res 44/39.

© EZEQUIEL JIMÉNEZ MARTINEZ, 2026 | DOI:10.1163/9789004749979_004

Rapporteur for the topic 'Draft Code of Crimes Against the Peace and Security of Mankind', focused his yearly reports on options available to States.[5] The task to develop a draft statute, however, was expertly executed by a smaller working group within the framework of the Draft Code of Crimes in 1992, 1993 and most importantly in 1994.[6] Under the leadership of James Crawford,[7] the working group developed a draft statute for an international criminal court in 1993, which was discussed by the General Assembly and obtained political support to submit a final draft for consideration in 1994.[8] To fully understand the emergence of the Assembly of States Parties to the Rome Statute, the 1993 and 1994 draft statutes provide an insight into the complex governance and oversight challenges that determined the institutional design of the proposed court. They also show States' concerns over the role and responsibility of the United Nations and the need to establish an impartial court devoid from real-politik and meddling. In this context, McCormack and Simpson writing at the time and offering professional advice to the Australian government, argued that institution-building had to correspond with a 'commitment to legality and the rule of law in the face of political pressure'.[9] The debates of the International Law Commission during this period build on the language and drafting choices made in 1937, 1943, and 1981, thus, revealing a continuum in the question how best to provide effective governance and oversight to an international criminal court.

---

5 Eighth Report on the Draft Code of Crimes Against the Peace and Security of Mankind, by Mr Doudou Thiam, Special Rapporteur, UN Doc. A/CN.4/430 and Add.1 (1990); Ninth report on the draft Code of Crimes against the Peace and Security of Mankind, by Mr. Doudou Thiam, Special Rapporteur, UN Doc. A/CN.4/435 and Add.l (1991); Tenth Report on the Draft Code of Crimes Against the Peace and Security of Mankind, by Mr. Doudou Thiam, Special Rapporteur, UN Doc. A/CN.4/442 (1992); Eleventh Report on the Draft Code of Crimes Against the Peace and Security of Mankind, by Mr. Doudou Thiam, Special Rapporteur. UN Doc. A/CN.4/449 and Corr.1 (1993).

6 Report of the International Law Commission on the Work of its Forty-Fourth Session, 4 May – 24 July 1992, UN Doc. A/47/10 (1992); Report of the International Law Commission on the Work of its Forty-Fifth Session, 3 May – 23 July 1993, UN Doc. A/48/10 (1993); Report of the International Law Commission on the Work of its Forty-Sixth Session, 2 May – 22 July 1994, UN Doc. A/49/10 (1994).

7 Crawford, James, 'The Drafting of the Rome Statute' in Sands, Philippe (ed), From Nuremberg to The Hague: The Future of International Criminal Justice (Cambridge University Press 2003) 129; Crawford, James, 'A Conversation with Emeritus Professor Judge James Richard Crawford Part 1: Early Life and Career' (2018) Eminent Scholars Archive, the Squire Law Library and the Faculty of Law 4.

8 UNGA Res 48/31 (1993).

9 McCormack, Timothy LH and Simpson, Gerry J, 'A New International Criminal Law Regime?' (1995) 42 (2) Netherlands International Law Review 206.

Thiam's eleventh report for the 45th session of the International Law Commission in 1993 was his lengthiest on the matter and included a draft statute. Overall, Thiam's draft considered necessary for the court to be a United Nations organ, without full-time judges, and with concurrent jurisdiction with States.[10] Thiam's choice to embed the court within the United Nations architecture meant there was no discussion about an express governance and oversight role for States.[11] It is notable, however, that Thiam delivered his drafting choices even after relying in part on Bassiouni's work, disregarding the role assigned to the Standing Committee of States Parties.[12]

Upon receiving the report, the members of the Commission disagreed with the direction of travel presented by Thiam and reaffirmed the need to establish the court by a 'multilateral convention'.[13] In fact, only discussing Thiam's report briefly,[14] the Commission decided to establish a working group to propose a consolidated text for the General Assembly.[15] Chaired by Abdul Koroma, and with the active participation of Professor James Crawford,[16] the working group held 22 meetings in the span of one month.[17] To aid their work, the Secretariat made available past statutes, which included Bassiouni's work.[18] The draft statute produced by the working group consisted of 67 articles divided in seven parts covering comprehensively provisions dealing with the establishment of the court, jurisdiction, investigation, prosecution, trial, appeals, cooperation, and enforcement.[19] Of these, Part 1 dealing with the establishment and composition of the tribunal and Part 6 on international cooperation and judicial assistance are relevant to the study of the Assembly of States Parties to the Rome Statute.

In summary, Article 2 in Part 1 covered the relationship between the court and the United Nations with the working group arguing for the first time the need of a 'separate treaty providing for the election of judges by the General

10 Eleventh Report on the Draft Code of Crimes Against the Peace and Security of Mankind, by Mr. Doudou Thiam, Special Rapporteur. UN Doc. A/CN.4/449 and Corr.1.

11 Schabas, The International Criminal Court: A Commentary on the Rome Statute 16.

12 Eleventh Report on the Draft Code of Crimes Against the Peace and Security of Mankind, by Mr. Doudou Thiam, Special Rapporteur. UN Doc. A/CN.4/449 and Corr.1 115.

13 Report of the International Law Commission on the Work of its Forty-Fifth Session, 3 May – 23 July 1993, UN Doc. A/48/10 16.

14 Schabas, The International Criminal Court: A Commentary on the Rome Statute 16.

15 Report of the International Law Commission on the Work of its Forty-Fifth Session, 3 May – 23 July 1993, UN Doc. A/48/10 20.

16 Ibid 10.

17 Ibid 100.

18 Ibid.

19 Ibid.

Assembly, or another organ'.[20] The conclusion pointed towards the need to create a political forum where States, within or outside the membership structure of the United Nations, could make governance and oversight decisions. This became evident when analysing the framework proposed for the election of judges and the Prosecutor. In both cases, the working group assigned the responsibility to 'States Parties to the statute' to nominate and elect by majority vote the 18 judges, the Prosecutor, and a Deputy.[21] The working group was unconvinced to require all members of the United Nations to have authority over institutional aspects of the court, yet no single provision on governance by States Parties appeared in the draft. The absence of such framework becomes apparent also when reading Article 60 on judicial cooperation with the court (See Table 3.2).

The briefest provision in Part 6 covering international judicial cooperation and assistance, Article 60 called for a meeting of States Parties to 'consult promptly, at the request of any one of them, concerning the application or the carrying out of the provisions on international cooperation and judicial assistance, either generally or in relation to a particular case'.[22] In other words, Article 60 set out a process to consider non-cooperation by States Parties with the court. For the experts, Article 60 was required to 'avoid undue delays in the functioning of the Tribunal which may require the cooperation of a number of States to effectively perform its functions'.[23] A number of practical and procedural questions arise when considering the absence of a permanent forum for States Parties to consider instances of non-cooperation. The lack of an effective oversight body to manage this political process surely would have curtailed the rationale to 'avoid undue delays' in the work of the court. Article 60 revealed that even if the working group considered establishing the court via a treaty, their analysis of the required governance arrangements was mostly wanting. The usual lack of time for the full Commission to discuss and adopt each article might be a plausible explanation for the contradictions found in the draft statute in relation to the role and responsibilities of States Parties.[24]

The Sixth Committee's reception of the draft statute was positive and commended the International Law Commission for moving from 'the realm of

20 Ibid 101–102.

21 Ibid 103–104.

22 Ibid 128.

23 Ibid.

24 Crawford, James, 'The ILC's Draft Statute for an International Criminal Tribunal' (1994) 88 (1) American Journal of International Law 142.

academic debate to concrete drafting'.[25] However, there was no in-depth discussion on required governance structures to a treaty. In view of the progress achieved, the General Assembly mandated the International Law Commission to 'continue its work as a matter of priority' to present a draft statute in 1994.[26]

2.1 *The International Law Commission 1994 Draft Statute*

The 1994 draft statute was considerably less ambitious than in 1993.[27] As the discussions progressed, it became evident concerns about the independence of the court, the jurisdictional architecture and the perceived encroachment on State sovereignty required changes reflecting larger control by the Security Council over the court.[28] In essence, the 1994 statute created a permanent but intermittent court via a multilateral treaty but without compulsory jurisdiction of crimes 'under general international law', except for the crime of genocide, and on active on matters referred by the Security Council. It applied a doctrine of maximum consent requiring States Parties to accept the jurisdiction of the court. All of which was not applicable to the Security Council if it acted under Chapter VII. Furthermore, no prosecutions were to be advanced if the Council was seized with the matter.[29] As James Crawford, chairman of the 1994 International Law Commission working group[30] put it, negotiations 'needed to be tempered by a strong sense of practicality'.[31] For Sadat, the Commission deliberately changed posture from 1993 due to the 'politics involved'.[32] For Bassiouni and Schabas, the choices made by the Commission to 'placate political opposition'[33] were reminiscent of the 1953 diluted statute.

---

25 Topical Summary of the Discussion held in the Sixth Committee of the General Assembly during its Forty-Eight Session, prepared by the Secretariat, UN Doc. A/CN.4/L.457 (1994) 6.

26 UNGA Res 48/31.

27 Bassiouni and Schabas, 70 at footnote 105.

28 Schabas, The International Criminal Court: A Commentary on the Rome Statute 18.

29 Report of the International Law Commission on the Work of its Forty-Sixth Session, 2 May – 22 July 1994, UN Doc. A/49/10; Berg, Bradley E, 'The 1994 ILC Draft Statute for an International Criminal Court: A Principled Appraisal of Jurisdictional Structure' (1996) 28 Case Western Reserve Journal of International Law 221.

30 Crawford, James, 'The ILC Adopts a Statute for an International Criminal Court' (1995) 89 (2) American Journal of International Law 390.

31 Crawford, James, 'The Work of the International Law Commission' in Cassese, Antonio, Gaeta, Paola and Jones, John RWD (eds), The Rome Statute of the International Criminal Court: A Commentary, vol 1 (2002) 27.

32 Sadat, 40.

33 Bassiouni and Schabas, 70 at footnote 105.

While clauses on applicable law, jurisdiction and elements of cooperation changed from 1993 to 1994, the International Law Commission developed new language about the 'role of States Parties in greater detail in the statute'.[34] The Commission agreed the court should be established by a treaty, in close relationship with the United Nations and introduced language illustrating the role of States Parties to such convention.[35] The first provision referring to the collective of States Parties was the preamble. An innovation from previous drafts, the inclusion of the preamble set out a locus of power for States Parties to govern the proposed court.[36] The subsequent provisions in Part 1 illustrated this point.

Articles 2 and 3 demanded 'States Parties to the Statute'[37] to approve the relationship agreement with the United Nations and the host State as negotiated by the President of the Court.[38] For the working group, such agreement, following the preamble, required the collective of States Parties to enter them as they assumed 'responsibility for the operation'[39] of the court. Acting in assembly, States Parties were required to take joint action as the governance body of the court. In this sense, logically, the preamble and Articles 2 and 3 made the creation of an assembly of States Parties capable of discussing and providing consent to these agreements indispensable. However, the Commission chose not to draft a provision to this effect opting to leave governance clauses 'as part of the process of adoption of the statute'.[40] This drafting choice explains the absence of the precedent of Article 112 on the Assembly of States Parties to the Rome Statute in 1994. An inapt choice that made the reading of the 1994 draft cumbersome from an institutional logic.

To bridge the governance gaps, as illustrated above, the Commission submitted a brief appendix to the General Assembly, for study by the Sixth Committee, outlining 'a number of matters which it will be necessary to resolve in

34 Report of the International Law Commission on the Work of its Forty-Sixth Session, 2 May – 22 July 1994, UN Doc. A/49/10 22.

35 Crawford, 'The ILC Adopts a Statute for an International Criminal Court' 416.

36 Klabbers, Jan, 'Treaties and Their Preambles' in Kritsiotis, Dino and Bowman, Michael J. (eds), Conceptual and Contextual Perspectives on the Modern Law of Treaties (Cambridge University Press 2018) 172.

37 Report of the International Law Commission on the Work of its Forty-Sixth Session, 2 May – 22 July 1994, UN Doc. A/49/10 28.

38 Ibid 27–28.

39 Ibid 28.

40 Ibid.

concluding such a treaty'.[41] Among the priorities listed was the crux of the governance responsibilities of the collective of States Parties to the statute:

> (b) Administration: The administration of the court as an entity is entrusted to the Presidency (see art. 8). However, States Parties will need to meet from time to time to deal with such matters as the finances and administration of the court, and to consider periodic reports from the court, etc. The means by which States Parties will act together will need to be established.[42]

The limits of the term 'administration' are evident when recalling the responsibilities assigned to States Parties in the draft statute; however, it does consider the substantive nature of their role noting States Parties needed to 'act together' to give effect to innate functions of the proposed court. In other words, it is not administrative matters what occupied States Parties but governance duties to render the court operational.

The International Law Commission adopted the 1994 draft and recommended to the General Assembly 'that it convene an international conference of plenipotentiaries to study the draft statute and to conclude a convention on the establishment of an international criminal court'.[43] The statements of most delegations in the Sixth Committee signalled agreement to a permanent court created by a treaty between States Parties and in relationship with the United Nations.[44] However, after the intervention of the United States, the Committee ultimately decided to reject the International Law Commission's recommendation to organize a diplomatic conference. Instead, it proposed an ad hoc committee 'to gain a full understanding of the draft provisions and their ramifications'.[45] Momentum towards an international criminal court was further energised as the Security Council finalized the creation of the International Tribunal for Rwanda.[46] Notably, resolution 49/53 of the General Assembly also requested the Secretary General to provide 'estimates of the staffing, structure and costs of the establishment and operation of an inter-

41 Ibid 69.

42 Ibid.

43 Ibid.

44 Topical Summary of the Discussion Held in the Sixth Committee of the General Assembly During its Forty-ninth Session Prepared by the Secretariat, Addendum, UN Doc. A/CN.4/464/Add.1 (1995) 10.

45 Ibid 8.

46 Crawford, 'The ILC Adopts a Statute for an International Criminal Court' 406.

national criminal court'.[47] While the General Assembly agreed with the Sixth Committee, as Schabas argued, 'it would take some time for those involved in promoting the project to realize just to what extent they were pushing on an open door'.[48]

3 1995: The Sessions of the Ad Hoc Committee on the Establishment of an International Criminal Court

The Ad Hoc Committee on the Establishment of an International Criminal Court met at the United Nations Headquarters from 3 to 13 April and from 14 to 25 August 1995.[49] The Committee was open to all United Nations members States, specialized agencies and accredited civil society.[50] An examination of the Committee's membership reveals that a mere 38% of member States participated in proceedings.[51] Out of the 185 United Nations membership in 1995,[52] only 75 sent a delegate, led primarily by the group of Western European and Other States. The membership of the Ad Hoc Committee, and that of subsequent working groups, is important to note because key delegates present in 1995 will go on to play a critical role in Rome in 1998 and in the institutional life of the International Criminal Court, and the Assembly of States Parties. For example, Professor Cherif Bassiouni, advising Egypt, Silvia Fernández de Gurmendi, from Argentina, and Sankurathripati Rama Rao from India, played a significant role in the Ad Hoc Committee and in Rome.[53] Indeed, as Benedetti, Bonneau and Washburn have established, 'at least 33 delegates from the Ad Hoc Committee where in Rome'.[54] For them, the continuity of key delegates[55] throughout the negotiations 'were an important reason for the

47 UNGA Res 49/53 (1994).

48 Schabas, The International Criminal Court: A Commentary on the Rome Statute 19.

49 Report of the Ad Hoc Committee on the Establishment of an International Criminal Court, UN Doc. A/50/22 (1995).

50 Benedetti, Fanny, Bonneau, Karine and Washburn, John, Negotiating the International Criminal Court: New York to Rome, 1994–1998 (Martinus Nijhoff Publishers 2014) 22.

51 Membership of the Ad Hoc Committee on the Establishment of an International Criminal Court, UN Doc. A/AC.244/INF/2 (1995).

52 United Nations, 'Growth in United Nations Membership' (United Nations, 2022) <https://www.un.org/en/about-us/growth-in-un-membership> accessed January 28, (2022).

53 Report of the Ad Hoc Committee on the Establishment of an International Criminal Court, UN Doc. A/50/22 (1995).

54 Benedetti, Bonneau and Washburn, 27.

55 Apart from Bassiouni, Fernández de Gurmendi and Rao, several other delegates present at the 1995 Ad Hoc Committee played a critical role during the negotiations and after,

speed, the psychological and emotional vigour and for the success in finding compromises'.[56] The chairmanship by Adriaan Bos, from the Netherlands, in 1995 and in the 1996–1998 Preparatory Committee should also be 'counted as part of the unusually good luck the negotiations enjoyed'.[57]

The work of the Committee did not commence ab initio. Apart from the International Law Commission's 1994 draft, it also considered a summary of the deliberations of the Sixth Committee, comments by governments, a report by the Secretary General on provisional estimates for the operations of the proposed court,[58] and observations by civil society.[59] These documents were the source to 'review the major substantive and administrative issues'.[60] As McCormack and Simpson argued at the time, the mandate of the Ad Hoc Committee did not include negotiating a new statute.[61] Rather, it was mandated to surface all key considerations that a future diplomatic conference would be tasked on negotiating.

In relation to the role of States Parties to the proposed court created by a multilateral treaty, the Committee had before it comments from Belarus, Venezuela, and the United States.[62] In particular, the United States argued

---

including Rolf Einar Fife (Norway), Mauro Politi (Italy), Herman von Hebel (Netherlands), Adriaan Bos (Netherlands), Elizabeth Wilmshurst (United Kingdom) and David Scheffer (United States).

56 Benedetti, Bonneau and Washburn, 27.

57 Ibid 18–19.

58 Report of the Ad Hoc Committee on the Establishment of an International Criminal Court, UN Doc. A/50/22 (1995) 1–2.

59 International Commission of Jurists, The International Criminal Court: Third ICJ Position Paper (1995) 11; Association Internationale de Droit Pénal, Istituto Superiore Internazionale di Scienze Criminali and Max Planck Institute for Foreign and International Criminal Law, Draft Statute for an International Criminal Court (Siracusa Draft) (1995) 1; Armstead, J Holmes, Jr., 'The International Criminal Court: History, Development and Status' (1997) 38 (3) Santa Clara Law Review 745.

60 UNGA Res 49/53.

61 McCormack and Simpson, 205.

62 Comments Received Pursuant to paragraph 4 of General Assembly Resolution 49/53 on the Establishment of an International Criminal Court, Report of the Secretary-General, UN Doc. A/AC.244/1 (1995); Comments Received Pursuant to paragraph 4 of General Assembly Resolution 49/53 on the Establishment of an International Criminal Court, Report of the Secretary-General, UN Doc. A/AC.244/1/Add.1 (1995); Comments Received Pursuant to paragraph 4 of General Assembly Resolution 49/53 on the Establishment of an International Criminal Court, Report of the Secretary-General, UN Doc. A/AC.244/1/Add.2 (1995); Comments Received Pursuant to paragraph 4 of General Assembly Resolution 49/53 on the Establishment of an International Criminal Court, Report of the Secretary-General, UN Doc. A/AC.244/1/Add.3 (1995); Comments Received Pursuant to paragraph 4 of General Assembly Resolution 49/53 on the Establishment of an Inter-

financial and oversight matters were 'of the highest priority'.[63] In doing so, their commentary advanced that:

> States Parties should also have a residual power, in exceptional circumstances, to make or overturn management decisions. While it is not desirable for States to interfere in the operations of the court or its independence as a judicial body, in case of serious need there should be some mechanism other than amendment of the statute for States Parties to take necessary measures as may be required. Our comments above are intended to highlight our major conceptual concerns.[64]

The concern voiced by the United States describing an all-encompassing role for States Parties warranted considerable debate, however, the opportunity to create the Assembly of States Parties, even after such acute commentary, would not materialize during the deliberations of the Ad Hoc Committee.[65] Instead, the Committee only briefly discussed an accessory role for States Parties in the 'budget and administration'[66] of the court. States questioned whether the United Nations or 'States Parties to the statute'[67] had to financially support the new institution. In neither possibility; however, the role of an assembly of States Parties was discussed. Indeed, the only reference assuming a responsibility for all States Parties was in relation to a 'possibility of establishing a supervisory mechanism to oversee the administration of the court'.[68]

The absence of any substantive discussion in the Ad Hoc Committee about the role of States Parties to a multilateral treaty is important for the study of

---

national Criminal Court, Report of the Secretary-General, UN Doc. A/AC.244/1/Add.4 (1995).

63 Comments Received Pursuant to paragraph 4 of General Assembly Resolution 49/53 on the Establishment of an International Criminal Court, Report of the Secretary-General, UN Doc. A/AC.244/1/Add.2 23.

64 Ibid 25. See also: Leigh, Monroe, 'Evaluating Present Options for an International Criminal Court' (1995) 149 Military Law Review 113.

65 Report of the Ad Hoc Committee on the Establishment of an International Criminal Court, UN Doc. A/50/22 1995; Summary of the Proceedings of the Ad Hoc Committee During the Period 3–13 April 1995, UN Doc. A/AC.244/2 (1995); Suikkari, Satu, 'Debate in the United Nations on the International Law Commission's Draft Statute for an International Criminal Court' (1995) 64 (2) Nordic Journal of International Law.

66 Report of the Ad Hoc Committee on the Establishment of an International Criminal Court, UN Doc. A/50/22 (1995) 45.

67 Ibid.

68 Ibid 46.

the Assembly of States Parties to the Rome Statute because it confirms States seldom considered the oversight and governance arrangements needed for the practical functioning of a court. With notable exceptions of proposals introduced in 1937, 1943, and 1981, contemporary approaches to statutes based on multilateral treaties have not considered the oversight role of States Parties. The absence of such debate in 1995 is equally remarkable given the presence of Cherif Bassiouni in the Ad Hoc Committee.

The Committee report suggested to the Sixth Committee to combine 'further discussions with the drafting of texts'[69] in preparation for a diplomatic conference. The Sixth Committee agreed with the recommendation.[70] However, Venezuela,[71] the United States,[72] and Sri Lanka asked that future discussions finally focus on how 'States Parties would participate in the administration of the treaty and of the court'.[73] Welcoming the report,[74] the General Assembly agreed to establish a Preparatory Committee to draft a consensus statute for consideration at a diplomatic conference.[75]

4 1996: The First and Second Sessions of the Preparatory Committee on the Establishment of an International Criminal Court

The 1996 Preparatory Committee, benefiting from the educational value of the Ad Hoc experience, moved from general discussion to 'the text itself'.[76] Led mostly by the same Bureau, under the chairmanship of Bos, the Committee met from 25 March to 12 April 1996 and from 12 to 30 August 1996 in New York.[77] Key people relevant for the study of the Assembly of States Parties to the Rome Statute participated in supporting functions or as delegates. For example, Renan Villacis, Director of the Secretariat of the Assembly of States

69 Ibid 49.

70 Report of the Sixth Committee, Establishment of an International Criminal Court, UN Doc. A/50/639 (1995).

71 UN Doc. A/C.6/50/SR.26 (1995) 4.

72 UN Doc. A/C.6/50/SR.27 (1995) 7.

73 UN Doc. A/C.6/50/SR.30 (1995) 3.

74 UN Doc. A/50/PV.87 (1995).

75 UNGA Res 50/46 (1995).

76 Sadat, 41.

77 Report of the Preparatory Committee on the Establishment of an International Criminal Court, Volume 1, Proceedings of the Preparatory Committee during March-April and August 1996, UN Doc. A/51/22 (1996) 1.

Parties until 2024, acted as an assistant secretary to the Committee.[78] Christian Wenaweser (Liechtenstein), later President of the Assembly from 2008 to 2011,[79] and Sankurathripati Rama Rao coordinator of Part 11 in Rome continued from 1995. Out of the 185 United Nations membership in 1996,[80] 85 delegations (46%) participated, mostly from the Western and Other States group.[81] For delegates from the Least Developed Countries, working exclusively in English was a barrier to participation.[82] As Hall argued, the absence of universality and adequate support for full participation was a disappointing aspect of the preparatory process.[83] In addition, during the sessions of the Committee two relevant actors with tangible impact in the Rome Conference emerged. The first actor was the Like-Minded group of States under the auspices of New Zealand.[84] This group initially comprised Canada, South Africa, Senegal, Germany, Argentina, the Netherlands and Australia.[85] As Bos explained, the group was initially established to assist him 'in organizing and completing the work in the most positive and efficient way',[86] but they would continue to influence negotiations all the way to Rome. The second

78 Ibid.

79 Report of the Sixth Session of the Assembly of States Parties to the Rome Statute of the International Criminal Court, New York, 30 November–14 December, Volume I, ICC-ASP /6/20 (2007) 5.

80 United Nations, 'Growth in United Nations Membership' (United Nations, 2022) <https://www.un.org/en/about-us/growth-in-un-membership> accessed January 28, (2022).

81 Preparatory Committee on the Establishment of an International Criminal Court, List of Delegations, 25 March – 12 April 1996, UN Doc. A/AC.249/INF/1, A/AC.249/INF/1/Add.1, A/AC.249/INF/1/Add.2 (1996); Preparatory Committee on the Establishment of an International Criminal Court, List of Delegations, 12–30 August 1996, UN Doc. A/AC.249/INF/2 and A/AC.249/INF/2/Add.1 (1996).

82 Benedetti, Fanny and Washburn, John L, 'Drafting the International Criminal Court Treaty: Two Years to Rome and an Afterword on the Rome Diplomatic Conference' (1999) 5 (1) Global Governance 15.

83 Hall, Christopher Keith, 'The First Two Sessions of the UN Preparatory Committee on the Establishment of an International Criminal Court' (1997) 91 (1) American Journal of International Law 186–187.

84 Benedetti, Bonneau and Washburn, 79;Eikel, Markus, "Germany's Global Responsibility' and the Creation of the International Criminal Court, 1993–1998' (2018) 16 (3) Journal of International Criminal Justice 551.

85 Glasius, Marlies, The International Criminal Court: A Global Civil Society Achievement (Routledge 2006) 21.

86 Bos, Adriaan, 'From the International Law Commission to the Rome Conference (1994–1998)' in Cassese, Antonio and others (eds), The Rome Statute of the International Criminal Court: A Commentary, vol 1 (Oxford University Press 2002) 50–51.

relevant actor was the Coalition for the International Court, made of 46 organizations in 1996,[87] which effectively influenced negotiations.[88]

In this context, specific proposals to locate a governance function for States Parties in the statute emerged timidly during the sessions of the Committee in 1996 (See Table 3.1). Agreeing in August 1996 the establishment of a permanent court via a multilateral treaty,[89] States in the Committee considered useful a 'general assembly of the States Parties could be held annually to consider administrative and financial issues and approve the budget'.[90] The issues put forward by States included a role in limiting the powers of the Presidency,[91] retaining control and approval over the Rules of the Court,[92] utilizing the meeting of States Parties to expand the jurisdiction of the court over time,[93] and a role by States Parties to vet candidacies to the court.[94] While these proposals envisioned a role for the collective of States Parties in a piecemeal fashion, a French working paper in August 1996[95] and a

---

87 Pace, William R and Schense, Jennifer, 'The Role of Non-Governmental Organizations' in Cassese, Antonio, Gaeta, Paola and Jones, John RWD (eds) Cassese, Antonio and others (eds), The Rome Statute of the International Criminal Court: A Commentary, vol 1 (Oxford University Press 2002) 115.

88 Bos, Adriaan, 'The Experience of the Preparatory Committee' in Mauro Politi and Nesi, Giuseppe (eds), The Rome Statute of the International Criminal Court: a Challenge to Impunity (Routledge 2001) 27.

89 Report of the Preparatory Committee on the Establishment of an International Criminal Court, Volume 1, Proceedings of the Preparatory Committee during March-April and August 1996, UN Doc. A/51/22 8.

90 Ibid 10.

91 Ibid 13; Proposals on the Organization of the Court, Working Paper Submitted by Japan, UN Doc. A/AC.249/L.8 (1996).

92 Report of the Preparatory Committee on the Establishment of an International Criminal Court, Volume 1, Proceedings of the Preparatory Committee during March-April and August 1996, UN Doc. A/51/22 15; Proposal Submitted by Finland for Articles 6, 12 And 19, UN Doc. A/AC.249/WP.30 (1996); Draft Set of Rules of Procedure and Evidence for the International Criminal Court, Working Paper Submitted by Australia and the Netherlands, UN Doc. A/AC.249/L.2 (1996).

93 Report of the Preparatory Committee on the Establishment of an International Criminal Court, Volume 1, Proceedings of the Preparatory Committee during March-April and August 1996, UN Doc. A/51/22 27; Note to the Bureau from the Delegations of Argentina, Austria, Belgium, Czech Republic, Denmark, Finland, Iceland, Norway, Poland, Portugal, Slovenia, South Africa, Sweden and Trinidad and Tobago, Review Clause: Adding of Crimes to the Jurisdiction of the Court, available at: <https://www.legal-tools.org/doc/83ee13/> (1996).

94 Proposal Submitted by Algeria, Egypt, Jordan, Kuwait, the Libyan Arab Jamahiriya and Qatar on the Organization of the Court, UN Doc. A/AC.249/WP.43 (1996) 2.

95 Draft Statute of the International Criminal Court, Working Paper Submitted by France, UN Doc. A/AC.249/L.3 (1996).

draft statute presented by civil society[96] introduced a complete provision creating an assembly of States Parties.

As Bos argued, the French working paper was the 'single place where a reference was made to an Assembly of States Parties'[97] during the negotiations in August 1996. The French draft statute contained 153 articles, taking the 1994 International Law Commission draft as a starting point, but reliant on civil law principles.[98] It assumed the court as a specialized agency of the United Nations thus requiring a governing body to enter into such relationship agreement.[99] Article 2, in Part 1 on the establishment of the court, described the role and responsibility of the 'General Assembly States Parties'.[100] However, the French proposal was not the only paper in front of the Committee with a detailed provision for States Parties' governance. A second submission by civil society and legal experts under the title of 'Updated Siracusa Draft'[101] also considered how States Parties to the court would enable its mandate. The Updated Siracusa Draft was the result of an intersessional meeting at the International Institute of Higher Studies in Criminal Sciences in Siracuse, Italy, under the leadership of Bassiouni.[102] Indeed, subsequent intersessional meetings in Siracuse between 1995 and 1998 would prove decisive to build consensus and forge creative solutions on the International Criminal Court statute.[103]

One of the main differences between the drafts was the Siracusa version assumed a court created by a multilateral treaty and the French paper a court as a specialized agency of the United Nations. However, both submissions created a governance and oversight role for the collective of States Parties responsible for interrelated policy and administrative duties. Article C describing the 'Standing Committee of States Parties' in the Updated Siracusa Draft was identical to the governing body proposed by Bassiouni and

96 Association Internationale de Droit Pénal and others, Draft Statute for an International Criminal Court (Updated Siracusa Draft) (1996).

97 Bos, 'Assembly of States Parties' (2002) 300.

98 Hall, 'The First Two Sessions of the UN Preparatory Committee on the Establishment of an International Criminal Court' 183.

99 Draft Statute of the International Criminal Court, Working Paper Submitted by France, UN Doc. A/AC.249/L.3 23.

100 Ibid.

101 Association Internationale de Droit Pénal and others, 13.

102 Ibid v.

103 Bassiouni, M Cherif, 'Observations Concerning the 1997–98 Preparatory Committee's Work' (1996) 25 Denver Journal of International Law & Policy 405 at footnote 33.

Derby in the context of the Apartheid Convention in 1981.[104] Article 2 in the French draft, on the other hand, extended a role for States Parties in decision–making, elections, loss of office, budgetary concerns, settlement of disputes, the approval of the relationship agreement with the United Nations and the removal of voting rights for States in arrears.[105]

Neither of these proposals submitted to the Preparatory Committee in 1996 attracted substantive discussion among delegations.[106] In fact, neither Bassiouni's presence in the Bureau[107] nor the extensive suggestions made by France were sufficient to make a specific note in the report of the Committee about the role of the collective of States Parties. Only once, and in passing, the report referred to a suggestion that 'a general assembly of the States Parties could be held annually to consider administrative and financial issues and approve the budget'.[108] In this context, Bassiouni argued in 1997 that from all topics pending involving substantial technical discussions, the question of the role and responsibilities of the of States Parties was 'probably the most important'.[109]

The report to the Sixth Committee suggested a work schedule of the Preparatory Committee over nine weeks up to April 1998 by focusing, beyond legal issues, on the 'establishment and relationship with the United Nations and final clauses and financial matters';[110] all relevant matters for the creation of the Assembly of States Parties to the Rome Statute. The Sixth Committee adopted by consensus a resolution in line with the Preparatory Committee report.[111] At its 88th plenary meeting in December 1996, during the same session inaugurating Kofi Annan as the seventh Secretary General of the United

---

104 Study on Ways and Means of Insuring the Implementation of International Instruments such as the International Convention on the Suppression and Punishment of the Crime of Apartheid, including the establishment of the International Jurisdiction Envisaged by the Convention, UN Doc. E/CN.4/1426 29.

105 Draft Statute of the International Criminal Court, Working Paper Submitted by France, UN Doc. A/AC.249/L. 3.

106 Benedetti and Washburn, 13.

107 Bassiouni, 'Observations Concerning the 1997–98 Preparatory Committee's Work' 416.

108 Report of the Preparatory Committee on the Establishment of an International Criminal Court, Volume 1, Proceedings of the Preparatory Committee during March-April and August 1996, UN Doc. A/51/22 10.

109 Bassiouni, 'Observations Concerning the 1997–98 Preparatory Committee's Work' 406.

110 Report of the Preparatory Committee on the Establishment of an International Criminal Court, Volume 1, Proceedings of the Preparatory Committee during March-April and August 1996, UN Doc. A/51/22 76.

111 Report of the Sixth Committee, Establishment of an International Criminal Court, UN Doc. A/51/627 (1996) 1.

TABLE 3.1 Preparatory Committee (1996)

Function	Proposals	Rome Statute (1998)
Governance and Management Oversight	France – Article 2 General Assembly of the States Parties (1) A General Assembly of the States Parties to this Statute ("the States Parties") is hereby established. Each State Party shall have a representative on the General Assembly. (2) The General Assembly of the States Parties shall elect a President and a Vice-President, for one year, as well as any other official it deems necessary. (3) The General Assembly of the States Parties shall hold annual sessions and, when circumstances so require, special sessions. The latter shall be convened by the President on his motion or at the request of a majority of the members. (4) The General Assembly of the States Parties shall be competent: (a) To perform the functions assigned to it under this Statute. (b) To rule on any budget questions. (c) To increase, if necessary, the number of judges or members of the Procuracy or the Registry, for the period that it shall determine. (5) The General Assembly of the States Parties may prevent the representative of a State Party from participating in its deliberations when the State Party: (a) Is in arrears in the payment of its contribution to the costs of the Court and the amount of its arrears is the same as or more than the contribution payable for the past two years; however, the General Assembly of the States Parties may in that event, authorize participation in its deliberations if it finds that such default is due to circumstances beyond the State Party's control. (b) Persistently violates the principles set forth in this Statute. (6) The decisions of the General Assembly of the States Parties shall be taken by secret ballot, by an absolute majority of the States Parties. However, decisions taken under paragraph 4 (c) and paragraph 5 (a) and (b) of this article shall be taken by a two-thirds majority of the States Parties. Updated Siracusa Draft – Article C[a] [Identical provision in Article 17 of the 1981 Draft Convention on the Establishment of an International Penal Tribunal for the Suppression and Punishment of the Crime of Apartheid and Other International Crimes[b]]	Article 112(1)–(10)

a Association Internationale de Droit Pénal and others, 13–14.

b Study on Ways and Means of Insuring the Implementation of International Instruments such as the International Convention on the Suppression and Punishment of the Crime of Apartheid, including the establishment of the International Jurisdiction Envisaged by the Convention, UN Doc. E/CN.4/1426.

Nations,[112] the General Assembly adopted without a vote[113] resolution 51/207 reaffirming the mandate of the Preparatory Committee to meet over nine weeks until April 1998, culminating in a diplomatic conference in the same year in Rome. For Benedetti and Washburn, 'fixing the date of the diplomatic conference ... was a major turning point'.[114] With a deadline set-out, the negotiations in 1997–1998 intensified.

5 1997: The Third, Fourth, and Fifth Sessions of the Preparatory Committee on the Establishment of an International Criminal Court

The Preparatory Committee met in February, August, and December 1997, the most sessions of any year.[115] As Bos explained, in 1997 the 'discussions became much more intensive, substantive, and technical and also more negotiation–like'.[116] The impetus to consolidate hundreds of pages, dubbed as a 'telephone book', was a direct response to the pressing timeline to get a draft ready by 1998.[117] To achieve this objective, the Bureau employed working groups and topic coordinators to draft rolling texts.[118] Yet, as the Committee began deliberations, only 71 (38%) delegations participated, the lowest of any previous session,[119] mostly led by Asia Pacific States and the Western and Other States groups. The Preparatory Committee had before it the 1996 compendium report with a plethora of proposals to consider in February, August, and December.[120] For the purpose of this study, however, the discussions on international cooperation and judicial assistance in December 1997 are the most relevant for the study of the Assembly of States Parties to the Rome

112 UN Doc. A/51/PV.88 (1996) 13.

113 Ibid 26.

114 Benedetti and Washburn, 19.

115 Ibid 6.

116 Bos, 'From the International Law Commission to the Rome Conference (1994–1998)' (2002) 54.

117 Hall, Christopher Keith, 'The Third and Fourth Sessions of the UN Preparatory Committee on the Establishment of an International Criminal Court' (1998) 92 (1) American Journal of International Law 124–125.

118 Benedetti and Washburn, 8.

119 United Nations, 'Growth in United Nations Membership' (United Nations, 2022) <https://www.un.org/en/about-us/growth-in-un-membership> accessed January 28, (2022).

120 Preparatory Committee on Establishment of International Criminal Court to Meet at Headquarters, 11–21 February, UN Doc. L/2819 (1997).

Statute because they clearly stipulated the need for a fora where States could consider instances of non-cooperation with the court (See Table 3.2).

An intersessional meeting in Siracuse had already proposed a consolidated text setting out a general obligation for States to cooperate with the court 'without undue delay'.[121] However, influenced by the emerging views on complementarity and the increasing realisation that cooperation from States was a determining factor for the success of the court,[122] the Siracuse compilation added a section giving the Security Council a role to 'take the measures necessary to enable the Court to exercise its jurisdiction' when non-cooperation 'prevents the Court from performing its duties under this Statute'.[123] During the December session, as opposition to the all-encompassing role of the Security Council increased, the delegations of Lesotho, Malawi, Namibia, South Africa, and Zimbabwe proposed to assign the role determining non-cooperation of States Parties to a yet-to-be-determined 'Council of States'.[124] The proposal was discussed at length, with Libya, Mexico, Peru, Venezuela, and Lebanon[125] voicing their preference a 'Council of States Parties' was seized with addressing instances of non-cooperation over any role for the Security Council, except for cases referred to the court by the Security Council.[126] The draft provision also included a footnote clarifying the role of such 'standing committee of the Council of States ... needs to be further addressed in the organization of the Court'.[127] As the Preparatory Committee sessions

121 Report of the International Law Commission on the Work of its Forty-Sixth Session, 2 May – 22 July 1994, UN Doc. A/49/10 62.

122 Hall, Christopher Keith, 'The Fifth Session of the UN Preparatory Committee on the Establishment of an International Criminal Court' (1998) 92 (2) American Journal of International Law 338.

123 Abbreviated Compilation of Proposals on International Cooperation and Judicial Assistance (ILC Draft Statute Part 7) and Enforcement (ILC Draft Statute Part 8), Working Group On International Cooperation and Judicial Assistance Preparatory Committee on the Establishment of an International Criminal Court during the period 1–12 December 1997, UN Doc. A/AC.249/1997/WG.5/CRP.l (1997) 4.

124 Proposal Submitted by Lesotho, Malawi, Namibia, South Africa and Zimbabwe on Article 51–52, UN Doc. A/AC.249/1997/WG.5/DP.6 (1997).

125 Miskowiak, Kristina, Preparatory Committee on the Establishment of an International Criminal Court, 54th Meeting, 1–2 December 1997, Articles 51 and 52, available at: <https://www.legal-tools.org/doc/f844e3/> (1997).

126 Mochochoko, Phakiso, 'International Cooperation and Judicial Assistance' in Lee, Roy S. (ed), The International Criminal Court: the Making of the Rome Statute: Issues, Negotiations and Results (Martinus Nijhoff Publishers 1999) 306.

127 Decisions Taken by the Preparatory Committee at its Session Held from 1 to 12 December 1997, UN Doc. A/AC.249/1997/L.9/Rev.1 (1997) 43.

TABLE 3.2 Preparatory Committee (1997)

Function	Proposals, chronologically	Rome Statute (1998)
Enforcement of Cooperation	Syracuse Compilation – Article 52 Requests for Cooperation: General Provisions (November 25, 1997)[a] (5) Where non-cooperation by [States] [States Parties] with requests by the Court prevents the Court from performing its duties under this Statute, the Court may [refer the non-cooperation to the Security Council] [request the Security Council to take the measures necessary to enable the Court to exercise its jurisdiction] [in relation to States Parties and States not parties to this Statute] Proposal Submitted by Lesotho, Malawi, Namibia, South Africa And Zimbabwe – Article 52 Requests for Cooperation: General Provisions (December 2, 1997)[b] (5) Where non-cooperation by [States] [States Parties] with requests by the Court prevents the Court from performing its duties under this Statute, the Court may [refer the non-cooperation to *the Council of States referred to in article* ... or to the General Assembly except where the Security Council referred the matter to the Court in which case the referral decided upon shall be to the Security Council] Rolling Text – Article 52 Requests for Cooperation: General Provisions (December 10, 1997)[c] (6) Where a State Party fails to comply with a request by the Court contrary to the provisions of the Statute, thereby preventing the Court from performing its duties under this Statute, the Court may make a finding to that effect and refer the matter to [*the Council of States Parties*] [or] [the United Nations General Assembly] [or, where the Security Council referred the matter to the Court] [to the Security Council] [so that necessary measures may be taken to enable the Court to exercise its jurisdiction]	Article 87(5)(b) and (7)

a Abbreviated Compilation of Proposals on International Cooperation and Judicial Assistance (ILC Draft Statute Part 7) and Enforcement (ILC Draft Statute Part 8), Working Group On International Cooperation and Judicial Assistance Preparatory Committee on the Establishment of an International Criminal Court during the period 1–12 December 1997, UN Doc. A/AC.249/1997/WG.5/CRP.l 4.

b Proposal Submitted by Lesotho, Malawi, Namibia, South Africa and Zimbabwe on Article 51–52, UN Doc. A/AC.249/1997/WG.5/DP.6 2.

c Rolling Text of Articles 51 and 52, UN Doc. A/AC.249/1997/WG.5/CRP.2 (1997) 3.

in 1997 concluded, the body responsible to assure cooperation as an obligation among States Parties was yet to be negotiated.

While Hall, Benedetti, Bonneau, and Washburn characterized the third and fourth sessions with 'an air of excitement and a new dedication by all concerned'[128] and as a 'psychological tipping point',[129] the December meeting only 'produced an unstructured and substantially unusable compilation of all governmental proposals'.[130] By the end of 1997 with a few months left to the diplomatic conference, and despite the efforts at consolidation, wide disagreements remained among delegations.[131] Aware of the possibility of failure, Bos closed the December session announcing an intersessional gathering in Zutphen, the Netherlands, for January 1998 with the aim to 'compile all the draft texts into a logical form' and so 'facilitate the adoption of a consolidated text at the final three-week session of the committee in March and April 1998'.[132]

6 1998: The Zutphen Draft

A few months before the Bureau, together with the chairs of working groups and coordinators met in Zutphen in January 1998, the Secretariat circulated two reports alerting of required actions by the collective of States Parties to a court established by a treaty. The first paper outlined options for an agreement between the court and the United Nations. Within the option to establish the court as an independent organization, it cautioned the agreement required approval 'by the States Parties to the Statute'.[133] Providing the example of the International Seabed Authority and the International Tribunal for the Law of the Sea, the Secretariat explained that 'a treaty concluded between two independent international organizations would therefore be appropriate in such case'.[134] To give effect to the relationship agreement, an assembly of States Parties negotiating and agreeing to the treaty became

128 Hall, 'The Third and Fourth Sessions of the UN Preparatory Committee on the Establishment of an International Criminal Court' 133.

129 Benedetti, Bonneau and Washburn, 45.

130 Bassiouni, M Cherif, 'Negotiating the Treaty of Rome on the Establishment of an International Criminal Court' (1999) 32 (3) Cornell International Law Journal 445.

131 Benedetti, Bonneau and Washburn, 45.

132 Hall, 'The Fifth Session of the UN Preparatory Committee on the Establishment of an International Criminal Court' 338.

133 Establishment of the Court and Relationship with the United Nations, UN Doc. A/AC.249/1998/L.10 (1997) 3.

134 Ibid 11.

apparent. Perhaps concerned States had not yet allocated time to the organizational set up of the court, the Secretariat requested 'suggestions on this subject'[135] by early 1998 for consideration by Preparatory Committee.

The second paper advanced draft final clauses for a treaty, the Final Act of the Diplomatic Conference, and a proposal for a Preparatory Commission post-Rome. According to Benedetti, Bonneau, and Washburn, the Secretariat circulated these documents 'on its own initiative',[136] perhaps weary of the short time left before the diplomatic conference. Within the final clauses, a 'meeting of States Parties' was crucially mentioned to give effect to amendments and to 'convene a special meeting to review the Statute'.[137] The Final Act was briefly mentioned as a conduit to summarize the proceedings of the diplomatic conference and include decisions to pave the way for the operationalization of the court.[138] In this regard, the draft text establishing a Preparatory Commission via the Final Act included essential elements yet to be negotiated by States Parties after Rome.[139] Crucially for the Assembly of States Parties, the Preparatory Commission was tasked with developing the 'relationship agreement between the Court and the United Nations and the rules of procedure of the Meeting of States Parties'.[140] The paper signalled the vital role the 'Meeting of the States Parties' would come to play as the main governance and oversight body of the Court, requiring the Commission to 'remain in existence' until the first Assembly meeting.[141]

Yet, even as the Zutphen attendees had the two papers of the Secretariat at their disposal together with other formative proposals, including from the International Law Commission,[142] States,[143] civil society,[144] and even histor-

---

135 Ibid 1.

136 Benedetti, Bonneau and Washburn, 44.

137 Draft Text Relating to Final Clauses, Final Act and Establishment of a Preparatory Commission, UN Doc. A/AC.249/1998/L.11 (1997) 4.

138 Ibid 5.

139 Ibid 6.

140 Ibid 6–7.

141 Ibid 7.

142 Report of the International Law Commission on the Work of its Forty-Sixth Session, 2 May – 22 July 1994, UN Doc. A/49/10 69.

143 Comments Received Pursuant to paragraph 4 of General Assembly Resolution 49/53 on the Establishment of an International Criminal Court, Report of the Secretary-General, UN Doc. A/AC.244/1 3; Comments Received Pursuant to paragraph 4 of General Assembly Resolution 49/53 on the Establishment of an International Criminal Court, Report of the Secretary-General, UN Doc. A/AC.244/1/Add.2 24–25; Proposal Submitted by Finland for Articles 6, 12 And 19, UN Doc. A/AC.249/WP.30; Proposal Submitted by Algeria, Egypt, Jordan, Kuwait, the Libyan Arab Jamahiriya and Qatar on the Organization of the Court,

ical precedent,[145] their draft statute did not contain a provision on the assembly of States Parties (See Table 3.3). As Rao and Ambach argued, the barrier to craft a governance provision resided in the ongoing debate about the exact relationship between the court and the United Nations, which would only be decided in the last preparatory session in March-April 1998.[146] Nonetheless, as Bos confirmed, no serious consideration was given to the Assembly during the Zutphen meeting.[147] The Zutphen meeting did succeed, however, in assembling a new text for negotiation, firmly leaving behind the 1994 International Law Commission draft.[148] For Bassiouni, the January 1998 meeting 'advanced the process in spite of differences of opinion'.[149]

With full knowledge of the state of negotiations and pending critical issues for States, the Zutphen draft consisted of eleven parts, provisionally titled 'Statute for the International Criminal Court'.[150] By providing an orderly overview of the statute, the group intended 'to make it easier to identify the relationship between the articles'.[151] It is curious that this objective was con-

---

UN Doc. A/AC.249/WP.43; Proposal Submitted by the United States of America for Article 6, UN Doc. A/AC.249/WP.22 (1996); Draft Statute of the International Criminal Court, Working Paper Submitted by France, UN Doc. A/AC.249/L.3; Proposal Submitted by Lesotho, Malawi, Namibia, South Africa and Zimbabwe on Article 51–52, UN Doc. A/AC.249/1997/WG.5/DP. 6.

144 Association Internationale de Droit Pénal, Istituto Superiore Internazionale di Scienze Criminali, Max Planck Institute for Foreign and International Criminal Law, Parliamentarians for Global Action, World Federalist Movement, International Scientific and Professional Advisory Council and International Human Rights Law Institute, De Paul University, Draft Statute for an International Criminal Court (Updated Siracusa Draft) (1996) 2.

145 Convention for the Creation of an International Criminal Court (16 November 1937) LoN Doc. C.547.M384.1937.V; Historical Survey of the Question of International Criminal Jurisdiction, UN Doc. A/CN.4/7 1949; Study on Ways and Means of Insuring the Implementation of International Instruments such as the International Convention on the Suppression and Punishment of the Crime of Apartheid, including the establishment of the International Jurisdiction Envisaged by the Convention, UN Doc. E/CN.4/1426.

146 Ambach, Philipp, 'Article 2 Relationship of the Court with the United Nations' in Ambos, Kai and Triffterer, Otto (eds), The Rome Statute of the International Criminal Court: A Commentary (3 edn, Beck/Hart 2016) 27.

147 Bos, 'Assembly of States Parties' 2002 300.

148 von Hebel, Herman, Lammers, Johan G and Schukking, Jolien, Reflections on the International Criminal Court: Essays in Honour of Adriaan Bos (TMC Asser Press 1999) 35.

149 Bassiouni, 'Negotiating the Treaty of Rome on the Establishment of an International Criminal Court' 455.

150 Report of the Inter-sessional Meeting from 19 to 30 January 1998 in Zutphen, The Netherlands, Preparatory Committee on the Establishment of an International Criminal Court, UN Doc. A/AC.249/1998/L.13 (1998) 9.

151 Ibid 8.

TABLE 3.3 Zutphen Draft (1998)

Function	Articles
Governance and Management Oversight	Article 2 – Relationship of the Court with the United Nations Article 3 – Seat of the Court Article 29 – Organs of the Court Article 34 – Independence of Judges (decision for full–time judges) Article 39 – Loss of Office (decision applicable to Judges, Prosecutor and Deputy Prosecutors) Article 55 – Place of Trial (decision to authorize functions outside the seat of the Court) Article 86 – Role of States in enforcement [and supervision] of sentences of imprisonment (elaboration of principles to govern States Parties' role in enforcement and supervision of imprisonment) Article 89 – Pardon, parole and commutation of sentences (decision on pardon by Permanent Committee of States Parties)
Election of Judges	Article 30 – Qualification and Election of Judges Article 31 – Judicial Vacancies
Election of the Prosecutor and Deputy	Article 36 – The Procuracy
Auxiliary Judicial Instruments Oversight	Article 43 – Rules of the Court
Enforcement of Cooperation	Article 78(4) – Cooperation by non-States Parties (decision on necessary measures to address non-cooperation) Article 78(6) – States Parties' Failure to Cooperate [Comply] (decision on necessary measures to address non-cooperation)
Amendments and Review of the Statute	Article 93[C] – Amendments Article 94[D] – Simplified Amendment Procedure Article 95[E] – Review of the Statute

sidered attained when the critical role of an assembly of States Parties was inherently missing. This point asserts itself when analysing the broad responsibilities assigned to States Parties across the Zutphen statute despite the absence of a provision regulating their mandate. The statute contained 16 articles requiring a specific action by a 'General Assembly', 'Standing Committee', 'Council', 'Permanent Committee' or 'Assembly of States Parties' for the functioning of the court.

Perhaps in reference to the inconsistencies arising from the new text, the final report highlighted the need to further examine the 'interrelationship between the various articles'.[152] On this same point, writing in 1999, Bassiouni characterized the results from Zutphen as 'essentially a cumbersome accumulation of alternative governmental proposals requiring additional technical work and more extensive negotiations'.[153] Further technical work was indeed needed to create a provision on the Assembly of States Parties. For Bos, aware of the little time left to the diplomatic conference, the Zutphen draft was 'an eye opener, showing clearly what still needed to be done'.[154]

7 1998: The Sixth Session of the Preparatory Committee on the Establishment of an International Criminal Court

The sixth and last session of the Preparatory Committee took place from 16 March to 3 April 1998, using the Zutphen draft as the basis for negotiation.[155] The final moment before the diplomatic conference attracted the participation of 90 States, 49% of United Nations membership at the time, the most of any previous session. The participation of delegates from African States[156], followed by Asia Pacific[157] contrasted with the lowest number of States from

152 Ibid 18.

153 Bassiouni, 'Negotiating the Treaty of Rome on the Establishment of an International Criminal Court' 444.

154 Preparatory Committee Convenes Final Session Before June/July Rome Conference on Establishing International Criminal Court, UN Doc. L/2859 (1998).

155 Report of the Preparatory Committee on the Establishment of an International Criminal Court, UN Doc. A/CONF.183/2 (1998) 3.

156 Gissel, Line Engbo, 'A Different Kind of Court: Africa's Support for the International Criminal Court, 1993–2003' (2018) 29 (3) European Journal of International Law 725.

157 Mahaseth, Harsh and Bansal, Ayushi, 'Asia and the ICC: The Development of International Criminal Law in a World Changing Order' (2021) 21 (2) International and Comparative Law Review 166.

the Western Europe and Other States.[158] At the same time the session began in New York, the United States Department of Defence began a campaign of 'hostile briefings to roughly one hundred foreign attachés'[159] in Washington. As Eikel argues, the 'court-sceptical camp felt that it urgently needed to put the brakes on'.[160]

For the first time in the preparatory process, a new working group was formed solely to deal with the question of an assembly of States Parties, in the context of the relationship between the court and the United Nations.[161] A second novel working group, intimately related, was led by Lionel Yee from Singapore negotiating articles on composition and administration.[162] Equally, the working group drafting the final clauses, chaired by Bos, also considered the role of States Parties.[163] During the second week of sessions, working group eight, chaired by Rao was tasked to draft articles pertaining to 'the establishment of the court and its relationship with the United Nations, the financing of the court; States Parties meetings and their organizations'.[164] The provision creating the Assembly of States Parties would emanate from this group; however, it would not be the only source of essential functions assigned to it.

The composition and administration working group, for their part, identified 11 articles where a specific action by an assembly of States Parties was required for, among other critical functions, the election and removal of the officers of the court, and approval of Rules of Procedure and Evidence.[165] One notable change occurred in relation to the organs of the court. Although in brackets, the Zutphen draft had listed 'an Assembly of States Parties'[166] as an

158 Preparatory Committee on the Establishment of an International Criminal Court, List of Delegations, 16 March – 3 April 1998, UN Doc. A/AC.249/INF/4 and A/AC.249/INF/4/Corr.1 (1998).

159 Benedetti, Bonneau and Washburn, 47.

160 Eikel, 557.

161 Preparatory Committee for International Criminal Court Concludes Session; to Meet Again in March 1998, UN Doc. L/2847 (1997).

162 Report of the Preparatory Committee on the Establishment of an International Criminal Court, UN Doc. A/CONF.183/2 3.

163 Ibid.

164 Preparatory Committee on Establishment of International Criminal Court to Hold Sixth Session at Headquarters, 16 March-3 April, UN Doc. L/2858 (1998).

165 Report of the Working Group on the Composition and Administration of the Court, UN Doc A/AC.249/1998/L.14 (1998).

166 Report of the Inter-sessional Meeting from 19 to 30 January 1998 in Zutphen, The Netherlands, Preparatory Committee on the Establishment of an International Criminal Court, UN Doc. A/AC.249/1998/L.13 66.

organ of the court in Article 29. During the working group session, the United States vowed to keep and further detail this arrangement[167] but the proposal was ultimately discarded.[168] This change was by no means simply a 'matter of nomenclature'[169] but rather an incisive reshaping of the constitutive parts of the court and the treaty. The revision signalled the strong opposition of the majority of States to any degree of influence over the independence of the court by any political actor, including an assembly. However, by existing outside the institutional framework of the court, the assembly retained a degree of governing 'autonomy'[170] that received some clarity during the deliberations of working group eight led by Rao.[171]

Before the provision addressing the governing body could be drafted, the working group needed first to determine the relationship between the court and the United Nations. During the preparatory process the predominant view from States favoured an independent organization, based on a treaty, with close ties to the United Nations.[172] On 26 March, the working group discussed proposals by France,[173] Spain,[174] and Switzerland[175] considering the general aspects of the court as an independent international organization.[176] As Roberts explained, by 27 March when the consolidated text was agreed, the working group had resolved with 'a clear preference'[177] that the court should be an international organization with a relationship agreement with the United Nations.[178] The immediate effect to establish an international organ-

167 Proposals submitted by the United States of America, UN Doc. A/AC.249/1998/DP.l (1998).

168 Consolidated Text for Articles 29,38 and 40–42, UN Doc. A/AC.249/1998/WG.7/CRP.2/Add.l (1998).

169 Khan, Karim A. A., 'Article 34 Organs of the Court' in Ambos, Kai and Triffterer, Otto (eds), The Rome Statute of the International Criminal Court: A Commentary (3 edn, Beck/Hart 2016) (1197).

170 Schabas, The International Criminal Court: A Commentary on the Rome Statute 677.

171 Bos, 'Assembly of States Parties' (2002) 300.

172 Schabas, The International Criminal Court: A Commentary on the Rome Statute 76.

173 Comments from Governments with regard to document A/AC.249/1998/L.10 entitled "Establishment of the Court and Relationship with the United Nations", UN Doc. A/AC.249/1998/L.12 (1998).

174 Proposal Submitted by Spain, UN Doc. A/AC.249/1998/DP.6 (1998).

175 Proposal Submitted by Switzerland, Comments on the Background Paper Prepared by the Secretariat Entitled "Establishment of the Court and Relationship with the United Nations" A/AC.249/1998/L.10, UN Doc. A/AC.249/1998AVG.7/DP. l (1998).

176 Bos, 'Assembly of States Parties' (2002) 300.

177 Roberts, 2013 496.

178 Consolidated Text for Articles 2 and 4, and A to E, on Financing, UN Doc. A/AC.249/1998/WG.8/CRP.1 (1998).

ization was the need for a provision governing the role and responsibilities of States Parties to the institution.

The working group negotiated the article on the Assembly of States Parties on 27 March,[179] and 31 March,[180] adopting and transmitting to the Bureau the consolidated text later the same day.[181] By then, the group had available specific proposals from France,[182] the United States,[183] and commentary from Switzerland[184] and Japan.[185] The French proposal remitted their detailed 1996 'General Assembly of the States Parties'[186] to the group. The extensive submission from the United States covered a host of organizational oversight issues.[187] The Swiss paper referred to the Assembly in regard to the authority to receive activity reports from the court and approve the relationship agreement with the United Nations.[188] Finally, for Japan, the financial sustainability of the institution supervised by 'oversight mechanisms' was key to ensure the 'effective functioning of the system'.[189] With these proposals, as Rao

---

179 Informal Group on the Establishment of the Court and Relationship with the United Nations, Rolling Text Assembly of States Parties, 27 March 1998, UN Doc. A/AC.249/1998/WG.8/IP (1998).

180 Informal Group on the Establishment of the Court and Relationship with the United Nations, Rolling Text Assembly of States Parties, 31 March 1998, UN Doc. A/AC.249/1998/WG.8/IP (1998).

181 Working Group on the Establishment of the Court and Relationship with the United Nations, Consolidated Text of Part 10 bis Assembly of States Parties, UN Doc. A/AC.249/1998/WG.8/CRP.l/Add.3 (1998).

182 Comments from Governments with regard to document A/AC.249/1998/L.10 entitled "Establishment of the Court and Relationship with the United Nations", UN Doc. A/AC.249/1998/L.12 3–4.

183 Proposals submitted by the United States of America, UN Doc.A/AC.249/1998/DP.l.

184 Proposal Submitted by Switzerland, Comments on the Background Paper Prepared by the Secretariat Entitled "Establishment of the Court and Relationship with the United Nations" A/AC.249/1998/L.10, UN Doc. A/AC.249/1998AVG.7/DP. l 1.

185 Statement by H.E. Mr. Hisashi Owada Permanent Representative of Japan, Establishment of the Court and Relationship with the United Nations, available at <https://www.legal-tools.org/doc/7bec05/> (1998).

186 Draft Statute of the International Criminal Court, Working Paper Submitted by France, UN Doc. A/AC.249/L. 3.

187 Proposals submitted by the United States of America, UN Doc. A/AC.249/1998/DP.l 2–3.

188 Proposal Submitted by Switzerland, Comments on the Background Paper Prepared by the Secretariat Entitled "Establishment of the Court and Relationship with the United Nations" A/AC.249/1998/L.10, UN Doc. A/AC.249/1998AVG.7/DP. l 2.

189 Statement by H.E. Mr. Hisashi Owada Permanent Representative of Japan, Establishment of the Court and Relationship with the United Nations, available at <https://www.legal-tools.org/doc/7bec05/> 4.

explained, the working group held a 'well-informed but non-controversial debate' towards agreements about the functions of the Assembly of States Parties.[190] For Bos, the debate intended to craft an Assembly respectful of the independence of the court but with discrete ability for States to govern the 'administrative and operational activities'[191] of the institution.

While Rao was aware that interrelated articles dealing with the structure and administration happening elsewhere required specific actions by the Assembly, the focus of the discussion was on 'participants, specific functions and powers of the organization, and the method of adoption of its decisions'.[192] Overall, by 31 March, the article dealing with the governance body of the treaty was situated in Part 1 of the statute, on the Establishment of the Court.[193] The consolidated text, transmitted to the Bureau, moved the provision to Part 10bis under Enforcement.[194] By the time the Committee adopted the Draft Statute in its entirety, 'a new, largely unbracketed Part 11'[195] establishing the Assembly of States Parties appeared as Article 102.[196] As Gradoni argued, Article 102 prefigured Article 112 in the Rome Statute.[197]

8 Governance and Management Oversight: Establishment and Membership of the Assembly of States Parties

Article 102(1), the first of twelve provisions describing the governance and management oversight of the Assembly of States Parties, dealt with the establishment and membership of the Assembly, providing it 'shall consist of rep-

190 Rao, (1999) 409.

191 Bos, 'Assembly of States Parties' (2002) 301.

192 Rao, (1999) 408.

193 Informal Group on the Establishment of the Court and Relationship with the United Nations, Rolling Text Assembly of States Parties, 27 March 1998, UN Doc. A/AC.249/1998/WG.8/IP; Informal Group on the Establishment of the Court and Relationship with the United Nations, Rolling Text Assembly of States Parties, 31 March 1998, UN Doc. A/AC.249/1998/WG.8/IP.

194 Report of the Working Group on the Establishment of the Court and Relationship with the United Nations, UN Doc. A/AC.249/1998/L.19 (1998).

195 Hall, Christopher Keith, 'The Sixth Session of the UN Preparatory Committee on the Establishment of an International Criminal Court' (1998) 92 (3) The American Journal of International Law 554.

196 Report of the Preparatory Committee on the Establishment of an International Criminal Court, Part 1 and Part 2, UN Doc. A/CONF.183/2/Add.1 (1998) 157–159.

197 Gradoni, (2012) (2008).

resentatives from each State Party to this Statute'.[198] What appeared unexceptionable in the context of a multilateral treaty became a point of tension between the group of Like-Minded States and other delegations on whether non-Party States could participate in the Assembly. As Rao explained, Like-Minded States refused widening membership arguing it 'would be a disincentive for States to become parties to the Statute'.[199] Neither the proposals from France nor the United States included an option for non-Party States participation. The inspiration came from a brand-new amendment in a completely different international organization. In May 1997, the seventh Meeting of States Parties to the United Nations Convention on the Law of the Sea agreed to amend its rules of procedure to allow observer participation to 'not Parties to the Convention'.[200] For Bos, the inclusion of States Parties and observers in the Assembly was an incentive to achieve universality of ratifications.[201] By the end of the 1998 session, the first clause was adopted without further changes.[202] However, it impacted Article 102(5) on decision-making majorities.

Established that only States Parties had the right to vote, Article 102(5) set out the modes for decision-making. As Bos and Rao agreed, all delegations supported decision making by consensus as the primary objective of the Assembly.[203] In the event a vote was required over substantive issues, the working group transmitted three options to the Rome Conference combining formulas for the number of States Parties required for quorum[204] and for adopting decisions.[205] While the working group disagreed over voting majorities, it was consistent across the different versions of Article 102(5) that the three modalities to reach a decision would apply, 'except as other-

198 Informal Group on the Establishment of the Court and Relationship with the United Nations, Rolling Text Assembly of States Parties, 27 March 1998, UN Doc. A/AC.249/1998/WG.8/IP 1.

199 Rao, (1999) 408.

200 Report of the Seventh Meeting of States Parties to the United Nations Convention on the Law of the Sea, New York, 19–23 May 1997, UN Doc. SPLOS/24 (1997) 8.

201 Bos, 'Assembly of States Parties' (2002) 302.

202 Report of the Preparatory Committee on the Establishment of an International Criminal Court, Part 1 and Part 2, UN Doc. A/CONF.183/2/Add.1 157.

203 Bos, 'Assembly of States Parties' (2002) 312; Rao, (1999) 411.

204 Bos, 'From the International Law Commission to the Rome Conference (1994–1998)' (2002) 59.

205 Informal Group on the Establishment of the Court and Relationship with the United Nations, Rolling Text Assembly of States Parties, 27 March 1998, UN Doc. A/AC.249/1998/AC.8/IP 1.

wise provided in the Statute'.[206] Cognizant that elsewhere in the statute the Assembly had a role, the exceptional rule to voting majorities in Article 102(5) intended to safeguard further requirements for decision making in the Statute. For example, Article 43(4) only required an 'an absolute majority of the States Parties'[207] for the election of the Prosecutor and deputies. The inconsistencies across the Statute, according to Rao, were the results of complex overlapping negotiations and the lack of time for 'even informal agreement during the PrepCom'.[208]

Articles 102(4) and 102(7) completed the provisions outlining the establishment of the Assembly. Envisaged in 102(4) to meet annually or more frequently, as required, in special sessions convened by the Bureau, the working group introduced several amendments during the 1998 session. In the second version of the rolling text, on 31 March, the power to convene special sessions by a request of one third of States Parties was added. However, the consolidated text included a bracketed option regarding the power of the Bureau to call for special sessions at its own initiative. The disagreements over the composition of the Bureau reflected a degree of mistrust over a smaller number of States Parties controlling the trigger for special sessions to deal, for example, with the review of the statute. Thus, the text transmitted to the Diplomatic Conference left the exclusive role of the Bureau only as an option. In contrast, Article 102(4) included language opening the possibility to convene special sessions of the Assembly of States Parties 'as otherwise specified in the Statute'.[209] The possibility to convene a special session beyond the requirements in Article 102(4) appeared in Article 111 on the review of the statute. Originating in a proposal by the United States,[210] both options in Article 111 asked for a qualified vote to organize a 'special meeting of the Assembly of States Parties to review the Statute'.[211] Thus, reading these two Articles together it is possible to distinguish two types of special sessions: one for the regular governance and

206 Working Group on the Establishment of the Court and Relationship with the United Nations, Consolidated Text of Part 10 bis Assembly of States Parties, UN Doc. A/AC.249/1998/WG.8/CRP.l/Add.3 2.

207 Report of the Preparatory Committee on the Establishment of an International Criminal Court, Part 1 and Part 2, UN Doc. A/CONF.183/2/Add.1 68.

208 Rao, (1999) 409.

209 Working Group on the Establishment of the Court and Relationship with the United Nations, Consolidated Text of Part 10 bis Assembly of States Parties, UN Doc. A/AC.249/1998/WG.8/CRP.l/Add.3 2.

210 Proposals Submitted by the United States of America, UN Doc. A/AC.249/1998/DP.l 8.

211 Report of the Preparatory Committee on the Establishment of an International Criminal Court, Part 1 and Part 2, UN Doc. A/CONF.183/2/Add.1 163.

management oversight tasks of the Assembly, and a second type exclusively to consider a review of the statute. However, as Schabas, Rao, and Ambach argued, it is still an open question what the definitive meaning or legal weight of this language is in the Rome Statute.[212]

Finally, the working group introduced late in the 1998 session the possibility for the Assembly to meet elsewhere than the seat of the Court or the United Nations. Draft Article 62 contained an option requiring the Assembly of States Parties to grant a change of location of trial proceedings for efficiency and interest of justice reasons.[213] The same argument could have been employed to foster cooperation, complementarity or even as a political statement to back the utility of the court closer to victims of crimes. In any event, to govern the powers and activities of the collective of States Parties, including changing the location for meetings, Article 102(7) set out the adoption of the Rules of Procedure of the Assembly.[214] For Amnesty International, the rules of procedure of the Assembly of States Parties had to address the participation of 'intergovernmental organizations and non-governmental organizations' and should mandate 'prompt public reports of their sessions'.[215] The draft Final Act establishing the Preparatory Commission included the creation of the Rules of Procedure of the Assembly of States Parties as one of the key auxiliary documents of the Statute.[216]

9 Governance and Management Oversight: Responsibilities of the Assembly of States Parties

Article 102(2) described the majority of responsibilities of the Assembly of States Parties across seven sections, with two of them entirely unresolved by the end of the session, including the first clause (see Table 3.4). The task to 'consider and adopt' the results from the Preparatory Commission only appeared for the first time in full brackets in the consolidated text transmitted

---

212 Rao and Ambach, (2016) 2241; Schabas, The International Criminal Court: A Commentary on the Rome Statute 1448.

213 Report of the Preparatory Committee on the Establishment of an International Criminal Court, Part 1 and Part 2, UN Doc. A/CONF.183/2/Add.1 99.

214 Ibid 159.

215 Amnesty International, The International Criminal Court: Making the Right Choices – Part IV, AI Index: IOR 40/04/98 (Amnesty International 1998) 57.

216 Report of the Preparatory Committee on the Establishment of an International Criminal Court, Part 1 and Part 2, UN Doc. A/CONF.183/2/Add.1 173.

to the Bureau on 31 March 1998.[217] The change corresponded with draft Part B of the Final Act in the Zutphen report required the Preparatory Commission to prepare all the auxiliary documents to the Statute. Draft Part B further instructed the Commission to 'remain in existence until the conclusion of the first Meeting of the States Parties to the Statute'[218], thus creating a programmatic and temporal link with the Assembly. In this context, Article 102(2)(a) guaranteed the Assembly's decision on essential instruments aiding the Statute.[219] Although there was 'general agreement'[220] with the provision, as Schabas explained, the source of disagreement emanated from the desire of some delegations to negotiate the Rules of Procedure and Evidence and the Elements of Crimes at the Diplomatic Conference citing their relevance to the Statute.[221]

Article 102(2)(b) was at the core of the governance and management role of the Assembly of States Parties. Emerging from the United States, the Assembly was to 'provide management oversight … regarding the organization of the Court'.[222] The United States had consistently called throughout the preparatory process for a 'mechanism of oversight by States Parties'.[223] France, on the other hand, argued that oversight issues did not belong in the statute but should be dealt in the Preparatory Commission.[224] The working group agreed with a role to oversee the administration by the Presidency, Prosecutor and Registrar but did not extend the same role to decisions about internal organization or operations of each organ. As Bos explained, delegations desired to avoid 'interference by the Assembly with the judicial functions of the Court'.[225] The undefined interpretation of administrative management oversight linked this provision with Article 102(3)(c) granting the Assembly the power to create subsidiary bodies, chiefly among them 'an independent over-

217 Working Group on the Establishment of the Court and Relationship with the United Nations, Consolidated Text of Part 10 bis Assembly of States Parties, UN Doc. A/AC.249/1998/WG.8/CRP.l/Add.3.

218 Report of the Inter-sessional Meeting from 19 to 30 January 1998 in Zutphen, The Netherlands, Preparatory Committee on the Establishment of an International Criminal Court, UN Doc. A/AC.249/1998/L.13 174.

219 Rao and Ambach, (2016) 2219.

220 Rao, 1999 409.

221 Schabas, The International Criminal Court: A Commentary on the Rome Statute 1437.

222 Proposals Submitted by the United States of America, UN Doc. A/AC.249/1998/DP.l 2.

223 UN Doc. A/C.6/52/SR.13 (1997) 6–7.

224 Comments from Governments with regard to document A/AC.249/1998/L.10 entitled "Establishment of the Court and Relationship with the United Nations", UN Doc. A/AC.249/1998/L.12 5.

225 Bos, 'Assembly of States Parties' (2002) 305.

sight mechanism for inspection, evaluation, and investigation in order to enhance the efficiency and economy of [non-judicial administration] [operations] of the Court'.[226]

Article 37ter in the proposal submitted by the United States described in detail the tasks assigned to the oversight mechanism, making it accountable to the Assembly to audit and assure the administration by organs of the court act in accordance with, presumably, the Statute.[227] Recalling Bos' explanation above, the second version of the rolling text added a bracket intended to clarify the oversight mechanism would cover exclusively the '[non judicial administration] [operations]'[228] of the court. The same language was transmitted to the Bureau and the Diplomatic Conference.[229] This provision probed difficult for States Parties to the Rome Statute to materialize due to possible inherence over the independence of the Court. In fact, it would not be until the 12th Assembly of States Parties in 2012 for the Independent Oversight Mechanism to obtain a definitive mandate fully respectful of 'the judicial and prosecutorial independence'[230] of the Court.

Article 102(2)(c) and 102(3)(a) and (b) should be analysed together because they pertained to the establishment and composition of the Bureau and the required action by the Assembly in relation to its activities. Before the United States put forward the creation of a smaller executive group of States Parties to 'assist the Assembly in carrying out its functions',[231] writing in 1997, Warrick and Bassiouni proposed an 'Executive Council ... as a means for more frequent management meetings to assist the work of the ICC'.[232] The composition of the Bureau in 102(3)(b) borrowed from the French proposal in relation to the leadership position of a President and one Vice-President;[233] and from the

226 Report of the Preparatory Committee on the Establishment of an International Criminal Court, Part 1 and Part 2, UN Doc. A/CONF.183/2/Add.1 158.

227 Proposals Submitted by the United States of America, UN Doc. A/AC.249/1998/DP.l 3.

228 Informal Group on the Establishment of the Court and Relationship with the United Nations, Rolling Text Assembly of States Parties, 31 March 1998, UN Doc. A/AC.249/1998/WG.8/IP.

229 Report of the Preparatory Committee on the Establishment of an International Criminal Court, Part 1 and Part 2, UN Doc. A/CONF.183/2/Add.1 157–158.

230 ICC-ASP/12/Res.6 Independent Oversight Mechanism (2013) 5.

231 Proposals Submitted by the United States of America, UN Doc. A/AC.249/1998/DP.l 3.

232 Warrick, Thomas S and Bassiouni, M Cherif, 'Organization of the International Criminal Court: Administrative and Financial Issues' (1997) 25 (2) Denver Journal of International Law and Policy 376–377.

233 Draft Statute of the International Criminal Court, Working Paper Submitted by France, UN Doc. A/AC.249/L.3 22.

United States the election of the remainder membership for a period of years.[234] The working group modified the years of service in the Bureau from five, proposed by the United States, to three; however, it left the total original number of members to 20 despite calls for expanding to two Vice-President roles.[235] Nothing in the drafting paper trail or the secondary literature points at a discussion about the required qualifications of Bureau members, including its leadership. Given the wide-range and essential tasks assigned to the executive organ, the omission was significant.

In contrast, the representative character of the Bureau was debated, inserting a bracket for elections to reflect geographical and legal diversity. However, as Rao notes, there were competing views whether the Bureau should follow convention of similar organs as 'administrative in nature' or be an active body able to make 'recommendations and reports to the Assembly on matters before the Assembly, including the non-cooperation of States'.[236] To this effect, the United States suggested an active Bureau able to 'hire persons to provide administrative and technical support'[237] independent from the court. While United Nations Secretariat had signalled the need for specialized support, the proposal by the United States was the first one to request the creation of a secretariat for the Assembly of States Parties.[238]

The third element of the composition of the Bureau considered if the President of the Court, the Prosecutor, and the Registrar should participate in the work led by States Parties. The second version of the rolling text questioned their participation in brackets,[239] but the consolidated text signalled consensus for their inclusion as '[observers] [members]'[240] in the deliberations of the Bureau. Recalling Bos' warning to States against politicizing the court by meddling with its independence, the option of membership, which assumed voting rights, for the officers of the court is worth noting.

---

234 Proposals Submitted by the United States of America, UN Doc. A/AC.249/1998/DP.l 3.

235 Working Group on the Establishment of the Court and Relationship with the United Nations, Consolidated Text of Part 10 bis Assembly of States Parties, UN Doc. A/AC.249/1998/WG.8/CRP.l/Add.3.

236 Rao, (1999) 410.

237 Proposals submitted by the United States of America, UN Doc. A/AC.249/1998/DP.l 2.

238 Establishment of the Court and Relationship with the United Nations, UN Doc. A/AC.249/1998/L.10 10.

239 Informal Group on the Establishment of the Court and Relationship with the United Nations, Rolling Text Assembly of States Parties, 31 March 1998, UN Doc. A/AC.249/1998/WG.8/IP

240 Working Group on the Establishment of the Court and Relationship with the United Nations, Consolidated Text of Part 10 bis Assembly of States Parties, UN Doc. A/AC.249/1998/WG.8/CRP.l/Add.3.

Article 102(2)(e), derived from France's 1996 proposal,[241] granted the Assembly of States Parties the power to alter the number of judges and their modality of service. As Rao explains, the working group agreed with the provision without much debate.[242] The question of the appropriate number of judges and whether they should serve in a full-time capacity featured throughout the preparatory period and was tied to the expectations of workload.[243] Moreover, the provision contained a bracketed option to exercise the same power in relation to '[members of the Office of the Prosecutor or the Registry]'.[244] In practice, this meant an intrusion of the Assembly of States Parties over the administration in the Office of the Prosecutor and the Registry. Therefore, both versions of the rolling text, and only in brackets in the consolidated draft, retained this power by the Assembly.

The last section describing the responsibilities of the Assembly of States Parties was Article 102(2)(g), a residual omnibus provision with the power to act in conformity with the Statute and the Rules of Procedure and Evidence as required and not envisioned at the moment of drafting. This provision was also necessary to set a boundary around potential decisions by the Assembly compromising the independence of the court, but more importantly, for the implementation of additional essential functions assigned to the Assembly elsewhere in the Statute and not captured in Article 102. The implied powers of the Assembly expand over 21 Articles across the Draft Statute.

Article 102(2)(g) also contained two bracketed clauses addressing the review of the statute and the Rules of Procedure and Evidence, and, saliently, a power by the Assembly to grant pardons. Both bracketed clauses were only introduced in the consolidated text the last day of deliberations.[245] There was no agreement whether the Assembly was the appropriate forum to grant reduction of sentences or pardons. As Rao explained, the substantive issue of the administration of penalties 'raised substantive issues beyond the role of the Assembly that needed to be dealt with in other relevant working

241 Draft Statute of the International Criminal Court, Working Paper Submitted by France, UN Doc. A/AC.249/L.3 22.

242 Rao, (1999) 409.

243 Rwelamira, Medard R, 'Composition and Administration of the Court' in Lee, Roy S. (ed), The International Criminal Court: the Making of the Rome Statute: Issues, Negotiations and Results (Martinus Nijhoff Publishers 1999) 153.

244 Report of the Preparatory Committee on the Establishment of an International Criminal Court, Part 1 and Part 2, UN Doc. A/CONF.183/2/Add.1 157.

245 Working Group on the Establishment of the Court and Relationship with the United Nations, Consolidated Text of Part 10 bis Assembly of States Parties, UN Doc. A/AC.249/1998/WG.8/CRP.l/Add.3 2.

TABLE 3.4 Draft Statute for the International Criminal Court (1998)

Function		**Rome Statute (1998)**
Governance and Management Oversight	Article 2 – Relationship of the Court with the United Nations Article 3 – Seat of the Court Article 36 – Judges Serving on a Full-time Basis Article 47 – Removal from Office Article 62 – Place of Trial Article 102 – Assembly of States Parties (new from Zutphen Draft) Article 108 – Settlement of Disputes (new from Zutphen Draft)	Articles 2, 3(2), 46(2), 112 and 119(2)
Election of Judges	Article 37 – Qualification and Election of Judges Article 38 – Judicial Vacancies Article 102 – Assembly of States Parties	Articles 36, 37 and 112
Election of the Prosecutor and Deputy	Article 43 – The Office of the Prosecutor	Article 42(4)
Election of the Registrar	Article 44 – The Registry (new from Zutphen Draft)	Article 43(4)
Auxiliary Judicial Instruments Oversight	Article 45 – Staff (new from Zutphen Draft) Article 52 – Rules of Procedure and Evidence Article 53 – Regulations of the Court (new from Zutphen Draft) Article 102 – Assembly of States Parties	Articles 44(3), 51, 52(3) and 112
Financial Oversight (new Articles from Zutphen Draft)	Article 50 – Salaries, Allowances, and Expenses Article 102 – Assembly of States Parties Article 103 – Payment of Expenses of the Court Article 105 – Voluntary Contributions	Articles 49, 112, 114 and 116

TABLE 3.4 Draft Statute for the International Criminal Court (1998) (*cont.*)

Function		Rome Statute (1998)
Enforcement of Cooperation	Article 71 – Sensitive National Security Information (new from Zutphen Draft) Article 86(4) – Cooperation by non-States Parties Article 86(6) – States Parties' Failure to Cooperate [Comply] Article 102 – Assembly of States Parties	Articles 87(5)(b), (7) and 112
Amendments and Review of the Statute	Article 110 – Amendments Article 111 – Review of the Statute	Articles 121 and 123

groups'.[246] Thus, only a footnote signalled a role for the Assembly of States Parties, as a political body, to 'decide on an application for pardon'.[247] For civil society, the political nature of the Assembly was enough reason to reject their role in granting pardons.[248]

By the end of the 1998 session, the seven sections of Article 102 describing the majority of responsibilities of the Assembly of States Parties were adopted (see Table 3.5).[249] One notable exception from the Draft Statute extending to the current Article 112 was the absent political characterization of the Assembly of States Parties. In other words, as du Plessis and Gevers argued, the provisions describe the functional role of the Assembly but avoided outlining the overall political responsibility of States Parties in relation to objectives of the statute.[250] In this context, civil society envisioned an Assembly of States Parties able to isolate the court from 'political interfer-

246 Rao, (1999) 410.

247 Report of the Preparatory Committee on the Establishment of an International Criminal Court, Part 1 and Part 2, UN Doc. A/CONF.183/2/Add.1 155.

248 Amnesty International, The International Criminal Court Making the Right Choices – Part V Recommendations to the Diplomatic Conference, AI Index: IOR 40/10/98 (Amnesty International 1998) 84.

249 Report of the Preparatory Committee on the Establishment of an International Criminal Court, Part 1 and Part 2, UN Doc. A/CONF.183/2/Add.1 157–158.

250 du Plessis and Grevers, (2016).

TABLE 3.5 Draft Statute for the International Criminal Court (1998)

Function	Article 102
Governance and Management Oversight	(1) There is hereby established an Assembly of States Parties to this Statute. Each State Party shall have one representative in the Assembly who may be accompanied by alternates and advisers. The signatories of the [Statute] [Final Act] may be [observers] [members] in the Assembly | Origin of the provision: France, Working Group 8 (2) The Assembly shall: [(a) consider and adopt recommendations of the preparatory commission;] | Origin of the provision: Working Group 8 (b) provide management oversight to the Presidency, Prosecutor and Registrar regarding the administration of the Court; | Origin of the provision: United States (c) consider the reports and activities of the Bureau and take appropriate action in regard thereto. | Origin of the provision: United States (e) determine whether to alter, as appropriate, the number of judges [or members of the Office of the Prosecutor or the Registry], serving on a full- or part–time basis, for such period as it shall determine. | Origin of the provision: France (g) perform any other function or take any other action as specified in this Statute or the Rules of Procedure and Evidence [including consideration of requests for a review of these instruments] [including consideration of applications relating to pardon submitted to it.] | Origin of the provision: Working Group 8 (3)(a) The Assembly shall have a Bureau consisting of a President, a Vice-President and [18] members elected by the Assembly for three-year terms. The President of the Court, the Prosecutor and the Registrar or their representatives may, as appropriate, participate as [observers] [members] in meetings of the Bureau.| Origin of the provision: France, United States, Working Group 8 (b) The Bureau shall [have a representative character] [be elected on the basis of ensuring its representative character], taking into account, in particular, equitable geographical distribution and bearing in mind the adequate representation of the principal legal systems of the world [as far as possible]. The Bureau shall meet as often as necessary, but at least once a year, and shall assist the Assembly in the discharge of its responsibilities. | Origin of the provision: Working Group 8

TABLE 3.5 Draft Statute for the International Criminal Court (1998) (*cont.*)

Function	Article 102
	(c) The Assembly may also establish other subsidiary bodies as may be necessary, including an independent oversight mechanism for inspection, evaluation, and investigation in order to enhance the efficiency and economy of [non-judicial administration] [operations] of the Court. | Origin of the provision: United States, Working Group 8
	(4) The Assembly shall meet at the seat of the Court or at the Headquarters of the United Nations [or in any other place as it may decide] once a year and, when circumstances so require, hold special sessions. Except as otherwise specified in the Statute, special sessions shall be convened [by the Bureau on its own initiative or] at the request of one third of the States Parties. | Origin of the provision: France, United States, Working Group 8
	(5) Each State Party shall have one vote. Every effort shall be made to reach decisions on matters of substance by consensus in the Assembly and in the Bureau. If consensus cannot be reached, decisions on matters of substance must be approved by [a two-thirds majority of those present and voting, representing the absolute majority of States Parties] [a two-thirds majority of those present and voting] [an absolute majority of States Parties] except as otherwise provided in the Statute. | Origin of the provision: France, United States, Working Group 8
	(7) The Assembly shall adopt its own Rules of Procedure. | Origin of the provision: Working Group 8

ence and pressure when it adopts unpopular decisions',[251] but, equally failed to table specific wording for inclusion of such language in Article 102.

10 Enforcement of Cooperation

Bearing in mind the jurisdictional set-up in the Zutphen draft, the role of the Assembly of States Parties in relation to the enforcement of cooperation was

251 Amnesty International, The International Criminal Court: Making the Right Choices – Part IV, AI Index: IOR 40/04/98 14.

a source of wide disagreement in the working group.[252] In fact, together with Article 102(2), dealing with the membership of non-Party States, Article 102 (2)(f) was transmitted to the Diplomatic Conference in full brackets (see Table 3.6).[253] Already in 1997, and reaffirmed in Article 86 of the Draft Statute, the Preparatory Committee identified the Assembly of States Parties as the forum for addressing non-cooperation by parties and non-Party States when a 'finding from the Court'[254] referred the matter to it. As Kreß and Prost explained, the missing element in the cooperation regime before the Diplomatic Conference was the determination of appropriate remedies in instances of non-cooperation.[255] Article 102(2)(f) only addressed a degree of '[necessary] [appropriate] measures' by giving the Assembly the power to 'consider any question'[256] or refer the matter to the United Nations Security Council or General Assembly. However, no remedies were outlined. In addition, there were two areas of wide disagreement in the working group.

The first one related to the power to consider questions of non-cooperation by non-Party States.[257] Provided that third parties to a treaty do not carry obligations under the statute, delegations questioned the Assembly's ability to take any measure towards them. The second version of the rolling text only referred to this power exclusively in relation to States Parties.[258] Only in the consolidated text a bracket referencing non-Party States was added.[259] Thus, while there was disagreement in the working group over the role of the Assembly, there was also a clear recognition that for the court to function, cooperation by all States was crucial.[260] The second dispute related the trigger to seize the Assembly with non-cooperation questions.[261]

252 Rao, (1999) 409.

253 Report of the Preparatory Committee on the Establishment of an International Criminal Court, Part 1 and Part 2, UN Doc. A/CONF.183/2/Add.1 157.

254 Ibid 132–133.

255 Kreß, Claus and Prost, Kimberly, 'Article 87 Requests for Cooperation: General Provisions' in Ambos, Kai and Triffterer, Otto (eds), The Rome Statute of the International Criminal Court: A Commentary (3 edn, Beck/Hart 2016) (2021).

256 Report of the Preparatory Committee on the Establishment of an International Criminal Court, Part 1 and Part 2, UN Doc. A/CONF.183/2/Add.1 157.

257 Bos, 'Assembly of States Parties' (2002) 308.

258 Informal Group on the Establishment of the Court and Relationship with the United Nations, Rolling Text Assembly of States Parties, 31 March 1998, UN Doc. A/AC.249/1998/WG.8/IP 2.

259 Working Group on the Establishment of the Court and Relationship with the United Nations, Consolidated Text of Part 10 bis Assembly of States Parties, UN Doc. A/AC.249/1998/WG.8/CRP.l/Add.3 1.

260 Mochochoko, (1999).

261 Rao, (1999) 409–410.

TABLE 3.6 Draft Statute for the International Criminal Court (1998)

Function	Article 102
Enforcement of Cooperation	(2) [(f) consider, upon recommendation [of the Court] [of the Bureau], any question relating to non-cooperation by States Parties [and non-States Parties] and take [necessary] [appropriate] measures, including referring the matter to [the Security Council] [the United Nations General Assembly] as provided in article 86.] | Origin of the provision: Working Group 8

In the second version of the rolling text, the Bureau was tasked with recommending to the Assembly how to address an instance of non-cooperation. In the consolidated text, the bracketed options included the court. The addition was significant because it better aligned with draft Article 86(5) and (6) requiring a judicial finding to trigger an action from the Assembly. However, Rao's working group also added in the consolidated text the ability of the Assembly to refer matters to the Security Council or the General Assembly as a specific measure to address non-cooperation.[262] The link with the Security Council corresponded with Article 10 in the Draft Statute providing the Council with referring power to the Prosecutor.[263] Accordingly, the working group identified the Security Council, the source of the referral, as the forum to address non-cooperation. The link with the General Assembly, as in other parts of the Draft Statute, intended to provide the nascent court with political and diplomatic backing to carry out its mandate[264] and to craft an alternative to the Security Council in case one of its permanent members 'is the recalcitrant State'.[265]

262 Rao and Ambach, (2016) 2226.

263 Report of the Preparatory Committee on the Establishment of an International Criminal Court, Part 1 and Part 2, UN Doc. A/CONF.183/2/Add.1 34.

264 Ciampi, Annalisa, 'Legal Rules, Policy Choices and Political Realities in the Functioning of the Cooperation Regime of the International Criminal Court' in Bekou, Olympia and Birkett, Daley (eds), Cooperation and the International Criminal Court (Brill Nijhoff 2016).

265 Women's Caucus for Gender Justice in the International Criminal Court, Recommendations and Commentary For December 1997 PrepCom on the Establishment of an International Criminal Court (1997) 7.

11 Financial Oversight

The financial oversight powers attracted its own set of disagreements when drafting provisions 102(2)(d) and (6) (see Table 3.7). As referenced in this chapter, financial support to the Court was a recurrent question among States, including in the Sixth Committee. In Zutphen, the Bureau, while not discussing the topic, envisioned the Preparatory Commission would prepare the 'financial regulations'[266] of the Court. As such, financial questions were discussed 'briefly'[267] and 'its treatment was purely synoptical'[268] in the working group. The working group had before it the French proposal granting the Assembly the power to 'rule on any budget question'.[269] France's Article 75 listed when States or the court were liable to cover expenses, and assumed the United Nations would provide the budget required. On the other hand, the United States, echoing comments made by Japan and Switzerland, put forward draft articles allocating to the Bureau the responsibility to craft the budget and to the Assembly the power to approve it. In addition, it suggested the funding originate from States Parties or 'from other sources'[270] but that any financial question be regulated by specific rules. The United States favoured the use of alternative funding scales to that of the United Nations. As Hall shows, the United States preferred, if Party to the court, to use the appropriation scales of the International Telecommunication Union or the Universal Postal Union in order to contribute much less to the budget of the court.[271]

Overall, two camps emerged. One group, led by the United States, argued States Parties had to fund the court. Another group, led by the Like-Minded States, proposed using the United Nations budget as the Court would 'be acting on behalf of the entire international community'.[272] The financial bar-

---

266 Report of the Inter-sessional Meeting from 19 to 30 January 1998 in Zutphen, The Netherlands, Preparatory Committee on the Establishment of an International Criminal Court, UN Doc. A/AC.249/1998/L.13 174.

267 Arsanjani, Mahnoush, 'Financing' in Cassese, Antonio, Gaeta, Paola and Jones, John RWD (eds), The Rome Statute of the International Criminal Court: a Commentary, vol 1 (Oxford University Press 2002) 322.

268 Rao, (1999) 403.

269 Draft Statute of the International Criminal Court, Working Paper Submitted by France, UN Doc. A/AC.249/L.3 22.

270 Proposals submitted by the United States of America, UN Doc. A/AC.249/1998/DP.l 3.

271 Hall, 'The Sixth Session of the UN Preparatory Committee on the Establishment of an International Criminal Court' 555.

272 Ibid 554.

rier to ratifications of the Statute was also considered.[273] To this effect, Warrick and Bassiouni argued for a tiered approach to appropriation of funds from States Parties,[274] and civil society even suggested a global levy on arms sales to fund the court.[275] As Arsanjani argued, the working group reverted back to the three options that appeared in the Ad Hoc Committee: funding by States Parties, by the United Nations or a combination of both.[276] The three options did not preclude the appropriation of funds from voluntary contributions from 'governments, international organizations, individuals, corporations and other entities'.[277] In this context, while there was no overall agreement on the sources or scales to appropriate funding,[278] the working group reached consensus about the role of the Assembly of States Parties to 'consider and approve the budget for the Court'.[279]

Proposals by France and the United States contained an explicit power for the Assembly to oversee the financial health of the institution.[280] The main change from the first version of the rolling text to the consolidated draft Article 102(2)(d) was the removal of the Bureau as the exclusive organ to review the budget.[281] In fact, by virtue of Article 44 on the Registry, working group eight did not make the link between the administrative role of the Registrar in developing the budget of the Court and the power of the Assembly to consider and approve it. The addition of a bracket in Article 102(2)(d) requiring the Assembly to consult with the main administrator of the Court on the

---

273 Amnesty International, The International Criminal Court: Making the Right Choices – Part IV, AI Index: IOR 40/04/98 20; Human Rights Watch, Commentary for the March-April 1998 Preparatory Committee Meeting on a Permanent International Criminal Court (1998) 3.

274 Warrick and Bassiouni, 385.

275 Amnesty International, The International Criminal Court: Making the Right Choices – Part IV, AI Index: IOR 40/04/98 26.

276 Arsanjani, (2002) 322.

277 Consolidated Text for Articles 2 and 4, and A to E, on Financing, UN Doc. A/AC.249/1998/WG.8/CRP. 1.

278 Preparatory Committee on Establishment of International Criminal Court Concludes Work by Adopting Draft Statute, UN Doc. L/2864 (1998) 22; Proposals submitted by the United States of America, UN Doc. A/AC.249/1998/DP.l 2.

279 Working Group on the Establishment of the Court and Relationship with the United Nations, Consolidated Text of Part 10 bis Assembly of States Parties, UN Doc. A/AC.249/1998/WG.8/CRP.l/Add.3 1.

280 Draft Statute of the International Criminal Court, Working Paper Submitted by France, UN Doc. A/AC.249/L.3.

281 Working Group on the Establishment of the Court and Relationship with the United Nations, Consolidated Text of Part 10 bis Assembly of States Parties, UN Doc. A/AC.249/1998/WG.8/CRP.l/Add.3 1.

budget was only added in the plenary of the Preparatory Committee on 3 April 1998.[282] In practice, a consultation stage with the Registrar was introduced in the process for approval.[283] The late introduction of the bracket signalled the anxiety of Like-Minded States to afford the court organs with a degree of independence to carry out their mandate while at the same time giving the Assembly of States Parties some overall budgetary control. Thus, the second bracket of Article 102(2)(d), as transmitted to the Bureau, also provided an option for the Assembly to '[rule on any financial issue]'.[284] This provision was also linked to Article 105 in Part 12 requiring the Assembly to develop the criteria for acceptance of funds, for example, voluntary contributions,[285] but also as another signal of the delicate balance between financial controls by the Registrar and financial oversight by States Parties, as for example, required by Japan.[286] In the context of donor fatigue during the late 1990s, including to the Ad Hoc Tribunals,[287] the question of financial oversight remained unresolved and a latent issue in Rome.[288]

The second provision dealing with the financial oversight responsibility of the Assembly was in Article 102(6) regulating the loss of voting rights for States in arrears. Originating from the French proposal,[289] States Parties in arrears equalling '[two full] [three] [five] years'[290] of their assessed contribution were not able to vote in the Bureau or the Assembly. However, still following the French proposal, the Assembly could decide to waive the sanction if the non–

282 Report of the Preparatory Committee on the Establishment of an International Criminal Court, UN Doc. A/CONF.183/2 3.

283 Bos, 'Assembly of States Parties' 2002 306.

284 Working Group on the Establishment of the Court and Relationship with the United Nations, Consolidated Text of Part 10 bis Assembly of States Parties, UN Doc. A/AC.249/1998/WG.8/CRP.l/Add.3 1.

285 Report of the Preparatory Committee on the Establishment of an International Criminal Court, Part 1 and Part 2, UN Doc. A/CONF.183/2/Add.1 161.

286 Statement by H.E. Mr. Hisashi Owada Permanent Representative of Japan, Establishment of the Court and Relationship with the United Nations, available at <https://www.legal-tools.org/doc/7bec05/> 4.

287 Zacklin, Ralph, 'The Failings of Ad Hoc International Tribunals Symposium: The ICTY 10 Years On: The View from Inside – A Tentative Appraisal' (2004) 2 (2) Journal of International Criminal Justice 543.

288 O'Donohue, Jonathan, 'Financing the International Criminal Court' in Rothe, Dawn L, Meernik, James and Ingadóttir, Þórdís (eds), The Realities of International Criminal Justice (Brill Nijhoff 2013) 269.

289 Draft Statute of the International Criminal Court, Working Paper Submitted by France, UN Doc. A/AC.249/L.3 23.

290 Report of the Preparatory Committee on the Establishment of an International Criminal Court, Part 1 and Part 2, UN Doc. A/CONF.183/2/Add.1 158–159.

TABLE 3.7 Draft Statute for the International Criminal Court (1998)

Function	Article 102
Financial Oversight	(2)(d) consider and approve the budget for the Court [in consultation with the Registrar] [and rule on any financial issue]. | Origin of the provision: France, United States, Plenary of the Preparatory Committee
	(6) [A State Party that is in arrears in the payment of its financial contributions to the costs of the Court shall have no vote in the Assembly and in the Bureau if the amount of its arrears equals or exceeds the amount of the contributions due from it for the preceding [two full] [three] [five] years. The Assembly may, nevertheless, permit such a State Party to vote in the Assembly and in the Bureau if it is satisfied that the failure to pay is due to conditions beyond the control of the State Party] | Origin of the provision: France, Working Group 8

payment reason pointed at a lack of capacity due to 'conditions beyond the control of the State Party'.[291] While the practice of disfranchisement of voting rights to non–compliant financial backers of international organizations was relevant to the working group, Article 102(6) did not reach consensus.[292] In fact, together with 102(2)(a) and (f), this was the third fully bracketed provision transmitted to the Diplomatic Conference. As Rao explained, the divergent views related to financial barriers of developing countries to fulfil financial obligations versus the need to achieve universality of ratifications.[293]

12 Conclusion

The working group led by Rao had, considering their mammoth task, less than a week to negotiate the governance provisions of the court. Echoing the same

291 Ibid.
292 Schabas, The International Criminal Court: A Commentary on the Rome Statute 1449.
293 Rao, (1999) 411.

sentiment from Zutphen, regretting the partial approach to the negotiations establishing the Assembly of States Parties, Bos acknowledged, 'it was clearly a handicap that the discussions of various parts of the Statute were not yet completed'.[294] The strategy to create silos to tackle complex judicial and non-judicial issues in the Statute achieved the final objective to adopt a draft text for negotiation, but at the expense of a comprehensive and detailed provision setting out the role and responsibility of the Assembly of States Parties. Neither the process at the International Law Commission nor the Ad Hoc Committee had resolved this question. Thus, while the text developed by the working group led by Rao finally created a governance forum for States Parties, the layered unresolved issues left to the Diplomatic Conference were far from simple.[295] By the end of the 1998 session, the Draft Statute contained 173 pages, 116 Articles and 1,300 pending language in brackets.[296] The key issues for the Diplomatic Conference to resolve included the jurisdictional regime, the proprio motu power of the Prosecutor, the role of the Security Council, the definition of war crimes,[297] and, as explained in this section, the membership, funding, arrears and non-cooperation enforcement by the Assembly of States Parties.[298]

On the 61st meeting of the Committee, on 3 April 1998, States approved the Draft Statute, the draft Final Act of the Diplomatic Conference, its draft Rules of Procedure and the draft schedule of work for Rome.[299] It also agreed on the list of civil society organizations credited to participate[300] and noted the nomination of Giovanni Conso (Italy) as President of the Conference, Bos as Chairman of the Committee of the Whole and Cherif Bassiouni to lead the Drafting Committee.[301] As negotiations moved from New York to the warm Italian summer, Warrick and Bassiouni's warning set the tone for drafting of Article 112 in Rome:

> For the International Criminal Court to succeed, considerable efforts and talents from States Parties and from the best jurists, prosecutors,

294 Bos, 'Assembly of States Parties' (2002) 301.

295 Rao and Ambach, (2016) 2217.

296 Bassiouni and Schabas, 80.

297 Preparatory Committee on Establishment of International Criminal Court Concludes Work by Adopting Draft Statute, UN Doc. L/2864.

298 Rao, (1999) 411.

299 Report of the Preparatory Committee on the Establishment of an International Criminal Court, UN Doc. A/CONF.183/2 4.

300 Ibid.

301 Ibid 5.

> investigators, and administrators will be essential. The Statute of the International Criminal Court must provide a sound administrative and financial foundation to ensure that the International Criminal Court becomes an effective instrument of international justice.[302]

302 Warrick and Bassiouni, 387.

CHAPTER 4

The Birth of the Assembly of States Parties to the Rome Statute

1 Introduction

The period between the Rome Conference in June–July 1998 and the sessions of the Preparatory Commission in 1999–2002 is the embryonic moment for the Assembly of States Parties to the Rome Statute. The diplomatic negotiations created the final legal text regulating the existence of the Assembly, and by 2002 the formative steps and documents for its establishment were completed. This chapter traces the choices that shaped the debate during this period giving birth to the Assembly. Doing so reveals that providing the International Criminal Court with an effective governing body was isolated to specific junctures during the negotiations in Rome, without considering the function of such body in the larger institution and effort to create a system of international justice. The work of the Preparatory Commission tried to rectify this outcome albeit only focusing on procedural steps to the creation of the Assembly rather than its significance as the governing body of the newly operational Court. In this context, this chapter first examines the negotiating outcomes of draft Article 102 on the Assembly of States Parties during the 1998 Rome Conference. Secondly, it examines the operational requirements imposed onto the Assembly as the Preparatory Commission built the architecture of the International Criminal Court between 1999 and 2002. Both parts of this chapter emphasize the expectations States put on the Assembly as they planned the first session in September 2002 in New York.

2 1998: The United Nations Diplomatic Conference of Plenipotentiaries on the Establishment of an International Criminal Court

The 1998 Diplomatic Conference in Rome was the culminating point for a centenary effort to create an international criminal court. The literature covering the Diplomatic Conference in Rome has expertly described the context, the critical issues, the factors influencing States' policy preferences and the

© EZEQUIEL JIMÉNEZ MARTINEZ, 2026 | DOI:10.1163/9789004749979_005

dramatic negotiations timeline.[1] The long-desired objective of ending impunity for atrocity crimes served as a powerful draw for States and civil society alike.[2] For Schabas, for example, what the United Nations War Crimes Commission called for in October 1944 was finally taking place in Rome.[3] Nonetheless, as Mégret suggests, unlike the 'excessively clean narrative of the Court's genesis',[4] the process to achieve the Rome Statute was charged with difficulties. For Gissel, the literature tends to reflect a history 'written by the victors of the negotiations in Rome'.[5] However, for Bassiouni, many of those 'victors' lacked expertise in the areas of discussion as governments favoured sending diplomats over legal experts.[6] In Kirsch and Oosterverld's view, finding common ground even at the expense of legal clarity was the main task in Rome.[7] For Sadat, delegates in Rome were 'framers of a new international organiza-

1 Kirsch, Philippe and Holmes, John T, 'The Rome Conference on an International Criminal Court: The Negotiating Process' (1999) 93 (1) The American Journal of International Law 2; Lee, Roy S, The International Criminal Court: The Making of the Rome Statute: Issues, Negotiations and Results (Martinus Nijhoff Publishers 1999); Kirsch, Philippe and Robinson, Darryl, 'Reaching Agreement at the Rome Conference' in Cassese, Antonio, Gaeta, Paola and Jones, John RWD (eds), The Rome Statute of the International Criminal Court: a Commentary, vol 1 (Oxford University Press Oxford 2002); Benedetti, Fanny, Bonneau, Karine and Washburn, John, Negotiating the International Criminal Court: New York to Rome, 1994–1998 (Martinus Nijhoff Publishers 2014); Bassiouni, M Cherif and Schabas, William A, The Legislative History of the International Criminal Court, vol 1 (2 edn, Brill | Nijhoff 2016); Conso, Giovanni, 'Some Reflections on the Rome Conference' in Politi, Mauro and Nesi, Guiseppe (eds), The Rome Statute of the International Criminal Court: a Challenge to Impunity (Routledge 2001); Mégret, Frédéric, 'The Rome Conference: Institutional Design and the Constraints of Diplomacy' in deGuzman, Margaret and Oosterveld, Valerie (eds), The Elgar Companion to the International Criminal Court (Edward Elgar Publishing 2020); Gissel, Line Engbo, 'Nomos and Narrative in International Criminal Justice: Creating the International Criminal Court' (2022) 20 (1) Journal of International Criminal Justice 117.

2 Deitelhoff, Nicole and Wallbott, Linda, 'Beyond Soft Balancing: Small States and Coalition-Building in the ICC and Climate Negotiations' (2012) 25 (3) Cambridge Review of International Affairs 353.

3 Schabas, 'The United Nations War Crimes Commission's Proposal for an International Criminal Court' 188.

4 Mégret, 'The Rome Conference: Institutional Design and the Constraints of Diplomacy' (2020) 22.

5 Gissel, 'Nomos and Narrative in International Criminal Justice: Creating the International Criminal Court' 137.

6 Bassiouni, 'Negotiating the Treaty of Rome on the Establishment of an International Criminal Court' 460.

7 Kirsch, Philippe and Oosterveld, Valerie, 'Negotiating an Institution For The Twenty-First Century: Multilateral Diplomacy and The International Criminal Court' (2001) 46 (4) McGill Law Journal (1153).

tion'[8] as they detailed legal provisions and created a whole new institution for enforcement. For Washburn, the fact delegates were creating a 'new international institution including its governance, administration, structure, financing, and fundamental procedures' meant 'a venture so new that it seemed to open the future'.[9] The creation of the Assembly of States Parties was part of the reckoning at the Diplomatic Conference.

2.1 *Arriving in Rome: Context and Key Actors*

A delay in translation from English to other languages of the Draft Statute meant governments had a very narrow window to analyse its contents and develop policy positions.[10] The complexity and size of the Draft Statute did not help. As Bassiouni noted, it ran at '173 pages and consisted of 116 articles with some 1300 brackets for optional provisions and word choices'.[11] For Rosenne, the basic text was not conducive for negotiations.[12] To add complexity, the vast diplomatic task ahead suffered a setback when Ambassador Adriaan Bos, the long-serving and respected Chairman of the preparatory process, became ill preventing his participation in Rome.[13] At the recommendation from Bos, Ambassador Philippe Kirsch of Canada was proposed as a replacement.[14] Ambassador Kirsch was only able to assume leadership two days before the Diplomatic Conference began.[15] The Diplomatic Conference attracted the most participating States from any moment in the period creating the International Criminal Court. A total of 160 States were accredited,[16]

8 Sadat, Leila Nadya and Carden, S Richard, 'The New International Criminal Court: An Uneasy Revolution' (2000) 88 (3) Georgetown Law Journal 390 at footnote 335.

9 Washburn, John, 'The Negotiation of the Rome Statute for the International Criminal Court and International Lawmaking in the 21st Century' (1999) 11 (2) Pace International Law Review 365–366.

10 Bassiouni, 'Negotiating the Treaty of Rome on the Establishment of an International Criminal Court' 444–445.

11 Ibid 445.

12 Rosenne, Shabtai, 'Poor Drafting and Imperfect Organization: Flaws to Overcome in the Rome Statute' (2000) 41 (1) Virginia Journal of International Law 167.

13 Benedetti and Washburn, 27.

14 United Nations Diplomatic Conference of Plenipotentiaries on the Establishment of an International Criminal Court, Reports and Other Documents, UN Doc. A/CONF.183/13 (Vol. III) (1998) 190.

15 Bassiouni, 'Negotiating the Treaty of Rome on the Establishment of an International Criminal Court' 448.

16 United Nations Diplomatic Conference of Plenipotentiaries on the Establishment of an International Criminal Court, Reports and Other Documents, UN Doc. A/CONF.183/13 (Vol. III) 3.

representing 86% of membership of the United Nations,[17] with 67 countries participating for the first time in negotiations.[18] A total of 48 African[19] and 37 Asian States led the number of delegations in Rome.[20] As Lee explained, the number of participating States in Rome was the highest of any United Nations-led conference.[21] However, the majority of delegates were new to the complex Draft Statute, which 'slowed the negotiations'.[22] In this sense, the 236 civil society organizations, under the umbrella of the Coalition for an International Criminal Court, played a decisive role in assisting States.[23] Beyond States and civil society organizations, 20 intergovernmental organizations, 14 specialized agencies of the United Nations, 474 journalists and 80 interpreters participated in Rome.[24]

For a Conference attended by hundreds of people dealing with a mammoth task of resolving 1300 brackets in the Draft Statute, compounded by some 200 additional written proposals over five weeks, the 'fact that the Conference succeeded in adopting the Rome Statute was in itself an outstanding achievement'.[25] A key reason for the completion of negotiations in Rome was the continuity of a core group of diplomats since the Ad Hoc Committee in 1995. As Bassiouni explained, the companionship despite their differences, 'fostered cooperation and a collegial atmosphere'.[26] This group included the designated

---

17 United Nations, 'Growth in United Nations Membership' (United Nations, 2022) <https://www.un.org/en/about-us/growth-in-un-membership> accessed January 28, (2022).

18 Bhutan, Cook Islands, Democratic Republic of Korea, Equatorial Guinea, Granada, Kiribati, Laos, Lebanon, Malaysia, Maldives, Mauritania, Micronesia, Myanmar, Palau, Papa New Guinea, Rwanda, Saint Kitts and Nevis, Saint Vincent and the Grenadines, Somalia, Suriname, Swaziland, Tonga, Turkmenistan, Tuvalu, and Vanuatu.

19 Nimigan, Sarah, 'The Problems Facing the International Criminal Court: African Perspectives' (The University of Western Ontario 2021) 95.

20 United Nations Diplomatic Conference of Plenipotentiaries on the Establishment of an International Criminal Court, Final Documents, UN Doc. A/CONF.183/13 (Vol. I) (1998) 74.

21 Lee, Roy S, 'Creating an International Criminal Court: Of Procedures and Compromises' in Hebel, Herman A.M. von, Lammers, J. G. and Schukking, Jolien (eds), Reflections on the International Criminal Court: Essays in Honour of Adriaan Bos (TMC Asser Press 1999) 143.

22 Bassiouni, 'Negotiating the Treaty of Rome on the Establishment of an International Criminal Court' 446.

23 Benedetti, Bonneau and Washburn, 95.

24 Lee, The International Criminal Court: The Making of the Rome Statute: Issues, Negotiations and Results 14.

25 Ibid 13.

26 Bassiouni, 'Negotiating the Treaty of Rome on the Establishment of an International Criminal Court' 455.

Bureau in Rome,[27] delegates from States, United Nations officials,[28] civil society leaders[29] and academics.[30] For Mégret, representing France, the 'transgovernmental solidarities' developed across the preparatory process 'would prove extremely useful in the final days of the Rome Conference'.[31] In this sense, the Coalition for an International Criminal Court was integral to the adoption of the Rome Statute.[32] Indeed, there were more civil society organizations (236) registered than States (160).[33] Civil society were key in providing technical papers overnight on solutions jamming negotiations between States.[34] As Benedetti, Bonneau and Washburn explained, 'that kind of rapid reaction earns you respect, earns you access and was a key to the NGO power, access and influence in the negotiations'.[35] John Washburn form the Washington Working Group on the International Criminal Court led the monitoring of Part 11 on the Assembly of States Parties.[36]

As Schabas showed, the pending issues in the Draft Statute were mostly political in nature.[37] The priority issues included the jurisdictional regime and definition of crimes, including aggression, complementarity, the role of the Prosecutor, the involvement of the United Nations Security Council, cooperation with the court, its funding, and governance via the Assembly of States Parties.[38] The degree of political will was more important than the

27 United Nations Diplomatic Conference of Plenipotentiaries on the Establishment of an International Criminal Court, Final Documents, UN Doc. A/CONF.183/13 (Vol. I) 68.

28 Ibid 69.

29 Washburn, John, 'The Formation and Nature of the International Criminal Court' (2006) 14 (1) Michigan State Journal of International Law 16.

30 Washburn, 'The Negotiation of the Rome Statute for the International Criminal Court and International Lawmaking in the 21st Century' 364.

31 Mégret, 'The Rome Conference: Institutional Design and the Constraints of Diplomacy' (2020) 26.

32 Pace and Schense, (2002).

33 United Nations Diplomatic Conference of Plenipotentiaries on the Establishment of an International Criminal Court, Final Documents, UN Doc. A/CONF.183/13 (Vol. I) 74.

34 Benedetti, Bonneau and Washburn, 85.

35 Washburn, 'The Formation and Nature of the International Criminal Court' 17.

36 World Federalist Movement/Institute for Global Policy, Center for the Development of International Law, Center for UN Reform Education, Rome Report of the Coalition for an International Criminal Court (2018) 274.

37 Schabas, The International Criminal Court: A Commentary on the Rome Statute 22.

38 United Nations Diplomatic Conference to Establish International Criminal Court to Convene in Rome, 15 June – 17 July, UN Doc. L/2867 (1998).

technical difficulty of drafting of the statute.[39] As such, given the perceived erosion of sovereignty, States focused on particular issues with more emphasis than others. Mégret helpfully distinguished them between 'high politics' priorities dealing with 'jurisdiction, trigger mechanisms, complementarity and the Security Council' versus 'institutional aspects [like the] Assembly of States Parties, election of office-holders'.[40] While inherently political, the Assembly of States Parties discussion did not enter the roam of 'high politics' as governments' concerns laid primarily in Part 2 of the Draft Statute. Nonetheless, as Lee also argued, there were 'inseparable linkages' between 'high politics' areas of the Draft Statute and the role of the Assembly to afford the nascent court with its most basic functions.[41]

2.2 *The Organization of Article 102 Negotiations*

As agreed by the Preparatory Committee, the Conference was governed by the interplay of committees assigned specific tasks.[42] Of these, the Committee of the Whole and the Drafting Committee were of particular importance for the negotiation of the Assembly of States Parties. The Committee of the Whole was principally in charge of concluding agreements on pending issues of the Draft Statute. It was comprised of Chairman Philippe Kirsch (Canada), Vice-Chairmen Silvia Fernández de Gurmendi (Argentina), Constantin Virgil Ivan (Romania), Phakiso Mochochoko (Lesotho) and Yasumasa Nagamine (Japan) as rapporteur.[43] Rule 57 was relevant as it permitted public meetings of the Committee of the Whole.[44] Similarly, Rule 34 endeavoured decision-making by consensus but also stipulated direct voting if 'all feasible efforts to reach

39 Bassiouni, M Cherif, 'Enforcing Human Rights Through International Criminal Law and Through an International Criminal Tribunal' (1994) 26 Studies in Transnational Legal Policy 362.

40 Mégret, 'The Rome Conference: Institutional Design and the Constraints of Diplomacy' (2020) 41.

41 Lee, The International Criminal Court: The Making of the Rome Statute: Issues, Negotiations and Results 21.

42 United Nations Diplomatic Conference of Plenipotentiaries on the Establishment of an International Criminal Court, Organization of Work, Memorandum of the Secretary-General on the Methods of Work and Procedures for the Conference, UN Doc. A/CONF.183/3 (1998) 1.

43 United Nations Diplomatic Conference of Plenipotentiaries on the Establishment of an International Criminal Court, Final Documents, UN Doc. A/CONF.183/13 (Vol. I) 68.

44 United Nations Diplomatic Conference of Plenipotentiaries on the Establishment of an International Criminal Court, Summary Records of the Plenary Meetings and of the Meetings of the Committee of the Whole, UN Doc. A/CONF.183/13 (Vol. II) (1998) 59.

general agreement have failed'.[45] Between 16 June and 17 July 1998, the Committee of the Whole met 42 times.[46]

Rule 49 of the Conference created the Drafting Committee in charge of, 'without altering their substance',[47] provide overall legal and linguistic cohesiveness to the final statute. The Drafting Committee comprised of 25 States led by Cherif Bassiouni (Egypt).[48] As Chairman, Bassiouni commanded respect from States as a towering figure in making the Conference a reality.[49] Sadat wondered 'if there would even be an ICC had not Bassiouni made its establishment a goal of his life and work'.[50] Over the period of five weeks, it would receive a variance of articles, whole parts and intricate options to make sense in a final statute. Bassiouni described the task of the Drafting Committee as the 'assembly of a large jigsaw puzzle'.[51] Enabling the Committee of the Whole and the Drafting Committee, the United Nations Secretariat, in particular the Codification Division of the Office of Legal Affairs played a significant role in Rome, for example Renan Villacis, later the Director of the Secretariat of the Assembly of States Parties to the Rome Statute, acted as an Assistant Secretary of the Conference.[52]

To overcome the political pending issues in the Draft Statute, the Committee of the Whole continued with the preparatory process tactic of assigning contentious questions to working groups led by coordinators.[53] In its second meeting, the Committee of the Whole formally created five working groups covering parts 4–10 of the Draft Statute led by delegates with a leadership

---

45 Report of the Preparatory Committee on the Establishment of an International Criminal Court Addendum, Part 3, UN Doc. A/CONF.183/2/Add.2/Rev.1 (1998) 12.

46 United Nations Diplomatic Conference of Plenipotentiaries on the Establishment of an International Criminal Court, Reports and Other Documents, UN Doc. A/CONF.183/13 (Vol. III) 93.

47 United Nations Diplomatic Conference of Plenipotentiaries on the Establishment of an International Criminal Court, Summary Records of the Plenary Meetings and of the Meetings of the Committee of the Whole, UN Doc. A/CONF.183/13 (Vol. II) 58.

48 United Nations Diplomatic Conference of Plenipotentiaries on the Establishment of an International Criminal Court, Final Documents, UN Doc. A/CONF.183/13 (Vol. I) 69.

49 de La Cuesta and Ottenhof, 1247.

50 Sadat, Leila Nadya, 'The International Criminal Court and the Transformation of International Law' in Scharf, Michael and Sadat, Leila Nadya (eds), The Theory and Practice of International Criminal Law (Brill Nijhoff 2008) 310.

51 Bassiouni, 'Negotiating the Treaty of Rome on the Establishment of an International Criminal Court' 452–453.

52 United Nations Diplomatic Conference of Plenipotentiaries on the Establishment of an International Criminal Court, Final Documents, UN Doc. A/CONF.183/13 (Vol. I) 69.

53 Benedetti, Bonneau and Washburn, 95–96.

track record since the 1995 Ad Hoc Committee.[54] Part 11 in the Draft Statute, on the Assembly of States Parties, was not treated through a formal working group created by the Committee of the Whole, but rather 'coordinated'[55] by Rama Rao. This is confirmed in the existing record, noting, simply, 'a number of remaining articles and parts were referred to informal consultations after discussions in the Committee of the Whole'.[56] Article 102 was referred exclusively for informal consultations. The allocation of formal working groups to parts of the Draft Statute signalled which articles required political assertiveness to solve pending issues. This, on the other hand, affected the conception of the Assembly of States Parties beyond a mere statutory governance requirement in a multilateral treaty. A decision that impacted the inherent relationship of Article 112 with other parts of the Rome Statute.

In this context, Part 11 on the Assembly of States Parties was discussed seven times at variable length and depth by the Committee of the Whole.[57] In fact, the 18th and 24th meeting on 29 June and 6 July respectively, were the most consequential to the creation of Article 112 in the Rome Statute. Throughout the negotiating period, only four proposals from States were introduced,[58] and the Drafting Committee resolved any imprecisions in two reports.[59] As Rao recalls, the debate was 'lengthy and relatively uncontroversial',[60] and 'proceeded in a business-like manner'.[61] The uncontested creation of the Assembly of States Parties was logical comparing with issues in Part 2 of the Draft Statute, but also revealed a shallow attempt at considering the function of such body and inherent relationship with the larger institution being created.

2.3 *The Pending Issues and Timeline of Article 102 Negotiations*

In the context of the long-history of the Assembly of States Parties to the Rome Statute covered earlier in this book, the Rome Conference gave birth to the

54 United Nations Diplomatic Conference of Plenipotentiaries on the Establishment of an International Criminal Court, Summary Records of the Plenary Meetings and of the Meetings of the Committee of the Whole, UN Doc. A/CONF.183/13 (Vol. II) 138.

55 Kirsch and Robinson, (2002) 73 at footnote 18.

56 United Nations Diplomatic Conference of Plenipotentiaries on the Establishment of an International Criminal Court, Reports and Other Documents, UN Doc. A/CONF.183/13 (Vol. III) 93–94.

57 Ibid 346.

58 Ibid 138.

59 Bassiouni, 'Negotiating the Treaty of Rome on the Establishment of an International Criminal Court' 451.

60 Rao and Ambach, (2016) 2217.

61 Rao, 1999 411.

governance provision of the International Criminal Court in a matter of days. Led by Rama Rao from India, States had already agreed in the last session of the Preparatory Committee to establish the International Criminal Court as an independent organization, albeit, in a close relationship with the United Nations.[62] For Sadat, by establishing the court as an independent organization, the Diplomatic Conference was akin to a constitutional moment in international law, 'albeit sotto voce'.[63] However, as Bos argued, it also reminded States of the clear contour between a purely judicial function led by the organs of the Court, and States Parties exclusive oversight over 'administrative and operational activities'[64] of the institution. For Warrick and Bassiouni, resolving well the functions of the Assembly of States Parties provision, 'was certain to determine, in the long run, the effectiveness of the Court'.[65] Thus, as Gradoni and Roberts agreed, Article 102, embodying the nature of the Statute as the charter of an independent organization, prefigured Article 112 in the Rome Statute.[66]

Article 102 in the Draft Statute in Rome consisted of seven clauses (see Table 4.1). Of these, three were fully bracketed denoting lack of consensus in their entirety. Clause (2)(a) on the interplay between the Assembly and the Preparatory Commission, (2)(f) on the powers of the Assembly over non-cooperation, and (6) on loss of voting rights due to arrears arrived in Rome unresolved. On the other hand, (2)(b) on the Assembly's management oversight over the organs of the court, (2)(c) on consideration of reports and activities of the Bureau, and (7) granting the Assembly its own Rules of Procedure gathered full consensus. In between, nine sections in Article 102 contained 32 brackets with options for the Diplomatic Conference to resolve.[67] The contention over clause (2)(a) on the interplay between the Assembly and the Preparatory Commission emanated from the desire of some delegations to negotiate in Rome the Rules of Procedure and Evidence and the Elements of Crimes, citing their relevance to the statute.[68]

Clause (2)(f) on the powers of the Assembly over non-cooperation attracted more disagreement than any of the three unresolved clauses. This clause was

62 Ambach, 'Article 2 Relationship of the Court with the United Nations' (2016) 27.
63 Sadat, The International Criminal Court and the Transformation of International Law: Justice for the New Millennium 79.
64 Bos, 'Assembly of States Parties' (2002) 301.
65 Warrick and Bassiouni, 333.
66 Gradoni, (2012) 2008; Roberts, (2013) 495.
67 Report of the Preparatory Committee on the Establishment of an International Criminal Court, Part 1 and Part 2, UN Doc. A/CONF.183/2/Add.1 157–159.
68 Schabas, The International Criminal Court: A Commentary on the Rome Statute (1437).

intimately related with parallel negotiations over the cooperation regime in Article 86(5) and (7). In fact, the conclusion of the Assembly of States Parties provision in Rome was delayed due to dissent in Part 9.[69] Finally, clause (6) on loss of voting rights due to arrears arrived in Rome only after minimal engagement in the last preparatory session.[70] While the practice of disfranchisement of voting rights to non-compliant financial backers of international organizations was well established, the main source of controversy resided in the financial barriers of developing countries to fulfil financial obligations versus the need to achieve universality of ratifications.[71]

The Committee of the Whole did not formally establish a working group for Part 11.[72] Instead, after considering Article 102 for the first time in its 18th meeting on 29 June, it entrusted Rama Rao to 'coordinate informal consultations on the text'.[73] Lee characterized Rao's role as 'magnificently'[74] performed. The meetings of the informal working group were private,[75] but in practice they allowed engagement from civil society.[76] The available written record of negotiations on Part 11 does not clarify how many informal meetings Rao led nor the composition of States debating its content. The decision by the Bureau to utilize an informal arrangement meant the available documents only describe the grand contour of what happened to Article 102. As Schabas notes, formal proposals from States or the coordinator and the agreed texts remain as authorities of the drafting process.[77] In this context, secondary sources such as reports from civil society are an important complement. Through reporting from the Coalition for an International Criminal Court it is possible to uncover that Denmark, Germany, Sweden, Australia, United

---

69 Sluiter, Göran, 'Enforcing Cooperation: Did the Drafters Approach It the Wrong Way?' (2018) 16 (2) Journal of International Criminal Justice 384.

70 Arsanjani, (2002) 322.

71 Rao, 1999 411.

72 United Nations Diplomatic Conference of Plenipotentiaries on the Establishment of an International Criminal Court, Reports and Other Documents, UN Doc. A/CONF.183/13 (Vol. III) 93–94.

73 Ibid 346.

74 Lee, The International Criminal Court: The Making of the Rome Statute: Issues, Negotiations and Results 22.

75 United Nations Diplomatic Conference of Plenipotentiaries on the Establishment of an International Criminal Court, Summary Records of the Plenary Meetings and of the Meetings of the Committee of the Whole, UN Doc. A/CONF.183/13 (Vol. II) 59.

76 Benedetti, Bonneau and Washburn, 99.

77 Schabas, William A, 'The Dynamics of the Rome Conference' in deGuzman, Margaret and Oosterveld, Valerie (eds), The Elgar Companion to the International Criminal Court (Edward Elgar Publishing 2020) 7.

TABLE 4.1 Rome Conference (1998)

Function	Draft Statute article 102	Pending issues
Governance and Management Oversight	(1) There is hereby established an Assembly of States Parties to this Statute. Each State Party shall have one representative in the Assembly who may be accompanied by alternates and advisers. The signatories of the [Statute] [Final Act] may be [observers] [members] in the Assembly. (2) The Assembly shall: [(a) consider and adopt recommendations of the preparatory commission;]	(1) Assembly membership. 4 brackets. (2)(a) Interplay between the Assembly and the Preparatory Commission. *Provision without consensus (fully bracketed).*
Governance and Management Oversight	(b) provide management oversight to the Presidency, Prosecutor and Registrar regarding the administration of the Court; (c) consider the reports and activities of the Bureau and take appropriate action in regard thereto.	
Financial Oversight	(2)(d) consider and approve the budget for the Court [in consultation with the Registrar] [and rule on any financial issue].	(2)(d) Assembly budget oversight powers, role of the Registrar. 2 brackets.
Governance and Management Oversight	(e) determine whether to alter, as appropriate, the number of judges [or members of the Office of the Prosecutor or the Registry], serving on a full– or part-time basis, for such period as it shall determine.	(2)(e) Assembly power to alter staffing of the Office of the Prosecutor and Registry. 1 bracket.
Enforcement of Cooperation	(2) [(f) consider, upon recommendation [of the Court] [of the Bureau], any question relating to non-cooperation by States Parties [and non-States Parties] and take [necessary] [appropriate] measures, including referring the matter to [the Security Council] [the United Nations General Assembly] as provided in article 86.]	(2)(f) Assembly power on non-cooperation. 7 brackets. *Provision without consensus (fully bracketed)*

TABLE 4.1 Rome Conference (1998) (*cont.*)

Function	Draft Statute article 102	Pending issues
Governance and Management Oversight	(g) perform any other function or take any other action as specified in this Statute or the Rules of Procedure and Evidence [including consideration of requests for a review of these instruments] [including consideration of applications relating to pardon submitted to it.]	(2)(g) Assembly power to review the Statute and the Rules of Procedure and Evidence, and granting pardons. 2 brackets.
	(3)(a) The Assembly shall have a Bureau consisting of a President, a Vice-President and [18] members elected by the Assembly for three-year terms. The President of the Court, the Prosecutor and the Registrar or their representatives may, as appropriate, participate as [observers] [members] in meetings of the Bureau.	(3)(a) Bureau membership and participation of Court officers in Bureau meetings. 3 brackets.
	(b) The Bureau shall [have a representative character] [be elected on the basis of ensuring its representative character], taking into account, in particular, equitable geographical distribution and bearing in mind the adequate representation of the principal legal systems of the world [as far as possible]. The Bureau shall meet as often as necessary, but at least once a year, and shall assist the Assembly in the discharge of its responsibilities.	(3)(b) Representative composition of the Bureau. 3 brackets. (3)(c) Independent oversight over Court organs. 2 brackets
	(c) The Assembly may also establish other subsidiary bodies as may be necessary, including an independent oversight mechanism for inspection, evaluation, and investigation in order to enhance the efficiency and economy of [non-judicial administration] [operations] of the Court.	(4) Location of Assembly meetings and authority to convene special sessions.2 brackets.
	(4) The Assembly shall meet at the seat of the Court or at the Headquarters of the United Nations [or in any other place as it may decide] once a year and, when circumstances so require, hold special sessions. Except as otherwise specified in the Statute, special sessions shall be convened [by the Bureau on its own initiative or] at the request of one third of the States Parties.	(5) Voting majority requirements for decision-making. 3 brackets.

TABLE 4.1 Rome Conference (1998) (*cont.*)

Function	Draft Statute article 102	Pending issues
	(5) Each State Party shall have one vote. Every effort shall be made to reach decisions on matters of substance by consensus in the Assembly and in the Bureau. If consensus cannot be reached, decisions on matters of substance must be approved by [a two-thirds majority of those present and voting, representing the absolute majority of States Parties] [a two-thirds majority of those present and voting] [an absolute majority of States Parties] except as otherwise provided in the Statute.	
Financial Oversight	(6) [A State Party that is in arrears in the payment of its financial contributions to the costs of the Court shall have no vote in the Assembly and in the Bureau if the amount of its arrears equals or exceeds the amount of the contributions due from it for the preceding [two full] [three] [five] years. The Assembly may, nevertheless, permit such a State Party to vote in the Assembly and in the Bureau if it is satisfied that the failure to pay is due to conditions beyond the control of the State Party]	(6) Loss of voting rights due to arrears. 3 brackets. *Provision without consensus* (*fully bracketed*)
Governance and Management Oversight	(7) The Assembly shall adopt its own Rules of Procedure.	

Kingdom, France, United States and New Zealand were active in negotiating Article 102.[78] France and the United States continued their engagement from 1996–1998, and in particular the United States projected a more flexible and helpful position than in other areas of the Draft Statute.[79] Ambassadors Arnold Skibsted (Denmark) and Ulrike Sundberg (Sweden) represented the views of the Like-Minded States as topic coordinators.[80] United Nations officials Mahnoush Arsanjani and Christiane Bourloyannis-Vrailas assisted the informal group;[81] however, 'there was very little interest otherwise … by IOs [International Organizations] and NGOs'.[82] Although more States became engaged in negotiating Article 102 in meetings of the Committee of the Whole, it appears a negligible number of States and civil society assisted Rao. Lack of participation from entire regional groups was equally problematic.

The newness of Article 102 in the Draft Statute, the lack of time for preparation and general novelty of a governance provision for an international criminal court could have contributed to explaining why it 'did not much interest either governments or NGO'.[83] Given the perceived erosion of sovereignty, it is logical States focused on particular 'high politics' issues than on 'institutional aspects'.[84] In this context, the assertion in the literature that negotiating Article 102 was 'uncontroversial',[85] or 'reached without difficulty',[86] should be caveated minding the degree of participation from States and civil society in its crafting. More so when there were 'inseparable linkages'[87] between 'high politics' areas of the Draft Statute and the role of the Assembly to afford the

78 World Federalist Movement/Institute for Global Policy, (2018) 282.

79 Scheffer, David, Developments at the Rome Treaty Conference (Department of State Dispatch, 1998) 20; Scheffer, David, 'The United States and the International Criminal Court' (1999) 93 (1) American Journal of International Law 13.

80 World Federalist Movement/Institute for Global Policy, (2018) 275.

81 Arsanjani, Mahnoush, 'The Rome Statute of the International Criminal Court' (1999) 93 (1) The American Journal of International Law 41.

82 World Federalist Movement/Institute for Global Policy, (2018) 282.

83 Ibid 283.

84 Mégret, 'The Rome Conference: Institutional Design and the Constraints of Diplomacy' (2020) 41.

85 Jarasch, Frank, 'Establishment, Organization and Financing of the International Criminal Court (Parts I, IV, XI–XIII)' (1998) 6 (4) European Journal of Crime Criminal Law and Criminal Justice 339; Roberts, (2013) 495; Rao and Ambach, (2016) 2217.

86 Barberini, (2006) 1562; Gradoni, (2012) 2010.

87 Lee, The International Criminal Court: The Making of the Rome Statute: Issues, Negotiations and Results 21.

nascent Court with its most basic functions, for example in the election of the Prosecutor.

In this context, Part 11 was revised throughout the five-week Diplomatic Conference (see Table 4.2).[88] It was discussed seven times by the Committee of the Whole, at its 18th (29 June), 24th (6 July), 30th (9 July), 37th (14 July), 38th (15 July), 39th (15 July), 41st meeting (16 July), and adopted at the 42nd meeting on 17 July 1998.[89] The plenary adopted Part 11 during its final 9th meeting, late, on the same day.[90] The Statute adopted by the final plenary transformed Article 102 into 112 after revised numbering.[91] Rao responded to discussions from the Committee of the Whole by preparing a Coordinator Text report on 3 July, and three Recommendation reports to solve outstanding disagreements on Article 102(5) on voting majorities for decision-making and Article (2)(f) on non-cooperation.[92] The Drafting Committee reviewed Part 11 and reported back to the Committee of the Whole in two instances: on 14 July containing the final language of Article 102(5), and on 16 July, at the penultimate meeting of the Committee of the Whole, considering the language of Article 102(2)(f).[93]

Part 11 received four amendment proposals.[94] Two amendments were received by the Committee of the Whole in time for its 18th meeting, on 29 June, discussing the Assembly of States Parties for the first time. The amendments received were from Mexico (proposed on 22 June) and Andorra, Argentina, Bolivia, Chile, Colombia, Dominican Republic, El Salvador, Guatemala, Panama, Paraguay, Peru, Spain, Uruguay and Venezuela (proposed on 23 June). In the same meeting, Mexico withdrew its amendment from consideration. The third amendment originated from Ukraine on 29 June and was

88 United Nations Diplomatic Conference of Plenipotentiaries on the Establishment of an International Criminal Court, Reports and Other Documents, UN Doc. A/CONF.183/13 (Vol. III) 346.

89 Ibid.

90 Ibid.

91 United Nations Diplomatic Conference of Plenipotentiaries on the Establishment of an International Criminal Court, Rome Statute of the International Criminal Court, UN Doc. A/CONF.183/9* (1998) 81–83.

92 United Nations Diplomatic Conference of Plenipotentiaries on the Establishment of an International Criminal Court, Reports and Other Documents, UN Doc. A/CONF.183/13 (Vol. III) 138.

93 Bassiouni, 'Negotiating the Treaty of Rome on the Establishment of an International Criminal Court' 451.

94 United Nations Diplomatic Conference of Plenipotentiaries on the Establishment of an International Criminal Court, Reports and Other Documents, UN Doc. A/CONF.183/13 (Vol. III) 138.

TABLE 4.2 Rome Conference (1998)

Timeline	Negotiation body	Outcome
29 June	Committee of the Whole, 18th meeting	Introduction of Draft Statute Part 11 by Rao. Substantial discussion across articles.[a]
2 July	Coordinator's Text for Article 102 (L.41)	Changes across articles.[b]
3 July	Coordinator's Text for Article 102 (L.41/Corr.1)	Corrigendum text for Article 102(2)(g).[c]
3 July	Recommendations of the Coordinator (L.47)	Report on informal negotiations for the Committee of the Whole. Article 102(2)(f) pending.[d]
6 July	Committee of the Whole, 24th meeting	Discussion of Coordinator's Report (L.47). Discussion across articles. Article 102(2)(f) on non-cooperation and (5) on voting majorities pending further negotiations.[e]
6 July	Recommendations of the Coordinator (L.47/Corr.1)	Corrigendum report reflecting the outcome of discussions at the 24th meeting of the Committee of the Whole.[f]
7 July	Drafting Committee (R.87)	Reception of transmitted Article 102, except 102(2)(f) and (5), from the Committee of the Whole.[g]

a United Nations Diplomatic Conference of Plenipotentiaries on the Establishment of an International Criminal Court, Summary Records of the Plenary Meetings and of the Meetings of the Committee of the Whole, UN Doc. A/CONF.183/13 (Vol. II) 244.

b Committee of the Whole, Coordinator's Text for Article 102 Assembly of States Parties, UN Doc. A/CONF.183/C.1/L.41 (1998).

c Committee of the Whole, Coordinator's Text for Article 102 Assembly of States Parties, Corrigendum, UN Doc. A/CONF.183/C.1/L.41/Corr.1 (1998).

d Committee of the Whole, Recommendations of the Coordinator, Article 102 Assembly of States Parties, UN Doc. A/CONF.183/C.1/L.47 (1998).

e United Nations Diplomatic Conference of Plenipotentiaries on the Establishment of an International Criminal Court, Summary Records of the Plenary Meetings and of the Meetings of the Committee of the Whole, UN Doc. A/CONF.183/13 (Vol. II) 266.

f Committee of the Whole, Recommendations of the Coordinator, Article 102 Assembly of States Parties, UN Doc. A/CONF.183/C.1/L.47/Corr.1 (1998).

g Drafting Committee, Articles Referred by the Committee of the Whole, UN Doc. A/CONF.183/DC/R.87 (1998) 41–42.

TABLE 4.2 Rome Conference (1998) (*cont.*)

Timeline	Negotiation body	Outcome
8 July	Recommendations of the Coordinator (L.47/Add.1)	Report on informal negotiations on 102(5) for the Committee of the Whole.[h]
9 July	Committee of the Whole, 30th meeting	Discussion of Coordinator's Report (L.47/Add.1). Agreement on Article 102(5) on voting majorities. Transmission of Article 102(5) to the Drafting Committee.[i]
9 July	Drafting Committee (L.58)	Compendium of Draft Articles referred to the Drafting Committee by the Committee of the Whole as of 9 July. Article 102(5) included and (2)(f) on non-cooperation pending.[j]
13 July	Drafting Committee (L.66)	Report of the Drafting Committee to the Committee of the Whole. Part 11 language and structure refined. Article 102(2)(f) on non-cooperation pending.[k]
14 July	Committee of the Whole, 37th meeting	Consideration of the Drafting Committee Report (L.66). Article 102(2)(f) on non-cooperation pending.[l]
14 July	Recommendations of the Coordinator (L.47/Add.2)	Report on informal negotiations on 102(2)(f) for the Committee of the Whole.[m]

h Committee of the Whole, Recommendations of the Coordinator, Article 102 Assembly of States Parties, UN Doc. A/CONF.183/C.1/L.47/Add.1 (1998).

i United Nations Diplomatic Conference of Plenipotentiaries on the Establishment of an International Criminal Court, Summary Records of the Plenary Meetings and of the Meetings of the Committee of the Whole, UN Doc. A/CONF.183/13 (Vol. II) 305.

j Draft Statute for the International Criminal Court, Compendium of Draft Articles Referred to the Drafting Committee by the Committee of the Whole as of 9 July 1998, UN Doc. A/CONF.183/C.1/L.58 (1998) 63–64.

k Report of the Drafting Committee to the Committee of the Whole Part 11 Assembly of States Parties, UN Doc. A/CONF.183/C.1/L.66 (1998).

l United Nations Diplomatic Conference of Plenipotentiaries on the Establishment of an International Criminal Court, Summary Records of the Plenary Meetings and of the Meetings of the Committee of the Whole, UN Doc. A/CONF.183/13 (Vol. II) 350.

m Committee of the Whole, Recommendations of the Coordinator, Article 102 Assembly of States Parties, UN Doc. A/CONF.183/C.1/L.47/Add.2 (1998).

TABLE 4.2 Rome Conference (1998) (*cont.*)

Timeline	Negotiation body	Outcome
15 July (3pm)	Committee of the Whole, 38th meeting	Discussion of Coordinator's Report (L.47/ Add.2). Adoption of Article 102(2)(f) on non-cooperation. Transmission of Article 102(2) (f) to the Drafting Committee.[n]
15 July (6:25pm)	Committee of the Whole, 39th meeting	Adoption of Drafting Committee Report on Part 11 (L.66), except Article 102(2)(f) as drafting pending.[o]
15 July	Drafting Committee (L.66/ Add.1)	Addendum Report of the Drafting Committee to the Committee of the Whole with drafted Article 102(2)(f).[p]
16 July (3:15pm)	Committee of the Whole, 41st meeting	Adoption of Article 102(2)(f) as per L.47/ Add.2.[q]
16 July	Bureau	Bureau package deal (L.76/Add.1–14) shared with delegations. Part 11 on the Assembly of States Parties (L.76/Add.11) included as Article 102.[r]
17 July (7:15pm)	Committee of the Whole, 42nd meeting	Adoption of L.76/Add.1–14, including Article 102.[s]

n United Nations Diplomatic Conference of Plenipotentiaries on the Establishment of an International Criminal Court, Summary Records of the Plenary Meetings and of the Meetings of the Committee of the Whole, UN Doc. A/CONF.183/13 (Vol. II) 352.

o A/CONF.183/C.1/SR.39 (1998) 4.

p Committee of the Whole, Recommendations of the Coordinator, Article 102 Assembly of States Parties, UN Doc. A/CONF.183/C.1/L.47/Add.2.

q United Nations Diplomatic Conference of Plenipotentiaries on the Establishment of an International Criminal Court, Summary Records of the Plenary Meetings and of the Meetings of the Committee of the Whole, UN Doc. A/CONF.183/13 (Vol. II) 357.

r Draft Statute for the International Criminal Court, Part 11. Assembly of States Parties, Article 102 Assembly of States Parties, UN Doc. A/CONF.183/C.1/L.76/Add.11 (1998).

s United Nations Diplomatic Conference of Plenipotentiaries on the Establishment of an International Criminal Court, Summary Records of the Plenary Meetings and of the Meetings of the Committee of the Whole, UN Doc. A/CONF.183/13 (Vol. II) 462.

TABLE 4.2 Rome Conference (1998) (*cont.*)

Timeline	Negotiation body	Outcome
17 July (10:35pm)	Plenary, 9th meeting	Adoption[t] of Rome Statute of the International Criminal Court (CONF.183/9), including Part 11, Article 112 on the Assembly of States Parties.[u] Adoption of Final Act and resolutions of the Diplomatic Conference.[v]

t Ibid 121.

u United Nations Diplomatic Conference of Plenipotentiaries on the Establishment of an International Criminal Court, Rome Statute of the International Criminal Court, UN Doc. A/CONF.183/9* 81–83.

v Final Act of the United Nations Diplomatic Conference of Plenipotentiaries on the Establishment of an International Criminal Court [with an Annex Containing the Resolutions Adopted by the Conference], UN Doc. A/CONF.183/10 (1998).

discussed informally. The final amendment was introduced by Mexico on 15 July, two days before the end of the Conference (see Table 4.3). It intended to remove any reference to the United Nations Security Council throughout the Statute and instead replace it with a generic phrase that a 'relevant principal organ of the United Nations'[95] might act instead. This amendment was a Mexican policy position, shared among many delegations,[96] against any Security Council involvement with the Court, citing it would 'contravene the principle of the independence of the judiciary and the right of everyone to a hearing by an independent tribunal'.[97] While not captured in the official Conference records under amendments considered for Article 102,[98] it was, nonetheless, relevant to Article 102(2)(f) as it listed the Security Council as a bracket for referral of non-cooperation with the Court.[99] In the end, as the final hours of

95 Amendment Submitted by Mexico to the Draft Statute for the International Criminal Court, UN Doc. A/CONF.183/C.1/L.81 (1998).

96 Schabas, 'The Dynamics of the Rome Conference' 2020 10.

97 United Nations Diplomatic Conference of Plenipotentiaries on the Establishment of an International Criminal Court, Summary Records of the Plenary Meetings and of the Meetings of the Committee of the Whole, UN Doc. A/CONF.183/13 (Vol. II) 361.

98 United Nations Diplomatic Conference of Plenipotentiaries on the Establishment of an International Criminal Court, Reports and Other Documents, UN Doc. A/CONF.183/13 (Vol. III) 138.

99 Report of the Preparatory Committee on the Establishment of an International Criminal Court, Part 1 and Part 2, UN Doc. A/CONF.183/2/Add.1 157.

TABLE 4.3 Rome Conference (1998)

Timeline	State	Proposal
22 June	Mexico (L.14)	Advisory opinion from the International Court of Justice to examine a controversy between a State Party and the International Criminal Court.[a] Proposal withdrawn on June 29 at the 18th meeting of the Committee of the Whole.[b]
23 June	Andorra, Argentina, Bolivia, Chile, Colombia, Dominican Republic, El Salvador, Guatemala, Panama, Paraguay, Peru, Spain, Uruguay and Venezuela (L.16)	Addition of paragraph 8 in Article 102: "8. The official and working languages of the Assembly of States Parties shall be those of the General Assembly of the United Nations'[c]
29 June	Ukraine (L.28)	Composition of the Assembly of States Parties' Bureau from among candidates nominated from each geographical group as defined by the General Assembly.[d]
15 July	Mexico (L.81)	Replace the words 'Security Council' in any article of the Draft Statute with 'the relevant principal organ of the United Nations'.[e]

a Proposal Submitted by Mexico, Article 12 bis, Article 15 Issues of Admissibility, Article 102 Assembly of States Parties, Article 108 Settlement of Disputes, UN Doc. A/CONF.183/C.1/L.14 (1998) 2.

b United Nations Diplomatic Conference of Plenipotentiaries on the Establishment of an International Criminal Court, Summary Records of the Plenary Meetings and of the Meetings of the Committee of the Whole, UN Doc. A/CONF.183/13 (Vol. II) 251.

c Proposal Submitted by Andorra, Argentina, Bolivia, Chile, Colombia, Dominican Republic, El Salvador, Guatemala, Panama, Paraguay, Peru, Spain, Uruguay and Venezuela, Proposals Relating to Official and Working Languages, UN Doc. A/CONF.183/C.1/L.16 (1998) 2.

d Proposal Submitted by Ukraine Article 102 Assembly of States Parties, UN Doc. A/CONF.183/C.1/L.28 (1998).

e Amendment Submitted by Mexico to the Draft Statute for the International Criminal Court, UN Doc. A/CONF.183/C.1/L.81.

the Conference became an ultimatum for delegations, Mexico did not put the amendment to a vote.[100]

If compared with States' engagement in similar institutional questions such as the election of judges or the cooperation regime, the timeline shows a shallow attempt at considering the function of the Assembly of States Parties and its inherent relationship with the larger institution. Rao's four reports are underwhelming in contrast to eight[101] and 19[102] reports discussing the election of judges and cooperation respectively. In fact, of the seven Committee of the Whole meetings on Article 102, the 18th (29 June) and 24th (6 July) meetings were the most consequential, and the first recommendation report by Rao managed to solve most outstanding questions by 3 July.[103] Furthermore, of the three fully bracketed provisions and 32 options needing resolution, only two clauses emerged as the most problematic to solve. Article 102(5) on voting majorities for decision-making was only settled at the 30th meeting of the Committee of the Whole on 9 July, and (2)(f) on non-cooperation at the 38th meeting on 15 July. In this context, the following section traces each hurdle to Article 112 in the Rome Statute.

2.4 *The First Hurdle of Article 102 Negotiations: A General Agreement (29 June–9 July)*

The first hurdle in negotiating the Assembly of States Parties was the divergent views on voting majorities needed for decision-making. Between 29 June and 9 July, when 102(5) was agreed, States modified the draft article solving most of the 32 brackets at hand. By the time of the 29 June meeting, overall negotiations were in their third week. Parts of the Draft Statute bearing a close relationship with the Assembly of States Parties had made initial progress as the Conference 'turned into a marathon'.[104]

---

100 United Nations Diplomatic Conference of Plenipotentiaries on the Establishment of an International Criminal Court, Summary Records of the Plenary Meetings and of the Meetings of the Committee of the Whole, UN Doc. A/CONF.183/13 (Vol. II) 361.

101 United Nations Diplomatic Conference of Plenipotentiaries on the Establishment of an International Criminal Court, Reports and Other Documents, UN Doc. A/CONF.183/13 (Vol. III) 372.

102 Ibid 383.

103 Committee of the Whole, Recommendations of the Coordinator, Article 102 Assembly of States Parties, UN Doc. A/CONF.183/C.1/L. 47.

104 Benedetti, Bonneau and Washburn, 120.

2.4.1 The 18th Meeting of the Committee of the Whole (29 June)

On Monday 29 June 1998, the Committee of the Whole began its 18th meeting. The meeting was open to all delegations with 32 States voicing a policy statement on Article 102.[105] Part 11 arrived, as explained before, with three clauses with and without consensus. In between, nine sections contained 32 brackets with options. Rao briefly introduced each paragraph without summarizing each bracket but focusing on certain elements for agreement. On clause 102(1), on the Assembly's membership, Rao asked delegates to decide which States should be members or observers.[106] To aid the discussion, Rao noted non-party States to the United Nations Convention on the Law of the Sea participated as observers in their governance meetings.[107] Delegates agreed States Parties should make the membership. However, no overall consensus emerged whether by virtue of signing the Statute or Final Act, a State could become an observer, albeit only Mali was against 'signatories of the Final Act participating in the Assembly'.[108] China and the United States, both reticent about the Draft Statute but eager to influence the Rules of Procedure and Evidence, argued States signing the Final Act should be observers as 'potential parties'.[109] No State proposed civil society or intergovernmental organizations should be part of the Assembly of States Parties in any capacity.[110]

Rao introduced 102(2) as the 'functions of the Assembly'.[111] Clause 102(2)(a)–(g) afforded the Assembly with governance and management, financial oversight as well as enforcement of cooperation with the court. Article 102 (2)(a), on the interplay between the Assembly and the Preparatory Commission, was fully bracketed. This was the case because the United States preferred the Rules of Procedure and Evidence to enter into force with the Statute

---

105 China, Democratic Republic of the Congo, Denmark, Germany, Ghana, Guinea, Iraq, Japan, Kazakhstan, Lesotho, Libya, Malawi, Mali, Mexico, Mozambique, Namibia, Nepal, Oman, Peru, Portugal, Republic of Korea, Senegal, Slovakia, Spain, Sweden, Syrian Arab Republic, Togo, Ukraine, United Arab Emirates, United Kingdom of Great Britain and Northern Ireland, United States of America and Venezuela.

106 United Nations Diplomatic Conference of Plenipotentiaries on the Establishment of an International Criminal Court, Summary Records of the Plenary Meetings and of the Meetings of the Committee of the Whole, UN Doc. A/CONF.183/13 (Vol. II) 244.

107 Report of the Seventh Meeting of States Parties to the United Nations Convention on the Law of the Sea, New York, 19–23 May 1997, UN Doc. SPLOS/24 8.

108 United Nations Diplomatic Conference of Plenipotentiaries on the Establishment of an International Criminal Court, Summary Records of the Plenary Meetings and of the Meetings of the Committee of the Whole, UN Doc. A/CONF.183/13 (Vol. II) 248.

109 Ibid 246.

110 Ibid 244.

111 Ibid.

rather by adoption by the Assembly on the recommendation of the Preparatory Commission.[112] No other State spoke in favour of this position but Lesotho, Mali, Senegal and the United Kingdom agreed with the Spanish proposal to accept (2)(a) as written.[113] The following unbracketed provision in (2)(b) on the Assembly's management oversight of the administration of the Court by the Presidency, Prosecutor and the Registrar received comments from Lesotho and Senegal alerting about the importance of the independence of judges and the Prosecutor as per Article 41.[114] The next unbracketed provision, (2)(c) was not discussed, confirming consensus.

Presenting clause 102(2)(d), considering the Assembly's financial oversight powers and the role of the Registrar, Rao suggested the Court, presumably via the Registrar, should prepare the budget for Assembly approval.[115] Rao made no comment on the second bracket in this provision giving the Assembly the power to '[rule on any financial issue],[116] nor he linked it with Article 105 in Part 12 requiring the Assembly to develop the criteria for acceptance of funds, for example, voluntary contributions.[117] Article 102(2)(d) and (6) belonged to the unresolved question who should finance the Court: States Parties, the United Nations or a combination of both options. In this context, Sweden, on behalf of the Like-Minded States, agreed the Assembly should consider the budget but the 'United Nations should finance the Court'.[118] On the other hand, Japan and Nepal preferred States Parties financed the Court and the Assembly consulted the President of the Court than the Registrar on the budget,[119] a view, Namibia disagreed with.[120]

On clause 102(2)(e), Rao explained the Assembly could alter the number of judges.[121] He did not, more importantly, refer to the bracket providing the power to alter staffing in the Office of the Prosecutor or Registry. As Bos argued, States wanted to retain a 'discrete ability…to govern the administrative and

---

112 Ibid 246.

113 Ibid 244.

114 Ibid 246.

115 Ibid 244.

116 Report of the Preparatory Committee on the Establishment of an International Criminal Court, Part 1 and Part 2, UN Doc. A/CONF.183/2/Add.1 157.

117 Ibid 161.

118 United Nations Diplomatic Conference of Plenipotentiaries on the Establishment of an International Criminal Court, Summary Records of the Plenary Meetings and of the Meetings of the Committee of the Whole, UN Doc. A/CONF.183/13 (Vol. II) 246.

119 Ibid 247.

120 Ibid 249.

121 Ibid 244.

operational activities'[122] of the institution, however without compromising the independence enshrined in Article 41, as noted by Senegal.[123] No delegations referred to the second bracket. Instead, Iraq requested the reference to part-time judges be rejected and Ghana alerted about the financial implications of additional judges. However, the question of increasing the number of judges belonged to Part 4, in turn, referencing the Assembly of States Parties in Article 37(2)(b).[124] This is an example how the negotiation of the Rome Statute and its governing body was isolated to specific junctures in the Committee of the Whole without considering its overall function across all its institutional responsibilities.

The same argument applied to the fully bracketed Article 102(2)(f), which Rao accepted 'would have to be coordinated with article 86, in Part 9 of the Draft Statute',[125] a statement Japan, Ghana, Mexico and United States agreed with.[126] Yet, nine States decidedly supported the Assembly was the appropriate forum to consider and take measures on non-cooperation.[127] To complete Article 102(2), Rao briefly mentioned clause (2)(g), a residual omnibus provision, to insure the Assembly of additional responsibilities 'which could not be foreseen at present'.[128] Rao did not explain the implied powers of the provision expanded to over 21 Articles across the Draft Statute. In addition, Rao did not reference the outstanding brackets regarding the power to review the statute and the Rules of Procedure and Evidence nor the ability to grant pardons by the Assembly. The Committee of the Whole did not comment on any of these questions either.[129] The available record does not explain why Rao selectively highlighted certain areas of disagreement over others, or why issues debated in the last preparatory session did not attract the same level

122 Bos, 'Assembly of States Parties' (2002) 301.

123 United Nations Diplomatic Conference of Plenipotentiaries on the Establishment of an International Criminal Court, Summary Records of the Plenary Meetings and of the Meetings of the Committee of the Whole, UN Doc. A/CONF.183/13 (Vol. II) 249.

124 Report of the Preparatory Committee on the Establishment of an International Criminal Court, Part 1 and Part 2, UN Doc. A/CONF.183/2/Add.1 62.

125 United Nations Diplomatic Conference of Plenipotentiaries on the Establishment of an International Criminal Court, Summary Records of the Plenary Meetings and of the Meetings of the Committee of the Whole, UN Doc. A/CONF.183/13 (Vol. II) 244.

126 Ibid 246.

127 In order of oral statements: Spain, Sweden, Libya, Iraq, Lesotho, Togo, Nepal and Senegal.

128 United Nations Diplomatic Conference of Plenipotentiaries on the Establishment of an International Criminal Court, Summary Records of the Plenary Meetings and of the Meetings of the Committee of the Whole, UN Doc. A/CONF.183/13 (Vol. II) 244.

129 Ibid.

of commentary from States. Plausible explanations reside in unreported progress achieved in informal meetings, the lack of time to delve into each option and the overall lack of interest in Article 102 from States and civil society.

Moving to 102(3)(a)–(c), on the Bureau of the Assembly, Rao only highlighted the bracket with the pending number of members, and recalled the suggestion there should be an additional Vice-President in (3)(a).[130] He did not address the bracket whether Court officers should be members or observers in Bureau meetings.[131] In fact, States[132] were more vocal about this issue than Rao, strongly suggesting the President, Prosecutor or Registrar should be observers, as the 'judicial functions of the Court must be kept separate from political and administrative considerations and the functions of the Assembly of States Parties'.[133] In contrast, only Guinea and Togo referred to the expansion to two Vice-Presidents.[134]

When turning to (3)(b) on the representative composition of the Bureau, Rao linked the discussion to 'decisions taken concerning other bodies mentioned in the Statute'.[135] This claim is not further substantiated opening the question whether Rao meant Article 37(8) requesting the Assembly consider the principal legal systems of the world, the main forms of civilization, equitable geographical distribution and gender balance when electing the bench.[136] No State pursued Rao's requirement to link 102(3)(b) with 37(8) but similar conditions were used by Iraq, Guinea, Mali, Oman[137] and Ukraine[138] (equitable geographical distribution), Syria[139] (principal legal sys-

130 Working Group on the Establishment of the Court and Relationship with the United Nations, Consolidated Text of Part 10 bis Assembly of States Parties, UN Doc. A/AC.249/1998/WG.8/CRP.L/Add.3.

131 United Nations Diplomatic Conference of Plenipotentiaries on the Establishment of an International Criminal Court, Summary Records of the Plenary Meetings and of the Meetings of the Committee of the Whole, UN Doc. A/CONF.183/13 (Vol. II) 244.

132 In order of oral statements: Spain, Venezuela, Guinea, Mali, Republic of Korea, Libya, United Arab Emirates and Senegal.

133 United Nations Diplomatic Conference of Plenipotentiaries on the Establishment of an International Criminal Court, Summary Records of the Plenary Meetings and of the Meetings of the Committee of the Whole, UN Doc. A/CONF.183/13 (Vol. II) 245.

134 Ibid 247–248.

135 Ibid 244.

136 Report of the Preparatory Committee on the Establishment of an International Criminal Court, Part 1 and Part 2, UN Doc. A/CONF.183/2/Add.1 63–64.

137 United Nations Diplomatic Conference of Plenipotentiaries on the Establishment of an International Criminal Court, Summary Records of the Plenary Meetings and of the Meetings of the Committee of the Whole, UN Doc. A/CONF.183/13 (Vol. II) 245.

138 Ibid 247.

139 Ibid 248.

tems of the world) and Nepal[140] and United Kingdom[141] (representative character). Beyond the representative characterization of the Bureau, the Committee of the Whole did not consider the manner to assure the composition and election conditions of the Bureau, an issue the Preparatory Commission was forced to solve. In fact, the Preparatory Commission regretted in 2001 the Statute did not permit the staggered election of Bureau members, changing its total membership every three years.[142] Furthermore, the desired qualifications of Bureau members, including its leadership, were not considered. Given the wide-range and essential tasks assigned to the executive organ, the omission in Rome was significant, more so when Rao considered Article 37, which set out specific qualification requirements for judges.

Lastly, when introducing Article 102(3)(c), giving the Assembly the ability to establish subsidiary organs, Rao requested clarity whether the oversight mechanism 'should deal with all the operations of the Court or only with non-judicial administration'.[143] Only Nepal voiced its preference for the wording 'non-judicial'.[144] Although the provision appeared in brackets, the last preparatory session had decided the oversight mechanism would not encroach in the independence of the Court.[145]

Rao presented Article 102(4) requesting a decision whether the Bureau or a third of States Parties could convene special sessions.[146] He did not reference an additional bracket allowing the Assembly to meet in a location of its preference. The Committee of the Whole did not provide any guidance on either question. On the other hand, Article 102(5), on voting majorities for decision-making, would require several rounds of negotiation but remarkably was not mentioned by Rao during his introduction of Part 11 on 29 June 1998.[147] As Bos

140 Ibid.

141 Ibid 249.

142 Yengejeh, Saeid Mirzaee, 'Rules of Procedure of the Assembly of States Parties to the Rome Statute of the International Criminal Court' (2002) 25 (3) Fordham International Law Journal 681.

143 United Nations Diplomatic Conference of Plenipotentiaries on the Establishment of an International Criminal Court, Summary Records of the Plenary Meetings and of the Meetings of the Committee of the Whole, UN Doc. A/CONF.183/13 (Vol. II) 244.

144 Ibid 248.

145 Informal Group on the Establishment of the Court and Relationship with the United Nations, Rolling Text Assembly of States Parties, 31 March 1998, UN Doc. A/AC.249/1998/WG.8/IP.

146 United Nations Diplomatic Conference of Plenipotentiaries on the Establishment of an International Criminal Court, Summary Records of the Plenary Meetings and of the Meetings of the Committee of the Whole, UN Doc. A/CONF.183/13 (Vol. II) 244.

147 Ibid.

and Rao agreed, all delegations supported consensus as the primary vehicle for decision making at the Assembly,[148] but three options for voting remained unresolved when consensus was not viable. Seven States[149] agreed with the United States[150] favouring the first option of '[two-thirds majority of those present and voting, representing the absolute majority of States Parties]'.[151] However, Spain[152] and the Democratic Republic of the Congo[153] supported alternative solutions, leaving the clause unresolved.

Article 102(6) on loss of voting rights due to arrears was also contested. Being the third fully bracketed provision in Part 11, Rao reminded States the link with Part 12.[154] The main source of controversy resided in the financial barriers of developing countries to fulfil financial obligations versus the need to achieve universality of ratifications.[155] As such, the options for financing the Court in Article 104 (the United Nations, States Parties or a combination) became a dependency for 102(6). States like Spain, Denmark, Sweden, Lesotho and Germany favoured the inclusion of the provision 'as an incentive for payment of contributions on time and in full'.[156] In fact, Germany proposed to impose penalties for arrears.[157] On the other hand, Mexico welcomed the ability of the Assembly to condone late-payers[158] and Senegal insisted on a distinction between States in dire economic conditions and opulent governments in arrears, which 'should be punished more severely'.[159] Looking at the issue of arrears more than two decades later, it is striking the issue has not evolved much. In this context, the bracket triggering the loss of voting

148 Rao, (1999) 411; Bos, 'Assembly of States Parties' (2002) 312.
149 In order of oral statements: United States, Ukraine, Senegal, United Kingdom, Mozambique, Republic of Korea and United Arab Emirates.
150 United Nations Diplomatic Conference of Plenipotentiaries on the Establishment of an International Criminal Court, Summary Records of the Plenary Meetings and of the Meetings of the Committee of the Whole, UN Doc. A/CONF.183/13 (Vol. II) 246.
151 Report of the Preparatory Committee on the Establishment of an International Criminal Court, Part 1 and Part 2, UN Doc. A/CONF.183/2/Add.1 158.
152 United Nations Diplomatic Conference of Plenipotentiaries on the Establishment of an International Criminal Court, Summary Records of the Plenary Meetings and of the Meetings of the Committee of the Whole, UN Doc. A/CONF.183/13 (Vol. II) 245.
153 Ibid 248.
154 Ibid 244.
155 Rao, (1999) 411.
156 United Nations Diplomatic Conference of Plenipotentiaries on the Establishment of an International Criminal Court, Summary Records of the Plenary Meetings and of the Meetings of the Committee of the Whole, UN Doc. A/CONF.183/13 (Vol. II) 245.
157 Ibid 250.
158 Ibid 251.
159 Ibid 249.

rights after two years' worth of arrears carried most support from States making an oral statement.[160] Lastly, Rao did not introduce Article 102(7) on Rules of Procedure for the Assembly to the Committee of the Whole.[161] As a clause without any brackets, it denoted full consensus and received no comments from States. As an auxiliary document regulating the Assembly of States Parties, the formulation of the Rules of Procedure was included in the Final Act for elaboration by the Preparatory Commission.[162]

During the 18th meeting on 29 June, the Committee of the Whole discussed two amendments. Spain, on behalf of Andorra, Argentina, Bolivia, Chile, Colombia, Dominican Republic, El Salvador, Guatemala, Panama, Paraguay, Peru, Uruguay and Venezuela proposed the official and working languages of the Assembly mirror the United Nations General Assembly.[163] The proposal received support from other regional groups without any State opposing it.[164] On the other hand, Mexico announced the withdrawal of their 22 June amendment allowing a State Party in conflict with the Court to seek an advisory opinion from International Court of Justice.[165] As explained by the Mexican delegate, negative feedback from governments to this proposal as 'inappropriate',[166] resulted in its repeal. As the treatment of Article 102 ended at the 18th meeting of the Committee, Ukraine introduced an amendment on the same day reacting to the earlier discussions on Article 102(3)(b) on the composition of the Bureau.[167] It proposed Bureau candidates be 'nominated from each geographical group as defined by the General Assembly'.[168] Thus, this late

160 In order of oral statements: Japan, Nepal, Syria, Mali, United Kingdom, Malawi, Libya and United Arab Emirates.

161 United Nations Diplomatic Conference of Plenipotentiaries on the Establishment of an International Criminal Court, Summary Records of the Plenary Meetings and of the Meetings of the Committee of the Whole, UN Doc. A/CONF.183/13 (Vol. II) 244.

162 Report of the Preparatory Committee on the Establishment of an International Criminal Court, Part 1 and Part 2, UN Doc. A/CONF.183/2/Add.1 173.

163 Proposal Submitted by Andorra, Argentina, Bolivia, Chile, Colombia, Dominican Republic, El Salvador, Guatemala, Panama, Paraguay, Peru, Spain, Uruguay and Venezuela, Proposals Relating to Official and Working Languages, UN Doc. A/CONF.183/C.1/L.16 2.

164 World Federalist Movement/Institute for Global Policy, (2018) 276.

165 Proposal Submitted by Mexico, Article 12 bis, Article 15 Issues of Admissibility, Article 102 Assembly of States Parties, Article 108 Settlement of Disputes, UN Doc. A/CONF.183/C.1/L.14 2.

166 United Nations Diplomatic Conference of Plenipotentiaries on the Establishment of an International Criminal Court, Summary Records of the Plenary Meetings and of the Meetings of the Committee of the Whole, UN Doc. A/CONF.183/13 (Vol. II) 251.

167 Ibid 247.

168 Proposal Submitted by Ukraine Article 102 Assembly of States Parties, UN Doc. A/CONF.183/C.1/L.28.

amendment and the overall feedback from the 18th meeting served as the basis for Rao to conduct further informal consultations to reconcile the brackets remaining in Part 11.

2.4.2 The First Coordinator's Recommendation Report (2–3 July)

The available record does not indicate how many informal meetings Rao led.[169] However, his Recommendation report for the 24th meeting of the Committee of the Whole was issued on 3 July, meaning the informal working group met, at least, for four days between 30 June and 3 July. Furthermore, the memorandum describing the Conference's organization of the work stipulated six meetings per day without counting those of the Conference's organs.[170] Assuming the informal group met six times over four days, the Recommendation report to the 24th meeting of the Committee of the Whole solving most pending issues was the product of 24 informal meetings. The literature confirms delegates were engaged in arduous and lengthy debates in the third week of negotiations. Bassiouni recalls 'as many as a dozen'[171] simultaneous informal groups, and Tallgren remembers 'some 15 to 20 hours of everyday drafting'.[172] In this context, Rao issued a report on July 2[173] and a further corrigendum text with a minor language change for 102(2)(g) on July 3.[174] The reports showed a new version of Part 11, summarizing the progress achieved in resolving most pending issues (see Table 4.4).[175] The first Recommendations report (L.47) resolved all fully-bracketed provisions except (2)(f) on non-cooperation, reducing the number of pending options

169 Rao, (1999) 411.

170 United Nations Diplomatic Conference of Plenipotentiaries on the Establishment of an International Criminal Court, Organization of Work, Memorandum of the Secretary-General on the Methods of Work and Procedures for the Conference, UN Doc. A/CONF.183/3 4.

171 Bassiouni, 'Negotiating the Treaty of Rome on the Establishment of an International Criminal Court' 449.

172 Tallgren, Immi, 'We did it? The Vertigo of Law and Everyday Life at the Diplomatic Conference on the Establishment of an International Criminal Court' (1999) 12 (3) Leiden Journal of International Law 692.

173 Committee of the Whole, Coordinator's Text for Article 102 Assembly of States Parties, UN Doc. A/CONF.183/C.1/L.41.

174 Committee of the Whole, Coordinator's Text for Article 102 Assembly of States Parties, Corrigendum, UN Doc. A/CONF.183/C.1/L.41/Corr.1.

175 Committee of the Whole, Recommendations of the Coordinator, Article 102 Assembly of States Parties, UN Doc. A/CONF.183/C.1/L.47.

from 32 to 7. It was the largest revision of draft Article 102 during the Rome Conference.[176]

On clause 102(1), on the Assembly's membership, all four brackets were solved by agreeing observer status for signatories of the Statute or the Final Act.[177] Rao characterized this agreement as 'a compromise'[178] to allow for a wide circle of observers but with States Parties retaining exclusive voting rights.[179] Gradoni[180] recalled some States, like Mali, would have preferred to reserve observer status for signatories of the Statute but as Schabas noted, it was deemed appropriate to accommodate States like the United States or China seeking to influence the Rules of Procedure and Evidence as potential parties.[181] Clause 102(2)(a), in full brackets in the Draft Statute, was solved in line with Spain's proposal to accept the wording as presented.[182] Negotiations benefited from progress made by a different informal working group finalizing the Final Act and annexed resolutions.[183] For this reason, the agreement was quick[184] as States recognized the Assembly had the prerogative to vote on recommendations from the Preparatory Commission. As stipulated in the Final Act, critical auxiliary documents such as the Rules of Procedure and Evidence, the Elements of Crimes and the Rules of Procedure of the Assembly would be prepared by the Commission but adopted by States Parties.[185] As Rao and Ambach explained, the Commission was the 'precursor to the Assembly'.[186] Clauses 102(2)(b) and (c) were not modified from the original draft article.[187] In regard to (2)(b) on the Assembly's financial oversight, Rao, Ambach and Barberini agreed States indisputably precluded the Assembly

176 Report of the Preparatory Committee on the Establishment of an International Criminal Court, Part 1 and Part 2, UN Doc. A/CONF.183/2/Add.1 157–159.

177 Committee of the Whole, Recommendations of the Coordinator, Article 102 Assembly of States Parties, UN Doc. A/CONF.183/C.1/L.47.

178 Rao and Ambach, (2016) 2218.

179 Bos, 'Assembly of States Parties' (2002) 303.

180 Gradoni, (2012) 2011.

181 Schabas, The International Criminal Court: A Commentary on the Rome Statute 1435.

182 United Nations Diplomatic Conference of Plenipotentiaries on the Establishment of an International Criminal Court, Summary Records of the Plenary Meetings and of the Meetings of the Committee of the Whole, UN Doc. A/CONF.183/13 (Vol. II) 244.

183 World Federalist Movement/Institute for Global Policy, (2018) 278.

184 Schabas, The International Criminal Court: A Commentary on the Rome Statute (1437).

185 Final Act of the United Nations Diplomatic Conference of Plenipotentiaries on the Establishment of an International Criminal Court [with an Annex Containing the Resolutions Adopted by the Conference], UN Doc. A/CONF.183/10 9.

186 Rao and Ambach, (2016) 2219.

187 Bos, 'Assembly of States Parties' (2002) 309; Gradoni, (2012) 2017.

from any interference into the judicial activities of the Presidency, Prosecutor and the Registrar.[188]

Clause 102(2)(d) was resolved by removing the two pending brackets, on the role of the Registrar and ruling on any financial issue, and changing a keyword from 'approval' to 'decide' on the Court's budget. The revised clause incorporated a footnote linking it with ongoing negotiations in Part 12.[189] States decided to remove the reference to the Registrar in the first bracket because the Presidency, not the Assembly, exerted management over the position.[190] To avoid any confusion, States agreed the Registrar would prepare the budget of the Court, and if any questions arose, these could be dealt in the Bureau as per Article 102(3)(a).[191] Furthermore, this provision had a direct link with the Final Act asking the Preparatory Commission to prepare the first budget of the Court.[192] While not addressed in the Committee of the Whole, the informal group removed the second bracket on the Assembly's power to rule on any financial issue. Cognizant all financial matters would be regulated by financial rules in Article 103 in Part 12 and the requirement the Preparatory Commission develop them, States deleted the bracket 'because it was considered superfluous'.[193] Nonetheless, together with Article 102(6), the overall question about financing was unresolved at this stage. In this sense, the footnote linking it (2)(d) with Part 12 was notable as negotiations stalled.[194]

Clause 102(2)(e) was thoroughly revised removing the bracket allowing the Assembly to alter the staffing of the Office of the Prosecutor and the Registry and deleting the possibility of part-time judges as proposed by Iraq.[195] Rao explained there was no agreement to allow the Assembly to alter the staffing of the Prosecution or Registry.[196] In fact, the provision was controversial as it impacted the independence of the Court enshrined in Article 41, as noted

188 Barberini, (2006) 1571–1572; Rao and Ambach, (2016) 2220.

189 Committee of the Whole, Recommendations of the Coordinator, Article 102 Assembly of States Parties, UN Doc. A/CONF.183/C.1/L.47 2.

190 Rao, (1999) 412; Bos, 'Assembly of States Parties' (2002) 306; Gradoni, (2012) 2018; Schabas, The International Criminal Court: A Commentary on the Rome Statute (1438).

191 Rao and Ambach, (2016) 2222.

192 Barberini, (2006) 1572.

193 Ibid 1572–1573; Rao and Ambach, (2016) 2222.

194 World Federalist Movement/Institute for Global Policy, (2018) 471.

195 United Nations Diplomatic Conference of Plenipotentiaries on the Establishment of an International Criminal Court, Summary Records of the Plenary Meetings and of the Meetings of the Committee of the Whole, UN Doc. A/CONF.183/13 (Vol. II) 249.

196 Rao, (1999) 412.

by Senegal.[197] In any event, this article would be further modified at a later stage as negotiations for Article 37(2)(b) in Part 4 continued.[198] Regarding non-cooperation, while nine States[199] agreed the Assembly was an appropriate forum to take measures under Article 102(2)(f), Rao was unable to advance any solutions. The clause remained pending in the report.

Clause 102(2)(g), the residual omnibus provision, was simplified by removing the bracket on a review mechanism of the Statute or the Rules of Procedure and Evidence, and granting pardons. The informal group received no steer from the Committee of the Whole in neither of these areas.[200] Because the mechanism to review the Statute was negotiated in Part 13, States decided to remove it from Article 102. However, the review of the Statute ultimately depended on a decision by the Assembly.[201] The power to grant pardons, in the context of draft Article 41 and the overall political nature of the Assembly of States Parties, was removed.[202] Overall, the omnibus clause allowed the Assembly to carry out other functions not explicitly mentioned in Article 102 and critical for the functioning of the Court, such as the election of the Prosecutor or the amendment of the Rules of Procedure and Evidence.[203] In effect, by virtue of (2)(g), the Assembly of States Parties had a 'quasi-political role in the making of international criminal law'.[204]

Clause 102(3)(a) appeared in Rao's report with a bis part. The first part resolved the first bracket, confirming the Bureau would have 18 members and two Vice-Presidents as requested by Guinea, Togo,[205] and the United Kingdom.[206] The bis part removed the options whether Court officials could

---

197 United Nations Diplomatic Conference of Plenipotentiaries on the Establishment of an International Criminal Court, Summary Records of the Plenary Meetings and of the Meetings of the Committee of the Whole, UN Doc. A/CONF.183/13 (Vol. II) 249.

198 Report of the Preparatory Committee on the Establishment of an International Criminal Court, Part 1 and Part 2, UN Doc. A/CONF.183/2/Add.1 62.

199 In order of oral statements: Spain, Sweden, Libya, Iraq, Lesotho, Togo, Nepal and Senegal.

200 United Nations Diplomatic Conference of Plenipotentiaries on the Establishment of an International Criminal Court, Summary Records of the Plenary Meetings and of the Meetings of the Committee of the Whole, UN Doc. A/CONF.183/13 (Vol. II) 244.

201 Rao and Ambach, (2016) 2230.

202 Rao, 1999 412; Bos, 'Assembly of States Parties' (2002) 307–308.

203 Barberini, (2006) 1562.

204 Gallant, 559.

205 United Nations Diplomatic Conference of Plenipotentiaries on the Establishment of an International Criminal Court, Summary Records of the Plenary Meetings and of the Meetings of the Committee of the Whole, UN Doc. A/CONF.183/13 (Vol. II) 247–248.

206 Kim, Young Sok, The Law of the International Criminal Court (2nd edn, William S. Hein & Co., Inc. 2019) 389.

be observers or members in the Bureau and instead qualified their participation in the Bureau and Assembly 'as appropriate'.[207] While States warned about the separation of judicial and political roams, Rao simply mentioned the question was 'left out'.[208] However, in a later publication, Rao mentioned drafters decided to keep the clause 'silent'.[209] Bos, on the other hand, explained the inserted phrase meant to allow for flexibility when their participation might be required to 'facilitate the decision-making in the Assembly'.[210] In any event, Rao and Ambach, Bos, Gradoni and Barberini agreed the silent provision did not entail voting rights for the President, Prosecutor or Registrar.[211] Gradoni further argued the structure of the Statute did not lend itself to make the Court an observer as an organ under Article 34 in the Rome Statute.[212] Interestingly, however, there is no mention in the drafting history of this clause whether States considered if representation from defence counsel should have any specific role in the Bureau and Assembly meetings.[213]

The main unresolved question in clause 102(3)(b) was the formula to determine the representative character of the Bureau membership.[214] The three brackets were combined providing an equal footing for geographical distribution and legal systems of the world.[215] Iraq, Guinea, Mali, Oman[216] (equitable geographical distribution) and Syria[217] (principal legal systems of the world) had voiced their steer in the Committee of the Whole. In this context, Ukraine's amendment requiring Bureau candidates be 'nominated from each geographical group as defined by the General Assembly'[218] was not incorporated. Nonetheless, it proved helpful to guide the Preparatory Commission to establish the Bureau in 2002. The representative character of the Bureau was

207 Committee of the Whole, Recommendations of the Coordinator, Article 102 Assembly of States Parties, UN Doc. A/CONF.183/C.1/L.47 2.

208 Rao, (1999) 412.

209 Rao and Ambach, (2016) 2240.

210 Bos, 'Assembly of States Parties' (2002) 310.

211 Ibid; Barberini, 2006 1570; Gradoni, (2012) 2012–2013; Rao and Ambach, (2016) 2240.

212 Gradoni, (2012) 2013.

213 Roberts, (2013) 398.

214 Schabas, The International Criminal Court: A Commentary on the Rome Statute 1442.

215 Rao and Ambach, (2016) 2232.

216 United Nations Diplomatic Conference of Plenipotentiaries on the Establishment of an International Criminal Court, Summary Records of the Plenary Meetings and of the Meetings of the Committee of the Whole, UN Doc. A/CONF.183/13 (Vol. II) 245.

217 Ibid 248.

218 Proposal Submitted by Ukraine Article 102 Assembly of States Parties, UN Doc. A/CONF.183/C.1/L.28 1.

important to afford its actions with legitimacy and support, as the clause refers, to 'assist the Assembly in the discharge of its responsibilities'.[219]

Clause 102(3)(c) had two brackets related to the independent oversight mechanism as a subsidiary body of the Assembly. An original idea presented by the United States in the last preparatory session, the intention of this subsidiary body was to enhance the effectiveness of the Court by a third-party evaluation but brackets remained to confine evaluations to non-judicial functions.[220] As Kim explained, the revised clause removed both brackets at the insistence of the United States although the United Kingdom and Sweden favoured to keep 'non-judicial administration'.[221] In this sense, it was clear States agreed to preserve the limits between the Assembly and the Court, however, the language in the provision did not aid its implementation. In fact, it would not be until 2013 the Assembly of States Parties established the Independent Oversight Mechanism fully respectful of 'judicial and prosecutorial independence'.[222] The core power in the clause, nonetheless, gave the Assembly a wide prerogative to establish subsidiary organs, which the working group on Part 4 considered for screening judgeship nominations.[223]

The two pending brackets in 102(4) were resolved in Rao's report despite receiving no specific guidance from the Committee of the Whole. The first option allowing the Assembly to meet elsewhere than the seat of the court or the United Nations was 'discreetly'[224] removed due to financial considerations.[225] The second bracket, whether the Bureau could convene a special session was adopted in the revised text together with the possibility a third of States Parties; however, with 'except as otherwise specified in the Statute'[226] as a chapeau. In essence, this meant the possibility to distinguish two types of special sessions by virtue of draft Article 111 on the review of the Statute.[227] One for the regular governance and management oversight tasks of the

---

219 Committee of the Whole, Recommendations of the Coordinator, Article 102 Assembly of States Parties, UN Doc. A/CONF.183/C.1/L.47 2; Bos, 'Assembly of States Parties' (2002) 307.

220 Proposals submitted by the United States of America, UN Doc. A/AC.249/1998/DP.L.

221 Kim, 390.

222 ICC-ASP/12/Res.6 Independent Oversight Mechanism 5.

223 World Federalist Movement/Institute for Global Policy, (2018) 274; United Nations Office of Legal Affairs, Daily Summary 24 June 1998, United Nations Diplomatic Conference of Plenipotentiaries on the Establishment of an International Criminal Court (1998) 1.

224 Gradoni, (2012) 2026.

225 Bos, 'Assembly of States Parties' (2002) 311.

226 Committee of the Whole, Recommendations of the Coordinator, Article 102 Assembly of States Parties, UN Doc. A/CONF.183/C.1/L.47 2.

227 Report of the Preparatory Committee on the Establishment of an International Criminal Court, Part 1 and Part 2, UN Doc. A/CONF.183/2/Add.1 165.

Assembly, and a second type exclusively to consider a review of the Statute, which required a two-third vote by the Assembly. In fact, as Schabas, Rao and Ambach argued, it is still an open question what the definitive meaning or legal weight of this language is in the Rome Statute.[228]

Despite Rao not formally introducing clause 102(5) on voting majorities for decision-making in the Committee of the Whole, the informal group agreed on the version of the bracket requiring a '[two-thirds majority of those present and voting, representing the absolute majority of States Parties]',[229] clarifying the 'absolute majority of States Parties constitutes the quorum for voting'.[230] This approach was favoured by the United States, Ukraine, Senegal, United Kingdom, Mozambique, Republic of Korea and United Arab Emirates.[231] However, in the informal group, Germany, Norway and the United Kingdom warned the compromise wording was 'unintelligible, made no sense mathematically and did not cover procedural votes'.[232] Rao 'brushed aside'[233] their complaints but was confronted about his choice during the 24th meeting of the Committee of the Whole. Furthermore, as with Article 102(4), the revised version qualified the provision with 'except as otherwise provided in the Statute'.[234] This meant to safeguard different voting requirements by the Assembly, for example, in draft Article 43(4) where a simple 'absolute majority of the States Parties'[235] was required to elect the Prosecutor. This provision, nonetheless, would attract further negotiations in the Committee of the Whole as it connected with the larger discussion on the Statute's amendment regime.[236] In fact, Article 102(5) was only settled at the 30th meeting of the Committee of the Whole on 9 July.

228 Rao and Ambach, (2016) 2241; Schabas, The International Criminal Court: A Commentary on the Rome Statute (1448).

229 Report of the Preparatory Committee on the Establishment of an International Criminal Court, Part 1 and Part 2, UN Doc. A/CONF.183/2/Add.1 158.

230 Committee of the Whole, Recommendations of the Coordinator, Article 102 Assembly of States Parties, UN Doc. A/CONF.183/C.1/L.47 2.

231 United Nations Diplomatic Conference of Plenipotentiaries on the Establishment of an International Criminal Court, Summary Records of the Plenary Meetings and of the Meetings of the Committee of the Whole, UN Doc. A/CONF.183/13 (Vol. II) 246.

232 World Federalist Movement/Institute for Global Policy, (2018) 283.

233 Ibid.

234 Committee of the Whole, Recommendations of the Coordinator, Article 102 Assembly of States Parties, UN Doc. A/CONF.183/C.1/L.47 2.

235 Report of the Preparatory Committee on the Establishment of an International Criminal Court, Part 1 and Part 2, UN Doc. A/CONF.183/2/Add.1 68.

236 Rao, (1999) 412.

The informal group also resolved Article 102(6), the third clause arriving in Rome without consensus. The Committee of the Whole had signalled the agreement to include the loss of voting rights for States in arrears, and a majority of States spoke in favour of triggering the sanction at an amount equivalent to two full years. Spain, Denmark, Sweden, Lesotho and Germany maintained this policy position.[237] As Schabas, Rao and Ambach, and Gradoni explained, the informal group acted by following the standard in Article 19 of the United Nations Charter,[238] almost 'word by word'.[239] This included the ability of the Assembly to condone arrears for States under financial stress, as Mexico and Senegal had supported.[240] Finally, while Germany proposed[241] to introduce an amendment to penalize late-payers, there is no trace of it in the available record.

Rao's report did not modify Article 102(7), on the Rules of Procedure of the Assembly of States Parties. In light of Article 102(5), however, it is odd the informal group negotiating the clause did not indicate the voting majority for its adoption.[242] Finally, the Recommendation report incorporated the Spain et al. amendment making the official and working languages of the Assembly of States Parties the same as the United Nations General Assembly.[243] The amendment, supported in the informal group,[244] was added as paragraph 102(8).

Rao's first Recommendation report shows a very productive negotiating outcome resolving all fully-bracketed provisions except (2)(f) on non-cooperation. It is plausible to imagine the informal group could have proposed a revised

237 United Nations Diplomatic Conference of Plenipotentiaries on the Establishment of an International Criminal Court, Summary Records of the Plenary Meetings and of the Meetings of the Committee of the Whole, UN Doc. A/CONF.183/13 (Vol. II) 245.

238 Charter of the United Nations and Statute of the International Court of Justice, 24 October 1945, 1 UNTS XVI (1945).

239 Gradoni, (2012) 2030;Rao and Ambach, 2016 2243; Schabas, The International Criminal Court: A Commentary on the Rome Statute (1449).

240 United Nations Diplomatic Conference of Plenipotentiaries on the Establishment of an International Criminal Court, Summary Records of the Plenary Meetings and of the Meetings of the Committee of the Whole, UN Doc. A/CONF.183/13 (Vol. II) 249.

241 Ibid 250.

242 Schabas, The International Criminal Court: A Commentary on the Rome Statute (1450).

243 Proposal Submitted by Andorra, Argentina, Bolivia, Chile, Colombia, Dominican Republic, El Salvador, Guatemala, Panama, Paraguay, Peru, Spain, Uruguay and Venezuela, Proposals Relating to Official and Working Languages, UN Doc. A/CONF.183/C.1/L.16 2.

244 United Nations Diplomatic Conference of Plenipotentiaries on the Establishment of an International Criminal Court, Summary Records of the Plenary Meetings and of the Meetings of the Committee of the Whole, UN Doc. A/CONF.183/13 (Vol. II) 266.

TABLE 4.4 Rome Conference (1998)

Functions	Draft Statute article 102	Coordinator recommendation report L.47
Governance and Management Oversight	(1) There is hereby established an Assembly of States Parties to this Statute. Each State Party shall have one representative in the Assembly who may be accompanied by alternates and advisers. The signatories of the [Statute] [Final Act] may be [observers] [members] in the Assembly	(1) There is hereby established an Assembly of States Parties to this Statute. Each State Party shall have one representative in the Assembly who may be accompanied by alternates and advisers. Other States which have signed the Statute or the Final Act may be observers in the Assembly
	(2) The Assembly shall: [(a) consider and adopt recommendations of the preparatory commission;]	(2) The Assembly shall: (a) Consider and adopt recommendations of the Preparatory Commission;
	(b) provide management oversight to the Presidency, Prosecutor and Registrar regarding the administration of the Court; (c) consider the reports and activities of the Bureau and take appropriate action in regard thereto.	
Financial Oversight	(d) Consider and approve the budget for the Court [in consultation with the Registrar] [and rule on any financial issue]	(d) Consider and decide the budget for the Court. At footnote 1: 'This paragraph is without prejudice to the final decision on article 104'.[a]
Governance and Management Oversight	(e) determine whether to alter, as appropriate, the number of judges [or members of the Office of the Prosecutor or the Registry], serving on a full– or part-time basis, for such period as it shall determine.	(e) Determine whether to alter, as appropriate, the number of judges;

a Committee of the Whole, Recommendations of the Coordinator, Article 102 Assembly of States Parties, UN Doc. A/CONF.183/C.1/L.47 2.

TABLE 4.4 Rome Conference (1998) (*cont.*)

Functions	Draft Statute article 102	Coordinator recommendation report L.47
Enforcement of Cooperation	[(f) consider, upon recommendation [of the Court] [of the Bureau], any question relating to non-cooperation by States Parties [and non-States Parties] and take [necessary] [appropriate] measures, including referring the matter to [the Security Council] [the United Nations General Assembly] as provided in article 86.]	(*f*) *Pending*
Governance and Management Oversight	(g) perform any other function or take any other action as specified in this Statute or the Rules of Procedure and Evidence [including consideration of requests for a review of these instruments] [including consideration of applications relating to pardon submitted to it.] (3)(a) The Assembly shall have a Bureau consisting of a President, a Vice-President and [18] members elected by the Assembly for three-year terms. The President of the Court, the Prosecutor and the Registrar or their representatives may, as appropriate, participate as [observers] [members] in meetings of the Bureau. (b) The Bureau shall [have a representative character] [be elected on the basis of ensuring its representative character], taking into account, in particular, equitable geographical distribution and bearing in mind the adequate representation of the principal legal systems of the world [as far as possible]. The Bureau shall meet as often as necessary, but at least once a year, and shall assist the Assembly in the discharge of its responsibilities.	(g) Perform any other function in accordance with this Statute or the Rules of Procedure and Evidence. 3(a) The Assembly shall have a Bureau consisting of a President, two Vice-Presidents and eighteen members elected by the Assembly for three-year terms. (b) The Bureau shall have a representative character, taking into account, in particular, equitable geographical distribution and the adequate representation of the principal legal systems of the world as far as possible. The Bureau shall meet as often as necessary, but at least once a year, and shall assist the Assembly in the discharge of its responsibilities.

TABLE 4.4 Rome Conference (1998) (*cont.*)

Functions	Draft Statute article 102	Coordinator recommendation report L.47
	(c) The Assembly may also establish other subsidiary bodies as may be necessary, including an independent oversight mechanism for inspection, evaluation, and investigation in order to enhance the efficiency and economy of [non-judicial administration] [operations] of the Court.	(c) The Assembly may also establish other subsidiary bodies as may be necessary, including an independent oversight mechanism for inspection, evaluation, and investigation in order to enhance the efficiency and economy of the Court. 3 bis. The President of the Court, the Prosecutor and the Registrar or their representatives may participate, as appropriate, in meetings of the Assembly of States Parties or of the Bureau.
	(4) The Assembly shall meet at the seat of the Court or at the Headquarters of the United Nations [or in any other place as it may decide] once a year and, when circumstances so require, hold special sessions. Except as otherwise specified in the Statute, special sessions shall be convened [by the Bureau on its own initiative or] at the request of one third of the States Parties.	(4) The Assembly shall meet at the seat of the Court or at the Headquarters of the United Nations once a year and, when circumstances so require, hold special sessions. Except as otherwise specified in the Statute, special sessions shall be convened by the Bureau on its own initiative or at the request of one third of the States Parties.

TABLE 4.4 Rome Conference (1998) (*cont.*)

Functions	Draft Statute article 102	Coordinator recommendation report L.47
	(5) Each State Party shall have one vote. Every effort shall be made to reach decisions on matters of substance by consensus in the Assembly and in the Bureau. If consensus cannot be reached, decisions on matters of substance must be approved by [a two-thirds majority of those present and voting, representing the absolute majority of States Parties] [a two-thirds majority of those present and voting] [an absolute majority of States Parties] except as otherwise provided in the Statute.	(5) Each State Party shall have one vote. Every effort shall be made to reach decisions on matters of substance by consensus in the Assembly and in the Bureau. If consensus cannot be reached, decisions on matters of substance must be approved by a two-thirds majority of those present and voting, provided that an absolute majority of States Parties constitutes the quorum for voting, except as otherwise provided in the Statute.
Financial Oversight	[(6) A State Party that is in arrears in the payment of its financial contributions to the costs of the Court shall have no vote in the Assembly and in the Bureau if the amount of its arrears equals or exceeds the amount of the contributions due from it for the preceding [two full] [three] [five] years. The Assembly may, nevertheless, permit such a State Party to vote in the Assembly and in the Bureau if it is satisfied that the failure to pay is due to conditions beyond the control of the State Party].	(6) A State Party that is in arrears in the payment of its financial contributions to the costs of the Court shall have no vote in the Assembly and in the Bureau if the amount of its arrears equals or exceeds the amount of the contributions due from it for the preceding two full years. The Assembly may, nevertheless, permit such a State Party to vote in the Assembly and in the Bureau if it is satisfied that the failure to pay is due to conditions beyond the control of the State Party.

TABLE 4.4 Rome Conference (1998) (*cont.*)

Functions	Draft Statute article 102	Coordinator recommendation report L.47
Governance and Management Oversight	(7) The Assembly shall adopt its own Rules of Procedure. Clause not included in the Draft Statute.	(8) The official and working languages of the Assembly of States Parties shall be those of the General Assembly of the United Nations.[b]

b Proposal Submitted by Andorra, Argentina, Bolivia, Chile, Colombia, Dominican Republic, El Salvador, Guatemala, Panama, Paraguay, Peru, Spain, Uruguay and Venezuela, Proposals Relating to Official and Working Languages, UN Doc. A/CONF.183/C.1/L.16.

version of the non-cooperation clause if it was co-negotiated or coordinated with the working group on Part 9. This is an example how the negotiation of the Rome Statute and its governing body was isolated to specific junctures without considering its overall function across all its institutional responsibilities.

2.4.3 The 24th Meeting of the Committee of the Whole (6 July)

The Committee of the Whole received a substantially modified Part 11 for its 24th meeting on 6 July 1998.[245] There is a discrepancy in the official documents of the Conference in this regard. The summary record compiled in Volume III[246] mistakenly marks the Committee also considered the corrigendum (L.47/Corr.1) report, which was only issued after the 24th meeting, as correctly captured in the individual summary record.[247] As the Committee considered Part 11, contingent articles to the Assembly of States Parties in Part 4 were also agreed in the same day.[248] For example, the Assembly had now a direct responsibility to elect and increase the number of judges (Article 37), elect the Prosecutor and deputies (Article 43), make a recommendation to the judges for the election of the Registrar (Article 44), approve the staff terms and conditions (Article 45), remove judges, the Prosecutor and deputies (Article 47), adopt and amend the Rules of Procedure and Evidence (Article 52) and consider the regulations of the Court (Article 53).[249] Clauses 102(2)(e) and (g) provided the basis of these powers. In this sense, by proxy of other articles, the role and responsibilities of the Assembly were discussed and agreed beyond Rao's work. This confirms States were more concerned with individual articles than with a comprehensive institutional view of the Assembly across the Statute. In this context, seven States[250] made statements in response to Rao's report. In comparison to the 18th meeting on June 29, only Spain, Syria and Ukraine spoke again. In fact, the number of States making a statement on the Assembly of States Parties decreased by 25. Nonetheless, by the end of the 24th meeting, Chairman Kirsch, proposed to transfer most clauses to the Drafting Commit-

245 A/CONF.183/C.1/SR.24 (1998) 4.

246 United Nations Diplomatic Conference of Plenipotentiaries on the Establishment of an International Criminal Court, Summary Records of the Plenary Meetings and of the Meetings of the Committee of the Whole, UN Doc. A/CONF.183/13 (Vol. II) 266.

247 A/CONF.183/C.1/SR.24 4.

248 World Federalist Movement/Institute for Global Policy, (2018) 278.

249 Recommendations of the Coordinator Part 4. Composition and Administration of the Court, UN Doc. A/CONF.183/C.1/L.45 (1998).

250 Algeria, Dominican Republic, Netherlands, Spain, Switzerland, Syrian Arab Republic and Ukraine.

tee, except 102(2)(f) on non-cooperation and 102(5) on voting majorities for decision-making.[251]

As with the previous meeting, Rao did not introduce the changes comprehensively. He focused on Article 102(3)(a), (b), (4), (5), (6) and (8), of which all but two comments from States were directed at voting majorities for decision-making.[252] Neither the summary records nor the literature explains Rao's choice. For example, if the strategy was to demonstrate substantial agreement reached, Rao could have briefed the Committee on 102(1) determining which States could be observers in the Assembly, a point that was debated at length at the 18th meeting and had the most brackets (four) from any clause except non-cooperation. In his introduction, Rao only asked once the Committee to endorse further changes to his report. This was the case of the removal of the wording 'as far as possible' in Article 102(3)(b) on the representative character of the Bureau. By removing the phrase, the clause put equal and sustained emphasis on geographical distribution and representation of the principal legal systems, without leaving the criteria to political negotiation in the Assembly.

The Netherlands, supported by Ukraine, made an observation about the footnote linking clause 102(2)(d), on the decision of the budget, with Article 104 on financing sources, in Part 12. Of the seven comments received, these are the only ones not focusing on 102(5). The Dutch delegate required the same footnote when referring to arrears in Article 102(6),[253] although, as replied by Rao,[254] the two clauses were distinct in intent. One referred to the Assembly's power to afford the Court with a budget and the second on the voting mechanism for States in arrears. Beyond this comment, States centred on voting majorities for decision-making in clause 102(5).

Rao explained the informal group's compromise.[255] He did not, however, acknowledge that Germany, Norway and the United Kingdom who had warned the wording was 'unintelligible, made no sense mathematically and did not cover procedural votes'.[256] The resulting confrontation was fully at display during the meeting. Algeria, the Dominican Republic, Spain, Switzerland, Syrian Arab Republic and Ukraine asked for clarifications. The crux of the confusion

251 United Nations Diplomatic Conference of Plenipotentiaries on the Establishment of an International Criminal Court, Summary Records of the Plenary Meetings and of the Meetings of the Committee of the Whole, UN Doc. A/CONF.183/13 (Vol. II) 267.

252 Ibid 266.

253 Ibid.

254 Ibid.

255 Ibid.

256 World Federalist Movement/Institute for Global Policy, (2018) 283.

resided in understanding the number of States constituting a quorum for voting (absolute majority of States), the number of States casting a valid vote, not counting abstentions (two-thirds majority of those present and voting) and the threshold needed for voting on substance or procedural matters. Spain asked Rao a clarification whether 'the two-thirds majority of those present and voting had also to constitute an absolute majority of States Parties'.[257] As the delegate from Algeria expressed, 'it was important to be precise'.[258] Rao was unable to respond with clarity to the question, suggesting 'the two kinds of majority referred to should be seen as an integral whole'.[259] At this stage, Kirsch also requested a further clarification but Rao refused to answer, 'to the Chairman's astonishment and accompanied sotto voce derision from delegates'.[260]

To further complicate matters, Spain, Syria and Ukraine raised concerns about the lack of clarity over voting majorities for procedural questions as they read the wording 'except as otherwise provided in the Statute' in the 102(5) clause. The phrase was meant to safeguard different voting requirements by the Assembly in other parts of the Statute like the amendment regime. Article 110(3) in the Draft Statute contained a footnote alerting it was necessary to consider different voting majorities for issues of substance versus 'institutional matters',[261] different, in the context of 102(5) from procedural questions. In this sense, Rao accepted his report had not addressed the issue while suggesting the Drafting Committee could be tasked with elucidating 'any remaining ambiguities'.[262] At this stage, in an already difficult meeting for the coordinator, a representative of the Drafting Committee, the delegate from the Dominican Republic, 'pointed out that it was not the task of that Committee to divine the intentions underlying the articles of the Statute'.[263] Seeing the unfolding situation, Chairman Kirsch proposed 102(5) be returned to the infor-

---

257 United Nations Diplomatic Conference of Plenipotentiaries on the Establishment of an International Criminal Court, Summary Records of the Plenary Meetings and of the Meetings of the Committee of the Whole, UN Doc. A/CONF.183/13 (Vol. II) 266.

258 Ibid.

259 Ibid 267.

260 World Federalist Movement/Institute for Global Policy, (2018) 283.

261 Report of the Preparatory Committee on the Establishment of an International Criminal Court, Part 1 and Part 2, UN Doc. A/CONF.183/2/Add.1 64.

262 United Nations Diplomatic Conference of Plenipotentiaries on the Establishment of an International Criminal Court, Summary Records of the Plenary Meetings and of the Meetings of the Committee of the Whole, UN Doc. A/CONF.183/13 (Vol. II) 267.

263 Ibid.

mal group for further negotiations while transmitting the rest of the Article, except the clause on non-cooperation, to the Drafting Committee.[264]

On the same day, Rao issued a corrigendum report reflecting the decisions from the Committee of the Whole. It showed the modification of clause 102(3)(b) and replaced the text on 102(5) with 'pending'.[265] The non-cooperation clause remained undecided. The next day, on 7 July, the Drafting Committee accused receipt of Article 102 and began its revision.[266] Resolution of voting majorities for decision-making, the first hurdle of the Assembly of States Parties Article, was settled only at the 30th meeting of the Committee of the Whole on 9 July, considering Rao's second Recommendation report.

2.4.4 The Second Coordinator's Recommendation Report (8 July) and the 30th Meeting of the Committee of the Whole (9 July)

Rao's second Recommendation report clarified voting majorities and decision making for procedural questions (see Table 4.5). The informal group decided to restructure the clause adding a part (a) on substantive, and (b) on procedural matters respectively. Both new parts were under the understanding the Assembly and Bureau would primarily seek consensus, and their application was 'except as otherwise provided in the Statute'.[267] In practice the reorganization of the clause allowed for the distinction requested by Syria and safeguarded different voting requirements by the Assembly, for example, in Article 43(4) where a simple 'absolute majority of the States Parties'[268] was required to elect the Prosecutor and deputies.

For part 102(5)(a) on matters of substance, Rao recalled the new language was similar to Rule 36 of the Conference procedure.[269] As Bos explained, 'a double majority'[270] of two-thirds of those present and voting, provided that an absolute majority of States constituted the quorum for voting, was now required. For part 102(5)(b) on matters of procedure, a simple majority of States Parties present and voting was sufficient. Voting majorities for decision-

264 Ibid; World Federalist Movement/Institute for Global Policy, (2018) 278.

265 Committee of the Whole, Recommendations of the Coordinator, Article 102 Assembly of States Parties, UN Doc. A/CONF.183/C.1/L.47/Corr.1.

266 Drafting Committee, Articles Referred by the Committee of the Whole, UN Doc. A/CONF.183/DC/R.87 41–42.

267 Committee of the Whole, Recommendations of the Coordinator, Article 102 Assembly of States Parties, UN Doc. A/CONF.183/C.1/L.47/Add.1.

268 Report of the Preparatory Committee on the Establishment of an International Criminal Court, Part 1 and Part 2, UN Doc. A/CONF.183/2/Add.1 68.

269 Rao, (1999) 412.

270 Bos, 'Assembly of States Parties' (2002) 312.

TABLE 4.5 Rome Conference (1998)

Functions	Coordinator recommendations report L.47	Coordinator recommendations report L.47/Add.1
Governance and Management Oversight	(5) Each State Party shall have one vote. Every effort shall be made to reach decisions on matters of substance by consensus in the Assembly and in the Bureau. If consensus cannot be reached, decisions on matters of substance must be approved by a two-thirds majority of those present and voting, provided that an absolute majority of States Parties constitutes the quorum for voting, except as otherwise provided in the Statute.	5. Each State Party shall have one vote. Every effort shall be made to reach decisions by consensus in the Assembly and in the Bureau. If consensus cannot be reached, except as otherwise provided in the Statute: (a) Decisions on matters of substance must be approved by a two-thirds majority of those present and voting provided that an absolute majority of States Parties constitutes the quorum for voting; (b) Decisions on matters of procedure shall be taken by a simple majority of States Parties present and voting.

making on procedural questions was not part of the Draft Statute and had not featured as an area of concern during the preparatory process. Rao called the result a 'more comprehensive formula'[271] and judging by the number of negotiating days remaining, States were satisfied with the outcome. The second Recommendations report was transmitted to the 30th meeting of the Committee of the Whole, albeit without resolution on clause 102(2)(f) on non-cooperation.

Rao's report was discussed in the Committee of the Whole on 9 July. It was brief and no State made any oral statements. Rao introduced the revision as

271 Rao, (1999) 412.

'self-explanatory',[272] recommending its adoption. Subsequently, upon silent agreement, the Committee transferred the text to the Drafting Committee.[273] On the same day, the Drafting Committee issued a compendium report of draft Articles referred by the Committee of the Whole.[274] Part 11, giving birth to the Assembly of States Parties, was complete except its role in dealing with non-cooperation. Affording the Assembly with a role dealing with non-cooperation depended on negotiations in the International Cooperation and Judicial Assistance working group led by Phakiso Mochochoko (Lesotho). Indeed, by resolving pending brackets in Article 86, the second and final hurdle to Article 112 was solved.

2.5 *The Second Hurdle of Article 102 Negotiations: Non-Cooperation and Final Approval (10–17 July)*

The days between 10 July and the closing of the Conference on 17 July 1998 were hectic and dramatic. The delays experienced in the last week of the Conference were rooted in profound divergent views about jurisdiction, admissibility, applicable laws and the degree of autonomy of the Court.[275] A compromise proposal put forward by the Bureau on 10 July was criticised to the point a frustrated Chairman Kirsch noted 'give us slack if you like, but do some work too'.[276] Hans Corell pleaded States to show flexibility in creating 'an international institution to serve the world at large'.[277] The inflexible position of the United States was a barrier. As Scheffer noted, seeking consensus within his government consumed most of his efforts.[278] Bassiouni shared the same level of frustration as other States opting 'to go ahead with Kirsch's proposed compromise package rather than to have it unravel due to last minute U.S.

272 United Nations Diplomatic Conference of Plenipotentiaries on the Establishment of an International Criminal Court, Summary Records of the Plenary Meetings and of the Meetings of the Committee of the Whole, UN Doc. A/CONF.183/13 (Vol. II) 305.

273 Ibid.

274 Draft Statute for the International Criminal Court, Compendium of Draft Articles Referred to the Drafting Committee by the Committee of the Whole as of 9 July 1998, UN Doc. A/CONF.183/C.1/L.58.

275 Kirsch, Philippe and Holmes, John T, 'The Birth of the International Criminal Court: The 1998 Rome Conference' (1999) 36 Canadian Yearbook of International Law/Annuaire Canadien de Droit International 29.

276 Meeting of Key Conference Committee Shows Continuing Differences on Important Provisions of International Criminal Court Statute, UN Doc. L/ROM/16 (1998).

277 United Nations Secretary-General's Representative Urges all out Effort to Achieve Consensus on International Criminal Court Treaty, UN Doc. L/ROM/17 (1998).

278 Scheffer, David, 'A Negotiator's Perspective on the International Criminal Court' (2001) 167 (1) Military Law Review 3.

demands'.[279] In this context, a new version of the Draft Statute was published by the Drafting Committee on 13 July (see Table 4.6).[280]

The new version of Article 102 consisted of ten paragraphs, taking the shape of what would become Article 112 in the Rome Statute. Furthermore, eight provisions were re-drafted to provide overall legal and linguistic cohesiveness, all under the careful watch of Bassiouni. Three refinements are notable. The wording 'as appropriate', was added to Article 102(2)(a) on the adoption of reports from the Preparatory Commission to further emphasize the power of the Assembly of States Parties to assess them without conditionalities.[281] Secondly, Article 102(2)(e) on the power to increase the number of judges now referenced Article 37 in Part 4 to further guide the Assembly's nomination and election process. In addition, the key action word changed from 'determine' to 'decide', as Rao and Ambach explained, to recognize the 'finality of the competence of the Assembly'.[282] Finally, two new paragraphs were introduced to clarify the set-up of subsidiary bodies and the participation 'as appropriate'[283] of the President, the Prosecutor and the Registrar in the Bureau and Assembly. In sum, by 13 July, except provision 102(2)(f) on non-cooperation, the evolution of Article 102 into 112 was complete.

Negotiations over the cooperation regime in Part 9 were 'generally troublesome'.[284] The Court was fully dependent on cooperation from States to carry out its most basic functions. Lacking its own police force, a revised version of Article 86 considered measures for non-cooperation for non-party States (5) and States Parties (7) respectively. Already in 1997, the working group on International Cooperation and Judicial Assistance had provided the Assembly with a role to consider non-cooperation with the Court.[285] However, while 'technical aspects'[286] were solved then, the political questions about the trigger to seize the Assembly, whether it also applied to non-party States Parties and which remedies it could take, were still pending days before the end of the

279 Bassiouni, 'Negotiating the Treaty of Rome on the Establishment of an International Criminal Court' 457.

280 Report of the Drafting Committee to the Committee of the Whole Part 11 Assembly of States Parties, UN Doc. A/CONF.183/C.1/L.66.

281 Kim, 388.

282 Rao and Ambach, (2016) 2224.

283 Report of the Drafting Committee to the Committee of the Whole Part 11 Assembly of States Parties, UN Doc. A/CONF.183/C.1/L.66.

284 World Federalist Movement/Institute for Global Policy, (2018) 260.

285 Decisions Taken by the Preparatory Committee at its Session Held from 1 to 12 December 1997, UN Doc. A/AC.249/1997/L.9/Rev.1 40.

286 Kreß and Prost, (2016) 2021.

TABLE 4.6 Rome Conference (1998)

Functions	Drafting committee, part 11. assembly of States Parties L.66 (1998)
Governance and Management Oversight	(1) An Assembly of States Parties to this Statute is hereby established. Each State Party shall have one representative in the Assembly who may be accompanied by alternates and advisers. Other States which have signed the Statute or the Final Act may be observers in the Assembly. |Refined by Drafting Committee (2) The Assembly shall: (a) Consider and adopt, as appropriate, recommendations of the Preparatory Commission.[1] Footnote 1: See document A/CONF.183/2/Add.l, annex to Final Act. |Refined by Drafting Committee (b) provide management oversight to the Presidency, Prosecutor and Registrar regarding the administration of the Court; (c) Consider the reports and activities of the Bureau established under paragraph 3 and take appropriate action in regard thereto. |Refined by Drafting Committee
Financial Oversight	(d) Consider and decide the budget for the Court
Governance and Management Oversight	(e) Decide whether to alter, in accordance with article 37, the number of judges. |Refined by Drafting Committee
Enforcement of Cooperation	(f) *Pending*
Governance and Management Oversight	(g) perform any other function consistent with this Statute or the Rules of Procedure and Evidence. (3)(a) The Assembly shall have a Bureau consisting of a President, two Vice-Presidents and eighteen members elected by the Assembly for three-year terms.

TABLE 4.6 Rome Conference (1998) (*cont.*)

Functions	Drafting committee, part 11. assembly of States Parties L.66 (1998)
	(b) The Bureau shall have a representative character, taking into account, in particular, equitable geographical distribution and the adequate representation of the principal legal systems of the world. (c) The Bureau shall meet as often as necessary, but at least once a year, and shall assist the Assembly in the discharge of its responsibilities. | Refined by Drafting Committee (4) The Assembly may establish such subsidiary bodies as may be necessary, including an independent oversight mechanism for inspection, evaluation and investigation of the Court, in order to enhance the efficiency and economy. |Refined by Drafting Committee (5) The President of the Court, the Prosecutor and the Registrar or their representatives may participate, as appropriate, in meetings of the Assembly and of the Bureau. |Refined by Drafting Committee (6) The Assembly shall meet at the seat of the Court or at the Headquarters of the United Nations once a year and, when circumstances so require, hold special sessions. Except as otherwise specified in the Statute, special sessions shall be convened by the Bureau on its own initiative or at the request of one third of the States Parties. (7) Each State Party shall have one vote. Every effort shall be made to reach decisions by consensus in the Assembly and in the Bureau. If consensus cannot be reached, except as otherwise provided in the Statute:

TABLE 4.6 Rome Conference (1998) (*cont.*)

Functions	Drafting committee, part 11. assembly of States Parties L.66 (1998)
	(a) Decisions on matters of substance must be approved by a two-thirds majority of those present and voting provided that an absolute majority of States Parties constitutes the quorum for voting; (b) Decisions on matters of procedure shall be taken by a simple majority of States Parties present and voting.
Financial Oversight	(8) A State Party which is in arrears in the payment of its financial contributions towards the costs of the Court shall have no vote in the Assembly and in the Bureau if the amount of its arrears equals or exceeds the amount of the contribution due from it for the preceding two full years. The Assembly may, nevertheless, permit such a State Party to vote in the Assembly and in the Bureau if it is satisfied that the failure to pay is due to conditions beyond the control of the State Party.
Governance and Management Oversight	(9) The Assembly shall adopt its own Rules of Procedure. (10) The official and working languages of the Assembly shall be those of the General Assembly of the United Nations. |Refined by Drafting Committee

Conference.[287] Following a similar trend as in Part 2, States objected any duty imposed on non-party States and the involvement of the United Nations

287 Schabas, The International Criminal Court: A Commentary on the Rome Statute 1274. Ciampi, Annalisa, 'The Obligation to Cooperate' in Antonio, Cassese, Paola, Gaeta and John, RWD Jones (eds), The Rome Statute of the International Criminal Court: a Commentary (Oxford University Press 2002); Swart, Bert and Sluiter, Goran, 'The ICC and International Criminal Cooperation' in von Hebel, Herman, Lammers, Johan G and

Security Council.[288] These two issues were considered by a sub-group led by French delegate Beatrice Le Fraper du Hellen.[289]

As Mégret explained, the 'intensification'[290] of talks during the last week of the Conference focused the will of States. The provision dealing with State Party failure to cooperate received overwhelming support from delegations on 1 July to, upon a finding from the Court, refer the matter to the Assembly or the Security Council if the latter referred a situation.[291] Similarly, after several rounds of informal negotiations, on 9 July, the majority of States agreed to 'invite'[292] non-party States to cooperate with the Court and if they failed to do so, authorize the Court to 'inform' the Assembly of States Parties or the Security Council.[293] The main distinction was informing a non-party States lack of compliance versus referring instances of non-cooperation of States Parties to the Assembly or Security Council. Even with these two options, by 14 July, Mexico, Libya, the United Arab Emirates, India, Sri Lanka, Yemen, Pakistan and Sudan maintained their refusal over any role for the Security Council.[294]

The impasse was resolved by agreeing to adjust Article 86(5) and (7) based on the resolution of Part 2 (see Table 4.7).[295] Logically, the role of the Security Council in triggering the jurisdiction of the Court had a direct bearing with Part 9. Part 2 would be finalized by 16 July as Chairman Kirsch and the Bureau proposed a 'final package'[296] as a last compromise. In the Bureau's package, all provisions were untangled, including keeping a role for the Security Council in

---

Schukking, Jolien (eds), Reflections on the International Criminal Court: Essays in Honour of Adriaan Bos (TMC Asser Press 1999).

288 Ciampi, 'Legal Rules, Policy Choices and Political Realities in the Functioning of the Cooperation Regime of the International Criminal Court' 2016.

289 Mochochoko, (1999) 305. She later served as Head of the Jurisdiction, Complementarity and Cooperation Division of the Office of the Prosecutor.

290 Mégret, 'The Rome Conference: Institutional Design and the Constraints of Diplomacy' (2020) 32.

291 Rolling Text Of Articles 85 and 86, UN Doc. A/CONF.183/C.1/WGIC/L.10 (1998) 2; World Federalist Movement/Institute for Global Policy, (2018) 249.

292 Report of the Working Group on International Cooperation and Judicial Assistance, UN Doc. A/CONF.183/C.1/WGIC/L.11/Add.2 (1998) 2.

293 World Federalist Movement/Institute for Global Policy, (2018) 249.

294 United Nations Diplomatic Conference of Plenipotentiaries on the Establishment of an International Criminal Court, Summary Records of the Plenary Meetings and of the Meetings of the Committee of the Whole, UN Doc. A/CONF.183/13 (Vol. II) 368; World Federalist Movement/Institute for Global Policy, (2018) 248.

295 World Federalist Movement/Institute for Global Policy, (2018) 249.

296 United Nations Diplomatic Conference of Plenipotentiaries on the Establishment of an International Criminal Court, Summary Records of the Plenary Meetings and of the Meetings of the Committee of the Whole, UN Doc. A/CONF.183/13 (Vol. II) 360.

TABLE 4.7 Rome Conference (1998)

Functions	Coordinator recommendations report (L.47)	Coordinator recommendations report (L.47/Add.2)
Enforcement of Cooperation	102(2)(f) *Pending*	(2)(f) Consider any question relating to non-cooperation pursuant to article 86, paragraphs 5 and 7.

Article 86 (5) and (7).[297] The package deal, on the other hand, failed to precisely include the steps and measures the Assembly of States Parties was to follow acting under Part 9 to address non-cooperation. Civil society characterized this innocuous absence of detail as 'baby teeth'[298] enforcement. Kaul and Kreß pointed out Article 102(2)(f) represented a lax non-compliance regime devoid of details for enforcing cooperation.[299]

In this context, Rao's third Recommendations report (L.47/Add.2) containing 102(2)(f) on non-cooperation was transmitted to the Committee of the Whole on 14 July.[300] The available record does not indicate the level of coordination between Rao, Le Fraper du Hellen and Mochochoko, but the Assembly's informal group benefited from the agreement to link Article 86 with resolving Part 2. The language proposed, after 'further informal consultations',[301] was purely synoptical:

As Rao explained, the informal group 'resolved the problem'[302] by referring to Part 9 in general terms without offering a substantive definition of the power to consider any question relating to non-cooperation by the Assembly (see Table 4.8). Doing so, as Schabas[303] argued, plainly removed any complex-

297 Draft Statute for the International Criminal Court, Part 9, International Cooperation and Judicial Assistance, UN Doc. A/CONF.183/C.1/L.76/Add.9 (1998); World Federalist Movement/Institute for Global Policy, (2018) 249.

298 World Federalist Movement/Institute for Global Policy, (2018) 264.

299 Kaul, Hans-Peter and Kreß, Claus, 'Jurisdiction and Cooperation in the Statute of the International Criminal Court: Principles and Compromises' (1999) 2 Yearbook of International Humanitarian Law 169.

300 Committee of the Whole, Recommendations of the Coordinator, Article 102 Assembly of States Parties, UN Doc. A/CONF.183/C.1/L.47/Add.2.

301 Ibid.

302 Rao, (1999) 412;Rao and Ambach, (2016) 2226.

303 Schabas, The International Criminal Court: A Commentary on the Rome Statute 1439.

TABLE 4.8 Rome Conference (1998)

Functions	Drafting committee report (L.66)	Drafting committee report (L.66/Add.1)
Enforcement of Cooperation	(2)(f) *Pending*	(2)(f) Consider any question relating to non-cooperation pursuant to article 86, paragraphs 5 and 7.

ity, and as Sluiter confirmed, the drafting history did not reveal 'what powers or concrete measures'[304] the Assembly could pursue in enforcing cooperation. In fact, several questions remained. Bos[305] wandered how the Assembly could take-up non-cooperation questions, Cassese[306] regretted the Statute did not authorize States Parties to seek countermeasures towards non-compliant States, and Sluiter warned the Assembly lacked sufficient means to enact Article 102(2)(f).[307] Some of these doubts would be partially resolved by the Assembly of States Parties in 2011, establishing a procedure to improve compliance with cooperation orders from the Court.[308]

The Committee of the Whole agreed at its 38th meeting on 15 July to transmit Article 102(2)(f) to the Drafting Committee, as proposed by Rao.[309] There were no oral statements from States. Rao only informed the Committee the clause 'had been reformulated in the light of the decisions taken in relation to article 86'.[310] Thus, the Committee of the Whole formally adopted the Drafting Committee's report on the Assembly of States Parties,[311] and later the same day an addendum with a slightly rewritten Article 102(2)(f).[312]

304 Sluiter, 388.

305 Bos, 'Assembly of States Parties' (2002) 307.

306 Cassese, Antonio, 'The Statute of the International Criminal Court: Some Preliminary Reflections' (1999) 10 (1) European Journal of International Law 166.

307 Sluiter, Göran, 'Appendix II: "An International Criminal Court is Hereby Established"' (1998) 16 (3) Netherlands Quarterly of Human Rights 419.

308 ICC-ASP/10/Res.5 Strengthening the International Criminal Court and the Assembly of States Parties (2011).

309 United Nations Diplomatic Conference of Plenipotentiaries on the Establishment of an International Criminal Court, Summary Records of the Plenary Meetings and of the Meetings of the Committee of the Whole, UN Doc. A/CONF.183/13 (Vol. II) 352.

310 Ibid.

311 A/CONF.183/C.1/SR.39 4.

312 Committee of the Whole, Recommendations of the Coordinator, Article 102 Assembly of States Parties, UN Doc. A/CONF.183/C.1/L.47/Add.2.

At the 41st meeting of the Committee of the Whole, on 16 July, the Assembly of States Parties Article was finally adopted.[313] In fact, while the Bureau rushed to craft the final compromise Statute in the final hours of 16 July, Part 11 was released early to States together with the preamble text.[314] The Bureau's compromise proposal was only available to States in the morning of the last day of the Conference on 17 July.[315] The Assembly of States Parties Article was duly incorporated into the Bureau's take it or leave it deal.[316]

On the last meeting of the Committee on 17 July 1998, Chairman Kirsch pleaded States to accept the 'very delicate balance between the views of delegations'[317] and adopt the text from the Bureau as a complete package. However India and the United States introduced last minute amendments threatening to re-open unresolved viewpoints among delegations.[318] At this stage, acting under Rule 25[319] of the Conference procedure and aiming to protect the compromises reached, Norway proposed a motion of no-action for each amendment.[320] In brief, the non-action motion triggered a vote to adjourn the debate precluding discussion of the amendments. As Lee explains, no-motion procedure was a long-standing Nordic tradition in the United Nations to avoid 'a showdown on substance'.[321] Norwegian delegate Rolf Einar Fife justified his intervention to 'avoid destroying the balance achieved with such difficulty and making it impossible to achieve the ultimate goal of an independent, effective and credible international court'.[322] Both amendments were defeated when the adjournment of debate was put to a vote.[323] As Bassiouni described,

---

313 United Nations Diplomatic Conference of Plenipotentiaries on the Establishment of an International Criminal Court, Summary Records of the Plenary Meetings and of the Meetings of the Committee of the Whole, UN Doc. A/CONF.183/13 (Vol. II) 357.

314 World Federalist Movement/Institute for Global Policy, (2018) 690.

315 Kirsch and Holmes, 'The Birth of the International Criminal Court: The 1998 Rome Conference' 34.

316 Draft Statute for the International Criminal Court, Part 11. Assembly of States Parties, Article 102 Assembly of States Parties, UN Doc. A/CONF.183/C.1/L.76/Add.11.

317 United Nations Diplomatic Conference of Plenipotentiaries on the Establishment of an International Criminal Court, Summary Records of the Plenary Meetings and of the Meetings of the Committee of the Whole, UN Doc. A/CONF.183/13 (Vol. II) 360.

318 Ibid.

319 Ibid 56.

320 Ibid 360–361.

321 Lee, The International Criminal Court: The Making of the Rome Statute: Issues, Negotiations and Results 25 at footnote 45.

322 United Nations Diplomatic Conference of Plenipotentiaries on the Establishment of an International Criminal Court, Summary Records of the Plenary Meetings and of the Meetings of the Committee of the Whole, UN Doc. A/CONF.183/13 (Vol. II) 360.

323 Ibid 362.

the second vote triggered a 'spontaneous standing ovation' marking 'one of the most extraordinary emotional scenes ever to take place at a diplomatic conference'.[324] Hans Corell duly communicated the result to Kofi Annan who rushed from Buenos Aires to Rome.[325] Kirsch's detailed account of these final moments has been captured in the literature.[326] By 10.30pm on 17 July the Statute moved to the plenary for adoption.[327] In the final plenary, upon instructions from the White House,[328] the United States requested a vote.[329] The Statute and Final Act were adopted by 120 votes to 7, with 21 abstentions.[330] The meeting closed, among jubilation,[331] well into the early hours of 18 July.[332] The Rome Statute of the International Criminal Court was issued in all six languages after needed re-numbering of different parts.[333] In this moment, the Assembly of States Parties emerged as Article 112.[334] The closing ceremony took place at Il Campidoglio, with Mauritius and Bolivia signing the Statute first.[335]

---

324 Bassiouni, 'Negotiating the Treaty of Rome on the Establishment of an International Criminal Court' 459.

325 Kofi Annan and Mousavizadeh, Nader, Interventions: A Life in War and Peace (Penguin 2013) 150.

326 Kirsch and Holmes, 'The Rome Conference on an International Criminal Court: The Negotiating Process' 3; Kirsch and Holmes, 'The Birth of the International Criminal Court: The 1998 Rome Conference' 4; Kirsch and Oosterveld, 1142; Kirsch and Robinson, (2002) 67.

327 United Nations Diplomatic Conference of Plenipotentiaries on the Establishment of an International Criminal Court, Summary Records of the Plenary Meetings and of the Meetings of the Committee of the Whole, UN Doc. A/CONF.183/13 (Vol. II) 462.

328 Scheffer, David, All the Missing Souls (Princeton University Press 2012) 260;Strijards, Gerard, 'The Institution of the International Criminal Court' (1999) 12 (3) Leiden Journal of International Law 671.

329 United Nations Diplomatic Conference of Plenipotentiaries on the Establishment of an International Criminal Court, Summary Records of the Plenary Meetings and of the Meetings of the Committee of the Whole, UN Doc. A/CONF.183/13 (Vol. II) 121.

330 Ibid.

331 World Federalist Movement/Institute for Global Policy, (2018) 698.

332 United Nations Diplomatic Conference of Plenipotentiaries on the Establishment of an International Criminal Court, Summary Records of the Plenary Meetings and of the Meetings of the Committee of the Whole, UN Doc. A/CONF.183/13 (Vol. II) 129.

333 Bassiouni, 'Negotiating the Treaty of Rome on the Establishment of an International Criminal Court' 458.

334 United Nations Diplomatic Conference of Plenipotentiaries on the Establishment of an International Criminal Court, Rome Statute of the International Criminal Court, UN Doc. A/CONF.183/9* 81–83.

335 Secretary-General Says Establishment of International Criminal Court is Major Step In March Towards Universal Human Rights, Rule Of Law, UN Doc. L/2890 (1998); World Federalist Movement/Institute for Global Policy, (2018) 706.

The appraisal of what was accomplished in Rome varies and continues to be analysed. At the time, Bassiouni agreed the 'method'[336] of the drafters would be criticised but also hoped the jurisprudence developed by the Court and the action of the Assembly of States Parties would remedy issues in the Statute. For Rosenne the 'haste' of the Conference added up to a 'sorry story'.[337] Kirsch, Holmes and Oosterverld have recognized the Statute was not perfect but the result of multilateral diplomacy and politics.[338] Cassese thought the final agreement was a 'luminous page in world history',[339] while Lee emphasized no State could claim victory or defeat altogether.[340] For critics like Mumford, the Court was bound to fail without consensus from major powers.[341] Contemporary discussion, more than twenty years after the Conference, still wonders if the compromises reached were 'as brilliant as was once thought'.[342] This is certainly true about the failure to agree on the crime of aggression.[343] When it comes to Article 112, Gradoni argued the appearance of simplicity in the text masked critical responsibilities of States Parties in the Statute.[344] Nesi pointed to the finance needs and adaptability of the Court in the long term.[345] Mundis and Gallant agreed the Assembly, as the driver of a new international organization, would be consequential to implementing the desires of the drafters in Rome.[346] Nonetheless, the agreed text was only a step in the process to establish the International Criminal Court and the Assembly of States Parties as the Rome Conference tasked a

336 Bassiouni, 'Negotiating the Treaty of Rome on the Establishment of an International Criminal Court' 466.

337 Rosenne, 'Antecedents of the Rome Statute of the International Criminal Court Revisited' 405–406.

338 Kirsch and Holmes, 'The Birth of the International Criminal Court: The 1998 Rome Conference' 38; Kirsch and Oosterveld, (1153).

339 Cassese, 171.

340 Lee, 'Creating an International Criminal Court: Of Procedures and Compromises' 1999 147.

341 Mumford, Marcus R, 'Building Upon a Foundation of Sand: A Commentary on the International Criminal Court Treaty Conference' (1999) 8 (1) Journal of International Law and Practice 216.

342 Schabas, 'The Dynamics of the Rome Conference' (2020) 19.

343 Heller, Kevin Jon, 'Options for Prosecuting Russian Aggression Against Ukraine: A Critical Analysis' (2022) Journal of Genocide Research 13.

344 Gradoni, (2012) 2010.

345 Nesi, (1999) 248.

346 Mundis, Daryl A, 'The Assembly of States Parties and the Institutional Framework of the International Criminal Court' (2003) 97 (1) American Journal of International Law 132; Gallant, 560.

Preparatory Commission to negotiate and prepare key auxiliary documents as the required 60 ratifications triggering the operations of the Court arrived.

3 1999–2002: The Preparatory Commission for the International Criminal Court

The Final Act of the Rome Conference established in Resolution F a Preparatory Commission under the authority of the United Nations General Assembly.[347] The Commission was charged with negotiating and preparing key auxiliary documents for the International Criminal Court to begin operations after the required 60 ratifications. The Commission was open to signatories of the Statute, the Final Act and other States invited to participate. As Schabas argued, besides the temporal and programmatic connection between the two bodies, the Commission looked 'very much like the continuation of the Rome Conference'.[348] This was the case in terms of membership and leadership. By virtue of the General Assembly resolution on the matter, civil society and other organizations were invited as observers.[349] The leadership of the Preparatory Commission also mirrored the Rome Conference. Ambassador Philippe Kirsch chaired the Bureau together with Rome participants, such as Medard R. Rwelamira, and several experienced delegates coordinating key aspects of the programme of work.[350]

As per Resolution F in the Final Act, the Preparatory Commission was tasked with preparing eight critical auxiliary documents.[351] In particular, the Rules of Procedure and Evidence and the Elements of Crimes had a hard deadline of 30 June 2000 for completion.[352] As Kirsch and Oosterverld noted, the deadline intended to avoid endless negotiations on two critical constitutive

347 UNGA Res 53/105 (1998) 2.

348 Schabas, William A, 'Follow up to Rome: Preparing for Entry into Force of the Statute of the International Criminal Court' in Politi, Mauro and Nesi, Guiseppe (eds), The Rome Statute of the International Criminal Court: a Challenge to Impunity (Routledge 2001) 206.

349 UNGA Res 53/105; Hall, Christopher Keith, 'The First Five Sessions of the UN Preparatory Commission for the International Criminal Court' (2000) 94 (4) American Journal of International Law 774.

350 Proceedings of the Preparatory Commission at its First Session (16–26 February), UN Doc. PCNICC/1999/L.3/Rev.1 (1999) 2.

351 United Nations Diplomatic Conference of Plenipotentiaries on the Establishment of an International Criminal Court, Final Documents, UN Doc. A/CONF.183/13 (Vol. I) 72.

352 Ibid.

instruments for the Court.[353] Other documents included an agreement on the privileges and immunities of the Court, the basic principles governing a headquarters agreement, the relationship agreement between the Court and the United Nations, and critically for the Assembly of States Parties: its rules of procedure, the financial regulations and rules and the budget for the first year.[354] In addition, as a last-minute concession in Rome, the Commission was tasked to prepare a definition and jurisdictional trigger for the crime of aggression.[355] Resolution F mandated the Commission to submit proposals on the crime of aggression to a Review Conference, by virtue of Article 123(1), seven years after the entry into force of the Statute.[356]

However, the Commission was only tasked with the preparation of proposals for an ultimate decision by States Parties.[357] This mandate was rather elusive as the Commission was forced to decide on operational requirements for the Court and the Assembly.[358] For example, while the staff regulations in Article 44(3) were removed[359] from of the list of documents developed by the Commission, the crafting of the budget for the first financial period determined, among other operational issues, a staff pension scheme.[360] The ambivalence of the Commission between an incubator for the Court and an embryonic form of the Assembly of States Parties was present across the 10 sessions between 1999 and 2002. For Rosenne, the ample remit was 'far beyond what is usual for a preparatory commission'.[361] In this sense, as with the Rome Conference, the absence of a complete preparatory record might

353 Kirsch, Philippe and Oosterveld, Valerie, 'The Post-Rome Conference Preparatory Commission' in Cassese, Antonio, Gaeta, Paola and Jones, John RWD (eds), The Rome Statute of the International Criminal Court: A Commentary, vol 1 (Oxford University Press Oxford 2002) 95.

354 United Nations Diplomatic Conference of Plenipotentiaries on the Establishment of an International Criminal Court, Final Documents, UN Doc. A/CONF.183/13 (Vol. I) 72.

355 Rao, (1999) 416.

356 United Nations Diplomatic Conference of Plenipotentiaries on the Establishment of an International Criminal Court, Final Documents, UN Doc. A/CONF.183/13 (Vol. I) 73.

357 Rao, (1999) 415.

358 United Nations Diplomatic Conference of Plenipotentiaries on the Establishment of an International Criminal Court, Final Documents, UN Doc. A/CONF.183/13 (Vol. I) 73.

359 Kirsch and Oosterveld, 'The Post-Rome Conference Preparatory Commission' (2002) 94.

360 Preparatory Commission for the International Criminal Court (1–12 July), UN Doc. PCNICC/2002/2 (2002).

361 Rosenne, 'Antecedents of the Rome Statute of the International Criminal Court Revisited' 409.

obscure the degree of trespassing from the original mandate to focus on proposals rather than operational arrangements.[362]

A final factor in the Commission was the position of the United States. The United States displayed a less intransigent negotiation posture ending in the signature of the Statute on the last day of the Clinton administration in December 2000[363] during the sixth session of the Commission. However, by 2002 the new Bush government reversed Clinton's decision and enacted the American Servicemembers' Protection Act, effectively authorizing the use of force to retrieve service personnel in the custody of the Court.[364] Further criticism particularly singled out the Assembly of States Parties as a barrier for accession. Casey disagreed the United States should have 'a single vote in the Assembly, the exact same representation enjoyed by His Serene Highness, the Prince of Liechtenstein'.[365] Lieutenant Colonel Newton, a member of the United States' delegation to the Commission, reminded delegates asking 'why we do not just shrug and join in the gang',[366] the Assembly, as a political body, was vulnerable to 'abuse'.[367] Neither Casey nor Newton's arguments have prevented the United States from engaging with the Court and the Assembly under different administrations, albeit with spectacular inconsistency.[368]

Despite opposition from powerful States, to the surprise of many delegations, the Statute reached the required 60 ratifications on 11 April 2002,[369] in the middle of the ninth session of the Preparatory Commission. By virtue of Article 126, the Statute came into force on 1 July 2002, at the beginning of the last session of the Commission.[370] Kirsch and Oosterverld credited the demon-

---

362 Hall, 'The First Five Sessions of the UN Preparatory Commission for the International Criminal Court' 775.

363 President Clinton Statement on Signature of the International Criminal Court Treaty, December 31, 2000 (State Department, 2000) <https://1997–2001.state.gov/www/global/swci/001231_clinton_icc.html> accessed 24 January 2018.

364 Benedetti, Bonneau and Washburn, 172.

365 Casey, Lee A, 'The Case Against the International Criminal Court' (2001) 25 (3) Fordham International Law Journal 844.

366 Newton, Michael A, 'The International Criminal Court Preparatory Commission: The Way It Is & The Way Ahead' (2001) (1) Virginia Journal of International Law 208.

367 Ibid 209.

368 Schabas, William A, 'International War Crimes Tribunals and the United States' (2011) 35 (5) Diplomatic History 769; Sterio, Milena, 'The Trump Administration and the International Criminal Court: A Misguided New Policy' (2019) 51 (1) Case Western Reserve Journal of International Law 201.

369 International Criminal Court will Enter Into Force on 1 July 2002, as 10 States Deposit Ratification Instruments at Headquarters, UN Doc. L/3000 (2002).

370 With Today's Entry Into Force of Rome Statute of Global Court, Speakers Hail 'Day of Hope' for Seekers of Justice, UN Doc. L/3007 (2002).

strative effect of the Commission for the 'widespread acceptance of not only the documents but of the Court itself'.[371] In this context, and in particular to study the establishment and operations of the Assembly of States Parties, the following sections provide an overview of the Commission's programme of work and elaboration of documents required in Resolution F. However, it focuses on relevant actions to set-up the governance and oversight role of the Assembly of States Parties towards its first session in September 2002.

3.1 *The Preparatory Commission's Work Programme*

The Preparatory Commission held 10 sessions between 1999 and 2002 at the United Nations Headquarter in New York and continued with the tactic of gatherings in between sessions.[372] Between 87 (first session) and 150 States (third session) attended the preparatory process, together with international organizations and civil society under the umbrella of the Coalition for an International Criminal Court.[373] According to Kirsch, the chair of the Bureau across all 10 sessions, the Commission worked in a collaborative way, 'much better than the Diplomatic Conference, despite all the difficulties it encountered'.[374] The Commission elected its Bureau during the first session in February 1999 with Philippe Kirsch (Canada) as Chair.[375] The first session between 16 and 26 February 1999 was opened by Kofi Annan and Hans Corell, both urging all States to join Senegal as the first State to accede to the Rome Statute.[376]

Indeed, the speed of ratifications surpassed the expectations of States and civil society alike.[377] Starting with one ratification (Senegal) and 75 signatories in February 1999, the Commission ended its mandate in July 2002 with 76 ratifications and 139 signatories.[378] While by the end of the fifth session

371 Kirsch, Philippe and Oosterveld, Valerie, 'The Preparatory Commission for the International Criminal Court' (2001) 25 (3) Fordham International Law Journal 587–588.

372 Hall, 'The First Five Sessions of the UN Preparatory Commission for the International Criminal Court' 774.

373 Welch, Claude E and Watkins, Ashley F, 'Extending Enforcement: The Coalition for the International Criminal Court' (2011) 33 (4) Human Rights Quarterly 992.

374 Kirsch and Oosterveld, 'Negotiating an Institution For The Twenty-First Century: Multilateral Diplomacy and The International Criminal Court' (1157).

375 Proceedings of the Preparatory Commission at its First Session (16–26 February), UN Doc. PCNICC/1999/L.3/Rev.1 2.

376 Ibid.

377 Schabas, William A, 'International Criminal Court: The Secret of Its Success' (2001) 12 (4) Criminal Law Forum 417.

378 United Nations Treaty Collection, Depositary of Notifications, Rome Statute of the International Criminal Court, available at <https://treaties.un.org/>' accessed 5 January 2024.

in June 2000, when the Commission adopted the Rules of Procedure and Evidence and the Elements of Crimes, there were 12 ratifications,[379] the next three sessions obtained 24,[380] 29,[381] and 42[382] new States Parties. With the presence Arthur Robinson, then President of Trinidad and Tobago, the Rome Statute obtained the needed 60 ratifications for activation during a ceremony organized by the United Nations in April 2002, days before the beginning of the ninth session of the Preparatory Commission.[383]

Across all 10 sessions, the pace of ratifications exacerbated the need to focus on operational requirements to setup the Court and the work of the Assembly. The programme of work shows how the Commission tackled these practical arrangements culminating in the first Assembly of States Parties in September 2002. In particular, it is notable the Commission decided in its eighth session in September 2001 to establish a subcommittee of the Bureau, led by Silvia Fernández de Gurmendi (Argentina), to coordinate suitable arrangements with the host country to establish the Court without delay.[384] By the following session in April 2002, the Commission had set up an advance team made of experts to 'ensure custody of information received after the entry into force of the Rome Statute and allow for the Court to rapidly recruit personnel and procure the goods and services necessary for its effective functioning'.[385] In the same meeting, a working group tasked with developing the core documentation needed for the first Assembly of States Parties was established.[386] When the Commission concluded its work in July 2002, the preparations by the advance team and the core documents for the first Assembly were in place.[387]

379 Preparatory Commission for International Criminal Court Adopts Rules of Procedure and Evidence and Text on Elements of Crimes, UN Doc. L/2963 (2000).

380 Preparatory Commission for International Criminal Court is Told Definition of Crime of Aggression Still Under Review, UN Doc. L/2967 (2000).

381 Preparatory Commission for International Criminal Court Opens Seventh Session at Headquarters, UN Doc. L/2975 (2001).

382 At Eighth Session of Preparatory Commission for International Criminal Court, Four Working Groups Announce Completion of Assignments, UN Doc. L/2988 (2001).

383 International Criminal Court will Enter Into Force on 1 July 2002, as 10 States Deposit Ratification Instruments at Headquarters, UN Doc. L/3000.

384 Proceedings of the Preparatory Commission at its Eighth Session (24 September–5 October), UN Doc. PCNICC/2001/L.3/Rev.1 (2001) 4.

385 Proceedings of the Preparatory Commission at its Ninth Session (8–19 April), UN Doc. PCNICC/2002/L.1/Rev.1 (2002) 3.

386 Ibid.

387 Proceedings of the Preparatory Commission at its Tenth Session (1–12 July), UN Doc. PCNICC/2002/L.4/Rev.1 (2002) 2.

TABLE 4.9 Preparatory Commission (1999–2002)

Session	Work programme, attendance and ratifications
1999 (1) 16–26 February	*Work Programme*: Rules of Procedure and Evidence (Part 5, 6 and 8), Element of Crimes, crime of aggression. *Attendance*: 87 / 188 (46%) United Nations membership *Ratifications*: 1
1999 (2) 26 July – 13 August	*Work Programme*: Rules of Procedure and Evidence (Part 4, 5, 6 and 8), Element of Crimes, crime of aggression. *Attendance*: 121 / 188 (64%) United Nations membership *Ratifications*: 3 (total 4)
1999 (3) 29 November – 17 December	*Work Programme*: Rules of Procedure and Evidence (Part 2, 4, 6–10), Element of Crimes, crime of aggression. *Attendance*: 150 / 188 (80%) United Nations membership *Ratifications*: 2 (total 6)
2000 (4) 13–31 March	*Work Programme*: Rules of Procedure and Evidence (Part 2, 4–6 and 8–10), Element of Crimes, crime of aggression. *Attendance*: 112 / 189 (59%) United Nations membership *Ratifications*: 1 (total 7)
2000 (5) 12–30 June	*Work Programme*: Adoption of Rules of Procedure and Evidence and Element of Crimes. Crime of aggression. *Attendance*: 99 / 189 (52%) United Nations membership *Ratifications*: 6 (total 13)
2000 (6) 27 November – 8 December	*Work Programme*: Relationship Agreement Court and United Nations, Financial Regulations and Rules, Privileges and Immunities Agreement, crime of aggression. *Attendance*: 103 / 189 (54%) United Nations membership *Ratifications*: 14 (total 27)
2001 (7) 26 February – 9 March	*Work Programme*: Relationship Agreement Court and United Nations, Financial Regulations and Rules, Privileges and Immunities Agreement, Assembly of States Parties Rules of Procedure, crime of aggression. *Attendance*: 114 / 189 (60%) United Nations membership *Ratifications*: 2 (total 29)

TABLE 4.9 Preparatory Commission (1999–2002) (*cont.*)

Session	Work programme, attendance and ratifications
2001 (8) 24 September – 5 October	*Work Programme*: Relationship Agreement Court and United Nations, Financial Regulations and Rules, Privileges and Immunities Agreement, Assembly of States Parties Rules of Procedure, crime of aggression, Basic Principles of the Headquarters Agreement, first year budget. *Attendance*: 102 / 189 (54%) United Nations membership *Ratifications*: 14 (total 43)
2002 (9) 8–19 April	*Work Programme*: Basic Principles of the Headquarters Agreement, preparatory documents for the Assembly of States Parties, first year budget, Financial Rules, crime of aggression. *Attendance*: 100 / 191 (52%) United Nations membership *Ratifications*: 23 (total 66)
2002 (10) 1–12 July	*Work Programme*: preparatory documents for the Assembly of States Parties, first year budget, Victims Trust Fund, remuneration of judges, the Prosecutor and the Registrar, crime of aggression, Bureau Advance Team report. *Attendance*: 113 / 191 (59%) United Nations membership *Ratifications*: 10 (total 76) *Ratifications by the first Session of the Assembly of States Parties*: 78 *Ratifications by the end of 2002*: 87

3.2 *The Rules of Procedure and Evidence and the Elements of Crimes*

The Rules of Procedure and Evidence were discussed between the first (1999) and fifth (2000) sessions of the Preparatory Commission. Together with the Elements of Crimes, they represented the first milestone of the Commission approving them by the 30 June 2000 deadline. As Hall noted, their timely completion surprised States and commentators.[388] Article 51 in the Rome Statute allocated to the Assembly of States Parties their adoption and approval of

388 Hall, 'The First Five Sessions of the UN Preparatory Commission for the International Criminal Court' 788.

amendments.[389] Unlike the Ad Hoc Tribunals leaving the Rules to the judges, the Rome Conference decided to afford States the responsibility of their elaboration.[390] Building on the preparatory process and the Diplomatic Conference, Silvia Fernández de Gurmendi (Argentina) led the working group in the Commission. For her and Friman (Sweden), the Rules of Procedure and Evidence covered 'almost all aspects referred to in the Rome Statute and necessary for the operation of the Court'.[391] For Lee, the key purpose of the Rules was to 'clarify the inter-relationships of all the parties involved in the proceedings before the Court'.[392] In this regard, as the governing body of the International Criminal Court, the Assembly of States Parties retained, by virtue of Article 112(2)(g), authority to agree any amendment proposed by the judges, the Prosecutor or a State Party.[393]

The 225 draft Rules, based on a proposal by Australia,[394] were organized in 12 chapters covering Part 2 to 10 of the Statute (see Table 4.10). As Kirsch and Oosterverld explained, the level of detail varied according to the need to develop clarity compared to provisions in the Statute. In general, they note negotiations were 'lengthy and difficult', and in particular, 'investigation and prosecution of crimes, the pre-trial regime, disclosure and evidence and fundamental notions of justice, fair trial, and rights of the accused' were especially complex.[395] Across the five sessions, the Commission elaborated nine Rules with a defined role for the Assembly of States Parties grouped in Chapter 1 (General Provisions) and 2 (Composition and Administration of the Court). Rule 3 on amendments, the only one in Chapter 1, was discussed between 1999 and 2000.[396] It referenced the procedure laid out in Article 51 of the Statute and assigned to the President of the Bureau of the Assembly of

389 Article 51(2), Rome Statute of the International Criminal Court (2002) 2187 UNTS 90.

390 Schabas, 'Follow up to Rome: Preparing for Entry into Force of the Statute of the International Criminal Court' (2001) 207.

391 Fernández de Gurmendi, Silvia and Friman, Håkan, 'The Rules of Procedure and Evidence of the International Criminal Court' (2000) 3 Yearbook of International Humanitarian Law 289.

392 Lee, Roy S, The International Criminal Court: Elements of Crimes and Rules of Procedure and Evidence (Transnational Publishers 2001) iv-vi.

393 Fernández de Gurmendi and Friman, 290.

394 Proposal Submitted by Australia, Draft Rules of Procedure and Evidence of the International Criminal Court, UN Doc. PCNICC/1999/DP.I (1999).

395 Kirsch and Oosterveld, 'The Post-Rome Conference Preparatory Commission' (2002) 100.

396 Report of the Preparatory Commission for the International Criminal Court, UN Doc. PCNICC/2000/1 (2000) 9–30.

States Parties the responsibility of translation and transmission of amendments.[397] As the executive body, the Bureau was tasked in the Statute with assisting the Assembly 'in the discharge of its responsibilities'.[398] However, operationally, the Assembly Secretariat, established in the Rules of Procedure of the Assembly, retained the duty to translate and transmit documentation to all States Parties.[399]

The remaining eight draft Rules appeared in Chapter 2 and were discussed throughout the five sessions.[400] These referred to the solemn undertaking of Court officials (Rule 5), the Code of Professional Conduct (Rule 8 and 20), qualifications and election of the Registrar and its Deputy (Rule 12), procedure for removal of office of Court officials (Rule 29), procedure for disciplinary measures (Rule 30), and the procedure in the event of death (Rule 36) or resignation (Rule 37) of a judge, Prosecutor, Deputy Prosecutor, Registrar or Deputy Registrar.[401] Rule 29 and 30 are of notable significance for the Assembly of States Parties as the Rome Statute provided specific voting majorities for the removal of a judge, Prosecutor or Deputy Prosecutor. In particular, Section IV in the draft Rules of Procedure and Evidence under the title 'Situations that may affect the functioning of the Court',[402] outlined in Rules 23–31 the principles and procedures to remove such Court officials. By virtue of draft Rule 26, the Assembly President decided which complaints were deemed justified for a 'competent organ'[403] to consider them. All complaints remained confidential.

The Bureau, rather than the Assembly, was identified as the competent organ to assess the removal of a judge, the Prosecutor or the Deputy Prosecutor. This is especially notable given the general lack of guidance regarding the skills and experience required for electing the Bureau, and the political nature of assessing complaints by a State-led organ. In this context, under draft Rule

397 Report of the Preparatory Commission for the International Criminal Court, Addendum, Finalized Draft Text of the Rules of Procedure and Evidence, UN Doc. PCNICC/2000/INF/3/Add.1 (2000) 12.

398 Article 112(3)(c), Rome Statute of the International Criminal Court (2002) 2187 UNTS 90.

399 Preparatory Commission for the International Criminal Court (24 September–5 October), Part IV Draft Rules of Procedure of the Assembly of States Parties, UN Doc. PCNICC/2001/1/Add.4 (2001) 13.

400 Report of the Preparatory Commission for the International Criminal Court, UN Doc. PCNICC/2000/1 9–30.

401 Report of the Preparatory Commission for the International Criminal Court, Addendum, Finalized Draft Text of the Rules of Procedure and Evidence, UN Doc. PCNICC/2000/INF/3/Add.1 13–26.

402 Ibid 23.

403 Ibid.

81 in the Procedure of the Assembly, the Bureau performed the first filter to test the alleged reasons for removal, including hearing the person under query, to then transmit 'a recommendation'[404] on the matter to an ordinary or special session of the Assembly. At which point, States Parties voted by secret ballot and qualifying majorities to remove each of the three senior officials.

The important role of a capable Bureau is more evident in the event of imposing disciplinary measures under Article 47 in the Statute and draft Rule 30. The Presidency of the Court remained the authority for disciplinary measures against a judge, the Registrar or the Deputy Registrar. For the Deputy Prosecutor, the Prosecutor could issue 'a reprimand', but needed an 'absolute majority of the Bureau of the Assembly of States Parties'[405] to impose a financial penalty. The same Bureau majority was required for any disciplinary measure, pecuniary or not, against the Prosecutor. Draft Rule 82 in the Procedure of the Assembly required a meeting of the Bureau to make a decision by an absolute majority.[406] Neither decision by the Bureau required transmission to all States Parties nor a report assuring the conduct at penalty. In essence, a political body acted as the arbiter to impose disciplinary measures and recommend a removal.

The power of the Bureau of the Assembly, and in a similar way the conference of judges, to assess, determine and issue recommendations or decisions for removal or penalties for Court officials was completely absent from the preparatory process debating the ideal conformation of such bodies to lead a robust and proper process. In fact, to safeguard against possible perceptions of undue activities for removal or sanction, France proposed in 1999 a 'disciplinary chamber' made of judges and representatives of the Assembly to 'deal with all proceedings brought on grounds of misconduct'.[407] Akin to national systems requiring a degree of representation from key constituencies in the organ responsible for sanction of judicial officials, the French proposal was not taken forward. Although Rule 26 was modified in 2018 to transfer the power of inves-

---

404 Preparatory Commission for the International Criminal Court (24 September – 5 October), Part IV Draft Rules of Procedure of the Assembly of States Parties, UN Doc. PCNICC/2001/1/Add.4 22.

405 Report of the Preparatory Commission for the International Criminal Court, Addendum, Finalized Draft Text of the Rules of Procedure and Evidence, UN Doc. PCNICC/2000/INF/3/Add.1 24.

406 Preparatory Commission for the International Criminal Court (24 September – 5 October), Part IV Draft Rules of Procedure of the Assembly of States Parties, UN Doc. PCNICC/2001/1/Add.4 22.

407 Working Paper Submitted by France, Comments on the Proposal by Australia Contained in Document PCNICC/1999/DP.I, UN Doc. PCNICC/1999/DP.3 (1999) 4.

TABLE 4.10 Preparatory Commission (1999)

	Draft rules of procedure and evidence	
Chapter	**Rule**	**ASP function**
Chapter 1. General Provisions	Rule 3 – Amendments 1. Amendments to the rules that are proposed in accordance with article 51, paragraph 2, shall be forwarded to the President of the Bureau of the Assembly of States Parties. 2. The President of the Bureau of the Assembly of States Parties shall ensure that all proposed amendments are translated into the official languages of the Court and are transmitted to the States Parties. 3. The procedure described in sub-rules 1 and 2 shall also apply to the provisional rules referred to in article 51, paragraph 3.	Auxiliary Judicial Instruments Oversight
Chapter 2. Composition and administration of the Court	Rule 5 – Solemn undertaking under article 45 2. The undertaking, signed by the person making it and witnessed by the President or a Vice-President of the Bureau of the Assembly of States Parties, shall be filed with the Registry and kept in the records of the Court	Governance and Management Oversight
	Rule 8 – Code of Professional Conduct 2. The draft Code shall then be transmitted to the Assembly of States Parties, for the purpose of adoption, according to article 112, paragraph 7.	Auxiliary Judicial Instruments Oversight
	Rule 12 – Qualifications and election of the Registrar and the Deputy Registrar 1. As soon as it is elected, the Presidency shall establish a list of candidates who satisfy the criteria laid down in article 43, paragraph 3, and shall transmit the list to the Assembly of States Parties with a request for any recommendations.	

TABLE 4.10 Preparatory Commission (1999) (*cont.*)

Draft rules of procedure and evidence

Chapter	Rule	ASP function
	2. Upon receipt of any recommendations from the Assembly of States Parties, the President shall, without delay, transmit the list together with the recommendations to the plenary session.	
	Rule 20 – Responsibilities of the Registrar relating to the rights of the defence. 3. For purposes such as the management of legal assistance in accordance with rule 21 and the development of a Code of Professional Conduct in accordance with rule 8, the Registrar shall consult, as appropriate, with any independent representative body of counsel or legal associations, including any such body the establishment of which may be facilitated by the Assembly of States Parties.	Auxiliary Judicial Instruments Oversight
	Rule 29 – Procedure in the event of a request for removal from office 2. The Presidency shall advise the President of the Bureau of the Assembly of States Parties in writing of any recommendation adopted in the case of a judge, and any decision adopted in the case of the Registrar or a Deputy Registrar. 3. The Prosecutor shall advise the President of the Bureau of the Assembly of States Parties in writing of any recommendation he or she makes in the case of a Deputy Prosecutor.	Governance and Management Oversight
	Rule 30 – Procedure in the event of a request for disciplinary measures	Governance and Management Oversight

TABLE 4.10 Preparatory Commission (1999) (*cont.*)

Draft rules of procedure and evidence		
Chapter	**Rule**	**ASP function**
	2. In the case of the Prosecutor, any decision to impose a disciplinary measure shall be taken by an absolute majority of the Bureau of the Assembly of States Parties. 3. In the case of a Deputy Prosecutor: (a) Any decision to give a reprimand shall be taken by the Prosecutor; (b) Any decision to impose a pecuniary sanction shall be taken by an absolute majority of the Bureau of the Assembly of States Parties upon the recommendation of the Prosecutor. 4. Reprimands shall be recorded in writing and shall be transmitted to the President of the Bureau of the Assembly of States Parties.	
	Rule 36 – Death of a judge, the Prosecutor, a Deputy Prosecutor, the Registrar or a Deputy Registrar The Presidency shall inform, in writing, the President of the Bureau of the Assembly of States Parties of the death of a judge, the Prosecutor, a Deputy Prosecutor, the Registrar or a Deputy Registrar.	Governance and Management Oversight
	Rule 37 – Resignation of a judge, the Prosecutor, a Deputy Prosecutor, the Registrar or a Deputy Registrar 1. A judge, the Prosecutor, a Deputy Prosecutor, the Registrar or a Deputy Registrar shall communicate to the Presidency, in writing, his or her decision to resign. The Presidency shall inform, in writing, the President of the Bureau of the Assembly of States Parties.	Governance and Management Oversight

tigation from the Presidency to the newly instituted Independent Oversight Mechanism, the Bureau retained its original role and complaints continued to be secret.[408] As Schabas explains, 'everything about the process is quite opaque'.[409]

The Elements of Crimes were discussed between the first and fifth session of the Preparatory Commission as per Resolution F. The Elements of Crimes are described in the Statute as an instrument to 'assist the Court in the interpretation and application of articles 6, 7, 8 and 8 bis'.[410] A two-third majority of States Parties was required for their adoption. Given the technical nature of the document, there is no reference to the Assembly of States Parties in the Elements of Crimes.[411] As Hall notes, the absence of wording to the effect of the Elements entering into force denoted the desire of States in Rome to give flexibility to the Court when using the instrument.[412] Kirsch and Oosterverld clarified 'the Elements of Crimes would guide, but not bind, the Court'.[413] Despite the guiding nature of the Elements, States Parties retained the responsibility to adopt them and approve amendments by a State Party, a majority of the judges and the Prosecutor. In this regard, draft Rule 74 in the Procedure for the Assembly assigned to the President of the Bureau the responsibility to translate and forward any proposed amendment.[414] Nonetheless, the oversight of auxiliary judicial instruments by the Assembly, via the Bureau, appeared as a critical function for both the Rules of Procedure and Evidence and the Elements of Crimes.

3.3 *The Agreement on Privileges and Immunities*

The Agreement on Privileges and Immunities of the Court was discussed between the sixth (2000) and eighth (2001) sessions of the Preparatory Commission. Article 48 in the Rome Statute provided privileges and immunities

---

408 ICC-ASP/17/Res.2 Amendments to Rule 26 of the Rules of Procedure and Evidence (2018).

409 Schabas, The International Criminal Court: A Commentary on the Rome Statute 778.

410 Article 9, Rome Statute of the International Criminal Court (2002) 2187 UNTS 90.

411 Report of the Preparatory Commission for the International Criminal Court, Addendum, Finalized Draft Text of the Elements of Crimes, UN Doc. PCNICC/2000/INF/3/Add.2 (2000).

412 Hall, 'The First Five Sessions of the UN Preparatory Commission for the International Criminal Court' 774.

413 Kirsch and Oosterveld, 'The Post-Rome Conference Preparatory Commission' (2002) 97.

414 Preparatory Commission for the International Criminal Court (24 September – 5 October), Part IV Draft Rules of Procedure of the Assembly of States Parties, UN Doc. PCNICC/2001/1/Add.4 20.

for Court officials 'necessary for the fulfilment of its purposes'.[415] For Nilsson, the agreement should be read together with Article 48 and the headquarter agreement between the Court and the host country to arrive at a standard and desired framework for international organizations.[416] Although Nilsson regarded the privileges and immunity agreement 'rather standard',[417] Kirsch and Oosterverld described the negotiations as 'unprecedented ... necessitating long hours (including many evenings) of discussions to reach consensus'.[418] For Phakiso Mochochoko, coordinator of the topic and later serving as an official in the Office of the Prosecutor, the agreement was a 'milestone in the codification of international law of criminal tribunals'[419] given the permanent nature of the International Criminal Court.

States were aided by a United Nations Secretariat paper borrowing from the Agreement on the Privileges and Immunities of the International Tribunal for the Law of the Sea and the Yugoslavia Tribunal Headquarters Agreement.[420] The initial draft during the sixth and seventh session consisted of 28 articles,[421] with the final instrument expanding to 38 clauses.[422] Draft Articles 13 (States participating in the Assembly and subsidiary organs), 24 (waiver) and 35 (amendments) were relevant for the Assembly of States Parties. Naturally, representatives of States Parties seized with activities of the Assembly under Article 112(1) of the Statute, were afforded privileges and immunities in Article 13, with minor modifications between the sixth and eighth sessions.[423] The most important modification took place in the sev-

415 Article 48, Rome Statute of the International Criminal Court (2002) 2187 UNTS 90.

416 Nilsson, Cecilia, 'Contextualizing the Agreement on the Privileges and Immunities of the International Criminal Court' (2004) 17 (3) Leiden Journal of International Law 572.

417 Ibid 578.

418 Kirsch and Oosterveld, 'The Preparatory Commission for the International Criminal Court' 580–581.

419 Mochochoko, Phakiso, 'The Agreement on Privileges and Immunities of the International Criminal Court' (2001) 25 Fordham International Law Journal 663.

420 Draft Agreement on the Privileges and Immunities of the International Criminal Court, Prepared by the Secretariat, UN Doc. PCNICC/2000/WGAPIC/L.1 (2000).

421 Preparatory Commission for the International Criminal Court (27 November–8 December), Annex IV, Draft Agreement on the Privileges and Immunities of the Court, Discussion Paper Proposed by the Coordinator, UN Doc. PCNICC/2000/L.4/Rev.1/Add.3 (2000).

422 Preparatory Commission for the International Criminal Court (24 September–5 October), Part III Draft Agreement on the Privileges and Immunities of the Court, UN Doc. PCNICC/2001/1/Add.3 (2001).

423 Preparatory Commission for International Criminal Court Opens Seventh Session at Headquarters, UN Doc. L/2975.

enth session in February–March 2001, adding the coverage to representatives under duty in subsidiary organs of the Assembly, as per Article 112(4) of the Rome Statute.[424] Article 24 outlined the procedure to waive immunity of representatives of States Parties to the agreement. States had the 'duty' to waive the immunity of their representative to avoid impeding 'the course of justice'.[425] To this effect, States modified the clause in the eighth session by specifically singling out the provision earlier nested under Article 19 covering also senior officers of the Court.[426]

Finally, Article 35 on amendments only appeared in the final version during the eighth session in September-October 2001.[427] The Secretary General, as depositary of the agreement, was tasked with the circulation of any amendment by a State Party. However, Article 35(1) asked the Secretary General to alert the Bureau of the Assembly of any change, triggering in Article 35(2) a discussion of such amendment proposal at a regular or forthcoming special session of the Assembly.[428] In essence, any amendment to the agreement became an item for consideration for the Assembly despite not all States being party to the privileges and immunity agreement. Article 35(2) further stipulated a Review Conference to consider amendments putting an additional burden to the Bureau and Assembly beyond its statutory responsibilities. Presumably, although not mentioned in the draft or final agreement, the Bureau could pursue the additional task by virtue of Article 112(2)(g). Mochochoko did not address this issue in his writing[429] and no further clarity can be found in the draft and final Relationship Agreement between the International Criminal Court and the United Nations outlining the responsibility

424 Preparatory Commission for the International Criminal Court (26 February – 9 March 2001), Annex IV Draft Agreement on the Privileges and Immunities of the Court, Discussion Paper Proposed by the Coordinator, UN Doc. PCNICC/2001/L.1/Rev.1/Add.3 (2001).

425 Preparatory Commission for the International Criminal Court (24 September – 5 October), Part III Draft Agreement on the Privileges and Immunities of the Court, UN Doc. PCNICC/2001/1/Add.3 13.

426 Mochochoko, 'The Agreement on Privileges and Immunities of the International Criminal Court' 650.

427 Preparatory Commission for the International Criminal Court (24 September – 5 October), Part III Draft Agreement on the Privileges and Immunities of the Court, UN Doc. PCNICC/2001/1/Add.3 16–17.

428 Ibid 16.

429 Mochochoko, 'The Agreement on Privileges and Immunities of the International Criminal Court' 638.

of the United Nations Secretary General,[430] nor in the draft and final Rules of Procedure of the Assembly of States Parties.[431]

3.4 *The Court-United Nations Relationship Agreement*

The Relationship Agreement between the Court and the United Nations was discussed between the sixth (2000) and eighth (2001) sessions of the Preparatory Commission. As Yañez-Barnuevo and Escobar Hernández argued, the relationship agreement between the Court and United Nations refers to the 'nature of the ICC itself'.[432] In other words, by virtue of creating the International Criminal Court as an independent international organization, any constituent agreement had to be overseen and approved by the Assembly of States Parties. Indeed, Article 2 in the Rome Statute sequentially mandated States Parties to craft an agreement for its conclusion at a later stage 'by the President of the Court on its behalf'.[433] Together with Article 1 in the Statute, as Gallant points out, the Assembly had to 'partake'[434] in all aspects regarding the legal personality of the Court. The Preparatory Commission, as the prologue to the Assembly, carefully envisaged a draft agreement considering standard and innovative aspects in its relationship with the United Nations, all within the Assembly's 'important role in the life of the ICC as an international institution'.[435]

At the request of the Bureau of the Preparatory Commission, the United Nations Secretariat prepared a draft agreement largely inspired in past practice and examples, including the Agreement on Cooperation and Relationship between the United Nations and the International Tribunal for the Law of the Sea.[436] Yañez-Barnuevo and Escobar Hernández noted the 'curious' situation the Secretariat 'serving two masters'[437] as part of the United Nations Legal

430 ICC-ASP/3/Res.1 Negotiated Relationship Agreement Between the International Criminal Court and the United Nations (2004).

431 Preparatory Commission for the International Criminal Court (24 September – 5 October), Part IV Draft Rules of Procedure of the Assembly of States Parties, UN Doc. PCNICC/2001/1/Add.4;Rules of Procedure of the Assembly of States Parties, ICC-ASP/1/3.

432 Yáñez-Barnuevo, Juan Antonio and Escobar Hernández, Concepción, 'The International Criminal Court and the United Nations: a Complex and Vital Relationship' in Lattanzi, Flavia and Schabas, William A (eds), Essays on the Rome Statute of the International Criminal Court, vol 2 (Editrice il Sirente 2003) 42.

433 Article 2, Rome Statute of the International Criminal Court (2002) 2187 UNTS 90.

434 Gallant, 559.

435 Yáñez-Barnuevo and Escobar Hernández, (2003) 44.

436 Draft Relationship Agreement Between the United Nations and the International Criminal Court, Prepared by the Secretariat, UN Doc. PCNICC/2000/WGICC-UN/L.1 (2000).

437 Yáñez-Barnuevo and Escobar Hernández, (2003) 66.

Office. Nonetheless, the authors claim such dual exercise impacted positively in building a close relationship between the two organizations 'from the very beginning'.[438] The initial Secretariat[439] and Coordinator[440] draft report contained 20 articles finally settling in 24 articles,[441] four of which specifically mentioned the Assembly of States Parties beyond its ultimate governance responsibility as described in Article 2 of the Rome Statute.

Three of the four draft articles specifically mentioning the Assembly of States Parties were under 'Institutional Relations'[442] in the second chapter, with the remainder article, on amendments, in the 'Final Provisions'.[443] As carefully examined by Schabas, the draft agreement suffered modifications during the sixth and eighth sessions.[444] This is true for article 10 (conference services and facilities), 11 (access to United Nations Headquarters) and 13 (financial matters) under the 'Institutional Relations' heading. Draft articles 10 and 11 were intimately related as they referred to the Assembly and Bureau's meeting at the United Nations Headquarters by virtue of Article 112(3) and (6) in the Rome Statute. The level of conference servicing provided under draft article 10 suffered modifications in the Preparatory Commission by clarifying its scope, availability and financing. The Secretariat and Coordinator paper primarily focused on conference services 'as may be required for'[445] the Assembly and Bureau, while the final draft article expanded such scope to 'including'[446] governance meeting but not limited to them. In other words, any of the organs of the Court could access conference services like the Assem-

438 Ibid.

439 Draft Relationship Agreement Between the United Nations and the International Criminal Court, Prepared by the Secretariat, UN Doc. PCNICC/2000/WGICC-UN/L.1.

440 Preparatory Commission for the International Criminal Court (27 November – 8 December 2000), Annex II, Draft Relationship Agreement between the Court and the United Nations, Discussion Paper Proposed by the Coordinator, UN Doc. PCNICC/2000/L.4/Rev.1/Add.1 (2000).

441 Preparatory Commission for the International Criminal Court (24 September – 5 October), Part I, Draft Relationship Agreement between the Court and the United Nations, UN Doc. PCNICC/2001/1/Add.1 (2001).

442 Ibid 6.

443 Ibid 10.

444 Schabas, The International Criminal Court: A Commentary on the Rome Statute 78–90.

445 Preparatory Commission for the International Criminal Court (27 November – 8 December 2000), Annex II, Draft Relationship Agreement between the Court and the United Nations, Discussion Paper Proposed by the Coordinator, UN Doc. PCNICC/2000/L.4/Rev.1/Add.1.

446 Preparatory Commission for the International Criminal Court (24 September – 5 October), Part I, Draft Relationship Agreement between the Court and the United Nations, UN Doc. PCNICC/2001/1/Add.1 6.

bly, Bureau and its subsidiary bodies. The expansion of scope was particularly useful for the Court to pursue technical meetings with specialized agencies of the United Nations for example. However, any conference services were conditional to availability or capacity to deliver them, and a supplementary agreement on financing.[447] Logically following from draft article 10, access to State Party and observer representatives to the United Nations Headquarters was stipulated in draft article 11, appearing for the first time in the finalized text of the agreement.[448] Draft article 11 was necessary to guarantee compliance with Article 112(1) of the Rome Statute.

Finally, draft article 13 on financial matters covered three distinct purposes: regulating Article 115 in the Rome Statute, any expense in relation to cooperation between the two organizations, and a statement of intent by the United Nations to 'provide advice on financial and fiscal questions'[449] as requested by the Court. Of these, the first purpose is worth highlighting as it disproportionally affected the financial sustainability of the Court. Draft article 13(1) governed the 'conditions' of a 'separate agreement' on funding contributions from the United Nations to the Court within Article 115(b) in the Rome Statute. As agreed in Rome, the United Nations General Assembly retained the right to fund the Court, 'in particular in relation to the expenses incurred due to referrals by the Security Council'.[450] The Registrar was tasked to reach such agreement and inform the Assembly accordingly. By 2021, the agreement stipulated by the Preparatory Commission was still pending costing States Parties €81.43 million in relation to Security Council referrals.[451] The lack of compliance by the United Nations General Assembly despite regular resolutions calling for a solution by the Assembly of States Parties was not foreseen at all by the Preparatory Commission.[452]

3.5 *The Basic Principles for the Headquarter Agreement*

The Preparatory Commission concluded the basic principles governing a headquarters agreement to be negotiated between the Court and the host country between the eighth (2001) and ninth sessions (2002). The bid of the city of The Hague to host the Court was successful and accepted by the Diplo-

447 Ibid.

448 Ibid.

449 Ibid 7.

450 Article 115(b), Rome Statute of the International Criminal Court (2002) 2187 UNTS 90.

451 ICC-ASP/21/Res.1 Programme Budget for 2023, the Working Capital Fund for 2023, the Scale of Assessment for the Apportionment of Expenses of the International Criminal Court, Financing Appropriations for 2023 and the Contingency Fund (2022) 10.

452 Yáñez-Barnuevo and Escobar Hernández, (2003).

matic Conference.[453] In fact, the Netherlands devoted substantial resources during the eighth to tenth sessions of the Commission to prepare the ground for the Court to become operational at the earliest.[454] By the time the Commission began its work on the headquarter agreement in September 2001, the Netherlands was already a State Party.[455]

Similar to the relationship between the Court and the United Nations, Article 3(2) in the Rome Statute assigned to the Assembly of States Parties the power to approve a headquarter agreement with the Netherlands for later conclusion by the President of the Court on its behalf.[456] The agreement was meant to 'regulate on a bilateral basis the legal status of the ICC-organisation in its host State'.[457] In other words, an 'all-encompassing'[458] regulatory framework outlining 'guarantees'[459] across 12 specific issues ranging from the legal status and juridical personality of the Court, privileges and immunities to the amendment regime and the procedure for dispute settlement.[460]

The only direct mention of the Assembly of States Parties was in relation to a dispute settlement scheme calling for the agreement to contain a provision 'without prejudice to the powers and responsibilities'[461] in the Statute. The clause meant to safeguard resolving disputes with private actors, like suppliers, and retaining the applicability of Article 119(2) of the Rome Statute. A set of 'general principles'[462] also accompanied the document prepared by the Com-

453 Harmsen, Robert O and Strijards, Gerard AM, 'Article 3 Seat of the Court' in Ambos, Kai and Triffterer, Otto (eds), Rome Statute of the International Criminal Court: A Commentary (3rd edn, Beck/Hart 2016) 42.

454 Preparatory Commission for the International Criminal Court (24 September–5 October), Statement by the Minister for Foreign Affairs of the Kingdom of the Netherlands Jozias J. van Aartsen, UN Doc. PCNICC/2001/INF/3 (2001).

455 Bevers, Hans, Blokker, Niels and Roording, Jaap, 'The Netherlands and the International Criminal Court: On Statute Obligations and Hospitality' (2003) 16 (1) Leiden Journal of International Law 136.

456 Article 3(2), Rome Statute of the International Criminal Court (2002) 2187 UNTS 90.

457 Harmsen and Strijards, (2016) 44.

458 Preparatory Commission for the International Criminal Court (24 September – 5 October), Basic Principles Governing an Agreement to be Negotiated Between the International Criminal Court and the Kingdom of the Netherlands Regarding the Headquarters of the Court, UN Doc. PCNICC/2001/WGHQA/L.1 (2001) 3.

459 Bevers, Blokker and Roording, 148.

460 Preparatory Commission for the International Criminal Court (8–19 April), Part I, Draft Basic Principles Governing a Headquarters Agreement to be Negotiated Between the Court and the Host Country, UN Doc. PCNICC/2002/1/Add.1 (2002) 3–9.

461 Ibid 9.

462 Ibid 1–2.

mission. In particular, the principle calling for a 'provisional application'[463] clause while negotiations proceeded meant the conclusion of an interim arrangement between the Netherlands and the United Nations to apply the norms reserved for the International Criminal Tribunal for the former Yugoslavia.[464] The interim arrangement stayed in place until 2008 when the headquarter agreement came into force.[465]

The reasoning behind the conclusion of basic principles rather than a full-fledged agreement, as done for the relationship with the United Nations, was due to practical considerations. Building on the experience of the International Criminal Tribunal for the former Yugoslavia and owing lack of time during the Rome Conference, States decided to 'let the judges build the edifice of the Court themselves'.[466] The Rome Statute identified the President as the competent organ to conclude the agreement to protect the Court against unforeseen operational matters directly with the host State that would have not been efficiently solved by a governing body like the Assembly. Timing was equally important. Even if the Bureau of the Assembly could make decisions more frequently than the Assembly, the number of pending issues with the host State remained closely aligned with the operations of the Court, a responsibility for the Presidency, the Registrar and Prosecutor. While recognizing the negotiating role of the Presidency as 'unusual', Harmsen and Strijards argued the Assembly's only task was to 'decide on the approvability of the Headquarters Agreement'.[467] In that regard, States Parties retained the ultimate governance responsibility as envisaged by the Rome Statute.

3.6 *The Financial Regulations and Rules and the Budget for the First Financial Year*

The Financial Regulations and Rules were discussed between the sixth (2000) and ninth (2002) sessions of the Preparatory Commission. Hiroshi Kawamura (Japan) was initially designated in 1999[468] as the contact point for financial questions but by the sixth session, Georg Witschel (Germany) led the working group, which focused first on the Regulations until the eighth session, and the

463 Ibid 2.

464 Bevers, Blokker and Roording, 149.

465 ICC-ASP/7/Res.3 Strengthening the International Criminal Court and the Assembly of States Parties (2008) 2.

466 Bevers, Blokker and Roording, 148.

467 Harmsen and Strijards, (2016) 45.

468 Criminal Court's Preparatory Commission Winds up Session with General Agreement on Key Texts, UN Doc. L/2939 (1999).

Rules during the ninth session.[469] According to Witschel, the working group came up with a 'State-of-the-art' financial framework in a 'very limited period of time'.[470] As with other auxiliary documents in Resolution F, the Bureau of the Commission required[471] the United Nations Secretariat to prepare a discussion paper, which rested on the experience of the General Assembly's Advisory Committee on Administrative and Budgetary Questions and the International Tribunal for the Law of the Sea.[472] Witschel, furthermore, credited the Coalition for an International Criminal Court for their expert advice.[473]

Part 12 of the Rome Statute detailed the financing of the Court as an international organization. Rao recalled a 'delicate debate'[474] over funding. Article 113 referred 'all financial matters'[475] to the Financial Regulations and Rules governing the organs of the Court and the Assembly of States Parties. The Assembly was responsible for their adoption and by virtue of its financial oversight responsibility in Article 112(2)(d), to 'consider and decide the budget for the Court',[476] in turn, governed by the Financial Regulations and Rules. The Registrar was responsible for the operational management of financial matters as the 'principal administrative officer of the Court'.[477] The need to develop 'relevant criteria adopted by the Assembly of States Parties'[478] for voluntary contributions to the Court was also tackled by the Financial Regulations and Rules. A thorough reading of the Rome Statute demonstrates that additional financial aspects appear beyond Part 12 such as salaries, allowances and expenses of Court officials (Article 49) and the Trust Fund for Victims (Article 79). These considerations were part of the remit of the working group.[479]

---

469 Proceedings of the Preparatory Commission at its Sixth Session (27 November-8 December), UN Doc. PCNICC/2000/L.4/Rev.1 (2000) 3.

470 Witschel, Georg, 'Financial Regulation and Rules of the Court' (2001) 25 (3) Fordham International Law Journal 673.

471 Proceedings of the Preparatory Commission at its Fifth Session (12–30 June), UN Doc. PCNICC/2000/L.3/Rev.1 (2000) 3.

472 Byron, Christine and Turns, David, 'The Preparatory Commission for the International Criminal Court' (2001) 50 (2) International & Comparative Law Quarterly 433.

473 Witschel, 667.

474 Rao, S Rama, 'Article 113 Financial Regulations' in Ambos, Kai and Triffterer, Otto (eds), The Rome Statute of the International Criminal Court: A Commentary (3 edn, Beck/Hart 2016) 2247.

475 Article 113, Rome Statute of the International Criminal Court (2002) 2187 UNTS 90.

476 Article 112(2)(d), Rome Statute of the International Criminal Court (2002) 2187 UNTS 90.

477 Article 42(2), Rome Statute of the International Criminal Court (2002) 2187 UNTS 90.

478 Article 116, Rome Statute of the International Criminal Court (2002) 2187 UNTS 90.

479 Preparatory Commission for the International Criminal Court (26 February – 9 March), Annex III Draft Financial Regulations and Rules, UN Doc. PCNICC/2001/L.1/Rev.1/Add.2 (2001) 15.

Building from 14 draft regulations prepared by the Secretariat[480] and a coordinator paper,[481] the Financial Rules, flowing from the Regulations, were only finalized during the ninth session in April 2002.[482] The Secretariat's report signalled two main questions: how should the Registrar build the programme budget, and which competent body should be tasked with its examination on behalf of the Assembly of States Parties.[483] Unlike the Tribunal of the Law of the Sea, the International Criminal Court consisted of four distinct organs, each requiring a degree of independence around budgetary questions. Certainly, by virtue of Article 42(2) in the Rome Statute, the Prosecutor had 'full authority over the management and administration of the Office',[484] as the Presidency was tasked with the 'proper administration of the Court'[485] via the Registry. The finalized Regulations and Rules described a thorough process to afford the Court and Assembly with sound financial management within the contours of the Rome Statute. Specifically, as Rao explained, the Regulations and Rules placed a 'clear responsibility for financial management'[486] in the Registrar to consult 'with the other organs of the Court'[487] and the Assembly on resource allocation and financial management. However, the ultimate power to fund the Court stayed firmly with States Parties.

The finalized financial framework covered the original question posed by the Secretariat across 13 Regulations and 65 Rules.[488] Notably, the Regulations, and associated operative Rules, referred to the mechanism to consolidate a budget across the organs of the Court, including salaries (Regulation 3, Rules 103.1–103.5),[489] provision of funds, including voluntary contributions[490]

480 Draft Financial Regulations of the International Criminal Court, Prepared by the Secretariat, UN Doc.PCNICC/2000/WGFIRR/L.1 (2000).

481 Preparatory Commission for the International Criminal Court (27 November-8 December), Annex III, Draft Financial Regulations and Rules, Discussion Paper Proposed by the Coordinator, UN Doc. PCNICC/2000/L.4/Rev.1/Add.2 (2000).

482 Preparatory Commission for the International Criminal Court (8–19 April), Part II, Draft Financial Rules, UN Doc. PCNICC/2002/1/Add.2 (2002) 1.

483 Draft Financial Regulations of the International Criminal Court, Prepared by the Secretariat, UN Doc.PCNICC/2000/WGFIRR/L.1 5–6.

484 Article 42(2), Rome Statute of the International Criminal Court (2002) 2187 UNTS 90.

485 Article 38(3)(a), Rome Statute of the International Criminal Court (2002) 2187 UNTS 90.

486 Rao, 'Article 113 Financial Regulations' (2016) 2249.

487 Preparatory Commission for the International Criminal Court (24 September – 5 October), Part II, Draft Financial Regulations, UN Doc. PCNICC/2001/1/Add.2 (2001) 3.

488 Preparatory Commission for the International Criminal Court (8–19 April), Part II, Draft Financial Rules, UN Doc. PCNICC/2002/1/Add.2.

489 Ibid 3–5.

490 Report of the Preparatory Commission for the International Criminal Court (continued) *, UN Doc. PCNICC/2001/1 (2001), Annex II, Draft Resolution of the Assembly of States

(Regulation 5, Rules 105.1–105.2),[491] internal controls (Regulation 10, Rule 110.1–110.2)[492] and audit of accounts (Regulation 12).[493] Though synoptically, Regulation 6(5) governed the Trust Fund for Victims envisaged in Article 79 of the Statute insofar 'the purposes and limits of each trust fund…shall be clearly defined by the appropriate authority'.[494] Indeed, during the tenth and last session of the Preparatory Commission, a dedicated working group finalized a draft resolution for the first Assembly of States Parties meeting creating a Board of Directors to 'develop suggestions for further criteria for the management of the Trust Fund'[495] in line with Article 79 of the Rome Statute.

Once the working group resolved the budget machinery, the preliminary examination and final approval at the Assembly of States Parties was next. Following the practice of the Tribunal for the Law of the Sea, the Secretariat proposed the creation of a Committee on Budget and Finance to offer 'comments and recommendations'[496] to the Assembly. While not mentioned in the Rome Statute, the creation of the 'Committee on Budget and Finance'[497] was the first subsidiary organ of the Assembly proposed by the Preparatory Commission under Article 112(4). The Committee on Budget and Finance satisfied, in part, the responsibility of the Assembly to 'provide management oversight to the Presidency, the Prosecutor and the Registrar regarding the administration of the Court'.[498] During the eighth session in September-October 2001, the working group finalized a draft resolution of the Assembly of States Parties for the establishment of the Committee.[499] The annex to the draft resolution mandated the Committee the 'technical examination of any document submitted to the Assembly that contains financial or budgetary implications or

Parties on Relevant Criteria for Voluntary Contributions to the International Criminal Court.

491 Preparatory Commission for the International Criminal Court (8–19 April), Part II, Draft Financial Rules, UN Doc. PCNICC/2002/1/Add.2 8–9.

492 Ibid 15–16.

493 Ibid 29.

494 Ibid 10.

495 Preparatory Commission for the International Criminal Court (1–12 July), UN Doc. PCNICC/2002/2, Annex XIII.

496 Draft Financial Regulations of the International Criminal Court, Prepared by the Secretariat, UN Doc.PCNICC/2000/WGFIRR/L.1 5.

497 Preparatory Commission for the International Criminal Court (26 February–9 March), Annex III Draft Financial Regulations and Rules, UN Doc. PCNICC/2001/L.1/Rev.1/Add.2 15.

498 Article 112(2)(b), Rome Statute of the International Criminal Court (2002) 2187 UNTS 90.

499 Report of the Preparatory Commission for the International Criminal Court (continued)*, UN Doc. PCNICC/2001/1, Annex I.

any other matter of a financial, budgetary or administrative nature, as may be entrusted to it by the Assembly of States Parties'.[500] As Ambach argues, the Committee had a 'relatively wide mandate' that has expanded over time to areas 'beyond the consideration of the budget'.[501] The 12 members from and elected for a period of three years by States Parties had to be 'experts of recognized standing and experience'.[502] The recommendation from the Committee was not binding in the Assembly, but in practice it became the basis for discussion and approval of the budget of the Court.[503] As the working group led by Witschel concluded its work, it also inputted[504] in the negotiations to build the budget for the first financial period of the International Criminal Court, initially coordinated by Saeid Mirzaei Yengejeh (Iran)[505] but finally steered by Rolf Fife (Norway).[506]

The budget for the first financial year of the Court was discussed between the eighth (2001) and final (2002) session of the Preparatory Commission. Unlike the Ad Hoc Tribunals' jurisdiction predicting a certain volume of work, the International Criminal Court depended, initially, on referrals from States or the United Nations Security Council. If the tribunals for the former Yugoslavia and Rwanda costed $85 and $78 million, respectively, in the year 2000, the International Criminal Court's budget was forecasted to be between $15.7 and $30 million depending on a referral situation.[507] In addition, the budget discussions had to consider different costing models depending if the Assembly met in New York or The Hague.[508] In this context, Fife appealed to States to understand the budget 'as a policy and management tool, rather than any particular mathematical insight'.[509] Fife, a long-standing supporter of the

---

500 Ibid.

501 Ambach, 'Article 112 Assembly of States Parties' (2022) 2791.

502 Report of the Preparatory Commission for the International Criminal Court (continued)*, UN Doc. PCNICC/2001/1, Annex I.

503 Ambach, 'Article 112 Assembly of States Parties' (2022) 2792.

504 International Criminal Court Now Has Two Thirds of Necessary Ratifications, Preparatory Commission Told, UN Doc. L/2986 (2001).

505 Proceedings of the Preparatory Commission at its Sixth Session (27 November–8 December), UN Doc. PCNICC/2000/L.4/Rev.1 3.

506 Proceedings of the Preparatory Commission at its Eighth Session (24 September–5 October), UN Doc. PCNICC/2001/L.3/Rev.1 3.

507 Draft Budget for the First Financial Year of the Court, Prepared by the Secretariat, UN Doc. PCNICC/2001/WGFYB/L.1 (2001) 4.

508 Ibid 4–5.

509 Fife, Rolf Einar, 'The Draft Budget for the First Financial Period of the Court' (2001) 25 (3) Fordham International Law Journal 609.

Court, rightly predicted in 2001 the Court's 'reputation' depended on its 'ability to respond' to 'international perceptions and the political environment'.[510]

The Secretariat paper distributed during the eighth session in September-October 2001 envisaged a two-scenario framework under several assumptions. If the Court received no referrals the calculation included 83 staff posts totalling an operational cost of $9,731,100 versus 191 posts and a cost of $24,076,500 if proceedings took place.[511] In a similar way, if the Assembly, the Bureau and the Inaugural Meeting of the Court took place in The Hague, the cost was $6,056,900 versus $5,947,800 in New York.[512] The best guess estimate by the Secretariat put the first budget of the International Criminal Court between $15.7 and $30 million. The coordinator's paper provided further clarity by affirming the assumption the first session of the Assembly would take place in New York, and the Inaugural Meeting of the Court in The Hague.[513] A generous financial offer by the Netherlands to support both meetings secured consensus among States Parties.[514] However, the Commission was not prepared to endorse the two-scenario framework based on the receipt of referrals. Instead, the coordinator proposed a set of guidelines to 'provide for a stronger capacity for the Court and the Assembly of States Parties to respond to various challenges'.[515] These guidelines included the strategic focus on core functions rather than staff posts, speedy recruitment at the right seniority level and financial contingency mechanisms.[516] The Commission asked the Secretariat to review the budget based on the coordinator's guidelines.[517]

The Secretariat prepared a revised budget for the ninth session in April 2002 moving away from the two-scenario framework. Instead, the new budget emphasized procedures 'responsive to the necessity … to recruit the required

510 Ibid 615.

511 Draft Budget for the First Financial Year of the Court, Prepared by the Secretariat, UN Doc. PCNICC/2001/WGFYB/L.1 24.

512 Ibid 4–5.

513 Preparatory Commission for the International Criminal Court (24 September–5 October), Annex II, Draft First-year Budget, Discussion Paper Proposed by the Coordinator, UN Doc. PCNICC/2001/L.3/Rev.1/Add.1 (2001) 4.

514 Ibid 2.

515 At Eighth Session of Preparatory Commission for International Criminal Court, Four Working Groups Announce Completion of Assignments, UN Doc. L/2988.

516 Preparatory Commission for the International Criminal Court (24 September–5 October), Annex II, Draft First-year Budget, Discussion Paper Proposed by the Coordinator, UN Doc. PCNICC/2001/L.3/Rev.1/Add.1 5–7.

517 Preparatory Commission for the International Criminal Court (8–19 April), Annex II, Revised Draft Budget for the First Financial Period of the Court, Discussion Paper Prepared by the Coordinator, UN Doc. PCNICC/2002/L.1/Rev.1/Add.1 (2002) 2.

staff at short notice'.[518] In other words, building flexible contingency budget lines in each organ of the Court to respond rapidly to a referral or other situation in front of the Chambers. To do so, the Secretariat relied on the experience of the Ad Hoc Tribunals, the International Court of Justice and the International Tribunal for the Law of the Sea.[519] It also asked experts, such as Morten Bergsmo from the Office of the Prosecutor in the Tribunal for the former Yugoslavia, for advice, albeit, in a personal capacity.[520] Reflecting on Bergsmo's work, Klaus Rackwitz, who together with Bergsmo became part of the advance team to set up the International Criminal Court, affirmed that the 'impact of a budget on a public institution goes beyond governance; it is an important policy tool'.[521]

In addition to the operational budget of the Court organs, the revised Secretariat paper costed required meetings of the Assembly, the Bureau and the Budget and Finance Committee. The coordinator paper adopted the recommendations from the Secretariat reaching a new price tag of €39,891,300 if meetings were held in The Hague versus €39,696,900 if held in New York.[522] Without the associated cost of required meetings, the Court's operation totalled €30,764,200, an increase from the first scenario in 2001. Noticeably, the working group shifted the currency for budget calculations from United States dollars to euros following a decision by the Financial Regulations and Rules working group.[523] Consensus over the budget was also possible thanks to the Netherland's financial commitments to the Court as the host State. During the ninth session, the Netherlands confirmed financial support for rent free interim premises for a decade, interior design and equipment investments of €10 million, contribution towards the initial meetings of the Assem-

518 Preparatory Commission for the International Criminal Court (8–19 April), Working Group on a Draft Budget for the First Financial Year of the Court, Revised Draft Budget for the First Financial Period of the Court, Prepared by the Secretariat, UN Doc. PCNICC/2002/WGFYB/L.1 (2002) 3.

519 Ibid.

520 Bergsmo, Morten, 'Institutional History, Behaviour and Development' in Bergsmo, Morten, Rackwitz, Klaus and Tianying, SONG (eds), Historical Origins of International Criminal Law, vol 5 (Torkel Opsahl Academic EPublisher 2017) 4.

521 Bergsmo, Morten and Rackwitz, Klaus, 'The First Budget of the Office of the Prosecutor' in Bergsmo, Morten, Rackwitz, Klaus and Tianying, Song (eds), ibid. (1009).

522 Preparatory Commission for the International Criminal Court (8–19 April), Annex II, Revised Draft Budget for the First Financial Period of the Court, Discussion Paper Prepared by the Coordinator, UN Doc. PCNICC/2002/L.1/Rev.1/Add.1 4.

523 Witschel, 669.

bly and the Bureau, and fully financing the Inaugural Meeting of the Court in The Hague.[524]

The draft budget for the first financial year for the Court and the Assembly was adopted at the tenth and last session of the Preparatory Commission in July 2002.[525] After the Rules of Procedure and Evidence, the draft budget was the lengthiest document produced by the Commission. The draft budget moved several assumptions to certainties and added new aspects for consideration. First, States agreed the first financial period of the Court would be for 16 months (September 2002 to December 2003) to cover the first and second sessions of the Assembly of States Parties.[526] Second, the Commission confirmed the first (September 2002), resumed (February and April 2003) and second (September 2003) meeting of the Assembly would take place in New York.[527] Third, the Inaugural Meeting of the Court and two additional plenary sessions of the judges would take place in February 2003 in The Hague, together with subsequent meetings later in 2003 to elect the Registrar and adopt the Regulations of the Court.[528] Fourth, the budget contained a meeting for the Bureau (June 2003) in preparation of the Assembly's second session and a five-day gathering for the Committee on Budget and Finance (August 2003). Additionally, the new version of the accounts showed a meeting of the Board of Directors of the Victims Trust Fund in 2003 in The Hague.[529] The budget also determined the judges' salary at €180,000 per year, with special allowances for the President and Vice-President.[530]

Based on these decisions by the Preparatory Commission, the draft budget for the International Criminal Court for the first financial period was €30,893,500, of which €6,852,700 covered meeting requirements.[531] Beyond

---

524 Preparatory Commission for the International Criminal Court (8–19 April), Statement by the Director-General, ICC Task Force, Ministry of Foreign Affairs of the Government of the Kingdom of the Netherlands, Mr. Edmond Wellenstein, on the Revised Draft Budget for the First Financial Period of the International Criminal Court, UN Doc. PCNICC/2002/INF/5 (2002).

525 Preparatory Commission for the International Criminal Court (1–12 July), A Guide to the Report of the Preparatory Commission, Prepared by the Secretariat, UN Doc. PCNICC/2002/3 (2002) 8.

526 Preparatory Commission for the International Criminal Court (1–12 July), Part I, Draft Budget for the First Financial Period of the Court, UN Doc. PCNICC/2002/2/Add.1 (2002) 3.

527 Ibid 4.

528 Ibid.

529 Ibid.

530 Ibid 34.

531 Ibid 28.

the financial calculations, as Treves, Fife and Rackwitz alerted, but unlike future years, the budget became the policy vehicle to chart the organizational development of the Court, including the first two regular sessions of the Assembly of States Parties.

3.7 *The Rules of Procedure of the Assembly of States Parties*

The Rules of Procedure of the Assembly of States Parties were discussed between the seventh and eighth sessions (2001) of the Preparatory Commission. The rules are examined last in this section because of their importance to regulate the work of the Assembly towards its first session in September 2002. Customary to international organizations, the collective of States Parties to a constitutive treaty undertake its supervision based on certain organizational guidelines. At the Rome Conference, as Rao explained,[532] States decided to establish the International Criminal Court as an independent international organization, and by virtue of Article 112(9), gave the power to the Assembly to 'adopt its own rules of procedure'.[533] With a view to 'prepar [ing] proposals for practical arrangements for the establishment and coming into operation of the Court',[534] the Rules of Procedure in Resolution F exclusively governed the Assembly of States Parties. It is the only auxiliary document in Resolution F not applicable to the organs of the Court.

While the Rules of Procedure assumed a rather technical exercise to regulate the conduct of the Assembly, Saeid Mirzaei Yengejeh (Iran), the coordinator, characterized the negotiation as 'not easy' due to the 'unprecedented nature of the issues under discussion'.[535] At one level, as argued in this book, a rich history outlining governance responsibilities towards an international criminal court could have assisted the Commission. At another level, however, the experience of the United Nations General Assembly or the Meeting of States Parties to the Convention on the Law of the Sea was partially inadequate for the International Criminal Court.[536] At Rome, States afforded the Assembly powers to exert close oversight over the Court in the context of a perceived erosion of sovereignty. As Yengejeh continues, the Assembly received 'unmatched powers' to regulate 'its various functions as provided

532 Rao, 'Financing of the Court, Assembly of States Parties and the Preparatory Commission' (1999).

533 Article 112(9), Rome Statute of the International Criminal Court (2002) 2187 UNTS 90.

534 Final Act of the United Nations Diplomatic Conference of Plenipotentiaries on the Establishment of an International Criminal Court [with an Annex Containing the Resolutions Adopted by the Conference], UN Doc. A/CONF.183/10 8.

535 Kirsch and Oosterveld, 'The Post-Rome Conference Preparatory Commission' (2002) 102.

536 Yengejeh, 678.

for in the Statute'.[537] Thus, States participated actively in the drafting of the rules, aided by the United Nations Secretariat and the precedent of the law of the sea process.[538]

The draft Rules of Procedure for the Assembly contained 96 rules in 21 chapters (see Table 4.11).[539] The rules satisfied a dual objective. First, it provided guidance to the conduct of business of the Assembly during a meeting. On a more relevant level, however, they detailed powers to oversee the Court beyond a meeting framework. In particular it described the function of the Bureau (Chapter V), President and Vice-Presidents (Chapter VI), Assembly Secretariat (Chapter IX), decision-making procedures (Chapter XV), disciplinary procedures against a judge, the Prosecutor or a Deputy Prosecutor (Chapter XVI), election of the bench and the Office of the Prosecutor (Chapter XVIII), financial oversight powers (Chapter XIX) and participation of observers and other participants in the work of the Assembly (Chapter XX).[540] The United Nations Secretariat paper prepared for the seventh session of the Commission in February-March 2001 allowed States to build the draft rules with the dual objective in mind.[541] Given the uninterrupted governance and management responsibility of States Parties towards the Court beyond their regular sessions, it is worth focusing on the rules describing the continuous mandate of the Assembly.

Draft Rule 2 describing the scope the procedure of the Assembly was important to subsequently analyse other powers. Rule 2 noted the application of the framework to the 'work of the Assembly'[542] encompassing the Bureau and subsidiary bodies regardless of a meeting format. It also stipulated its preliminary application during a review conference unless States Parties decide otherwise.[543] In 2010, the Kampala Review Conference employed its

537 Ibid 677.

538 Preparatory Commission for International Criminal Court Holds Seventh Session at Headquarters 26 February – 9 March, UN Doc. L2973 (2001).

539 Preparatory Commission for the International Criminal Court (24 September – 5 October), Part IV Draft Rules of Procedure of the Assembly of States Parties, UN Doc. PCNICC/2001/1/Add.4.

540 Ibid.

541 Draft Rules of Procedure of the Assembly of States Parties, Prepared by the Secretariat, UN Doc. PCNICC/2001/WGRPASP/L.1 (2000).

542 Preparatory Commission for the International Criminal Court (24 September – 5 October), Part IV Draft Rules of Procedure of the Assembly of States Parties, UN Doc. PCNICC/2001/1/Add.4 6.

543 Flexibility Must be Cornerstone of Administration of International Criminal Court, Preparatory Commission Told, UN Doc. L/2976 (2001).

TABLE 4.11 Preparatory Commission (2001)

Draft rules of procedure of the assembly of States Parties

Chapter	Rules	Rome Statute reference
I General	1–2	112, 121(2), 123
II Sessions	3	112(6)
	4–7	112(6)
	8–9	112(6)
III Agenda	10–13	112(6), 112(2)(f)
	14–17	112(6)
	18–22	112(6)
IV Representation and Credentials	23–28	112(1)
V Bureau	29	112(3)(a)
VI President and Vice-Presidents	30–33	112(3)(a)
VII Participation of the President of the Court, the Prosecutor and the Registrar	34	112(5)
VIII Participation of the United Nations	35–36	112(6)
IX Secretariat	37	112(2)(g)
X Languages	38–40	112(10)
XI Records	41	112(2)(g)
XII Public and private meetings	42	112(6)
XIII Minute of silent prayer or meditation	43	112(6)
XIV Conduct of business	44–59	112(6), 112(5)
XV Decision-making	60–80	112(7)(a)(b), 112(8), 112(2)(g), 51(1)–(3), 9(1)–(2), 112(2)(e), 121(1), 122(1)
XVI Disciplinary proceedings	81–82	112(3), 46(2), 47
XVII Subsidiary bodies	83–84	112(4), 112(9)
XVIII Elections of the judges, the Prosecutor and the Deputy Prosecutors	85–86	112(2)(g), 36, 37, 42(2)–(4)
XIX Administrative and budgetary questions	87–91	112(2)(g), 44(3), 113, 116, 79, 112(2)(d)
XX Participation of observers and other participants	92–95	112(1), 112(2)(g)
XXI Amendments	96	112(2)(g), 112(9)

own version of procedural rules, however, under the authority of Rule 2.[544] Thus, as Yengejeh conclusively explained, the rules covered 'activities of the Assembly and its Bureau, for which meetings will not be required'.[545] In this context, the rules applied to States Parties and observer States by virtue of Article 112(1) and (7). Chapter IV (Rules 23–28) regulated both types of membership. However, Chapter XX in the rules included a third category for 'observers and other participants'[546] absent from the Rome Statute. The Commission agreed to extend participation rights to entities (such as Palestine), intergovernmental organizations and other entities (such as the International Committee of the Red Cross) with a standing invitation from the United Nations General Assembly (Rule 92, observers), civil society organizations invited to the Rome Conference or accredited by the United Nations Economic and Social Council (Rule 93, other participants), and States without observer status, pending an invitation of the President with subsequent approval from the Assembly (Rule 94, States not having observer status).

Of these, given the history of the preparatory process, it is not surprising international organizations, other entities and civil society had recourse to participate in the Assembly. In fact, Argentina[547] and France[548] tabled amendments to strengthen Rules 92 and 93. Rule 94, on the other hand, emerged in the Commission due to 'political considerations'.[549] States had placed considerable importance to the universality of the Court.[550] As Yengejeh explained, the working group 'felt'[551] a new mechanism to accommodate States outside Article 112(1) was 'highly desirable' given the Court was 'intended to be a universal criminal court'.[552] Rule 94 emerged after three informal meetings dur-

544 Draft Rules of Procedure of the Review Conferences, RC/3 (2010).

545 Yengejeh, 678–679.

546 Preparatory Commission for the International Criminal Court (24 September – 5 October), Part IV Draft Rules of Procedure of the Assembly of States Parties, UN Doc. PCNICC/2001/1/Add.4 24–25.

547 Proposal Submitted by Argentina, Australia, Belgium, Brazil, Canada, Denmark, Finland, Germany, Lesotho, Liechtenstein, Mali, New Zealand, the Philippines, Portugal, South Africa, Spain, the Sudan, Sweden, Switzerland, the Syrian Arab Republic, Trinidad and Tobago, and the United Kingdom of Great Britain and Northern Ireland, Rule 88 Observers, UN Doc. PCNICC/2001/WGRPASP/DP.1 (2001).

548 Proposal Submitted by France, Rule 11, Rule 88, Rule 88bis, Rule 88ter, UN Doc. PCNICC/2001/WGRPASP/DP.3 (2001).

549 Yengejeh, 683–684.

550 Ibid.

551 Ibid 684.

552 Ibid 683–684.

ing the eighth session.[553] Despite its absence from the Statute or the preparatory paper by the United Nations Secretariat, for the Commission, Chapter XX entailed a 'comprehensive and well-balanced'[554] mechanism for States outside Article 112(1). Invited States under Rule 94 were only allowed to participate in the meetings of the Assembly on a case-by-case basis under the purview of the Assembly President.[555]

The draft rules on the Bureau (Chapter V), President and Vice-Presidents (Chapter VI), and the Assembly's permanent Secretariat (Chapter IX) can be studied together as they form the 'executive body'[556] and corresponding support structure. The provision on the Bureau in the United Nations' Secretariat paper[557] only referenced the Rome Statute and changed minimally by the eighth session of the Commission. Following the same order as Article 112(3)(a)–(c), draft Rule 29 indicated the composition of 21 States, the representative character and meeting frequency.[558] The working group was unable to add further details to the function of the Bureau in the absence of discussions on the matter throughout the preparatory process and in Rome. As opposed, for example, to the Budget and Finance Committee, the lack of specificity on the responsibilities of Bureau left the working group hoping they would be 'developed in practice'.[559] This decision by States was part of a trend observed throughout the history of the Assembly of States Parties paying scant attention to the operational requirements needed to govern and manage the first ever permanent international criminal court.

A second area of concern was the term of service of the Bureau. In Rome, States had decided to create three-year mandates for the 21 members, however, without a staggering system to retain expertise, institutional memory and continuity in the Bureau. The working group led by Yengejeh recognized this issue but failed to gather consensus that a third of members only serve

553 International Criminal Court Now Has Two Thirds of Necessary Ratifications, Preparatory Commission Told, UN Doc. L/2986.

554 At Eighth Session of Preparatory Commission for International Criminal Court, Four Working Groups Announce Completion of Assignments, UN Doc. L/2988.

555 Ambach, 'Article 112 Assembly of States Parties' (2022) 2771.

556 Ibid 2775.

557 Draft Rules of Procedure of the Assembly of States Parties, Prepared by the Secretariat, UN Doc. PCNICC/2001/WGRPASP/L.1 13.

558 Preparatory Commission for the International Criminal Court (24 September – 5 October), Part IV Draft Rules of Procedure of the Assembly of States Parties, UN Doc. PCNICC/2001/1/Add.4 11.

559 Yengejeh, 681.

one year as the 'proposal contradicts the Statute provision'.[560] The Rome Statute did not preclude the re-election of members albeit at the mercy of political dynamics rather than a transparent election process. The risk of total renewal of the Bureau every three years was at odds with Article 36(8)(b) providing a staggered election of judges and in remarkable contrast to the cadence of the term of office for members of the Budget and Finance Committee, a subsidiary body of the Assembly.[561]

Draft Rules 30–33 in Chapter VI outlined the powers of the President of the Assembly and the circumstances when one of the Vice-Presidents might step-in as acting President exclusively in the context of a meeting.[562] The working group did not change the advice from the United Nations Secretariat.[563] In fact, neither the Statute nor the draft Rules of Procedure of the Assembly describe in detail the role of the President and Vice-Presidents outside a meeting format. There is no mention of the acute need to 'assist the Assembly'[564] in the regular 'management oversight to the Presidency, the Prosecutor and the Registrar'.[565] Nor the political responsibility to protect the Court against backlash, promote universality, call for the speedy payments of arrears and pursue effective cooperation. The draft rules reflected the desire from the architects of the Rome Statute to envisage a Bureau mainly focused on the regular meetings of the Assembly. However, if the Court is analysed through the lens of an international organization, the weak role afforded to the presidency is a barrier to a comprehensive governance function within the remit of the Assembly, for example, in fostering effective cooperation with the Court among other key roles.

To enable and support the Assembly, Bureau and subsidiary bodies, the United Nations' paper[566] proposed a permanent secretariat, reproducing almost identically Rule 26 of the Rules of Procedure for Meetings of States

560 Ibid.

561 Report of the Preparatory Commission for the International Criminal Court (continued)*, UN Doc. PCNICC/2001/1 5.

562 Preparatory Commission for the International Criminal Court (24 September – 5 October), Part IV Draft Rules of Procedure of the Assembly of States Parties, UN Doc. PCNICC/2001/1/Add.4 11–12.

563 Draft Rules of Procedure of the Assembly of States Parties, Prepared by the Secretariat, UN Doc. PCNICC/2001/WGRPASP/L.1 13–14.

564 112(3)(c), Rome Statute of the International Criminal Court (2002) 2187 UNTS 90.

565 112(2)(b), Rome Statute of the International Criminal Court (2002) 2187 UNTS 90.

566 Draft Rules of Procedure of the Assembly of States Parties, Prepared by the Secretariat, UN Doc. PCNICC/2001/WGRPASP/L.1 15.

Parties to the Convention on the Law of the Sea.[567] Rule 37 in the final document described the duties of the secretariat along the traditional lines of conferencing services except in the last sentence including the task to 'perform all other work which the Assembly or the Bureau may require'.[568] Analogous to the flexibility given to the Assembly in Article 112(2)(g) in the Rome Statute, the last sentence of Rule 37 is particularly important for enabling the Bureau and subsidiary bodies outside a meeting framework. In fact, the working group led by Yengejeh agreed the Assembly could not depend on the United Nations as a separate organization and would require technical support to carry out its mandate under the Statute.[569] The need for an independent and permanent Assembly secretariat became more evident when the Financial Rules and Regulations working group proposed the creation of the Budget and Finance Committee during the same session.[570] However, citing the Statute was silent on the permanent secretariat for the Assembly, the working group forwarded the ultimate decision for establishment to the Commission.[571] This decision firmly contradicted the approach taken to create the Budget and Finance Committee, equally inexistent in the Statute.

During the ninth session of the Commission, the United Nations prepared an exhaustive paper with options to create the permanent secretariat, alerting the Assembly that it 'will require a wide range of secretariat services to enable it to perform various functions which are inherent in the establishment and operation of an institution of this nature'.[572] During the tenth and last session, Belgium[573] and Spain[574] tabled proposals to maintain the United Nations' secretariat function on a preliminary basis while tasking the Bureau under Article

567 United Nations Convention on the Law of the Sea, Rules of Procedure for Meetings of States Parties, UN Doc. SPLOS/2/Rev.3 (1995) 14.

568 Preparatory Commission for the International Criminal Court (24 September–5 October), Part IV Draft Rules of Procedure of the Assembly of States Parties, UN Doc. PCNICC/2001/1/Add.4 13.

569 Yengejeh, 679.

570 Report of the Preparatory Commission for the International Criminal Court (continued)*, UN Doc. PCNICC/2001/1, Annex I.

571 At Eighth Session of Preparatory Commission for International Criminal Court, Four Working Groups Announce Completion of Assignments, UN Doc. L/2988.

572 Preparatory Commission for the International Criminal Court (8–19 April), Secretariat of the Assembly of States Parties of the International Criminal Court, Information Paper by the Secretariat, UN Doc. PCNICC/2002/WGASP-PD/L.3 (2002) 3.

573 Proposal Submitted by Belgium, Secretariat of the Assembly of States Parties: Organization of a Permanent Secretariat, UN Doc. PCNICC/2002/WGASP-PD/DP.7 (2002).

574 Proposal Submitted by Spain, Permanent Secretariat of the Assembly of States Parties, UN Doc. PCNICC/2002/WGASP-PD/DP.6 (2002).

112(3)(c) to make a proposal to establish the permanent Assembly secretariat in time for the 2003 session.[575] This proposal became a draft resolution for the first session of the Assembly of States Parties in September 2002.[576]

Draft Chapter XV on decision-making contained 20 Rules (60–80) without distinguishing modes of agreement within or outside a meeting framework of the Assembly.[577] Thus, certain draft rules such as 66 (meaning of the phrase "States Parties present and voting"), 69 (explanation of vote), and 79–80 on restricted balloting for elections were exclusively for the application during sessions of the Assembly with little relevance in the constant and ongoing governance and management of the Court. On the other hand, draft Rules 60 and 61 outlining voting rights under Article 112 and the objective to agree by consensus if not voting, were of use beyond a meeting framework. Another example of the uneven application of the draft rules for decision making was the direct reference to the voting requirements for the Rules of Procedure and Evidence, Elements of Crimes, number of judges and amendments to the Statute in Rules 73–76 but not for the Financial Rules and Regulations or the Staff Regulations.[578]

In fact, draft Chapter XIX on 'Administrative and Budgetary Questions' contained the rules to approve the Staff Regulations (87), Financial Regulations and Rules (88), and criteria to manage the Trust Fund for Victims (89). Equally important to give effect to the Statute, these draft rules did not specify the voting majorities required for their approval by the Assembly at the same time Chapter XV on decision-making did not clarify this issue. Absent from the United Nations' Secretariat paper,[579] If any conflict or confusion arose, the President of the Assembly under draft Rule 64 was tasked to decide if a decision was a matter of substance or procedure.[580] In a similar confusing manner, draft Rule 62 required that any 'decision having financial implications' be

575 Report of the Preparatory Commission for the International Criminal Court (continued) (8–19 April), UN Doc. PCNICC/2002/1 (2002) 6.

576 Preparatory Commission for the International Criminal Court (1–12 July), UN Doc. PCNICC/2002/2 20.

577 Preparatory Commission for the International Criminal Court (24 September – 5 October), Part IV Draft Rules of Procedure of the Assembly of States Parties, UN Doc. PCNICC/2001/1/Add.4 17–21.

578 Ibid 23.

579 Draft Rules of Procedure of the Assembly of States Parties, Prepared by the Secretariat, UN Doc. PCNICC/2001/WGRPASP/L.1 13–14.

580 Preparatory Commission for the International Criminal Court (24 September–5 October), Part IV Draft Rules of Procedure of the Assembly of States Parties, UN Doc. PCNICC/2001/1/Add.4 18.

accompanied by a report from the Assembly secretariat or the Registrar before a determination could be made. Taken textually from Rule 50 in the Rules of Procedure for Meetings of States Parties Law of the Sea,[581] draft Rule 62 appeared in Chapter XV on decision-making instead of Chapter XIX, presumably governing 'Administrative and Budgetary Questions'. This issue shows the working group faced challenges to envision the Assembly of States Parties within the uniqueness of the International Criminal Court versus simply taking precedent from other institutions. The challenge to copy provisions without applying a degree of adaptation meant that the meeting format of the Assembly dominated its procedure and conduct over a more comprehensive, constant and insightful set of provisions foreseeing a body able to govern the Court outside a meeting format. This is certainly the case in regard to securing payment of arrears, effective cooperation and political backing for the universality of the Court.

The same issue appeared in Chapter XVIII on the election of the bench, Prosecutor and Deputy Prosecutor. Draft Rules 85 and 86 synoptically reproduced the relevant provisions in the Rome Statute but were silent about the significant responsibility of the Assembly to establish a robust nomination process, including the Advisory Committee on Nominations, one of the only two subsidiary bodies actually mentioned in the Statute.[582] Similarly, while Article 43(4) required the judges take into consideration 'any recommendation by the Assembly of States Parties'[583] on the election of the Registrar, the draft Rules of Procedure contain no reference to this responsibility. On the other hand, draft Rules 81 and 82 on disciplinary procedures against a judge, the Prosecutor or a Deputy Prosecutor in Chapter XVI offered better guidance to the actions required by the Bureau and the Assembly. The level of detail in disciplinary procedures stands in contrast with other provisions because the finalized Rules of Procedure and Evidence adopted by the Commission in June 2000 clearly stated what was expected of the Bureau and Assembly.[584] Thus, draft Rule 81 identified the President of the Bureau as the recipient of a recommendation to remove or consider a complaint against a judge, Prosecutor or Deputy Prosecutor. It required the Assembly President to circulate the

581 United Nations Convention on the Law of the Sea, Rules of Procedure for Meetings of States Parties, UN Doc. SPLOS/2/Rev.3 19.

582 Article 36(4)(c) and Article 112(4), Rome Statute of the International Criminal Court (2002) 2187 UNTS 90.

583 Article 43(4), Rome Statute of the International Criminal Court (2002) 2187 UNTS 90.

584 Report of the Preparatory Commission for the International Criminal Court, Addendum, Finalized Draft Text of the Rules of Procedure and Evidence, UN Doc. PCNICC/2000/INF/3/Add.1, see Rules 26, 29 and 30.

information and call a meeting of the Bureau, hear fairly the person under scrutiny and transmit the same materials and a recommendation for ultimate decision by the Assembly.[585] A similar procedure applied to disciplinary measures against the Prosecutor or Deputy Prosecutor according to draft provision 30 in the Rules of Procedure and Evidence.[586] This procedure would be modified by the Assembly with the establishment of the Independent Oversight Mechanism.

4 2002: Setting Up the Assembly of States Parties

The Preparatory Commission developed the required auxiliary documents listed in Resolution F in the Final Act by its tenth session in July 2002. By this time, the Rome Statute had 76 States Parties, 16 more than required to activate the Court and call the first Assembly meeting. In response to the growing number of States Parties, the Commission began making the necessary arrangements for the first session of the Assembly of States Parties. Already during the seventh session in February-March 2001, Kirsch was aware the Commission had to deal 'in some fashion' with an 'orderly transition'[587] to an established Court and Assembly. In the same session, the Dutch representative called on States to establish an advance unit to plan for the new institution in The Hague.[588] Verweij, the Deputy Head of the Dutch task force to prepare the ground for the International Criminal Court, argued that even without a straight blueprint to follow, there was an urgent need to plan the basic operational requirements of the Court and the Assembly.[589] Schense alerted the Assembly would be required to take 'unique'[590] decisions governing the set-up of the Court. Several of these decisions revolved around administrative, finan-

585 Preparatory Commission for the International Criminal Court (24 September–5 October), Part IV Draft Rules of Procedure of the Assembly of States Parties, UN Doc. PCNICC/2001/1/Add.4 22.

586 Report of the Preparatory Commission for the International Criminal Court, Addendum, Finalized Draft Text of the Rules of Procedure and Evidence, UN Doc. PCNICC/2000/INF/3/Add.1, see Rules 30.

587 International Criminal Court Preparatory Commission Concludes Seventh Session, UN Doc. L/2977 (2001).

588 Ibid.

589 Verweij, Harry, 'The International Criminal Court: Alive, Soon Kicking' (2001) 25 (3) Fordham International Law Journal 739.

590 Schense, Jennifer, 'Necessary Steps for the Creation of the International Criminal Court' (2001) 25 (3) Fordham International Law Journal 725.

cial and human resource questions. However, by design in the Rome Statute, the Registrar could only be in place after the full bench was elected. In essence, creating a vacuum in the early days of the Court. For Verweij, the situation was 'awkward'[591] at best while suspecting delegates in Rome had made a mistake. Outside the remit of the Registrar, the coming into force of the Statute by virtue of Article 126 on 1 July 2002 created concerns about the prosecutorial activities during the emergence of the new institution, which in turn, required supervision by judges and a Prosecutor yet to be elected.[592] The Final Act did not provide helpful guidance on how to construct the sequence of events required to build the organs of the Court. While the Commission could propose practical arrangements, ultimately, decisions belonged to the Assembly of States Parties. In this context, this last section outlines the main actions taken by the Commission to enable an orderly establishment process, culminating in the first session of the Assembly from 3 to 10 September 2002.[593]

Pressured by the speed of ratifications, the Bureau of the Commission prepared for the eighth session in 2001 a roadmap setting out the 'assessment of the most effective way to prepare for the establishment of the Court upon the entry into force of the Statute' (see Table 4.12).[594] The roadmap described the desired sequence of decisions by the Assembly and the Court, pending procedural documents and the relationship with the host State. To aid the actions of the Assembly of States Parties, the Commission charged Saied Mirzaei Yengejeh to develop the preparatory documents of the first session.[595] To solve pending internal rules of the Court on human resources and administration, financial frameworks and operational issues, Phakiso Mochochoko, Christian Much (Germany) and Sivu Maqungo (South Africa) were appointed respectively as focal points.[596] A meeting with experts aided their work.[597]

591 Verweij, 741.

592 Muller, Sam, 'Setting up the International Criminal Court: Not One Moment but a Series of Moments' (2004) 1 International Organization Law Review 192.

593 Proceedings of the Preparatory Commission at its Tenth Session (1–12 July), UN Doc. PCNICC/2002/L.4/Rev.1 3.

594 Preparatory Commission for the International Criminal Court (24 September–5 October), Road map Leading to the Early Establishment of the International Criminal Court, UN Doc. PCNICC/2001/L.2 (2001) 1.

595 Proceedings of the Preparatory Commission at its Eighth Session (24 September–5 October), UN Doc. PCNICC/2001/L.3/Rev.1 4.

596 Ibid.

597 Preparatory Commission for the International Criminal Court, Provisional Internal Rules and Regulations of the International Criminal Court, Inter-sessional Meeting of Experts Held at The Hague from 11 to 15 March 2002, UN Doc. PCNICC/2002/INF/2 (2002).

However, a separate sub-committee of the Bureau, led by Silvia Fernández de Gurmendi, had additional and extensive powers to set-up the Court on time. First, the sub-committee managed the relationship with the Netherlands.[598] In fact, during the eighth session, the Dutch Minister for Foreign Affairs announced the establishment of a dedicated planning unit and a substantial financial package to enable operations.[599] Secondly, it created and managed an advance team in charge of developing the bulk of the operational work to set-up the Court.[600] The advance team was coordinated by Sam Muller, seconded to the role from the Registry of the former Yugoslavia tribunal, and remained in place between June and November 2002, when Bruno Cathala was appointed Director of Common Services at the Court.[601] The genesis of the advance team to 'ensure the early and effective establishment of the Court'[602] was between the 38th and 42nd meeting of the last session of the Commission as reported by Silvia Fernández de Gurmendi. Unlike the roadmap for the establishment of the Court, the decision was very briefly explained in a single paragraph in the Commission's report. The 'engine room'[603] proposed was not fully backed by all States which remained suspicious it could be used to favour appointments of certain nationals to high office in the Court.[604]

The question of legal personality and supervision of the advance team emerged as an issue for the sub-committee. Aware the Court could not afford wasting time for its set-up, the United Nations, the Netherlands and the Carnegie Foundation agreed to host the team under a framework of secondments, reimbursements and accounting support.[605] For the Netherlands in particular as the host State it was a risk to only begin operational preparations after the first Assembly session.[606] Nonetheless, the decision by States Parties was

598 Proceedings of the Preparatory Commission at its Eighth Session (24 September – 5 October), UN Doc. PCNICC/2001/L.3/Rev.1 4.

599 Preparatory Commission for the International Criminal Court (24 September – 5 October), Statement by the Minister for Foreign Affairs of the Kingdom of the Netherlands Jozias J. van Aartsen, UN Doc. PCNICC/2001/INF/3 3.

600 Muller, 192.

601 Bergsmo, (2017) 2.

602 Proceedings of the Preparatory Commission at its Tenth Session (1–12 July), UN Doc. PCNICC/2002/L.4/Rev.1 2–3.

603 Holthuis, Hans, 'Operational Aspects of Setting Up the International Criminal Court: Building on the Experience of the International Criminal Tribunal for the Former Yugoslavia' (2001) 25 (3) Fordham International Law Journal 712.

604 Muller, 192.

605 Ibid.

606 Bevers, Blokker and Roording, 148.

opaque and lacked the necessary governance and policy framework that benefited and made the whole negotiation process of the Commission successful. In fact, while charged with providing 'guidance and assistance to the Court during its initial stages',[607] the advance team did not submit a report or an account of its activities to the Assembly of States Parties.[608]

On the other hand, the working group on preparatory documents for the Assembly of States Parties, led by Saied Mirzaei Yengejeh, followed a known pattern of discussion among States, guided by the roadmap to activate the Court.[609] By the end of 2001, the United Nations General Assembly asked the Secretary General to make the necessary arrangements to convene the first session of the Assembly of States Parties, as required by Article 126 in the Statute.[610] After the receipt of the required 60 ratifications, the Commission focused on the organization of the first session of the Assembly utilizing a roadmap of six steps necessary for the 'smooth operation'[611] of the Assembly. The roadmap contained at least three meetings of the Assembly of States Parties. The sequence respected the constraints of the Statute dictating the layout of the Bureau, subsidiary bodies, election of Court officials and consideration of the annual budget. Several decisions made by the Commission were included. For example, the establishment of the Committee on Budget and Finance as a subsidiary body[612] and the criteria to govern voluntary contributions to the Court.[613] However, several others were missing and entrusted to the working group on preparatory documents for the Assembly of States Parties to finalize in the last two sessions of the Commission in 2002. These included the composition of the Bureau, the procedure for nomination and election of Court officials, the interim period awaiting a Registrar and the

607 Proceedings of the Preparatory Commission at its Ninth Session (8–19 April), UN Doc. PCNICC/2002/L.1/Rev.1 4.

608 Report of the First Session of the Assembly of States Parties to the Rome Statute of the International Criminal Court, New York, 3–10 September 2002, ICC-ASP/1/3 (2002) 4.

609 Preparatory Commission for the International Criminal Court (24 September – 5 October), Road map Leading to the Early Establishment of the International Criminal Court, UN Doc. PCNICC/2001/L.2 1.

610 UNGA Res 56/85 (2001) 3.

611 Preparatory Commission for the International Criminal Court (24 September – 5 October), Road map Leading to the Early Establishment of the International Criminal Court, UN Doc. PCNICC/2001/L.2 2.

612 Preparatory Commission for the International Criminal Court (26 February – 9 March), Annex III Draft Financial Regulations and Rules, UN Doc. PCNICC/2001/L.1/Rev.1/Add.2 15.

613 Report of the Preparatory Commission for the International Criminal Court (continued)*, UN Doc. PCNICC/2001/1 6.

preparatory meeting documents for the first session of the Assembly, including its first agenda.[614]

To assist the Assembly in its discharge of responsibilities, the establishment of the Bureau became pressing. The Rome Statute and the draft Rules of Procedure of the Assembly required a composition of 21 members, with one President and two Vice-Presidents. Neither document described in detail the functional role of the Bureau. There were no references in the preparatory process as to the qualification of members or the executive positions. On composition, the only guiding reference was in Article 112(3)(b) 'equitable geographical distribution and the adequate representation of the principal legal systems of the world'.[615] As discussed in this chapter, the Bureau was primarily described to support a meeting format of the Assembly. However, as the operationalization of the Assembly became urgent, the Commission tasked the Bureau with responsibilities outside a regular session, for example in reporting back options to establish a permanent secretariat of the Assembly,[616] and setting the date for the nomination and election process of Court officers.[617]

In this context, the working group on preparatory documents for the Assembly of States Parties paid special attention to Article 112(3)(b) ensuring geographical representation was assured while drawing States from different legal traditions. To do so, it took into consideration the total number of member States. By the first session, 76 States had deposited instruments of ratification under Article 126: 24 represented the Western Europe and other States regional group, 17 Africa, 15 Latin America and the Caribbean, 12 Eastern Europe and 8 from Asia Pacific.[618] The composition of the Bureau resulted in six seats for Western Europe and other States, five seats for African States, four seats for Latin American and Caribbean States, and three seats each for Asian and Eastern European States.[619] Once the allocation was determined, the working group identified and proposed the allotment of 'core functions' to

614 Preparatory Commission for the International Criminal Court (24 September – 5 October), Road map Leading to the Early Establishment of the International Criminal Court, UN Doc. PCNICC/2001/L.2 2.

615 Article 112(2)(b), Rome Statute of the International Criminal Court (2002) 2187 UNTS 90.

616 Preparatory Commission for the International Criminal Court (1–12 July), UN Doc. PCNICC/2002/2 20.

617 Ibid 23.

618 United Nations Treaty Collection, Depositary of Notifications, Rome Statute of the International Criminal Court, available at <https://treaties.un.org/>.

619 Preparatory Commission for the International Criminal Court (1–12 July), A Guide to the Report of the Preparatory Commission, Prepared by the Secretariat, UN Doc. PCNICC/2002/3 9.

TABLE 4.12 Preparatory Commission (2001)

Roadmap leading to the early establishment of the International criminal court

Steps	Outcome	Body
(1) Reception of sixtieth instrument of ratification	Statute enters into force 60 days after the deposit of the sixtieth instrument of ratification. Trigger to convene the first Assembly of States Parties to the Rome Statute	United Nations Secretary General
(2) United Nations General Assembly adopts a resolution to convene the first Assembly of States Parties to the Rome Statute	Secretary-General to notify States and to make arrangements for the preparation and circulation of the relevant documents	United Nations General Assembly, Secretary General
(3) First Session of the Assembly of States Parties	Establishment of the Bureau and the election of its President Adoption the documents recommended by the Preparatory Commission Adoption, inter alia, the nomination and election procedures for the judges and the Prosecutor. Call for nominations.	Assembly of States Parties
(4) Subsequent Session of the Assembly of States Parties	Election of judges and Prosecutor	Assembly of States Parties
(5) Inaugural Meeting of the Court	Judges and the Prosecutor sworn in. Election of the Presidency. Establishment of the Chambers. Presidency transmits list of candidates for Registrar for any recommendation by the Assembly of States Parties.	Court

TABLE 4.12 Preparatory Commission (2001) (*cont.*)

Roadmap leading to the early establishment of the International criminal court

Steps	Outcome	Body
(6) Subsequent Session of the Assembly of States Parties	Transmission of any recommendation regarding the list of candidates for Registrar. Election of Registrar by the judges.	Assembly of States Parties, Court

regional groups. The terminology was only accurate if the role of the President and two Vice-Presidents is understood in the context of an Assembly meeting. The remaining two 'functions' were for a rapporteur and the Chair of the Credentials Committee.[620] Although absent from the Statute, the draft procedure for the Assembly and the preparatory proceedings, the working group added the rapporteur and Credential Committee chairmanship to avoid a political problem in the representation of the Bureau.[621] The result was a fully representative Bureau made up of the five United Nations regional groups. The Commission also endorsed the principle of rotation for future renditions of the Bureau.[622] Before the end of its mandate, the Commission's Bureau led the political work to identify the first President of the Assembly. After consultation among States, and aware the preparatory process had been primarily led by delegates from Western Europe and other States, Africa and Latin America and the Caribbean, the Bureau proposed Prince Zeid Raíad Zeid Al-Hussein from Jordan as the first President of the Assembly.[623]

With the composition of the Assembly Bureau in place, the procedure for nomination and election of the judges, the Prosecutor and Deputy Prosecutor could proceed.[624] During the ninth session in April 2002, the working group discussed a United Nations Secretariat paper outlining the building blocks to

620 Ibid 10.
621 Ibid 9.
622 Ibid 10.
623 Ibid 9.
624 Preparatory Commission for the International Criminal Court (1–12 July), UN Doc. PCNICC/2002/2 23.

elect the officers of the Court.[625] As with previous advice, the practice of the Ad Hoc Tribunals, the International Court of Justice and the International Tribunal for the Law of the Sea offered a starting point for the working group.[626] However, the procedure had to comply with Articles 36, 37, 42 and 43 of the Rome Statute, and draft Rule 12 of the Procedure and Evidence in regard to the Registrar.[627] Only Article 36 on the 'qualifications, nomination and election of judges'[628] had the necessary detail for the Assembly, including guidance for the first round of election. This was not the case for the Prosecutor, Deputy Prosecutor and Registrar where the Statute did not offer the same level of guidance.

Curiously, however, States did not discuss the establishment of the Advisory Committee on Nominations in Article 36(4)(c). Together with the Independent Oversight Mechanism in Article 112(4), it was the only subsidiary body referred in the Statute directed to assuring the election of judges. More so, nothing in the clause prevented States to utilize the Advisory Committee on Nominations for other elected positions. The United Nations flagged this possibility but it was not taken by States.[629] In fact, the Advisory Committee would only be agreed at the tenth session of the Assembly in 2011.[630] In this context, writing in 2001, Schabas warned States Parties faced 'considerable international embarrassment'[631] if they pursued unqualified candidates for the bench. He further alerted a Prosecutor without the necessary skillset 'could quickly destroy the entire institution'.[632]

Left with 'certain practical questions'[633] at the end of the April session, the working group accepted the recommendation by the United Nations for the

625 Preparatory Commission for the International Criminal Court (8–19 April), Election of Judges, the Prosecutor and the Registrar of the International Criminal Court, Working Paper by the Secretariat, UN Doc. PCNICC/2002/WGASP-PD/L.1 (2002).

626 Ibid 3.

627 Report of the Preparatory Commission for the International Criminal Court, Addendum, Finalized Draft Text of the Rules of Procedure and Evidence, UN Doc. PCNICC/2000/INF/3/Add.1.

628 Article 36, Rome Statute of the International Criminal Court (2002) 2187 UNTS 90.

629 Preparatory Commission for the International Criminal Court (8–19 April), Election of Judges, the Prosecutor and the Registrar of the International Criminal Court, Working Paper by the Secretariat, UN Doc. PCNICC/2002/WGASP-PD/L.1 7.

630 ICC-ASP/10/Res.5 Strengthening the International Criminal Court and the Assembly of States Parties 31.

631 Schabas, 'International Criminal Court: The Secret of Its Success' 425.

632 Ibid.

633 Secretary-General Addresses Preparatory Commission for International Criminal Court as it Concludes Ninth Session, UN Doc. L/3003 (2002).

Assembly to adopt a nomination and election procedure for all officers of the Court.[634] An updated procedure, based on the United Nations paper, received several proposals during the final session of the Commission. For example, Switzerland asked to publicise all nominations on the internet,[635] Greece and Switzerland proposed a minimum number of supporting States for any Prosecution nomination,[636] and Belgium added language requiring nominations contain a written statement explaining the fulfilment of judgeship criteria as per the Statute.[637] The Coordinator's paper addressed each proposal setting out a detailed procedure for the nomination and election of judges with the expectation it would also apply mutatis mutandis to the nomination of the Prosecutor and Deputy Prosecutor.[638] The system formulated by States included timely periods for nomination, with a role for the Bureau and the forthcoming permanent secretariat of the Assembly to coordinate the receipt and distribution of documents. It also described the steps to elect judges following closely the criteria laid out in Article 36(8)(a)(i)–(iii) and the voting requirements in Article 112(7) of the Statute. It finally clarified the same steps applied to a judicial vacancy.[639] The guidance for the Prosecutor changed insofar it required nominations had the backing of several States and, if possible, the election took place by consensus.[640] The process for the Deputy Prosecutor followed closely Article 42(4), placing the responsibility for nominations on the Prosecutor.[641] By the end of the tenth session in 2002, the Commission transmitted a draft resolution on the matter to the Assembly, but signalled lack of agreement in the procedure for the election of judges.[642]

634 Preparatory Commission for the International Criminal Court (8–19 April), Election of Judges, the Prosecutor and the Registrar of the International Criminal Court, Working Paper by the Secretariat, UN Doc. PCNICC/2002/WGASP-PD/L.1 4.

635 Proposal Submitted by Switzerland, Election of Judges, the Prosecutor and the Registrar of the International Criminal Court, UN Doc. PCNICC/2002/WGASP-PD/DP.1 (2002).

636 Proposal Submitted by Greece and Switzerland, Nomination of the Prosecutor, UN Doc. PCNICC/2002/WGASP-PD/DP.3 (2002).

637 Proposal Submitted by Belgium, UN Doc. PCNICC/2002/WGASP-PD/DP.2 (2002).

638 Preparatory Commission for the International Criminal Court (8–19 April), Draft Resolution of the Assembly of States Parties on the Procedure for the Nomination and Election of Judges, the Prosecutor and the Deputy Prosecutors of the International Criminal Court, Rolling Text Prepared by the Coordinator, UN Doc. PCNICC/2002/WGASP-PD/RT .2 (2002).

639 Preparatory Commission for the International Criminal Court (1–12 July), UN Doc. PCNICC/2002/2 23–25.

640 Ibid 25–26.

641 Ibid 26–27.

642 Ibid 25 at footnote a.

During the first session of the Assembly of States Parties in New York, States addressed concerns regarding thresholds of judicial candidates per regional grouping and agreed to an election system.[643]

However, while noted by the United Nations,[644] States did not include the election of the Registrar in the draft resolution transmitted to the Assembly. The sequence of events to elect the judges meant they would only realistically be in a position to submit a list of nominations to the Assembly of States Parties in mid-2003.[645] In the interim, the working group on the budget for the first financial year of the Court proposed the position of Director of Common Services be appointed by the Assembly until a Registrar was in place.[646] The Common Services Division had the task to provide joint administrative services to the Chambers, Prosecution and Registry.[647] Once all elected positions were in place, the Director of Common Services would transfer all relevant duties as appropriate.[648] Patricio Ruedas from Spain was tasked with overseeing the process, including drafting the job description and coordinating nominations for the first Assembly meeting.[649] By June 2003, after consulting the Assembly, Bruno Cathala was elected by the judges as the first Registrar.[650]

During the tenth and final session in 2002, the Commission turned to the finalization of the budget for the first financial year as the remaining document listed in Resolution F. The draft budget determined the financial infrastructure by deciding on scales of assessed contributions from States, the programme budget of the Court and Assembly, the establishment of the Working Capital Fund and the crediting of States' contributions to the United Nations Trust Fund to Support the Establishment of the International Criminal Court. In addition, it determined the participation of the Court in United Nations

643 ICC-ASP/1/Res.2 Procedure for the Nomination and Election of Judges, the Prosecutor and Deputy Prosecutors of the International Criminal Court (2002).

644 Preparatory Commission for the International Criminal Court (8–19 April), Election of Judges, the Prosecutor and the Registrar of the International Criminal Court, Working Paper by the Secretariat, UN Doc. PCNICC/2002/WGASP-PD/L.1 19.

645 Preparatory Commission for the International Criminal Court (1–12 July), UN Doc. PCNICC/2002/2 16.

646 Proceedings of the Preparatory Commission at its Tenth Session (1–12 July), UN Doc. PCNICC/2002/L.4/Rev.1 3.

647 Preparatory Commission for the International Criminal Court (1–12 July), Part I, Draft Budget for the First Financial Period of the Court, UN Doc. PCNICC/2002/2/Add.1 24.

648 Ibid.

649 Preparatory Commission for International Criminal Court Concludes Tenth and Final Session, UN Doc. L/3010 (2002).

650 Report of the International Criminal Court, ICC-ASP/2/5 (2003) 8.

Joint Staff Pension Fund.[651] Each of these decisions was put forward to the Assembly in draft decisions or resolutions in the Preparatory Commission's final report.[652]

Beyond the preparation of required auxiliary documents in Resolution F, the Commission also developed remaining critical preparatory document for the first Assembly of States Parties (see Table 4.13). For example the provisional agenda for the first session, which was based on advice from the United Nations and precedence from the Conference of the Parties to the Convention on Biological Diversity (1992), the Conference of the Parties to the United Nations Convention to Combat Desertification (1994) and Meeting of States Parties to the United Nations Convention on the Law of the Sea (1995), among others.[653] While the primary task of the first session of the Assembly was the consideration of the Preparatory Commission's report, it was also tasked with constructing the institutional organization of the Assembly. Thus, in the final agenda transmitted to States Parties, the Commission listed the election of the President, the adoption of the Rules of Procedure and the establishment of the Bureau before any other substantive report.[654] In fact, beyond the eight draft texts listed in the Final Act, the first session of the Assembly received 22 draft resolutions or decisions to operationalize the Court and the Assembly.

5 Conclusion

After decades of joint effort by governments, civil society, academia and other partners, the International Criminal Court was finally established in 1998. The Rome Conference succeeded in finding policy and legal compromises among divergent views from States from every regional group. As difficult concessions emerged in Part 2 of the Statute, the Assembly of States Parties was also created by solving outstanding issues inherited from the Zutphen Draft.

---

651 Preparatory Commission for the International Criminal Court (1–12 July), A Guide to the Report of the Preparatory Commission, Prepared by the Secretariat, UN Doc. PCNICC/2002/3 8.

652 Ibid 18–20.

653 Preparatory Commission for the International Criminal Court (8–19 April), Provisional Agenda for the First Meeting of the Assembly of States Parties, Working Paper by the Secretariat, UN Doc. PCNICC/2002/WGASP-PD/L.2 (2002).

654 Preparatory Commission for the International Criminal Court (1–12 July), Annex I, Provisional Agenda for the First Meeting of the Assembly of States Parties, to be Held at United Nations Headquarters from 3 to 10 September 2002, UN Doc. PCNICC/2002/2/Add.3 (2002) 1–2.

TABLE 4.13 Preparatory Commission (2002)

Practical arrangements	Action for establishment and operations	Function
Crime of aggression	Draft resolution of the Assembly of States Parties on the continuity of work in respect of the crime of aggression.[a]	Amendments and Review of the Statute
Issues relating to the meeting of the Assembly of States Parties	Draft recommendation of the Assembly of States Parties concerning seating arrangements for States Parties.[b]	Governance and Management Oversight
	Provisional agenda for the first meeting of the Assembly of States Parties, to be held at United Nations Headquarters from 3 to 10 September 2002.[c]	Governance and Management Oversight
	Composition of the Bureau at the first meeting of the Assembly of States Parties.[d]	Governance and Management Oversight
	Draft resolution of the Assembly of States Parties concerning the provisional arrangements for the Secretariat of the Assembly of States Parties.[e]	Governance and Management Oversight
	Draft resolution of the Assembly of States Parties relating to the permanent secretariat of the Assembly of States Parties.[f]	Governance and Management Oversight

a Preparatory Commission for the International Criminal Court (1–12 July), Part II, Proposals for a Provision on the Crime of Aggression, UN Doc. PCNICC/2002/2/Add.2 (2002).

b Preparatory Commission for the International Criminal Court (1–12 July), UN Doc. PCNICC/2002/2.

c Preparatory Commission for the International Criminal Court (1–12 July), Annex I, Provisional Agenda for the First Meeting of the Assembly of States Parties, to be Held at United Nations Headquarters from 3 to 10 September 2002, UN Doc. PCNICC/2002/2/Add.3.

d Preparatory Commission for the International Criminal Court (1–12 July), UN Doc. PCNICC/2002/2.

e Report of the Preparatory Commission for the International Criminal Court (continued) (8–19 April), UN Doc. PCNICC/2002/1.

f Preparatory Commission for the International Criminal Court (1–12 July), UN Doc. PCNICC/2002/2.

TABLE 4.13 Preparatory Commission (2002) (*cont.*)

Practical arrangements	Action for establishment and operations	Function
Establishment of subsidiary bodies	Draft resolution of the Assembly of States Parties on the establishment of the Committee on Budget and Finance.[g]	Financial Oversight
	Draft resolution of the Assembly of States Parties relating to the establishment of a fund for the benefit of victims of crimes within the jurisdiction of the Court, and of the families of such victims.[h]	Auxiliary Judicial Instruments Oversight
Procedures for nomination and for conduct of elections	Draft resolution of the Assembly of States Parties relating to the procedure for the nomination and election of members of the Committee on Budget and Finance.[i]	Governance and Management Oversight
	Draft resolution of the Assembly of States Parties relating to the procedure for the nomination and election of members of the Board of Directors of the Trust Fund for the benefit of victims.[j]	Governance and Management Oversight
	Draft resolution of the Assembly of States Parties relating to the procedure for the nomination and election of judges, the Prosecutor and Deputy Prosecutors of the International Criminal Court.[k]	Election of Judges, Election of the Prosecutor and Deputy

g Report of the Preparatory Commission for the International Criminal Court (continued)*, UN Doc. PCNICC/2001/1.
h Preparatory Commission for the International Criminal Court (1–12 July), UN Doc. PCNICC/2002/2.
i Ibid.
j Ibid.
k Ibid.

TABLE 4.13 Preparatory Commission (2002) (*cont.*)

Practical arrangements	Action for establishment and operations	Function
Issues relating to financing for the Court and the budget for the first financial period	Draft resolution of the Assembly of States Parties relating to budget appropriations for the first financial period and financing of appropriations for the first financial period.[l]	Financial Oversight
	Draft resolution of the Assembly of States Parties relating to the Working Capital Fund for the first financial period.[m]	Financial Oversight
	Draft resolution of the Assembly of States Parties relating to scales of assessments for the apportionment of the expenses of the International Criminal Court.[n]	Financial Oversight
	Draft resolution of the Assembly of States Parties on crediting contributions to the United Nations Trust Fund to Support the Establishment of the International Criminal Court.[o]	Financial Oversight
	Draft decision of the Assembly of States Parties relating to the provision of funds for the Court.[p]	Financial Oversight
	Draft resolution of the Assembly of States Parties on relevant criteria for voluntary contributions to the International Criminal Court.[q]	Financial Oversight

l Ibid.

m Ibid.

n Ibid.

o Report of the Preparatory Commission for the International Criminal Court (continued) (8–19 April), UN Doc. PCNICC/2002/1.

p Preparatory Commission for the International Criminal Court (1–12 July), UN Doc. PCNICC/2002/2.

q Report of the Preparatory Commission for the International Criminal Court (continued)*, UN Doc. PCNICC/2001/1.

TABLE 4.13 Preparatory Commission (2002) (*cont.*)

Practical arrangements	Action for establishment and operations	Function
	Draft decision of the Assembly of States Parties relating to interim arrangements for the exercise of authority pending the assumption of office by the Registrar.[r]	Governance and Management Oversight
Issues relating to officials and staff as well as to the establishment of the International Criminal Court	Conditions of service and compensation of judges of the International Criminal Court.[s]	Governance and Management Oversight
	Draft decision of the Assembly of States Parties relating to the participation of the International Criminal Court in the United Nations Joint Staff Pension Fund.[t]	Governance and Management Oversight
	Draft resolution of the Assembly of States Parties relating to selection of the staff of the International Criminal Court.[u]	Auxiliary Judicial Instruments Oversight
	Establishment of an international criminal bar.[v]	Governance and Management Oversight

r Preparatory Commission for the International Criminal Court (1–12 July), UN Doc. PCNICC/2002/2.

s Preparatory Commission for the International Criminal Court (1–12 July), Part I, Draft Budget for the First Financial Period of the Court, UN Doc. PCNICC/2002/2/Add.1.

t Preparatory Commission for the International Criminal Court (1–12 July), UN Doc. PCNICC/2002/2.

u Ibid.

v Ibid.

In fact, the birth of Article 112 was uncontroversial compared with other clauses dealing with the definition of crimes, jurisdiction and the role of the independent Prosecutor. The definitions required for the governance body of Court were resolved in a matter of days under the leadership or Rao Rama from India with the assistance of small group of States and civil society. The clauses under Article 112 benefited from the preparatory process but the bulk of the negotiation was only done in Rome. The drafting managed to balance views about membership, decision-making, voting rights, resolving non-cooperation issues and financial oversight responsibilities. However, the political role of the Assembly was not discussed jointly with other parts of the Statute that would have benefited from a stronger correlation. This is the case with Article 112(2)(f) and Part 9 on the cooperation regime. While Part 9 assigned a role to the Assembly, Article 112 did not capture the exact procedural steps States Parties could take to foster adequate cooperation with the Court. This issue would become a source of disagreement as the Assembly of States Parties developed over time.

Post-Rome and after four years and ten sessions, the Preparatory Commission concluded on 12 July 2002 the compendium of documents for the Assembly's operationalization and the completion of all draft texts under Resolution F as requested by the Rome Conference and the United Nations General Assembly.[655] States decided to hold the first meeting of the Assembly of States Parties from 3 to 10 September 2002 in New York,[656] and planned for two resumed sessions in February and April 2003, leading to the second session of the Assembly in September 2003.[657] As 76 States Parties prepared to gather in New York, Secretary General Kofi Annan predicted during the fourth anniversary of the adoption of the Statute in Rome on 17 July 2002, that 'an exciting but challenging journey now lies ahead of us'.[658] An accurate statement that would survive the test of time.

---

655 Proceedings of the Preparatory Commission at its Tenth Session (1–12 July), UN Doc. PCNICC/2002/L.4/Rev.1 3.

656 Ibid.

657 Preparatory Commission for the International Criminal Court (1–12 July), Part I, Draft Budget for the First Financial Period of the Court, UN Doc. PCNICC/2002/2/Add.1 4.

658 'Exciting but Challenging Journey' Lies Ahead, Says Secretary-General on Fourth Anniversary of Adoption of ICC Statute, UN Doc. L/3011 (2002).

CHAPTER 5

The Practice of the Assembly of States Parties: Governance and Management Oversight

1 Introduction

The first meeting of the Assembly of States Parties to the Rome Statute in New York on 3–10 September 2002 was an end and a beginning. The end of the long negotiating process to create the International Criminal Court and the beginning of the governance and management responsibility of States Parties to steward the Court so 'the most serious crimes of concern to the international community as a whole'[1] do not go unpunished. For the next 20 years the Assembly of States Parties would be confronted with political, policy and operational challenges affecting the Court's purpose, effectiveness and reputation. More so as the institution faced internal existential questions[2] as well as serious external challenges from powerful States.[3] By virtue of their governance and management oversight role enshrined primarily in Articles 112(1)–(10), the Assembly confronted these questions while developing its own institutional practices. With a nascent Court, the emerging Assembly expanded its membership, created subsidiary bodies, elected its leadership and learnt how to implement powers assigned to it by the Rome Statute. This organizational development process was not without challenges. Indeed, tracing the Assembly's governance and management oversight practice across 20 sessions delivers a complex but rich understanding of the dynamics among States Parties and with the Court. For States Parties, governing the Court required a delicate balance between fulfilling statutory responsibilities while preserving the independence of the judicial body. For the Court, engaged with accomplishing the promises of the Rome Statute, the Assembly and its Bureau represented a gatekeeper of its ability to pursue these aims. The delicate balance set in the Statute became manifest as the Assembly of States Parties met

1 Preamble, Rome Statute of the International Criminal Court (2002) 2187 UNTS 90.

2 Report of the Independent Expert Review of the International Criminal Court and the Rome Statute System, ICC-ASP/19/16.

3 ASP President O-Gon Kwon Rejects Measures Taken Against ICC, ICC-ASP-20200611-PR1527 (2020); The Presidency of the Assembly of States Parties Stands Firmly by the International Criminal Court, its Elected Officials, and its Personnel, ICC-ASP-20230520-PR1721 (2023).

© EZEQUIEL JIMÉNEZ MARTINEZ, 2026 DOI:10.1163/9789004749979_006 for the first time in New York in 2002 and developed its practice as the 'management oversight and legislative body of the International Criminal Court'[4] over 20 years.

In this context, this chapter examines the governance and management practice of the Assembly of States Parties between its first and twentieth sessions. This function of the Assembly can be found in Articles 112(1)–(10) and 119(2) in terms of structure and overall powers, Articles 2 and 3(2) for the approval of the relationship agreements with the United Nations and the host country, and Articles 46(2), 47 and 112(2)(b) for the responsibility to provide management oversight to elected officials. The aim of this chapter is to trace these statutory responsibilities within the governance and management oversight function of the Assembly to offer an appraisal of the International Criminal Court from the under-examined point of view of the practice of States Parties. In this sense, subsequent chapters focus on other important statutory responsibilities across elections, financial oversight, disciplinary measures and removal of elected officials, oversight of auxiliary judicial instruments, enforcement of cooperation and the review and amendments of the Rome Statute. Therefore, this chapter begins with a description of the main decisions taken during the first session of the Assembly of States Parties in order to understand the institutional set-up that has prevailed since 2002. Secondly, it describes the main governance and management oversight actions taken by the Assembly and its Bureau between 2002 and 2021. In doing so, the chapter also reflects on the relevant findings of the 2020 Independent Expert Review report commissioned by the Assembly.[5]

2 Becoming the Institution: The First Assembly of States Parties (2002)

Pursuing the challenge described by Schabas[6] wondering when the real birthday of the International Criminal Court is, one worthy contestant date is 3 September 2002, when the first session of the Assembly of States Parties to the Rome Statute commenced. Held at the United Nations Headquarter in

4 Assembly of States Parties to the Rome Statute, 'ICC – Assembly of States Parties' (2020) <https://asp.icc-cpi.int/assembly> accessed 20 March 2020.

5 Report of the Independent Expert Review of the International Criminal Court and the Rome Statute System, ICC-ASP/19/16.

6 Schabas, William A, 'The International Criminal Court at Ten' (2011) 22 (4) Criminal Law Forum 493.

New York until 10 September, 76 States Parties, gathered in assembly, were the first to act under the Rome Statute.[7] Indeed, only after the constitution of the Assembly of States Parties under Article 112, the treaty became alive, and a new international organization destined to fight impunity was created.[8] The act of creation, as planned by the Preparatory Commission, also included two resumed sessions in February and April 2003 in New York.[9] Under Rule 7 of the Rules of Procedure of the Assembly, a meeting could 'adjourn temporarily'[10] and resume at a later date. A practice that continued over the 20 sessions of the Assembly, the use of Rule 7 was needed in 2002 to chart a sequential path providing the Court with its Assembly President, Bureau, Rules of Procedure and Evidence, budget, external auditor, judges, Registrar and Prosecutor, among other critical institutional requirements.[11]

Bearing in mind Article 112(1) and relevant Rules of Procedure of the Assembly,[12] the first meeting was attended by representatives of 76 States Parties,[13] 63 observer States and 16 entities and intergovernmental organizations under Rule 92.[14] In addition, to promote the universality of the nascent Court, the Assembly decided to invite 27 non-party States and without observer status under Rule 94 and accredit 68 civil society organizations under Rule 93.[15] Out of the 76 inaugural States Parties, 24 represented the Western Europe and Other States regional group, 17 Africa, 15 Latin America and the Caribbean, 12 Eastern Europe and eight from Asia Pacific.[16] By other metrics, only 40% of United Nations membership in 2002 was represented in the Assembly.

---

7 Report of the First Session of the Assembly of States Parties to the Rome Statute of the International Criminal Court, New York, 3–10 September 2002, ICC-ASP/1/3.

8 Gallant, Kenneth S, 'The International Criminal Court in the System of States and International Organizations' (2003) 16 Leiden Journal of International Law 553.

9 Preparatory Commission for the International Criminal Court (1–12 July), Part I, Draft Budget for the First Financial Period of the Court, UN Doc. PCNICC/2002/2/Add.1 4.

10 Rule 7, Rules of Procedure of the Assembly of States Parties, ICC-ASP/1/3.

11 Provisional Agenda, First Session, ICC-ASP/1/1 (2002); Provisional Agenda, First Session (First and Second Resumptions), ICC-ASP/1/1/Add.1 (2002).

12 Rule 23, 92–94, Rules of Procedure of the Assembly of States Parties, ICC-ASP/1/3.

13 Report of the First Session of the Assembly of States Parties to the Rome Statute of the International Criminal Court, New York, 3–10 September 2002, ICC-ASP/1/3, Annex II, Report of the Credentials Committee.

14 Delegations to the First Session of the Assembly of States Parties to the Rome Statute of the International Criminal Court, New York, 3–10 September 2002, ICC-ASP/1/INF.1 (2002).

15 Ibid. See also Rules 92–94 in Rules of Procedure of the Assembly of States Parties, ICC-ASP/1/3.

16 United Nations Treaty Collection, Depositary of Notifications, Rome Statute of the International Criminal Court, available at <https://treaties.un.org/>.

Overwhelmingly, the 42 States Parties making statements urged for the universality of the Rome Statute and an effective International Criminal Court.[17] The first session of the Assembly was chaired its first President Prince Zeid Raíad Zeid Al-Hussein of Jordan.[18] Unlike the strict criteria set out for judges or the Prosecutor in the Rome Statute,[19] the election of the highest authority for the Assembly of States Parties was purely a political and diplomatic act. By the time of the inaugural plenary of the session, the Preparatory Commission had identified through political negotiations that Prince Zeid should be elected as the first President of the Assembly[20] for a three-year term, as stipulated in Article 112(3)(a).[21] The election of Prince Zeid demonstrated the intention of States active in the Commission to guarantee equitable geographical distribution of power after the preparatory process had been primarily led by delegates from Western Europe and Other States, Africa and Latin America and the Caribbean.[22] In fact, Jordan was one of eight States Parties to the Statute from the Asia Pacific group, the least represented region.[23] Prince Zeid Raíad Zeid Al-Hussein, in his capacity as President, vowed to transfer the 'greater responsibilities for the future success of the Court from the Assembly to the Court itself'.[24]

Accompanying Prince Zeid, the Assembly elected its first Bureau made of two Vice-Presidents and 18 members of the Assembly as per Article 112(3)(a)–(b). On composition, the only guiding reference was in Article 112(3)(b) requiring 'equitable geographical distribution and the adequate representation of the principal legal systems of the world'.[25] While the Bureau was tasked with

---

17 First Session of Assembly of States Parties to International Criminal Court Concludes Work, UN Doc. L/3014 (2002).

18 Report of the First Session of the Assembly of States Parties to the Rome Statute of the International Criminal Court, New York, 3–10 September 2002, ICC-ASP/1/3 165.

19 See Articles 36 and 42, Rome Statute of the International Criminal Court (2002) 2187 UNTS 90.

20 Report of the First Session of the Assembly of States Parties to the Rome Statute of the International Criminal Court, New York, 3–10 September 2002, ICC-ASP/1/3 2–3.

21 Article 112(3)(a), Rome Statute of the International Criminal Court (2002) 2187 UNTS 90.

22 Preparatory Commission for the International Criminal Court (1–12 July), A Guide to the Report of the Preparatory Commission, Prepared by the Secretariat, UN Doc. PCNICC/2002/3 9.

23 United Nations Treaty Collection, Depositary of Notifications, Rome Statute of the International Criminal Court, available at <https://treaties.un.org/>.

24 Polli, Maura, 'What Can 92 Countries Agree On' (2003) 12 International Law Students Association Quarterly 8.

25 Article 112(2)(b), Rome Statute of the International Criminal Court (2002) 2187 UNTS 90.

assisting the 'Assembly in the discharge of its responsibilities',[26] Rule 29 of the procedure of the Assembly on 'Composition and function'[27] repeated the language from the Statute. Nonetheless, the Assembly proceeded in electing Allieu Ibrahim Kanu (Sierra Leone) and Felipe Paolillo (Uruguay) as Vice-Presidents and Austria, Croatia, Cyprus, Democratic Republic of the Congo, Ecuador, Gabon, Germany, Mongolia, Namibia, Netherlands (the host State), New Zealand, Nigeria, Norway, Peru, Romania, Trinidad and Tobago, United Kingdom of Great Britain and Northern Ireland and Yugoslavia, later Serbia and Montenegro,[28] as the remainder members of the Bureau.[29] The election of the Bureau aligned with the geographical distribution requirement among States Parties whereas six seats corresponded to the Western Europe and other States group, five seats for African States, four seats for Latin American and Caribbean States, and three seats each for Asian and Eastern European States.[30] To further the objective of regional balance, the Assembly designated Alexander Marschik from Austria, representing the group of Western Europe and other States as Rapporteur and Dejan Šahović from Yugoslavia, representing the Eastern European States, as Chairman of the Credentials Committee.[31] This way, all regional groups represented in the Bureau had a leadership role within the Assembly. The newly elected Bureau received secretariat support from the Office of Legal Affairs of the United Nations,[32] which included Renan Villacis[33] from Ecuador, later Director of Secretariat of the Assembly of States Parties between 2006 and 2024.[34]

---

26 Article 112(3)(c), Rome Statute of the International Criminal Court (2002) 2187 UNTS 90.

27 Report of the First Session of the Assembly of States Parties to the Rome Statute of the International Criminal Court, New York, 3–10 September 2002, ICC-ASP/1/3 165.

28 Report of the First Session (First and Second Resumptions) of the Assembly of States Parties to the Rome Statute of the International Criminal Court, New York, 3–7 February and 21–23 April 2003, ICC-ASP/1/3/Add.1 footnote 4 at page 10. 4 February 2003, the Federal Republic of Yugoslavia officially informed the Secretary– General of the United Nations that it had changed its name to Serbia and Montenegro.

29 Report of the First Session of the Assembly of States Parties to the Rome Statute of the International Criminal Court, New York, 3–10 September 2002, ICC-ASP/1/3 2–3.

30 Preparatory Commission for the International Criminal Court (1–12 July), A Guide to the Report of the Preparatory Commission, Prepared by the Secretariat, UN Doc. PCNICC/2002/3 9.

31 Report of the First Session of the Assembly of States Parties to the Rome Statute of the International Criminal Court, New York, 3–10 September 2002, ICC-ASP/1/3 2–3.

32 Ibid 3.

33 Delegations to the First Session of the Assembly of States Parties to the Rome Statute of the International Criminal Court, New York, 3–10 September 2002, ICC-ASP/1/INF.1 56.

34 See: Bureau of the Assembly of States Parties, 13th Meeting, 5 April 2006 (2006); 'Job Title: Director of the Secretariat of the Assembly of States Parties (D-1), Requisition ID

Under the leadership of the newly elected Bureau, the Assembly pursued the agenda at hand containing 17 items[35] covering the necessary steps to 'consider and adopt, as appropriate, recommendations of the Preparatory Commission'[36] and operationalize the Court, for example by approving the budget for the first financial period.[37] Indeed, the Assembly had before it eight draft texts listed in the Final Act and 22 draft resolutions or decisions to operationalize the Court and the Assembly (see Table 5.1).[38] Each resolution built, one by one, the necessary sequence of events required to resource the organs of the Court and the Assembly. While some commentators present in New York described the first Assembly session as 'fairly uneventful',[39] the reach of decisions made then still shape the life of the Court 20 sessions later. In fact, the 16 resolutions, four decisions and one recommendation adopted between 2002[40] and 2003,[41] essentially created the Court. For example, Resolution 2 set the procedure for the nomination and election of judges, the Prosecutor and Deputy Prosecutors,[42] and Resolutions 11–16 regulated the financing of the Court.[43]

23198, available at: <https://www.icc-cpi.int/vacancy/director-secretariat-assembly-states-parties-d-1'> (2023) accessed 17 December 2023.

35 Report of the First Session of the Assembly of States Parties to the Rome Statute of the International Criminal Court, New York, 3–10 September 2002, ICC-ASP/1/3 3.

36 Article 112(2)(a), Rome Statute of the International Criminal Court (2002) 2187 UNTS 90.

37 Symonides, Janusz, 'Towards the Launch of the International Criminal Court' (2002) 11 The Polish Quarterly of International Affairs 60.

38 Report of the First Session of the Assembly of States Parties to the Rome Statute of the International Criminal Court, New York, 3–10 September 2002, ICC-ASP/1/3 4.

39 Schense, Jennifer, Summary of the Fist Assembly of States Parties (Coalition for the International Criminal Court 2002) 1.

40 Report of the First Session of the Assembly of States Parties to the Rome Statute of the International Criminal Court, New York, 3–10 September 2002, ICC-ASP/1/3 328–357.

41 Report of the First Session (First and Second Resumptions) of the Assembly of States Parties to the Rome Statute of the International Criminal Court, New York, 3–7 February and 21–23 April 2003, ICC-ASP/1/3/Add.1 11–12.

42 ICC-ASP/1/Res.2 Procedure for the Nomination and Election of Judges, the Prosecutor and Deputy Prosecutors of the International Criminal Court.

43 ICC-ASP/1/Res.11 Relevant Criteria for Voluntary Contributions to the International Criminal Court (2002); ICC-ASP/1/Res.12 Budget Appropriations for the First Financial Period and Financing of Appropriations for the First Financial Period (2002); ICC-ASP/1/Res.13 Working Capital Fund for the First Financial Period (2002); ICC-ASP/1/Res.14 Scales of Assessments for the Apportionment of the Expenses of the International Criminal Court (2002); ICC-ASP/1/Res.15 Crediting Contributions to the United Nations Trust Fund to Support the Establishment of the International Criminal Court (2002); ICC-ASP /1/Res.16 Commencement of Functions by the Committee on Budget and Finance; Election of Two Members from the Eastern European States; and Deferment of Drawing of Lots (2003).

TABLE 5.1 First Session of the Assembly of States Parties (2002–2003)

Meeting	Resolutions, decisions and recommendations	Function
1st plenary meeting, 3 September 2002	Decision 4 – Seating arrangements for States Parties	Governance and Management Oversight
	Resolution 4 – Establishment of the Committee on Budget and Finance	Financial Oversight
	Resolution 5 – Procedure for the nomination and election of members of the Committee on Budget and Finance	Financial Oversight
2nd plenary meeting, 3 September 2002	Decision 1 – Provision of funds for the Court	Financial Oversight
	Decision 2 – Interim arrangements for the exercise of authority pending the assumption of office by the Registrar	Governance and Management Oversight
	Resolution 11 – Relevant criteria for voluntary contributions to the International Criminal Court	Financial Oversight
	Resolution 12 – Budget appropriations for the first financial period and financing of appropriations for the first financial period	Financial Oversight
	Resolution 13 – Working Capital Fund for the first financial period	Financial Oversight
	Resolution 14 – Scales of assessments for the apportionment of the expenses of the International Criminal Court	Financial Oversight
	Resolution 15 – Crediting contributions to the United Nations Trust Fund to Support the Establishment of the International Criminal Court	Financial Oversight
3rd plenary meeting, 9 September 2002	Decision 3 – Participation of the International Criminal Court in the United Nations Joint Staff Pension Fund	Governance and Management Oversight
	Resolution 1 – Continuity of work in respect of the crime of aggression	Amendments and Review of the Statute

TABLE 5.1 First Session of the Assembly of States Parties (2002–2003) (*cont.*)

Meeting	Resolutions, decisions and recommendations	Function
	Resolution 2 – Procedure for the nomination and election of judges, the Prosecutor and Deputy Prosecutors of the International Criminal Court	Election of Judges, Election of the Prosecutor and Deputy
	Resolution 3 – Procedure for the election of the judges for the International Criminal Court	Election of Judges
	Resolution 6 – Establishment of a fund for the benefit of victims of crimes within the jurisdiction of the Court, and of the families of such victims	Auxiliary Judicial Instruments Oversight
	Resolution 7 – Procedure for the nomination and election of members of the Board of Directors of the Trust Fund for the benefit of victims	Auxiliary Judicial Instruments Oversight
	Resolution 8 – Provisional arrangements for the Secretariat of the Assembly of States Parties	Governance and Management Oversight
	Resolution 9 – Permanent secretariat of the Assembly of States Parties	Governance and Management Oversight
	Resolution 10 – Selection of the staff of the International Criminal Court	Auxiliary Judicial Instruments Oversight
10th plenary meeting, 21 April 2003	Resolution 16 – Commencement of functions by the Committee on Budget and Finance; election of two members from the Eastern European States; and deferment of drawing of lots	Financial Oversight
12th plenary meeting, 23 April 2003	Recommendation 1 – Recommendation concerning the election of the Registrar of the International Criminal Court	Election of the Registrar

To arrive at these decisions, the Assembly created a 'Working Group of the Whole'.[44] The Working Group met six times[45] between 3 and 6 September to consider and approve the report of the Preparatory Commission and other draft resolutions. As Mundis explained, the Working Group 'adopted virtually every document prepared by the Preparatory Commission without change and by consensus, with just a few minor exceptions'.[46] The adoption of all preparatory documents made by the Commission effectively constructed the governance architecture for the Court and within the Assembly. What follows is a summary discussion of these key decisions.

One of the first decisions taken by the Assembly related to the creation of the first subsidiary body of the Assembly under Article 112(4), namely the Committee on Budget and Finance.[47] While not mentioned in the Rome Statute, the Assembly passed two resolutions on the Committee on Budget and Finance. Resolution 4[48] formally established the Committee and Resolution 5 the procedure for the nomination and election its members.[49] The Assembly of States Parties acted decisively on these resolutions for two main reasons. First, the Committee satisfied, in part, the responsibility of the Assembly to 'provide management oversight to the Presidency, the Prosecutor and the Registrar regarding the administration of the Court'.[50] Secondly, to meet the required time for nominations so the election of the 12 members could take place during the second resumed session in April 2003.[51] The urgency to elect the Committee also resided in their responsibility to examine the budget in time for the second session of the Assembly in September 2003.[52]

Next, to complete the financial oversight architecture, the Assembly approved two decisions and four resolutions.[53] Decision 1 and Resolutions 11 to 15 satisfied requirements in Part 11 and 12 of the Statute, including a request to

44 Report of the First Session of the Assembly of States Parties to the Rome Statute of the International Criminal Court, New York, 3–10 September 2002, ICC-ASP/1/3 4.

45 Ibid 358.

46 Mundis, 132.

47 Report of the First Session of the Assembly of States Parties to the Rome Statute of the International Criminal Court, New York, 3–10 September 2002, ICC-ASP/1/3 4.

48 ICC-ASP/1/Res.4 Establishment of the Committee on Budget and Finance (2002).

49 ICC-ASP/1/Res.5 Procedure for the Nomination and Election of Members of the Committee on Budget and Finance (2002).

50 Article 112(2)(b), Rome Statute of the International Criminal Court (2002) 2187 UNTS 90.

51 Report of the First Session of the Assembly of States Parties to the Rome Statute of the International Criminal Court, New York, 3–10 September 2002, ICC-ASP/1/3 5.

52 ICC-ASP/1/Res.4 Establishment of the Committee on Budget and Finance 2.

53 Provisional Work Programme (Revised), First Session, available at <https://legal.un.org/icc/asp/aspfra.htm> (2002).

the United Nations Secretary General to 'inform States Parties of their commitments in respect of their assessed contributions for the first financial period of the Court'.[54] Although the Financial Regulations and Rules prepared by the Preparatory Commission giving effect to Article 113 of the Statute had not been discussed yet in the Assembly, Resolutions 11–15 dealt with criteria for voluntary contributions, budget appropriations, the Working Capital Fund, scales of assessments for the apportionment of the expenses and crediting contributions to the United Nations Trust Fund to Support the Establishment of the International Criminal Court. Importantly, Resolution 12 set the budget of the Court at €30,893,500.[55] Out of the budget approved, 22.7% was assigned to meetings of the Assembly of States Parties, subsidiary bodies and the inaugural meeting of judges.[56] To provide financial oversight to the Court in the absence of the Registrar, the Assembly agreed to appoint Bruno Cathala (France), the Deputy Registrar of the International Criminal Tribunal for the former Yugoslavia (ICTY), as Director of Common Services for the Court, effectively as interim Registrar.[57] Decision 2 regulated the scope of Cathala's responsibilities which excluded him from attending Bureau meetings, as the Registrar would do, under Article 112(5).[58]

After deciding on the financial architecture of the Court, the Working Group of the Whole turned to the report of the Preparatory Commission resulting in one decision and eight resolutions.[59] On 9 September, during the third plenary meeting, the Assembly adopted, under Article 112(2)(a), the Rules of Procedure and Evidence, Elements of Crimes, the draft relationship agreement between the Court and the United Nations, the basic principles governing a headquarters agreement to be negotiated between the Court and the host country, the Financial Regulations and Rules and the Agreement on the Privileges and Immunities of the Court.[60] Only the Rules of Procedure and Evidence, the Agreement on the Privileges and Immunities of the Court and the draft relationship agreement between the Court and the United Nations received

---

54 ICC-ASP/1/Decision 1 Provision of Funds for the Court (2002).

55 ICC-ASP/1/Res.12 Budget Appropriations for the First Financial Period and Financing of Appropriations for the First Financial Period 1.

56 Ibid.

57 Report of the First Session of the Assembly of States Parties to the Rome Statute of the International Criminal Court, New York, 3–10 September 2002, ICC-ASP/1/3 6.

58 ICC-ASP/1/Decision 2 Interim Arrangements for the Exercise of Authority Pending the Assumption of Office by the Registrar (2002) 1.

59 Report of the First Session of the Assembly of States Parties to the Rome Statute of the International Criminal Court, New York, 3–10 September 2002, ICC-ASP/1/3 5–6.

60 Ibid.

friendly amendments or comments from States, which were resolved without requiring in-depth negotiations.[61]

The Assembly concluded its third plenary meeting on 9 September by passing one decision and eight resolutions. Resolution 1 created a Special Working Group on the Crime of Aggression tasked with seeking an acceptable definition in time for the Review Conference under Article 123.[62] Resolution 1 would kick-off a lengthy negotiating process on the crime of aggression culminating in 2017 with the activation of the crime by the Assembly of States Parties.[63] While Ambach,[64] Blokker and Muller[65] argue the Special Working Group was constituted as a subsidiary body of the Assembly, unlike the Budget and Finance Committee, Resolution 1 did not invoke Article 112(4). Furthermore, given the Special Working Group was open to 'all States Members of the United Nations or members of specialized agencies',[66] it is unclear how the Assembly retained exclusive authority over its procedure and negotiated results.[67]

Resolution 2 set the overall steps for nomination and election of judges, the Prosecutor and Deputy Prosecutors,[68] and Resolution 3 the specific procedure for the election of judges.[69] The Assembly had agreed to ask the Working Group of the Whole to consider minimum voting requirements in the election of judges, partially unresolved from the Preparatory Commission.[70] To arrive at consensus, the Assembly discussed constructive amendments from France[71] and a group of States led by Brazil.[72] To resolve the impasse the agreed require-

61 Ibid 358.

62 ICC-ASP/1/Res.1 Continuity of Work in Respect of the Crime of Aggression (2002).

63 ICC-ASP/16/Res.5 Activation of the Jurisdiction of the Court Over the Crime of Aggression (2017); Kreß, Claus and Barriga, Stefan, The Crime of Aggression: A Commentary (Cambridge University Press 2016).

64 Ambach, 'Article 112 Assembly of States Parties' (2022) 2801.

65 Blokker, Niels and Muller, Sam, 'International Criminal Court' (2004) 16 Hague Yearbook of International Law/Annuaire de La Haye de Droit International 182.

66 ICC-ASP/1/Res.1 Continuity of Work in Respect of the Crime of Aggression.

67 Barriga, Stefan and Kreß, Claus, The Travaux Préparatoires of the Crime of Aggression (Cambridge University Press 2012).

68 ICC-ASP/1/Res.2 Procedure for the Nomination and Election of Judges, the Prosecutor and Deputy Prosecutors of the International Criminal Court.

69 ICC-ASP/1/Res.3 Procedure for the Election of the Judges for the International Criminal Court (2002).

70 Report of the First Session of the Assembly of States Parties to the Rome Statute of the International Criminal Court, New York, 3–10 September 2002, ICC-ASP/1/3 4.

71 Proposal Submitted by France, Election of Judges, ICC-ASP/1/L.1 (2002).

72 Proposal Submitted by Brazil, Chile, Costa Rica, Ecuador, Mexico, Nauru, Nigeria, Mongolia, Paraguay, Peru, Republic of Korea, Trinidad and Tobago and Uruguay, Election of Judges, ICC-ASP/1/L.2 (2002).

ments included a minimum number of ballots per State per judges in List A and List B, and minimum voting conditions to achieve balanced gender and geographical representation.[73] Not without confusion,[74] Nigeria, France and Spain alerted about the 'complicated nature of the voting mechanism'[75] expecting the Assembly to review it over time. In fact, the Assembly made changes to the election procedure of judges in 2004,[76] 2007[77] and 2019.[78] As the nominations period opened for judges and the Prosecutor, the Bureau warned States against the common practice[79] in international organization elections of vote trading 'in order to ensure the integrity of the electoral process'.[80]

After adopting the texts from the Preparatory Commission, creating subsidiary bodies, assembling the financial architecture of the Court, and taking action on the process to elect the bench and Prosecutor, States Parties decided on other auxiliary requirements. First, under Resolution 6 and 7, the Assembly established the Trust Fund for Victims[81] and its Board of Directors,[82] as stipulated in Article 79(1) of the Rome Statute.[83] Secondly, under Decision 3 the Assembly agreed the participation of the Court in the United Nations Joint Staff Pension Fund, including the acceptance of the jurisdiction of the United

73 ICC-ASP/1/Res.3 Procedure for the Election of the Judges for the International Criminal Court.

74 Jones, John R. W. D, 'Composition of the Court' in Cassese, Antonio, Gaeta, Paola and Jones, John RWD (eds), The Rome Statute of the International Criminal Court: a Commentary, vol 1 (Oxford University Press 2002) 246.

75 Report of the First Session of the Assembly of States Parties to the Rome Statute of the International Criminal Court, New York, 3–10 September 2002, ICC-ASP/1/3 363–364.

76 ICC-ASP/3/Res.6 Procedure for the Nomination and Election of Judges, the Prosecutor and Deputy Prosecutors of the International Criminal Court (2004).

77 ICC-ASP/5/Res.5 Procedure for the Nomination and Election of Judges, the Prosecutor and Deputy Prosecutors of the International Criminal Court: Amendment to Operative Paragraph 27 of Resolution ICC-ASP/3/Res.6 (2007).

78 ICC-ASP/18/Res.4 Resolution on the Review of the Procedure for the Nomination and Election of Judges (2019).

79 Voeten, Erik, 'The Politics of International Judicial Appointments' (2009) 9 Chicago Journal of International Law; Bosco, David, Rough Justice: The International Criminal Court in a World of Power Politics (Oxford University Press 2013) 82.

80 Report of the First Session of the Assembly of States Parties to the Rome Statute of the International Criminal Court, New York, 3–10 September 2002, ICC-ASP/1/3 7.

81 ICC-ASP/1/Res.6 Establishment of a Fund for the Benefit of Victims of Crimes Within the Jurisdiction of the Court, and of the Families of Such Victims (2002) 1.

82 ICC-ASP/1/Res.7 Procedure for the Nomination and Election of Members of the Board of Directors of the Trust Fund for the Benefit of Victims (2002).

83 Article 79(1), Rome Statute of the International Criminal Court (2002) 2187 UNTS 90.

Nations Administrative Tribunal.[84] Also related to staff issues, Resolution 10 set the basic criteria for hiring personnel, including expectations around selection, standards, competency and gender and geographical representation favouring nationals of States Parties but allowing employment of non-party State nationals.[85] Finally, Resolutions 8 and 9 asked the Bureau to make the necessary arrangements to provide secretariat services to the Assembly of States Parties,[86] while asking the United Nations to continue to provide services 'on the basis of full reimbursement'.[87] As Blokker and Muller argued, a secretariat arm for the Assembly was a necessary 'passarelle'[88] between the Court and States Parties. At the second session in 2003, the permanent Secretariat of the Assembly of States Parties was established.[89]

Undoubtedly, and far from irrelevant, the first session of the Assembly between 3 and 10 September laid the groundwork for the creation of a new international organization and shaped several of its policies and practices in the long term. As the first meeting came to a close on 10 September and the preparations for the first (February 2003) and second resumed sessions (April 2003) began, Sierra Leone reminded delegations 'the world was analysing the new international judicial institution. It was up to the Assembly to make it a success'.[90]

2.1 *Becoming a Court: The First Resumed Session (February 2003)*

The first resumption of the first session of the Assembly of States Parties took place on 3–7 February 2003 in New York. By then, the Rome Statute had added nine new States taking the Assembly from 76 to 85 members.[91] The addition of new States Parties did not alter the composition of the Bureau, except

84 ICC-ASP/1/Decision 3 Participation of the International Criminal Court in the United Nations Joint Staff Pension Fund (2002).

85 ICC-ASP/1/Res.10 Selection of the Staff of the International Criminal Court (2002) 2.

86 ICC-ASP/1/Res.9 Permanent Secretariat of the Assembly of States Parties (2002).

87 ICC-ASP/1/Res.8 Provisional Arrangements for the Secretariat of the Assembly of States Parties (2002).

88 Blokker and Muller, 183.

89 ICC-ASP/2/Res.3 Establishment of the Permanent Secretariat of the Assembly of States Parties to the International Criminal Court (2003).

90 First Session of Assembly of States Parties to International Criminal Court Concludes Work, UN Doc. L/3014.

91 Report of the First Session (First and Second Resumptions) of the Assembly of States Parties to the Rome Statute of the International Criminal Court, New York, 3–7 February and 21–23 April 2003, ICC-ASP/1/3/Add.1 3.

the decision by Germany to relinquish its seat.[92] Germany was replaced by Malta.[93] Endowed with a governance body, a budget, procedures for electing judges and the Prosecutor, an interim registrar function, an interim secretariat, the selection criteria for staff recruitment and a privileges and immunities framework, the set-up of the Court moved from institutional arrangements to electing the individuals in charge of realizing the expectations of the Rome Statute. The election of the first 18 judges and preparations for the election of the first Prosecutor were the main items in the agenda of the first resumption.[94]

The election of the first 18 judges of the Court was regulated by Article 36 of the Rome Statute and Assembly Resolutions 2 and 3 from September 2002. Nominations had to conform with specific criteria set out in Article 36(3)–(4) of the Rome Statute, briefly: high moral character, established competence in criminal law and procedure (List A) or relevant areas of international law (List B) and excellent knowledge of working languages of the Court.[95] However, Article 36(7)–(8) placed additional conditions on States Parties for the first election, namely: selecting nine candidates from List A, five from List B, ensuring no two judges were from the same nationality, and taking into consideration 'representation of the principal legal systems of the world, equitable geographical representation, fair representation of female and male judges',[96] and expertise in violence against women and children.[97] Based on these requirements, a candidate obtaining the highest number of votes and a two-thirds majority of States Parties present and voting was elected. In the words of President Prince Zeid, the election of judges was indeed a 'gruelling procedure'.[98]

By the end of the nomination period, all 43 candidacies fulfilled the minimum requirements.[99] Nominations across List A and B were fairly balanced with 23 and 22 respectively. Across regions, the majority of candidacies came

92 Assembly of States Parties to Rome Statute of International Criminal Court Opens Resumed First Session, UN Doc. L/3020 (2003). The available public record and literature does not address the reasons why Germany decided to exit the Bureau in (2003).

93 Report of the First Session (First and Second Resumptions) of the Assembly of States Parties to the Rome Statute of the International Criminal Court, New York, 3–7 February and 21–23 April 2003, ICC-ASP/1/3/Add.1 2.

94 Ibid.

95 Election of the Judges of the International Criminal Court, Note by the Secretariat, ICC-ASP/1/4 (2002) 1.

96 Ibid 2.

97 Article 36(8)(b), Rome Statute of the International Criminal Court (2002) 2187 UNTS 90.

98 Polli, 7.

99 Letter H.R.H. Prince Zeid Raíad Zeid Al-Hussein, President Assembly of States Parties to the Rome Statute of the International Criminal Court, Status of Nomination for Judges

from the Western Europe and Other States group (12) followed by Africa (10), Latin American and Caribbean (8), Eastern Europe (7) and Asia (6). Gender balance was skewed towards male candidates with only 10 nominations for female judges.[100] Curiously, only Elizabeth Odio Benito, from Costa Rica, was nominated by another State Party than her own, in this case by Panama.[101] To facilitate the election procedure, the interim secretariat prepared, as requested by Resolution 3, a guide and the ballot card containing all the voting requirements, bearing in mind that if a State Party did not comply with them, their vote would be invalid.[102] Before the election took place, President Prince Zeid reiterated, on behalf of the Bureau, that States Parties should 'refrain from entering into reciprocal arrangements for exchange of support in respect of the election'.[103] To limit any unwanted intrusion, the Assembly also agreed to bar judicial candidates from the voting venue during the election process. In 2003, President Prince Zeid maintained that the election was free from 'reciprocal agreements',[104] however, Schiff[105] and Bosco[106] have argued the opposite took place based on interviews with key witness of the election. In fact, Bosco quotes Sam Muller, a seasoned German diplomat, expecting a direct connection between budget contributions and judgeships regardless of merit.[107] As Bosco shows, the top five financial backers of the Court in 2002–2003, Germany, France, the United Kingdom, Italy and Canada, all had a judge each in the inaugural bench.[108]

Between 4 and 7 February, the Assembly delivered the first bench of the International Criminal Court after 33 rounds of balloting (see Table 5.2).[109]

---

and Prosecutor, available at: <https://legal.un.org/icc/electionsjudges/noticeletter_30%20november(e).pdf> (2002) 1.

100 Election of the Judges of the International Criminal Court, Note by the Secretariat, ICC-ASP/1/4 3–7.

101 Ibid.

102 Election of the Judges for the International Criminal Court: Guide for the First Election, Note by the Secretariat, ICC-ASP/1/5 (2002) 1.

103 Report of the First Session (First and Second Resumptions) of the Assembly of States Parties to the Rome Statute of the International Criminal Court, New York, 3–7 February and 21–23 April 2003, ICC-ASP/1/3/Add.1 3.

104 Polli, 7.

105 Schiff, 107.

106 Bosco, 82.

107 Ibid.

108 Ibid.

109 Report of the First Session (First and Second Resumptions) of the Assembly of States Parties to the Rome Statute of the International Criminal Court, New York, 3–7 February and 21–23 April 2003, ICC-ASP/1/3/Add.1 4.

Several factors were at play during the first election: satisfying statutory requirements, ticking all conditions for a valid vote, a primer experience at elections for the Assembly, the large quantity of vacancies and the seemingly short allocation of time for a complex procedure.[110] Another key element to consider was the recurring adjustment of the two-third majority needed from States Parties as 24 candidates withdrew across the 33 rounds of ballots.[111] For example, French candidate Claude Jorda was elected at the 33rd round with the lowest number of States Parties needed for the two-third majority (54) after four abstentions were received, and only after the Croatian candidate withdrew at the last moment.[112] Confusion over minimum List A/B, gender, regional and expertise requirements meant that States Parties introduced invalid votes in three of the eight rounds where candidates were successfully elected (rounds 1, 3 and 4).[113] Nevertheless, the results delivered the 18 judges during the planned resumed session and historically elected seven women, an achievement in gender parity within international courts, and international criminal courts in particular.[114] Once the inaugural judges were elected, following Article 36(9)(b) and Resolution 2 from 2002, the Assembly President drew lots to determine which individuals should serve a 3, 6 and 9 year term.[115]

Once the election of judges was concluded, the Assembly turned to preparations for the election of the Prosecutor. After receiving no nominations for the position of Prosecutor by November 2002,[116] under the procedure described in Resolution 2,[117] the President of the Assembly extended the nomination period twice until 4 April 2003.[118] While official Assembly documents describe a certain apathy among States Parties to put forward a candidate for the Office of the Prosecutor, in reality, President Prince Zeid was

---

110 States Parties to International Criminal Court Elect Final Four Judges; in Total, 18 Selected, Requiring 33 Ballots Over Four Days, UN Doc. L/3026 (2003).

111 Election of the Judges of the International Criminal Court, Results First Election, First Resumed Session of the Assembly of States Parties, 3–7 February, available at: <https://legal.un.org/icc/asp/aspfra.htm> (2003).

112 Ibid.

113 Ibid.

114 Grossman, Nienke, 'Achieving Sex-Representative International Court Benches' (2016) 110 (1) American Journal of International Law 83.

115 Ibid.

116 Ibid 6.

117 ICC-ASP/1/Res.2 Procedure for the Nomination and Election of Judges, the Prosecutor and Deputy Prosecutors of the International Criminal Court.

118 Report of the First Session (First and Second Resumptions) of the Assembly of States Parties to the Rome Statute of the International Criminal Court, New York, 3–7 February and 21–23 April 2003, ICC-ASP/1/3/Add.1 6.

TABLE 5.2 First election of judges (2003)

Day	Round	Votes / required majority	Candidate[a]	Nationality	Gender	List	Term of office
4 February	1	65/56	Maureen Harding Clark	Ireland	Female	A	9
	1	65/56	Fatoumata Dembele Diarra	Mali	Female	A	9
	1	60/56	Elizabeth Odio Benito	Costa Rica	Female	A	9
	1	63/56	Sang-hyun Song	Republic of Korea	Male	A	3
	1	61/56	Sylvia H. de Figueiredo Steiner	Brazil	Female	A	9
	1	60/56	Akua Kuenyehia	Ghana	Female	B	3
	1	56/56	Navanethem Pillay	South Africa	Female	B	6
5 February	3	56/56	Karl T. Hudson-Phillips	Trinidad and Tobago	Male	A	9
6 February	4	60/56	Gheorghios M. Pikis	Cyprus	Male	A	6
	4	57/56	Philippe Kirsch	Canada	Male	B	6
	4	56/56	Erkki Kourula	Finland	Male	B	3
7 February	9	59/57	Adrian Fulford	United Kingdom	Male	A	9
	9	57/57	Hans-Peter Kaul	Germany	Male	B	3
	9	59/57	Anita Usacka	Latvia	Female	B	3
	13	57/56	René Blattmann	Bolivia	Male	B	6
	21	58/57	Mauro Politi	Italy	Male	B	6
	28	58/57	Tuiloma Neroni Slade	Samoa	Male	A	3
	33	57/54	Claude Jorda	France	Male	A	6

a Report of the First Session (First and Second Resumptions) of the Assembly of States Parties to the Rome Statute of the International Criminal Court, New York, 3–7 February and 21–23 April 2003, ICC-ASP/1/3/Add.1 5.

leading informal consultations with Luis Moreno Ocampo from Argentina for the position since November 2002.[119] As Moreno Ocampo retells, he visited the Jordanian embassy in New York on 'a cold morning in December 2002' to

119 Moreno Ocampo, Luis, War and Justice in the 21st Century: A Case Study on the International Criminal Court and its Interaction with the War on Terror (Oxford University Press 2022) 17.

'discuss whether I would be interested in the job'.[120] However, due to lack of consensus among States Parties in January and February 2003, President Prince Zeid asked Moreno Ocampo to 'keep considering the possibility'.[121] After the inaugural meeting and swearing-in of the judges on 11 March 2003, Moreno Ocampo obtained the backing from Argentina and toured several European capitals to gather support.[122] Shortly after, on 24 March, Assembly President Prince Zeid issued a press release announcing 'on Friday 21 March 2003, the States Parties to the Rome Statute of the International Criminal Court agreed informally, and on the basis of consensus, to elect at the forthcoming resumed session of the Assembly of States Parties, Mr. Luis Moreno Ocampo, of Argentina, as prosecutor of the International Criminal Court'.[123] In this context, 87 States Parties[124] met in New York between 21 and 23 April to elect the first Prosecutor of the Court.[125]

2.2 *Completing the Court: The Second Resumed Session (April 2003)*

By the time the second resumption took place in New York between 21 and 23 April 2003, the first 18 judges of the International Criminal Court were more than a month into their assignment[126] and 22 staff members from 18 countries were employed in The Hague.[127] In this context of rapid operational development, the most important task of the second resumption of the first session of the Assembly was to complete the Court's organigram with the election of the Prosecutor and to transmit a recommendation to the judges for the election of

120 Ibid.

121 Ibid 23.

122 Ibid.

123 Statement by the President of the Assembly of States Parties Prince Zeid Raíad Zeid Al-Hussein, Press Release, ICC-20030411-5 (2003).

124 Delegations to the Second Resumed First Session of the Assembly of States Parties to the Rome Statute of the International Criminal Court, New York, 3–7 February 2003, ICC-ASP/1/INF.I/Add.2 (2003).

125 Report of the First Session (First and Second Resumptions) of the Assembly of States Parties to the Rome Statute of the International Criminal Court, New York, 3–7 February and 21–23 April 2003, ICC-ASP/1/3/Add.1 6.

126 States Parties to International Criminal Court to Meet at Headquarters, 21–23 April, UN Doc. L/3034 (2003).

127 Statement by Judge Philippe Kirsch, President of the International Criminal Court, Assembly of States Parties to the Rome Statute of the International Criminal Court, New York, 22 April 2003, available at <https://legal.un.org/icc/asp/firstresumed.Apr03.htm> (2003) 2.

the Registrar.[128] Compared to the February meeting, the Assembly welcomed two new States Parties: Barbados and Saint Vincent and the Grenadines, taking it to a total of 87 members.[129] There was no change in the Bureau.[130]

The election of the first Prosecutor of the International Criminal Court was a closely watched event by States Parties and non-party States alike. The complex negotiations from Rome still reverberated in the United Nations Headquarters and the known opposition from the United States to the Court, partly due to the role of the Prosecutor, was palpable.[131] By 21 March 2003, States Parties had agreed by consensus to the election of Luis Moreno Ocampo.[132] The press release from Assembly President Prince Zeid described a selection process made up of 'lengthy consultations between governments' focusing on a 'number of strong contenders'.[133] The public record from the Assembly of States Parties does not reveal which candidates were considered; however, there was media speculation about 'six or seven'[134] options, including Carla del Ponte, Reginald Blanch and unnamed nominees from Brazil, Canada, Gambia and South Africa. Before the last nomination window opened on 24 March 2003,[135] States Parties settled on Moreno Ocampo describing him as a 'gifted prosecutor with proven abilities; a man of recognized integrity'.[136] On 4 April 2003, the closing day for candidacies, Argentina formally nominated Moreno Ocampo.[137] Although the Assembly had signalled a preference that nominations be supported by several States Parties and Resolution 2 included

128 Report of the First Session (First and Second Resumptions) of the Assembly of States Parties to the Rome Statute of the International Criminal Court, New York, 3–7 February and 21–23 April 2003, ICC-ASP/1/3/Add.1 2.

129 Ibid 3.

130 Ibid 1.

131 Ferencz, Benjamin B, 'The International Criminal Court: the First Year and Future Prospects' (2003) 97 America Society of International Law Proceedings 259.

132 Statement by the President of the Assembly of States Parties Prince Zeid Raíad Zeid Al-Hussein, Press Release, ICC-20030411-5.

133 Ibid.

134 Report of the First Session (First and Second Resumptions) of the Assembly of States Parties to the Rome Statute of the International Criminal Court, New York, 3–7 February and 21–23 April 2003, ICC-ASP/1/3/Add.1 6.

135 Ibid.

136 Statement by the President of the Assembly of States Parties Prince Zeid Raíad Zeid Al-Hussein, Press Release, ICC-20030411-5.

137 Mision Permanente de la Republica Argentina ante las Naciones Unidas, Carta al Sr Secretario General de las Naciones Unidas, Kofi Annan, NU 60/03/619 701 RLB/jlI, available at <http://legal.un.org/icc/elections/prosecutor/moreno_ocampo/moreno_ocampo.htm> (2003).

the same wording,[138] Moreno Ocampo was only nominated by his home nation.[139]

The election of the Prosecutor was regulated by Article 42(4) of the Rome Statute, Rule 86 of the Rules of Procedure of the Assembly of States Parties, and Resolution 2 from 2002 on the procedure for voting. The interim secretariat prepared a paper for States Parties describing the regulatory framework and highlighted the statutory requirements for the post.[140] The Prosecutor should be a person of 'high moral character, be highly competent in and have extensive practical experience in the prosecution or trial of criminal cases, as well as having an excellent knowledge of and be fluent in at least one of the working languages of the Court'.[141]

Unlike subsequent elections for the Office of the Prosecutor, in 2003, there was no vetting procedure to evaluate how Moreno Ocampo fulfilled the criteria in the Rome Statute.[142] While Rule 86[143] of Assembly procedure and Resolution 2[144] required a statement of qualifications, they were silent on the need for an assessment of any kind. A note by the interim secretariat was available to States Parties detailing how 'the candidate fulfils the requirements of paragraph 3 of Article 42 of the Statute'.[145] However, the document only described Moreno Ocampo's curriculum vitae only. It was far from an assessment of alignment to statutory criteria for the position. For Morten Bergsmo the election process of the first Prosecutor of the Court was done in 'an almost careless manner'.[146]

---

138 ICC-ASP/1/Res.2 Procedure for the Nomination and Election of Judges, the Prosecutor and Deputy Prosecutors of the International Criminal Court 4.

139 Election of the Prosecutor of the International Criminal Court, Note by the Secretariat, Addendum, ICC-ASP/1/6/Add.1 (2003) 1.

140 Election of the Prosecutor of the International Criminal Court, Note by the Secretariat, ICC-ASP/1/6 (2002) 1.

141 Ibid.

142 Mudukuti, Angela, 'The Procedure for Appointing the International Criminal Court Prosecutor: High Moral Character and the Need for Comprehensive Vetting' (2021) 19 (4) Journal of International Criminal Justice

143 Rule 86, Rules of Procedure of the Assembly of States Parties, ICC-ASP/1/3.

144 ICC-ASP/1/Res.2 Procedure for the Nomination and Election of Judges, the Prosecutor and Deputy Prosecutors of the International Criminal Court 4.

145 Election of the Prosecutor of the International Criminal Court, Note by the Secretariat, Addendum, ICC-ASP/1/6/Add.1

146 Bergsmo, (2017) 25.

On 21 April 2003, the President of the Assembly thanked States Parties for avoiding a 'contested election',[147] and proceeded to opening the secret balloting. The Rome Statute mandated an absolute majority for the election of the Prosecutor. At the second resumed meeting, the International Criminal Court had 87 States Parties, which meant 44 represented an absolute majority. Luis Moreno Ocampo was successfully elected after receiving 78 votes out of 78 valid ballots.[148] Since votes were secret it is not possible to uncover who were the remaining eight States Parties that did not participate. The Assembly further decided on 21 April, following Article 42(4), to afford a nine-year term to Moreno Ocampo marking the beginning of his term of office from 16 June 2003.[149] In his speech to the Assembly of States Parties, the newly elected Prosecutor wished the 'Assembly to rest assured that I will indeed exercise my functions with caution and within the strict limits provided for in the Statute'.[150] Learning from this experience, the Bureau devised a different and more robust process for the election of the second and third Prosecutor of the Court in 2011 and 2021.[151]

After electing the Prosecutor, the Assembly completed the organigram by making their recommendation to the judges regarding the election of the Registrar. Article 43(4) in the Rome Statute required the judges to take into account 'any recommendation by the Assembly of States Parties',[152] before electing a Registrar by absolute majority during a plenary session 'as soon as possible'[153] as per Rule 12 of the Rules of Evidence and Procedure of the Court. The President of the Court, Philippe Kirsch, was responsible for transmitting to the Assembly 'a list of candidates who satisfied the criteria laid down in article 43, paragraph 3'[154] requesting States Parties to make a recommendation

147 States Parties to Rome Statute Elect Luis Moreno Ocampo as Prosecutor of International Criminal Court, UN Doc. L/3035 (2003).

148 Report of the First Session (First and Second Resumptions) of the Assembly of States Parties to the Rome Statute of the International Criminal Court, New York, 3–7 February and 21–23 April 2003, ICC-ASP/1/3/Add.1 6.

149 Ibid.

150 Statement Made by Mr. Luis Moreno Ocampo, Assembly of States Parties to the Rome Statute of the International Criminal Court, New York, 22 April 2003, available at <https://legal.un.org/icc/asp/firstresumed.Apr03.htm> (2003) 6.

151 Search Committee for the Position of the Prosecutor of the International Criminal Court, Terms of Reference, ICC-ASP/9/INF.2 (2010);'Assembly of States Parties to the Rome Statute, Election of Prosecutor (2020), available at: <https://asp.icc-cpi.int/elections/prosecutor/Prosecutor2020>' accessed 5 January 2024.

152 Article 43(4), Rome Statute of the International Criminal Court (2002) 2187 UNTS 90.

153 Rule 12, Rules of Procedure and Evidence, ICC-PIOS-LT-03-004/19.

154 Rule 12, Rules of Procedure and Evidence, ICC-PIOS-LT-03-004/19.

to the judges. To curate the list of candidates, the President of the Court had to assess each nominee be a person of high moral character, highly competent and have proficient command and fluency of at least one working language of the Court.[155] To this effect, on 15 April 2003, Kirsch transmitted two nominations to the Assembly: Bruno Cathala (France), the interim Registrar of the Court, and that of Bert Maan, President of Zwolle-Lelystad District Court in the Netherlands.[156] Neither the Statute nor the Rules of Procedure of the Assembly granted any vetting powers to States Parties and limited their action to issuing a recommendation. Led by Vice President Felipe Paolillo from Uruguay, the Assembly agreed the judges proceed with the election based on the two candidates put forward.[157] For Blokker and Muller, in reality, the Assembly simply 'took note'[158] of the candidates without any intervention. On 24 June 2003, Bruno Cathala was elected for a five-year term by the plenary of the judges.[159] As Muller showed, with the appointment of Cathala, 'the three most senior managers of the Court were in place one year and four days after work had started'.[160]

Apart from completing the organigram of the Court, the Assembly also appointed the external auditor,[161] proceeded with the election of the 12 members of the Committee on Budget and Finance,[162] and opened the nomination period for the Trust Fund for Victims Board of Directors.[163] With the conclusion of the second resumed meeting on 23 April 2003, the first session of the Assembly of States Parties culminated. The construction plan for the Court devised by the Preparatory Commission was closely actioned by States Parties setting-up the regulatory framework of the Assembly and by placing all elected officials in post. The International Criminal Court was ready, as Assembly President Prince Zeid Raíad Zeid Al-Hussein explained in the clos-

---

155 Article 43(3), Rome Statute of the International Criminal Court (2002) 2187 UNTS 90.

156 Election of the Registrar of the International Criminal Court, Note by the Secretariat, ICC-ASP/1/11 (2003) 1.

157 Report of the First Session (First and Second Resumptions) of the Assembly of States Parties to the Rome Statute of the International Criminal Court, New York, 3–7 February and 21–23 April 2003, ICC-ASP/1/3/Add.1 7.

158 Blokker and Muller, 180.

159 Bruno Cathala of France Elected Registrar of International Criminal Court, UN Doc. L/3041 (2003).

160 Muller, 195.

161 Report of the First Session (First and Second Resumptions) of the Assembly of States Parties to the Rome Statute of the International Criminal Court, New York, 3–7 February and 21–23 April 2003, ICC-ASP/1/3/Add.1 7.

162 Ibid 7–8.

163 Ibid 9.

ing meeting, to 'set in motion the criminal justice processes that had been carefully elaborated in the Rome Statute'.[164] In a similar way, the Assembly and its Bureau were dully established to provide 'management oversight to the Presidency, the Prosecutor and the Registrar regarding the administration of the Court'.[165] For the next 20 years, the Assembly would find governing the expectations and possibilities afforded in the Rome Statute a challenging venture.[166]

3 Governance and Management Oversight Practice (2002–2021)

By virtue of the Rome Statute, the Assembly of States Parties is the 'management oversight and legislative body of the International Criminal Court'.[167] This function of the Assembly can be found across the Statute. Articles 112 (1)–(10) and 119(2) in terms of structure and overall powers, Articles 2 and 3(2) for the approval of the relationship agreements with the United Nations and the host country and Articles 46(2), 47 and 112(2)(b) for the responsibility to provide management oversight to elected officials. In this context, this section focuses on these provisions in order to situate the key aspects how States Parties are organized as a collective. Additional relevant powers such as financial oversight, elections and enforcement of cooperation will be tackled separately given their prominence in the Assembly's governance towards the Court.

3.1 *Governance Structure*

A joint reading of Articles 112(1), (6), (7), (9) and (10) describes the overall structure of the Assembly of States Parties (see Table 5.3). Membership is determined by States that have ratified the Rome Statute whereas each State Party has one vote. Article 112(1) allows States that have signed the Statute or the Final Act of the Rome Conference to become non-voting observers of the Assembly. As per Article 112(6), the Assembly meets annually or in special

---

164 States Parties to International Criminal Court Conclude Session With Adoption of Draft Report, UN Doc. L/3038 (2003).

165 Article 112(2)(b), Rome Statute of the International Criminal Court (2002) 2187 UNTS 90.

166 Prince Zeid Raíad Zeid Al-Hussein, Stagno Ugarte, Bruno, Wenaweser, Christian and Intelman, Tiina, 'The International Criminal Court Needs Fixing' (Atlantic Council, 2019) <https://www.atlanticcouncil.org/blogs/new-atlanticist/the-international-criminal-court-needs-fixing> accessed 24 April 2019.

167 'Assembly of States Parties to the Rome Statute, About, available at: <https://asp.icc-cpi.int/assembly>' accessed 4 January 2024.

TABLE 5.3 Governance and management oversight

Function	Responsibilities	Relevant articles
Governance Structure	Membership, Rules of Procedure, sessions, leadership, subsidiary bodies and working groups, decision-making, settlement of disputes, political role and permanent Secretariat	112(1)–(10), 119(2)
Relationships Agreements	Relationship with the United Nations and the host State	2, 3(2)
Management of Elected Officials	Management oversight of the President, Prosecutor and Registrar	112(2)(b), 112(4), 112(5)

sessions at the seat of the Court or at the United Nations. The working languages of the Assembly, covered in Article 112(10), correspond with those of the General Assembly of the United Nations. The Assembly under Article 112(9) has the power to agree on its own rules of procedure to guide its work and of any subsidiary body. To assist the Assembly, the governance structure includes a 21–member elected Bureau and the power to create subsidiary bodies under Article 112(4). Between 2002 and 2021 the governance structure of the Assembly remained stable albeit its membership evolved significantly.

3.1.1 Membership and Universality

In terms of membership, the rapid pace of ratifications after 1998 did not recede immediately after the first session, but it did find an attrition point after 2011. By the end of the 20th session of the Assembly in 2021, there were 123 States Parties. The pinnacle of membership occurred in 2016 during the 15th session with 124 members. In 2017 and 2019 Burundi and the Philippines withdrew from the Rome Statute as per Article 127. At the moment of writing in January 2024, but outside the scope of this book, the Assembly welcomed Armenia as the 124th member during the 23rd session. As shown in Figure 5.1, the pace of accession concentrated in the 1999–2002 period with a slower pace every year between 2002 and 2021 with an exception in 2011.[168]

168 United Nations Treaty Collection, Depositary of Notifications, Rome Statute of the International Criminal Court, available at <https://treaties.un.org/>.

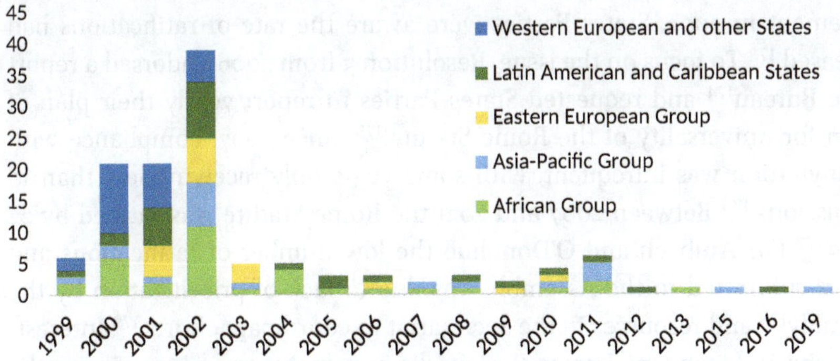

FIGURE 5.1 Accession to the Rome Statute (until 2021)

Of the 123 members in 2021, the Africa regional group was the largest represented in the Assembly with 33 States. The regional composition of the Assembly mattered greatly as it affected the allocation of seats in the Bureau, subsidiary bodies and the election of judges. However, States Parties faced challenges to adhere to the principle of regional rotation agreed in 2002. For example, during the 19th session, the Africa regional group voiced concerns at the proposal to elect Canada and Czech Republic as Vice-Presidents, noting the same regional groups had already performed the role between 2018 and 2021. As the largest regional group in the Assembly, African States Parties hoped to be included in the Bureau as 'many cases before the Court were from the African continent'.[169] Ultimately, Canada and Czech Republic were elected by the Assembly by consensus without dispelling the appropriate question raised by the Africa regional group. In addition, the Assembly consensus building mechanism was highly dependent on agreements and tactical arrangements within regional groups. For example, nominations for the Budget and Finance Committee tended to be uncontested because of prior tactical agreements.[170] However, as with the Bureau, African States Parties questioned the imbalance of regional representation in the Budget and Finance Committee.[171] In 2023, the Assembly rectified this issue by expanding the Committee's membership to 17 seats.[172]

The Assembly of States Parties made the universality of the Rome Statute a strategic objective in 2005 during the fourth session. Past the point of

169 Bureau of the Assembly of States Parties, 20th Meeting, 5 February 2021 (2021) 2.

170 de Hoon and Lohne, (2019) 60.

171 Bureau of the Assembly of States Parties, 9th Meeting, 9 November 2022 (2022) 2.

172 ICC-ASP/22/Res.8 Resolution on the Election of Members to the Committee on Budget and Finance of the International Criminal Court (2023).

excitement in 2002, States Parties were aware the rate of ratifications had decreased.[173] To focus on the issue, Resolution 3 from 2006 endorsed a report of the Bureau[174] and requested States Parties to report yearly their plan of action for universality of the Rome Statute.[175] Since 2007, compliance with this invitation was infrequent, with some years only receiving less than 10 submissions.[176] Between 2007 and 2021 the Rome Statute was ratified by 22 States.[177] For Ambach and O'Donohue the low number of ratifications and reports submitted to the Assembly was due to lack of prioritization by the Assembly[178] and resources in the Secretariat to coordinate efforts.[179] Interestingly, the Independent Expert Review did not make any comment on the challenges of the Assembly to increase its membership.[180]

Article 112(1) is also relevant to describe the membership of the Assembly of States Parties between 2002 and 2021 (see Table 5.4). Each State Party has one representative accompanied by alternates and advisers. The composition of delegations heavily featured diplomats based in The Hague or New York rather than a specific and permanent post for matters in the Assembly, Bureau or wider Court.[181] Unlike the preparatory process when a relatively permanent group of government officials participated sustainably for many years, delegates to the Assembly tended to rotate or share their appointment with other Hague or New York-based international organizations.[182] As with any diplomatic posting, the Assembly, Bureau and subsidiary bodies have been

173 ICC-ASP/4/Res.4 Strengthening the International Criminal Court and the Assembly of States Parties (2005) 2.

174 Report of the Bureau on Ratification and Implementation of the Rome Statute and on Participation in the Assembly of States Parties, ICC-ASP/5/26 (2006) 4.

175 ICC-ASP/5/Res.3 Strengthening the International Criminal Court and the Assembly of States Parties 1.

176 Assembly of States Parties to the Rome Statute, Plan of Action (Replies), Election Results, available at: <https://asp.icc-cpi.int/sessions/plan-of-action> accessed 5 January 2024.

177 United Nations Treaty Collection, Depositary of Notifications, Rome Statute of the International Criminal Court, available at <https://treaties.un.org/>.

178 Ambach, 'Article 112 Assembly of States Parties' (2022) 2785.

179 O'Donohue, 'The ICC and the ASP' (2015) 134–135.

180 Report of the Independent Expert Review of the International Criminal Court and the Rome Statute System, ICC-ASP/19/16 13.

181 Assembly of States Parties to the Rome Statute, Composition of the Bureau 2002–2019, available at: <https://asp.icc-cpi.int/sites/asp/files/asp_docs/Bureau/ASP1-17_Bureau Members-ENG.pdf> accessed 5 January 2024.

182 Václav, Vlček, 'How Many and Why? Size Variation of National Delegations to Plenary Meetings of International Organizations' (2021) 56 (1) Czech Journal of International Relations 8.

TABLE 5.4 States Parties to the Rome Statute (December 2021)

Total	123	Withdrawals
African Group	33	Burundi (2017)
Asia-Pacific Group	19	Philippines (2019)
Eastern European Group	18	
Latin American and Caribbean States	28	
Western European and other States	25	

impacted by departures during regular meetings and the intersessional period.[183] Bergsmo has argued the combination of insufficient skills to oversee a 'multi-faceted international criminal jurisdiction'[184] coupled with the diplomatic practice of rotating personnel has affected the adequate governance quality of the Court.

3.1.2 Rules of Procedure

The Rules of Procedure of the Assembly applied to the Assembly, Bureau and any subsidiary body, effectively regulating all States Parties' activities.[185] In other words, the Rules administered the 'functioning of the organization'.[186] In this context, between 2001 and 2021, the Assembly made three modifications to its procedural rules in 2008, 2013 and 2019. During the seventh session in 2008, Rule 40 on 'languages of decisions and other documents'[187] was amended so publications reflected 'all languages of the Assembly which are also the official languages of at least one State Party'.[188] In effect, the amend-

183 See for example: Bureau of the Assembly of States Parties, 9th Meeting, 7 July 2008 (2008); Bureau of the Assembly of States Parties, 13th Meeting, 13 September 2010 (2010); Bureau of the Assembly of States Parties, 4th Meeting, 23 March 2011 (2011); Bureau of the Assembly of States Parties, 6th Meeting, 19 September 2016 (2016); Bureau of the Assembly of States Parties, 4th Meeting, 9 March 2018 (2018); Bureau of the Assembly of States Parties, 20th Meeting, 5 February 2021.

184 Bergsmo, Morten, Buis, Emiliano J, Gordon, Gregory S, Inder, Brigid, Kaleck, Wolfgang, Ekeløve-Slydal, Gunnar M and Tianying, Song, 'ICC State-Party Governance in Times of Disunity' (2023) Policy Brief Series No. 146 Torkel Opsahl Academic EPublisher 3.

185 Rules of Procedure of the Assembly of States Parties, ICC-ASP/1/3 316.

186 Karns, Margaret P, 'General Assemblies and Assemblies of States Parties' in Cogan, Jacob Katz, Hurd, Ian and Johnstone, Ian (eds), The Oxford Handbook of International Organizations (Oxford University Press 2016) 780.

187 Rules of Procedure of the Assembly of States Parties, ICC-ASP/1/3 323.

188 Ibid.

ment limited Article 112(10) applying the working languages of the United Nations General Assembly,[189] as no State Party in 2008 had Russian or Chinese as an official language. Resolution 6[190] represented 'substantial savings by avoiding unnecessary translations of documents' amounting to '€254,000'.[191]

The second amendment during the 12th session in 2013 modified Rule 29 in order to allow more time for an effective transition between different compositions of the Bureau between regular sessions.[192] As per Rule 96, the Bureau supported the amendment to 'allow an incoming President of the Assembly and Bureau members to commence preparations for the next Assembly well in advance of the date of that session'.[193] The third amendment occurred in 2019 also on Bureau composition, allowing an interim election of a Vice-President should a vacancy arise during the intersessional period.[194] Faced with the resignation of Momar Diop (Senegal) as first Vice-President in March 2018,[195] the Bureau had to deal with a substantial absence of a key executive position. To remedy the situation, the Assembly approved the amendment at the 18th session.[196]

3.1.3 Meetings of the Assembly

In terms of typology of meetings of the Assembly, Article 112(6) in the Rome Statute mandates States Parties to gather annually 'at the seat of the Court or at the Headquarters of the United Nations' (see Table 5.5).[197] It also allows the Assembly to 'hold special sessions'[198] when circumstances require, and Article 123(1) stipulates a Review Conference as a third kind of meeting.[199] The typ-

189 Article 112(10), Rome Statute of the International Criminal Court (2002) 2187 UNTS 90.

190 ICC-ASP/7/Res.6 Amendment to the Rules of Procedure of the Assembly of States Parties (2008).

191 Report of the Seventh Session of the Assembly of States Parties to the Rome Statute of the International Criminal Court, The Hague, 14–22 November 2008, Volume II, ICC-ASP /7/20 (2008) 230.

192 ICC-ASP/12/Res.8 Strengthening the International Criminal Court and the Assembly of States Parties (2013) 68.

193 Bureau of the Assembly of States Parties, 2nd Meeting, 20 March 2013 (2013) 4.

194 Bureau of the Assembly of States Parties, 10th Meeting, 12 November 2019 (2019) 5.

195 Assembly of States Parties to the Rome Statute, Composition of the Bureau 2002–2019, available at: <https://asp.icc-cpi.int/sites/asp/files/asp_docs/Bureau/ASP1-17_Bureau Members-ENG.pdf> 7.

196 ICC-ASP/18/Res.6 Strengthening the International Criminal Court and the Assembly of States Parties (2019) 13, 25.

197 Article 112(6), Rome Statute of the International Criminal Court (2002) 2187 UNTS 90.

198 Article 112(6), Rome Statute of the International Criminal Court (2002) 2187 UNTS 90.

199 Article 123(1), Rome Statute of the International Criminal Court (2002) 2187 UNTS 90.

TABLE 5.5 Assembly of States Parties meetings (2002–2021)

Total	32
Regular sessions	20
Resumed sessions	11
Special sessions	–
Review conference	1
Sessions in The Hague	14
Sessions in New York	17
Session elsewhere	1 (Kampala, Uganda)

ology of meeting including regular, special or the Review Conference are distinct from resumed sessions under Rule 7. A resumed session corresponds to a temporary adjournment of a regular session. Thus, between 2002 and 2021, the Assembly held 32 meetings in total: 20 regular sessions plus 11 resumed sessions and one Review Conference.

In terms of location, following Article 112(6), the Assembly has favoured meeting in New York (17) over The Hague (14), albeit not disproportionally. Sessions in New York have been favoured due to a larger presence of diplomatic missions than in the Netherlands, especially during elections.[200] The only case of a meeting outside Article 112(6) was during the Review Conference in 2010, hosted by the government of Uganda in Kampala. However, during the Covid-19 pandemic, the Assembly was forced to adapt to a hybrid situation.[201] In terms of gathering in a special session, the Assembly had not utilized this option between 2002 and 2021 although the Bureau received requests from Kenya (2013[202] and 2014),[203] Uganda (2013)[204] and the State of Palestine (2019)[205] ultimately deciding against organizing them. Finally, the Assembly of States Parties debated between the 18th and 20th session the 'challenges

200 Villacis, 565.

201 ICC-ASP/19/Res.4 Resolution on the Procedure for Adoption of Decisions by the Assembly During the Nineteenth Session of the Assembly of States Parties to the Rome Statute Owing to the Coronavirus Disease (COVID-19) Pandemic (2020).

202 Bureau of the Assembly of States Parties, 7th Meeting, 8 July 2013 (2013) 3.

203 Bureau of the Assembly of States Parties, 15th Meeting, 5 December 2014 (2014) 1.

204 Bureau of the Assembly of States Parties, 18th Meeting, 26 November 2013 (2013) 1.

205 Bureau of the Assembly of States Parties, 4th Meeting, 7 May 2019 (2019) 4.

and benefits'[206] of its meeting in The Hague and New York.[207] States Parties were concerned about the lengthy timeline to approve the Court's budget and the difficulty of attracting high-level delegates during the month of December.[208] However, up until the 20th session in 2021 no final decision was made to change the organization of Assembly meetings.

3.1.4 Election of the President, Vice-Presidents and Bureau

Article 112(3)(a) created a Bureau composed of an elected President, two Vice-Presidents and 18 members at large. Between 2002 and 2021, the Assembly elected seven Bureau compositions following a three-year term as per Article 112(3)(a), albeit taking into account an anomaly due to the Covid-19 pandemic (see Table 5.6). In 2020, the Assembly agreed to extend the Bureau's mandate beyond 'the completion of the Bureau's three-year term falls'[209] in order to complete overseeing the election of the third Prosecutor and six new judges.[210] The Statute and the Rules of Procedure of the Assembly are silent on the possibility of re-election of the Bureau, including the President and two Vice-Presidents, for subsequent three-year terms. In the first 20 sessions, States Parties have followed regional rotation every three years, however, in 2017 some States considered re-appointing Sidiki Kaba from Senegal to a second term as President to focus on repairing the Court's relationship with the African Union.[211]

The presidency of the Assembly has been held by each regional group, with the Asia-Pacific and Latin American and Caribbean groups exerting the position twice (see Table 5.7). On the other hand, the vice-presidencies have been held by all regional groups except Asia-Pacific. Although, unlike judgeships, gender parity is not part of the election requirements of the Bureau, it is worth pointing out that of 24 diplomats playing a leadership role in the Assembly,

206 ICC-ASP/18/Res.6 Strengthening the International Criminal Court and the Assembly of States Parties 13.

207 Report of the Bureau on the Scheduling of Assembly Sessions, ICC-ASP/20/33 (2021).

208 Report of the Bureau on the Scheduling of Assembly Sessions, ICC-ASP/19/36 (2020).

209 ICC-ASP/19/Res.5 Resolution Concerning a Possible Second Resumption of the Nineteenth Session of the Assembly and the Term of the Current Bureau in Relation Thereto (2020) 1.

210 Report of the Nineteenth Session (First and Second Resumptions) of the Assembly of States Parties to the Rome Statute of the International Criminal Court, New York, 17–23 December 2020 and 12 February 2021, ICC-ASP/19/20/Add.1 (2021).

211 Diplomatic Row Over Possible Second Term for Kaba as President of ICC States (Journalists For Justice, 2017) <https://jfjustice.net/diplomatic-row-over-possible-second-term-for-kaba-as-president-of-icc-states/#> accessed 15 June 2019.

TABLE 5.6 Assembly of States Parties Bureau Leadership (2002–2021)

Sessions	President	First Vice President	Second Vice President
ASP 1–3 (2002–2004)	H.R.H. Prince Zeid Raíad Zeid Al-Hussein (Jordan)	Mr. Allieu Ibrahim Kanu (Sierra Leone)	Mr. Felipe Paolillo (Uruguay)
ASP 4–6 (2005–2008)	Mr. Bruno Stagno Ugarte (Costa Rica)	Mr. Erwin Kubesch (Austria)	Ms. Hlengiwe Mkhize (South Africa)
ASP 7–9 (2008–2010)	Mr. Christian Wenaweser (Liechtenstein)	Mr. Jorge Lomonaco (Mexico)	Mr. Zachary D. Muburi-Muita (Kenya), Ms. Simona Mirela Miculescu (Romania)
ASP 10–12 (2011–2013)	Ms. Tiina Intelmann (Estonia)	Mr. Markus Börlin (Switzerland)	Mr. Ken Kanda (Ghana)
ASP 13–16 (2014–2017)	Mr. Sidiki Kaba (Senegal)	Mr. Álvaro Moerzinger (Uruguay), Mr. Sergio Ugalde (Costa Rica)	Mr. Sebastiano Cardi (Italy)
ASP 17–19 (2018–2020)	Mr. O-Gon Kwon (Republic of Korea)	Mr. Momar Diop (Senegal), Mr. Jens-Otto Horslund (Denmark)	Mr. Michal Mlynár (Slovakia)
ASP 20 (-22) 2021 (-2023)[a]	Ms. Silvia Fernández de Gurmendi (Argentina)	Mr. Robert Keith Rae (Canada)	Ms. Kateřina Sequensová (Czech Republic)

a Report of the Nineteenth Session (First and Second Resumptions) of the Assembly of States Parties to the Rome Statute of the International Criminal Court, New York, 17–23 December 2020 and 12 February 2021, ICC-ASP/19/20/Add.1 6, 19.

TABLE 5.7 Leadership composition by regional group (2002–2021)

Regional group	States Parties	President	First Vice President	Second Vice President	Bureau member	Total States Parties holding a leadership position
Total	124	7	7	7	57	61
African Group	33	1	1	3	13	14
Asia-Pacific Group	19	2			7	7
Eastern European Group	18	1		3	9	9
Latin American and Caribbean States	28	2	3	1	12	13
Western European and other States	25	1	3	2	16	18

five were women whereas only two took the presidency.[212] Furthermore, due to political changes within States affecting the availability of diplomats to serve in the Assembly, elections to fill vice presidency vacancies took place in 2010, 2016 and 2018.[213]

212 Report of the Tenth Session of the Assembly of States Parties to the Rome Statute of the International Criminal Court, New York, 12–21 December, Volume I, ICC-ASP/10/20 (2011) 9.

213 Assembly of States Parties to the Rome Statute, Composition of the Bureau 2002–2019, available at: <https://asp.icc-cpi.int/sites/asp/files/asp_docs/Bureau/ASP1-17_Bureau Members-ENG.pdf>.

In keeping with the requirement to reflect geographical distribution and legal systems in the Bureau, the Assembly elected 61 States Parties to serve in the Bureau between the first and twentieth sessions.[214] Looking at regional participation, although the group of Western European and other States made the third constituency of the Assembly, between 2002 and 2021 this group has concentrated most leadership roles in the Bureau (18), followed by the African (14) and Latin American and Caribbean States (13).

3.1.5 Organization of the Bureau

As the Bureau provides continuous management oversight to the Court, it is further organized in two geographical working groups, one in New York and another in The Hague, open to all States Parties and other States requesting observer status.[215] The reason to create this Bureau mechanism in 2005 emanated from the desire to intensify the 'dialogue with the Court as it moves into the next phase of its establishment and operations'.[216] Thus, during the first iteration of the working groups, States Parties in The Hague dealt with 'permanent premises, host country issues and the draft Code of Professional Conduct for Defence Counsel'.[217] In New York, on the other hand, States Parties focused on the relationship agreement with the United Nations and States on arrears, for example.[218] The split of thematic focus evolved between 2002 and 2021, with the Bureau utilizing its own decision-making powers and the Assembly omnibus resolution to allocate specific mandates to each location and appoint ambassadorial-level coordinators, all under the purview of the President and vice-presidencies.[219] In fact, the Bureau has adopted the practice to assign to the Vice-Presidents the coordination of a working group.[220]

---

214 Assembly of States Parties to the Rome Statute, Composition of the Bureau 2002–2019, available at: <https://asp.icc-cpi.int/sites/asp/files/asp_docs/Bureau/ASP1-17_BureauMembers-ENG.pdf> Report of the Nineteenth Session (First and Second Resumptions) of the Assembly of States Parties to the Rome Statute of the International Criminal Court, New York, 17–23 December 2020 and 12 February 2021, ICC-ASP/19/20/Add.1 6, 19.

215 Assembly of States Parties to the Rome Statute, Terms of Reference Bureau Working Groups, available at: <https://asp.icc-cpi.int/bureau/ToR-Working-Groups> (2006).

216 ICC-ASP/3/Res.8 Intensifying Dialogue Between the Assembly of States Parties and the International Criminal Court (2004) 1.

217 Assembly of States Parties to the Rome Statute, Terms of Reference for the Subsidiary Bodies of the Bureau, available at: <https://asp.icc-cpi.int/bureau/ToR-Working-Groups> (2005).

218 Ibid.

219 de Hoon and Lohne, (2019) 64–65.

220 Villacis, 567.

Originally, the mandate of the working groups extended to the end of the fourth session, but in 2006, under the Presidency of Bruno Stagno Ugarte from Costa Rica, they were agreed 'until the Bureau decides otherwise'.[221] As Trahan argues, the working groups, in effect, enable the Bureau to comply with Article 112(3)(c).[222]

In practice, however, the Bureau struggled to manage several aspects of its governance structure, including: the proliferation of mandates assigned to States Parties, the level of engagement from topic coordinators, quality of reports and unexpected vacancies in facilitations or coordinator roles.[223] The mix of mandates for The Hague and New York Working Groups resulted in as little of 10 facilitators in 2006, to 39 in 2013,[224] and 24 in 2021.[225] Given the Bureau's role in appointing facilitators for each theme allocated to The Hague or New York, between 2006 and 2021, it issued 77 decisions to fill vacancies.[226] To govern this complex arrangement, the Assembly embarked in a process of reform in 2012 to re-organize the allocation of mandates and provide a timeline in which the Bureau should assign topic facilitators.[227] In 2016, it agreed on a roadmap to this effect, which continued to apply in the 20th session.[228]

3.1.6 Subsidiary Bodies

To enable governance and management oversight of the Court, Article 112(4) provided the Assembly the power to establish subsidiary bodies 'as may be necessary … in order to enhance its efficiency and economy'. Between 2002 and 2021, the Assembly established six subsidiary bodies (see Table 5.8), although this number is disputed.[229] On the one hand, strictly only four subsidiary bodies were established under Article 112(4), namely the Budget and Finance Committee, the Oversight Committee, the Working Group on Amendments and the Independent Oversight Mechanism. However, the Assembly's

221 Assembly of States Parties to the Rome Statute, Terms of Reference Bureau Working Groups, available at: <https://asp.icc-cpi.int/bureau/ToR-Working-Groups>.

222 Trahan, (2020) 234.

223 Villacis, 569.

224 Ibid 568.

225 Bureau of the Assembly of States Parties, 2nd Meeting, 8 April 2021 (2021) 6–7.

226 Assembly of States Parties to the Rome Statute, Bureau Decisions, available at: <https://asp.icc-cpi.int/bureau/decisions> accessed 5 January 2024.

227 Villacis, 571.

228 ICC-ASP/15/Res.5 Strengthening the International Criminal Court and the Assembly of States Parties (2016) 57.

229 Gradoni, (2012) 2022.

organigram published in the official website also shows the Board of Directors of the Trust Fund for Victims and the Advisory Committee on Nominations.[230] The issue of identification is further complicated as the Assembly established other bodies outside Article 112(4) but under its purview, for example the Special Working Group on the Crime of Aggression,[231] the Audit Committee,[232] the Staff Pension Committee[233] and the Review Mechanism.[234] It is unclear which identification criteria should be employed. In view of the 'labyrinthine and fragmented'[235] organization of subsidiary bodies, this book follows the Assembly's public record, as does Villacis,[236] Director of the Secretariat of the Assembly of States Parties between 2006 and 2024.

Chronologically, the Assembly established the Budget and Finance Committee under Article 112(4) during the first session in 2002. The Committee was tasked with the 'technical examination of any document submitted to the Assembly that contains financial or budgetary implications or any other matter of a financial, budgetary or administrative nature'.[237] Following the principles of fair geographical representation and expertise on relevant matters, the Committee consisted of 12 members with a renewable three-year term.[238] Between the first and twentieth sessions, the Assembly amended operational aspects of the Committee but left its mandate untouched. The changes included: travel and expenses for members,[239] duration of the terms

230 Assembly of States Parties to the Rome Statute, ASP Organigramme, available at: <https://asp.icc-cpi.int/assembly/asp_organigramme>.

231 ICC-ASP/1/Res.1 Continuity of Work in Respect of the Crime of Aggression.

232 ICC-ASP/14/Res.1 Programme Budget for 2016, the Working Capital Fund and the Contingency Fund for 2016, Scale of Assessments for the Apportionment of Expenses of the International Criminal Court and Financing Appropriations for 2016 (2015) 23.

233 ICC-ASP/3/Res.3 Strengthening the International Criminal Court and the Assembly of States Parties (2004) 14.

234 ICC-ASP/19/Res.7 Review of the International Criminal Court and the Rome Statute System (2020).

235 Vasiliev, 'Judicial Governance Entities as Power-Holders in International Criminal Justice: A Plea for a Socio-Legal Enquiry' (2020) 537.

236 Villacis, 565.

237 ICC-ASP/1/Res.4 Establishment of the Committee on Budget and Finance 2.

238 ICC-ASP/1/Res.5 Procedure for the Nomination and Election of Members of the Committee on Budget and Finance.

239 ICC-ASP/2/Res.4 Travel and Subsistence Expenses of Members of the Committee on Budget and Finance (2003).

TABLE 5.8 Assembly of States Parties subsidiary bodies (2002–2021)

Subsidiary body	Membership / term	Temporal mandate
Budget and Finance Committee	12 / 3 years	ASP 1 (2002) –
Board of Directors of the Trust Fund for Victims	5 / 3 years	ASP 1 (2002) –
Oversight Committee for Permanent Premises	10 / 2 years	ASP 6 (2007)–ASP 15 (2016)
Working Group on Amendments	All States Parties	ASP 8 (2009) –
Independent Oversight Mechanism	–	ASP 8 (2009) –
Advisory Committee on Nominations	9 / 3 years	ASP 10 (2011) –

in office,[240] travel arrangements,[241] election procedure for vacancies[242] and translation of official documents.[243] The Budget and Finance Committee played a vital role in recommending to the Assembly the approval of the Court's budget, operational issues across human resources, IT, legal, the external audit and financial assessments for its subsidiary bodies. In fact, as Gradoni[244] and Ambach agree, the Committee's weight in the workings of the Assembly has expanded over time 'within the framework of the Assembly's governance of the Court'.[245]

The Board of Directors of the Trust Fund for Victims' establishment also took place during the first session of the Assembly, but under Article 79(1) of the Statute.[246] The five-member Board was tasked with directing the 'activities and projects of the Trust Fund and the allocation of the property and money available to it, bearing in mind available resources and subject to the decisions

240 ICC-ASP/2/Res.5 Term of Office of the Members of the Committee on Budget and Finance (2003).

241 ICC-ASP/3/Res.5 Travel of Members of the Committee on Budget and Finance (2004).

242 ICC-ASP/4/Res.6 Procedure for Filling Vacancies in the Committee on Budget and Finance (2005).

243 ICC-ASP/7/Res.7 Amendment to the Rules of Procedure of the Committee on Budget and Finance (2008).

244 Ambach, 'Article 112 Assembly of States Parties' (2022) 2792.

245 Ibid 2791.

246 Article 79(1), Rome Statute of the International Criminal Court (2002) 2187 UNTS 90.

taken by the Court'.[247] Pursuant to Article 79(2), the Board was also required to develop and seek approval on the Fund's management and criteria to direct reparations. Between the first and twentieth sessions, the Assembly amended operational aspects of the Board but left its mandate untouched. The changes included the establishment of its own permanent Secretariat,[248] the approval of its operational regulations,[249] election procedure for vacancies,[250] duration of the terms in office[251] and rules for earmarked voluntary contributions.[252]

The Oversight Committee for Permanent Premises was established by the Assembly of States Parties under Article 112(4) during the sixth session in 2007 and concluded its work in 2016.[253] The purpose of the Committee was to provide 'strategic oversight' in the 'construction of the permanent premises of the International Criminal Court'.[254] Ten States Parties, respecting geographical representation, were members of the Committee with renewable two-year terms. Between the first and seventeenth session, the Assembly issued 12 resolutions to address vacancies, project design issues, hiring of the Project Director, budget management, oversight of payments by States Parties and the relationship with the Host Country.[255] After the inauguration of the permanent premises, the ongoing oversight function was allocated to The Hague Working Group of the Bureau.[256]

As amendments to the subject-matter jurisdiction were not permitted for seven years after entry into force of the Statute, the Working Group on Amendments emerged in the context of the Review Conference under Article 123(1). Amendments of an institutional nature covered by Article 122 were permitted at any time. As States Parties gathered in Kampala in 2010, the Working Group was instructed to 'consider' from its ninth session onwards, proposals for

247 ICC-ASP/1/Res.6 Establishment of a Fund for the Benefit of Victims of Crimes Within the Jurisdiction of the Court, and of the Families of Such Victims 2.

248 ICC-ASP/3/Res.7 Establishment of the Secretariat of the Trust Fund for Victims (2004).

249 ICC-ASP/4/Res.3 Regulations of the Trust Fund for Victims (2005).

250 ICC-ASP/4/Res.5 Procedure for Filling Vacancies in the Board of Directors of the Trust Fund for Victims (2005).

251 ICC-ASP/4/Res.7 Amendment Regarding the Term of Office of Members of the Board of Directors of the Trust Fund for Victims (2005).

252 ICC-ASP/6/Res.3 Amendment to the Regulations of the Trust Fund for Victims (2007).

253 ICC-ASP/15/Res.2 Permanent Premises (2016) 29.

254 ICC-ASP/6/Res.1 Permanent Premises (2007) 11,13.

255 See Resolutions ICC-ASP/6/Res.1 (2007); ICC-ASP/7/Res.1 (2008); ICC-ASP/8/Res.5 (2009); ICC-ASP/8/Res.8 (2009); ICC-ASP/9/Res.1 (2010); ICC-ASP/10/Res.6 (2011); ICC-ASP/11/Res.3 (2012); ICC-ASP/12/Res.2 (2013); ICC-ASP/13/Res.2 (2014); ICC-ASP/13/Res.6 (2014); ICC-ASP/14/Res.5 (2015) and ICC-ASP/15/Res.2 (2016).

256 ICC-ASP/15/Res.2 Permanent Premises 29.

amending the Statute and the Rules of Procedure and Evidence 'with a view to identifying amendments to be adopted'.[257] The membership of the group was opened to all States Parties but only in 2012 the Assembly of States Parties agreed to its terms of reference under Article 112(4).[258] Importantly, the terms of reference required that amendment proposals to the crimes listed in the Statute be 'characterized as one of the most serious crimes of concern to the international community as a whole and whether the crime is based on an existing prohibition under international law'.[259] Between 2010 and 2021, the subsidiary body issued regular reports but it did not suffer any structural amendments.[260] However, its work has been increasingly influenced by another committee of the Assembly: the Study Group on Governance. Created by the Assembly in 2010 to strengthen the 'institutional framework both within the Court and between the Court and the Assembly',[261] the Study Group was initially established with a one-year mandate. Its mandate was to seek a constructive dialogue with the Court on changes via amendments by the Assembly.[262] For example, in 2011, the Group was successful in proposing the amendment of Rule 4 of the Procedure and Evidence to grant the President of the Court the power to speedily assign judges to divisions without waiting for a plenary decision.[263] Between 2010 and 2021, the Assembly renewed the mandate of Study Group on Governance every year.[264]

The Independent Oversight Mechanism was directly mentioned in Article 112(4), however, the Assembly only turned to its creation in 2009.[265] As the Rome Conference travaux préparatoires reveal, the Independent Oversight Mechanism was introduced in the Statute akin to an internal audit function of the Court. It was equally clear the Mechanism had non-judicial oversight

---

257 ICC-ASP/8/Res.6 Review Conference (2009) 2.

258 ICC-ASP/11/Res.8 Strengthening the International Criminal Court and the Assembly of States Parties (2012) 55.

259 Ibid 56.

260 See Resolutions ASP/14/Res.2 (2015), ICC-ASP/15/Res.4 (2016), ICC-ASP/16/Res.4 (2017), ICC-ASP/17/Res.2 (2018), ICC-ASP/18/Res.5 (2019), ICC-ASP/19/Res.6 (2020) and ICC-ASP /20/Res.5 (2021).

261 ICC-ASP/9/Res.2 Establishment of a Study Group on Governance (2010).

262 Ambach, 'Article 112 Assembly of States Parties' (2022) 2799.

263 ICC-ASP/10/Res.1 Amendments to Rule 4 of the Rules of Procedure and Evidence (2011).

264 See Resolutions ASP/14/Res.2 (2015); ICC-ASP/15/Res.4 (2016); ICC-ASP/16/Res.4 (2017); ICC-ASP/17/Res.2 (2018); ICC-ASP/18/Res.5 (2019); ICC-ASP/19/Res.6 (2020) and ICC-ASP /20/Res.5 (2021).

265 ICC-ASP/7/Decision 1 Decision Concerning an Independent Oversight Mechanism (2009) 1.

powers respecting the independence of the organs.[266] As the Independent Oversight Mechanism was established to comply with the tripartite mandate of 'investigation, inspection and evaluation of the Court',[267] the Assembly developed it over two phases. The first phase of implementation, until 2013, focused on conducting 'investigations on allegations of misconduct and to ensuring effective and meaningful oversight thereof'.[268] To do so, the Mechanism's independent investigative function ensured undue conduct by elected officials and their staff were 'investigated and an effective remedy provided'.[269] Due to disagreements with Prosecutor Moreno Ocampo,[270] the investigate powers of the Mechanism were only agreed after several setbacks and eight years after the establishment of the Court. By 2013, a three people independent unit came into operation, seconding expertise from the United Nations Office of Internal Oversight.[271] The second phase in 2013 further specified the inspection, evaluation and investigation roles by clarifying their purpose and legal mandate.[272] In doing so, the Assembly also developed a dispute settlement scheme in the event any Court organ head disagreed with an investigation. Furthermore, the Assembly created a reporting procedure to the Bureau and provided a stable budget and staffing to the Mechanism.[273] Thus, by 2017, at the 16th session of the Assembly, the investigation, inspection and evaluation functions were fully functional.[274] In 2020, during the 19th session, the Assembly agreed to expand the investigative function of the Mechanism to cover 'alleged conduct of former elected officials and staff both while they were in office and when they separated from service'.[275] Such change allowed the Mechanism to investigate media allegations against former Court officials like those against the first Prosecutor of the Court.[276]

---

266 Vasiliev, 'Judicial Governance Entities as Power-Holders in International Criminal Justice: A Plea for a Socio-Legal Enquiry' (2020) 519.

267 Article 112(4), Rome Statute of the International Criminal Court (2002) 2187 UNTS 90.

268 ICC-ASP/8/Res.1 Establishment of an Independent Oversight Mechanism (2009) 3.

269 Schabas, The International Criminal Court: A Commentary on the Rome Statute (1446).

270 Vasiliev, 'Judicial Governance Entities as Power-Holders in International Criminal Justice: A Plea for a Socio-Legal Enquiry' (2020) 519.

271 ICC-ASP/8/Res.1 Establishment of an Independent Oversight Mechanism 3.

272 ICC-ASP/12/Res.6 Independent Oversight Mechanism 3.

273 Ibid.

274 ICC-ASP/16/Res.6 Strengthening the International Criminal Court and the Assembly of States Parties (2017) 49.

275 ICC-ASP/19/Res.6 Strengthening the International Criminal Court and the Assembly of States Parties (2020) 17.

276 ICC Statement on Recent Media Allegations, Press Release: 5 October 2017, available at: <https://www.legal-tools.org/doc/babdf6/> (2017).

Beyond the critical investigation function, the Independent Oversight Mechanism played a role to vet candidates for Prosecutor and Deputy Prosecutor in 2020 and 2021, and has carried out evaluations into the Registry and the Trust Fund for Victims.[277] During the period between 2013 and 2021, the Independent Oversight Mechanism shared seven annual reports with the Assembly.[278]

The Advisory Committee on Nominations was established in 2011, giving life to Article 36(4)(c) of the Statute to 'facilitate that the highest-qualified individuals are appointed as judges of the International Criminal Court'.[279] While Article 112(4) was not referenced, the Committee was created as 'an independent organism in the very structure of the Assembly'.[280] Despite the mandate to assess nominations as per Article 36, States Parties routinely deviated from the recommendations made by this subsidiary body, including in the 2014 and 2017 elections.[281] The Advisory Committee on Nominations issued its first recommendation report in 2013.[282] The composition consisted of an appointed nine-member panel from States Parties, respecting geographical and legal systems of the world representation, and acting in a personal capacity. The Bureau retained the responsibility to recommend to the Assembly names for the panel for their final appointment. Each member had to possess 'established competence and experience in criminal or international law'.[283] Upon finishing his term as a judge, Philippe Kirsch became the inaugural chair of the Advisory Committee.[284] Between 2011 and 2021, the Committee's terms of reference was amended in 2014[285] and 2019. Notably, the 2019 amendments strengthened the 'screening mechanisms as to the suitability of judge candidates'.[286] Changes included baring any member from assessing

277 Annual Report of the Head of the Independent Oversight Mechanism, ICC-ASP/20/16 (2021).

278 Assembly of States Parties to the Rome Statute, Independent Oversight Mechanism, available at: <https://asp.icc-cpi.int/IOM> accessed 5 January (2024).

279 Report of the Bureau on the Establishment of an Advisory Committee on Nominations of Judges of the International Criminal Court, ICC-ASP/10/36 (2011) 4.

280 Ibid 2.

281 Ambach, 'Article 112 Assembly of States Parties' 2022 (2793).

282 Report of the Advisory Committee on Nominations of Judges on the Work of its First Meeting, ICC-ASP/12/23 (2013).

283 Report of the Bureau on the Establishment of an Advisory Committee on Nominations of Judges of the International Criminal Court, ICC-ASP/10/36 4.

284 Report of the Advisory Committee on Nominations of Judges on the Work of its First Meeting, ICC-ASP/12/23.

285 ICC-ASP/13/Res.5 Strengthening the International Criminal Court and the Assembly of States Parties (2014) 51.

286 Ambach, 'Article 112 Assembly of States Parties' 2022 (2794).

nominations of its own nationality, a common assessment questionnaire, signed declarations from nominees acknowledging no allegations of misconduct or sexual harassment, and the possibility for States Parties to request a confidential provisional assessment of candidates before their effective nomination.[287] Between 2011 and 2021, the Advisory Committee on Nominations rendered five assessment reports to the Assembly of States Parties.[288]

3.1.7 Decision-making in the Assembly and Bureau

Between 2002 and 2021, the Assembly of States Parties considered 517 agenda items and adopted 154 resolutions, seven decisions, four recommendations and two declarations, these, exclusively at the Review Conference in 2010 (see Table 5.9).[289] Remarkably, all 167 decisions were passed by consensus as stipulated under Article 112(7)[290] and Rule 61 of the procedure of the Assembly.[291] Given the legislative role of the Assembly,[292] arriving at each resolution by consensus should not be confused with total and inherent agreement among States Parties.[293] By modelling the governance procedures of the Assembly after the United Nations, consensus can represent the absence of insisting on voting rather than absolute support.[294] The length and complexity over the negotiations of the crime of aggression is a notable example.[295]

In this context, when observing the practice of the Assembly, States Parties considered the most agenda items during the 19th session. The reason of the heavy work programme of the Assembly across 39 items in 2020 was the combination of disruption of the normal meeting procedure by the Covid-19 pan-

---

287 ICC-ASP/18/Res.4 Resolution on the Review of the Procedure for the Nomination and Election of Judges 4–5.

288 Assembly of States Parties to the Rome Statute, Advisory Committee on Nominations of Judges of the International Criminal Court, available at: <https://asp.icc-cpi.int/ACN> accessed January 5 (2024).

289 Assembly of States Parties to the Rome Statute, Resolutions, available at: <https://asp.icc-cpi.int/resolutions> accessed 5 January (2024).

290 Article 112(7), Rome Statute of the International Criminal Court (2002) 2187 UNTS 90.

291 Rule 61, Rules of Procedure of the Assembly of States Parties, ICC-ASP/1/3.

292 Birdsall, Andrea and Lang Jr, Anthony F, 'The International Criminal Court and Global Constitutionalism' in Lang Jr, Anthony F and Wiener, Antje (eds), Handbook on Global Constitutionalism (Edward Elgar 2017).

293 Ruffert, Matthias and Walter, Christian, Institutionalised International Law (Bloomsbury 2015) 155.

294 Wang, Chen, 'Issues on Consensus and Quorum at International Conferences' (2010) 9 (4) Chinese Journal of International Law 719.

295 Schabas, William A, 'La Cour Pénale Internationale à Vingt Ans. Un Bilan Géopolitique' (2023) Annuaire Français de Relations Internationales 911.

demic as well as the concurrent election of the Assembly Presidency and Bureau, third Prosecutor of the Court, six judges, six members of the Committee on Budget and Finance, and the follow-up to the Independent Expert Review report.[296] The Assembly also considered a lengthy agenda in 2008 and 2013, with 32 items in each session. Beyond these notable years with a lengthy meeting agenda, the Assembly considered in average 24 items per session between 2002 and 2021. When focusing on resolutions between 2002 and 2021, the highest number corresponded to the inaugural session in 2002–2003 with 16.[297] The majority of resolutions from the first session created the regulatory framework, subsidiary bodies and completed steps taken by the Preparatory Commission since 1999. The second highest number of resolutions passed by States Parties took place during the 14th session with 12 resolutions, including plans for the permanent premises of the Court.[298] Moreover, in terms of decision-making via resolutions, the customary annual omnibus resolution 'Strengthening the International Criminal Court and the Assembly of States Parties' had a particular role in the Assembly. First issued in 2003, the purpose of the omnibus resolution, as Villacis explained, evolved from a 'repository of texts which did not have their own resolution' to a mechanism to centralize the 'key decisions of the Assembly'.[299] In fact, the omnibus resolution guided the governance and oversight actions for the subsequent session at the same time in regulated operational aspects of the Bureau, such as assigning the mandates of its working groups and specific technical requests to subsidiary bodies and the Court.[300] On average, between 2002 and 2021, the Assembly passed seven resolutions per session.

While neither the Rome Statute nor the Rules of Procedure of the Assembly offer clarity on the distinction between decisions, recommendations and dec-

---

296 See: Report of the Nineteenth Session of the Assembly of States Parties to the Rome Statute of the International Criminal Court, The Hague, 14–16 December, Volume I, ICC-ASP/19/20 (2020); Report of the Nineteenth Session (First and Second Resumptions) of the Assembly of States Parties to the Rome Statute of the International Criminal Court, New York, 17–23 December 2020 and 12 February 2021, ICC-ASP/19/20/Add.1.

297 Assembly of States Parties to the Rome Statute, Resolutions, available at: <https://asp.icc-cpi.int/resolutions>.

298 See: Report of the Fourth Session of the Assembly of States Parties to the Rome Statute of the International Criminal Court, The Hague, 28 November-3 December, ICC-ASP/4/L.32 (2005); Report of the Fourth Session (Resumed) of the Assembly of States Parties to the Rome Statute of the International Criminal Court, New York, 26–27 January, ICC-ASP/4/37 (2006).

299 Villacis, 568, at footnote 531.

300 Ambach, 'Article 112 Assembly of States Parties' (2022) 2790.

TABLE 5.9 Assembly of States Parties decisions (2002–2021)

Session	Agenda items	Resolutions	Decisions	Recommendations	Declarations
Total	**517**	**154**	**7**	**4**	**2**
ASP 1 (2002)	15	16	4	1	
ASP 2 (2003)	19	9			
ASP 3 (2004)	18	8			
ASP 4 (2005)	31	12			
ASP 5 (2006)	29	6			
ASP 6 (2007)	29	8		1	
ASP 7 (2008)	32	7	1		
ASP 8 (2009)	25	9			
Kampala Review (2010)	12	6			2
ASP 9 (2010)	21	5			
ASP 10 (2011)	25	6			
ASP 11 (2012)	24	8		1	
ASP 12 (2013)	22	8			
ASP 13 (2014)	32	6	2		
ASP 14 (2015)	25	5			
ASP 15 (2016)	24	5			
ASP 16 (2017)	27	6		1	
ASP 17 (2018)	23	5			
ASP 18 (2019)	22	7			
ASP 19 (2020)	39	7			
ASP 20 (2021)	23	5			

larations as a mode of decision-making,[301] between 2002 and 2021, the Assembly issued seven decisions, four recommendations and two declarations. The use of recommendations has been constantly applied to the election of the Registrar under Article 43(4) of the Statute and Rule 12 of the Rules of Procedure and Evidence. This has been the case in 2003, 2007, 2012 and 2017.[302] Lastly,

301 Gradoni, 2012 (2014).

302 Assembly of States Parties to the Rome Statute, Election of the Registrar, available at: <https://asp.icc-cpi.int/elections/Registrar> accessed 5 January 2024.

the Assembly only issued declarations in the context of the Review Conference in Kampala in 2010.[303]

At the level of the Bureau, Article 112(3)(c) in the Statute described its functional role and the Rules of Procedure of the Assembly regulated its ways of working, including decision-making, under Rule 2.[304] However, neither the Rules of Procedure of the Assembly nor any other operational document of the Bureau described the exact mode of decision-making and how decisions should be recorded. In other words, while the Assembly issued resolutions, decisions, recommendations and declarations, the Bureau did not develop a mechanism to record decisions. Between 2002 and 2021, at each session, the President of the Bureau delivered an oral report to the Assembly describing the number of meetings since the last regular session, and a summary of the main actions.[305] However, in the absence of regulations for the mode of decision-making and lacking recorded decisions, it is challenging to correctly map the volume of work done by the Bureau. In this context, the oral reports of the Bureau in the first 20 sessions count 255 meetings, in contrast with the 266 meeting records available in the ICC Legal Tools Database (see Table 5.10).[306] The discrepancy might be partially explained by an incomplete oral report by the Bureau not accounting for meetings during the proper Assembly session in addition to the intersessional period.

Accounting for the issues with the available record of meetings of the Bureau, the 1081 items contained across 266 meetings were analysed to catalogue whether a specific decision was made or if it was simply noted. In this sense, of the 1081 matters, the Bureau discussed and actively decided on a future action in 541 agenda items. The remaining 450 agenda topics without a specific future action by the Bureau referred to subjects such as activities of the President, general updates, statements by the Court and subsidiary bodies, logistical preparatory information about upcoming sessions, and financial notifications, among other topics.[307]

3.1.8 Settlement of Disputes

Although not located in Article 112, the Assembly had a role in settling disputes among States Parties. Article 119 clearly differentiates between the responsi-

303 Review Conference of the Rome Statute of the International Criminal Court, Kampala, 31 May – 11 June 2010, Official Records, RC/11 (2010) 23.

304 Rule 2, Rules of Procedure of the Assembly of States Parties, ICC-ASP/1/3.

305 Assembly of States Parties to the Rome Statute, ASP Sessions, available at: <https://asp.icc-cpi.int/sessions>.

306 ICC Legal Tools Database, available at <https://www.legal-tools.org>.

307 Assembly of States Parties to the Rome Statute, Bureau Decisions, available at: <https://asp.icc-cpi.int/bureau/decisions>.

TABLE 5.10 Assembly of States Parties Bureau meetings (2002–2021)

Session	Reported by Bureau	Available public record	Agenda items	Decisions
Total	255	266	1081	541
ASP 1 (2002)	–	–	–	–
ASP 2 (2003)	10	Not available	Not available	Not available
ASP 3 (2004)	8	Not available	Not available	Not available
ASP 4 (2005)	19	2	9	5
ASP 5 (2006)	9	19	67	29
ASP 6 (2007)	11	17	55	35
ASP 7 (2008)	13	14	43	20
ASP 8 (2009)	15	12	33	28
Kampala Review	Not available	Not available	Not available	Not available
ASP 9 (2010)	19	14	85	32
ASP 10 (2011)	20	19	100	48
ASP 11 (2012)	18	17	79	49
ASP 12 (2013)	19	21	74	39
ASP 13 (2014)	16	33	111	64
ASP 14 (2015)	11	13	24	14
ASP 15 (2016)	8	9	41	20
ASP 16 (2017)	7	11	44	20
ASP 17 (2018)	18	22	92	40
ASP 18 (2019)	11	12	72	34
ASP 19 (2020)	14	20	91	33
ASP 20 (2021)	9	11	61	31

bility of the Court to decide on questions of 'judicial functions' and the Assembly to resolve disputes around the 'interpretation or application' of the Statute.[308] As Klamberg argued, the dispute settlement clause was appropriate and ordinary in multilateral treaties.[309] However, none of the constitutive

308 Article 119(1)–(2), Rome Statute of the International Criminal Court (2002) 2187 UNTS 90.

309 Klamberg, Mark, Nilsson, Jonas and Angotti, Antonio (eds), Commentary on the Law of the International Criminal Court: The Statute, vol 2 (Torkel Opsahl Academic EPublisher 2023) 1039.

instruments, namely the Statute, Rules of Procedure and Evidence and Rules of Procedure of the Assembly described carefully the difference between judicial functions and interpretation or application in Article 119(1) and (2). It is clear States Parties are barred by the Statute to interfere with the judicial independence of the Court,[310] in the words of Clark, the 'Court is master of its own house'.[311] Nonetheless, the absence of auxiliary clauses setting out the prerogative under Article 119(2) can meddle with the protection of judicial and prosecutorial autonomy.[312] Thus, as Schabas argued, 'it is not at all apparent how the line is to be drawn'.[313] While Ochoa[314] and Clark[315] offered tentative areas of distinction, including the power of the Assembly under Article 119(2) to settle concerns over financial aspects, the Trust Fund for Victims and qualifications required for election of judges and the Prosecutor, this issue remained untested between 2002 and 2021.

Procedurally, unlike other treaties, the Rome Statute assigned to the Assembly a mediation role under Article 119(2) before recommending the involvement of the International Court of Justice as an impartial third party.[316] A three-step process included a three-month deadline for parties to the dispute to reach a conclusion amicably, a referral to the Assembly for further mediation, presumably under the offices of the President, and lastly a recommendation of the Assembly to defer the dispute to other 'means of settlement',[317] including the International Court of Justice. If parties to the dispute accepted a recommendation by the Assembly to involve the International Court of Justice, these, presumably, would also need to recognize its jurisdiction.[318]

310 Wenaweser, Christian, 'The Assembly of States Parties of the Rome Statute: Perspectives on the Years Ahead, 2009–2011'2009 (Consultative Conference on International Criminal Justice) 2.

311 Clark, Roger S, 'Article 119 Settlement of Disputes' in Triffterer, Otto and Ambos, Kai (eds), Rome Statute of the International Criminal Court: a Commentary (3 edn, Beck/Hart 2016) 2279.

312 Trahan, (2020) 245.

313 Schabas, The International Criminal Court: A Commentary on the Rome Statute (1483).

314 Ochoa, Juan Carlos S, 'Settlement of Disputes Concerning States Arising from the Application of the Statute of the International Criminal Court: Balancing Sovereignty and the Need for an Effective and Independent ICC' (2007) 7 International Criminal Law Review 26.

315 Clark, (2016) 2282.

316 Gradoni, (2012) 2009.

317 119(2), Rome Statute of the International Criminal Court (2002) 2187 UNTS 90.

318 Pellet, Alain, 'Settlement of Disputes' in Cassese, Antonio, Gaeta, Paola and Jones, John RWD (eds), The Rome Statute of the International Criminal Court A Commentary, vol 2 (Oxford University Press 2002) (1845).

Despite the inaction by the Assembly under Article 119(2) between 2002 and 2021, suggestions have been made to trigger a dispute settlement process targeting non-cooperation with the Court[319] and outstanding financial contributions of withdrawing States Parties.[320]

3.1.9 Article 112(2)(g): Political Support?

Article 112(2)(g) in the Statute assigned to the Assembly the power to 'perform any other function consistent with this Statute or the Rules of Procedure and Evidence'.[321] Indeed, States Parties must perform several functions mandated elsewhere in the Statute besides those listed in Article 112. For example, the election of judges (Article 36) or the amendments of the Rules of Procedure and Evidence (Article 51). This omnibus clause provided inherent powers to the Assembly to guarantee the adequate governance and management of the Court. It also served as a safeguard against 'unforeseen developments'.[322] A chief example of unforeseen events revolved around providing political support to the Court in the face of severe challenges between 2001 and 2021. Indeed, as the Court developed its judicial practice and the Assembly familiarized itself with its governance role, several high-stakes issues challenged the perception, legitimacy and efficiency of the Rome Statute system, that is, the ecosystem of an independent criminal court governed by States influenced by geopolitical interests. In particular, the role of the President of the Assembly became important. In the words of Assembly President between the seventh and ninth sessions, Christian Wenaweser from Liechtenstein, 'the issue of political support for and cooperation with the Court is certainly of the highest order'.[323]

In fact, President Wenaweser was not alone in singling the political role of the Assembly in providing support for the Court. President Prince Zeid Raíad Zeid Al-Hussein (2002–2004) noticed early on 'the ASP must function and exist in a style that conveys an impression to the international community that it, the ASP, is the chief champion of the Court',[324] while President Bruno Stagno Ugarte (2005–2008) warned 'the ICC cannot afford to have its moral

319 Schabas, The International Criminal Court: A Commentary on the Rome Statute (1440).

320 Options for Securing Payment of Withdrawing States Parties' Contributions to the Loan Granted by the Host State, ICC-ASP/17/24 (2018) 4–5.

321 Article 112(2)(g), Rome Statute of the International Criminal Court (2002) 2187 UNTS 90.

322 Bos, 'Assembly of States Parties' (2002) 308.

323 Wenaweser, (2009) 5.

324 Interview with H.R.H. Prince Zeid Raíad Zeid Al-Hussein (Jordan), First President of the Assembly of States Parties. Interview with H.E. Ambassador Bruno Stagno Ugarte (Costa Rica), Second President of the Assembly of States Parties. (2005) 31 ICC Monitor 13.

legitimacy and authority tainted by the failings of a few'.[325] In fact over time, the Assembly asserted its political defence of the Rome Statute but also turned inwards alerting, as President Tiina Intelmann (Estonia, 2011–2013) explained, 'the Court has to be mindful of the fact that the political support of States Parties is not limitless'.[326] An appropriate example was the fraught relationship with African States Parties and the African Union at the time the docket of the Court was solely directed at situations in that particular geography. The confrontation with the African Union was exacerbated as the Court started proceedings against Heads of State in Sudan and Kenya.[327]

President Sidiki Kaba (Senegal, 2014–2017) complained of 'deux poids, deux mesures' in the treatment of the Court when called to play a role in his continent but not in Syria or elsewhere, emphasizing, 'there are Africans who feel not listened to and humiliated by the ICC'.[328] In this challenging political context, President Kaba precluded further withdrawals by African States and persistently maintained the 'need for this Court'.[329] A Court also confronted by geopolitical interests at the time the State of Palestine joined the Rome Statute as a member in 2015.[330] Several Bureau members at the time denounced the 'designation'[331] of the State of Palestine in official Assembly documents. The membership of the State of Palestine brought into light the political role of the Assembly in 2021 when the Chambers determined the circumspect question of territorial jurisdiction responding to a request by the Prosecutor.[332] By the time President O-Gon Kwon (Republic of Korea, 2018–2020) began his tenure, several issues mounted.[333] Burundi and the

325 Ibid 3.

326 Intelmann, Tiina, 'Keynote Address Lectures' (2014) 47 Studies in Transnational Legal Policy 12.

327 Leslie, Vinjamuri, 'The ICC and the Politics of Peace and Justice' in Carsten, Stahn (ed), The Law and Practice of the International Criminal Court (Oxford University Press 2015).

328 Exclusive Interview with Sidiki Kaba on Withdrawals from the ICC (Journalists For Justice, 2016) <https://jfjustice.net/exclusive-interview-with-asp-president-sidiki-kaba-on-withdrawals-from-the-icc/> accessed 22 May (2018).

329 Ibid.

330 Imseis, Ardi, 'State of Exception: Critical Reflections on the Amici Curiae Observations and Other Communications of States Parties to the Rome Statute in the Palestine Situation' (2020) Journal of International Criminal Justice.

331 Bureau of the Assembly of States Parties, 7th Meeting, 15 November 2016 (2016).

332 Situation in the State of Palestine (Decision on the 'Prosecution Request Pursuant to Article 19(3) for a Ruling on the Court's Territorial Jurisdiction in Palestine) ICC-01/18-143 (5 February 2021).

333 Exclusive Interview: New ASP President Kwon Seeks to Expand the ICC Family (Journalists for Justice, 2018) <https://jfjustice.net/diplomatic-row-over-possible-second-term-for-kaba-as-president-of-icc-states/#> accessed 2 August (2018).

Philippines withdrew from the Rome Statute and Malaysia did not complete the accession to the Court.[334] On the judicial front, allegations of misconduct surrounded the former Prosecutor Moreno Ocampo and Bensouda. In addition, the perception of slow and expensive proceedings gave way to speculations about political motives influencing the Court as it decided not to investigate alleged crimes in Afghanistan due to lack of resources.[335] And for the first time, a non-party State, the United States imposed sanctions on staff of the Court.[336]

In this charged and evolving political context, former Assembly Presidents Prince Zeid, Ugarte, Wenaweser and Intelmann wrote in 2019 they were 'disappointed by the quality of some of its judicial proceedings, frustrated by some of the results, and exasperated by the management deficiencies that prevent the Court from living up to its full potential'.[337] Unprecedented in the practice of dissent within the diplomatic community that surrounds the Assembly, the letter called for an urgent external assessment of the Rome Statute system: Court and States Parties. President Kwon oversaw the design process of the assessment exercise and negotiation to follow up on the recommendations of the Independent Expert Review.[338] He did so in a heightened context as the Trump administration in the United States imposed unprecedented sanctions against Court officials for their involvement in the situation of Afghanistan.[339] Reacting to the sanctions by the United States, the Bureau held in June 2020 the first ever emergency meeting.[340] Calling the Court a 'young institution' and a 'project in progress',[341] Kwon passed the baton to President Silvia Fernández de Gurmendi (Argentina) in 2021.

---

334 United Nations Treaty Collection, Depositary of Notifications, Rome Statute of the International Criminal Court, available at <https://treaties.un.org/>.

335 Guilfoyle, Douglas, 'Lacking Conviction: Is the International Criminal Court Broken? An Organisational Failure Analysis' (2020) 20 (2) Melbourne Journal of International Law 1.

336 Sterio, Milena, 'The Trump Administration and the International Criminal Court: A Misguided New Policy' (2019) 51 Case Western Reserve Journal of International Law 201.

337 Prince Zeid Raíad Zeid Al-Hussein, Stagno Ugarte, Bruno, Wenaweser, Christian and Intelman, Tiina, 'The International Criminal Court Needs Fixing' (Atlantic Council, 2019) <https://www.atlanticcouncil.org/blogs/new-atlanticist/the-international-criminal-court-needs-fixing> accessed 24 April 2019.

338 Report of the Independent Expert Review of the International Criminal Court and the Rome Statute System, ICC-ASP/19/16.

339 ASP President O-Gon Kwon Rejects Measures Taken Against ICC, ICC-ASP-20200611-PR 1527.

340 Bureau of the Assembly of States Parties, 7th Meeting, 15 November 2016.

341 Medina, Romina and Opinion, Ann Clarice, 'Interview with Judge O-Gon Kwon' (2021) 2 (1) Asia-Pacific Journal of International Humanitarian Law 7.

President Silvia Fernández de Gurmendi's extensive involvement with the International Criminal Court began as a diplomat during the negotiations before and after the Rome Conference. She later worked for the first Prosecutor and was elected a judge in 2009 and later President of the Court in 2015.[342] President Fernández de Gurmendi was fully aware that 'despite all this movement and growth, the enthusiasm of the negotiating years gradually turned into disappointment'.[343] Although Fernández de Gurmendi focused on effective trial procedures and collegiality during her tenure as Court President, at the time she was elected by the Assembly as President, 'some institutional and judicial setbacks triggered, again, serious concerns. By then, patience had run out'.[344] Powderly[345] and Vasiliev have described this period of crisis and backlash on the legitimacy and utility of the Court finding a neat role for States Parties to 'mobilize political support and have their differences arbitrated in a more open and inclusive manner'.[346] In essence, Article 112(2)(g) averted this situation affording States Parties an inherent power to revise and perfect their governance role towards the Court offering sobering support and productive feedback, all in the spirit of judicial independence as enshrined in the Rome Statute. By the 20th session in 2021, the recommendations of the Independent Expert Review received praise by States Parties and found an institutional mechanism for implementation, both at the Assembly and the Court.[347] In fact, the first meeting of the Bureau chaired by Fernández de Gurmendi explicitly focused on the review follow-up mechanism.[348]

3.1.10 Permanent Secretariat of the Assembly

As part of an international organization, it is a normal feature the Assembly of States Parties to be assisted by a permanent secretariat.[349] The Rome Statute did not contain any clause in relation to its establishment but the Preparatory

342 Judge Silvia Fernández de Gurmendi (International Criminal Court) <https://www.icc-cpi.int/courtstructure/pages/judge.aspx?name=judge%20silvia%20fernández%20de%20gurmendi> accessed 13 October 2021.

343 Fernández de Gurmendi, Silvia, 'A Path to Global Justice: My Insider's View' (2022) 9 (1) The International Journal of Ethical Leadership 9.

344 Ibid 11.

345 Powderly, Joseph, 'International Criminal Justice in an Age of Perpetual Crisis' (2019) 32 (1) Leiden Journal of International Law 1.

346 Vasiliev, 'The Crises and Critiques of International Criminal Justice' (2020) 636.

347 ICC-ASP/20/Res.3 Review of the International Criminal Court and the Rome Statute System (2021).

348 Bureau of the Assembly of States Parties, 1st Meeting, 18 February 2021 (2021).

349 Ruffert and Walter, 163.

Commission[350] included in Rule 37 of the procedure of the Assembly a list of 'normal functions carried out by the secretariats'.[351] Broadly, Rule 37 outlined duties on information management, conference services, record keeping and 'all other work which the Assembly or the Bureau may require'.[352] As Blokker explained, while 'far from spectacular,' these duties were 'indispensable for making the work of the organization successful'.[353] In fact, the literature[354] generally identifies the vital role of secretariats for successful treaty implementation, including that of the Rome Statute Assembly.[355]

Resolution 3 from 2003 established the permanent secretariat together with an annex outlining its operational procedure.[356] The secretariat was located in The Hague and managed by a Director, overseen by the Bureau. It performed duties across four areas: conference servicing, providing legal and substantive advise, financial expertise and administrative support.[357] In the Bureau report to the Assembly, the secretariat was also tasked with monitoring non-cooperation, but this duty was not included in the final resolution.[358] Conceived operationally a part of the Registry, the initial staff resources and budget plan for the secretariat was of seven members and €531,145.[359] By the 20th session in 2021, the secretariat consisted of 22 staff members and a budget of €1,911,200.[360] Between 2003 and 2021, the number of roles expanded to cover an increasing workload to service the Assembly, Assembly President, Bureau and subsidiary bodies while providing legal and technical advice on substantive and organizational governance issues.[361] As Blokker[362] and Piipar-

350 Proceedings of the Preparatory Commission at its Eighth Session (24 September-5 October), UN Doc. PCNICC/2001/L.3/Rev.1.

351 Yengejeh, 673.

352 Rule 37, Rules of Procedure of the Assembly of States Parties, ICC-ASP/1/3.

353 Blokker, Niels, 'International Organizations or Institutions, Secretariats' in Wolfrum, Rüdiger (ed), Max Planck Encyclopedia of Public International Law, vol V (Oxford University Press 2008) para. 10.

354 Bauer, Steffen, 'Does Bureaucracy Really Matter? The Authority of Intergovernmental Treaty Secretariats in Global Environmental Politics' (2006) 6 (1) Global Environmental Politics 50.

355 Karns, (2016) 780.

356 ICC-ASP/2/Res.3 Establishment of the Permanent Secretariat of the Assembly of States Parties to the International Criminal Court 3–4.

357 Ibid 2.

358 Draft Programme Budget for 2004, ICC-ASP/2/2 (2003) 123.

359 Ibid 134.

360 Proposed Programme Budget for 2022 of the International Criminal Court, ICC-ASP/20/10 (2021) 153.

361 Ibid 149.

362 Blokker, 'International Organizations or Institutions, Secretariats' (2008) para. 9.

inen[363] have established, the ever-growing functions assigned to the secretariat pointed at their bureaucratic expertise developed over time. For example, the Assembly required the active involvement of the secretariat in enhancing complementarity,[364] cooperation between States Parties,[365] and the Independent Expert Review.[366]

The mandate of the secretariat has not varied between 2003 and 2021; however, its workload has increased significantly. In 2017 during the 16th session, States Parties acknowledged this fact and asked the Bureau to assess the functions of the secretariat in 'assisting and servicing the current needs of the Assembly'.[367] In 2018, the Bureau delivered the assessment outlining 12 recommendations to improve the efficiency of the secretariat.[368] The recommendations covered all the points of concern of States Parties after the Bureau spent nine meetings in 2018 on the topic.[369] In 2021, during the 20th session, the Assembly requested the President to report in the next session the level of progress implementing the recommendations accepted in 2018.[370]

Up until 2021, the Bureau appointed two Directors of the Secretariat. In late 2003, Medard Rwelamira from South Africa was selected as inaugural Director.[371] Rwelamira was a well-known figure among States Parties as Chief Legal Advisor to South Africa during the Rome Conference coordinating the negotiations of Part 4 on composition and administration of the Court.[372] In April 2006, Medard Rwelamira passed away and Renan Villacis was seconded from the United Nations Office of Legal Affairs as interim Director.[373] After

363 Piiparinen, Touko, 'Secretariats' in Cogan, Jacob Katz, Hurd, Ian and Johnstone, Ian (eds), The Oxford Handbook of International Organizations (Oxford University Press 2016) 842.

364 RC/Res.1 Complementarity (2010).

365 ICC-ASP/18/Res.3 Cooperation (2019).

366 ICC-ASP/18/Res.7 Review of the International Criminal Court and the Rome Statute System (2019).

367 ICC-ASP/16/Res.6 Strengthening the International Criminal Court and the Assembly of States Parties 53.

368 ICC-ASP/17/Res.5 Strengthening the International Criminal Court and the Assembly of States Parties (2018) 43.

369 Report of the Bureau on the Assessment of the Secretariat, ICC-ASP/17/39 (2018) 5.

370 ICC-ASP/20/Res.5 Strengthening the International Criminal Court and the Assembly of States Parties (2021) 22.

371 Report of the Third Session of the Assembly of States Parties to the Rome Statute of the International Criminal Court, The Hague, 6–10 September, ICC-ASP/3/25 (2004) 5.

372 Passing of Dr. Medard Rwelamira, ICC-CPI-20060431-130 (2006) <https://www.icc-cpi.int/news/icc-passing-dr-medard-rwelamira> accessed 12 May 2019.

373 Bureau of the Assembly of States Parties, 13th Meeting, 5 April 2006

receiving 59 applications and involving the New York Working Group,[374] in February 2007, the Bureau appointed Renan Villacis as the second Director of the Secretariat.[375] At the of writing in 2024, the Bureau circulated a vacancy call for the Director position of the Secretariat during its 22nd session in 2023.[376]

4 Relationship Agreement with the United Nations and Host State

The Rome Statute created an international organization in which States Parties were called to approve a relationship agreement with the United Nations and with the host State, the Kingdom of the Netherlands.[377] The link between the International Criminal Court and the United Nations can be traced throughout the negotiation history and within the Statute specifically in Article 2.[378] Although Article 112 did not contain a clause giving to the Assembly the power to approve the relationship agreement with the United Nations, Article 2 added 'yet another function'[379] to States Parties bearing in mind their 'treaty-making power'.[380] Similarly, and as a direct consequence of its establishment as an independent organization, Article 3(2) in the Statute assigned to the Assembly the power to approve the headquarter agreement with the Netherlands, the host State.[381]

In relation to the agreement with the United Nations, after its role creating the Court was recognized during the second session in 2003,[382] the relationship agreement was concluded in 2004.[383] The Rules of Procedure of the Assembly also contained a number of provisions that regulated the participa-

---

374 Report of the Sixth Session of the Assembly of States Parties to the Rome Statute of the International Criminal Court, New York, 30 November – 14 December, Volume I, ICC-ASP/6/20 7.

375 Bureau of the Assembly of States Parties, 4th Meeting, 1 February 2007 (2007).

376 See: Bureau of the Assembly of States Parties, 13th Meeting, 5 April 2006; 'Job Title: Director of the Secretariat of the Assembly of States Parties (D-1), Requisition ID 23198, available at: <https://www.icc-cpi.int/vacancy/director-secretariat-assembly-states-parties-d-1'>.

377 Gradoni, (2012) 2009.

378 Preamble, Article 2, Rome Statute of the International Criminal Court (2002) 2187 UNTS 90.

379 Ambach, 'Article 2 Relationship of the Court with the United Nations' (2016)

380 Yáñez-Barnuevo and Escobar Hernández, (2003) 44.

381 Article 3(2), Rome Statute of the International Criminal Court (2002) 2187 UNTS 90.

382 ICC-ASP/2/Res.9 Role of the United Nations in the Establishment of the International Criminal Court (2003) 1.

383 UNGA Res 58/318 (2004).

tion of the United Nations, including its ability to add items to the agenda, the role of the Secretary General, and its engagement with subsidiary bodies.[384] While Rule 36 extended a standing invitation for the Secretary General or a delegate to attend Bureau meetings, this had not occurred between 2005 and 2021.[385] Further to the agreement, the United Nations Office of Legal Affairs issued in 2016 a best practice manual to guide the engagement with the Court.[386] Since the relationship agreement in 2004, the connection between the Assembly and the United Nations has rendered mixed results. On the positive side, States Parties have benefitted greatly from conference and logistical services as well as the inclusion of Court staff members to the United Nations pension system.[387] The Bureau also received assistance with developing the Independent Oversight Mechanism[388] and the vetting system for the election of judges.[389] The Assembly, in turn, has summarized and recognized the work of the United Nations in a separate section of the annual omnibus resolution since 2012.[390]

On the other hand, the financial implication of referrals from the Security Council to the Court remained unresolved by the 20th session in 2021. Article 115(b) of the Statute stipulated that, subject to the approval of the General Assembly, the Court shall receive funds from the United Nations 'in particular in relation to the expenses incurred due to referrals by the Security Council'.[391] Article 13 of the relationship agreement outlines that any provision of funds as decided by the General Assembly 'shall be subject to separate arrangements'.[392] However, despite the Security Council referring two situations

384 See Rules 6, 9, 11, 12, 14, 16, 35 and 36, Rules of Procedure of the Assembly of States Parties, ICC-ASP/1/3.

385 Assembly of States Parties to the Rome Statute, Bureau Decisions, available at: <https://asp.icc-cpi.int/bureau/decisions>.

386 United Nations Office of Legal Affairs, Best Practices Manual for United Nations – International Criminal Court Cooperation, available at: <https://legal.un.org/ola/media/UN-ICC_CooperationBest%20Practice%20Guidance%20for%20UN-ICC%20cooperation%20-public.docx.pdf> (2016).

387 ICC-ASP/8/Res.3 Strengthening the International Criminal Court and the Assembly of States Parties (2009) 6.

388 See for example Bureau of the Assembly of States Parties, 16th Meeting, 28 October 2010 (2010).

389 Bureau of the Assembly of States Parties, 3rd Meeting, 12 May 2021 (2021) 3.

390 ICC-ASP/11/Res.8 Strengthening the International Criminal Court and the Assembly of States Parties 48.

391 Article 115, Rome Statute of the International Criminal Court (2002) 2187 UNTS 90.

392 ICC-ASP/3/Res.1 Negotiated Relationship Agreement Between the International Criminal Court and the United Nations 100.

to the Office of the Prosecutor amounting to €75 million[393] in 2021, no funding agreement was in place by the 20th session. In this regard, the Assembly of States Parties noted 'with concern' the financial gap for the first time in 2013[394] and in every omnibus resolution in the period analysed in this book.[395]

In regard to the relationship agreement with the host State, the Court remained the contracting party with the Kingdom of the Netherlands.[396] The Assembly, by virtue of Article 3(2), approved the agreement in 2005[397] and in 2007 the President of the Court signed the treaty with the Dutch Minister of Foreign Affairs.[398] On 1 March 2008 the agreement came into force after the ratification of the host State parliament.[399] Given the treaty outlined arrangements relevant for the Court, the Rules of Procedure of the Assembly did not contain any reference to the host State. However, the Assembly has noted 'with appreciation the ongoing commitment of the host State to the Court with a view to its more efficient functioning',[400] in each omnibus resolution between 2011 and 2021. In practice, between 2002 and 2021, the relationship between the Assembly, the Bureau and the host State evolved around logistical support for meetings of States Parties in The Hague, notably during the Covid-19 pandemic,[401] and the interim[402] and permanent premises of the Court.[403] In addition, the host State provided valuable security assistance to

393 ICC-ASP/20/Res.5 Strengthening the International Criminal Court and the Assembly of States Parties 7.

394 ICC-ASP/12/Res.8 Strengthening the International Criminal Court and the Assembly of States Parties 57–58.

395 Report of the Registry on the Approximate Costs Allocated so far within the Court in Relation to Referrals by the Security Council, ICC-ASP/20/11 (2021) 1.

396 Harmsen and Strijards, (2016) 71.

397 Headquarters Agreement Between the International Criminal Court and the Host State, ICC-ASP/5/Res.3, Annex II. (2006) 5.

398 ICC-ASP/6/Res.2 Strengthening the International Criminal Court and the Assembly of States Parties (2007).

399 ICC-ASP/7/Res.3 Strengthening the International Criminal Court and the Assembly of States Parties (2008).

400 ICC-ASP/10/Res.5 Strengthening the International Criminal Court and the Assembly of States Parties 30.

401 Bureau of the Assembly of States Parties, 14th Meeting, 11 December 2020 (2020).

402 Report on Interim Premises, Note by the Secretariat, ICC-ASP/4/INF.2 (2006).

403 ICC-ASP/15/Res.2 Permanent Premises.

the Court in 2022 and 2023 responding to a case of espionage[404] and a cyber-attack[405] respectively.

5 Management Oversight of Elected Officials

The Rome Statute assigned to the Assembly of States Parties the 'management oversight to the Presidency, the Prosecutor and the Registrar regarding the administration of the Court'.[406] Article 112(2)(b) can be read together with 112(4) establishing the Independent Oversight Mechanism and 112(5) allowing elected officials to participate in meetings of the Assembly and the Bureau.[407] These three clauses indicate a conventional level of supervision by States Parties over the principals of the Court. The limits of supervision, however, are confined strictly to the non-judicial aspects of the Court. This is confirmed by reading Articles 40, 42 and 119 whereas the independence of judges and the Office of the Prosecutor is coupled with the Court's exclusive remit in settling any issue 'concerning the judicial functions'.[408] The drafting period confirms the 'delicate relationship'[409] between States Parties and the Court emerging from this clause. However, as Guilfoyle explained, respecting the independence of the organs of the Court does not necessarily preclude criticism by States Parties as the ultimate governance body of the Rome Statute.[410] The Assembly-mandated Independent Expert Review is a good example of Article 112(2)(b) in practice within the safeguards offered elsewhere in the Statute. In a broader sense, as Blokker showed, the tension between oversight and transparency risks wrong perceptions of accountability between States Parties and the Court.[411] In the opposite way, if oversight instruments are calibrated to provide a space for organizational development and excellence, the Assembly is the natural venue for management oversight discussions which, in turn, can build confidence between States Parties and the Court, preventing among

404 Reuters, 'Netherlands says Russian spy Caught Seeking War Crimes Court Internship' (2022) <https://www.reuters.com/world/europe/netherlands-says-russian-spy-caught-seeking-war-crimes-court-internship-2022-06-16/> accessed 18 June 2022.

405 Measures Taken Following the Unprecedented Cyber-attack on the ICC, International Criminal Court, Press Release: 20 October 2023 (2023).

406 112(2)(b), Rome Statute of the International Criminal Court (2002) 2187 UNTS 90.

407 112(4)–(5), Rome Statute of the International Criminal Court (2002) 2187 UNTS 90.

408 119(1), Rome Statute of the International Criminal Court (2002) 2187 UNTS 90.

409 Donat Cattin, (1999) 74.

410 Guilfoyle, 42.

411 Blokker, 'The Governance of International Courts and Tribunals' (2018) 40.

other consequences, misperceptions and possible withdrawals.[412] Thus, it is proper the Assembly examined annually the activities of the Court, its strategic plans, staffing priorities, budget expenditure, human resources and staff regulations in order to 'improve organizational efficiency and cost-effectiveness'.[413] As summarized by Assembly President Wenaweser in 2009, 'management oversight should be limited to issues that have an impact on the effective functioning of the Court and in particular that have budgetary consequences'.[414] The practice of the Assembly between 2002 and 2021 reveals key methods in which management oversight has manifested itself within the confines of non-judicial activities of the Court.

The first oversight method has been the application of Article 112(5) regulating the participation of the principals of the Court in Assembly and Bureau meetings. Between 2003 and 2021, the Court President, Prosecutor and Registrar have taken part of every session of the Assembly.[415] Aligned with Rule 34 of the procedure of the Assembly, the Court has presented an annual report as part of a standing agenda item since 2003. The annotated version of the Assembly's agenda has included a direct reference to Article 112(2)(b) and (5) since the second session in 2003.[416] As de Hoon and Lohne have observed, the participation of the Prosecutor in other events is more frequent than that of the judges as they appear to 'emphasize its independence from the political and managerial backstage'.[417] At the level of the Bureau, while Rule 34 applies in the same manner as in the Assembly, the principals of the Court have addressed the Bureau infrequently between 2005 and 2021. In total, the Court President addressed the Bureau in six occasions, the Prosecutor in three and the Registrar in four.[418] However, it is important to recall that the record of Bureau meetings in the public domain is incomplete and the agendas do not describe attendance, which might include representatives of the Court organs.

---

412 Guilfoyle, 42.

413 Clements, Richard, 'From Bureaucracy to Management: The International Criminal Court's Internal Progress Narrative' (2019) 32 (1) Leiden Journal of International Law 149.

414 Wenaweser, (2009) 2.

415 Assembly of States Parties to the Rome Statute, ASP Sessions, available at: <https://asp.icc-cpi.int/sessions>.

416 Second Session of the Assembly of States Parties to the Rome Statute of the International Criminal Court, New York, 8–12 September 2003, Annotated List of Items Included in the Provisional Agenda, ICC-ASP/2/1/Add.1 (2003).

417 de Hoon and Lohne, (2019) 71.

418 Assembly of States Parties to the Rome Statute, Bureau Decisions, available at: <https://asp.icc-cpi.int/bureau/decisions>.

A second method in which States Parties have fulfilled Article 112(2)(b) was by focusing on specific management themes in the Assembly and Bureau. For example, since 2005 the Assembly via the Bureau have commented on strategic planning processes in the Presidency, Office of the Prosecutor and Registry.[419] In 2006, the Assembly welcomed the Court's strategic plan and recommended further dialogue on 'cross-cutting issues such as location of the activities of the Court, position of victims, outreach and communication activities of the Court, and the relationship between the Strategic Plan and the budget'.[420] The list of issues showed wide interest by States Parties on the operations of the Court, albeit at a strategic oversight level.[421] Between 2006 and 2021, the Bureau remained seized with strategic planning matters across the organs of the Court, including with the development of key performance indicators,[422] receiving annual reports and noting their importance in the omnibus resolution.[423]

6 Conclusion

The governance and management practice of the Assembly of States Parties between 2002 and 2021 rendered a complex system of oversight, organizational accountability and decision-making, putting substantial pressure on States Parties. This chapter found that, between 2002 and 2021, the Assembly of States Parties considered 517 agenda items and adopted by consensus 154 resolutions, seven decisions, four recommendations and two declarations, these, exclusively at the Review Conference in 2010. Led by seven Bureau compositions, the Assembly held 32 meetings in total: 20 regular sessions plus 11 resumed sessions and one Review Conference. In the 20 sessions stud-

419 ICC-ASP/4/Res.4 Strengthening the International Criminal Court and the Assembly of States Parties 3.

420 ICC-ASP/5/Res.2 Strategic Planning Process of the Court (2006).

421 Clements, Richard 'ReVisiting the ICC Registry's ReVision Project'; Clements, Richard, '"Efficiency Is Paramount in This Regard": The Managerial Role of the ICC Presidency from Kirsch to Fernández' (2022) 21 (2) The Law & Practice of International Courts and Tribunals 342.

422 Carcano, Andrea, 'On the Governance of International Judicial Institutions: The Development of Performance Indicators for the International Criminal Court' (2019) 22 (1) Max Planck Yearbook of United Nations Law Online.

423 Assembly of States Parties to the Rome Statute, Strategic Planning (2010–2016), available at: <https://asp.icc-cpi.int/bureau/WorkingGroups/StrategicPlanning> accessed 5 January 2024.

ied, the pinnacle of membership occurred in 2016 during the 15th session with 124 members. Even as membership changed, however, States Parties faced challenges to adhere to the principle of regional rotation agreed in 2002, greatly affecting the quota of power entitled to the Africa Group of States. In addition, the chapter argued that structural changes to the Assembly corresponded with specific challenges facing States Parties in their governance and management responsibility towards the Court. The Independent Oversight Mechanism and the Study Group on Governance were notable examples how States Parties devolved to these bodies key responsibilities to oversee elected officials and examine the performance of the Court. In this context, the chapter found the Bureau struggled to manage the proliferation of mandates assigned to States Parties, the level of engagement from topic coordinators, quality of reports and unexpected vacancies as diplomats were reassigned to other duties by their respective States. In addition, Chapter 4 found the Assembly of States Parties benefitted from its relationship agreement with the United Nations and the host State. Although the Court led the operational details of these agreements, the Assembly's use of United Nations services and advice as well as financial support from the host State, facilitated respectively the organization of meetings and establishment of the permanent premises of the Court. The Assembly, however, did struggle to further negotiate with the United Nations the cost recovery of referrals by the Security Council to Court amounting to €75 million in 2021.

CHAPTER 6

The Practice of the Assembly of States Parties: Election, Disciplinary Measures and Removal of Court Officials

1 Introduction

The Assembly of States Parties retained the critical function to endow the Court with judges, a Prosecutor, Deputy Prosecutor, and indirectly, a Registrar. The power of States Parties to shape the fortunes of the Court via their election cannot be overstated. In the spirit of review and reflection, there is overwhelming consensus between the academic literature and practitioners of the need for competent principals with demonstrable integrity to lead the Court through its various obligations under the Rome Statute.[1] The practice of the Assembly between 2002 and 2021 revealed institutional deficits that precluded the election of the most suitable candidates. For example, the Assembly's slow-walk towards the establishment of the Advisory Committee on Nomination of Judges, the weak procedure for the election of the Prosecutor and a lacking permanent vetting system for elected officials. On the other hand, as the Assembly elected the principals of the Court, it also retained the power to impose disciplinary measures and decide on their removal from post. Indeed, States Parties' management oversight over elected officials included evaluating undesiring conduct and consequences thereof. Between 2002 and 2021, the Assembly was confronted with public exposes criticizing the conduct of elected officials, for example of the first Prosecutor, urging States Parties to take corrective action. In this sense, interrelated provisions located primarily across the Rome Statute,[2] Rules of Procedure of the Assembly,[3] Rules of Proce-

1 Fernández de Gurmendi, Silvia, 'Judges: Selection, Competence, Collegiality' (2018) 112 American Journal of International Law 163;Clements, 'From Bureaucracy to Management: The International Criminal Court's Internal Progress Narrative' 149; Bergsmo, Morten and Dittrich, Viviane E., 'Integrity as Safeguard Against the Vicissitudes of International Justice Institutions' in Bergsmo, Morten and Dittrich, Viviane E. (eds), Integrity in International Justice (Torkel Opsahl Academic EPublisher 2020) 1.

2 Articles 46(2) and 47, Rome Statute of the International Criminal Court (2002) 2187 UNTS 90.

3 Rules 11, 81 and 82, Rules of Procedure of the Assembly of States Parties, ICC-ASP/1/3.

© EZEQUIEL JIMÉNEZ MARTINEZ, 2026 | DOI:10.1163/9789004749979_007

dure and Evidence,[4] and the Regulations of the Court,[5] and secondarily in the Staff Regulations[6] and Rules,[7] guided the role of the Assembly in disciplinary measures and removal of elected officials. In this context, this chapter follows the practice of the Assembly of States Parties across its election function as well as its role in imposing disciplinary measures and dismissing the principals of the Court. To do so, the chapter begins with a brief discussion of the normative framework guiding the Assembly. Secondly, it offers an overview of the election of judges, the Prosecutor, Deputy Prosecutor and the Registrar. Finally, it discusses the disciplinary and dismissal framework.

2 Election of Court Officials Practice (2002–2021)

Starting with the normative framework, the election of judges by the Assembly of States Parties is regulated by Articles 36, 37 and 112(2)(e) (see Table 6.1).[8] Article 36 sets out the nomination and election criteria for the 18-member bench. The Assembly elects judicial candidates that obtain the highest number of votes from a two-third majority of States present and voting. To elect the bench, Article 36 further imposes on States qualifying requirements for putting forward candidates, such as the need to have 'established competence'[9] in criminal law and procedure (List A) or international law (List B). In the event of a vacancy, Article 37 stipulates the same application of nomination and election criteria as Article 36.[10] The normative framework is completed with Articles 36(2) and 112(2)(e) which enable the President of the Court to request an increase in the number of judges beyond the original 18 membership 'indicating the reasons why this is considered necessary and appropriate'.[11] Article 112(2)(e) is a mirror provision to that in Article 36(2), simply referencing the power of States Parties to 'decide whether to alter, in accordance with article

4 Rules 26, 29 and 30, Rules of Procedure and Evidence, ICC-PIOS-LT-03-004/19.

5 Regulations 121 and 123, Regulations of the Court, International Criminal Court, ICC-BD /01-05-16.

6 ICC-ASP/2/Res.2 Staff Regulations for the International Criminal Court.

7 Staff Rules of the International Criminal Court, ICC/AI/2015/004/Cor.1.

8 Bohlander, Michael, 'Article 36 Qualifications, Nomination and Election of Judges' in Triffterer, Otto and Ambos, Kai (eds), Rome Statute of the International Criminal Court: a Commentary (3rd edn, Beck/Hart 2016) 1217.

9 Article 36, Rome Statute of the International Criminal Court (2002) 2187 UNTS 90.

10 Article 37, Rome Statute of the International Criminal Court (2002) 2187 UNTS 90.

11 Article 36(2)(a), Rome Statute of the International Criminal Court (2002) 2187 UNTS 90.

36, the number of judges'.[12] Although judges have complained about issues of workload[13], the Presidency of the Court has not requested to the Assembly an increase in the bench between 2002 and 2021.[14] Finally, to 'facilitate that the highest-qualified individuals are appointed as judges of the International Criminal Court',[15] the Advisory Committee on Nominations under Article 36 (4)(c) was established in 2011.

The rules for the election of the Prosecutor and Deputy Prosecutor are located in Article 42.[16] The Assembly elects the Prosecutor by secret ballot and by absolute majority. The Deputy Prosecutor is elected in the same manner but from a list of three candidates nominated by the Prosecutor. The Assembly has the power to decide the duration of office up to a non-renewable term of nine years. Both positions must be held by 'persons of high moral character' and 'highly competent in and have extensive practical experience in the prosecution or trial of criminal cases'.[17] However, as Schabas noted, critical elements on leadership, political acumen and strategic management skills are not part of the normative framework.[18]

In regard to the election of the Registrar under Article 43, the Assembly of States Parties does not have a direct role but an advisory one.[19] Under the authority of the President of the Court,[20] the Registrar and Deputy Registrar are elected by an absolute majority of judges in a secret ballot, 'taking into account any recommendation by the Assembly of States Parties'.[21] The list transmitted to the Assembly of States Parties must comply the candidates are 'persons of high moral character, be highly competent and have an excel-

---

12 Article 112(2)(e), Rome Statute of the International Criminal Court (2002) 2187 UNTS 90.

13 The Prosecutor v Uhuru Muigai Kenyatta and Mohammed Hussein Ali (Annex I to Decision Replacing a Judge in Trial Chamber V(b)) ICC-01/09-02/11-890-AnxI (30 January 2014).

14 Assembly of States Parties to the Rome Statute, Election of Judges, available at: <https://asp.icc-cpi.int/elections/judges> accessed 5 January 2024.

15 Report of the Bureau on the Establishment of an Advisory Committee on Nominations of Judges of the International Criminal Court, ICC-ASP/10/36 4.

16 Article 42, Rome Statute of the International Criminal Court (2002) 2187 UNTS 90.

17 Article 42(3), Rome Statute of the International Criminal Court (2002) 2187 UNTS 90.

18 Schabas, The International Criminal Court: A Commentary on the Rome Statute 743.

19 Karagiannakis, Magda, 'Article 43 The Reigstry' in Ambos, Kai and Triffterer, Otto (eds), The Rome Statute of the International Criminal Court: A Commentary (3 edn, Beck/Hart 2016) 1284.

20 Lachowska, Anna, 'The Support Work of the Courts Registry' in Doria, José, Hans-Peter Gasser and M. Cherif Bassiouni (eds), The Legal Regime of the International Criminal Court: Essays in Honour of Professor Igor Blishchenko (Brill Nijhoff 2009) 387.

21 Article 43(4), Rome Statute of the International Criminal Court (2002) 2187 UNTS 90.

TABLE 6.1 Election of judges, prosecutor, deputy prosecutor and registrar

Function	Responsibilities	Relevant articles
Election of Judges, Prosecutor and Deputy Prosecutor	Nomination, assessment and election of Judges, judicial vacancies, Prosecutor and Deputy Prosecutor. Increase of number of Judges.	36, 37, 42(4), 112 (2)(e)
Recommendation on the election of the Registrar	Consideration and recommendation of proposed candidates for the position of Registrar by the Court President.	43(4)

lent knowledge of and be fluent in at least one of the working languages of the Court'.[22]

Within this statutory normative context, between 2002 and 2021, the Assembly of States Parties elected 54 judges,[23] three Prosecutors, five Deputy Prosecutors,[24] four Registrars and one Deputy Registrar (see Table 6.2).[25] Considering the criteria laid out in the Statute, States Parties elected 34 judges from List A and 20 from List B. Upon a proposal from the Prosecutor judging the needs of the Office, States Parties elected two deputies focused on prosecutions, one on investigations, one within a group of female candidates and one within a group of French speakers with a civil law background.[26]

Between 2002 and 2021, States Parties decided on elections in 14 sessions (see Table 6.3).[27] In other words, only in six sessions did the Assembly solely focus on other responsibilities and pressing issues besides the election of

22 Article 43(3), Rome Statute of the International Criminal Court (2002) 2187 UNTS 90.

23 Assembly of States Parties to the Rome Statute, Election of Judges, available at: <https://asp.icc-cpi.int/elections/judges>.

24 Assembly of States Parties to the Rome Statute, Election of the Office of the Prosecutor, available at: <https://asp.icc-cpi.int/elections/prosecutor> accessed 5 January 2024.

25 Assembly of States Parties to the Rome Statute, Election of the Registrar, available at: <https://asp.icc-cpi.int/elections/Registrar>.

26 Assembly of States Parties to the Rome Statute, Election of the Office of the Prosecutor, available at: <https://asp.icc-cpi.int/elections/prosecutor>.

27 Assembly of States Parties to the Rome Statute, ASP Sessions, available at: <https://asp.icc-cpi.int/sessions>.

TABLE 6.2 Assembly of States Parties elected officials (2002–2021)

Judges	List A – Criminal law and procedure	List B – international law	Total
	34	20	54
Prosecutor		3	
Deputy Prosecutor	Prosecution	Investigation	Total
	2	1	3
	List A – Female Only	List B – Francophone / Civil Law	Total
	1	1	2
Registrar		4	
Deputy Registrar		1	

judges, members of the Office of the Prosecutor or Registry. In fact, the Assembly resorted to eight resumed sessions in order to allow sufficient time for decisions on elections.[28] Bearing in mind that each cycle represented a substantial amount of time and consensus building for nominations, assessment and elections, it is notable that criticism persists about the Assembly's ability to elect the most competent and skilled officials for the Court.[29]

2.1 *Election of Judges*

Between 2002 and 2021 the Assembly passed eight resolutions addressing changes to the procedure for nomination and election of judges. The foundational Resolution 2 and 3 from 2002[30] set out the initial guidance and were

28 Ibid.

29 Report of the Independent Expert Review of the International Criminal Court and the Rome Statute System, ICC-ASP/19/16 213; see also: Bergsmo, Morten and others, 'A Prosecutor Falls, Time for the Court to Rise' (2017) 86 FICHL Policy Brief Series 1; Clements, Richard, 'Governing International Criminal Justice: Managerial Practices and the International Criminal Court' (University of Cambridge 2019) 14; Baetens, Freya, 'Identity and Diversity on the International Bench: Implications for the Legitimacy of International Adjudication' in Baetens, Freya (ed), Identity and Diversity on the International Bench: Who is the Judge? (Oxford University Press 2020) 1; Guilfoyle, 1; Kersten, Mark, 'The Next ICC Prosecutor, a Symposium' (Justice in Conflict, 2020) <https://justiceinconflict.org/2020/04/08/the-next-icc-prosecutor-a-symposium/> accessed 10 April 2020.

30 ICC-ASP/1/Res.2 Procedure for the Nomination and Election of Judges, the Prosecutor and Deputy Prosecutors of the International Criminal Court; ICC-ASP/1/Res.3 Procedure for the Election of the Judges for the International Criminal Court.

TABLE 6.3 Assembly of States Parties elective sessions (2002–2021)

Session	Judges (including vacancies)	Office of the Prosecutor	Registrar
ASP 1 (2002/ 2003)	Inaugural Election, 18 judges	Inaugural Election, Prosecutor	Inaugural Election, Registrar
ASP 2 (2003)	–	Inaugural Election, Deputy Prosecutor (Investigations)	–
ASP 3 (2004)		Inaugural Election, Deputy Prosecutor (Prosecutions)	–
ASP 4 (2005/ 2006)	Second Election, 6 judges		
ASP 5 (2006)			
ASP 6 (2007)	Vacancy Election, 3 judges	–	Second Election, Registrar
ASP 7 (2008/ 2009)	Third Election, 6 judges		Inaugural Election, Deputy Registrar
ASP 8 (2009)	Vacancy Election, 2 judges		–
ASP 9 (2010)			
ASP 10 (2011)	Fourth Election, 6 judges	Second Election, Prosecutor	
ASP 11 (2012)	–	Second Election, Deputy Prosecutor (Prosecutions)	Third Election, Registrar
ASP 12 (2013)	Vacancy Election, 1 judge	–	–

TABLE 6.3 Assembly of States Parties elective sessions (2002–2021) (*cont.*)

Session	Judges (including vacancies)	Office of the Prosecutor	Registrar
ASP 13 (2014/2015)	Fifth Election, 6 judges Vacancy Election, 1 judge		
ASP 14 (2015)			
ASP 15 (2016)			
ASP 16 (2017)	Sixth Election, 6 judges	–	Fourth Election, Registrar
ASP 17 (2018)			
ASP 18 (2019)			
ASP 19 (2020)	Seventh Election, 6 judges	Third Election, Prosecutor	–
ASP 20 (2021)	–	Third Election, Deputy Prosecutor (List A – Female Only) Third Election, Deputy Prosecutor (List B – Francophone / Civil Law Tradition)	

revised in 2004 during the third session of the Assembly. The review of the procedure took place in preparation for the election of six judges scheduled for the fourth session in 2005. Resolution 6 from 2004 amended integrally the process by specifying the time period for nominations, the triggers for extending the nomination period, and most importantly, the introduction of minimum voting requirements to assure the election was consistent with the requirements of Article 36, namely List A and B competence, gender and geographical representation.[31] States Parties also introduced a cut-off point of

31 ICC-ASP/3/Res.6 Procedure for the Nomination and Election of Judges, the Prosecutor and Deputy Prosecutors of the International Criminal Court.

four rounds of ballots after which minimum voting requirements ceased to apply, except the number of judges from List A and B.[32] Additionally, Resolution 6 from 2004 adjusted the procedure to fill judicial vacancies by specifying how judicial candidates must fill-in any incomplete diversity criteria.[33]

By the resumed fifth session in 2007, the Assembly further modified the procedure to fill a judicial vacancy by giving the Bureau the power to fix the election date beyond the prescribed 20 weeks, after consulting with the Court.[34] The issue of vacancies became urgent for the Bureau in 2006–2007 as judges Maureen Harding Clark (Ireland), Karl T. Hudson-Phillips (Trinidad and Tobago) and Claude Jorda (France) tendered their resignations.[35] However, as Schabas and Ogwuma have argued, further elections for judicial vacancies during the eighth, twelfth and thirteenth sessions have impacted the careful balance of Article 36 given the complexity of the minimum voting requirements.[36] Thus, in 2015 during the fourteenth Assembly, States Parties agreed to a series of provisions to join the regular election and that of vacancies by amending Resolution 3 from 2004.[37] To address the complex voting system, in 2016, the Bureau facilitator for the topic, Stefan Barriga (Liechtenstein), wrote an 'easy-to-understand overview'[38] aiming to explain the volatile procedure in simple terms. Barriga's document was circulated to States Parties for the sixth (2017) and seventh (2020) regular election of judges.[39]

Other notable changes by the Assembly to the procedure for nomination and election of judges took place in 2013, 2014 and 2019 further amending Resolution 6 from 2004. In 2013, the amendment sought to create an automatic vacancy if 'an elected judge does not make his or her solemn undertak-

32 Ibid.

33 Ibid 4.

34 ICC-ASP/5/Res.5 Procedure for the Nomination and Election of Judges, the Prosecutor and Deputy Prosecutors of the International Criminal Court: Amendment to Operative Paragraph 27 of Resolution ICC-ASP/3/Res.6.

35 Election of Judges to Fill Three Judicial Vacancies of the International Criminal Court, ICC-ASP/6/15 (2007) 1.

36 Ogwuma, Odo Annette, 'Article 37 Judicial Vacancies' in Ambos, Kai and Triffterer, Otto (eds), The Rome Statute of the International Criminal Court: A Commentary (3 edn, Beck/Hart 2016) 1232;Schabas, The International Criminal Court: A Commentary on the Rome Statute 698.

37 ICC-ASP/14/Res.4 Strengthening the International Criminal Court and the Assembly of States Parties (2015) 49.

38 Report to the Bureau on the Review of the Procedure for the Nomination and Election of Judges, ICC-ASP/15/23 (2016) 5.

39 Assembly of States Parties to the Rome Statute, Election of Judges, available at: <https://asp.icc-cpi.int/elections/judges>.

ing … within six months of his or her election'.[40] The amendment emerged as Miriam Defensor-Santiago (Philippines) did not assume her role as judge after the 2011 election.[41] Aware of the issue and disservice to the Court, the Bureau tabled the amendment in time for the regular session; however, it clarified it would not apply retroactively.[42] Resolution 6 from 2004 was amended again in 2014 to modify the period for nominations,[43] and further updated in 2019 with considerable changes to the nomination procedure and the role of the Advisory Committee on Nominations of Judges.[44] The nomination period was changed to leave ample time for the assessment as well as a mandatory request to States to clarify the national nomination procedure used for the selection of their candidate.[45] In addition a public roundtable to assess candidacies was included.[46]

The Advisory Committee rendered four reports between 2011 and 2021. If the purpose of the Committee was to guarantee the most competent and skilled judges become part of the Court, the four reports issued between 2011 and 2021 did not offer a thorough assessment of the nominees. For example, only in 2017 and 2020, in time for the sixth and seventh election of judges, the Committee employed a timid benchmark to assess candidates ranging from 'well qualified', 'particularly well qualified', 'highly qualified', 'qualified', 'formally qualified' and 'not qualified'.[47] While the Committee did add an 'entirely new dimension to the appointments process not seen before in an international court or tribunal',[48] the assessment only offered 'subtle semantic differentiation'[49] between candidates. This was partly due to the overall power by States Parties under Article 36 to nominate and elect judges unfettered of

40 ICC-ASP/12/Res.8 Strengthening the International Criminal Court and the Assembly of States Parties 67.

41 Assembly of States Parties to the Rome Statute, Election of Judges, available at: <https://asp.icc-cpi.int/elections/judges>.

42 Bureau of the Assembly of States Parties, 20th Meeting, 28 November 2013 (2013) 2.

43 ICC-ASP/13/Res.5 Strengthening the International Criminal Court and the Assembly of States Parties 50.

44 ICC-ASP/18/Res.4 Resolution on the Review of the Procedure for the Nomination and Election of Judges.

45 Ibid 3.

46 Ibid.

47 Report of the Advisory Committee on Nominations of Judges on the Work of its Sixth Meeting, ICC-ASP/16/7 (2017); Report of the Advisory Committee on Nominations of Judges on the Work of its Seventh Session, ICC-ASP/19/11 (2020) 6.

48 Powderly, Joseph, Judges and the Making of International Criminal Law (Brill | Nijhoff 2020) 83.

49 Ambach, 'Article 112 Assembly of States Parties' (2022) 2780.

disqualifying assessments and the diplomatic expectation to avoid confrontation among States. Indeed, as Ambos argued, without 'an actual filter function',[50] States could disregard their findings. For example, while a nominee 'did not have in-depth knowledge in a number of areas, including the participation of victims in the proceedings'[51] and civil society alerted of an improper national nomination procedure leading to the candidacy,[52] the aspirant judge was rated 'qualified'[53] and subsequently elected by the Assembly,[54] despite other candidates rated 'highly qualified' available within the mandated voting requirements.[55]

A closer look to the 12 judges elected in 2017 and 2020, shows that States Parties did not select only persons rated 'particularly well qualified'[56] and 'highly qualified'[57] across List A or B competence, gender and geographical representation. Of the 12 judges elected, nine received top marks.[58] Members of the Committee, which included former Court judges and eminent professionals,[59] were aware of their limitations asking for 'guidance' to the Assembly in 2015 to 'establish any form of ranking or other evaluation of the candidates'.[60] However, up to the 20th session in 2021, the Assembly had retained the 2019 procedure even as the Independent Expert Review report noted 'some Judges have owed their success in the ballot more to electoral horse-

50 Ambos, Kai, 'Interests of Justice? The ICC Urgently Needs Reforms' (EJIL Talk!, 2019) <https://www.ejiltalk.org/interests-of-justice-the-icc-urgently-needs-reforms/> accessed 6 September 2020.

51 Report of the Advisory Committee on Nominations of Judges on the Work of its Seventh Session, ICC-ASP/19/11 22.

52 Ibid 25.

53 Ibid 22.

54 Assembly of States Parties to the Rome Statute, Election of Judges, available at: <https://asp.icc-cpi.int/elections/judges>.

55 Report of the Advisory Committee on Nominations of Judges on the Work of its Seventh Session, ICC-ASP/19/11.

56 Report of the Advisory Committee on Nominations of Judges on the Work of its Sixth Meeting, ICC-ASP/16/7.

57 Report of the Advisory Committee on Nominations of Judges on the Work of its Seventh Session, ICC-ASP/19/11.

58 Report of the Advisory Committee on Nominations of Judges on the Work of its Sixth Meeting, ICC-ASP/16/7; Report of the Advisory Committee on Nominations of Judges on the Work of its Seventh Session, ICC-ASP/19/11 6.

59 Report of the Advisory Committee on Nominations of Judges on the Work of its Second Meeting, ICC-ASP/12/47 (2013) 3.

60 Report of the Advisory Committee on Nominations of Judges on the Work of its Fourth Meeting, ICC-ASP/13/46 (2015) 4.

trading than competence'.[61] This claim by the Independent Expert Review is supported by the literature.[62] For example, Nimigan found electoral success tied to financial contributions, campaigning and vote-trading and whether the candidate's State has an open situation at the Court.[63] While the Bureau has frequently asked States Parties to refrain from using judicial positions as political tools, the practice has taken place between 2002 and 2021. Judge-elect Defensor-Santiago describing her election to the media as 'a mutual exchange of favours or quid pro quo'[64] is a telling example.

2.2 *Election of the Prosecutor and Deputy Prosecutor*

Absent of any guiding clause in the Statute, the Assembly of States Parties established bespoke processes to identify, nominate and elect the principal of the Office of the Prosecutor for each of the three elections between 2002 and 2021. In turn, the three Prosecutors have designed their own procedure for selecting Deputies. Designating the Prosecutor for the Court is a highly political exercise by States Parties, conscious of the discretionary power of the position to pursue cases and bring charges and the symbolic role it plays in the overall international justice and accountability architecture.[65] As such, the statutory criteria and procedure laid out in corresponding Assembly resolutions only go so far as States Parties make their decision within a political body and without any effective assurance that Article 42(3) is rigorously

61 Report of the Independent Expert Review of the International Criminal Court and the Rome Statute System, ICC-ASP/19/16 213.

62 Eldar, Ofer, 'Vote-trading in International Institutions' (2008) 19 (1) European Journal of International Law 3; Voeten, 387; Mackenzie, Ruth and others, Selecting International Judges: Principle, Process, and Politics (Oxford University Press 2010) 1; Fife, Rolf Einar, 'Generating Incentives to Appoint Women to the International Bench: Experiences with State Practice' in Baetens, Freya (ed), Identity and Diversity on the International Bench: Who is the Judge? (Oxford University Press 2020) 50; Carcano, Andrea, 'On the Exercise of the Judicial Function at the International Criminal Court: Issues of Credibility and Structural Design' (Questions of International Law, 2020) 1. <http://www.qil-qdi.org/on-the-exercise-of-the-judicial-function-at-the-international-criminal-court-issues-of-credibility-and-structural-design/> accessed March 31 (2020).

63 Nimigan, Sarah, 'Electoral Success at the ICC: A State-Level Analysis' (2022) 3 (3) European Journal of International Law 1.

64 Ibid 18.The claim is publicly available in Youtube at: <https://www.youtube.com/watch?v=EVddIjMZUE0>.

65 Jenia Iontcheva, Turner, 'Accountability of International Prosecutors' in Carsten, Stahn (ed), The Law and Practice of the International Criminal Court (Oxford University Press 2015) 396; Crane, David M, Sadat, Leila N and Scharf, Michael P, The Founders: Four Pioneering Individuals Who Launched the First Modern-Era International Criminal Tribunals (Cambridge University Press 2018) 24.

applied.[66] The election of Luis Moreno Ocampo (Argentina) in 2003, Fatou Bensouda (The Gambia) in 2011 and Karim Khan (United Kingdom) in 2021 have amplified the question whether States Parties acting collectively in the Assembly ensured the 'the protection of the integrity and independence of the Court'.[67]

The Assembly did not institute a bespoke mechanism to identify candidates for the first election of the Prosecutor; instead, it left it exclusively to Assembly President Prince Zeid Raíad Zeid Al-Hussein to coordinate the process.[68] While official Assembly documents describe a certain apathy from States Parties to put forward a candidate for the Office of the Prosecutor, in reality, President Al-Hussein was leading informal consultations with Luis Moreno Ocampo for the position since November 2002.[69] On 24 March 2003, Assembly President Al-Hussein issued a press release announcing consensus among States Parties to elect Moreno Ocampo as the first Prosecutor of the Court.[70] In April 2003, Moreno Ocampo was elected after receiving 78 votes out of 78 valid ballots.[71] As Bergsmo and O'Donohue have argued, the process to select the first Prosecutor was neither transparent[72] nor received support from all States Parties.[73] Bergsmo and Gordon have further reflected on the role of Argentina, Canada, the United Kingdom and Germany in the lead up to Moreno Ocampo's election.[74]

---

66 Schabas, The International Criminal Court: A Commentary on the Rome Statute 743.

67 Donat Cattin, David and Verpile, Melissa, 'Integrity and the Preservation of Independence in International Criminal Justice' in Bergsmo, Morten and Dittrich, Viviane E (eds), Integrity in International Justice (Torkel Opsahl Academic EPublisher 2020) 1086.

68 Bergsmo, Morten, 'Unmasking Power in International Criminal Justice: Invisible College v. Visible Colleagues' in Bergsmo, Morten and others (eds), Power in International Criminal Justice (Torkel Opsahl Academic EPublisher 2020) 12.

69 Moreno Ocampo, 17.

70 Statement by the President of the Assembly of States Parties Prince Zeid Raíad Zeid Al-Hussein, Press Release, ICC-20030411-5.

71 Report of the First Session (First and Second Resumptions) of the Assembly of States Parties to the Rome Statute of the International Criminal Court, New York, 3–7 February and 21–23 April 2003, ICC-ASP/1/3/Add.1 6.

72 O'Donohue, 'The ICC and the ASP' (2015) 129.

73 Bergsmo, Morten, Buis, Emiliano J., Gordon, Gregory S., Inder, Brigid, Kaleck, Wolfgang, Ekeløve-Slydal, Gunnar M. and Tianying, Song, 'ICC State-Party Governance in Times of Disunity' (2023) Policy Brief Series No. 146 Torkel Opsahl Academic EPublisher 3.

74 Gordon, Gregory S., 'Selecting the ICC's Next ASP President: High Scrutiny for High Stakes' (Opinio Juris, 2020) <http://opiniojuris.org/2020/11/16/selecting-the-iccs-next-asp-president-high-scrutiny-for-high-stakes/> accessed 20 November 2020; Bergsmo, 'Unmasking Power in International Criminal Justice: Invisible College v. Visible Colleagues' (2020) 1.

Subsequent to his election, Moreno Ocampo informed the Assembly in August 2003 his nomination of Serge Brammertz (Belgium), Hassan Bubacarr Jallow (The Gambia) and Vladimir Tochilovsky (Ukraine) as candidates for the position of Deputy Prosecutor for investigations.[75] Acting under Article 42(2), the first Prosecutor received 130 applications and was assisted by prosecutors Carla Del Ponte, Louise Arbour and Richard Goldstone in reaching the final three nominations for the Assembly.[76] Moreno Ocampo lamented 'there were not many women candidates nor were there sufficient candidates from all regions and legal systems'.[77] Before the second session of the Assembly in 2003, States Parties were informed Hassan Bubacarr Jallow had withdrawn his candidacy and thus, elected Brammertz over Tochilovsky by 65 to 22 votes, whereas 46 was the threshold of the mandated secret majority vote under Article 42(4).[78] The Assembly decided to allocate a term of office of six years for Brammertz, until November 2009.[79] However, in December 2005, the Assembly was informed the United Nations Secretary General intended to appoint Brammertz as Commissioner of the United Nations International Independent Investigation into Lebanon.[80] After Moreno Ocampo agreed to his release in 2006,[81] Brammertz formally resigned as Deputy Prosecutor of the International Criminal Court in June 2007.[82] In July 2005, Moreno Ocampo informed the Assembly his intention to nominate a second Deputy Prosecutor in charge of prosecutions in time for an election during the third session in 2004.[83] After receiving 198 applications, he nominated Fatou Bensouda (The Gambia), Nicola Crutchley (New Zealand) and Josaia Naigulevu (Fiji).[84] Unlike the procedure to select Serge Brammertz, the first Prosecutor conducted interviews with 10 candidates unassisted.[85] On September 2004, the Assembly elected Bensouda with 58 votes whereas 48 were required by

75 Election of the Deputy Prosecutor of the International Criminal Court, Note by the Secretariat, ICC-ASP/2/8 (2003).

76 Ibid.

77 Ibid 2.

78 Report of the Second Session of the Assembly of States Parties to the Rome Statute of the International Criminal Court, New York, 8–12 September 2003, ICC-ASP/2/10 (2003) 6.

79 Ibid.

80 Bureau of the Assembly of States Parties, 8th Meeting, 21 December 2005 (2005).

81 Bureau of the Assembly of States Parties, 9th Meeting, 13 January 2006 (2006).

82 Bureau of the Assembly of States Parties, 7th Meeting, 6 July 2007 (2007) 2.

83 Election of the Deputy Prosecutor of the International Criminal Court, ICC-ASP/3/8 (2004).

84 Ibid.

85 Ibid 5.

Article 42(4).[86] The Assembly further decided a term of office of nine years from November 2004 for Fatou Bensouda.[87]

As the expiration for Moreno Ocampo's term neared, the Bureau began discussing in September 2010 the mode for the election of the second Prosecutor of the Court in time for the 10th session of the Assembly in 2011.[88] Aware of the issues around the first election in 2003, Assembly President Christian Wenaweser (Liechtenstein), presented a draft proposal to the Bureau in October 2010 to establish a Search Committee for the second Prosecutor.[89] A revised terms of reference document establishing the Committee was agreed by the Bureau in December 2010.[90] The Search Committee was tasked 'to facilitate the nomination and election, by consensus, of the next Prosecutor'[91] producing a 'shortlist of at least three suitable candidates'[92] for consideration by the Bureau. The Committee was composed by single representatives from each regional group, led by a coordinator, and was particularly mandated to keep States Parties appraised of their work in a confidential manner.[93] By March 2011, the Search Committee composition was in place[94] with former Assembly President Prince Zeid Raíad Zeid Al-Hussein selected as coordinator.[95] As the United Nations permanent representative of Jordan at the time, it is notable Al-Hussein's involvement in the election of the first and second Prosecutor of the Court. In light of direct criticism to the Court by Al-Hussein in 2019,[96] Bergsmo has questioned to what extent the issues voiced could be traced to his direct involvement.[97]

86 Report of the Third Session of the Assembly of States Parties to the Rome Statute of the International Criminal Court, The Hague, 6–10 September, ICC-ASP/3/25 6.

87 Ibid.

88 Bureau of the Assembly of States Parties, 13th Meeting, 13 September 2010.

89 Bureau of the Assembly of States Parties, 15th Meeting, 19 October 2010 (2010) 4.

90 Bureau of the Assembly of States Parties, 19th Meeting, 2 December 2010 (2010).

91 Search Committee for the Position of the Prosecutor of the International Criminal Court, Terms of Reference, ICC-ASP/9/INF.2 1.

92 Ibid 2.

93 Ibid 1–2.

94 Bureau of the Assembly of States Parties, 2nd Meeting, 1 February 2011 (2011).

95 Bureau of the Assembly of States Parties, 3rd Meeting, 1 March 2011 (2011).

96 Prince Zeid Raíad Zeid Al-Hussein, Stagno Ugarte, Bruno, Wenaweser, Christian and Intelman, Tiina, 'The International Criminal Court Needs Fixing' (Atlantic Council, 2019) <https://www.atlanticcouncil.org/blogs/new-atlanticist/the-international-criminal-co\urt-needs-fixing> accessed 24 April 2019.

97 Bergsmo, 'Unmasking Power in International Criminal Justice: Invisible College v. Visible Colleagues' (2020) 12.

The report of the Search Committee was transmitted to the Bureau in late October 2011, under two months before the 10th session of the Assembly in December.[98] After an 'extensive'[99] process, the Committee received 52 applications, with the majority coming from the African and the Western European and Other groups, and lamenting 'gender diversity was not as great as the Search Committee would have hoped'.[100] By the end of the process, the Search Committee proposed a shortlist of four candidates to the Bureau: Deputy Prosecutor Fatou Bensouda (The Gambia), Andrew T. Cayley (United Kingdom), Mohamed Chande Othman (Tanzania) and Robert Petit (Canada).[101] At the receipt of the report, the Bureau organized open sessions between States Parties and the four shortlisted candidates in November 2011.[102] After the Assembly President led informal consultations, States Parties agreed the second Prosecutor should originate from the African group, meaning, a choice between Fatou Bensouda and Mohamed Chande Othman.[103] Already in June 2011, the African Union had endorsed Bensouda as their preferred candidate, albeit undermining the search process installed by the Bureau.[104] Further informal consultations in early December resulted in the consensus nomination of Fatou Bensouda by 66 States Parties.[105] Although Article 42(4) of the Statute mandated the election of the Prosecutor by a secret ballot of the absolute majority of States Parties, Fatou Bensouda was elected by acclamation on 12 December 2011 for a nine year period.[106]

Article 42 of the Statute and Resolution 2 from 2002 did not indicate geographical origin of the Prosecutor as a criterion for appointment. While it was generally understood that regional rotation across the elected positions of the Court and the Assembly was expected, the decision to narrow the selection of the second Prosecutor to the African group of States corresponded more to the

98 Report of the Search Committee for the Position of the Prosecutor of the International Criminal Court, available at: <https://asp.icc-cpi.int/sites/asp/files/asp_docs/Elections/EP2011/EP2011-PSC-Report-complete-ENG.pdf> (2011).

99 Ibid 1.

100 Ibid 5.

101 Ibid 1.

102 Assembly of States Parties to the Rome Statute, Election of Prosecutor (2011), available at: <https://asp.icc-cpi.int/elections/prosecutor/prosecutor> accessed 5 January 2024.

103 Election of the Prosecutor of the International Criminal Court, Note by the Secretariat, ICC-ASP/10/38 (2011) 2.

104 O'Donohue, 'The ICC and the ASP' (2015) 130.

105 Election of the Prosecutor of the International Criminal Court, Note by the Secretariat, ICC-ASP/10/38 2.

106 Report of the Tenth Session of the Assembly of States Parties to the Rome Statute of the International Criminal Court, New York, 12–21 December, Volume I, ICC-ASP/10/20 11.

political context in 2011 than a rigorous application of the normative framework.[107] To this effect, when asked by reporters, Assembly President Wenaweser agreed that Bensouda's nationality was 'helpful' to 'increase acceptance of the Court on the continent'.[108] In this context, the Assembly requested the Bureau to 'examine ways of strengthening future elections of the Prosecutor, including an evaluation of such a process'.[109] At the 12th session in 2013, the evaluation report highlighted the utility of the procedure but criticized the terms of reference, imbalances in the composition, compliance with statutory regulations and lack of transparency.[110] Notably, it also underscored that by avoiding a competitive election it precluded 'trading of votes' in favour of a 'technical, merit-based evaluation of candidates'.[111] However, the report did not take into consideration the omnipresent political context as a contributing factor for the election. In addition, several States recommended an earlier starting point for any future rendition of a similar process, coupled with clearer criteria for the selection of candidates.[112] At the time the Assembly of States Parties embarked on the election of the third Prosecutor due in 2020, these recommendations were available to the Bureau.[113]

Despite Prosecutor Fatou Bensouda's term starting in June, the process to recruit a Deputy Prosecutor for prosecutions ran between February and April 2012.[114] The second Prosecutor received 120 applications and evaluated them in two rounds of interviews, assisted by two separate panels, including 'two persons from outside the Office of the Prosecutor',[115] and a group of senior trial lawyers. After the internal assessment, Bensouda transmitted to the Assembly the nomination of Paul Rutledge (Australia), James Stewart (Canada) and Raija Toiviainen (Finland), in time for an election to take place during the

107 du Plessis, Max, 'Reflections on a Storm: the International Criminal Court and its Work in Africa' (2012) 18 (2) Australian Journal of Human Rights 161.

108 Press Conference on Upcoming Session of Assembly of States Parties to Rome Statute, 1 December 2011, available at: <https://asp.icc-cpi.int/sites/asp/files/NR/rdonlyres/7755943C-E70A-4E43-B032-5416E6240029/0/UNPressCPASP01Dec2011ENG.pdf> (2011).

109 ICC-ASP/10/Res.5 Strengthening the International Criminal Court and the Assembly of States Parties 31.

110 Report on the Evaluation of the Process on the Election of the Prosecutor, ICC-ASP/12/58 (2013).

111 Ibid 2.

112 Ibid.

113 Bureau of the Assembly of States Parties, 11th Meeting, 9 July 2018 (2018) 4.

114 Election of the Deputy Prosecutor of the International Criminal Court, Note by the Secretariat, ICC-ASP/11/17 (2012) 2.

115 Ibid.

11th session in November 2012.[116] In contrast from the process ran by Moreno Ocampo, the three candidates were interviewed by States Parties between October and November 2012.[117] The election at the 11th session was competitive. Only after five rounds of ballots and the withdrawal of candidates, James Stewart was elected with 81 votes whereas 61 represented the absolute majority of States Parties.[118] This was the first time abstentions occurred in an election for a Deputy Prosecutor.[119] Stewart in 2016 recognized the politicization of his election and his shock to have to campaign for votes in New York, The Hague and Brussels.[120] The newly elected Deputy Prosecutor was afforded a nine-year term of office by the Assembly.[121]

As Fatou Bensouda's mandate was set to conclude in June 2021, the Bureau began charting in July 2018 the process to elect the third Prosecutor of the Court.[122] Learning from one of the key recommendations from the evaluation report of Bensouda's election in 2011,[123] the Bureau's early start aimed to 'depoliticize the election process' while seeking a consensus candidate in time for the 19th session of the Assembly in 2020.[124] Between 2018 and 2021, the Bureau engaged with the election process in 33 meetings as the aim for a consensus candidate suffered several setbacks and was finally not achieved.[125] During the 17th session in 2018, Assembly President O-Gon Kwon proposed draft terms of reference for a Committee on the Election of the Prosecutor,[126]

---

116 Ibid.

117 Assembly of States Parties to the Rome Statute, Election of Deputy Prosecutor [Prosecutions] (2012), available at: <https://asp.icc-cpi.int/elections/prosecutor/deputyprosecutor> accessed 5 January 2024.

118 Report of the Eleventh Session of the Assembly of States Parties to the Rome Statute of the International Criminal Court, The Hague, 14–22 November 2012, Volume I, ICC-ASP/11/20 (2012) 8.

119 Ibid 9.

120 Charania, Shehzad, 'A Test of Our Resilience – An Interview with the ICC Deputy Prosecutor' (Justice in Conflict, 2016) <https://justiceinconflict.org/2016/08/10/a-test-of-our-resilience-an-interview-with-the-icc-deputy-prosecutor/> accessed 3 June 2021.

121 Report of the Eleventh Session of the Assembly of States Parties to the Rome Statute of the International Criminal Court, The Hague, 14–22 November 2012, Volume I, ICC-ASP/11/20 8.

122 Bureau of the Assembly of States Parties, 11th Meeting, 9 July (2018) 4.

123 Report on the Evaluation of the Process on the Election of the Prosecutor, ICC-ASP/12/58 2.

124 Bureau of the Assembly of States Parties, 11th Meeting, 9 July (2018) 4.

125 Assembly of States Parties to the Rome Statute, Bureau Decisions, available at: <https://asp.icc-cpi.int/bureau/decisions>.

126 Bureau of the Assembly of States Parties, 1st Meeting, 7 February 2019 (2019).

which were discussed and further revised by the Bureau in March 2019[127] and finally adopted in April the same year.[128] The aim of the Committee was to 'facilitate the nomination and election of the next Prosecutor'.[129] It was composed of single representatives from regional groups and assisted by a five-person external panel of experts with 'extensive national or international criminal investigation, prosecution or judicial experience'.[130]

In June 2019, after consultation with States Parties, the Bureau appointed the members of the Committee[131] and the panel of experts.[132] The addition of external experts to the Committee was in response to the 2011 evaluation seeking to depoliticize the choice of candidates for a shortlist. In July 2019, the Committee and the panel designated Sabine Nölke and Charles Jalloh as their respective chairs.[133] Under the working methods, the Bureau entrusted the Committee with the drafting of the vacancy advert, the receipt of individual candidacies, competency-based interviews to determine a longlist of applicants and the transmission of a shortlist of three to six candidates to the Bureau.[134] Cryptically, it also asked the Committee to assure the 'best interests of the Court and the Assembly of States Parties as a whole'[135] during the process. This requirement was not part of the 2011 precedent and its location in the same paragraph considering diversity criteria for the selection of candidates opens up a question of undue political factors in what was established as a technical exercise.

The Committee on the Election of the Prosecutor handed its report and shortlist of candidates to the Bureau in June 2020. Despite operational challenges due to the Covid-19 pandemic, the Committee transmitted four candidacies: Morris A. Anyah (Nigeria), Fergal Gaynor (Ireland), Susan Okalany (Uganda) and Richard Roy (Canada).[136] This outcome emerged after the Com-

127 Bureau of the Assembly of States Parties, 3rd Meeting, 20 March 2019 (2019).

128 Bureau of the Assembly of States Parties, 4th Meeting, 7 May 2019 (2019).

129 Bureau of the Assembly of States Parties: Election of the Prosecutor Terms of Reference, ICC-ASP/18/INF.2 (2019) 2.

130 Ibid 1.

131 Bureau of the Assembly of States Parties, 5th Meeting, 7 June 2019 (2019).

132 Bureau of the Assembly of States Parties, 7th Meeting, 17 July 2019 (2019); President of the Assembly of States Parties Welcomes the Committee on the Election of the Prosecutor and its Panel of Experts, Press Release, 3 July 2019, ICC-ASP-20190703-PR1463 (2019).

133 Report of the Committee on the Election of the Prosecutor, ICC-ASP/19/INF.2 (2020) 4.

134 Bureau of the Assembly of States Parties: Election of the Prosecutor Terms of Reference, ICC-ASP/18/INF.2 2–3.

135 Ibid 2.

136 Report of the Committee on the Election of the Prosecutor, ICC-ASP/19/INF.2 4.

mittee received 89 applications.[137] As the Search Committee interviewed candidates, civil society called to vet all nominees for the high moral requirement in Article 42(3), making sure 'those with a history of workplace and/or sexual harassment would not advance to the shortlist'.[138] The request by 26 civil society actors, including Open Society Justice Initiative, Women's Initiatives for Gender Justice, International Federation for Human Rights and the Kenyan Section of the International Commission of Jurists, alerted of 'enormous reputational and financial risks for the Court' given it had 'suffered reputational damage in the past due to critical deficits of high moral character'.[139] In May 2020, in agreement with the Bureau[140] and with the 14 candidates under consideration, the Committee requested the Security and Safety Section of the Court to confidentially undertake a detailed background check for each nominee.[141] The report from the Committee did not reveal in which ways the vetting process affected its choice, only reporting it 'contributed to the Committee's ability to present to the Assembly a strong and credible list of the most highly qualified candidates, whose candidacy are likely to withstand the reputational scrutiny that the subsequent public process will bring with it'.[142] While short of 'full vetting', Mudukuti argues the 'Committee did their best within the confines of their mandate'.[143] Upon conclusion of the interview period, the vetting process and the receipt of a confidential assessment report by the experts, the Committee transmitted the shortlist of four names to the Bureau in June 2020.[144]

As per the terms of reference of the Committee, the expectation was to elect the third Prosecutor from the shortlist. However, already in July 2020, upon receipt of the report, members in the Bureau, the New York and Hague Working Groups, in particular Kenya, voiced concerns about the work of the Com-

137 Ibid 6.

138 Ibid 7.

139 Open Letter to Committee on the Election of the ICC Prosecutor: Zero Tolerance Must be Shown Towards Sexual Harassment (International Justice Monitor, 2020) <https://www.ijmonitor.org/2020/02/open-letter-to-committee-on-the-election-of-the-icc-prosecutor-zero-tolerance-must-be-shown-towards-sexual-harassment/> accessed 3 March 2020.

140 Bureau of the Assembly of States Parties, 3rd Meeting, 28 May 2020 (2020).

141 Report of the Committee on the Election of the Prosecutor, ICC-ASP/19/INF.2 8.

142 Ibid.

143 Mudukuti, Angela, 'The Procedure for Appointing the International Criminal Court Prosecutor: High Moral Character and the Need for Comprehensive Vetting' (2021) 19 Journal of International Criminal Justice 748.

144 Report of the Committee on the Election of the Prosecutor, ICC-ASP/19/INF.2 8.

mittee and the final result.[145] By September 2020 it was clear States Parties could not agree on a consensus candidate from the shortlist. The Bureau prolonged the period for consultation until October 2020 as 'some States Parties called for extending the group of candidates under consideration'.[146] By the end of October the Bureau reported a stalemate among States Parties. No agreement could be found to either endorse the shortlist as a vehicle for decision-making nor any of the four candidates. Faced with the looming date of the 19th session in December 2020, the Assembly President proposed[147] to reconstitute the Committee to expand the shortlist to 10 previously interviewed candidates, and created a consultative team of single regional representatives to assist the President and scheduled public hearings with all nominees.[148] Importantly, the additional guidance urged States to avoid nominating or endorsing any candidate and to 'refrain from campaigning or otherwise rallying support for the candidates'.[149]

The additional report by the Committee on the Election of the Prosecutor was transmitted to the Bureau on 25 November 2020. Out of the list of 10 remaining candidates, only five had agreed to be considered again by the Assembly of States Parties: Carlos Castresana Fernández (Spain), Karim A. A. Khan (United Kingdom), Francesco Lo Voi (Italy), Robert Petit (Canada) and Brigitte Raynaud (France).[150] Remarkably different from the original June 2020 report, the Committee decided to waive its auto-imposed confidentiality rules and shared the technical assessment of all additional candidates.[151] Then candidate Khan was initially not included in the shortlist due to limited 'familiarity with ICC budgetary processes', the 'probability of the need for multiple recusals' due to his defence work at the Court, and a seemingly 'coordinated write-in campaign by civil society organizations… despite the confidential nature of the process'.[152] These reasons can be helpful in the necessary and

145 Bureau of the Assembly of States Parties, 5th Meeting, 9 July 2020 (2020); Heller, Kevin Jon, 'The Coming Kerfuffle Over the Next ICC Prosecutor' (Opinio Juris, 2020) <http://opiniojuris.org/2020/07/17/the-coming-kerfuffle-over-the-next-icc-prosecutor/> accessed 8 September 2020.

146 Bureau of the Assembly of States Parties, 7th Meeting, 11 September 2020 (2020) 3.

147 Bureau of the Assembly of States Parties, 11th Meeting, 13 November 2020 (2020).

148 Brazil, Estonia, Jordan, Portugal and Sierra Leone were appointed as focal points. Interestingly, with this appointment, Jordan participated in every search process of the Prosecutor. Bureau of the Assembly of States Parties, 13th Meeting, 4 December 2020 (2020) 1.

149 Bureau of the Assembly of States Parties, 11th Meeting, 13 November 2020 3.

150 Report of the Committee on the Election of the Prosecutor, Addendum, Appraisals of Additional Candidates, ICC-ASP/19/INF.2/Add.3 (2020) 2.

151 Ibid 3.

152 Ibid 4.

holistic assessment of a candidate but they do not strictly amount as disqualifying factors within the requirements in Article 42 of the Statute. Even after conducting a new round of public hearings in 9–10 December 2020 with the nine candidates identified through the Committee's process, States Parties were unable to find consensus.[153] The situation forced the Assembly to pass Resolution 5 from 2020 requiring the Bureau to organize a resumed session in the first two months of 2021 to complete its statutory obligation.[154]

After four rounds of intense consultation between January and February 2021 led by the Bureau, States Parties still could not agree on a consensus candidate. The situation forced the Assembly President to pursue talks in extremis hours before the scheduled vote in the afternoon of 8 February in New York.[155] The complete inability to achieve consensus among States Parties required the Bureau to postpone the second resumed session to 12 February and to open the formal nomination process for the election of the Prosecutor until midday 10 February, in essence, abandoning the search process started in July 2018.[156] At the end of the period, the Secretariat received the nominations of Carlos Castresana Fernández (Spain), Fergal Gaynor (Ireland), Karim A. A. Khan (United Kingdom) and Francesco Lo Voi (Italy), with Gaynor as the only candidate originally in the shortlist produced by the election Committee.[157]

The election took place on 12 February at midday in New York and was competitive for the first time in the Assembly's history. The election required two rounds of ballots where Castresana Fernández and Lo Voi only obtained 12 and five out of 123 possible votes.[158] In the second round, Khan was finally elected as third Prosecutor for the Court after obtaining 72 votes whereas 62 was the required statutory majority.[159] The Assembly concluded the item and troubled process by affording Khan a nine-year term of office.[160] Far from

153 Bureau of the Assembly of States Parties, 14th Meeting, 11 December 2020 3.

154 ICC-ASP/19/Res.5 Resolution Concerning a Possible Second Resumption of the Nineteenth Session of the Assembly and the Term of the Current Bureau in Relation Thereto.

155 Bureau of the Assembly of States Parties, 20th Meeting, 5 February 2021.

156 Report of the Nineteenth Session (First and Second Resumptions) of the Assembly of States Parties to the Rome Statute of the International Criminal Court, New York, 17–23 December 2020 and 12 February 2021, ICC-ASP/19/20/Add.1 18.

157 Election of the Prosecutor of the International Criminal Court, Note by the Secretariat, ICC-ASP/19/19 (2021).

158 Assembly of States Parties to the Rome Statute, Election of Prosecutor (2020), available at: <https://asp.icc-cpi.int/elections/prosecutor/Prosecutor2020>.

159 Ibid.

160 Report of the Nineteenth Session (First and Second Resumptions) of the Assembly of States Parties to the Rome Statute of the International Criminal Court, New York, 17 – 23 December 2020 and 12 February 2021, ICC-ASP/19/20/Add.1 20.

agreeing the path to elect Khan was appropriate, the Assembly required the Bureau during the 19th and 20th sessions to conduct an evaluation of the process.[161] In 2021, the Bureau led by Assembly President Silvia Fernández de Gurmendi (Argentina) discussed in six meetings the modality and options to review the search process of a future Prosecutor for the Court.[162] At the 21st session of the Assembly in 2022, the lessons learnt report revealed 'politics, and lobbying, still played an influential role' in the election procedure, also noting the view of several States Parties arguing that the aim to 'remove the political element was impossible or undesirable'.[163]

As with his predecessors, Prosecutor Karim Khan moved swiftly to appoint his team, but unlike Moreno Ocampo and Bensouda, he opened the vacancy period for two positions to be jointly elected by the Assembly during the 20th session in December 2021. The selection process of the two Deputy Prosecutors introduced three innovations. First, Prosecutor Khan narrowed the selection of candidates to two categories: female only (List A) and francophone lawyers from a civil law tradition (List B).[164] For the Prosecutor, the two restricted categories put forward to States amounted to the 'requisite experience and qualifications to assist me in running an effective and efficient Office'.[165] However, some Bureau members raised concerns this procedure would alter the meaning of Article 42(4) in the Statute as the provision did not include the possibility of two lists in a single election.[166] The election of the two deputies from a single list of six candidates or two lists of three each had an impact in the overall balance of gender, geographical and legal tradition criteria. For this reason, and as an exception, the Bureau recommended the Assembly to maintain the two lists but draw lots to decide which list would be considered first.[167]

The second innovation referred to the involvement of the Independent Oversight Mechanism in vetting candidates for the high moral character

161 ICC-ASP/18/Res.6 Strengthening the International Criminal Court and the Assembly of States Parties 10;ICC-ASP/19/Res.6 Strengthening the International Criminal Court and the Assembly of States Parties 11.

162 Bureau of the Assembly of States Parties, 8th Meeting, 3 November 2021 (2021).

163 Report by the Facilitators on the Third Election of the Prosecutor of the ICC – Lessons Learnt, ICC-ASP/21/16 (2022) 15–16.

164 Election of the Deputy Prosecutor of the International Criminal Court, ICC-ASP/20/34 (2021) 3.

165 Ibid.

166 Bureau of the Assembly of States Parties, 9th Meeting, 24 November 2021 (2021).

167 Election of the Deputy Prosecutors of the International Criminal Court: Guide for the Fourth Election, ICC-ASP/20/37/Rev.1 (2021).

requirement in Article 42(3). Learning from Khan's election, Assembly President Fernández de Gurmendi agreed with the Prosecutor on the modalities for vetting candidates for 'human rights violations, incidents of sexual harassment, bullying in the workplace and other ethical or legal breaches of a serious nature such as fraud or corruption'.[168] The vetting process led by the Independent Oversight Mechanism did not find 'any information that would render any of the candidates ineligible pursuant to the article 42(3) requirement'.[169] The Prosecutor was assisted by Adama Dieng (Senegal) Special Adviser to the United Nations Secretary General on the Prevention of Genocide and Catherine Marchi-Uhel (France) Head of the International, Impartial and Independent Mechanism in determining the final six candidates.[170] The third innovation introduced in 2021 was the written and public appraisal of all six candidates in a similar a manner to the Advisory Committee on Nomination of Judges. In the end, the Assembly elected Mame Mandiaye Niang (Senegal), from List B and Nazhat Shameen Khan (Fiji), from List A in December 2021.[171] Both elected Deputy Prosecutors received a term of nine years.[172]

2.3 *Election of the Registrar*

The Assembly of States Parties has only an indirect role in the election of the Registrar. The Presidency of the Court has the role to identify and transmit a list of candidates to the Assembly, and subsequently, to share any recommendation by States Parties with the plenary of the judges for election.[173] Between the first and twentieth sessions of the Assembly, States Parties received four lists of candidates for Registrar and issued recommendations in 2003, 2007, 2012 and 2017.[174]

As detailed before, the first election of the Registrar took place during the second resumption of the first session of the Assembly in April 2003. Philippe Kirsch transmitted two nominations to the Assembly: Bruno Cathala

168 Bureau of the Assembly of States Parties, 5th Meeting, 7 July 2021 (2021) 5.

169 Election of the Deputy Prosecutor of the International Criminal Court, ICC-ASP/20/34 2.

170 Ibid.

171 Report of the Twentieth Session of the Assembly of States Parties to the Rome Statute of the International Criminal Court, The Hague, 6–11 December, Volume I, ICC-ASP/20/20 (2021) 9.

172 Assembly of States Parties to the Rome Statute, Election of Deputy Prosecutors (2021), available at: <https://asp.icc-cpi.int/elections/prosecutor/DeputyProsecutor2021> accessed 4 January 2024.

173 Rule 12, Rules of Procedure and Evidence, ICC-PIOS-LT-03-004/19.

174 Assembly of States Parties to the Rome Statute, Election of the Registrar, available at: <https://asp.icc-cpi.int/elections/Registrar>.

(France), the interim Registrar of the Court, and that of Bert Maan, President of Zwolle-Lelystad District Court in the Netherlands.[175] After a working group of the Bureau considered the candidates, the Assembly agreed with a recommendation the judges proceed with the election based on the two candidates put forward.[176] The recommendation did not include any preference or criteria to take into account for the election of Registrar.[177] On 24 June 2003, Bruno Cathala was elected for a five-year term by the plenary of the judges.[178]

In 2007, during the sixth session of the Assembly, the process to elect Cathala's successor changed. The first Vice-President of the Court, Akua Kuenyehia, oversaw an open application procedure that attracted 97 candidates for the post of Registrar.[179] Unlike the nomination of two candidates in 2003, the Presidency transmitted 10 nominations.[180] The Bureau considered the list and recommended to the Assembly the inclusion of further clarifications of statutory and other criteria applicable for the election of the Registrar.[181] While Recommendation 1 from 2007 did not deviate from 2003 insofar it agreed with the slate of candidates proposed, it added specific elements for the judges to select the next Registrar.[182] For example, the Assembly asked the Court to consider appointing exclusively a national of a State party with 'the highest standards of efficiency, competency and integrity…proven managerial skills'.[183] At the end of February 2008, the plenary of the judges elected Silvana Arbia (Italy) as the second Registrar of the Court for a five-year term.[184] Upon

175 Election of the Registrar of the International Criminal Court, Note by the Secretariat, ICC-ASP/1/11 1.

176 Report of the First Session (First and Second Resumptions) of the Assembly of States Parties to the Rome Statute of the International Criminal Court, New York, 3–7 February and 21–23 April 2003, ICC-ASP/1/3/Add.1 7.

177 ICC-ASP/1/Rec.1 Concerning the Election of the Registrar of the International Criminal Court (2003).

178 Bruno Cathala of France Elected Registrar of International Criminal Court, UN Doc. L/3041.

179 Election of the Registrar of the International Criminal Court, Note by the Secretariat, ICC-ASP/6/16 (2007) 3.

180 Ibid. Interestingly Rama Rao (India), the coordinator at the Rome Conference for Article 112, was a candidate.

181 Bureau of the Assembly of States Parties, 13th Meeting, 3 December 2007 (2007).

182 ICC-ASP/6/Rec.1 Concerning the Election of the Registrar of the International Criminal Court (2007).

183 Ibid 1.

184 Election of the Registrar of the International Criminal Court, Note by the Secretariat, ICC-ASP/11/19 (2012) 2.

taking office, Arbia recommended the election of a Deputy Registrar, which the judges elected in September 2008 for a period of five years.[185]

The Assembly provided a recommendation for the third Registrar election during the 11th session of the Assembly in November 2012.[186] Judge Sang-Hyun Song as President of the Court transmitted a shortlist of 11 names to States Parties after receiving 67 applications but finding only 30 met the vacancy criteria.[187] The incumbent Registrar, Silvana Arbia from Italy, was included in the list, seeking her re-election as per Article 43(5). Compared to 2007, the Bureau discussed the recommendation for the judges in four meetings, including providing feedback to the vacancy announcement as invited by the Presidency of the Court.[188] The Hague Working Group was tasked in July 2012 with consulting on a draft recommendation for the Assembly, which was transmitted to the Bureau in November.[189] As with 2007, the Assembly's recommendation endorsed the slate of 11 names but expanded the list of elements for the consideration of the judges.[190] In contrast with the 2007 recommendation, the Assembly suggested the elected candidate demonstrate qualifications or extensive experience with 'financial and budgetary competencies', 'ability to liaise effectively with the Assembly' and 'establishment of constructive interpersonal relationships in a multicultural setting'.[191] As Clements notes, the election of the Registrar took place in a context States Parties sought to bring efficiencies to the structures and processes of the Court. As such, the successful candidate, Herman von Hebel (Netherlands), 'ran on a promise'[192] to restructure the Registry, a project later known as ReVision and launched in 2013. Herman von Hebel was a known figure in the International Criminal Court given his participation in the negotiations of the Rome Statute.[193] In

---

185 Mr Didier Preira Newly Elected Deputy Registrar of the International Criminal Court, Press Release: 10 September 2008, ICC-CPI-20080910-PR352 (2008).

186 Report of the Eleventh Session of the Assembly of States Parties to the Rome Statute of the International Criminal Court, The Hague, 14–22 November 2012, Volume I, ICC-ASP /11/20 10.

187 Letter from the President of the Court to the President of the Assembly on the Shortlist of Candidates for Election to the Post of Registrar, 2012/PRES/00475/SHS/PD (2012) 1.

188 Bureau of the Assembly of States Parties, 12th Meeting, 29 May 2012 (2012) 2.

189 Bureau of the Assembly of States Parties, 14th Meeting, 9 July 2012 (2012) 2.

190 ICC-ASP/11/Rec.1 Recommendation Concerning the Election of the Registrar of the International Criminal Court (2012) 1.

191 Ibid.

192 Clements, 'ReVisiting the ICC Registry's ReVision Project' 265.

193 von Hebel, Lammers and Schukking, 33.

March 2013, the plenary of the judges elected Herman von Hebel as the third Registrar of the Court for a five-year term.[194]

The Assembly of States Parties was due to agree on a recommendation for the fourth Registrar during the 16th session in December 2017.[195] The President of the Court, judge Silvia Fernández de Gurmendi, distributed a shortlist of 14 candidates to the Assembly in September 2017 after receiving 73 applications.[196] Different from the 2012 process, the Presidency took special note of geographic and gender balance and distributed the shortlist for additional comments to the whole bench.[197] The recommendation by the Assembly did not divert from previous practice and endorsed the full slate of 14 candidates.[198] However, States Parties altered some elements for consideration by the judges. The Assembly recommended the judges consider a candidate that would convey information requested by the Assembly in an 'efficient, complete and timely manner', 'knowledge of another official language of the Court (Arabic, Chinese, Russian, Spanish)', and reminded the bench that 'equitable geographic and gender representation can be implemented by means of a rotation of the incumbents of the post of Registrar'.[199] Given the three previous Registrars had been elected from a single regional group, the note by the Assembly pursued to balance diversity requirements across all elected positions. Yet, the judges decided in March 2018 to elect Peter Lewis from the United Kingdom for a period of five years.[200]

The 2020 Independent Expert Review report singled out the lack of diversity and involvement of States Parties in the election of the Registrar and recommended the Assembly conduct the selection of the post and transmits a list to the judges.[201] The Study Group on Governance considered the recommendation of the independent review in 2021, agreeing to 'strengthen the role of the

194 Election of the Registrar of the International Criminal Court, Note by the Secretariat, ICC-ASP/16/28/Rev.1 (2017) 2.

195 Report of the Sixteenth Session of the Assembly of States Parties to the Rome Statute of the International Criminal Court, New York, 4–14 December, Volume I, ICC-ASP/16/20 (2017) 11.

196 Election of the Registrar of the International Criminal Court, Note by the Secretariat, ICC-ASP/16/28/Rev.1 3.

197 Ibid.

198 ICC-ASP/16/Rec.1 Recommendation Concerning the Election of the Registrar of the International Criminal Court (2017).

199 Ibid 1–2.

200 Election of the Registrar of the International Criminal Court, Note by the Secretariat, ICC-ASP/21/2 (2022) 2.

201 Report of the Independent Expert Review of the International Criminal Court and the Rome Statute System, ICC-ASP/19/16 43.

Assembly' in time for the fifth Registrar election in 2022.[202] To that effect, the Group proposed a series of changes that were included in Resolution 4 from 2021, during the 20th session. Resolution 4 called on the Court to 'consult with States Parties on the drafting of the vacancy announcement' and to 'take measures to encourage a wider diversity of eligible candidates'.[203] It further asked the Bureau to 'establish a due diligence process' in cooperation with the Court and the Independent Oversight Mechanism, facilitate 'public roundtable discussions with the candidates' and 'submit a report and any recommendation for consideration'[204] by the Assembly. The process for selecting the fifth Registrar in 2022 delivered some of these procedural changes[205] ending in the election of the first non-European candidate, Oswaldo Zavala Giler from Ecuador, an internal candidate from the Court, for a period of five years.[206]

3 Disciplinary Measures and Removal of Judges, Prosecutor and Deputy Prosecutor

Just as the Assembly of States Parties has the critical role to elect the principals of the Court, it is equally responsible to guarantee their conduct in no way contravenes assigned duties under the Rome Statute. It is also their governance role under Article 112(4), albeit avoiding undue interference with judicial independence as enshrined in Article 40, 42 and 43 (see Table 6.4). The provisions pertaining the role of the Assembly in disciplinary measures and removal of elected officials are located primarily across the Rome Statute,[207] Rules of Procedure of the Assembly,[208] Rules of Procedure and Evidence,[209]

202 Report of the Bureau on the Study Group on Governance, ICC-ASP/20/21 (2021) 3.

203 ICC-ASP/20/Res.4 Review of the International Criminal Court and the Rome Statute System, Outcome of the Work of the Study Group on Governance on Recommendations of the Group of Independent Experts (2021) 2.

204 Ibid.

205 ICC-ASP/21/Rec.1 Recommendation Concerning the Election of the Registrar of the International Criminal Court (2022).

206 Osvaldo Zavala Giler Elected as ICC Registrar, Press Release: 10 February 2023 (International Criminal Court, 2023) <https://www.icc-cpi.int/news/osvaldo-zavala-giler-elected-icc-registrar> accessed 24 February 2023.

207 Articles 46(2) and 47, Rome Statute of the International Criminal Court (2002) 2187 UNTS 90.

208 Rules 11, 81 and 82, Rules of Procedure of the Assembly of States Parties, ICC-ASP/1/3.

209 Rules 26, 29 and 30, Rules of Procedure and Evidence, ICC-PIOS-LT-03-004/19.

and the Regulations of the Court,[210] and secondarily in the Staff Regulations[211] and Rules.[212] Crucial across these texts are the principles of confidentiality and due process for any person facing disciplinary measures or removal. Interrelated clauses and procedural steps across these legal texts renders a complex system of accountability for wrongful acts by elected officials, and thus, this section cannot provide an extensive study. It does, nonetheless, provide an overview of the available normative framework involving an action by the Assembly of States Parties, and notable examples of its practice between 2002 and 2021.

Starting with the normative framework, Article 46(2)(a) assigns to the Assembly the power to remove a judge by secret ballot of two-third of States after a two-third majority of judges recommend the action. Article 46(2)(b) for the Prosecutor, lowers the threshold to a secret ballot of the absolute majority of States, without any previous qualified recommendation from any organ. For the Deputy Prosecutor, Article 46(2)(c) operates as in the case of the Prosecutor but only after the Head of the Organ recommends the removal of the Deputy. Article 46(3) affords to the judges the responsibility to dismiss the Registrar or Deputy Registrar. Article 46(1) stipulates the removal of elected officials in the event of 'serious misconduct or a serious breach of his or her duties' or whether the person is 'unable to exercise the functions required by this Statute'.[213] Section IV in the Rules of Procedure and Evidence describe the acts covered in Article 46(1) and the steps to request a removal in Article 46(2). In this context, Rules 26 and 29 of the Rules of Procedure and Evidence explain the crucial role to the Independent Oversight Mechanism in the receipt and investigation of grounds for removal and the actions required by the President of the Assembly in the transmission of such assessment to all States Parties.[214] Importantly, Rule 26 requires confidentiality on the receipt and assessment of any allegation. In 2019, during the 19th session, the Assembly agreed to expand the investigative function of the Mechanism to cover 'alleged conduct of former elected officials and staff both while they were in office and when they

210 Regulations 121 and 123, Regulations of the Court, International Criminal Court, ICC-BD /01-05-16.

211 ICC-ASP/2/Res.2 Staff Regulations for the International Criminal Court.

212 Staff Rules of the International Criminal Court, ICC/AI/2015/004/Cor.1.

213 Articles 46(1)(a)–(b), Rome Statute of the International Criminal Court (2002) 2187 UNTS 90.

214 ICC-ASP/17/Res.2 Amendments to Rule 26 of the Rules of Procedure and Evidence.

separated from service'.[215] In this way, by 2021, the normative framework has covered the actions of present and past elected officials.

The regulation regarding disciplinary measures is located in Article 47, whereas the action under review amounts to 'misconduct of a less serious nature'[216] than the grounds for removal. In this instance, Rules 24 and 25 in the Rules of Procedure and Evidence provide an aid to define acts of serious misconduct and breach of duty and those in this threshold.[217] In fact, Chapter 8 of the Regulations of the Court further elaborates on the steps and due diligence procedure necessary to trigger a removal or impose disciplinary measures.[218] The consequences of a finding under Article 47 are a reprimand or a financial sanction against the person involved. Slightly different from the hierarchy in Article 46(1), the Assembly, through its Bureau, can only reprimand the Prosecutor or impose a pecuniary sanction to both the Prosecutor and Deputy.[219] The Court's Presidency retains the power to sanction judges and personnel from the Registry, and the Prosecutor can reprimand the Deputy Prosecutor. The Assembly, thus, cannot impose disciplinary measures on any judge, Registrar and Deputy Registrar, and cannot reprimand the Deputy Prosecutor. Nonetheless, all reprimands must be informed to the Bureau,[220] and the Independent Oversight Mechanism is responsible to report to the Assembly the overall use of the normative framework for disciplinary measures or removal of elected officials. In the first 20 sessions of the Assembly, no disciplinary measures or removal of elected officials by the States Parties occurred.

The normative framework reveals a complex set of procedural steps, which has been characterized as 'opaque'.[221] In fact, in his study of these rules, Laucci, a former Legal Advisor in the Registry, argued it is 'failing to uphold the highest standards of integrity'.[222] Indeed, the Independent Expert Review

215 ICC-ASP/19/Res.6 Strengthening the International Criminal Court and the Assembly of States Parties 17.

216 Articles 47, Rome Statute of the International Criminal Court (2002) 2187 UNTS 90.

217 Rules 24 and 25, Rules of Procedure and Evidence, ICC-PIOS-LT-03-004/19.

218 Regulations 119–125, Regulations of the Court, International Criminal Court, ICC-BD/01-05-16.

219 Rule 30, Rules of Procedure and Evidence, ICC-PIOS-LT-03-004/19.

220 Rule 30 and 32, Rules of Procedure and Evidence, ICC-PIOS-LT-03-004/19.

221 Schabas, The International Criminal Court: A Commentary on the Rome Statute 777.

222 Laucci, Cyril, 'The Wider Policy Framework of Ethical Behaviour: Outspoken Observations from a True Friend of the International Criminal Court' in Bergsmo, Morten and Dittrich, Viviane E. (eds), Integrity in International Justice (Torkel Opsahl Academic EPublisher 2020) 848.

TABLE 6.4 Disciplinary measures and removal of judges, prosecutor and deputy prosecutor

Function	Responsibilities	Relevant articles
Disciplinary measures and removal of Judges, Prosecutor and Deputy Prosecutor	Consideration and decision on imposing disciplinary measures or removal of a Judge, Prosecutor or Deputy Prosecutor.	46(2), 47, 112(4)

harshly criticized the internal judicial system of the Court in relation to serious complaints of misconduct by elected officials and staff across all organs.[223] For the independent experts, the seemingly failing system should be replaced by 'an independent and impartial Judicial Council of the Court'[223] as a subsidiary body of the Assembly or by amending the Rome Statute. This recommendation emerged after the report found the system faced 'operational challenges and limitations'.[224] Their report uncovered a 'general reluctance, if not extreme fear'[225] to report elected officials. The past and current caseload of the International Labour Organization's Administrative Tribunal confirms a serious situation as it dealt with 61 cases between 2007 and 2021 related to the Court.[226] The interlinked issues of internal accountability, judicial independence and high moral character have been covered by the expert literature, describing a situation underserving of the purpose of an institution tasked with fighting impunity.[227]

Bearing in mind the duty of confidentiality it is not possible to obtain a full picture of the involvement of the Bureau and the Assembly. Nonetheless, the annual reports by the Head of the Independent Oversight Mechanism reveal the receipt of 6 out of 137 matters in relation to misconduct by elected officials (see Table 6.5). However, only since 2018 the report provided commentary

223 Ibid 69.

224 Ibid 66.

225 Ibid.

226 Administrative Tribunal of the International Labour Organization, International Criminal Court, Total Judgements, available at: <https://www.ilo.org/dyn/triblex/triblexmain.byOrg>.

227 Sadat, Leila Nadya, 'Reforming the International Criminal Court: "Lean In" or "Leave"' (2020) 62 (1) Washington University Journal of Law & Policy 51; Lovat, Henry, 'International Criminal Tribunal Backlash' in Heller, Kevin Jon and others (eds), The Oxford Handbook of International Criminal Law (2 edn, Oxford University Press 2020) 601.

TABLE 6.5 Head of independent oversight mechanism reports (2015–2021)[a]

Period	Total matters received	Matters regarding an elected official
	137	6
2015–2016	9	Not specified
2016–2017	15	Not specified
2017–2018	27	Not specified
2018–2019	43	4
2019–2020	19	1
2020–2021	24	1

a Report of the Independent Expert Review of the International Criminal Court and the Rome Statute System, ICC-ASP/19/16 Sections II, III, IV and XIX.

leading to the identification of which elected officials it referred.[228] Right or wrong, the full analysis of the role of the Assembly in dealing with these questions is severely limited by the principle of confidentiality.

However, beyond the Independent Oversight Mechanism reporting, certain situations of alleged misconduct have been made public between 2002 and 2021. In the absence of official proceedings by the Court or the Assembly, these instances cannot be taken as prima facie evidence for wrongdoing, but they do offer an insight into conduct criticized in the public fora. Notable examples involved two judges (Miriam Defensor-Santiago[230] and Kuniko Ozaki[231]), the first Prosecutor[232] and the third Registrar.[233]

228 Annual report of the Head of the Independent Oversight Mechanism, ICC-ASP/17/8 (2018) 3.

230 Report to the Bureau on the Review of the Procedure for the Nomination and Election of Judges, ICC-ASP/12/57 (2013) 5.

231 Heller, Kevin Jon, 'Judge Ozaki Must Resign – Or Be Removed' (Opinio Juris, 2019) <http://opiniojuris.org/2019/03/29/judge-ozaki-must-resign-or-be-removed/> accessed 29 March (2019).

232 ICC Statement on Recent Media Allegations, Press Release: 5 October 2017, available at: <https://www.legal-tools.org/doc/babdf6/>; Full Statement of the Prosecutor, Fatou Bensouda, on External Expert Review and Lessons Drawn from the Kenya Situation, 26 November 2019, available at: <https://www.legal-tools.org/doc/32p2hy/> (2019).

233 Inder, Brigid, 'Conformity, Leadership and the Culture of Integrity at the International Criminal Court' in Bergsmo, Morten and Dittrich, Viviane E (eds), Integrity in International Justice (Torkel Opsahl Academic EPublisher 2020) 309.

In relation to the two public allegations against the bench, the first case involved judge-elect Miriam Defensor-Santiago from the Philippines. After her election in 2011, Defensor-Santiago did not assume office for a period close to three years.[234] The delay effectively prevented the Court from properly functioning with a fully staffed bench. In fact, the Bureau discussed the matter and asked the President of the Court to persuade Defensor-Santiago to take office via 'administrative measures'.[235] In dealing with the issue, the Bureau facilitator on the topic of nomination and election of judges argued the case of Defensor-Santiago appeared to enter the 'area of disciplinary rules'.[236] The situation forced the Assembly to amend the procedure for vacancies in 2013 to prevent a similar situation in the future.[237] As Ogwuma argued, pending the 'legitimacy of the reasons given for such a deferral of full-time service',[238] the case could have been made for disciplinary or removal proceedings given the impeding normal functioning or impact on the standing of the Court.

The second example relates to Judge Kuniko Ozaki from Japan. Part of *the case of The Prosecutor v. Bosco Ntaganda*, Ozaki requested the plenary of judges in January 2019 to work part-time 'citing personal reasons'.[239] She later informed the Presidency she had taken up an ambassadorial position in Estonia. Upon the agreement of 14 judges, Ozaki was allowed to take an executive branch position, which triggered a petition by the Ntaganda's defence team to disqualify her from proceedings. The request outlined the dual role was 'not consistent with the appearance of judicial independence or impartiality'.[240] In April, the Japanese government informed the Court Judge Ozaki had resigned as an ambassador[241] and in June, the Court dismissed the motion for disqualification.[242] Nonetheless, in mind of the standard for disciplinary and removal

234 Bureau of the Assembly of States Parties, 4th Meeting, 4 June 2014 (2014) 1.

235 Bureau of the Assembly of States Parties, 20th Meeting, 28 November 2013 2.

236 Report to the Bureau on the Review of the Procedure for the Nomination and Election of Judges, ICC-ASP/12/57 5.

237 ICC-ASP/12/Res.8 Strengthening the International Criminal Court and the Assembly of States Parties 67.

238 Ogwuma, (2016) 1228.

239 International Criminal Court, Internal Memorandum, 2019/PRES/00003-21 (2019) 1.

240 The Prosecutor v Bosco Ntaganda (Annex I to the Notification of the Decision of the Plenary of Judges on the Defence Request for the Disqualification of Judge Kuniko Ozaki from the Case) ICC-01/04-02/06-2355-AnxI-Red (20 June 2019) 3.

241 The Prosecutor v Bosco Ntaganda (Notification Concerning Judge Kuniko Ozaki) ICC-01/04-02/06 (1 May 2019) 1.

242 The Prosecutor v Bosco Ntaganda (Annex I to the Notification of the Decision of the Plenary of Judges on the Defence Request for the Disqualification of Judge Kuniko Ozaki from the Case) ICC-01/04-02/06-2355-AnxI-Red (20 June 2019) 3.

actions in the normative framework, the unfolding saga was 'inherently problematic and could undermine the independence of the Court'.[243] The lack of transparency to disclose an ambassadorial appointment while asking to carry out judicial functions part-time could be interpreted to cause harm to the standing of the Court as the integrity of the bench was at the heart of the institution.[244]

The allegations of misconduct by the first Prosecutor, Luis Moreno Ocampo, have been covered by the media,[245] Court documents,[246] the International Labour Organizations' Administrative Tribunal[247] and academic commentary.[248] They range from actions taken during and after his time at the Office of the Prosecutor. Once Moreno Ocampo left the Court, the normative framework for disciplinary or removal procedures ceased to apply to him as a former employee. In 2019, during the 19th session, the Assembly amended the operational mandate of the Independent Oversight Mechanism to cover 'alleged conduct of former elected officials and staff both while they were in office and when they separated from service'.[249] The change was triggered after Prosecutor Fatou Bensouda and the Independent Oversight Mechanism reacted to media allegations about Moreno Ocampo in 2017.[250] The Assembly of States Parties was well aware of the inapplicability of available procedures to former staff but asked the Court to 'identify any necessary follow-up action for the Court and/or the Assembly'[251] by 2019. In her interim report of the situation,

243 Donat Cattin and Verpile, (2020) 1085.

244 Heller, 'Judge Ozaki Must Resign – Or Be Removed'.

245 European Investigative Collaborations, 'Court Secrets' (European Investigative Collaborations, 2017) <https://eic.network/projects/court-secrets.html>.

246 ICC Statement on Recent Media Allegations, Press Release: 5 October 2017, available at: <https://www.legal-tools.org/doc/babdf6/> Full Statement of the Prosecutor, Fatou Bensouda, on External Expert Review and Lessons Drawn from the Kenya Situation, 26 November 2019, available at: <https://www.legal-tools.org/doc/32p2hy/>.

247 Palme v ICC (Judgment) No. 2757 (9 July 2008) 2.

248 Bergsmo, 'Unmasking Power in International Criminal Justice: Invisible College v. Visible Colleagues' (2020) 11; Vasiliev, 'Judicial Governance Entities as Power-Holders in International Criminal Justice: A Plea for a Socio-Legal Enquiry' 2020 542; Wiley, William H, 'Effective Leadership, Management and Integrity in International Criminal Investigations' in Bergsmo, Morten and Dittrich, Viviane E (eds), Integrity in International Justice (Torkel Opsahl Academic EPublisher 2020) 416.

249 ICC-ASP/19/Res.6 Strengthening the International Criminal Court and the Assembly of States Parties 17.

250 ICC Statement on Recent Media Allegations, Press Release: 5 October 2017, available at: <https://www.legal-tools.org/doc/babdf6/>.

251 ICC-ASP/17/Res.5 Strengthening the International Criminal Court and the Assembly of States Parties 47.

Bensouda identified the legal lacuna and recommended legislative amendments.[252] Up until the 20th session in 2021 no official proceedings have opened in relation to the first Prosecutor. For Inder, States Parties are to blame as they 'have been consistently willing to look the other way, especially when the misconduct involved Court officials'.[253] Vasiliev, in his analysis of governance of international justice institutions, also concluded the Assembly 'failed to intervene proactively and swiftly enough to bridge the gaps of governance'.[254] Writing at the time the Office of the Prosecutor was being established, Schabas had already warned 'no single individual has more responsibility for the survival and success of the International Criminal Court than its prosecutor'.[255] Indeed, If serious allegations against elected officials are left unattended, there is a grave risk to the standing of the Court and its ability to confer trust into its judicial work. Although outside the scope of this book, in 2024 the Assembly of States Parties referred to the United Nations an external investigation into alleged misconduct by the third Prosecutor, Karim Khan.

The allegations against Herman von Hebel, the third Registrar of the Court, relate to the management of the ReVision project aimed at a complete restructure of the Registry between 2014 and 2015. As Clements explained, von Hebel was elected after campaigning on a proposal to increase efficiencies at the Court.[256] Once elected, von Hebel commissioned an external review of the Registry in 2013 that unveiled a 'complex organizational bricolage which had emerged over the previous decade'.[257] With the external report, von Hebel made the case to States Parties of the need for a thorough reform project, which was agreed by the Assembly in Resolution 1 from 2013 during the 12th session.[258] Clements, Inder[259] and the project auditor's report[260] have evalu-

---

252 Interim Report of the Office of the Prosecutor in Response to Paragraph 140 of Resolution ICC/ASP/17/Res.5, ICC-ASP/18/INF.5 (2019) 3.

253 Inder, (2020) 343.

254 Vasiliev, 'Judicial Governance Entities as Power-Holders in International Criminal Justice: A Plea for a Socio-Legal Enquiry' (2020) 541.

255 Schabas, William A, 'Interacting with Academic Institutions' in Bergsmo, Morten, Rackwitz, Klaus and Tianying, Song (eds), Historical Origins of International Criminal Law, vol 5 (Torkel Opsahl Academic EPublisher 2017) 377.

256 Clements, 'ReVisiting the ICC Registry's ReVision Project' 265.

257 Ibid 263.

258 ICC-ASP/12/Res.1 Programme Budget for 2014, the Working Capital Fund for 2014, Scale of Assessments for the Apportionment of Expenses of the International Criminal Court, Financing Appropriations for 2014 and the Contingency Fund (2013) 20.

259 Inder, (2020) 309.

260 Audit Report of the ReVision Project of the International Criminal Court's Registry, ICC-ASP/15/27 (2016).

ated whether the restructure achieved its objectives while also uncovering failures of leadership that can be analysed through the disciplinary and removal normative framework. One example related to the management of staff changes and financial stewardship. Although the project only reduced 10.4 posts, 'fear of job abolitions, followed by implementation of 120 separation procedures affected the morale of staff during the project'.[261] Furthermore, the restructure led to formal grievances in front of internal and external bodies, for example, 12 claims for a total of '€8,4m in indemnities'[262] at the International Labour Organization's Administrative Tribunal.

In the midst of the change process, Judges Marc Perrin de Brichambaut, Sanji Monageng, Geoffrey Henderson, Chile Eboe-Osuji and Cuno Tarfusser expressed concerns with ReVision to President Fernández de Gurmendi as the Registrar's superior, but without any result.[263] As staff claims for wrongful dismissal advanced, the International Labour Organization's Administrative Tribunal found in 2018 the inherent internal procedural steps within the Court were not followed and lacked legal standing.[264] In other words, the Registrar had presided over an expensive and possibly illegal process to search for efficiencies in the Registry as his position demanding financial stewardship and oversight of the human resources function of the Court. For Inder, 'ReVision both exposed and took advantage of the weaknesses in the oversight and governance system and brought the Court's institutional integrity crisis to a head'.[265] Despite a call to resign by Judge Tarfusser, von Hebel completed the project but did not succeed in his re-election as Registrar in 2017.[266]

4 Conclusion

This chapter examined the statutory practice of the Assembly on election, disciplinary measures and removal of Court officials between 2002 and 2021. The chapter found States Parties elected 54 judges (34 in List A and 20 in List B), three Prosecutors, five Deputy Prosecutors, four Registrars and one Deputy Registrar over 20 sessions. The Assembly did not impose disciplinary measures or removed any elected official between 2002 and 2021. The weight of the

261 Ibid 16.
262 Ibid 15.
263 Ibid 7.
264 Clements, 'ReVisiting the ICC Registry's ReVision Project' 278.
265 Inder, (2020) 360.
266 Clements, 'ReVisiting the ICC Registry's ReVision Project' 283.

statutory election role, however, meant the Assembly dedicated 16 sessions to this item. Bearing in mind that each cycle represented a substantial amount of time and consensus building for nominations, assessment and elections, it is notable that criticism persists about the Assembly's ability to elect the most competent and skilled officials for the Court. Specifically to the election of judges, the chapter found that even after establishing the Advisory Committee on Nomination of judges in 2010, the Assembly still favoured candidates without the full backing of the Committee. The election of the Prosecutor followed a similar pattern whereas the Assembly instituted a bespoke mechanism each time, albeit with grave difficulty to follow its own procedure. Most notable, the 2020 Committee on the Election of the Prosecutor faced severe criticism by States and civil society for their search, assessment and recommendation procedure to the Assembly. Thus, the chapter argued the inability of the Assembly of States Parties to manage a depoliticized and merit-based election for judges and the Prosecutor risked the legitimacy and operational capability of the Court.

In this sense, the chapter also noted the Assembly's effort to set up a permanent vetting system for elected officials. Next, when covering the election of the Registrar, the chapter explored the indirect yet important role of the Assembly of States Parties. It argued a more directive approach was required to guide the judges' election bearing in mind the integral role the Registry played in servicing the Assembly and enabling its governance role. Finally, while no elected official was reprimanded or removed by the Assembly, States Parties were confronted with public exposes criticizing the conduct of elected officials. Notable examples involved two judges, the first Prosecutor and the third Registrar. Despite the establishment of the Independent Oversight Mechanism, the available public record did not indicate any corrective action by the Assembly of States Parties. In fact, the chapter revealed that while the annual reports by the Head of the Independent Oversight Mechanism between 2015 and 2021 contained 6 out of 137 matters in relation to misconduct by elected officials, no action was necessary by States Parties. Overall, the chapter concluded the dual role of States Parties to elect and oversee the performance of senior officials has suffered from weak institutional oversight tools prone to political manoeuvres.

CHAPTER 7

The Practice of the Assembly of States Parties: Financial Oversight

1 Introduction

As an international organization, the financial oversight of the International Criminal Court rested with the Assembly of States Parties.[1] As such, States Parties retained control over budgetary approvals and rules that governed the financial system embedded in the Rome Statute. The financial oversight power of the Assembly originated from Article 112(2)(d), with corresponding clauses across other parts of the Statute, notably in Part 4 and 12. In this sense, complying with Article 112(2)(d), the Assembly approved 20 budgets between 2002 and 2021, totalling €2,22 billion. As a negotiated process between the Court and States Parties, the gap between what Court organs requested and the Assembly finally approved stood at a total of €79,9 million (3,6%) in 2021. In fact, the literature examining the relationship between the budget and the ability of the Court to perform its mandate agree the Assembly's tightened its financial oversight grip over time, possibly risking judicial independence.[2] To aid the financial oversight function of the Assembly, States Parties established during the first session in 2002 the Committee on Budget and Finance as the first subsidiary body under Article 112(4). In this context, this chapter follows

1 Halff, Maarten, Tolbert, David and Villacis, Renan, 'Article 115 Funds of the Court and of the Assembly of States Parties' in Ambos, Kai and Triffterer, Otto (eds), The Rome Statute of the International Criminal Court: A Commentary (3 edn, Beck/Hart 2016) 2257.

2 O'Donohue, Jonathan, 'Financing the International Criminal Court' (2013) 13 (1) International Criminal Law Review 269; Ford, Stuart, 'How Much Money Does the ICC Need?' in Carsten, Stahn (ed), The Law and Practice of the International Criminal Court (Oxford University Press 2015) 84; Kotecha, Birju, 'The ICC's Office of the Prosecutor and the Limits of Performance Indicators' (2017) 15 (3) Journal of International Criminal Justice 543; Cannock, Matt and O'Donohue, Jonathan, 'Don't Ask and You Won't Receive – Will the ICC Request the Resources it Needs in 2019?' (Amnesty International, Human Rights in International Justice, 2019) <https://hrij.amnesty.nl/icc-zero-growth-dont-ask-and-you-wont-receive/> accessed 10 May 2018; Wiebelhaus-Brahm, Eric and Ainley, Kirsten, 'The Evolution of Funding for the International Criminal Court: Budgets, Donors and Gender Justice' (2023) 22 (1) Journal of Human Rights 31; Ford, Stuart, 'Funding the ICC for Its Third Decade' in Stahn, Carsten and Braga da Silva, Rafael (eds), The International Criminal Court in Its Third Decade: Reflecting on Law and Practices (Brill | Nijhoff 2023) 368.

© EZEQUIEL JIMÉNEZ MARTINEZ, 2026 | DOI:10.1163/9789004749979_008

the practice of the Assembly of States Parties across financial oversight of the Court's budget. To do so, the chapter begins with a brief discussion of the normative framework guiding the Assembly. Secondly, it offers an overview of total financial investment between 2002 and 2021. Finally, it discusses the main challenges of the contested relationship between the Court and States Parties over the annual budget, including the issue of arrears and the failure of the United Nations Security Council to provide funds for the cost of referrals to the Court.

2 Financial Oversight Practice (2002–2021)

Starting with the normative framework, the financial oversight power of the Assembly is firmly located in Article 112(2)(d), with corresponding clauses across other parts of the Statute, notably in Part 4 and 12. An overall normative assessment shows States Parties have a role in budget governance (Article 112), management (Articles 113 and 116) and a decision over the salaries, allowances and expenses of elected officials (Article 49) (see Table 7.1).

The Assembly of States Parties passed 43 resolutions and two decisions under its financial oversight powers between 2002 and 2021.[3] Among these, 20 related to the annual approval of the budget as stipulated in Article 112(2)(d). To give effect to Article 113, the Assembly approved the Financial Regulations and Rules during the first session and proceeded to amend them three times in standalone resolutions in 2005, 2007 and 2008.[4] However, annual resolutions approving the budget have also been used by States Parties to refine the rules governing the movement of financial resources at the Court. In relation to Article 116, States Parties did not come back to the original resolution from 2002 establishing the criteria for voluntary contributions. On the other hand, complying with Article 49, the Assembly amended the remuneration and pension of judges seven times, in 2005, 2007, 2008, 2018, 2019 and 2020.[5] In this process, the Assembly involved the Committee on Budget and

3 Assembly of States Parties to the Rome Statute, Resolutions, available at: <https://asp.icc-cpi.int/resolutions>.

4 ICC-ASP/4/Res.10 Amendments to the Financial Regulations and Rules (2005); ICC-ASP/6/Res.5 Amendments to the Financial Regulations and Rules (2007); ICC-ASP/7/Res.5 Amendment to the Financial Regulations and Rules (2008).

5 ICC-ASP/4/Res.9 Pension Scheme for Judges (2005); ICC-ASP/5/Res.6 Conditions of Service and Compensation of Judges of the International Criminal Court: Amendment to the Pension Scheme Regulations for Judges of the International Criminal Court (2007); ICC-ASP/6/Res.6 Amendments to the Pension Scheme Regulations for Judges of the International

TABLE 7.1 Financial oversight

Function	Responsibilities	Relevant articles
Budget Governance	Consideration and decision on the budget of the Court, States in arrears	112(2)(d), 112(4), 112(8)
Budget Management	Approval of Financial Regulations and criteria for voluntary contributions	113, 116
Salaries, Allowances and Expenses	Pay package for judges, Prosecutor, Deputy Prosecutor, Registrar and Deputy Registrar	49

Finance and bespoke working groups to advice how to answer judges' calls for changes in salaries, allowances and pensions.[6]

Finally, to complete the overall financial oversight framework, the Assembly established the Budget and Finance Committee as a subsidiary body under Article 112(4) in 2002. Since the first session, the 12-member Committee has been tasked with the 'technical examination of any document submitted to the Assembly that contains financial or budgetary implications or any other matter of a financial, budgetary or administrative nature'.[7] Over the years, the Committee played a vital role in recommending to the Assembly the approval of the Court's budget and changes in operational issues across human resources, IT, legal, the external audit, performance indicators, management practices and financial assistance for its subsidiary bodies.[8] The Committee relayed its recommendations to States Parties after evaluating the budget from the Court. Between 2018 and 2020, the Committee sent approximately 100 inquiries to the Court per annual budget submitted.[9] Once the Committee submit-

Criminal Court (2007); ICC-ASP/6/Res.7 Funding of the Disability Pension of a Former Judge of the International Criminal Court (2008); ICC-ASP/17/Res.1 Resolution on the Remuneration of the Judges of the International Criminal Court (2018); ICC-ASP/18/Res.2 Resolution on the Remuneration of the Judges of the International Criminal Court (2019); ICC-ASP/19/Res.3 Resolution on the Remuneration of the Judges of the International Criminal Court (2020).

6 Bureau of the Assembly of States Parties, 14th Meeting, 11 December 2020.

7 ICC-ASP/1/Res.4 Establishment of the Committee on Budget and Finance 2.

8 Zavala, Osvaldo, 'The Budgetary Efficiency of the International Criminal Court' (2018) 18 (3) International Criminal Law Review 461.

9 Report of the Independent Expert Review of the International Criminal Court and the Rome Statute System, ICC-ASP/19/16 74.

ted its report to the Assembly, the Bureau's Hague Working Group and an appointed Assembly facilitator for the topic of budget conducted the final negotiations to conclude the approved budget.[10] Given the heavy scrutiny performed by the Court, the Committee and the Assembly, the Independent Expert Review recommended 'enhanced consultations' among these bodies to 'enable the States Parties' to dedicate more of its resources and attention on less-technical matters'.[11] In fact, the literature examining the relationship between the budget and the ability of the Court to perform its mandate agree the Assembly's tightened its financial oversight grip over time, possibly risking judicial independence.[12]

Taking into consideration the Statute, the Financial Regulations and Rules and the work of the Committee on Budget and Finance, the annual approval of the budget by the Assembly is the most important financial oversight action by States Parties. Complying with Article 112(2)(d), the Assembly has approved 20 budgets between 2002 and 2021, totalling €2,22 billion (see Table 7.2). As a negotiated process between the Court and States Parties, the gap between what Court organs requested and the Assembly finally approved stood at a total of €79,9 million (3,6%) in 2021. As O'Donohue and Zavala explained, the interaction between the Court, the Committee on Budget and Finance and, subsequently, the Assembly, determines the final amount of the budget not without extensive lobbying by the Court's President, Prosecutor and Registrar.[13]

The budget approved by the Assembly grew every year except between 2010 and 2011 even if slightly (€103,623,300 versus €103,607,900). Only in the approved budget for 2010 the Court received more funds than requested (€102,980,000 versus €103,623,300) due to the establishment of a new budget line for the Independent Oversight Mechanism and additional funding for the Secretariat of the Assembly as it prepared for the Review Conference in Kampala.[14] In other words, the organs of the Court did not benefit from the addi-

10 O'Donohue, 'The ICC and the ASP' (2015) 116.

11 Report of the Independent Expert Review of the International Criminal Court and the Rome Statute System, ICC-ASP/19/16 74.

12 O'Donohue, 'Financing the International Criminal Court' 269;Ford, 'How Much Money Does the ICC Need?' 2015 84; Kotecha, 543; Wiebelhaus-Brahm and Ainley, 31; Ford, 'Funding the ICC for Its Third Decade' (2023) 368.

13 O'Donohue, 'Financing the International Criminal Court' 276; Zavala, 470–471.

14 ICC-ASP/8/Res.7 Programme Budget for 2010, the Working Capital Fund for 2010, Scale of Assessments for the Apportionment of Expenses of the International Criminal Court, Financing Appropriations for the year 2010, the Contingency Fund, Conversion of a GTA Psychologist Post to an Established one, Legal aid (Defence) and the Addis Ababa Liaison Office.

TABLE 7.2 International Criminal Court budget (2002–2021)

Budget (€)	Requested[a]	Approved[b]	Difference
	2,307,147,400	2,227,187,946	79,959,454 (3,6%)

a Draft Programme Budget for 2004, ICC-ASP/2/2; Draft Programme Budget for 2005, ICC-ASP/3/2* (2004); Proposed Programme Budget for 2006 of the International Criminal Court, ICC-ASP/4/5 (2005); Proposed Programme Budget for 2007 of the International Criminal Court, ICC-ASP/5/9 (2006); Proposed Programme Budget for 2008 of the International Criminal Court, ICC-ASP/6/8 (2007); Proposed Programme Budget for 2009 of the International Criminal Court, ICC-ASP/7/9 (2008); Proposed Programme Budget for 2010 of the International Criminal Court, ICC-ASP/8/10 (2009); Proposed Programme Budget for 2011 of the International Criminal Court, ICC-ASP/9/10 (2010); Proposed Programme Budget for 2012 of the International Criminal Court, ICC-ASP/10/10 (2011); Proposed Programme Budget for 2013 of the International Criminal Court, ICC-ASP/11/10 (2012); Proposed Programme Budget for 2014 of the International Criminal Court, ICC-ASP/12/10 (2013); Proposed Programme Budget for 2015 of the International Criminal Court, ICC-ASP/13/10 (2014); Proposed Programme Budget for 2016 of the International Criminal Court, ICC-ASP/14/10 (2015); Proposed Programme Budget for 2017 of the International Criminal Court, ICC-ASP/15/10 (2016); Proposed Programme Budget for 2018 of the International Criminal Court, ICC-ASP/16/10 (2017); Proposed Programme Budget for 2019 of the International Criminal Court, ICC-ASP/17/10 (2018); Proposed Programme Budget for 2020 of the International Criminal Court, ICC-ASP/18/10 (2019); Proposed Programme Budget for 2021 of the International Criminal Court, ICC-ASP/19/10* (2020); Proposed Programme Budget for 2022 of the International Criminal Court, ICC-ASP/20/10.

b ICC-ASP/1/Res.12 Budget Appropriations for the First Financial Period and Financing of Appropriations for the First Financial Period; ICC-ASP/2/Res.1 Programme Budget for 2004, Working Capital Fund for 2004, Scale of Assessments for the Apportionment of Expenses of the International Criminal Court and Financing of Appropriations for 2004 (2003); ICC-ASP/3/Res. 4 Programme Budget for 2005, Contingency Fund, Working Capital Fund for 2005, Scale of Assessments for the Apportionment of Expenses of the International Criminal Court and Financing of Appropriations for the year 2005 (2004); ICC-ASP/4/Res.8 Programme Budget for 2006, the Working Capital Fund for 2006, Scale of Assessments for the Apportionment of Expenses of the International Criminal Court and Financing Appropriations for the Year 2006 (2005); ICC-ASP/5/Res.4 Programme Budget for 2007, the Working Capital Fund for 2007, Scale of Assessments for the Apportionment of Expenses of the International Criminal Court and Financing Appropriations for the Year 2007 (2006); ICC-ASP/6/Res.4 Programme Budget for 2008, the Working Capital Fund for 2008, Scale of Assessments for the Apportionment of Expenses of the International Criminal Court and Financing Appropriations for the Year 2008 (2007); ICC-ASP/7/Res.4 Programme Budget for 2009, the Working Capital Fund for 2009, Scale of Assessments for the Apportionment of Expenses of the International Criminal Court, Financing Appropriations for the Year 2009 and the Contingency Fund (2008); ICC-ASP/8/Res.7 Programme Budget for 2010, the Working Capital Fund for 2010, Scale of Assessments for the Apportionment of Expenses of the International Criminal Court, Financing Appropriations for the year 2010, the Contingency Fund, Conversion of a GTA Psychologist Post to an Established one, Legal aid (Defence) and the Addis Ababa Liaison Office (2009); ICC-ASP/9/Res.4 Programme Budget for 2011, the

TABLE 7.2 International Criminal Court budget (2002–2021) (*cont.*)

Working Capital Fund for 2011, Scale of Assessments for the Apportionment of Expenses of the International Criminal Court, Financing Appropriations for 2011 and the Contingency Fund (2010); ICC-ASP/10/Res.4 Programme Budget for 2012, the Working Capital Fund for 2012, Scale of Assessments for the Apportionment of Expenses of the International Criminal Court, Financing Appropriations for 2012 and the Contingency Fund (2011); ICC-ASP/11/Res.1 Programme Budget for 2013, the Working Capital Fund for 2013, Scale of Assessments for the Apportionment of Expenses of the International Criminal Court, Financing Appropriations for 2013 and the Contingency Fund (2012); ICC-ASP/12/Res.1 Programme Budget for 2014, the Working Capital Fund for 2014, Scale of Assessments for the Apportionment of Expenses of the International Criminal Court, Financing Appropriations for 2014 and the Contingency Fund; ICC-ASP/13/Res.1 Programme Budget for 2015, the Working Capital Fund for 2015, Scale of Assessments for the Apportionment of Expenses of the International Criminal Court, Financing Appropriations for 2015 and the Contingency Fund (2014); ICC-ASP/14/Res.1 Programme Budget for 2016, the Working Capital Fund and the Contingency Fund for 2016, Scale of Assessments for the Apportionment of Expenses of the International Criminal Court and Financing Appropriations for 2016; ICC-ASP/15/Res.1 Programme Budget for 2017, the Working Capital Fund for 2017, Scale of Assessment for the Apportionment of Expenses of the International Criminal Court, Financing Appropriations for 2017 and the Contingency Fund (2016); ICC-ASP/16/Res.1 Programme Budget for 2018, the Working Capital Fund for 2018, the Scale of Assessment for the Apportionment of Expenses of the International Criminal Court, Financing Appropriations for 2018 and the Contingency Fund (2017); ICC-ASP/17/Res.4 Programme Budget for 2019, the Working Capital Fund for 2019, Scale of Assessment for the Apportionment of Expenses of the International Criminal Court, Financing Appropriations for 2019 and the Contingency Fund (2018); ICC-ASP/18/Res.1 Programme Budget for 2020, the Working Capital Fund for 2020, Scale of Assessment for the Apportionment of Expenses of the International Criminal Court, Financing Appropriations for 2020 and the Contingency Fund (2019); ICC-ASP/19/Res.1 Programme Budget for 2021, the Working Capital Fund for 2021, Scale of Assessment for the Apportionment of Expenses of the International Criminal Court, Financing Appropriations for 2021 and the Contingency Fund (2020); ICC-ASP/20/Res.1 Programme Budget for 2022, the Working Capital Fund for 2022, Scale of Assessment for the Apportionment of Expenses of the International Criminal Court, Financing Appropriations for 2022 and the Contingency Fund (2021).

tional resources in 2010. By 2021, the gap between the proposed budget and the approved total, thus, accumulated to €79,9 million.

Out of the total budget approved between 2002 and 2021, the portion assigned for expenses of the Assembly of States Parties was €67 million. The expenses of the Assembly primarily covered the costs for the venue and logistics of the regular session and meetings of subsidiary bodies. The highest amounts allocated to the Assembly were in 2002 (€7,029,600) and 2010 (€4,272,800) corresponding to the inaugural session and expenses for the Review Conference in 2010 (see Figure 7.1). Besides these two outlier years,

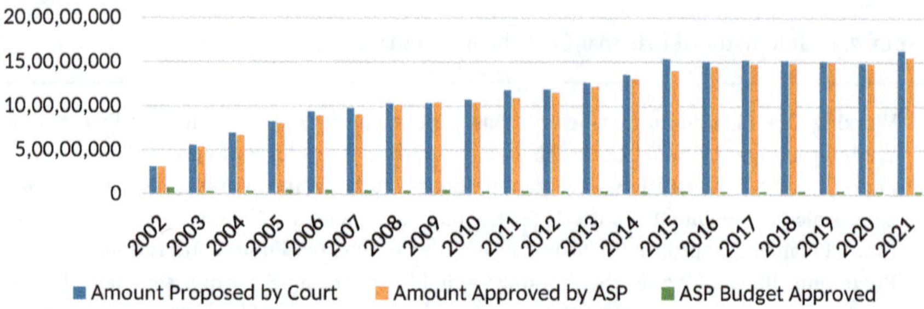

FIGURE 7.1 International Criminal Court budget 2002–2021 (in Euros)

TABLE 7.3 Assembly of States Parties budget (2002–2021)

Budget, Assembly of States Parties (€)	**Total approved budget**	**ASP approved budget**	**Percentage**
	2,227,187,946	67,287,272	3%

the budget of the Assembly has remained stable averaging 3% by 2021 (see Table 7.3).

The gap between the requested budget by the Court and the final approved amount by the Assembly might be explained by three interrelated arguments. First, States Parties' willingness to fund the budget was affected by practices at the Court and the external political and macroeconomic environment. Second, the substantial pending payments by States in arrears disproportionally affected the ability of the Court to access funds in a timely manner. Finally, the infringement of the United Nations Security Council to provide financial support for expenses incurred by referrals, as per Article 115(b), put undue pressure on States Parties to absorb the cost of activities in Sudan[15] and Libya.[16] In turn, this section provides an overview of each argument to uncover the key moments in the financial oversight practice of the Assembly of States Parties between 2002 and 2021.

2.1 *Balancing Financial Practices and the External Context*

As Ford explained, the Court experienced periods of 'greater growth' during 2002–2007 and 2013–2016 and 'slow growth'[17] between 2009 and 2012 and 2017

15 UNSC Res 1593 (2005).
16 UNSC Res 1970 (2011).
17 Ford, 'Funding the ICC for Its Third Decade' (2023) 381.

and 2021. The inaugural years of the Court saw the internal financial processes develop at the same time judicial activity commenced. Within a context of organizational immaturity but high political buy-in from States Parties, the budgets presented by the Court and approved by the Assembly differed due to a difficulty by the Court to calibrate its activity assumptions as cases were built from scratch. The Coordination Council, the highest body within the Court assembling the President, Prosecutor and Register, created a steering committee in 2004 dedicated to budget questions[18] but the Court was unable to predict or control its expenditure accurately. As Zavala, who became Registrar in 2022, noted, the 'recurrent challenges the Court has faced in developing fully reliable and accurate budget proposals ... was also the cause of the under-resourcing of activities which, in the light of their uncertainty were left as contingencies'.[19] Even in this context, Assembly President Prince Al-Hussein and Court President Kirsch were more concerned with endowing the Court with ample funding than 'the need for strategic planning and oversight'.[20]

To aid the budgetary planning process the Assembly agreed in 2004 to move its regular session later in the calendar year to allow more time for the Court to develop realistic funding assumptions and created a contingency fund.[21] The €10 million contingency fund was set up to cover unforeseen costs by the Prosecutor, overall judicial services or the Assembly.[22] The Court could only access the contingency fund upon the full implementation of the regular budget.[23] This way, the Assembly intended to provide flexibility to the Court while controlling the level of spending within the approved budget.[24] This also meant greater scrutiny by States Parties in the event the Prosecutor required access to contingency funding.[25] The Bureau reviewed and discussed the topic of contingency funding access by the Court in 19 meetings

18 Clements, '"Efficiency Is Paramount in This Regard": The Managerial Role of the ICC Presidency from Kirsch to Fernández' 352.

19 Zavala, Osvaldo, 'The Budgetary Efficiency of the International Criminal Court' (2018) 18 International Criminal Law Review 462.

20 Clements, 'Governing International Criminal Justice: Managerial Practices and the International Criminal Court' 127.

21 O'Donohue, 'Financing the International Criminal Court' 278.

22 Financial Regulations and Rules, ICC-ASP/1/3 and Corr.1 (2014).

23 Zavala, 473.

24 ICC-ASP/3/Res. 4 Programme Budget for 2005, Contingency Fund, Working Capital Fund for 2005, Scale of Assessments for the Apportionment of Expenses of the International Criminal Court and Financing of Appropriations for the year (2005).

25 O'Donohue, Jonathan, 'The 2005 Budget of the International Criminal Court: Contingency, Insufficient Funding in Key Areas and the Recurring Question of the Independence of the Prosecutor' (2005) 18 (3) Leiden Journal of International Law 593.

between 2011 and 2021.[26] States Parties' scrutiny over contingency funding amplified the issue of budget planning and mismatch at the Court. Indeed, in an attempt to predict future workload to efficiently allocate resources, President Kirsch introduced in 2006 the first strategic plan of the Court.[27] The plan included key performance indicators in the Office of the Prosecutor, which represented the largest portion of budget uncertainty given the complexity of building future-proof criminal cases.[28] However, by 2007, the Budget and Finance Committee complained of the 'substantial level of capacity that had not been utilized' and warned the situation diminished the 'ability of the Committee and the Assembly to assess budgetary needs'.[29] The increasing budget difficulties reached a natural point as the 2008 financial crisis hit national budgets across all States Parties. As O'Donohue explained, during the seventh session in 2008, the Assembly went €5 million further than the cuts adopted by the Committee noting the severe external financial situation but also recalling the Court had 'spent less than the full amount of the annual appropriations'.[30] In the same annual budget resolution, the Assembly requested the Court to fund any 'new investments and cost increases entirely from savings to administrative processes'.[31]

Since 2009–2011, the premise of efficiencies and savings became the primary narrative for budget discussions at the Assembly. With the accession of Japan to the Rome Statute in 2007, the group of highest contributors to the Court, namely France, Germany, Italy, Japan and the United Kingdom, pursued a policy of zero-growth and enhanced efficiency savings.[32] Given the baseline use of United Nations' scales for determining State Party contributions to the budget, this group of States was able to influence the language and tactics deployed to qualify the annual budget approval process.[33] Asserting their role, the group requested substantial reductions in real terms by asking

---

26 Assembly of States Parties to the Rome Statute, Bureau Decisions, available at: <https://asp.icc-cpi.int/bureau/decisions>.

27 Strategic Plan of the International Criminal Court, ICC-ASP/5/6 (2006).

28 Kotecha, Birju, 'The ICC's Office of the Prosecutor and the Limits of Performance Indicators' (2017) 15 Journal of International Criminal Justice 548.

29 Report of the Committee on Budget and Finance on the Work of its Ninth Session, ICC-ASP/6/12 (2007) 10.

30 ICC-ASP/7/Res.4 Programme Budget for 2009, the Working Capital Fund for 2009, Scale of Assessments for the Apportionment of Expenses of the International Criminal Court, Financing Appropriations for the Year 2009 and the Contingency Fund 3.

31 Ibid.

32 O'Donohue, 'Financing the International Criminal Court' 280.

33 Romano, Cesare, 'The Price of International Justice' (2005) 4 (2) The Law and Practice of International Courts and Tribunals 302.

for zero-based budgeting practices.[34] Presidents Kirsch, Song (Korea) and Fernández de Gurmendi sought to influence States Parties to approve budgets in line with the Court's request but nevertheless implemented a series of efficiency measures affecting the mandate of the Court.[35] In this regard, both Moreno Ocampo and Bensouda frequently warned States Parties of the outsized impact of budget cuts to their mandate.[36] As Clements argued, the decision by the Assembly to seek austere budgets with minimal growth in real terms, 'contributed to the notion that justice, however construed, was the outcome of the optimal application of institutional resources'.[37] In his detailed analysis of the budget process, Zavala showed how between 2009 and 2013 the Court made extensive savings that were, however, consumed by the nature of highly context dependent judicial activities. He argues that while 'the Court was being asked to be more efficient and was reporting accordingly ... what was really intended is for the Court to be cheaper.[38] In this context, the annual budgets remained flat while the caseload of the Court increased from nine in 2009 to 18 in 2013.[39]

Still within the efficiency mode, several procedural changes introduced since 2011 by the Study Group on Governance resulted in budget envelopes in line with the recommendation of the Committee on Budget and Finance.[40] The primary innovation was the inclusion of the Bureau's Hague Working Group in the approval process, which enabled an interim step for frank exchanges between States Parties and the Court before the highly politicised regular Assembly sessions.[41] However, as Wiebelhaus-Brahm and Ainley showed, even when budgets were not dramatically cut, the Office of the Prosecutor was €8 million less than its counterpart at the International Criminal Tribunal for the Former Yugoslavia was at the height of prosecutorial activity.[42] Even as the Court's Coordination Council took in 2016 an enhanced role in budget alignment and design,[43] the Assembly approved minimal increases

34 Ford, 'How Much Money Does the ICC Need?' (2015) 90.
35 Clements, '"Efficiency Is Paramount in This Regard": The Managerial Role of the ICC Presidency from Kirsch to Fernández' 361.
36 Ford, 'How Much Money Does the ICC Need?' (2015) 90.
37 Clements, 'Governing International Criminal Justice: Managerial Practices and the International Criminal Court' 143.
38 Zavala, 485.
39 Ford, 'How Much Money Does the ICC Need?' 2015 86–87.
40 O'Donohue, 'Financing the International Criminal Court' 282.
41 O'Donohue, 'The ICC and the ASP' 2015 115.
42 Wiebelhaus-Brahm, Eric and Ainley, Kirsten, 'The Evolution of Funding for the International Criminal Court: Budgets, Donors and Gender Justice' (2023) 22 Journal of Human Rights 34.
43 Zavala, 486–487.

between 2017 and 2021.[44] In fact, in 2018 the approved budget went further than the cuts recommended by the Budget and Finance Committee and was not even in line with the inflation rate of the Netherlands.[45] In 2019 and 2020 the increase was below 3% compared to the previous year[46] and in 2021, at the height of the Covid-19 pandemic, the Court's budget was actually reduced in nominal terms from €149,205,600 million to €148,259,000.[47]

The Independent Expert Review was attuned to the substantial gap between the Court's mandate and the available resources to implement it. The report found a relationship of deep mistrust between the Court and States Parties. While officials saw the Assembly as 'micro-managing' the operation of the Court, States Parties considered they were not getting 'full value for the funding their taxpayers provide'.[48] Other observers have equally voiced concerns about the use of budget negotiations to achieve political goals. Building on O'Donohue's analysis, Wiebelhaus-Brahm and Ainley questioned whether States Parties' willingness to fund the Court corresponded with opening investigations outside the African region or stalling progress in other situations like Palestine, Afghanistan and Georgia.[49] However, there is fair criticism aimed at the Court for not pursuing a robust budget request by confronting the Assembly on the limits of its mandate. Cannock and O'Donohue argued 'the Court appears to have developed its request based on a guess of what States are willing to pay'[50] rather a fully costed and mandate-led budget. It is surprising, however, that the defunding trend suddenly stopped in 2022 and 2023 after the findings from the Independent Expert Review and as Prosecutor Khan requested additional funds for his office's docket, including for the situation in Ukraine.[51] In summary, the financial oversight responsibility of the Assem-

44 Ford, 'Funding the ICC for Its Third Decade' 2023 369–370.

45 Hillebrecht, Courtney, Saving the International Justice Regime (Cambridge University Press 2021) 131.

46 Wiebelhaus-Brahm and Ainley, 35.

47 ICC-ASP/18/Res.1 Programme Budget for 2020, the Working Capital Fund for 2020, Scale of Assessment for the Apportionment of Expenses of the International Criminal Court, Financing Appropriations for 2020 and the Contingency Fund; ICC-ASP/19/Res.1 Programme Budget for 2021, the Working Capital Fund for 2021, Scale of Assessment for the Apportionment of Expenses of the International Criminal Court, Financing Appropriations for 2021 and the Contingency Fund.

48 Report of the Independent Expert Review of the International Criminal Court and the Rome Statute System, ICC-ASP/19/16 312.

49 Wiebelhaus-Brahm and Ainley, 35.

50 Cannock and O'Donohue, 1.

51 Ford, 'Funding the ICC for Its Third Decade' 2023 369–370.

bly was highly influenced by internal practices at the Court but also the external political and macroeconomic environment between 2002 and 2021.

2.2 *States and Budget in Arrears*

Lateness or non-payment of dues by States Parties is unfortunately a normal practice in multiple treaty-organizations, including international courts.[52] For the International Criminal Court the issue became evident at the fourth session in 2005. Article 112(8) considers a State Party in arrears if their pending payment 'equals or exceeds the amount of the contributions due from it for the preceding two full years'.[53] Without a reasonable explanation by a State Party in arrears, Article 112(8) removes their voting rights at the Bureau and Assembly. Faced with the normative framework in 2005, two financial cycles after the inauguration of the Court in 2002, the Assembly had to determine the loss of voting rights of States in arrears. A Bureau report outlined the statutory requirements, the practice of the United Nations and recommended criteria for the Assembly to agree on exceptions of removal of voting rights.[54] In effect, a decision by the Assembly upon a recommendation from the Committee on Budget and Finance was deemed sufficient to suspend the application of Article 112(8) if failure to pay was due to conditions beyond the control of the State in question.[55]

However, the same report already warned in 2005 that 11 States Parties had not settled their contributions since 2002, representing a total amount of €5,6 million (see Table 7.4).[56] As the Assembly decided to apply Article 112(8) from the fifth session onwards,[57] the situation of unpaid dues continued over time. By November 2021, the total amount of contributions pending to the regular budget, the Host State Loan for the permanent premises and other funds, increased to €49.9 million.[58] Taking the September 2021 Committee on Budget and Finance's report as an example, eight of the top 10 debtor States Par-

---

52 Romano, 281; Smeulers, Alette, Hola, Barbora and van den Berg, Tom, 'Sixty-Five Years of International Criminal Justice: The Facts and Figures' (2013) 13 (1) International Criminal Law Review 7; Cogan, Jacob Katz, 'Financing and Budgets' in Cogan, Jacob Katz, Hurd, Ian and Johnstone, Ian (eds), The Oxford Handbook of International Organizations (Oxford University Press 2016) 903.

53 Article 112(8), Rome Statute of the International Criminal Court (2002) 2187 UNTS 90.

54 Report of the Bureau on the Arrears of States Parties, ICC-ASP/4/14 (2005).

55 Ibid.

56 Ibid 2.

57 ICC-ASP/4/Res.4 Strengthening the International Criminal Court and the Assembly of States Parties 7.

58 Report of the Bureau on the Arrears of States Parties, ICC-ASP/20/27 (2021) 2.

TABLE 7.4 Top 10 States Parties with outstanding contributions as of 31 August 2021

States Party	Regional group	Outstanding periods	Total amount (€62,014,130)
Brazil	Latin American and Caribbean States	2019–2021	€24,054,755
Venezuela	Latin American and Caribbean States	2014–2021	€12,816,996
France	Western European and other States	2021	€12,528,181
Argentina	Latin American and Caribbean States	2020–2021	€4,857,998
Mexico	Latin American and Caribbean States	2021	€3,424,286
Nigeria	African Group	2019–2021	€1,402,877
Chile	Latin American and Caribbean States	2021	€1,078,689
Peru	Latin American and Caribbean States	2019–2021	€853,722
Colombia	Latin American and Caribbean States	2020–2021	€765,992
Uruguay	Latin American and Caribbean States	2020–2021	€230,634

ties primarily came from the group of Latin American and Caribbean States, however, France also owed the Court €12,5 million.[59]

To address this situation, the Bureau engaged with the issue of arrears and overdue payments in 22 meetings between 2007 and 2021.[60] The most serious financial episode took place in 2021 as the Court faced worrying crisis of liquidity. The Registrar reported that, by September 2021, the Court was considering deferring pension and medical insurance payments as €50,7 million

59 Report of the Committee on Budget and Finance on the Work of its Thirty-Seventh Session, ICC-ASP/20/15 (2021) 40.

60 Assembly of States Parties to the Rome Statute, Bureau Decisions, available at: <https://asp.icc-cpi.int/bureau/decisions>.

were outstanding by States Parties.[61] Several States decided to pay their dues in advance to avert the liquidity crisis but the Bureau agreed it 'should not become the norm'.[62] Indeed, utilizing funds from 2022 for the operations in 2021 only increased the likelihood of a liquidity crisis in 2022.[63] The Assembly has reaffirmed its focus on solving the issue of arrears by issuing an annual report since 2005 and the Court has extended financial solutions, such as payment plans, to avoid the application of Article 112(8). However, by the twentieth session in 2021 the problem was persistent and worsening. In this regard, the Independent Expert Review agreed with the Committee on Budget and Finance to seek alternative solutions to solve chronic situation, including lowering the amount that triggers arrears and barring noncompliant States from nominating candidates for elected positions.[64]

2.3 *United Nations Security Council Non-Payment*

In this context, the financial woes of the Court have been further worsened by the United Nations Security Council lack of financial support for expenses incurred by the Sudan and Libya referrals. While Article 115(b) describes in no uncertain terms an expectation the United Nations General Assembly would provide funds to the Court in relation to referrals, Security Council resolutions 1593 and 1970 precluded any financial support. Both resolutions mandated that 'none of the expenses incurred … shall be borne by the United Nations and that such costs shall be borne by the parties to the Rome Statute and those States that wish to contribute voluntarily'.[65] As O'Donohue argued, the clause preventing usage of United Nations funds was not consistent with the original intent of the Rome Statute negotiations, 'which included the five permanent members of the Security Council'.[66] Furthermore, as Halff, Tolbert and Villacis agreed, it was 'clearly justifiable' for the Court to expect reimbursement of expenses incurred in providing services to the 'referring organization'.[67] Thus, after receipt of the Libya referral in 2011, the Assembly requested the

61 Bureau of the Assembly of States Parties, 7th Meeting, 6 October 2021 (2021) 2.

62 Ibid.

63 Ford, 'Funding the ICC for Its Third Decade' (2023) 376.

64 Report of the Independent Expert Review of the International Criminal Court and the Rome Statute System, ICC-ASP/19/16 76.

65 UNSC Res 1593 para. 7; UNSC Res 1970 para. 8.

66 O'Donohue, 'Financing the International Criminal Court' 294.

67 Halff, Maarten, Tolbert, David and Villacis, Renan, 'Article 115 Funds of the Court and of the Assembly of States Parties' in Ambos, Kai and Triffterer, Otto (eds), The Rome Statute of the International Criminal Court: A Commentary (3 edn, Beck/Hart 2016) 2260.

Court to 'include this matter in its institutional dialogue'[68] with the United Nations and report back on any results on a yearly basis. In 2015, during the 14th session, the Assembly further asked the Registrar to 'report on the approximate costs allocated so far within the Court in relation to referrals by the Security Council'.[69] Relaying the information for the first time in 2016, the Registrar calculated the costs associated with the referrals of the Security Council at 'approximately €55 million'.[70] By November 2021, the costs had climbed to circa €75 million.[71] In comparable terms, the incurred costs due to the referred situations by the Security Council would more than suffice to cover the €49,9 million[72] gap in the budget of the Court in 2021.

3 Conclusion

This chapter examined the practice of the Assembly's financial oversight statutory role. The chapter found that between 2002 and 2021, States Parties approved 20 budgets totalling €2.22 billion. Of this allocation, the portion assigned for expenses of the Assembly of States Parties was €67 million. Overall, the budget approved by the Assembly grew every year except between 2010 and 2011 even if slightly (€103,623,300 versus €103,607,900). However, as a negotiated process between the Court and States Parties, the gap between what Court organs requested and the Assembly finally approved stood at €79,9 million (3,6%) in 2021. The chapter argued that this gap corresponded to three interrelated arguments. First, States Parties' willingness to fund the budget was affected by Court underspends during the first 10 years coupled with challenging external political and macroeconomic conditions. Noticeably, after the 2008 financial crisis, the premise of efficiencies and savings became the primary narrative for budget discussions at the Assembly. Even as Court organs, specially the Office of the Prosecutor, explained the impact of flat budgets and an increasing workload, States Parties pursued austere finan-

68 ICC-ASP/10/Res.4 Programme Budget for 2012, the Working Capital Fund for 2012, Scale of Assessments for the Apportionment of Expenses of the International Criminal Court, Financing Appropriations for 2012 and the Contingency Fund 26.

69 ICC-ASP/14/Res.4 Strengthening the International Criminal Court and the Assembly of States Parties 45.

70 Report of the Registry on the Approximate Costs Allocated so far Within the Court in Relation to Referrals by the Security Council, ICC-ASP/15/30 (2016) 2.

71 Report of the Registry on the Approximate Costs Allocated so far within the Court in Relation to Referrals by the Security Council, ICC-ASP/20/11 2.

72 Report of the Bureau on the Arrears of States Parties, ICC-ASP/20/27 2.

ces with minimal growth in real terms. In this regard, the chapter showed the outsized power of the Committee on Budget and Finance in determining the budget even as the Registry prepared substantive analysis to support funding increases. The other two reasons pointed at the chronic inability of the Assembly to recoup budget arrears from States Parties and funding from the United Nations for the Sudan and Libya referrals. By November 2021, the total amount of pending States Parties' contributions to the regular budget, the Host State Loan for the permanent premises and other fund was to €49,9 million. For Security Council referrals it stood at €75 million. Thus, the chapter argued that even as the Assembly's tightened its financial oversight grip over time, risking judicial independence, it did not engage effectively with cost recovery strategies aimed at States Parties in arrears as well as further negotiating a settlement with the United Nations.

CHAPTER 8

The Practice of the Assembly of States Parties: Enforcement of Cooperation

1 Introduction

Paraphrasing Antonio Cassese, the International Criminal Court is a giant without limbs.[1] To walk and work, the Court relies exclusively on the willingness and cooperation of States. The drafters in the Rome Conference purposedly crafted Part 9 of the Statute on cooperation and judicial assistance[2] locating the responsibility to enable the Court on States, and specifically, on States Parties.[3] The distinction was important as the Statute only created obligations to signatories but welcomed assistance from non-party States as well other entities like the United Nations.[4] In essence, for the Court to investigate and prosecute crimes under its jurisdiction, States Parties became the vehicle to provide a range of assistance from the investigatory stage to the enforcement of sentences.[5] As the former Registrar sustained, the Court relies on its States Parties in the absence of its own police force.[6] In this context, the statutory design puts a premium on compliance from States Parties to actively service the Court. States that accede to the Rome Statute do so fully aware of their obligations pacta sunt servanda under Article 86 describing the general duty

1 Cassese, Antonio, 'On the Current Trends Towards Criminal Prosecution and Punishment of Breaches of International Humanitarian Law' (1998) 9 (1) European Journal of International Law 13.

2 Report of the Working Group on International Cooperation and Judicial Assistance, UN Doc. A/CONF.183/C.1/WGIC/L.11/Add.2 2.

3 Bellelli, Roberto, 'Obligation to Cooperate and Duty to Implement' in Bellelli, Roberto (ed), International Criminal Justice: Law and Practice from the Rome Statute to its Review (Ashgate 2010) 236.

4 Schabas, The International Criminal Court: A Commentary on the Rome Statute 1439.

5 Ciampi, Annalisa, 'Legal Rules, Policy Choices and Political Realities in the Functioning of the Cooperation Regime of the International Criminal Court' in Bekou, Olympia and Birkett, Daley (eds), Cooperation and the International Criminal Court: Perspectives from Theory and Practice (Brill 2016) 8.

6 von Hebel, Herman, Opening Address at the High-Level Seminar for Fostering Cooperation with the International Criminal Court, Port of Spain, 10 January 2017, available at: <https://www.icc-cpi.int/sites/default/files/2022-04/20170110-remarks-registrar-eng.pdf> (2017) 3.

© EZEQUIEL JIMÉNEZ MARTINEZ, 2026 | DOI:10.1163/9789004749979_009

to cooperate with the Court. On the other hand, the request to cooperate for non-party States follows a different but important procedure. In both cases, nonetheless, given the damage non-compliance can cause to the work of the Court, the Assembly of States Parties has a critical role to foster cooperation. Yet, despite receiving 11 referrals of non-cooperation from the Court between 2010 and 2021, the Assembly has not succeeded in changing recalcitrant behaviour from non-compliant States.[7] Even as States Parties deployed a range of diplomatic measures to influence cooperation with the Court, these have remained largely ineffective. In this context, this chapter follows the practice of the Assembly of States Parties in enforcing cooperation with the Court. To do so, the chapter begins with a brief discussion of the normative framework guiding the Assembly. Secondly, it offers an overview of the referrals received from the Court and the tactics developed by States Parties to address non-cooperation.

2 Enforcement of Cooperation Practice (2002–2021)

Starting with the normative framework, Article 87(5)(b) refers to non-party States that have entered an ad hoc agreement with the Court, for example under Article 12(3) (see Table 8.1). Non-party States can be bound by Part 9 in situations referred by the United Nations Security Council under Chapter VII of the Charter or by virtue of their ad hoc agreement.[8] Non-party States outside these two conditions may cooperate with the Court but without any legal obligation.[9] In any case, it is for the Court to determine whether the State in question has failed to cooperate with a request. If such finding is sustained, it is equally for the Court to decide whether to 'inform the Assembly of States Parties or, where the Security Council referred the matter to the Court, the Security Council'.[10] In other words, the trigger for political bodies to consider non-cooperation situations of non-party States is purely judicial. The Court has the latitude to determine the elements of non-

7 Assembly of States Parties to the Rome Statute, Non Cooperation, available at: <https://asp.icc-cpi.int/non-cooperation> accessed 8 January 2024.

8 Ciampi, 'Legal Rules, Policy Choices and Political Realities in the Functioning of the Cooperation Regime of the International Criminal Court' (2016) 46.

9 Kreß, Claus and Prost, Kimberly, 'Article 87 Requests for Cooperation: General Provisions' in Ambos, Kai and Triffterer, Otto (eds), The Rome Statute of the International Criminal Court: A Commentary (3 edn, Beck/Hart 2016), (2030).

10 Article 87(5)(b), Rome Statute of the International Criminal Court (2002) 2187 UNTS 90.

compliance with requests and to subsequently decide whether to engage the Assembly, the Security Council, or both.[11]

On the other hand, Article 87(7) applies exclusively to States Parties. The Statute asks the Court to make a finding whether the lack of compliance with a cooperation request prevents it 'from exercising its functions and powers', and if so, to decide whether to 'refer the matter to the Assembly of States Parties or, where the Security Council referred the matter to the Court, to the Security Council.[12] The difference between informing non-party States and referring States Parties is important as it elevates the legal obligation of States Parties to cooperate within 'an intergovernmental organization'.[13] Similarly, the trigger to refer a situation to the Assembly or the Security Council is purely judicial. To make such determination, Court Regulation 109(3) affords an opportunity for the State Party in question to address the Chamber on the matter.[14] After hearing the requested State Party, the Court can make its legal finding and refer the matter, via the President of the Court, to the Assembly or Security Council.[15]

However, the Court is not empowered to determine which actions these political bodies may pursue.[16] In fact, nowhere in the Statute or the Rules of Procedure of the Assembly we can find a provision outlining consequences for non-cooperation unlike, for example, late payment to the budget. The absence of consequences for recalcitrant States Parties was the result of compromises made during the Rome Conference.[17] While France proposed removing voting rights for States Parties found in breach of their cooperation obligations,[18] the final and delicate agreement was devoid of specific consequences in order evade direct political confrontations at the Assembly, which in turn, presumably, would dissuade the universality of the Rome Statute.[19]

11 Kowalski, Mateus, 'Article 87: Requests for Cooperation' in Klamberg, Mark, Nilsson, Jonas and Angotti, Antonio (eds), Commentary on the Law of the International Criminal Court: The Statute, vol 2 (Torkel Opsahl Academic EPublisher 2023) 639.

12 Article 87(7), Rome Statute of the International Criminal Court (2002) 2187 UNTS 90.

13 Kreß and Prost, 2016 (2034).

14 Regulation 109(3), Regulations of the Court, International Criminal Court, ICC-BD/01-05-16.

15 Regulation 109(4), Regulations of the Court, International Criminal Court, ICC-BD/01-05-16.

16 Kreß and Prost, 2016 (2041).

17 Ibid 2021.

18 Draft Statute of the International Criminal Court, Working Paper Submitted by France, UN Doc. A/AC.249/L.3 23.

19 Smith-van Lin, Lorraine, 'Non-Compliance and the Law and Politics of State Cooperation: Lessons from the Al Bashir and Kenyatta Cases' in Bekou, Olympia and Birkett,

TABLE 8.1 Enforcement of cooperation

Function	Responsibilities	Relevant articles
Non State Party in ad hoc arrangement non-cooperation	Consider Court information of non-cooperation of non-party State in ad hoc arrangement with the Court.	87(5)(b)
State Party non-cooperation	Consider Court referral of non-cooperation of State Party.	87(7)
Assembly non-cooperation involvement	Consideration of non-cooperation pursuant to Article 87(5) and (7)	112(2)(f)

In this context, the role of the Assembly of States Parties in enforcing cooperation becomes key.[20] The Assembly is empowered to 'consider pursuant to article 87, paragraphs 5 and 7, any question relating to non-cooperation'.[21] As Bekou explained, it is proper for the Assembly deals with breaches of cooperation as it is the 'governance structure that underpins the Rome Statute regime'.[22] While Sluiter and Talontsi have argued the weakness and ambiguous usage of the term 'consider' in Article 112(2)(f), they equally point out at its flexibility.[23] Indeed, as former Assembly President Christian Wenaweser argued, upon a referral from the Court, States Parties are 'challenged to craft an appropriate response'.[24] Between 2002 and 2021, the Assembly has responded to 11 referrals of non-cooperation by deploying specific procedures to address the situation.[25] In addition, the Assembly passed 13 resolutions

Daley (eds), Cooperation and the International Criminal Court: Perspectives from Theory and Practice (Brill 2016) 135.

20 Bekou, Olympia, 'Dealing with Non-cooperation at the ICC: Towards a More Holistic Approach' (2019) 19 (6) International Criminal Law Review 916.

21 Article 112(2)(f), Rome Statute of the International Criminal Court (2002) 2187 UNTS 90.

22 Bekou, 916.

23 Sluiter, Göran and Talontsi, Stanislas, 'Credible and Authoritative Enforcement of State Cooperation with the International Criminal Court' in Bekou, Olympia and Birkett, Daley (eds), Cooperation and the International Criminal Court: Perspectives from Theory and Practice (Brill 2016) 80.

24 Wenaweser, Christian, 'The Assembly of States Parties of the Rome Statute: Perspectives on the Years Ahead, 2009–2011' (Consultative Conference on International Criminal Justice) 4.

25 Assembly of States Parties to the Rome Statute, Non Cooperation, available at: <https://asp.icc-cpi.int/non-cooperation>.

and made one declaration during the Review Conference in Kampala in 2010 on the overall importance of cooperation with the Court.[26] However, as Bekou,[27] Kreß and Prost,[28] Ambach,[29] and Sarkin[30] have observed, the practice of the Assembly has been both inefficient and inadequate to respond to a repetitive pattern of non-cooperation with the Court with no tangible consequences for recalcitrant States.[31] This has been the case specially but not exclusively in relation to the situation of Sudan after the referral of United Nations Security Council in 2005.[32] Lead Rome negotiator and former Court President Philippe Kirsch has linked the lack of cooperation to the overt concern to 'avoid turmoil in the Assembly'.[33] For Kirsch, the absolute accommodation of political realities over judicial findings was not 'the way the system is supposed to work'.[34]

2.1 *Assembly Non-Cooperation Procedures and Toolkit*

Up until 2011, coinciding with an increase of litigiousness from the situation in Sudan, non-cooperation with the Court was not a regular item in the Assembly. In fact, the main focus of States Parties between 2002 and 2005 was cooperation on institutional building aspects between the Court, States Parties and other entities like the United Nations or intergovernmental regional organizations.[35] After the United Nations Security Council referred the situation of

---

26 'Assembly of States Parties to the Rome Statute, Resolutions, available at: <https://asp.icc-cpi.int/resolutions>'.

27 Bekou, 914.

28 Kreß, Claus and Prost, Kimberly, 'Article 87 Requests for Cooperation: General Provisions' in Ambos, Kai (ed), The Rome Statute of the International Criminal Court: A Commentary (4 edn, Beck/Hart 2022) 2490.

29 Ambach, 'Article 112 Assembly of States Parties' (2022) 2784.

30 Sarkin, Jeremy Julian, 'Will the International Criminal Court Be Able to Secure the Arrest of Vladimir Putin When He Travels?: Understanding State Cooperation Through Other ICC Non-Arrest Cases Against Malawi, Chad, Nigeria, the Democratic Republic of Congo, South Africa, Djibouti, Uganda, and Jordan' (2023) 12 (1) International Human Rights Law Review 31.

31 Rastan, Rod, 'Can the ICC Function Without State Compliance?' in deGuzman, Margaret and Oosterveld, Valerie (eds), The Elgar Companion to the International Criminal Court (Edward Elgar Publishing 2020) 173.

32 UNSC Res 1593.

33 Kirsch, Philippe, 'Reflections on the 20th Anniversary of the International Criminal Court' in Stahn, Carsten and Braga Da Silva, Rafael (eds), The International Criminal Court in Its Third Decade: Reflecting on Law and Practices (Brill | Nijhoff 2023) 49.

34 Ibid.

35 ICC-ASP/4/Res.4 Strengthening the International Criminal Court and the Assembly of States Parties.

Sudan to the Court, the Assembly added language for the first time in 2006 urging 'States to comply with their obligations to cooperate with the Court'.[36] The same resolution requested the Bureau for the first time to present a report on the matter at the next meeting in 2007.[37] Recognizing the importance of cooperation among stakeholders, the Bureau proposed and the Assembly endorsed[38] 31 recommendations for States Parties and the Court and 35 recommendations 'in the United Nations context'.[39] The 66 recommendations proposed a series of actions to foster cooperation on all aspects of the Court's mandate.[40]

In 2009, with the first arrest warrant issued against Omar Al Bashir,[41] the Assembly passed the first resolution dedicated exclusively to cooperation. Resolution 2 from 2009 also noted for the first time the need for 'States Parties and those States under an obligation to do so'[42] to act on arrest warrants. However, the focus of States Parties was on the Review Conference in Kampala. Thus, the same resolution asked a 'stocktaking'[43] exercise on cooperation and in particular progress with the 66 recommendations from 2007. Overshadowed by the negotiations over the crime of aggression, the Kampala Review Conference only passed a declaration on cooperation which emphasized the 'crucial role that the execution of arrest warrants plays in ensuring the effectiveness of the Court's jurisdiction'.[44]

The focus of the Assembly towards non-cooperation began to shift in 2010 and 2011. Only in those two years, the Court made five referrals to the Assembly under Article 87(7) involving Chad (2010 and 2011), Kenya (2010), Djibouti (2011) and Malawi (2011).[45] The five referrals occurred in relation to the failure of these States Parties to arrest and surrender Al Bashir as he travelled to their territories. The situation unfolded after the African Union requested member States not to cooperate with the Court with the arrest of Al Bashir, considering

36 ICC-ASP/5/Res.3 Strengthening the International Criminal Court and the Assembly of States Parties 5.

37 Ibid.

38 ICC-ASP/6/Res.2 Strengthening the International Criminal Court and the Assembly of States Parties 6.

39 Report of the Bureau on Cooperation, ICC-ASP/6/21 (2007) 16.

40 Ambach, 'Article 112 Assembly of States Parties' (2022) 2784.

41 The Prosecutor v Omar Hassan Ahmad Al Bashir (Warrant of Arrest for Omar Hassan Ahmad Al Bashir) ICC-02/05-01/09-1 (4 March 2009).

42 ICC-ASP/8/Res.2 Cooperation (2009) 2.

43 Ibid 3.

44 RC/Decl.2 Declaration on Cooperation (2010) 1.

45 Assembly of States Parties to the Rome Statute, Non Cooperation, available at: <https://asp.icc-cpi.int/non-cooperation>.

him immune as a serving Head of State.[46] As O'Donohue explained, the inability to influence States Parties to execute the arrest warrants led to a change of strategy in the Assembly.[47] During the ninth session in 2010, the Bureau allocated the topic to The Hague Working Group and asked for concrete actions.[48] Ending a certain lethargy on the issue, the Bureau recommended the Assembly to put meaning behind the power endowed in Article 112(2)(f).[49] The Assembly agreed to establish a specific procedure to 'enable it to discharge its mandate to consider any question relating to non-cooperation'.[50] In other words, almost 10 years after its inception, the Assembly decided to establish in practice a mechanism to act under Article 112(2)(f).

The result was the 2011 Assembly procedures relating to non-cooperation (see Table 8.2).[51] The proposal located the authority of the Assembly under Article 112(2)(f) to deploy 'political and diplomatic efforts to promote cooperation and to respond to non-cooperation'.[52] It also clarified their non-judicial nature.[53] The procedures envisaged two scenarios with specific actions emanating from them. The first scenario stipulated a referral of non-cooperation by the Court requiring a 'formal response'[54] by the Assembly. The second scenario was more nuanced. The procedures would apply exceptionally and in the absence of a Court referral if the Assembly had 'reasons to believe' an imminent incident of non-cooperation 'in respect of a request for arrest and surrender of a person'.[55] In this case, the Assembly would deploy an urgent but 'entirely informal response'.[56] In sum, the Assembly procedures contained a dual track response: a formal one driven by the Court and an informal one driven by States Parties, and in particular by the good offices of the

46 Decision on the Meeting of African States Parties to the Rome Statute of the International Criminal Court, Assembly/AU/Dec.245(XIII) Rev.1 (2009).

47 O'Donohue, 'The ICC and the ASP' (2015) 131.

48 Report of the Bureau on Cooperation, ICC-ASP/9/24 (2010) 3.

49 Ibid 4.

50 ICC-ASP/9/Res.3 Strengthening the International Criminal Court and the Assembly of States Parties (2010) 3.

51 ICC-ASP/10/Res.2 Cooperation (2011).

52 Report of the Bureau on Potential Assembly Procedures Relating to non-Cooperation, ICC-ASP/10/37 (2011) 2.

53 Bekou, 928.

54 ICC-ASP/10/Res.5 Strengthening the International Criminal Court and the Assembly of States Parties 12.

55 Ibid.

56 Ibid.

President of the Assembly.[57] The Assembly procedures were amended, albeit minimally, in 2012 and 2018.

Either via a formal or informal route, the President of the Assembly and appointed regional focal points had a role to influence States Parties' behaviour through a range of mostly diplomatic methods. Bekou characterized the procedure as 'formalistic' and 'not very agile'[58] while Sluiter questioned the value of 'rehashing'[59] the merits of judicial findings in the context of the Assembly. Indeed, the formal or informal route, while expected in diplomatic circles, lacked steps for sanctioning or penalizing non-cooperation. Kreß and Prost[60] and Bekou[61] have shown the tacit possibility to impose collective countermeasures on a State Party failing to abide by their treaty obligation to cooperate with the Court. However, such radical option has never been seriously considered by the Assembly.

The informal route of the Assembly procedure was further strengthened during the 15th session in 2016 under the Presidency of Sidiki Kaba (Senegal). By then, the Court had referred 10 instances of non-cooperation by States Parties to the Assembly.[62] The Bureau recognized the need to refine their anticipatory procedure with additional tools to prevent via diplomatic means a situation of non-cooperation evolving to a referral by the Court. Thus, as President Omar Al Bashir visited Djibouti and Uganda in May 2016,[63] focal points finalized a 'toolkit for the implementation of the informal dimension of the non-cooperation procedures'.[64] The toolkit's principal aim was to 'encourage more standardized responses to potential instances of non-cooperation, and to depoliticize action taken to encourage States to meet their cooperation obligations'.[65] The document contained a range of ready to use materials including internet tools to monitor travel of fugitives, draft Statements and draft social

57 Schabas, The International Criminal Court: A Commentary on the Rome Statute (1440).

58 Bekou, 929.

59 Sluiter, 'Enforcing Cooperation: Did the Drafters Approach It the Wrong Way?' 395–396.

60 Kreß and Prost, 'Article 87 Requests for Cooperation: General Provisions' (2022) 2490.

61 Bekou, 927.

62 Assembly of States Parties to the Rome Statute, Non Cooperation, available at: <https://asp.icc-cpi.int/non-cooperation>.

63 Report of the Bureau on non-Cooperation, ICC-ASP/15/31 (2016) 3.

64 Ibid 6.

65 Report of the Bureau on non-Cooperation, Toolkit for the Implementation of the Informal Dimension of the Assembly Procedures Relating to non-Cooperation, ICC-ASP/15/31/Add.1 (2016) 3.

TABLE 8.2 Assembly procedures on non-cooperation (as amended in 2012 and 2018)

	FORMAL RESPONSE PROCEDURE
Trigger	Decision of the Court regarding non-cooperation addressed to the Assembly.
Procedure	Court decision should be forwarded to all States Parties without delay. The general public should be informed by way of a press release of the Secretariat of the Assembly of States Parties. (a) Emergency Bureau meeting. (b) Open letter from the President of the Assembly, on behalf of the Bureau, to the State concerned requesting its views on the matter within a specified time limit of no more than two weeks. Letter to all States Parties, encouraging them to raise the matter in bilateral contacts with the requested State. (c) Bureau meeting to hear views of the State concerned.[a] (d) If regular session more than three months away, New York Working Group to hold a public meeting on the matter with open dialogue with the requested State. (e) The Court's decision to be noted in the omnibus resolution adopted by the Assembly at its next (or on-going) session.[b] (f) Bureau report on actions taken at session plenary session. Bureau able to appoint a dedicated facilitator to consult on a draft resolution containing concrete recommendations on the matter.[c] (g) If the Court refers the non-cooperation situation to the Security Council, the Assembly President could write to the Council President asking the Security Council to follow up on its own referrals.[d]
	INFORMAL RESPONSE PROCEDURE: GOOD OFFICES BY THE PRESIDENT OF THE ASSEMBLY
Trigger	The President of the Assembly would become active on his or her own initiative upon a decision by the Court on the matter or if there are reasons to believe that a specific and serious incident of non-cooperation is about to occur or is currently ongoing.

a ICC-ASP/17/Res.5 Strengthening the International Criminal Court and the Assembly of States Parties, Annex II, Assembly Procedures Relating to non-Cooperation.

b Ibid, Annex II, Assembly Procedures Relating to non-Cooperation.

c Ibid, Annex II, Assembly Procedures Relating to non-Cooperation.

d Ibid, Annex II, Assembly Procedures Relating to non-Cooperation.

TABLE 8.2 Assembly procedures on non-cooperation (as amended in 2012 and 2018) (*cont.*)

Procedure	To assist the President, the Bureau would appoint among its members five focal points on the basis of the principle of equitable geographic representation. The President to raise the issue informally and directly with officials from the requested State and other relevant stakeholders. The President may request any of the regional focal points, or any other Bureau member, as appropriate, to provide assistance in this interaction. The President to report to the Bureau on his or her engagement on the matter, including any information from the United Nations. The regional focal points for non-cooperation should assist in the exercise of the President's good offices as outlined above by engaging, as appropriate, with officials from the requested State. The Secretariat of the Assembly should fully assist in the President's formal response procedure and the exercise of good offices. It should assist and share information, such as official contact point, with the regional focal points.

e ICC-ASP/11/Res.8 Strengthening the International Criminal Court and the Assembly of States Parties 11.
f ICC-ASP/17/Res.5 Strengthening the International Criminal Court and the Assembly of States Parties, Annex II, Assembly Procedures Relating to non-Cooperation.
g Ibid, Annex II, Assembly Procedures Relating to non-Cooperation.
h Ibid, Annex II, Assembly Procedures Relating to non-Cooperation.

media posts.[66] At the 15th session, the Assembly adopted the toolkit in the omnibus resolution[67] and amended them slightly in in 2018 (see Table 8.3).[68]

As with the overall Assembly procedures for non-cooperation, the toolkit for the informal route relied on the influence of States Parties to be ultimately effective. While Ambach argued the toolkit closed 'any operational gaps'[69] left by the Assembly procedure, Bekou was not convinced about the 'efficacity of

66 Ibid.
67 ICC-ASP/15/Res.5 Strengthening the International Criminal Court and the Assembly of States Parties 5.
68 ICC-ASP/17/Res.5 Strengthening the International Criminal Court and the Assembly of States Parties 6.
69 Ambach, 'Article 112 Assembly of States Parties' (2022) 2783.

TABLE 8.3 Toolkit for informal measures of the procedure on non-cooperation (as amended in 2018)

Area	Resource
II. Monitoring the travel of persons subject to warrants of arrest	(a) Monitoring through the diplomatic network. (b) Monitoring through other means (Google alerts and Twitter).[a] (c) Sharing information with the Court and the non-cooperation focal points. (d) Sharing information with States Parties. (e) Sharing information with civil society.
III. Preventing instances of non-cooperation	(a) Draft Statements. (b) Draft notes verbale. (c) Talking points. (d) Draft media release. (e) Draft Tweets.[b]
IV. Sensitizing interlocutors to non-cooperation issues	States Parties are encouraged to express their support for the Court in all relevant bilateral and multilateral meetings.
V. Security Council referrals (language)	(a) Security Council referral resolutions.> (b) The obligation to cooperate. (c) Future referral resolutions.

a Report of the Bureau on non-Cooperation, ICC-ASP/17/31 (2018).
b Ibid.

using Google alerts in stopping non-cooperation'.[70] Indeed, as the former facilitator for cooperation in The Hague Working Group argued, non-cooperation 'is not a question of lack of ability to comply with obligations, but lack of will'.[71] In this context, the toolkit fell short of becoming a tangible resource to change

70 Bekou, 931.

71 Ramberg Krutnes, Anniken 'Reflections of the Facilitator for Cooperation in the Hague Working Group, 2012–2015' in Bekou, Olympia and Birkett, Daley (eds), Cooperation and the International Criminal Court: Perspectives from Theory and Practice (Brill 2016) 260.

uncooperative State behaviour.[72] It does, however, widen the menu of options for States Parties to challenge non-cooperation in a more organized and cohesive way. While the Independent Expert Review only made a recommendation to the Assembly on the issue of arrests within their analysis of the issue of non-cooperation,[73] it also encouraged 'stronger political support for the Court by States Parties'.[74]

Besides the focus on specific procedures to operationalize Article 112(2)(f), the Assembly tackled additional themes, most notably through the informal working group on cooperation at The Hague.[75] Through this flexible body, opened to civil society, States Parties organized high-level events to promote a deeper understanding of Part 9 obligations and to provide political support to the Court, including in Africa.[76] The working group was also responsible to decide the theme for plenary sessions on cooperation, for example at the 11th session, States Parties discussed 'arrest and identification, freezing and seizing of assets'[77] In addition, the group considered the report of Roberto Bellelli (Italy) as rapporteur appointed by the Bureau on arrest strategies.[78] Furthermore, the annual cooperation resolution at the Assembly described the main areas of concern, such as the number of pending arrests, and reported back on activities by the working group and facilitators appointed by the Bureau.[79]

2.2 *Referrals to the Assembly*

Between 2010 and 2017, the Assembly of States Parties received 11 non-cooperation referrals from the Court (see Table 8.4).[80] There were no judicial

72 Sluiter, 'Enforcing Cooperation: Did the Drafters Approach It the Wrong Way?' 398.

73 Report of the Independent Expert Review of the International Criminal Court and the Rome Statute System, ICC-ASP/19/16 167.

74 Ibid 211.

75 Ramberg Krutnes, Anniken 'Reflections of the Facilitator for Cooperation in the Hague Working Group, 2012–2015' in Bekou, Olympia and Birkett, Daley (eds), Cooperation and the International Criminal Court: Perspectives from Theory and Practice (Brill 2016) 248.

76 Ibid 265.

77 Ibid 251.

78 Ibid 261.

79 See for example: ICC-ASP/14/Res.3 Cooperation (2015); ICC-ASP/17/Res.3 Cooperation (2018); ICC-ASP/18/Res.3 Cooperation; ICC-ASP/19/Res.2 Cooperation (2020); ICC-ASP /20/Res.2 Cooperation (2021).

80 Assembly of States Parties to the Rome Statute, Non Cooperation, available at: <https://asp.icc-cpi.int/non-cooperation>.

findings before 2010 and between 2018 and 2021.[81] Ten decisions were in relation to the situation in Sudan and one regarding the situation in Kenya. As such, for the situation in Sudan, the Court informed and referred uncooperative States Parties to the Security Council and the Assembly. The only non-cooperation finding sent solely to the Assembly was in relation to Kenya in 2016 within the case against Uhuru Kenyatta.[82] While there were 11 decisions of non-cooperation, these were directed to eight States Parties whereas only Chad, Djibouti and Kenya accounted for five decisions. Kenya was the only State Party found to be uncooperative in both the situation in Sudan[83] and Kenya. When analysing the material actions found by the Court preventing its functioning by uncooperative States, the referrals for the situation in Sudan outline the failure to arrest and surrender Al Bashir while the single case for Kenya relates to lacking meaningful steps to cooperate with the Prosecutor.[84] Overall, States Parties found to be in breach of their cooperation duty with the Court in the situation in Sudan alleged several issues impacting their inability to arrest Al Bashir. These included: his alleged immunity as a Head of State, a perceived conflict between Articles 27 and 98 of the Statute, the decision by the African Union not to cooperate with his arrest, the peace process in Sudan and unrealized consultations with the Court under Article 97. Of the 11 non-cooperation referrals by the Court, the case of Malawi and Chad in 2011 and Jordan in 2017 is worth exploring as telling examples of the challenges faced by the Assembly's power under Article 112(2)(f).

On 13 December 2011, as the 10th session was unfolding in New York, the Court referred Malawi and Chad to the Assembly and Security Council for failure to arrest and surrender Al Bashir. In both decisions, Pre-Trial Chamber I referenced Article 87(7) and Court Regulation 109(4) to seize the attention of

---

81 Report of the Bureau on non-Cooperation, ICC-ASP/17/31; Report of the Bureau on non-Cooperation, ICC-ASP/18/23 (2019); Report of the Bureau on non-Cooperation, ICC-ASP /19/23 (2020); Report of the Bureau on non-Cooperation, ICC-ASP/20/23 (2021).

82 The Prosecutor v Uhuru Muigai Kenyatta (Second Decision on Prosecution's Application for a Finding of non-Compliance under Article 87(7) of the Statute) ICC-01/09-02/11 (19 September 2016) 18.

83 The Prosecutor v Omar Hassan Ahmad Al Bashir (Decision Informing the United Nations Security Council and the Assembly of the States Parties to the Rome Statute About Omar Al-Bashir's Presence in the Territory of the Republic of Kenya) ICC-02/05-01/09 (27 August 2010) 3.

84 The Prosecutor v Uhuru Muigai Kenyatta (Second Decision on Prosecution's Application for a Finding of non-Compliance under Article 87(7) of the Statute) ICC-01/09-02/11 (19 September 2016) 18.

TABLE 8.4 Enforcement of cooperation (2002–2021)

Date / situation	Court decision	Identified State Party	Assembly action
27 August 2010 / Sudan[a]	Informed Security Council and Assembly[b]	Chad	Assembly President letter and meeting with Foreign Minister. Chad invited but no show to Bureau meeting.[c]
27 August 2010 / Sudan	Informed Security Council and Assembly[d]	Kenya	Assembly President letter and meeting with Foreign Minister. Kenya attended Bureau meeting on the matter.[e]
12 May 2011 / Sudan	Informed Security Council and Assembly[f]	Djibouti	Assembly President letter to Foreign Minister. Subsequent meeting with United Nations permanent representative. Bureau meeting on the matter.[g]
13 December 2011 / Sudan	Referred to Security Council and Assembly	Malawi	Assembly President letter to Foreign Minister. Meeting with Security Council President. Subsequent meeting with United Nations permanent representative.[h]
13 December 2011 / Sudan	Referred to Security Council and Assembly	Chad	Assembly President letter to Foreign Minister. Subsequent meeting with United Nations permanent representative. Assembly President requests States Parties to bring the matter on their bilateral relationship with Chad.[i]

a Assembly of States Parties to the Rome Statute, Non Cooperation, available at: <https://asp.icc-cpi.int/non-cooperation>.

b The Prosecutor v Omar Hassan Ahmad Al Bashir (Decision Informing the United Nations Security Council and the Assembly of the States Parties to the Rome Statute About Omar Al-Bashir's Presence in the Territory of the Republic of Chad) ICC-02/05-01/09 (27 August 2010).

c Bureau of the Assembly of States Parties, 1st Meeting, 11 January 2011 (2011) 2.

d The Prosecutor v Omar Hassan Ahmad Al Bashir (Decision Informing the United Nations Security Council and the Assembly of the States Parties to the Rome Statute About Omar Al-Bashir's Presence in the Territory of the Republic of Kenya) ICC-02/05-01/09 (27 August 2010).

e Bureau of the Assembly of States Parties, 14th Meeting, 5 October 2010 (2010).

f The Prosecutor v Omar Hassan Ahmad Al Bashir (Decision Informing the United Nations Security Council and the Assembly of the States Parties to the Rome Statute About Omar Al-Bashir's Recent Visit to Djibouti) ICC-02/05-01/09 (12 May 2011) 3.

g Bureau of the Assembly of States Parties, 7th Meeting, 7 June 2011 (2011) 4.

h Report of the Bureau on non-Cooperation, ICC-ASP/11/29 (2012) 2.

i Ibid 3–4.

TABLE 8.4 Enforcement of cooperation (2002–2021) (*cont.*)

Date / situation	Court decision	Identified State Party	Assembly action
26 March 2013 / Sudan	Referred to Security Council and Assembly[j]	Chad	Assembly President notification to States Parties. Press release. Letter to Foreign Minister. Subsequent meeting with United Nations permanent representative. Meeting of the New York Working Group on the matter. Meeting with Security Council President. Bureau meetings on the matter.[k]
9 April 2014 / Sudan	Referred to Security Council and Assembly[l]	Democratic Republic of the Congo	Assembly President notification to States Parties. Press release issued. Letter to Foreign Minister. Subsequent meeting with United Nations permanent representative. Social media Statement. Bureau meetings on the matter. United Nations Human Rights Council Universal Periodic Review comments on improving cooperation between the Democratic Republic of the Congo and the Court.[m]
11 July 2016 / Sudan	Referred to Security Council and Assembly[n]	Djibouti	Throughout the year, the President of the Assembly recalled the importance for States to spare no effort in executing the arrest warrants issued by the Court. The President transmitted to States Parties decisions of the Court related to non-cooperation.[o]

j The Prosecutor v Omar Hassan Ahmad Al Bashir (Decision on the non-compliance of the Republic of Chad with the Cooperation Requests Issued by the Court Regarding the Arrest and Surrender of Omar Hassan Ahmad Al-Bashir) ICC-02/05-01/09 (26 March 2013) 10–11.

k Report of the Bureau on non-Cooperation, ICC-ASP/12/34 (2013) 2.

l The Prosecutor v Omar Hassan Ahmad Al Bashir (Decision on the Cooperation of the Democratic Republic of the Congo Regarding Omar Al Bashir's Arrest and Surrender to the Court) ICC-02/05-01/09 (9 April 2014) 17.

m Report of the Bureau on non-Cooperation, ICC-ASP/13/40 (2014) 4.

n The Prosecutor v Omar Hassan Ahmad Al Bashir (Decision on the non-Compliance by the Republic of Djibouti with the Request to Arrest and Surrender Omar Al-Bashir to the Court and Referring the Matter to the United Nations Security Council and the Assembly of the State Parties to the Rome Statute) ICC-02/05-01/09 (11 July 2016) 10.

o Report of the Bureau on non-Cooperation, ICC-ASP/15/31 5; Report of the Bureau on non-Cooperation, ICC-ASP/16/36 (2017) 3.

TABLE 8.4 Enforcement of cooperation (2002–2021) (*cont.*)

Date / situation	Court decision	Identified State Party	Assembly action
11 July 2016 / Sudan	Referred to Security Council and Assembly[p]	Uganda	
19 September 2016 / Kenya	Referred to the Assembly[q]	Kenya	
11 December 2017 / Sudan	Referred to Security Council and Assembly (referral rescinded upon Appeal on 6 May 2019)	Jordan	

p The Prosecutor v Omar Hassan Ahmad Al Bashir (Decision on the non-Compliance by the Republic of Uganda with the Request to Arrest and Surrender Omar Al-Bashir to the Court and Referring the Matter to the United Nations Security Council and the Assembly of the State Parties to the Rome Statute) ICC-02/05–01/09 (11 July 2016) 9.

q The Prosecutor v Uhuru Muigai Kenyatta (Second Decision on Prosecution's Application for a Finding of non-Compliance under Article 87(7) of the Statute) ICC-01/09–02/11 (19 September 2016) 18.

the Assembly.[85] Malawi had asserted Al Bashir had immunity as a Head of State which precluded his arrest,[86] and Chad recalled the decision by the African Union to desist on cooperating with the Court.[87] While the Bureau had been alerted of the developing situation in November 2011, Assembly Presi-

85 The Prosecutor v Omar Hassan Ahmad Al Bashir (Corrigendum to the Decision Pursuant to Article 87(7) of the Rome Statute on the Failure by the Republic of Malawi to Comply with the Cooperation Requests Issued by the Court with Respect to the Arrest and Surrender of Omar Hassan Ahmad Al Bashir) ICC-02/05-01/09 (13 December 2011) 21; The Prosecutor v Omar Hassan Ahmad Al Bashir (Decision Pursuant to article 87(7) of the Rome Statute on the Refusal of the Republic of Chad to Comply with the Cooperation Requests Issued by the Court with Respect to the Arrest and Surrender of Omar Hassan Ahmad Al Bashir) ICC-02/05-01/09 (13 December 2011) 8.

86 The Prosecutor v Omar Hassan Ahmad Al Bashir (Corrigendum to the Decision Pursuant to Article 87(7) of the Rome Statute on the Failure by the Republic of Malawi to Comply with the Cooperation Requests Issued by the Court with Respect to the Arrest and Surrender of Omar Hassan Ahmad Al Bashir) ICC-02/05-01/09 (13 December 2011) 7.

87 The Prosecutor v Omar Hassan Ahmad Al Bashir (Decision Pursuant to article 87(7) of the Rome Statute on the Refusal of the Republic of Chad to Comply with the Cooperation Requests Issued by the Court with Respect to the Arrest and Surrender of Omar Hassan Ahmad Al Bashir) ICC-02/05-01/09 (13 December 2011) 5.

dent Tiina Intelmann formally engaged with Malawi and Chad in January 2012,[88] but had difficulty to make contact with the representative of Chad.[89] In its first report on non-cooperation, the Bureau noted there was no 'shift in attitude on the part of the government of Chad' from previous instances of non-cooperation.[90] On the other hand, the open dialogue probed productive and effective as Malawi declined to host an African Union summit in June 2012 where Al Bashir was expected to attend.[91] The contrast between Chad and Malawi's reaction to the Assembly's procedure in practice signalled the risk of only deploying diplomatic means to address non-cooperation. The lack of tangible consequences meant no adverse impact for Chad and no recompense for Malawi.[92]

Understandably frustrated, the Pre-Trial Chamber II argued when referring Djibouti in 2016 that absent of action by the Security Council and the Assembly, any further non-cooperation finding 'would become futile and incapable of achieving its ultimate goal of putting an end to impunity'.[93] In this context, it is remarkable the Bureau reports on non-cooperation for 2016 and 2017 did not outline the actions taken by President Sidiki Kaba (Senegal) under the Assembly procedures.[94] The report superficially mentioned Sidiki's transmission of Court referrals to States Parties and a rather obvious plea to 'spare no effort in executing the arrest warrants issued by the Court'.[95] Nothing in the public record or the expert literature explains fully the change of focus and detail in the non-cooperation report by the Bureau. However, O'Donohue[96] and Ciampi[97] have pointed out the inherently political dynamics in the Assembly with members of the African Union during this time, possibly precluding tangible actions to dissuade non-cooperation with the Court.

88 Bureau of the Assembly of States Parties, 17th Meeting, 1 November 2011 (2011) 3; Bureau of the Assembly of States Parties, 5th Meeting, 17 January 2012 (2012) 2.

89 Report of the Bureau on Non-Cooperation, ICC-ASP/11/29 2.

90 Ibid 3–4.

91 Ibid 3.

92 Bekou, 930.

93 The Prosecutor v Omar Hassan Ahmad Al Bashir (Decision on the non-Compliance by the Republic of Djibouti with the Request to Arrest and Surrender Omar Al-Bashir to the Court and Referring the Matter to the United Nations Security Council and the Assembly of the State Parties to the Rome Statute) ICC-02/05-01/09 (11 July 2016) 9.

94 Report of the Bureau on non-Cooperation, ICC-ASP/15/31; Report of the Bureau on non-Cooperation, ICC-ASP/16/36.

95 Report of the Bureau on non-Cooperation, ICC-ASP/15/31 5.

96 O'Donohue, 'The ICC and the ASP' (2015) 133.

97 Ciampi, 'Legal Rules, Policy Choices and Political Realities in the Functioning of the Cooperation Regime of the International Criminal Court' (2016) 46.

The next notable example is in regard to Jordan in 2017. In March 2017, Al Bashir attended the 28th Arab League Summit in Amman but was not arrested.[98] On 11 December 2017, the Court referred Jordan to the Assembly and Security Council.[99] A week later, Jordan requested the Pre-Trial Chamber II leave to appeal which was granted in February 2018.[100] The appeal was an opportunity to finally address non-cooperation on the basis of Al Bashir's immunity as a Head of State and the duty to cooperate with the Court created by a Security Council resolution.[101] In addition, a third ground of appeal considered whether the Pre-Trial Chamber erred in referring Jordan to the Assembly and Security Council.[102] Nothing in the Assembly procedures on non-cooperation precluded President Kwon from addressing Jordan's failure to arrest Al Bashir while an appeal took place. However, following the trend from 2016, the Bureau report on non-cooperation did not offer details on the actions pursued by the President.[103]

The Appeals Chamber gave its decision in May 2019. The decision held that Jordan had effectively violated its duty under Security Council resolution 1593 and the Statute to cooperate in the arrest of Al Bashir also dismissing the Head of State immunity argument.[104] However, on the third ground of appeal, it found the Pre-Trial Chamber had rushed to refer Jordan to the Assembly and Council by failing to adequately pursue consultations under Article 97 of the Statute. The Appeals Chamber accepted there was no standard procedure to fulfil Article 97 consultations but that Jordan had clearly indicated their desire to dialogue with the Court but this request was not corresponded. In this particular point, the decision noted inconsistencies with a separate case involving South Africa where Article 97 consultations had been correctly pursued by the same Chamber.[105] Thus, the judgement rescinded the non-cooperation referral from 2017 to the Assembly.[106]

98 The Prosecutor v Omar Hassan Ahmad Al Bashir (Decision Under Article 87(7) of the Rome Statute on the non-Compliance by Jordan with the Request by the Court for the Arrest and Surrender of Omar Al-Bashir) ICC-02/05-01/09 (11 December 2017) 21–22.

99 Ibid 21.

100 The Prosecutor v Omar Hassan Ahmad Al Bashir (Judgment in the Jordan Referral re Al-Bashir Appeal) ICC-02/05-01/09 OA2 (6 May 2019) 10.

101 Ibid.

102 Ibid 11.

103 Report of the Bureau on non-Cooperation, ICC-ASP/17/31 5.

104 Kreß, Claus, 'Preliminary Observations on the ICC Appeals Chamber's Judgment of 6 May 2019 in the Jordan Referral re Al-Bashir Appeal' (2019) (8) Torkel Opsahl Academic EPublisher 1.

105 The Prosecutor v Omar Hassan Ahmad Al Bashir (Judgment in the Jordan Referral re Al-Bashir Appeal) ICC-02/05-01/09 OA2 (6 May 2019) 97.

106 Ibid 98.

3 Conclusion

This chapter examined the statutory practice of the Assembly on enforcement of cooperation with the Court between 2002 and 2021. The chapter found that, despite receiving 11 referrals of non-cooperation from the Court, the Assembly did not succeeded in changing recalcitrant behaviour from non-compliant States. This was particularly problematic in the Sudan situation where the Court issued two arrest warrants against Omar Al Bashir. Despite referring 10 instances of a failure to arrest Al Bashir in the territory of a State Party, the Assembly did not take remedial action to motivate a change of behaviour. For example, even as the Assembly passed 13 resolutions and made one declaration during the Review Conference in Kampala in 2010 on the overall importance of cooperation with the Court, the situation never improved between 2010 and 2021. States Parties only focused on developing a range of diplomatic measures to influence cooperation with the Court, including a detailed procedure to respond to Court findings and a flexible toolkit of optional measures to encourage compliance. These measures were not effective. The chapter argued that while the Assembly procedures and toolkit on non-cooperation certainly had a role, without tangible and concrete actions to penalize non-compliant State Party behaviour, their utility was severely limited. In this context, alternatives have emerged to address this issue, including the creation of a dedicated subsidiary body, the imposition of penalties and fines and baring candidates for judicial elections from non-compliant States. In conclusion, the chapter insisted the severe issues with cooperation compliance should become a top priority of the Assembly of States Parties in order to avoid the paralyzing effect fighting impunity experienced between 2010 and 2017.

CHAPTER 9

The Practice of the Assembly of States Parties: Auxiliary Judicial Instruments Oversight, Statute Amendments and Review

1 Introduction

The Assembly of States Parties had a role to act on auxiliary instruments that go to the heart of the judicial capacity of the Court to exert its mandate.[1] This is the case as States Parties adopted and amended the Elements of Crimes, the Rules of Procedure and Evidence, approved the Staff Regulations, commented on the Regulations of the Court and established the Trust Fund for Victims within the overall context of reparations under Part 7. States Parties derived the power to act on these areas by virtue of Article 112(2)(g), whereas the Assembly performed other functions than those described in Part 11. Indeed, between 2002 and 2021, the Assembly passed 20 resolutions and two decisions on these statutory areas.[2] Closely linked to this responsibility, Part 13 afforded States Parties the sole power to amend the Rome Statute.[3] This is the case as the Rome Statute is both the foundation of an international criminal tribunal and the charter of an international organization, governed, naturally, by its States Parties.[4] Thus, amendments to the Statute, in particular to the crimes under the jurisdiction of the Court, have a natural effect on the Elements of Crimes and the Rules of Procedure and Evidence. As such, the Assembly had an important role to maintain all key legal texts in harmony when applying the amendment regime in the Statute, in particular Articles 121, 122 and 123. Indeed, between 2002 and 2021, States Parties have amended the Rome Stat-

1 Ambach, Philipp and Rackwitz, Klaus U, 'A Model of International Judicial Administration? The Evolution of Managerial Practices at the International Criminal Court' (2013) 76 (3–4) Law and Contemporary Problems 122.

2 Assembly of States Parties to the Rome Statute, Resolutions, available at: <https://asp.icc-cpi.int/resolutions>.

3 Gallant, Kenneth S, 'The International Criminal Court in the System of States and International Organizations' (2003) 16 Leiden Journal of International Law 553.

4 Galand, Alexandre Skander, 'The Nature of the Rome Statute of the International Criminal Court (and its Amended Jurisdictional Scheme)' (2020) 17 Journal of International Criminal Justice 1478.

© EZEQUIEL JIMÉNEZ MARTINEZ, 2026 | DOI:10.1163/9789004749979_010

ute in five opportunities.[5] As Schabas noted, given 'the enormous complexity'[6] and detailed provisions in the Statute, changes were expected as the Court became operational and fully functional. More so when the Statute itself asked the Assembly of States Parties to finalize the provision dealing with the crime of aggression and consider the fate of Article 124 on waving jurisdiction over war crimes for a period of seven years for States Parties lodging a declaration to that effect. The Final Act of the Rome Conference had also signalled an expectation from States to discuss expanding the jurisdiction of the Court to crimes related to drug-trafficking, terrorism and the use of nuclear weapons.[7] Thus, both from the point of view of the drafting history of the Statute and the natural need to amend a constitutive instrument to enhance the practice of the Court, the power of States Parties in the amendment regime is significant.

Besides amendments to the Statute between 2010 and 2021, the Assembly of States Parties have also instituted a mechanism to review and change institutional, legal and political practices emanating from the 2020 Independent Expert Review. The Independent Expert Review (IER) was called to 'make concrete, achievable, actionable recommendations aimed at enhancing the performance, efficiency and effectiveness of the Court and the Rome Statute system as a whole'[8] after public criticism about its mandate potential.[9] In fact, several recommendations from the Independent Expert Review have centred on auxiliary judicial instruments under the oversight of the Assembly of States Parties.

In this context, this chapter follows the practice of the Assembly of States Parties in overseeing key auxiliary judicial instruments, and, in close relationship, the amendment and review of the Rome Statute. To do so, the chapter first discusses the normative framework and main actions taken by States Parties in relation to the Elements of Crimes, the Rules of Procedure and Evidence, the Staff Regulations, the Regulations of the Court and the Trust Fund for Victims. Secondly, it traces the role of States Parties in the normative

5 Assembly of States Parties to the Rome Statute, Rome Statute and Other Agreements, available at: <https://asp.icc-cpi.int/assembly>.

6 Schabas, The International Criminal Court: A Commentary on the Rome Statute 1499.

7 Ibid 1513.

8 ICC-ASP/18/Res.7 Review of the International Criminal Court and the Rome Statute System 4.

9 Prince Zeid Raíad Zeid Al-Hussein, Stagno Ugarte, Bruno, Wenaweser, Christian and Intelman, Tiina, 'The International Criminal Court Needs Fixing' (Atlantic Council, 2019) <https://www.atlanticcouncil.org/blogs/new-atlanticist/the-international-criminal-court-needs-fixing> accessed 24 April 2019.

framework of the amendment regime, the 2010 Kampala amendment on the crime of aggression and the 2019 amendment on using starvation of civilians as a method of warfare in non-international armed conflict. The chapter ends with a discussion of the first report of the Review Mechanism established by the Assembly after the 2020 Independent Expert Review.

2 Auxiliary Judicial Instruments Oversight Practice (2002–2021)

Starting with the normative framework, the Elements of Crimes in Article 9 is described in the Statute as an instrument to 'assist the Court in the interpretation and application of Articles 6, 7, 8 and 8 bis'.[10] The auxiliary document functioned as a 'flexible instrument'[11] to aid the Court in the specification of the material and mental elements of the crimes listed in the Statute.[12] Despite the guiding nature of the Elements, States Parties retained the responsibility to adopt them by a two-third majority and approve subsequent amendments by a State Party, an absolute majority of the judges and the Prosecutor. In effect, during the first session in 2002, the Assembly of States Parties adopted the Elements of Crimes by consensus.[13] Between 2002 and 2021, the Elements of Crimes was modified to accommodate amendments to the Rome Statute in relation to Article 8 on war crimes and 8bis on the crime of aggression.

Article 44(3) asks the Registrar to present draft Staff Regulations to the Assembly on common agreement with the Presidency and Prosecutor. The Staff Regulations outline the 'terms and conditions upon which the staff of the Court shall be appointed, remunerated and dismissed'.[14] In other words, it is the basis for employment and management of human resources at the Court, and thus, falls under the purview of the Registrar to propose them.[15] In addition, Article 44(4) affords to the Court the possibility 'in exceptional

10 Article 9, Rome Statute of the International Criminal Court (2002) 2187 UNTS 90.

11 Schabas, The International Criminal Court: A Commentary on the Rome Statute 322.

12 Triffterer, Otto, 'Can the "Elements of Crimes" Narrow or Broaden Responsibility for Criminal Behaviour Defined in the Rome Statute?' in Stahn, Carsten and Sluiter, Göran (eds), The Emerging Practice of the International Criminal Court (Brill 2008) 383.

13 Report of the First Session of the Assembly of States Parties to the Rome Statute of the International Criminal Court, New York, 3–10 September 2002, ICC-ASP/1/3 5–6.

14 Article 44(3), Rome Statute of the International Criminal Court (2002) 2187 UNTS 90.

15 Karagiannakis, Magda, 'Article 44 Staff' in Ambos, Kai and Triffterer, Otto (eds), The Rome Statute of the International Criminal Court: A Commentary (3 edn, Beck/Hart 2016) 1292.

circumstances'[16] to employ gratis personnel from States Parties, intergovernmental organizations and civil society. However, it also asks the Assembly to establish guidelines on the employment of non-staff members under Article 44(4). Both actions, as will be discussed below, were taken by the Assembly during the second and fourth sessions in 2003 and 2005 respectively.[17]

The Assembly of States Parties also has a direct role in the approval and amendment of the Rules of Procedure and Evidence in Article 51 (1) to (3). The Preparatory Commission was in charge of their drafting as States agreed in Rome they would retain the prime role as legislators, unlike the experience of the Ad Hoc Tribunals.[18] The Rules of Procedure and Evidence were adopted by the Assembly of States Parties during the first session in 2002.[19] Articles 51(2) and (3) dealt with the amendment regime. Amendments could be proposed by any State Party, the judges after securing an absolute majority on the proposed change, and the Prosecutor. As with Article 51(1), a two-third majority of the members of the Assembly was required for their adoption. To assist the judges in proposing amendments to the Rules, the Advisory Committee of Legal Texts under Regulation 4 of the Regulations of the Court served as a platform to consult with the Registry, Prosecutor and defence counsel. To assist States Parties, although not precluding their statutory right to propose amendments, the Assembly established the Working Group on Amendments and subsequently the Study Group on Governance. The Prosecutor, as a member of the Advisory Committee of Legal Texts, could presumably use it as a vehicle for proposing amendments. However, Article 51(2)(c) did not require it and neither did the Regulations of the Court as the Office of the Prosecutor acted independently from the judges. In this context, between 2002 and 2021, the Assembly adopted 11 amendments to the Rules of Procedure and Evidence under Article 51(2) over five sessions in 2011, 2012, 2013, 2016 and 2018.[20]

Article 51(3) also referred to the amendment regime albeit it allows the judges acting in majority to draw up provisional Rules 'in urgent cases where

16 Article 44(4), Rome Statute of the International Criminal Court (2002) 2187 UNTS 90.

17 ICC-ASP/2/Res.2 Staff Regulations for the International Criminal Court; ICC-ASP/4/Res.4 Strengthening the International Criminal Court and the Assembly of States Parties, Annex II Guidelines for the Selection and Engagement of Gratis Personnel at the International Criminal Court.

18 Kreß, Claus, 'The Procedural Texts of the International Criminal Court' (2007) 5 (2) Journal of International Criminal Justice 539.

19 Report of the First Session of the Assembly of States Parties to the Rome Statute of the International Criminal Court, New York, 3–10 September 2002, ICC-ASP/1/3 5–6.

20 Assembly of States Parties to the Rome Statute, Working Group on Amendments, available at: <https://asp.icc-cpi.int/wga> accessed 5 January 2024.

the Rules do not provide for a specific situation before the Court'.[21] Upon the establishment of the provisional Rule, the Assembly by virtue of Article 51(2) must adopt, amend or reject it at the 'next ordinary or special session'.[22] In other words, denoting the transient nature of the Rule and the urgency to devote the Court with legal certainty, States Parties must act at speed at the soonest available meeting. Up until a decision by the Assembly, the provisional Rule perseveres. Broomhall has suggested a provisional Rule might be rejected 'by default'[23] if no consensus, even to call for a vote, can be reached; however, a plain reading of the Statute seems to confirm rejection is only viable with an effective vote carrying such decision. The issue of applying Article 51(3) came at full display in the Assembly in 2016 as the judges enacted provisional Rule 165.[24]

Article 52 sets out the establishment by the judges of the Regulations of the Court 'necessary for its routine functioning'.[25] Across nine chapters, the Regulations develop the expected routine practice of the Court across key issues such as composition and administration, proceedings, victims' participation, reparations, detention, cooperation, removal from office, disciplinary measures and the adoption of the Code of Judicial Ethics.[26] Like the Staff Regulations, the judges are called to consult with the Prosecutor and Registrar in their elaboration. However, unlike Article 44(3), States Parties are only invited to 'comment' on the Regulations for a period of six months and these shall remain in force only if there are no 'objections from a majority of States Parties'.[27] The Statute, Rules of Procedure and Evidence and the Regulations of the Court themselves are silent about the expected steps the judges should take upon the receipt of comments from States Parties or the procedure to resolve a majority objection. The lacuna is further exacerbated as the normative framework does not specify what majority of the Assembly is required to object to the Regulations of the Court. Presumably Article 112(7)(a) regulating voting majorities for matters of substance would apply, but it remains an

---

21 Article 51(3), Rome Statute of the International Criminal Court (2002) 2187 UNTS 90.

22 Article 51(3), Rome Statute of the International Criminal Court (2002) 2187 UNTS 90.

23 Broomhall, Bruce, 'Article 51 Rules of Procedure and Evidence' in Triffterer, Otto and Ambos, Kai (eds), Rome Statute of the International Criminal Court: A Commentary (3rd edn, Beck/Hart 2016) 1342–1343.

24 Report of the Study Group on Governance Cluster I in Relation to the Provisional Amendments to Rule 165 of the Rules of Procedure and Evidence, ICC-ASP/15/7 (2016).

25 Article 52(1), Rome Statute of the International Criminal Court (2002) 2187 UNTS 90.

26 Regulations of the Court, International Criminal Court, ICC-BD/01–05–16.

27 Article 52(3), Rome Statute of the International Criminal Court (2002) 2187 UNTS 90.

unknown factor in the practice of the Court and the Assembly as the Regulations were approved with no objections in May 2004.[28]

Lastly, the Assembly played a role within the overall architecture of reparations for victims under Part 7 of the Statute. While the mandate to provide reparations is firmly located with the Chambers, and to a great extent the Registry, the Assembly was called to establish a Trust Fund 'for the benefit of victims of crimes within the jurisdiction of the Court, and of the families of such victims'.[29] Upon the establishment of the Fund by the Assembly, any financial resources emanating from 'fines or forfeiture' were to 'be transferred, by order of the Court, to the Trust Fund'.[30] Later, in 2007, the Assembly decided the Trust Fund could also receive voluntary contributions from States, organizations and individuals.[31] As a financial instrument, the Fund required specific criteria for its administration and governance. Thus, during the first session in 2002, the Assembly established a Board of Directors,[32] which by 2004 and 2005 was supported by its own Secretariat and Regulations.[33] Despite not being established under 112(4), the Board of Directors is a subsidiary body of the Assembly, which in turn, is responsible for its oversight, election of members and overall inspection via the Committee on Budget and Finance.

In this context, the section below describes notable moments in the practice of the Assembly between 2002 and 2021 under each of these statutory roles that go to the heart of the judicial capacity of the Court to exert its mandate.

2.1 *Elements of Crimes*

The inaugural Elements of Crimes was adopted by the Assembly of States Parties during the first session in 2002.[34] In fact, the Assembly made no changes to the version transmitted by the Preparatory Commission and ado-

---

28 ICC-ASP/3/Res.3 Strengthening the International Criminal Court and the Assembly of States Parties 4.

29 Article 79(1), Rome Statute of the International Criminal Court (2002) 2187 UNTS 90.

30 Article 79(2), Rome Statute of the International Criminal Court (2002) 2187 UNTS 90.

31 ICC-ASP/6/Res.3 Amendment to the Regulations of the Trust Fund for Victims.

32 ICC-ASP/1/Res.6 Establishment of a Fund for the Benefit of Victims of Crimes Within the Jurisdiction of the Court, and of the Families of Such Victims.

33 ICC-ASP/3/Res.7 Establishment of the Secretariat of the Trust Fund for Victims; ICC-ASP/4/Res.3 Regulations of the Trust Fund for Victims.

34 Report of the First Session of the Assembly of States Parties to the Rome Statute of the International Criminal Court, New York, 3–10 September 2002, ICC-ASP/1/3 5–6.

TABLE 9.1 Auxiliary judicial instruments oversight

Function	Responsibilities	Relevant articles
Elements of Crimes	Adoption and amendments thereto of the Elements of Crimes.	9(1)–(2)
Staff Regulations	Approval of Staff Regulations for the Court and guidelines to employ gratis personnel.	44(3)–(4)
Rules of Procedure and Evidence	Adoption and amendments thereto of the Rules of Procedure and Evidence.	51(1)–(3)
Regulations of the Court	Consideration and commentary of Regulations and amendments thereto.	52(3)
Trust Fund for Victims	Establishment of Trust Fund for Victims and determination of management criteria.	79(1) and (3)

pted the Elements without a vote, disregarding Article 9(1).[35] Between 2002 and 2021, the auxiliary document was modified four times as the Statute itself was amended in 2010 (war crimes and aggression), in 2017 (war crimes) and 2019 (war crimes). In each of these instances, the modifications were introduced by States Parties. Neither the majority of judges nor the Prosecutor, as stipulated in Article 9(2), proposed changes to the Elements of Crimes between 2002 and 2021. While Article 9(1) mandates that amendments be adopted by a two-thirds majority of the Assembly, the four changes introduced in 2010, 2017 and 2019 passed by consensus. As in other parts of the Statute, the voting majority required in Article 9(1) is different from Article 112(7)(a) whereas the latter also asks, 'that an absolute majority of States Parties constitute the quorum for voting'.[36] As long as States Parties reached consensus on amendments to the Elements of Crimes, Article 9(1) has been superfluous in the practice of the Assembly between 2002 and 2021. However, the literature questions whether the Elements of Crimes should be at all part of the legislative domain of States Parties as judges are better placed to consider

35 Report of the Preparatory Commission for the International Criminal Court, Addendum, Finalized Draft Text of the Elements of Crimes, UN Doc. PCNICC/2000/INF/3/Add.2.

36 Article 112(7)(a), Rome Statute of the International Criminal Court (2002) 2187 UNTS 90.

the material and mental elements of genocide, crimes against humanity, war crimes and aggression.[37]

The Elements of Crimes have been modified four times as Part 2 in the Rome Statute was amended in 2010 (twice), 2017 and 2019. Amendments to the crimes under the jurisdiction of the Court are governed by Article 121(5) whereas they enter into force a year after a State Party deposits its instrument of ratification or acceptance. Only then the modified provision and jurisdiction of the Court applies exclusively to the ratifying State Party. In this sense, as explored later in this chapter, States Parties established the Working Group on Amendments in 2009 and the Study Group on Governance in 2010 to structure and gather consensus on proposed changes to the Rome Statute or other auxiliary instruments like the Rules of Procedure and Evidence and the Elements of Crimes. Thus, unlike amendments to other parts of the Statute outside Articles 5, 6, 7, 8 and 8bis, changes to the Elements of Crimes were inherently linked to Statute amendments while retaining their guiding purpose.

In summary, the first change to the Elements of Crimes took place during the Review Conference in Kampala in 2010 as States Parties agreed by consensus to amend Article 8 on war crimes and 8bis on the crime of aggression. Resolution 5 from the Review Conference amended provisions related to poisoned weapons, prohibited gases, liquids, materials or devices and prohibited bullets under Article 8(2)(e).[38] Resolution 6, on the other hand, contained the definition and jurisdictional triggers for the crime of aggression.[39] In each resolution, the corresponding changes to the Elements of Crimes appeared. The third and fourth changes in 2017 and 2019 took place in the context of a regular Assembly session. In 2017, during the 16th session, States Parties agreed to further amend Article 8(2)(b) and (e) on war crimes in relation to using microbial, biological or toxin weapons, weapons that injure by fragments undetectable by X-rays and laser blinding weapons in international armed conflict and in armed conflict not of an international character.[40] In 2019, during the 18th session, States Parties adopted an amendment to Article 8(2)(e) on the use of starvation as a war crime applicable in armed conflicts

---

37 Gadirov, Erkin and Clark, Roger S, 'Article 9 Elements of Crimes' in Triffterer, Otto and Ambos, Kai (eds), Rome Statute of the International Criminal Court: a Commentary (3 edn, Beck/Hart 2016) 642.

38 RC/Res.5 Amendments to Article 8 of the Rome Statute (2010).

39 RC/Res.6 The Crime of Aggression (2010).

40 ICC-ASP/16/Res.4 Amendments to Article 8 of the Rome Statute of the International Criminal Court (2017).

not of an international character. The same resolution annexed the required changes to the Elements of Crimes.[41]

2.2 *Staff Regulations, Rules and Gratis Personnel*

The Assembly of States Parties took several steps during the first session in 2002 to guide the recruitment, selection and terms of employment of staff members of the Court.[42] By the second session in 2003, the draft Staff Regulations were ready for consideration and approval by States Parties. The draft text contained 12 Articles with nested regulations covering a range of human resources issues such as duties and obligations, salaries and allowances, social security, separation of service and disciplinary measures.[43] Importantly, Regulation 12.2 allowed the Registrar to establish detailed staff rules consistent with the Assembly-approved Staff Regulations. In this sense, the same provision mandated the Registrar to circulate staff rules or any amendment annually to the Assembly for revision, who, upon examination, could 'direct that the rule and/or amendment be withdrawn or modified'.[44] The first edition of the Staff Rules was transmitted and considered by the Assembly during the fourth session in 2005.[45] Subsequently, by virtue of Regulation 12.2, the Registrar amended the rules in 2015 and 2017 but without specific changes requested by the Assembly. In 2018, however, the Assembly noted the need to align the Staff Rules with the United Nations 'education grant, special education grant and related benefits'.[46] But even after the Committee on Budget and Finance recommended these changes,[47] the administrative issuance updating the Rules was pending at the time of writing in 2024.

In terms of regulations for gratis personnel under Article 44(4), the Registrar prepared draft guidelines in time for the fourth session in 2005 after

41 ICC-ASP/18/Res.5 Amendments to Article 8 of the Rome Statute of the International Criminal Court (2019) 2.

42 ICC-ASP/1/Decision 2 Interim Arrangements for the Exercise of Authority Pending the Assumption of Office by the Registrar.

43 ICC-ASP/2/Res.2 Staff Regulations for the International Criminal Court.

44 Ibid 11.

45 Staff Rules of the International Criminal Court (Annex to ICC/AI/2005/003), ICC-ASP/4/3 (2005).

46 ICC-ASP/17/Res.4 Programme Budget for 2019, the Working Capital Fund for 2019, Scale of Assessment for the Apportionment of Expenses of the International Criminal Court, Financing Appropriations for 2019 and the Contingency Fund 27.

47 Report of the Committee on Budget and Finance on the Work of its Thirty-Second Session, ICC-ASP/18/5 (2019) 23.

consulting an inter-organ working group.[48] The guidelines included: the applicability of statutory requirements for efficiency, competency and integrity, confidentiality and that 'poor planning'[49] should not serve as a rationale for hiring gratis personnel. In essence, gratis personnel were not treated as regular staff members and their use was expected to be narrow, specific and time-bound.[50] The guidelines were adopted by the Assembly in 2005.[51] The Independent Expert Review in 2020 analysed the utility of the guidelines recommending the Court to revise them to allow for secondments from interested governments for 'positions of a non-managerial, technical or specialist nature'.[52] Notably, in 2022, the Office of the Prosecutor agreed to 74 seconded personnel from States and international organizations with expertise in 'judicial, law, military and law enforcement' to provide expert advice 'for all situations'.[53]

Independently if personnel corresponded to regular staff or pro-bono, Resolution 10 from 2002 continued to apply seeking to maintain equitable geographical, gender and State Party representation of human resources at the Court.[54] Between 2004 and 2021, the Assembly maintained a special focus whether the Court complied with Resolution 10.[55] During the 13th meeting of the Bureau in 2006, a topic facilitator for the matter was established for the first time,[56] and remained so between 2006 and 2021.[57] Subsequent reports from the Bureau and the Court between 2006 and 2021 showed the aim to achieve equitable representation across the diversity criteria of Resolution 10

---

48 Report on Draft Guidelines for the Selection and Engagement of Gratis Personnel at the International Criminal Court, ICC-ASP/4/15 (2005) 2.

49 Ibid 3.

50 Karagiannakis, 'Article 44 Staff' 2016 1293–1294.

51 ICC-ASP/4/Res.4 Strengthening the International Criminal Court and the Assembly of States Parties, Annex II Guidelines for the Selection and Engagement of Gratis Personnel at the International Criminal Court.

52 Report of the Independent Expert Review of the International Criminal Court and the Rome Statute System, ICC-ASP/19/16 55.

53 Report of the Twenty-First Session of the Assembly of States Parties to the Rome Statute of the International Criminal Court, The Hague, 5–10 December, Volume I, ICC-ASP/21/20 (2022) 87.

54 ICC-ASP/4/Res.4 Strengthening the International Criminal Court and the Assembly of States Parties, Annex I Amendment to Resolution ICC-ASP/1/Res.10.

55 Schabas, The International Criminal Court: A Commentary on the Rome Statute 767–768.

56 Bureau of the Assembly of States Parties, 13th Meeting, 5 April (2006) 1.

57 Bureau of the Assembly of States Parties, 1st Meeting, 18 February (2021) 2.

was poorly met.[58] As a baseline, in 2007 the Bureau reported that out of the 468 established posts, 43.7% were held by female staff and 56.3% male.[59] at 203 posts in the professional category, the Bureau found that female staff represented the majority of lower level professional posts (P-1 to P-3). At the highest professional level (D-1) the gap between female and male staff was of 60% in favour of the latter.[60] In terms of geographical representation, in 2007 the group of Western European and other States held 56.3% of staff positions, followed by 18% for the group of African States, 11.2% for Latin American and Caribbean States, 7.84% for Eastern European States and 6.37% for the group of Asian States.[61]

By the 20th session in 2021 the situation had not improved. By the end of December 2020, the Court employed 1041 people whereas 866 where in established posts and 175 in the General Temporary Assistance category.[62] Of this total, 53% were male and 47% female.[63] Focusing on the professional and higher staff category as reported by the Bureau in July 2021, a total of 439 staff worked at the Court. Of this total, 51.9% were male and 48,1% female; however the gap widened at senior level whereas only 11.1% of D-1 post holders were female.[64] Within the professional staff category, 68 State Party nationalities were represented and 24 corresponded to non-party States.[65] Of staff members from States Parties, the group of Western European and other States held 58.5% of staff positions, followed by 16.8% for the group of African States, 10.2% for Eastern European States, 7.5% for Latin American and Caribbean States and 7% for the group of Asian States.[66] Comparing to 2016, the Bureau noted geographical representation remained chronically 'imbalanced'.[67]

Alarmed by gender imbalances, especially within senior roles, the President, Prosecutor and Registrar adopted a high-level statement in April 2021 to outline 'areas where further action will be undertaken to promote gender

58 Assembly of States Parties to the Rome Statute, Geographical Representation and Gender Balance (GRGB), available at: <https://asp.icc-cpi.int/bureau/WorkingGroups/GRGB> accessed 4 January (2024).

59 Report of the Bureau on Equitable Geographical Representation and Gender Balance in the Recruitment of Staff of the International Criminal Court, ICC-ASP/6/22 (2007) 9–10.

60 Ibid.

61 Ibid 7–8.

62 Report of the Court on Human Resources Management, ICC-ASP/20/3 (2021) 17.

63 Ibid.

64 Report of the Bureau on Equitable Geographical Representation and Gender Balance in the Recruitment of Staff of the International Criminal Court, ICC-ASP/20/29 (2021) 3–4.

65 Ibid.

66 Ibid 4.

67 Ibid 5.

equality at the Court'.[68] The Independent Expert Review was equally concerned asking the Court and the Assembly to take decisive action on its commitment to achieve gender equality.[69] As Mudukuti showed, despite plans to bridge gaps in gender, geographical and State Party representation, the numbers show 'little progress'.[70] Mudukuti argued that part of the issue was the adoption of desirable ranges in Resolution 10 from 2002 following the practice of the United Nations. Such practice takes into consideration population size, membership and the financial contribution of States Parties. Each element puts a weigh to the likelihood of employment of applicants whereas 55% comes from how much the State of nationality contributes to the budget. In order words, nationals from wealthy States Parties receive a weighted benefit to be employed by the Court.[71] The structural flaw was noted by the Bureau in 2021, but it took no action to thoroughly assess the imbalances it creates.[72] As Mudukuti argues, the continuing practice by the Assembly and the Court is 'neither fair nor merit based'.[73]

2.3 *Rules of Procedure and Evidence*

The Assembly of States Parties adopted the Rules of Procedure and Evidence in the first session in 2002 by consensus. Between 2002 and 2021, the Assembly adopted 11 amendments to the Rules under Article 51(2) over five sessions in 2011, 2012, 2013, 2016 and 2018.[74] As discussed below, the 12th session in 2013 was particularly challenging for States Parties as Kenya and other African States voiced their dissatisfaction with proceedings against President Uhuru Muigai Kenyatta and Deputy President William Samoei Ruto. In 2016, the Assembly dealt with the first provisional Rule adopted by the judges under Article 51(3), not without controversy. In this context, to assist the Assembly in introducing amendments to the Rules of Procedure and Evidence, the

68 Report of the Court on Human Resources Management, ICC-ASP/20/3 8.

69 Report of the Independent Expert Review of the International Criminal Court and the Rome Statute System, ICC-ASP/19/16 20.

70 Mudukuti, Angela, 'The Gap: Gender and Geographical Imbalance at the ICC, 20 Years On' in Stahn, Carsten and Braga da Silva, Rafael (eds), The International Criminal Court in Its Third Decade: Reflecting on Law and Practices (Brill | Nijhoff 2023) 358.

71 Ibid 363.

72 Report of the Bureau on Equitable Geographical Representation and Gender Balance in the Recruitment of Staff of the International Criminal Court, ICC-ASP/20/29 2.

73 Mudukuti, 'The Gap: Gender and Geographical Imbalance at the ICC, 20 Years On' (2023) 363.

74 Assembly of States Parties to the Rome Statute, Working Group on Amendments, available at: <https://asp.icc-cpi.int/WGA>.

Working Group on Amendments and the Study Group on Governance became the interactive platform between States Parties and the Court. Connected, the Court's Advisory Committee of Legal Texts and the Working Group on Lessons Learnt also became part of a 'multi-layered process [that] has proven resource intensive and uniquely complex'.[75]

From the ninth session onwards, the Working Group on Amendments was instructed with 'identifying amendments to be adopted'.[76] However, only in 2012 the Assembly of States Parties agreed to the terms of reference under Article 112(4).[77] The Working Group was the previous step before the Assembly discussed and decided to adopt a change to the Rules of Procedure and Evidence, however, without precluding States to act under Article 51(2). To arrive at consensus-proof proposals, the Study Group on Governance became relevant after its establishment in 2010. The Group was created to strengthen the 'institutional framework both within the Court and between the Court and the Assembly'.[78] Acknowledging the 'complex institutional structure'[79] set by the Statute, the Group was initially established with a one-year mandate to seek a constructive dialogue with the Court on changes required to enhance the efficiency of judicial proceedings and to also build awareness and trust among States Parties of the amendments required by the Assembly.[80] As Ambach explained, the Study Group aimed to 'become a channel between the Court and States Parties to achieve appropriate changes, where necessary, to the legal framework of the Court'.[81]

In this sense, the Study Group on Governance motivated the Court to create in 2012 the Working Group on Lessons Learnt. The Court's Working Group aimed at recouping the main lessons from the completion of the first judicial cycle after the conclusion of the Lubanga trial. The objective, endorsed by the Assembly, was to identify 'potential improvements in current procedures'.[82]

---

75 Abtahi, Hirad and Charania, Shehzad, 'Expediting the ICC Criminal Process: Striking the Right Balance between the ICC and States Parties' (2018) 18 (3) International Criminal Law Review 8.

76 ICC-ASP/8/Res.6 Review Conference 2.

77 ICC-ASP/11/Res.8 Strengthening the International Criminal Court and the Assembly of States Parties 55.

78 ICC-ASP/9/Res.2 Establishment of a Study Group on Governance.

79 Ibid.

80 Ambach, 'Article 112 Assembly of States Parties' (2022) 2799.

81 Ambach, Philipp, 'A Look towards the Future – The ICC and 'Lessons Learnt'' in Carsten, Stahn (ed), The Law and Practice of the International Criminal Court (Oxford University Press 2015) 1286.

82 Ibid.

To do so, the Court's Advisory Committee of Legal Texts, as created in the Regulations of the Court, was identified by the President as the appropriate fora to agree on improvements. This was particularly the case because the Advisory Committee was made of the key constituencies of the Court, namely: judges, Registry, Office of the Prosecutor and counsel.[83] Thus, in the context of the interactive dialogue between the Assembly and the Court to enhance the efficiency of judicial proceedings and build trust, the Study Group on Governance and the Court agreed on a roadmap of priorities for amendments to the Rules of Procedure and Evidence in 2012.[84] With the agreed roadmap, the emerging amendment circuit first started at the Working Group on Lessons Learnt, then to the Advisory Committee of Legal Texts to reach the Study Group on Governance which clarified any outstanding issues with the Court before transmitting a recommendation to the Working Group of Amendments. Then, the Working Group on Amendments concluded a final assessment for final decision at the Assembly of States Parties.[85] While agreeing to keep the roadmap flexible, these inter Assembly-Court bodies became the bureaucratic vehicle and barrier to agree changes to the Rules of Procedure and Evidence between 2002 and 2021.[86]

This amendment circuit was not always utilized by States Parties or judges to amend the Rules, as seen in 2013 and 2016. For Fernandez de Gurmendi, writing as President of the Court, 'the amendment process was too complex and cumbersome due to the multiplication of groups'.[87] Indeed, the Independent Expert Review revealed the Court spent 100 hours of preparation for the interactive dialogue with States, which in turn, spent 50 hours per proposal per body involved in the amendment circuit.[88] Despite the resource intensity of the process, the literature and the Expert Review agreed the onus on consensus building at the Working Group on Amendments and the Assembly blocked the possibility to move at pace with changes supported by the majority of States Parties but held by a few delegations. While Article 51(2) and (3) stipulate a vote of the majority of members to adopt an amendment, the Assembly has been accused of taking 'Rule-making hostage' as 'one State's consensus is another

83 Ibid.

84 Report of the Bureau on the Study Group on Governance, ICC-ASP/11/31 (2012) 4.

85 Ambach, 'Article 112 Assembly of States Parties' (2022) 2800.

86 Ambach, 'A Look towards the Future – The ICC and 'Lessons Learnt'' (2015) 1291.

87 Fernández de Gurmendi, Silvia, 'Enhancing the Court's Efficiency: From the Drafting of the Procedural Provisions by States to their Revision by Judges' (2018) 16 (2) Journal of International Criminal Justice 349.

88 Report of the Independent Expert Review of the International Criminal Court and the Rome Statute System, ICC-ASP/19/16 219.

State's veto'.[89] Instrumentalizing lack of consensus to derail the amendment circuit designed by States Parties and the Court directly contravened the objective set out by the Study Group on Governance to build trust between the Court and the Assembly.[90] Indeed, the Independent Expert Review concluded in 2020 that 'foregoing history has demonstrated that driving progressive development of the RPE is not one of the strengths of the ASP'.[91] In this context, to illustrate the challenges faced by the Assembly, this section explores in detail the changes adopted by the States Parties in 2013 and 2016.

2.3.1 The 12th Assembly of States Parties: Rules 68, 100, 134bis, 134ter, and 134quater

The third set of amendments to the Rules of Procedure and Evidence took place in 2013 during the twelfth session.[92] As Assembly President Tiina Intelmann remarked, what transpired in the regular session was not 'business as usual'.[93] The background to the 12th session, in particular regarding the relationship between African States Parties, the African Union and the Court is important to understand the rules changes enacted by the Assembly. Already by 2009 after the Court issued an arrest warrant for Sudanese President Omar Al Bashir, the debate over immunity for heads of State and Article 27 in the Statute became a source of controversy among States Parties.[94] Coupled with public perceptions the Prosecutor was purposely targeting Africa, the opening of a propio motu investigation in 2010 into Kenyan Deputy Prime Minister and Minister of Finance Uhuru Kenyatta[95] and Minister of Higher Education William Ruto[96] for their involvement during the 2007–2008 post-election vio-

89 Ibid.
90 Ibid.
91 Ibid 220.
92 ICC-ASP/12/Res.7 Amendments to the Rules of Procedure and Evidence (2013)during the 12th session.
93 Report of the Twelfth Session of the Assembly of States Parties to the Rome Statute of the International Criminal Court, The Hague, 20–28 November, Volume I, ICC-ASP/12/20 (2013) 84.
94 Mills, Kurt, '"Bashir is Dividing Us": Africa and the International Criminal Court' (2012) 34 (2) Human Rights Quarterly 404.
95 The Prosecutor v Uhuru Muigai Kenyatta (Second Decision on Prosecution's Application for a Finding of non-Compliance under Article 87(7) of the Statute) ICC-01/09–02/11 (19 September 2016).
96 The Prosecutor v William Samoei Ruto and Joshua Arap Sang (Judgment on the appeals of Mr William Samoei Ruto and Mr Joshua Arap Sang against the decision of Trial Chamber V(A) of 19 August 2015 entitled "Decision on Prosecution Request for Admission of Prior Recorded Testimony) ICC-01/09–01/11 (12 February 2016).

TABLE 9.2 Amendments to the Rules of Procedure and Evidence (2002–2021)

Session	Amended rule	Proponent
ASP 10 (2011)	Rule 4: plenary session of judges for constitution of the Presidency.[a]	Study Group on Governance
	Rule 4bis: assignment of judges to divisions by the Presidency.[b]	Study Group on Governance
ASP 11 (2012)	Rule 132bis: designation of a judge for the preparation of the trial.[c]	Judges
ASP 12 (2013)	Rule 68: introduction of prior recorded testimony.	Judges
	Rule 100: change of location of the place of proceedings beyond seat of the Court.	Judges
	Rule 134bis: ability of the accused person to petition Trial Chamber to be present through the use of video technology during part or parts of his or her trial.	State Party
	Rule 134ter: ability of the accused person to petition Trial Chamber to be excused and to be represented by counsel only during part or parts of his or her trial.	State Party
	Rule 134quarter: ability of the accused person to petition Trial Chamber to be excused and to be represented by counsel if mandated to fulfil extraordinary public duties at the highest national level.	State Party
ASP 15 (2016)	Rule 101: commencement of time limits in relation to the notification of translations.	Judges
	Rule 144: provision of partial translations of decisions of the Court.	Judges
ASP 17 (2018)	Rule 26: receipt and admissibility of complaints against elected officials by the Independent Oversight Mechanism.[d]	Study Group on Governance

a ICC-ASP/10/Res.1 Amendments to Rule 4 of the Rules of Procedure and Evidence.
b Ibid.
c ICC-ASP/11/Res.2 Amendment of the Rules of Procedure and Evidence (2012) 1.
d ICC-ASP/17/Res.2 Amendments to Rule 26 of the Rules of Procedure and Evidence.

lence in the country, worsened the relationship between African States Parties and the Court.[97] As the proceedings in the situation of Kenya continued, in 2013 Kenyatta and Ruto were elected President and Deputy President in a joint ticket. Upon their election, the African Union decided to request a deferral of their case to the United Nations Security Council under Article 16.[98] As the Security Council rejected the deferral request on 15 November 2013, the regular session of the Assembly was due to open on 20 November 2013.[99]

In this charged political context, the Bureau agreed to hold a special segment during the meeting as requested by the African Union titled 'indictment of sitting Heads of State and government and its consequences on peace and stability and reconciliation'.[100] As some African States Parties actively pursued an amendment of Article 27 and publicly threatened to withdraw from the Rome Statute,[101] the Assembly agreed to 'consider looking into practical solutions consistent with the existing legal framework that would address concerns expressed by the African Union'.[102] Those 'practical solutions'[103] materialized in the introduction of Rules 134bis, 134ter and 134quater in the Rules of Procedure and Evidence. These amendments under Article 51(2)(a) were completely outside the roadmap established by the Court and the Study Group on Governance.[104] The inclusion of Rules 134bis, 134ter and 134quater contrasted greatly in terms of process and analysis with additional changes proposed, via the roadmap, to Rules 68 and 100, thus, creating a two-track process for rule amendments at the 12th session in 2013.

---

97 Maunganidze, Ottilia Anna, du Plessis, Anton and Stahn, Carsten, 'The ICC and the AU' in Stahn, Carsten (ed), The Law and Practice of the International Criminal Court (Oxford University Press 2015) 65.

98 Vasiliev, 'Judicial Governance Entities as Power-Holders in International Criminal Justice: A Plea for a Socio-Legal Enquiry' (2020) 524–525.

99 Security Council Resolution Seeking Deferral of Kenyan Leaders' Trial Fails to Win Adoption, with 7 Voting in Favour, 8 Abstaining, UN Doc. SC/11176 (2013). See also: Jalloh, Charles Chernor, Akande, Dapo and du Plessis, Max, 'Assessing the African Union Concerns about Article 16 of the Rome State of the International Criminal Court' (2011) 4 African Journal of Legal Studies 5.

100 Report of the Twelfth Session of the Assembly of States Parties to the Rome Statute of the International Criminal Court, The Hague, 20–28 November, Volume I, ICC-ASP/12/20 12.

101 Knottnerus, Abel, 'The International Criminal Court on Presence at Trial: The (in)validity of Rule 134quater' (2014) 5 International Crimes Database 11.

102 Report of the Twelfth Session of the Assembly of States Parties to the Rome Statute of the International Criminal Court, The Hague, 20–28 November, Volume I, ICC-ASP/12/20 12.

103 Ibid 84.

104 Ambach, Philipp, 'The "Lessons Learnt" Process at the International Criminal Court – a Suitable Vehicle for Procedural Improvements' (2016) 12 Zeitschrift für Internationale Strafrechtsdogmatik 865.

The States Parties-driven approach to amendments of Rules 134bis, 134ter and 134quater originated during the regular session. The Statute and the Rules of Procedure of the Assembly were silent regarding time limits or formal procedures for considering amendments under Article 51(2). In fact, any State Party could act at its own volition even without conferring with the Court.[105] Thus, draft proposals and other explanatory documents were circulated to States Parties but did not form part of the Assembly's public record.[106] At the receipt of the proposals, the Working Group on Amendments held two meetings during the session before transmitting its recommendation to the Assembly.[107] In contrast with the roadmap track for amendments, two formal meetings during the hectic session of the Assembly contrasted with the several months allocated to discussion and analysis of roadmap amendments in close consultation with the Court. Nonetheless, the Chair of the Working Group on Amendments celebrated the discussions took place in a 'spirit of understanding, cooperation and flexibility, in close consultation with the organs of the Court'.[108]

Without the definitive public record of the amendments proposed, we can infer from the speeches of delegations in the general debate and reports from civil society which States Parties proposed changes to Rule 134bis. Thus, it seems the United Kingdom,[109] Jordan, Liechtenstein and Botswana[110] proposed Rule 134bis on the ability of accused persons to be present at trial through video technology. Rule 134ter centred on the ability of the accused person to petition a Trial Chamber to be excused and to be represented by

105 Ibid 864.

106 Abtahi, Hirad and Charania, Shehzad, 'Expediting the ICC Criminal Process: Striking the Right Balance between the ICC and States Parties' (2018) 18 International Criminal Law Review 383.

107 Report of the Twelfth Session of the Assembly of States Parties to the Rome Statute of the International Criminal Court, The Hague, 20–28 November, Volume I, ICC-ASP/12/20 11.

108 Ibid 71.

109 Statement of the United Kingdom of Great Britain and Northern Ireland by Iain Macleod, Head of UK Delegation Assembly of States Parties of the International Criminal Court, Thursday 21 November 2013, available at: <https://asp.icc-cpi.int/sites/asp/files/asp_docs/ASP12/GenDeba/ICC-ASP12-GenDeba-UK-ENG.pdf> (2013) 2.

110 Statement by H.R.H Prince Zeid Raíad Zeid Al-Hussein of the Hashemite Kingdom of Jordan, Speaking Also on Behalf of H.E. Ambassador Christian Wenaweser of the Principality of Liechtenstein Before the Twelfth Session of the Assembly of State Parties to the Rome Statute of the International Criminal Court, The Hague, 20 November 2013, available at: <https://asp.icc-cpi.int/sites/asp/files/asp_docs/ASP12/GenDeba/ICC-ASP12-GenDeba-JordanLiechtenstein-ENG.pdf> (2013) 2.

counsel only during parts of his or her trial. As Ambach and Knottnerus argued, a previous ruling in the Ruto case had recognized this possibility within strict conditions and on a case-by-case basis.[111] Rule 134ter aimed at codifying the practice of the Chamber but in broad and expansive terms without the need to analyse the merits of each situation.[112] An unattributed working paper with such codification was circulated to States Parties which ended up serving as the template for all three amendments to Rule 134.[113]

Rule 134quater proved more controversial. According to Vasiliev, Kenya was the sole proponent of the amendment giving the accused person the ability to petition the Trial Chamber to be excused and to be represented by counsel if mandated to fulfil extraordinary public duties at the highest national level.[114] In practice, a few weeks after the Assembly session, by virtue of his role as Deputy President of Kenya, Ruto was able to invoke Rule 134quater to be solely represented by counsel during parts of his trial in The Hague.[115] Departing from the notion of separation of powers and judicial independence enshrined in the Statute, Ambach argued States Parties as legislators must not generate rules of specific case application, warning Rule 134quater could 'create an unhelpful precedent'.[116] Vasiliev agrees that even if the amendment was adopted within the statutory normative framework, the 'quality of the Rule is tainted by the circumstances of its adoption'.[117] By the end of the 12th session, Resolution 7 from 2013 enacted the three amendments to Rule 134 by consensus.[118]

The roadmap track approach following the amendment circuit established in 2012 was used to propose changes to Rule 68 on the introduction of prior recorded testimony and Rule 100 on a change of location of the place of proceedings beyond seat of the Court. Both Rules intended to achieve greater efficiencies of judicial proceedings and were put forward in agreement with

111 Knottnerus, 3–4.

112 Ambach, 'The "Lessons Learnt" Process at the International Criminal Court – a Suitable Vehicle for Procedural Improvements' 865.

113 Women's Initiatives for Gender Justice, Gender Report Card on the International Criminal Court (2013) 32–33.

114 Vasiliev, 'Judicial Governance Entities as Power-Holders in International Criminal Justice: A Plea for a Socio-Legal Enquiry' (2020) 548.

115 Knottnerus, 5.

116 Ambach, 'Article 112 Assembly of States Parties' (2022) (2800).

117 Vasiliev, 'Judicial Governance Entities as Power-Holders in International Criminal Justice: A Plea for a Socio-Legal Enquiry' (2020) 524–525.

118 ICC-ASP/12/Res.7 Amendments to the Rules of Procedure and Evidence.

the judges. Rule 68 aimed at reducing the time of proceedings and 'streamline evidence presentation by increasing the instances in which prior recorded testimony can be introduced instead of hearing the witness in person'.[119] In the context of the situation in Kenya, some delegations voiced concerns about the legality of the rule change seeking assurances it would not be applied retroactively.[120] Indeed, Article 51(4) already contained this guarantee. The Working Group on Amendments agreed with the Study Group on Governance and recommended the formal submission of the rule change by the judges under Article 51(2)(b).[121] To alleviate concerns on retroactive application of amended Rule 68, Resolution 7 from 2013 included a paragraph emphasizing the wording of Article 51(4).[122]

However, Rule 68 would become the source of conflict between Kenya and the Assembly in 2015. As the 14th session took place, the Appeals Chamber was deliberating the Trial Chamber's decision to grant the introduction of prior recorded testimony of four prosecution witnesses under amended Rule 68.[123] To voice its concerns Kenya requested and the Bureau agreed to add a new item in the session's agenda to 'review of the application and implementation of amendments to the Rules of Procedure and Evidence introduced at the 12th Assembly'.[124] For Vasiliev, the added agenda item risked the independence of the judiciary as 'Kenya sought to make the Court suppress that prior recorded evidence'.[125] The perceived intrusion by a State Party into a purely judicial remit motivated an unprecedented letter by the principals of the Court to the President of the Assembly noting 'with great concern that a number of issues have been proposed for discussion at the Assembly which relate to matters falling clearly within the judicial and prosecutorial competence of the Court'.[126] The President of the Court, the Prosecutor and the Registrar urged Sidiki Kaba to 'ensure that judicial and prosecutorial independence is

---

119 Report of the Bureau on Study Group on Governance, ICC-ASP/12/37 (2013) 4.

120 Ibid.

121 Report of the Working Group on Amendments, ICC-ASP/12/44 (2013) 2.

122 ICC-ASP/12/Res.7 Amendments to the Rules of Procedure and Evidence.

123 Vasiliev, 'Judicial Governance Entities as Power-Holders in International Criminal Justice: A Plea for a Socio-Legal Enquiry' (2020) 552.

124 Report of the Fourteenth Session of the Assembly of States Parties to the Rome Statute of the International Criminal Court, The Hague, 18–26 November, Volume I, ICC-ASP/14/20 (2015) 12.

125 Vasiliev, 'Judicial Governance Entities as Power-Holders in International Criminal Justice: A Plea for a Socio-Legal Enquiry' (2020) 552.

126 Letter to H.E. Mr Sidiki Kaba, President of the Assembly of States Parties, signed by Silvia Fernández de Gurmendi, Fatou Bensouda, and Herman von Hebel, 13 November 2015, available at: <https://www.legal-tools.org/doc/ragycx/> (2015) 1.

not undermined, or perceived to be undermined, by proceedings of the Assembly'.[127] The high-level segment did not deviate from the original text of Resolution 7 from 2013 as the Assembly simply 'reaffirmed its understanding that the amended rule 68 shall not be applied retroactively'.[128] However, the incongruent encroachment of the Assembly into ongoing judicial proceedings damaged the relationship with the Court.[129]

Rule 100 on a change of location of the place of proceedings beyond seat of the Court was part of the roadmap and formally proposed by the judges. Seeking to bring proceedings to the proximity of interested parties, the rule change added a role for the Registry and the Presidency to assess security and financial implications before a final relocation decision.[130] The Study Group on Governance discussed the amendment in May 2013 engaging with the Court to add a specific advisory role for the Registry.[131] In turn, the Working Group on Amendments recommended its adoption upon the formal introduction of the change by the judges under Article 51(2)(b).[132] Thus, as the charged 12th session came to a close in 2013, Resolution 7 from 2013 adopted amendments to Rule 68, 100 and 134bis, 134ter and 134quater by consensus.[133]

2.3.2 The 15th Assembly of States Parties: Rules 101, 144 and Provisional Rule 165

In 2016, during the 15th session, the Assembly of States Parties passed[134] amendments to Rule 101 and 144 in accordance with the Study Group on Governance roadmap and in agreement with the judges. Rules 101 and 144 were part of the so-called 'language cluster'[135] amendments aimed at reducing time and resources to translations and interpretation needs while preserving the rights of the accused.[136] However, the 15th session of the Assembly was confronted with a novel development as the judges acting under Article 51(3)

127 Ibid 2.
128 Report of the Fourteenth Session of the Assembly of States Parties to the Rome Statute of the International Criminal Court, The Hague, 18–26 November, Volume I, ICC-ASP/14/20 13.
129 Abtahi and Charania, 16.
130 Ibid 13.
131 Report of the Bureau on Study Group on Governance, ICC-ASP/12/37 4.
132 Report of the Working Group on Amendments, ICC-ASP/12/44 2.
133 ICC-ASP/12/Res.7 Amendments to the Rules of Procedure and Evidence.
134 ICC-ASP/15/Res.4 Amendments to Rule 101 and Rule 144, paragraph 2(b), of the Rules of Procedure and Evidence (2016).
135 Abtahi and Charania, 25.
136 Report of the Working Group on Amendments, ICC-ASP/15/24 (2016) 5.

enacted for the first time a provisional rule in February 2016.[137] Although not overtly, the judges resort to provisional rules can be linked to the dramatic departure from the roadmap during the 12th session in 2013. Provisional Rule 165 dealt with the procedure to regulate offences against the administration of justice in Article 70 of the Statute. In effect, the amended Rule allowed the Court to expedite Article 70 proceedings by assigning a single judge to the pre-trial and trial Chambers and to allow a panel of three judges to hear any appeal instead of the Appeals Chamber.[138] As per Article 51(3), the judges argued the rule change was urgent in the face of 'resource constraints facing the judiciary',[139] and in the absence of another rule allowing the same result. The provisional rule was transmitted to the Assembly President, which in turn asked the Study Group on Governance and the Working Group on Amendments for their assessment.

In the Study Group the majority of States Parties favoured the adoption of provisional Rule 165 except Kenya, who argued the changes were 'ultra vires'.[140] The provisional rule aimed at simplifying proceedings, including that against Paul Gicheru, charged in 2015 with offences against the administration of justice consisting in 'corruptly influencing witnesses in the situation in Kenya'.[141] The Working Group on Amendments received the report from the Study Group and concluded that while 'a large majority of States Parties supported the adoption of the provisional amendments by the Assembly',[142] it was not in a position to endorse it. The Working Group agreed to further consider the issue during the 15th session.

Akin to the 12th session, the 2016 meeting took place in a politically charged environment. For de Hoon and Lohne, the session was 'crucial for the ICC's future and its place in the geopolitical constellation'.[143] Indeed, by the time States Parties met in The Hague, Burundi, South Africa and Gambia disclosed their intention to leave the Court after perceiving a bias against

---

137 Report of the Bureau on the Study Group on Governance, ICC-ASP/15/21 (2016) 2–3.

138 Report of the Study Group on Governance Cluster I in Relation to the Provisional Amendments to Rule 165 of the Rules of Procedure and Evidence, ICC-ASP/15/7 2.

139 Ibid.

140 Ibid 12.

141 The Prosecutor v Paul Gicheru (Decision Terminating the Proceedings against Paul Gicheru) ICC-01/09-01/20 (14 October 2022).

142 Report of the Working Group on Amendments, ICC-ASP/15/24 7.

143 de Hoon and Lohne, 2019 72.

accused individuals from their regional group.[144] Under these circumstances, the opposition from Kenya to provisional Rule 165 added to the already challenging political context in the Assembly. Ultimately, the Assembly was unable to make a decision as required under Article 51(3) and requested the Working Group on Amendments to continue considering the issue. Kenya welcomed the further involvement of the Working Group but also requested the Court 'to continue not to apply the provisional rule while the matter of rule 165 is still under consideration ... as the best way to avoid legal absurdities'.[145] As Sharma has noted, neither Kenya nor the Assembly can constrain the actions of the Court in the pursuit and application of provisional rules under Article 51(3) except an effective vote rejecting it.[146] Indeed the failure of the Assembly to decide on a provisional rule does not preclude the Court to apply it in the interim, as a plain reading of Article 51(3) suggests.

The legal uncertainty spans from the Assembly's lack of resolution of this issue as the 'concerns of a few States'[147] continued to block the Rules of Procedure and Evidence between 2016 and 2021. Indeed, the Independent Expert Review acknowledged the issue and recommended the Assembly 'should vote on RPE amendments by two thirds majority, rather than consensus, in line with the provisions of Article 51(2)'.[148] In 2021, the Study Group on Governance agreed applying Article 112(7) would avoid the 'paralysis and enhance the efficiency and effectiveness of the Court'.[149] It also recognized that previous Assembly practice had sent 'a negative political signal for the Court'.[150] As of the time of writing in 2024, Rule 165 was still provisionally applied.

---

144 Ssenyonjo, Manisuli, 'State Withdrawal Notifications from the Rome Statute of the International Criminal Court: South Africa, Burundi and the Gambia' (2018) 29 (1) Criminal Law Forum 63.

145 Report of the Fifteenth Session of the Assembly of States Parties to the Rome Statute of the International Criminal Court, The Hague, 16–24 November, Volume I, ICC-ASP/15/20 (2016) 69.

146 Sharma, Kritika, 'The Curious Case of Rule 165 of the Rules of Procedure and Evidence: The Effect of Control Exercised by the Assembly of States Parties over the International Criminal Court' (2020) 20 (2) International Criminal Law Review 301.

147 Report of the Working Group on Amendments, ICC-ASP/16/22 (2017) 5.

148 Report of the Independent Expert Review of the International Criminal Court and the Rome Statute System, ICC-ASP/19/16 220.

149 Report of the Working Group on Amendments, ICC-ASP/20/28 (2021) 4.

150 Ibid.

2.4 *Regulations of the Court*

Article 52 sets out the establishment by the judges of the Regulations of the Court 'necessary for its routine functioning'.[151] Like the Staff Regulations, the judges are called to consult with the Prosecutor and Registrar in their elaboration. However, unlike Article 44(3), States Parties are only invited to 'comment' on the Regulations for a period of six months and these shall remain in force only if there are no 'objections from a majority of States Parties'.[152] The Assembly of States Parties had this opportunity in 2004.[153] Upon circulation of the Regulations, no State Party transmitted any objections to the text except minor corrections to the French version.[154] Between 2004 and 2022, the judges amended the Regulations of the Court in seven occasions.[155] As per Article 52(3), States Parties had six months to comment on amendments despite the clause not being entirely clear about the scope and procedure for transmitting a response.[156] Nonetheless, the public record of the Assembly shows no objections were made by any State Party or by the Assembly as a whole to the amended Regulations in 2007, 2011, 2016 (twice), 2017, 2018 and 2022.[157] Given the debate about this regulatory text in the literature,[158] at least in regard to Regulation 55 on the authority of the Chamber to modify the legal characterization of facts, the lack of engagement from States Parties, unlike in other auxiliary texts like the Rules of Procedure and Evidence, might point at a principled decision to avoid interference with judges' discretion to determine

151 Article 52(1), Rome Statute of the International Criminal Court (2002) 2187 UNTS 90.

152 Article 52(3), Rome Statute of the International Criminal Court (2002) 2187 UNTS 90.

153 ICC-ASP/3/Res.3 Strengthening the International Criminal Court and the Assembly of States Parties 4.

154 Report on the Activities of the Court, ICC-ASP/4/16 (2005) 7.

155 Regulations of the Court, International Criminal Court, ICC-BD/01–05–16.

156 Jacobs, Dov and Staker, Christopher, 'Article 52 Regulations of the Court' in Ambos, Kai and Triffterer, Otto (eds), The Rome Statute of the International Criminal Court: A Commentary (3 edn, Beck/Hart 2016) 1359.

157 Report of the Seventh Session of the Assembly of States Parties to the Rome Statute of the International Criminal Court, The Hague, 14–22 November 2008, Volume I, ICC-ASP/7/20 (2008); Report on the Activities of the Court, ICC-ASP/11/21 (2012); Report on the Activities of the Court, ICC-ASP/15/16 (2016); Bureau of the Assembly of States Parties, 5th Meeting, 22 September 2017 (2017); Bureau of the Assembly of States Parties, 18th Meeting, 4 December 2018 (2018); Bureau of the Assembly of States Parties, 10th Meeting, 2 December 2022 (2022).

158 Stahn, Carsten, 'Modification of the Legal Characterization of Facts in the ICC System: A Portrayal of Regulation 55' (2005) 16 (1) Criminal Law Forum 1; Heller, Kevin Jon, "A Stick to Hit the Accused With' The Legal Recharacterization of Facts under Regulation 55' in Carsten, Stahn (ed), The Law and Practice of the International Criminal Court (Oxford University Press 2015) 1006.

the routine functioning of the Court. The Assembly did, however, request the Court in 2018 to align the operational mandate of the Independent Oversight Mechanism, Rule 26 of the Rules of Procedure and Evidence and Regulations 129 and 130 of the Court in relation to receipt of complaints against elected officials.[159] By 2020, the Independent Expert Review also noted the need by the Court to revise the different regulatory texts on the matter.[160] While some progress was reported by the Head of the Mechanism, the required modifications had not yet taken place by the 20th session in 2021.[161]

2.5 *Trust Fund for Victims*

The unique provisions on victims' participation and reparations under Part 6 and 7 of the Statute connect with the role of the Assembly of States Parties only in Article 79. Article 79(1) and (3) on the Trust Fund for Victims mandates to the Assembly its establishment and management criteria. Between the first and twentieth sessions, States Parties passed 13 resolutions on the matter.[162] As the Court-driven reparation practice developed, the Assembly became engaged in two levels. First, States Parties, by virtue of Article 112(2)(g), directly influenced the institutional development of the Trust Fund for Victims via its establishment, approval of regulations, creation of a dedicated Secretariat, funding and election of the five-member Board of Directors. On a second level, States Parties probed challenges with participation of victims in proceedings, reparation principles by the Chambers and other closely linked issues. In this context, this section discusses these two levels to offer an overview of the notable moments in the practice of the Assembly between 2002 and 2021.

The Assembly of States Parties decided to establish the Trust Fund for Victims, a Board of Directors and the procedure for their election during the first session in 2002.[163] In doing so, the Assembly followed the expectation of the Rome Conference whereas the Fund would be a vehicle for pooling and using resources from 'fines or forfeiture'[164] for the benefit of victims. As a financial

159 ICC-ASP/17/Res.5 Strengthening the International Criminal Court and the Assembly of States Parties 47.

160 Report of the Independent Expert Review of the International Criminal Court and the Rome Statute System, ICC-ASP/19/16 66.

161 Annual Report of the Head of the Independent Oversight Mechanism, ICC-ASP/20/16 3.

162 Assembly of States Parties to the Rome Statute, Resolutions, available at: <https://asp.icc-cpi.int/resolutions>.

163 ICC-ASP/1/Res.6 Establishment of a Fund for the Benefit of Victims of Crimes Within the Jurisdiction of the Court, and of the Families of Such Victims.

164 Article 79(2), Rome Statute of the International Criminal Court (2002) 2187 UNTS 90.

instrument, the Board of Directors was tasked with developing further criteria for its management for approval by the Assembly.[165] To enable this objective, Resolution 7 from 2002 described the procedure for the nomination and election of the Board. Constituted with five members, each from a regional group striving to achieve gender and legal systems balance, the term of office was set at three years with one re-election possible.[166] The Board's nomination and election procedure was amended in 2005 to allow the Bureau to fill any vacancy between regular sessions of the Assembly and to guarantee Board members' terms ended in coincidence with the meeting of States Parties.[167] In 2019[168] and 2021,[169] the Bureau considered further amendments at the request of the Board of Directors, resulting in the extension of their mandate from three to four years and the introduction of staggered terms to guarantee continuity.[170]

Between 2003 and 2021, the Assembly undertook seven elections. The second and fifth rounds in 2006 and 2015 were the only disputed ballots.[171] Several prominent figures have been elected as Board members over the years, especially during in the early phase of the Fund.[172] While some elected individuals were recognized public figures, the criteria to 'have competence in the assistance to victims of serious crimes'[173] was not seriously vetted by the procedure enacted by the Assembly.[174] After requesting it in April 2004,[175] the

---

165 ICC-ASP/1/Res.6 Establishment of a Fund for the Benefit of Victims of Crimes Within the Jurisdiction of the Court, and of the Families of Such Victims.

166 ICC-ASP/1/Res.7 Procedure for the Nomination and Election of Members of the Board of Directors of the Trust Fund for the Benefit of Victims.

167 ICC-ASP/4/Res.5 Procedure for Filling Vacancies in the Board of Directors of the Trust Fund for Victims; ICC-ASP/4/Res.7 Amendment Regarding the Term of Office of Members of the Board of Directors of the Trust Fund for Victims.

168 Bureau of the Assembly of States Parties, 8th Meeting, 17 September 2019 (2019) 7.

169 Bureau of the Assembly of States Parties, 7th Meeting, 6 October 2021 4–5.

170 ICC-ASP/20/Res.5 Strengthening the International Criminal Court and the Assembly of States Parties 23.

171 Assembly of States Parties to the Rome Statute, Election of the Members of the Board of Directors of the Trust Fund for the Benefit of Victims, available at: <https://asp.icc-cpi.int/elections/trust-fund-for-victims> accessed 5 January 2024.

172 Ibid.

173 ICC-ASP/1/Res.6 Establishment of a Fund for the Benefit of Victims of Crimes Within the Jurisdiction of the Court, and of the Families of Such Victims.

174 Rauxloh, Regina E, 'Good Intentions and Bad Consequences: The General Assistance Mandate of the Trust Fund for Victims of the ICC' (2021) 34 (1) Leiden Journal of International Law 208–209.

175 Report to the Assembly of States Parties on the Activities and Projects of the Board of Directors of the Trust Fund for Victims, 2003–2004, ICC-ASP/3/14/Rev.1 (2004) 1.

Assembly agreed with the inaugural Board to create of a Secretariat 'to provide such assistance as is necessary for the proper functioning of the Board of Directors in carrying out its tasks'.[176] In establishing the Secretariat of the Trust Fund for Victims, the Assembly also agreed to fund it via the regular budget and to allocate an Executive Director as the principal officer. By the end of 2021, the Trust Fund had €22,2 millions of available resources[177] and in 2022, the Secretariat had larger budget than the Assembly's counterpart (€3,227,200 versus €3,025,600).[178] A key task of the Board of Directors, as mandated by the Assembly in 2002, was to propose further criteria to manage the Fund. In 2005, the Assembly adopted the proposed regulations of the Fund.[179] The five-part Regulations outlined the management and oversight of the Fund, including receipt of funds, voluntary contributions, beneficiaries and modes for implementing activities and projects, guidance for individual and collective awards and reporting required to the Committee on Budget and Finance, the external auditor and the Assembly.[180]

The Regulations, approved by the Assembly, also described a dual mandate for the Trust Fund. Under Regulation 50(a), the Board of Directors was called to 'provide physical or psychological rehabilitation or material support for the benefit of victims and their families'.[181] Before implementing any general assistance project, the judges could intervene, however, within a narrow timeline after which the Fund was able to proceed.[182] On the other hand, Regulation 50 (b) required the Trust Fund to implement Court-mandated reparation orders as per Article 75 of the Statute and Rules 85 and 98 of the Rules of Procedure and Evidence.[183] Outside the Court-mandated focus, the Trust Fund has been characterized as a humanitarian non-governmental organization.[184] In 2021,

176 ICC-ASP/3/Res.7 Establishment of the Secretariat of the Trust Fund for Victims.

177 Report to the Assembly of States Parties on the Projects and the Activities of the Board of Directors of the Trust Fund for Victims for the Period 1 July 2020 to 30 June 2021, ICC-ASP /20/14 (2021) 3.

178 ICC-ASP/20/Res.1 Programme Budget for 2022, the Working Capital Fund for 2022, Scale of Assessment for the Apportionment of Expenses of the International Criminal Court, Financing Appropriations for 2022 and the Contingency Fund 1.

179 Report to the Assembly of States Parties on the Activities and Projects of the Board of Directors of the Trust Fund for Victims, 2003–2004, ICC-ASP/3/14/Rev.1 1.

180 ICC-ASP/4/Res.3 Regulations of the Trust Fund for Victims.

181 Regulation 50(a), Regulations of the Trust Fund for Victims.

182 Regulation 50(b), Regulations of the Trust Fund for Victims.

183 Ibid. See Part 3 for example.

184 Schabas, The International Criminal Court: A Commentary on the Rome Statute 1182; Rauxloh, 207.

the budget for general assistance amounted to €4,199,087.[185] For Khan, writing before his appointment as the third Prosecutor, the general mandate might not be consistent with fair trial guarantees as the Trust Fund moves to identify victims before any final conviction.[186] The Independent Expert Review echoed similar criticisms in 2020 reporting States Parties, Court officials and civil society questioned 'whether the TFV was fit for purpose'.[187] For the Experts, the Board of Directors should restrict its functions to 'fundraising, administration of the funds, and release of the funds and property as ordered by the Court and complementing reparations awards'.[188] Already in 2019 a confidential evaluation of the administration of the Secretariat of the Trust Fund carried out by the Independent Oversight Mechanism revealed 'issues concerning the strategic focus with respect to reparations, and the interaction and prioritization of the assistance and reparation mandates'.[189]

On a second level, the Assembly of States Parties also engaged with the challenge of victims' identification, participation in proceedings and reparation principles to determine whether to award individual or collective awards in a context of insufficient funds to 'redress the totality of harm'.[190] As the Lubanga, Katanga, Al Mahdi and Ntaganda cases progressed through the different judicial stages towards a reparation order, as Vasiliev explained, the Court experienced 'managerial problems with the system for the victims to apply for participation, including delays with processing applications and resulting backlogs'.[191] It was not until the Kampala Review Conference in 2010 that the Assembly passed a specific resolution in relation to victims and reparations.[192] By the 10th session in 2011, States Parties were fully aware of the challenges with the participation of victims as well as the absence of repara-

185 Report to the Assembly of States Parties on the Projects and the Activities of the Board of Directors of the Trust Fund for Victims for the Period 1 July 2020 to 30 June 2021, ICC-ASP /20/14 13.

186 Khan, 'Article 79 Trust Fund' 2016 (1906).

187 Report of the Independent Expert Review of the International Criminal Court and the Rome Statute System, ICC-ASP/19/16 207.

188 Ibid 208.

189 Annual Report of the Head of the Independent Oversight Mechanism, ICC-ASP/19/26 (2020) 7.

190 Khan, 'Article 79 Trust Fund' 2016 (1905).

191 Vasiliev, Sergey, 'Victim Participation Revisited—What the ICC is Learning About Itself' in Carsten, Stahn (ed), The Law and Practice of the International Criminal Court (Oxford University Press 2015) (1188).

192 RC/Res.2 The Impact of the Rome Statute System on Victims and Affected Communities (2010).

tion principles as stipulated by Article 75 in the Statute.[193] Concluding that 'guidance and clarification from States Parties are essential',[194] the Assembly asked the Court to report back on progress by 2012. In the same session, States Parties further requested the Court to review the 'victim participation system with a view to ensuring its sustainability, effectiveness and efficiency'.[195] In subsequent resolutions in 2012, 2013 and 2014, the Assembly welcomed improvements to the system of victim participation,[196] acknowledged the reparation principles in the Lubanga case,[197] and reiterated only convicted persons were liable to fund any reparation award.[198] Indeed all three resolutions encouraged States Parties to cooperate with the Court in the identification and freezing of assets of accused individuals while clarifying no State 'shall be ordered'[199] to provide funds. Since 2014, the Assembly has reacted to the annual reports from the Fund and continued to press for improved victim participation via the annual omnibus resolution.[200]

3 Statute Amendments and Review Practice (2002–2021)

Part 13 affords States Parties the sole power to amend the Rome Statute.[201] In particular, Articles 121, 122 and 123 set out the procedure and format to effect changes. States Parties have amended the Rome Statute in five opportunities between 2002 and 2021.[202] As Schabas noted, given 'the enormous complexity'[203] and detailed provisions in the Statute, changes were expected as the

193 Vasiliev, 'Victim Participation Revisited—What the ICC is Learning About Itself' 2015 1187–1188.

194 ICC-ASP/10/Res.3 Reparations (2011) 1.

195 ICC-ASP/10/Res.5 Strengthening the International Criminal Court and the Assembly of States Parties 7.

196 ICC-ASP/12/Res.5 Victims and Affected Communities, Reparations and Trust Fund for Victims (2013) 1.

197 ICC-ASP/11/Res.7 Victims and Reparations (2012) 1.

198 ICC-ASP/13/Res.4 Resolution on Victims and Affected Communities, Reparations and Trust Fund for Victims (2014) 3.

199 Ibid 2.

200 Assembly of States Parties to the Rome Statute, Victims and Affected Communities, Reparations and Trust Fund for Victims, available at: <https://asp.icc-cpi.int/bureau/WorkingGroups/Victims> accessed 4 January 2024.

201 Gallant, Kenneth S, 'The International Criminal Court in the System of States and International Organizations' (2003) 16 Leiden Journal of International Law 553.

202 Assembly of States Parties to the Rome Statute, Rome Statute and Other Agreements, available at: <https://asp.icc-cpi.int/assembly>.

203 Schabas, The International Criminal Court: A Commentary on the Rome Statute 1499.

Court became operational and fully functional. More so when the Statute itself asked the Assembly of States Parties to finalize the provision dealing with the crime of aggression and consider the fate of Article 124 on preventing jurisdiction over war crimes for a period of seven years for States Parties lodging a declaration to that effect. Thus, both from the point of view of the drafting history of the Statute and the natural need to amend a constitutive instrument to enhance the practice of the Court, the power of States Parties in the amendment regime is significant. Besides amendments to the Statute between 2010 and 2021, the Assembly of States Parties have also instituted a mechanism to review and change organizational, legal and political practices emanating from the 2020 Independent Expert Review. The Independent Expert Review was called to 'make concrete, achievable, actionable recommendations aimed at enhancing the performance, efficiency and effectiveness of the Court and the Rome Statute system as a whole'[204] after public criticism about its mandate potential.[205]

In this context, to understand the power of the Assembly in amending and reviewing the Statute, this section first outlines the normative framework, secondly focuses on the 2010 amendment and 2017 activation of the crime of aggression and the 2019 amendment on using starvation of civilians as a method of warfare in non-international armed conflict. The section ends with a summary of the Review Mechanism established by the Assembly after the 2020 Independent Expert Review.

In terms of the normative framework, Part 13 outlines in detail the powers and steps to amend the Statute, specifically under Articles 121, 122 and 123. As Clark noted, every line of Article 121 was the result of 'hard negotiation'.[206] The balance was struck between States that preferred amendments introduced as soon as the Court was operational and those who preached calm to allow a certain degree of organizational solidification before agreeing to changes.[207] The compromise in 121(1), then, allowed States Parties to table amendments only seven years after the entry into force of the treaty. In practical terms, it meant no amendments until 1 July 2009. After this time limit, States Parties could submit proposals to the United Nations Secretary General for transmis-

---

204 ICC-ASP/18/Res.7 Review of the International Criminal Court and the Rome Statute System 4.

205 Prince Zeid Raíad Zeid Al-Hussein, Stagno Ugarte, Bruno, Wenaweser, Christian and Intelman, Tiina, 'The International Criminal Court Needs Fixing' (Atlantic Council, 2019) <https://www.atlanticcouncil.org/blogs/new-atlanticist/the-international-criminal-court-needs-fixing> accessed 24 April 2019.

206 Clark, 'Article 121 Amendments' (2016) 2299.

207 Klamberg, 'Article 121 Amendments' (2023) 1047.

sion to the Assembly.[208] After transmission and a period of three months for the proper study of the change proposed, the Assembly must decide by a majority of those present and voting whether to entertain the amendment. Article 121(2) outlines the Assembly might choose to discuss the merits of the change at its next meeting or 'if the issue involved so warrants'[209] at a Review Conference as per Article 123. The Statute does not guide the Assembly in deciding which issue warrants a Review Conference.[210] The practice of the Assembly, however, shows the first Review Conference in Kampala, Uganda in 2010 discussed the finalization of the crime of aggression, and amendments to Article 8 on war crimes and Article 124. The Kampala Conference also served as a vehicle for reflection in relevant issues surrounding the work of the Court.[211] Article 121(2) also signals the ability of the Assembly to use its powers under Article 112(6) to convene a special session, different from a Review Conference, to consider the tabled amendment. Between 2002 and 2021 the Assembly had not called for any special session under Article 112(6).

In the absence of consensus, Article 121(3) requires the Assembly to adopt any amendment under any meeting format by a two-thirds majority. In other words, Article 121(3) raises the standard to a positive vote of 75% of the full membership to adopt it.[212] In effect, as Clark noted, a third of States Parties plus one can block the adoption of amendments by voting negatively or being simply absent from the ballot.[213] In this context, the Working Group on Amendments created in 2010 served as the platform to build consensus before Article 121(1) was triggered by any State.[214] In fact, between 2009 and 2021, the five amendments to the Rome Statute have been agreed by consensus, albeit not without controversy.[215] Once an amendment has been adopted, Article 121(4), (5) and (6) governs their entry into force.

Naturally, any amendment to the Statute needs to be ratified or acceded by each State Party, including by new members. As Article 121(4) explains, such

208 Article 121(1), Rome Statute of the International Criminal Court (2002) 2187 UNTS 90.

209 Article 121(2), Rome Statute of the International Criminal Court (2002) 2187 UNTS 90.

210 Schabas, The International Criminal Court: A Commentary on the Rome Statute 1502.

211 Review Conference of the Rome Statute of the International Criminal Court, Kampala, 31 May – 11 June 2010, Official Records, RC/11.

212 Klamberg, Mark, 'Article 121 Amendments' in Klamberg, Mark, Nilsson, Jonas and Angotti, Antonio (eds), Commentary on the Law of the International Criminal Court: The Statute, vol 2 (Torkel Opsahl Academic EPublisher 2023) 1050.

213 Clark, 'Article 121 Amendments' (2016) 2301.

214 ICC-ASP/8/Res.6 Review Conference 2.

215 Assembly of States Parties to the Rome Statute, Rome Statute and Other Agreements, available at: <https://asp.icc-cpi.int/assembly>.

amendment enters into force a year after accession. Once the threshold of ratifications reaches seven-eighths of States Parties, such amendment becomes binding for all members. For States Parties outside the majority of seven-eights, Article 121(6) provides the opportunity to withdraw from the treaty with immediate effect after giving notice in writing to the United Nations Secretary General within 12 months after the amendment in question became binding. This withdrawal mechanism is an exception to Article 127 whereas the general exit notification may stipulate a departure date beyond 12 months.[216] In practice, a State Party outside the majority of seven-eighths has two years to withdraw: one year after the rule became binding plus 12 months under Article 121(6). The withdrawal of Burundi in 2017 and the Philippines in 2019 occurred exclusively under Article 127.[217]

Article 121(5), on the other hand, is 'a troublesome provision'.[218] Article 121(5) deals exclusively with the entry into force of amendments to the crimes under the jurisdiction of the Court, namely, any change to genocide, crimes against humanity, war crimes and the crime of aggression. States Parties must propose and adopt amendments via Articles 121(1)–(3) but those changes only become binding for ratifying members a year after such instrument is deposited. In doing so, the amendment regime for Articles 5, 6, 7 and 8 crafts an exception to the general rule discussed before.[219] Meaning, regardless if seven-eighths of States Parties ratify a change to an Article dealing with a crime, such change does not become binding for 'a State Party which has not accepted the amendment'.[220] Thus, the Court lacks jurisdiction over non-ratifying States Parties' nationals or on its territory in regard to such amendment.[221]

Article 122 regulates amendments of an institutional nature exclusively confined to certain Articles in Part 4 of the Statute on composition and administration of the Court. Article 122 lists 12 provisions over 10 Articles strictly considered of an institutional nature. These include for example, Article 36(8) and (9) in regard to judges' election and terms of office, Article 42(4)–(9) on the election and some qualifications of the Prosecutor and Deputy Prosecutor and the totality of Articles 46 and 47 on removal and disciplinary

216 Article 127(1), Rome Statute of the International Criminal Court (2002) 2187 UNTS 90.

217 Woolaver, Hannah, 'Withdrawal from the International Criminal Court: International and Domestic Implications' in Gerhard Werle and Zimmermann, Andreas (eds), The International Criminal Court in Turbulent Times (T.M.C. Asser Press 2019) 23.

218 Schabas, The International Criminal Court: A Commentary on the Rome Statute 1505.

219 Klamberg, 'Article 121 Amendments' 2023 1052.

220 Article 121(5), Rome Statute of the International Criminal Court (2002) 2187 UNTS 90.

221 Schabas, The International Criminal Court: A Commentary on the Rome Statute 1503.

measures against elected officials.[222] Oddly, Article 112 on the Assembly is not listed under Article 122 when it could be considered the heart of the institutional architecture of the Rome Statute. States Parties seeking an amendment to provisions listed in Article 122 were not barred to wait seven years as Article 121(1) entailed,[223] and, could transmit proposals to the Secretary General or 'other person designated by the Assembly'.[224] The Statute and the Rules of Procedure of the Assembly are silent about the relevant actor within the Assembly to receive and circulate amendments of an institutional nature. However, it is presumed, at least since 2010, the Assembly President and the Working Group on Amendments would play a significant role. An amendment under Article 122 does not require a preliminary vote by the Assembly to agree its discussion.[225] Rather, as with Article 121(3), in the absence of consensus, a positive vote of 75% of the full membership was required for adoption. However, unlike Article 121(4), the institutional amendment becomes binding for all States Parties six months after adoption discarding any accession threshold requirement. States Parties unable to agree with the binding agreement can resort to Article 127 to withdraw from the Statute.[226] Between 2002 and 2021, there were no amendments under Article 122 even when the Court faced significant institutional issues like, for example, questions about the high moral character of elected officials and staff-related grievances.[227]

Article 123(1) mandated the United Nations Secretary General to convene a Review Conference seven years after the entry into force of the Statute. In practice, the Review Conference in 2010 in Kampala satisfied Article 123(1). The purpose of a Review Conference is to consider amendments including to Articles 5, 6, 7 and 8. While amendments might be considered, nothing in Article 123(1) mandated their adoption. As Clark explained, the basic idea in Rome was to afford States Parties with the time and focus required to thoroughly consider amendments without the burden of other agenda items present at regular sessions.[228] The membership to a Review Conference is the same as with any meeting of the Assembly of States Parties. Article 121 governs the procedure to adopt a change and its entry into force. In essence then, as Bellelli argued, 'a Review Conference is nothing else than the Assembly of

222 Article 122(1), Rome Statute of the International Criminal Court (2002) 2187 UNTS 90.

223 Schabas, The International Criminal Court: A Commentary on the Rome Statute 1510.

224 Article 122(1), Rome Statute of the International Criminal Court (2002) 2187 UNTS 90.

225 Schabas, The International Criminal Court: A Commentary on the Rome Statute 1511.

226 Clark, 'Article 121 Amendments' (2016) 2307.

227 Report of the Independent Expert Review of the International Criminal Court and the Rome Statute System, ICC-ASP/19/16.

228 Clark, 'Article 123 Review of the Statute' (2016) 2308.

States Parties itself, although convened with a specific mandate'.[229] Since the Kampala Conference there has been no other equivalent meeting in the decade to 2021. A subsequent Review Conference can be requested by any State Party but requires the agreement of a majority of the Assembly. Upon approval by the Assembly, the United Nations Secretary General is responsible to convene the meeting.[230]

Outside the formal amendment regime, the Assembly of States Parties maintained a review focus on the efficiency and effectiveness of the Court throughout its first 20 sessions.[231] It did so via its statutory powers under Article 112(2)(b) and (g) whereas the Assembly provides 'management oversight to the Presidency, the Prosecutor and the Registrar regarding the administration of the Court' and can 'perform any other function consistent with this Statute or the Rules of Procedure and Evidence'.[232] Telling examples of this focus were the creation of the Study Group on Governance[233] and Assembly mandates in, for example, strategic planning and budget.[234] But perhaps the most ambitious reform project has been the 2019 Assembly decision to commission an external review of the Court and implement their recommendations through a Review Mechanism. The Independent Expert Review delivered a report with 384 recommendations to the Assembly in September 2020.[235]

Departing from the normative framework, the practice of the Assembly of States Parties resulted in five resolutions amending the Rome Statute. Two resolutions were adopted during the Kampala Review Conference in 2010, on the definition and jurisdiction of the crime of aggression and a second one on prohibited weapons within war crimes. In 2015, States Parties agreed to delete Article 124, in 2017 a further cadre of prohibited weapons was added to Article 8 and in 2019 the war crime of starvation in non-international armed conflict was adopted. Four amendments related to crimes under the Statute and thus were regulated under Article 121(5). Yet, the level of ratifications for these amendments up until January 2024 was

229 Bellelli, 'The Law of the Statute and its Practice Under Review' (2010) 395.

230 Article 123(2), Rome Statute of the International Criminal Court (2002) 2187 UNTS 90.

231 Fernández de Gurmendi, 'Enhancing the Court's Efficiency: From the Drafting of the Procedural Provisions by States to their Revision by Judges' 341.

232 Article 112(2)(b), Rome Statute of the International Criminal Court (2002) 2187 UNTS 90.

233 ICC-ASP/9/Res.2 Establishment of a Study Group on Governance.

234 Assembly of States Parties to the Rome Statute, Working Groups, available at: <https://asp.icc-cpi.int/bureau/WorkingGroups> accessed 4 January 2024.

235 Report of the Independent Expert Review of the International Criminal Court and the Rome Statute System, ICC-ASP/19/16.

TABLE 9.3 Statute amendment and review

Function	Responsibilities	Relevant articles
Statute amendment regime	Decision to take on amendment proposals and subsequent adoption and entry into force.	121(1)–(6)
Statute amendment to provisions of an institutional nature	Decision to take on amendment proposals to provisions of an institutional nature and subsequent adoption and entry into force.	122(1)–(2)
Review of the Statute	Set agenda for compulsory first Review Conference. Decision to convene and on the agenda of a subsequent Review Conference.	123(1)–(3)
Governance and management oversight	Ongoing governance and management oversight of the administration of the Court, including review of the Rome Statute system.	112(2)(b) and (g)

worryingly low, in the best case scenario, a mere 35% of States Parties. The low level of accession begs the question of the utility of the complex amendment procedure when States Parties are reticent to afford the Court widening jurisdiction. This is particularly important as States Parties face pressure to consider amending the jurisdictional regime of the crime of aggression in light of Russia's war on Ukraine and calls to add a new typology of crimes such as ecocide.[236]

236 Global Institute for the Prevention of Aggression, Proposal for the Amendment of the Conditions Under which the International Criminal Court Exercises Jurisdiction Over the Crime of Aggression (2023); Statement by H.E John H Licht, Ambassador of the Republic of Vanuatu to the European Union, General Debate of the 18th Session of the Assembly of States Parties to the Rome Statute, available at: <https://asp.icc-cpi.int/sites/asp/files/asp_docs/ASP18/GD.VAN.2.12.pdf> (2019); Sands, Phillipe and Sow, Dior Fall, Independent Expert Panel for the Legal Definition of Ecocide, Commentary and Core Text (2021).

TABLE 9.4 Statute amendments (2002–2021)

Year / Session	Amendments	Ratifications (2024)[a]
2010 / Review Conference	Article 8(2)(e)(xiii) War crime of employing poison or poisoned weapons	45
	Article 8(2)(e)(xiv) War crime of employing prohibited gases, liquids, materials or devices	
	Article 8(2)(e)(xv) War crime of employing prohibited bullets	
	Article 8bis Crime of Aggression	45
	Article 15bis Exercise of jurisdiction over the crime of aggression (State referral, proprio motu)	
	Article 15ter Exercise of jurisdiction over the crime of aggression (Security Council referral)	
2015 / ASP 14	Deletion Article 124 Transitional Provision	20
2017 / ASP 16	Article 8(2)(b)(xxvii) and (2)(e)(xvi) Employing weapons, which use microbial or other biological agents, or toxins, whatever their origin or method of production	17
	Article 8(2)(b)(xxviii) and (2)(e)(xvii) Employing weapons the primary effect of which is to injure by fragments which in the human body escape detection by X-rays	15
	Article 8(2)(b)(xxix) and (2)(e)(xviii) Employing laser weapons	15
2019 / ASP 18	Article 8(2)(e)(xix) Intentionally using starvation of civilians as a method of warfare in non-international armed conflict	13

a Assembly of States Parties to the Rome Statute, Rome Statute and Other Agreements, available at: <https://asp.icc-cpi.int/assembly>.

In this context, this section provides an overview of the 2010 amendment and 2017 activation of the crime of aggression and the 2019 amendment on using starvation of civilians as a method of warfare in non-international armed conflict. Then, it offers a summary of the context, results and progress of the Independent Expert Review process up to the 20th session.

3.1 *The 2010 Kampala and 2019 Starvation Amendments*

On 1 July 2009 the Rome Statute turned seven years since its adoption. On 7 August 2009, the United Nations Secretary General convened a Review Conference as mandated by Article 123(1).[237] Between 31 May and 11 June 2010, the 111 States Parties to the Rome Statute gathered in Kampala, Uganda together with other States signatory to the Statute or Final Act and civil society to consider three amendment proposals and take stock of learnings on cooperation, complementarity, enforcement of sentences and the role of victims.[238] Of the three amendments considered only a decision on Article 124 was required by the Conference as explicitly requested by the Statute.[239] The other two amendments, on the final adoption of the crime of aggression and the inclusion of a list of prohibited weapons to Article 8 on war crimes, were the result of intense negotiations between the fifth and eighth sessions of the Assembly.[240] The agenda of the Review Conference corresponded with a desire to reflect about the state of the Court after close to a decade in operation. In this sense, Triffterer helpfully distinguished between the rigid act of amending a legal document over a 'broader notion' of review 'covering all aspects which may play a role, in particular in the future'.[241] Yet, the main issue at hand was the final adoption of the crime of aggression, a project as old as the quest to establish the Court.[242] The negotiating journey within the Assembly had formally started in 2002,[243] and Kampala was its natural conclusion. According to participants, the mood as delegations arrived in Kampala was of scepticism, anxiety[244] and a feeling of 'might be now or never'.[245] Akin to the experi-

---

237 Review Conference of the Rome Statute of the International Criminal Court, Kampala, 31 May – 11 June 2010, Official Records, RC/11 1.

238 Clark, Roger S, 'Amendments to the Rome Statute of the International Criminal Court Considered at the First Review Conference on the Court, Kampala, 31 May-11 June 2010' (2010) 2 (2) Goettingen Journal of International Law 690.

239 Zimmermann, Andreas, 'Article 124 Transitional Provision' in Triffterer, Otto and Ambos, Kai (eds), Rome Statute of the International Criminal Court: a Commentary (3 edn, Beck/Hart 2016) 2316.

240 Report of the Bureau on the Review Conference, ICC-ASP/8/43 (2009) 8.

241 Triffterer, Otto, 'The Object of Review Mechanisms: Statutes' Provisions, Elements of Crimes and Rules of Procedure and Evidence' in Bellelli, Roberto (ed), International Criminal Justice: Law and Practice from the Rome Statute to its Review (Ashgate 2010) 357.

242 Kreß, Claus and Barriga, Stefan, The Crime of Aggression: A Commentary (Cambridge University Press 2016).

243 ICC-ASP/1/Res.1 Continuity of Work in Respect of the Crime of Aggression.

244 Wenaweser, Christian, 'Reaching the Kampala Compromise on Aggression: The Chair's Perspective' (2010) 23 (4) Leiden Journal of International Law 884.

245 McDougall, Carrie, The Crime of Aggression Under the Rome Statute of the International Criminal Court (2 edn, Cambridge University Press 2021) 24.

ence in Rome, delegations ran out the clock on the last day on 11 June 2010 as they agreed by consensus the definition and jurisdictional trigger for the crime of aggression.[246] For Blokker and Kreß, participants of the Conference, the Review Conference was a historic achievement.[247] To arrive at such conclusion, the Assembly began preparations for the Review Conference since 2006.[248] Indeed, Rolf Fife (Norway), a veteran of the Rome Conference, enabled much of the preparatory work.[249]

The eighth session of the Assembly in November 2009 and its resumed meeting in March 2010 were crucial for the Review Conference. Past the seven year mark stipulated in Article 121(1) in July 2009, States were able to table amendments for the Review Conference. To organize the stream of proposals in preparation for the eighth session, the Bureau agreed on a 30 September deadline and appointed two facilitators in the New York Working Group to consider and recommend a final slate of proposals to the Assembly.[250] The threshold for agreement was the ability to master broad consensus among States Parties. By the September deadline, Liechtenstein, Belgium, Mexico, the Netherlands, Norway, Trinidad and Tobago, and Belize had submitted proposals for amendments.[251] Over six meetings between March and November, the New York Working Group was able to agree which amendments to transmit to the Assembly for approval as per Article 121(2).[252] In November 2009 the Assembly agreed by consensus to transmit the fate of Article 124, the Liechtenstein-led Special Working Group proposal on the crime of aggression and Belgium's suggestion for adding prohibited weapons to Article 8(2)(e).[253] In the same resolution, the Assembly settled on the themes of complementarity, cooperation, the impact of the Rome Statute system on victims, and peace and justice for stocktaking sessions.[254] The resumed eighth session in March 2010 further refined the stocktaking exercise and set in motion a collection of pledges by States and other entities alike to support the work of

246 Ibid 31.

247 Blokker, Niels and Kreß, Claus, 'A Consensus Agreement on the Crime of Aggression: Impressions from Kampala' (2010) 23 (4) Leiden Journal of International Law 889.

248 Review Conference: Scenarios and Options, ICC-ASP/5/INF.2 (2006) 1.

249 Ibid 2.

250 Report of the Bureau on the Review Conference, ICC-ASP/8/43 3.

251 Ibid 6.

252 Ibid 3.

253 ICC-ASP/8/Res.6 Review Conference.

254 Ibid.

the Court.[255] As the final preparatory moment before Kampala, the resumed session finalized draft resolutions and papers ready for the Review Conference, including a high-level declaration to mark the historic moment.[256]

As per Article 123(1), the Review Conference was opened to States Parties, signatories of the Statute and the Rome Conference Final Act and to other entities like intergovernmental organizations and civil society. Non-party States like the United States, China, Russia and Iran had an active participation in the Conference.[257] In particular, the United States, China and Russia had an inherent interest in the crime of aggression as part of the United Nations Security Council.[258] Like Rome, civil society and academia played a significant role to influence States choices and in the stocktaking sessions.[259] Besides the work on amendments, States Parties adopted a resolution on complementarity, enforcement of sentences and victims.[260] The Conference also issued two high-level declarations, including on the need to increase cooperation with the Court,[261] and received 112 pledges on promises to improve the work of the Court.[262]

Only in the second week at Kampala States Parties focused solely on the three amendment proposals.[263] In the final two days, on 10 and 11 of June, the Conference adopted by consensus the amendment on the crime of aggression and Belgium's proposal on prohibited weapons in Article 8(2)(e).[264] While the decision to retain, modify or delete Article 124 was the only compulsory item at the Conference, States Parties could not reach agreement over the course of

255 Report of the Eighth (Resumed) Session of the Assembly of States Parties to the Rome Statute of the International Criminal Court, New York, 22–25 March, ICC-ASP/8/20/Add.1 (2010) 53.

256 ICC-ASP/8/Res.9 Review Conference (2010) 1–2.

257 Clark, 'Article 123 Review of the Statute' 2016 2310.

258 McDougall, 25.

259 de Hoon, Marieke, 'Negotiating the Crime of Aggression: Between Legal Autonomy and State Power' in Bergsmo, Morten and others (eds), Power in International Criminal Justice (Torkel Opsahl Academic EPublisher 2020) 445.

260 RC/Res.1 Complementarity; RC/Res.2 The Impact of the Rome Statute System on Victims and Affected Communities; RC/Res.3 Strengthening the Enforcement of Sentences (2010).

261 RC/Decl.1 Kampala Declaration (2010); RC/Decl.2 Declaration on Cooperation.

262 Review Conference of the Rome Statute of the International Criminal Court, Kampala, 31 May – 11 June 2010, Official Records, RC/11 7.

263 Schabas, William A, 'Documents of the Review Conference of the International Criminal Court; Introductory Note' (2010) 49 (5) International Legal Materials 1325.

264 Review Conference of the Rome Statute of the International Criminal Court, Kampala, 31 May – 11 June 2010, Official Records, RC/11 6.

action.[265] The main point of tension was over the utility of the transient clause to expand the membership of the Court. Iran and China suggested the waiver of jurisdiction over war crimes in Article 124 could persuade their accession to the Statute while 'an overwhelming majority of those taking the floor spoke in favour of its deletion'.[266] Blocked by a minority, the Conference agreed to a further review point during the 14th session of the Assembly of States Parties while keeping Article 124 intact.[267] Neither China nor Iran joined the Rome Statute in 2014 or after.

A day before the end of the Review Conference, Belgium's proposal on Article 8(2)(e) was adopted.[268] States Parties agreed to expand the jurisdiction of the Court in the context of non-international armed conflict to the crime of employing 'poison or poisoned weapons, employing asphyxiating, poisonous or other gases, and all analogous liquids, materials and devices, and employing bullets which expand or flatten easily in the human body'.[269] The Rome Conference tried unsuccessfully to craft a list of prohibited weapons 'which are of a nature to cause superfluous injury or unnecessary suffering or which are inherently indiscriminate in violation of the international law of armed conflict'[270] in the context of international armed conflict under Article 8(2)(b)(xx). The amendment at Kampala intended to complete the work in Rome but by applying the prohibition of Article 8(2)(b) on international armed conflict to Article 8(2)(e) on non-international armed conflict.[271] In other words, as Clark explained, 'the 'weapons' amendment' took the language currently in Article 8(2)(b) of the Statute concerning forbidden weapons in international armed conflict, and applied the same prohibitions in paragraph 2(e) to non-international armed conflict'.[272] Together with 19 co-sponsors Belgium's proposal was adopted by consensus under Article 121(5).[273]

265 Zimmermann, (2016) 2316.

266 Clark, 'Amendments to the Rome Statute of the International Criminal Court Considered at the First Review Conference on the Court, Kampala, 31 May-11 June 2010' 692.

267 RC/Res.4 Article 124 (2010) 1.

268 Review Conference of the Rome Statute of the International Criminal Court, Kampala, 31 May – 11 June 2010, Official Records, RC/11 6.

269 RC/Res.5 Amendments to Article 8 of the Rome Statute.

270 Article 8(b)(xx), Rome Statute of the International Criminal Court (2002) 2187 UNTS 90.

271 Schabas, 'Documents of the Review Conference of the International Criminal Court; Introductory Note' 1326.

272 Clark, 'Article 123 Review of the Statute' (2016) 2309.

273 Clark, 'Amendments to the Rome Statute of the International Criminal Court Considered at the First Review Conference on the Court, Kampala, 31 May-11 June 2010' 708.

At the last possible moment on 11 June 2010, after stopping the clock, the Conference adopted the crime of aggression package including its definition, the conditions for jurisdiction by the Court and the entry into force of the amendment.[274] The detailed history, politics and legal compromises reached by the Conference are in itself rich and have been expertly covered by the literature.[275] It is worth recalling the Rome Conference included the crime in the Statute but delayed its finalization pending a definition and conditions by which the Court could exercise its powers. In 2002, the Assembly of States Parties instructed a Special Working Group on the matter to find consensus on these questions in time for the Review Conference.[276] Led by Liechtenstein, the Working Group succeeded in presenting to the Kampala Conference a definition and options on the jurisdictional regime.[277] Welcoming the final report of the Special Working Group, the controversies in Kampala concentrated in the conditions for jurisdiction by the Court and the entry into force of the amendment. The definition, on the other hand, did not probe too controversial.[278]

The centre of dispute was the role of the Security Council given its prerogative under the United Nations Charter to determine cases of aggressive acts by States.[279] A Security Council-controlled architecture to activate the Court's involvement contravened the major gains of the Rome Conference in relation to the proprio motu powers of the Prosecutor and State referrals.[280] Secondly, the dispute over the entry into force of the amendment concerned non-party States, including members of the Security Council, wary about the Court's ability exert its jurisdiction over the crime of aggression in the event, for example, a national of a State Party ratifying the amendment committed the crime in a non-party State territory. The settlement of the competing views about the crime of aggression put a herculean emphasis on the need to arrive at a

274 Review Conference of the Rome Statute of the International Criminal Court, Kampala, 31 May – 11 June 2010, Official Records, RC/11 6.

275 Bassiouni, M Cherif, Ferencz, B Benjamin, 'The Crime against Peace and Aggression: From its Origins to the ICC' in Bassiouni, M Cherif (ed), International Criminal Law: Sources, Subjects and Contents, vol 1 (Brill Nijhoff 2008) 205; McDougall, 25.

276 ICC-ASP/1/Res.1 Continuity of Work in Respect of the Crime of Aggression.

277 Kreß, Claus and Barriga, Stefan, The Crime of Aggression: A Commentary (Cambridge University Press 2016).

278 Wenaweser, 'Reaching the Kampala Compromise on Aggression: The Chair's Perspective' 883–884.

279 Van Schaack, Beth, 'Negotiating at the Interface of Power and Law: the Crime of Aggression' (2010) 49 Columbia Journal of Transnational Law 591.

280 McDougall, 263.

consensus solution even if it meant difficult concessions.[281] Given the weight of the issue at hand, States Parties agreed early on to avoid 'divisive'[282] confrontation of views via the voting procedure in Article 121(3). As Van Schaack, representing the United States explained, agreeing on the crime of aggression by consensus was the 'only valid decision-making rule for issues of constitutional import such as the adding of a complex and controversial crime to the Court's subject matter jurisdiction'.[283]

In this context, to solve the impasse on triggers for jurisdiction and the entry into force of the amendment, the Conference adopted by consensus Articles 15bis regulating State referrals and the Prosecutors' proprio motu power, and Article 15ter in relation to Security Council referrals.[284] After a series of proposals by Argentina, Brazil, Switzerland, Slovenia, Canada, the United States, Germany[285] and France[286] both Articles outlined a complex set of conditions. Article 15bis authorized the Prosecutor to act under proprio motu powers or after a State Party referral pending a series of conditions. The first condition required the ratification of minimum 30 States Parties before the Court had jurisdiction under Article 15bis. Secondly, after satisfying the 30 ratifications and only after 1 January 2017, the majority of the Assembly had to subsequently decide to activate the jurisdiction of the crime. Upon the fulfilment of these two conditions, the Prosecutor had to inform the Security Council and wait minimum six months for a determination from that body if an act of aggression effectively occurred. In the event the Security Council made such determination, the Prosecutor could move forward with the investigation. In the negative scenario, and after six months, only a decision by the full Pre-Trial Division could authorize the investigation. As per Article 16, however, the Security Council could decide to defer such investigation for a renewable term of one year.[287]

Clauses 15bis(4) and (5) set out the jurisdiction covering States Parties and non-party States effectively creating an exception to Articles 12(3) and

---

281 Blokker and Kreß, 891.

282 Schermers, Henry G. and Blokker, Niels, International Institutional Law: Unity Within Diversity (5 edn, Martinus Nijhoff Publishers 2011) 780.

283 Van Schaack, 517.

284 Clark, 'Amendments to the Rome Statute of the International Criminal Court Considered at the First Review Conference on the Court, Kampala, 31 May-11 June 2010' 701.

285 Wenaweser, 'Reaching the Kampala Compromise on Aggression: The Chair's Perspective' 885.

286 Belliard, Edwige 'France' in Kreß, Claus and Barriga, Stefan (eds), The Crime of Aggression: A Commentary (2016) 1147–1148.

287 RC/Res.6 The Crime of Aggression.

121(5).[288] While both Articles granted the Court with jurisdiction over a crime committed by a national of a State Party that has ratified the amendment in the territory of a non-ratifying State Party, clause 15bis(4) blocked this avenue for any State Party after it lodged a declaration to that effect with the Registrar.[289] Clause 15bis(5), on the other hand, applied a similar logic but with respect to non-party States.[290] Article 15ter completed the picture regulating Security Council referrals. After satisfying the 30 ratifications and posterior decision by the Assembly in 2017, the Prosecutor could move ahead as per Article 13(b).[291] In practical terms, except a referral by the Security Council, the crime of aggression applied exclusively between the 45 States Parties that have ratified the Kampala amendment at the time of writing in 2024.

For Assembly President and Review Conference Chair Christian Wenaweser, the Kampala compromise on the crime of aggression was a 'big step to advance international criminal law'.[292] While the amendment certainly dispelled doubts about the Court's authority over the crime post-Nuremberg, as Ferencz wrote: 'the illusion of unanimity cloaked the reality of stalemate on key issues'.[293] Writing in 2024, the Kampala compromise reads as a grave mistake in light of ongoing aggression in Ukraine and elsewhere. Nonetheless, from an institutional point of view, the Assembly did succeed in complying with Article 123. As Ambach argued, the first Review Conference had a 'precedent-setting value'.[294] Indeed, it delivered the first two amendments of the Statute and Elements of Crimes, also spurring a rapid process of ratifications aided by a coalition of States and civil society.[295] In June 2017 Palestine ratified the Kampala amendment, marking the 30 required ratifications. As such, the

288 Schabas, The International Criminal Court: A Commentary on the Rome Statute 1504.

289 Barriga, Stefan and Blokker, Niels, 'Entry into Force and Conditions for the Exercise of Jurisdiction: Cross-Cutting Issues' in Kreß, Claus and Barriga, Stefan (eds), The Crime of Aggression: A Commentary (Cambridge University Press 2016).

290 Review Conference of the Rome Statute of the International Criminal Court, Kampala, 31 May – 11 June 2010, Official Records, RC/11 6.

291 RC/Res.6 The Crime of Aggression.

292 Wenaweser, 'Reaching the Kampala Compromise on Aggression: The Chair's Perspective' 887.

293 Ferencz, Benjamin B 'Epilogue. The Long Journey to Kampala: A Personal Memoir' in Kreß, Claus and Barriga, Stefan (eds), The Crime of Aggression: A Commentary (2016) 1511.

294 Ambach, 'Article 112 Assembly of States Parties' (2022) 2809.

295 Ferencz, Donald M, 'Aggression Is No Longer a Crime in Limbo' (2018) 88 FICHL Policy Brief Series 1.

Assembly gathered during the 16th session in December in New York to activate of the crime of aggression.[296]

The path towards activation was as fraught as the Kampala Conference. This time, the tension resided in the ultimate confirmation of a narrow interpretation of Article 15bis(4) and (5). In particular, the United Kingdom, France, Canada, Norway, Colombia and Japan pushed the Bureau to create a specific facilitation mandate to discuss the issue in 2016 in advance of the activation decision.[297] For this group of States, nothing but a restrictive understanding of the Kampala amendment sufficed to join a consensus resolution on the matter.[298] On the other hand, the majority of States Parties sustained a broad interpretation allowing the Court to exercise its jurisdiction under Article 12(3) barred only by the opt-out clause in Article 15bis (4). In other words as McDougall explains, the dispute was whether in the event a victim State had ratified the amendment 'the alleged aggressor State needed to have opted-out prior to a use of force in order to avoid the ICC's jurisdiction, or whether it was sufficient to have not ratified or accepted the amendments'.[299] Faced with a majority supporting the broad view, France and the United Kingdom tabled a draft resolution in October 2017 based on the narrow interpretation signalling their readiness to call for a vote on the matter.[300] In addition, Japan routinely reminded the Assembly of its contributions to the budget.[301]

The 16th session was tense.[302] Absent of consensus, the activation required a two-third majority of the full membership, as per Article 15bis(4).[303] Once again like Rome and Kampala, the matter in New York extended until the very end of the session as States Parties conducted heated negotiations with France and the United Kingdom over their inflexible approach to the interpretative options available.[304] In the end, the narrow interpretation, as McDougall describes, was the 'unpalatable price paid for activation'.[305] By consensus,

296 Barriga and Blokker, 2016 635.

297 McDougall, 33.

298 Ibid 34.

299 Ibid 36.

300 Ibid 37.

301 Ibid 39.

302 Ibid 38.

303 RC/Res.6 The Crime of Aggression.

304 Zimmermann, Andreas, 'A Victory for International Rule of Law? Or: All's Well that Ends Well? The 2017 ASP Decision to Amend the Kampala Amendment on the Crime of Aggression' (2018) 16 (1) Journal of International Criminal Justice 20.

305 McDougall, 39–40.

Resolution 5 from 2017 activated the jurisdiction of the crime of aggression from 17 July 2018, hypocritically coinciding with international justice day.[306]

The second paragraph of the resolution confirmed the narrow interpretation whereas 'in the case of a State referral or proprio motu investigation the Court shall not exercise its jurisdiction regarding a crime of aggression when committed by a national or on the territory of a State Party that has not ratified or accepted these amendments.[307] Paragraph 3 of Resolution 5 made a reference to Articles 40(1) and 119(1) signalling the power of the Court, and judges in particular, to settle any legal dispute emanating from the Statute in the event the aggression provisions and the narrow interpretation were ever challenged in Court. For Donald Ferencz, paragraph 3 reminded States that 'even if the ASP may be subject to bullying, the judges should not be'.[308] At the time of writing in 2024, the crime of aggression has been ratified by 45 States Parties[309] while only Kenya and Guatemala have opted-out as per Article 15bis(4).[310]

The 'distinctly bittersweet'[311] moment has been lauded as 'historic'[312] in the face of the journey to criminalize aggression. However, the sense of double standards[313] and unjust application of rules among States Parties[314] became patently evident as Russia invaded Ukraine in 2022.[315] Luckily, the Kampala resolution on the crime of aggression included a provision deciding to 'review the amendments on the crime of aggression seven years after the beginning of the Court's exercise of jurisdiction'.[316] Effectively, States Parties will have an

306 ICC-ASP/16/Res.5 Activation of the Jurisdiction of the Court Over the Crime of Aggression.

307 Ibid 1.

308 Ferencz, 3–4.

309 Assembly of States Parties to the Rome Statute, Rome Statute and Other Agreements, available at: <https://asp.icc-cpi.int/assembly>.

310 International Criminal Court, Referrals and Declarations, available at: <https://www.icc-cpi.int/resource-library> accessed 5 January 2024.

311 McDougall, 40.

312 Kreß, Claus, 'On the Activation of ICC Jurisdiction over the Crime of Aggression' in Šturma, Pavel (ed), The Rome Statute of the ICC at Its Twentieth Anniversary (Brill Nijhoff 2018) 60.

313 de Hoon, 2020 481.

314 Koskenniemi, Martti, "A Trap for the Innocent ..." in Kreß, Claus and Barriga, Stefan (eds), The Crime of Aggression: A Commentary (Cambridge University Press 2016) 1376–1377.

315 Dutton, Yvonne, 'Political Will to Amend the International Criminal Court's Aggression Regime After Russia's Invasion of Ukraine' (2023) 38 (1) Maryland Journal of International Law 41.

316 RC/Res.6 The Crime of Aggression 1.

opportunity in 2025 to trigger Article 121(1) to revise the current form of the crime of aggression.[317] A proposal to re-harmonize the jurisdictional regime of the Court by deleting clauses 15bis(4) and (5)[318] has emerged from civil society. Nothing precludes a State Party to table such proposal under Article 121(1). It would need, however, a substantial majority of the Assembly to entrain the change and ultimately approve it as well as considerable time until it enters into force.[319]

Beyond the Kampala Conference, the Assembly of States Parties amended the Statute in 2015, 2017 and 2019. For each of these instances, the Working Group on Amendments played a significant role to foster consensus building among States Parties before transmitting a proposal to the Assembly.[320] Established as a subsidiary body of the Assembly,[321] the Working Group did not preclude States Parties to act under Article 121(1); however, it managed to secure overall agreements to avoid the adoption of amendments via the voting procedure in Article 121(3). In fact, the 2015 amendment deleting Article 124,[322] the 2017 amendment adding a number of prohibited weapons to Article 8 for both international and non-international armed conflict,[323] and the 2019 amendment on starvation as a war crime[324] were adopted by consensus. Of these, the 2019 amendment on using starvation of civilians as a method of warfare in non-international armed conflict is relevant illustrative example to understand the Assembly's practice beyond a Review Conference.

Recalling a resolution from the Security Council on the matter, Switzerland suggested its proposal was 'in line with current international law, in particular international humanitarian law'.[325] The majority of States in the

---

317 Trahan, Jennifer, 'Amending the Kampala Amendments: A Proposal to Harmonize the ICC's Jurisdiction' (Opinio Juris, 2023) <https://opiniojuris.org/2023/10/02/amending-the-kampala-amendments-a-proposal-to-harmonize-the-iccs-jurisdiction/> accessed 3 November 2023

318 Global Institute for the Prevention of Aggression, 2023 5.

319 Trahan, Jennifer, 'The Need for an International Tribunal on the Crime of Aggression Regarding the Situation in Ukraine' (2023) 46 (5) Fordham International Law Journal 650.

320 ICC-ASP/8/Res.6 Review Conference 2.

321 ICC-ASP/11/Res.8 Strengthening the International Criminal Court and the Assembly of States Parties 55.

322 ICC-ASP/14/Res.2 Resolution on Article 124 (2015) 1.

323 ICC-ASP/16/Res.4 Amendments to Article 8 of the Rome Statute of the International Criminal Court.

324 ICC-ASP/18/Res.5 Amendments to Article 8 of the Rome Statute of the International Criminal Court.

325 Report of the Working Group on Amendments, ICC-ASP/18/32 (2019) 3.

Working Group on Amendments agreed with the Swiss proposal noting the drafters had not included the provision in the Rome Statute 'due to an oversight'.[326] However some States had reservations arguing 'successive amendments'[327] impaired the universality of the Statute while others argued the provision was already covered by virtue of customary law.[328] In addition, States questioned whether the timing for amendments was right as 'discussions about the reform of the Court were ongoing'.[329] Documenting these comments, the Working Group agreed to recommend to the Assembly the adoption of the Swiss proposal,[330] which was sponsored by 21 States Parties.[331] After adopting the amendment during the 9th plenary meeting on 6 December 2019, only Venezuela registered objections citing its 'very broad definition'.[332] Resolution 5 from 2019 made a direct reference to the narrow understanding of Article 121(5) in regard to the entry into force and jurisdiction of the Court over the amendment.[333] As of the time of writing in 2024, 13 States Parties had ratified it.[334]

The crime of aggression and starvation amendments demonstrate the premium attached to decision-making by consensus in the Assembly even when a small minority of States disagree with a change. The overly political concerns of disunity between States Parties have created challenges for the Court amendments related to the crimes listed in the Statute exist within a narrow understanding of their reach. The apparent situation of acts of aggression in Ukraine, where the Court retains jurisdiction, is a telling example. However, it is not the only case as the amendment for the crime of starvation is equally confined to ratifying States Parties. In this regard, the alarming low number of ratifications to Statute amendments questions the value of lengthy and complex debates at the Working Group on Amendments and the Assembly when

326 Ibid.

327 Ibid.

328 Ibid.

329 Ibid.

330 Ibid 5.

331 Report of the Eighteenth Session of the Assembly of States Parties to the Rome Statute of the International Criminal Court, The Hague, 2–7 December, Volume I, ICC-ASP/18/20 (2019) 99.

332 Ibid 96.

333 ICC-ASP/18/Res.5 Amendments to Article 8 of the Rome Statute of the International Criminal Court.

334 Assembly of States Parties to the Rome Statute, Rome Statute and Other Agreements, available at: <https://asp.icc-cpi.int/assembly>.

the uptake by members reaches, in the best case scenario, 35% of States Parties. In fact, neither the Bureau nor a dedicated mandate within the Assembly is tasked with promoting the universality of ratifications. In this context and bearing in mind the change process spurred by the 2020 Independent Expert Review report, the Assembly might be in a position to review its practice for agreeing and promoting amendments to the Rome Statute. Not doing so precludes the progressive evolution of international criminal law.

3.2 *The Independent Expert Review Report and Process*

Any international organization as complex as the International Criminal Court is bound to face challenges as it develops over time. This has been the case, for example, for the Ad Hoc Tribunals,[335] and the Special Court for Sierra Leone,[336] which in comparison to the Rome Statute system, are of a lesser degree of political, organizational, financial and legal complexity.[337] However, when the United Kingdom delegate to the seventeenth session of the Assembly lamented in 2017 that 'after 20 years, and 1.5 billion Euros spent we have only three core crime convictions',[338] the expectation for revision and improvement became paramount at the Court. The literature analysing the deficiencies of the Rome Statute system points at a diverse set of reasons for the perceived and real unmet expectations that prompted the Assembly to commission an independent expert review of the Court in 2019.[339] For Richard Goldstone, the chair of the group of independent experts, the interplay between States Parties and judicial officials to negotiate critical elements such as amendments to the legal regime, the budgetary investment, enforcement of non-cooperation, election of the principals of the Court and the

335 Report of the Expert Group to Conduct a Review of the Effective Operation and Functioning of the International Tribunal for the Former Yugoslavia and the International Criminal Tribunal for Rwanda, UN Doc. A/54/634 (1998) 9.

336 Retreat on Strengthening the Proceedings at the International Criminal Court, Glion, Switzerland, 3–5 September 2014, Chair's Summary, available at: <https://asp.icc-cpi.int/sites/asp/files/asp_docs/ASP19/ICCRetreatSept2014.pdf> (2014) 6.

337 Gallant, Kenneth S, 'The International Criminal Court in the System of States and International Organizations' (2003) 16 Leiden Journal of International Law 553.

338 Statement by Andrew Murdoch, Legal Director to the International Criminal Court Assembly of States Parties, at its 17th session in The Hague, available at: <https://www.gov.uk/government/speeches/uk-statement-to-icc-assembly-of-states-parties-17th-session>.

339 ICC-ASP/18/Res.7 Review of the International Criminal Court and the Rome Statute System.

approval of a host of key auxiliary documents were central challenges to the Court,[340] as also covered in this book.

Besides these institutional complexities, Evenson,[341] Wilmshurst,[342] Trahan,[343] Vasiliev,[344] Clements[345] and Smith[346] have pointed out at failures of management, prosecutorial discretion, trial strategies, outreach, participation of victims, judicial reasoning by judges and lack of collegiality affecting the performance of the Court. As the Court reached its 20th anniversary, scholars have pondered about the reasons of unmet expectations and how to reform the Rome Statute system.[347] A telling example of the collective frustration with the Court was in relation to the situation in Afghanistan in April 2019 when the Pre-Trial Chamber II rejected by majority the request of the Prosecutor to proceed with an investigation.[348] The reasons from the bench had nothing to do with the tests imposed by the Statute but were related to dire prospects of securing any convictions due to a predicted lack of cooperation from Afghanistan. As Trahan argued, the decision 'essentially rewarded non-cooperation by States' and set a 'hugely problematic precedent for the future of the ICC'.[349] Other judicial decisions, for example in the case of Jean-Pierre

340 Goldstone, Richard J, 'The International Criminal Court: Origins, Challenges and Desirable Reforms to Strengthen It' in Falk, Richard and Lopez-Claros, Augusto (eds), Global Governance and International Cooperation (Routledge 2024) 378.

341 Evenson, Elizabeth, 'Too Few Trials, Too Many Tribulations: The ICC's Terrible Year and Where to Go from Here' (2020) 52 Case Western Reserve Journal of International Law 442.

342 Wilmshurst, Elizabeth 'Strengthen the International Criminal Court' (Royal Institute of International Affairs, 2019) <https://www.chathamhouse.org/expert/comment/strengthen-international-criminal-court> accessed 12 June 2019.

343 Trahan, 'The Assembly of States Parties' 2020 259.

344 Vasiliev, 'The Crises and Critiques of International Criminal Justice' 2020 632.

345 Clements, 'ReVisiting the ICC Registry's ReVision Project' 259.

346 Smith, Stephen Eliot, 'Is the International Criminal Court Dying? An Examination of Symptoms' (2022) 23 Oregon Review of International Law 76.

347 Werle, Gerhard and Zimmermann, Andreas, The International Criminal Court in Turbulent Times (T.M.C. Asser Press 2019); deGuzman, Margaret and Oosterveld, Valerie (eds), The Elgar Companion to the International Criminal Court (Edward Elgar Publishing 2020); Steinberg, Richard H (ed), The International Criminal Court: Contemporary Challenges and Reform Proposals (Brill | Nijhoff 2020); Heinze, Alexander and Dittrich, Viviane E. (eds), The Past, Present and Future of the International Criminal Court (Torkel Opsahl Academic EPublisher 2021); Stahn, Carsten and Braga da Silva, Rafael, The International Criminal Court in Its Third Decade: Reflecting on Law and Practices (Brill | Nijhoff 2023).

348 ICC Judges Reject Opening of an Investigation Regarding Afghanistan Situation, Press Release, ICC-CPI-20190412-PR1448 (2019).

349 Trahan, 'The Assembly of States Parties' 2020 259.

Bemba,[350] Laurent Gbagbo,[351] Blé Goudé[352] and the situation in Kenya[353] have caused similar concerns by observers of the Court. Criticism of the Court was combined with a general deterioration of international politics and unprecedented sanctions against Court officials by the United States and Russia.[354] In this dire context, a few days after the Afghanistan decision by the Court, an online opinion piece penned by former Assembly presidents Prince Zeid Raíad Zeid Al-Hussein, Bruno Stagno Ugarte, Christian Wenaweser and Tiina Intelmann created a tipping point towards the Independent Expert Review process.

The former presidents wrote they were 'disappointed by the quality of some of its judicial proceedings, frustrated by some of the results, and exasperated by the management deficiencies that prevent the Court from living up to its full potential'.[355] To 'provide Court officials and all stakeholders with a common point of reference going forward, at a crucial moment for the Court', the former presidents recommended an 'independent assessment of the Court's functioning'.[356] The proposal was quickly endorsed by States Parties and civil society as way to conduct an integral assessment of the Rome Statute system.[357] As Vasiliev argued, the rhetoric of crisis helped to capture and focus the attention of 'decision-makers, commentators, and the general public'[358] towards a path for review and reform not without, however, warnings that such exercise should not be used as 'a trojan horse with which to impede judicial and prosecutorial independence'.[359]

350 Evenson, 442.

351 Wilmshurst, Elizabeth 'Strengthen the International Criminal Court' (Royal Institute of International Affairs, 2019) <https://www.chathamhouse.org/expert/comment/strengthen-international-criminal-court> accessed 12 June 2019.

352 Vasiliev, 'The Crises and Critiques of International Criminal Justice' 2020 632.

353 Mburu, Daniel M, 'The Lost Kenyan Duel: The Role of Politics in the Collapse of the International Criminal Court Cases Against Ruto and Kenyatta' (2018) 18 (6) International Criminal Law Review 1015.

354 ASP President O-Gon Kwon Rejects Measures Taken Against ICC, ICC-ASP-20200611-PR 1527;The Presidency of the Assembly of States Parties Stands Firmly by the International Criminal Court, its Elected Officials, and its Personnel, ICC-ASP-20230520-PR1721.

355 Prince Zeid Raíad Zeid Al-Hussein, Stagno Ugarte, Bruno, Wenaweser, Christian and Intelman, Tiina, 'The International Criminal Court Needs Fixing' (Atlantic Council, 2019) <https://www.atlanticcouncil.org/blogs/new-atlanticist/the-international-criminal-court-needs-fixing> accessed 24 April 2019.

356 Ibid.

357 Bekou, Olympia, 'The Independent Expert Review of the ICC: What Next for Cooperation?' (2022) 21 (1) Washington University Global Studies Law Review 17.

358 Vasiliev, 'The Crises and Critiques of International Criminal Justice' (2020) 635.

359 Evenson, 448.

In this context, a few short weeks after the publication of the opinion piece by the former presidents of the Assembly, the Bureau organized a retreat to 'focus on reforms and the challenges faced by the Court'.[360] At a preparatory meeting President Kwon transmitted to Bureau members a letter by the Court President Chile Eboe-Osuji on behalf of the Prosecutor and the Registrar 'calling for an independent comprehensive expert review of the Court's performance'.[361] There have been previous attempts at reviewing key aspects of the Rome Statute since 2012 with the establishment and reports of the Study Group on Governance[362] as well as State Party-led retreats focused on lessons learned. For example, a 2013 meeting on evaluating the working methods of the Assembly,[363] and a well-attended conference in 2014 on how to enhance the effectiveness at the Court[364] based on the findings of a commissioned report of independent experts.[365] However, none of these reflection moments had the same impact as the opinion piece by the former Assembly leadership.

The 2019 Bureau retreat in June focused on 'governance, management and leadership; investigations, prosecutions and the judicial process; and the external environment'.[366] The retreat arrived at the conclusion regulatory and political changes were needed as well as 'potential internal and external (expert) reviews'.[367] Moving rapidly, between August and the 18th session in December 2019, the Bureau consulted and finalized a matrix of issues,[368] a terms of reference document,[369] a draft resolution for the independent expert review,[370] and secured political and financial backing from States Parties and civil soci-

360 Bureau of the Assembly of States Parties, 4th Meeting, 7 May (2019) 5.

361 Bureau of the Assembly of States Parties, 5th Meeting, 7 June (2019) 3.

362 Study Group on Governance: Lessons Learnt: First Report of the Court to the Assembly of States Parties, ICC-ASP/11/31/Add.1 (2012) 1.

363 Report of the Bureau: Evaluation and Rationalization of the Working Methods of the Subsidiary Bodies of the Bureau, ICC-ASP/12/59 (2013) 3–4.

364 Retreat on Strengthening the Proceedings at the International Criminal Court, Glion, Switzerland, 3–5 September 2014, Chair's Summary, available at: <https://asp.icc-cpi.int/sites/asp/files/asp_docs/ASP19/ICCRetreatSept2014.pdf> 1.

365 Mettraux, Guénaël and others, Expert Initiative on Promoting Effectiveness at the International Criminal Court (2014) 2.

366 Bureau of the Assembly of States Parties, Summary Bureau Retreat – Meeting the Challenges of Today for a Stronger Court Tomorrow, available at: <https://asp.icc-cpi.int/iccdocs/asp_docs/Bureau/Bureau%20retreat%20summary.10Jul19.1000.pdf#search=Bureau%20Retreat> (2019) 1.

367 Ibid 12.

368 Bureau of the Assembly of States Parties, 8th Meeting, 17 September 2019 2–4.

369 Bureau of the Assembly of States Parties, 10th Meeting, 12 November 2019 2.

370 Ibid 3.

TABLE 9.5 Bureau matrix of possible changes (2019)[a]

Area	Topics	Topics assigned to IER
Total	41	23
Governance, management and leadership	19	12
Investigations, prosecutions and the judicial process	13	10
The external environment	9	1

a Bureau of the Assembly of States Parties, Draft Working Paper, Meeting the Challenges of Today for a Stronger Court Tomorrow, Matrix Over Possible Areas of Strengthening the Court and Rome Statute System, available at: <https://asp.icc-cpi.int/sites/asp/files/asp_docs/ASP18/ICC-review-Matrix-v2–27Nov19–1740.pdf> (2019).

ety.[371] Of these actions, the November 2019 finalized matrix of issues was particularly helpful for the subsequent external review.[372] Aware that some issues were part of ongoing reform discussions at the Court and within the bodies of the Assembly, the matrix showed which topics could be assigned to the independent experts. The matrix document proposed to assign 23 out of 41 topics to the review process mostly around governance, management and leadership; investigations, prosecutions and the judicial process.

By the eighteenth session in December 2019, after considering the matrix document,[373] the Assembly passed Resolution 7 by consensus establishing the Independent Expert Review 'with a view to making concrete, achievable and actionable recommendations aimed at enhancing the performance, efficiency and effectiveness of the Court and the Rome Statute system as a whole'.[374] To guide the work of the experts, the Assembly referred three clusters for review: governance; the judiciary and the judicial process; and preliminary examina-

371 Coalition for the International Criminal Court, Civil Society Observations on the "Matrix over Possible Areas of Strengthening the Court and the Rome Statute System", available at: <https://www.coalitionfortheicc.org/sites/default/files/cicc_documents/190826%20-%20CICC%20-%20Civil%20Society%20Submissions%20on%20the%20Matrix.pdf> (2019) 2.

372 Bureau of the Assembly of States Parties, 11th Meeting, 28 November 2019 (2019) 3.

373 Report of the 18th Session of the Assembly of States Parties to the Rome Statute of the International Criminal Court, The Hague, 2–7 December, Volume I, ICC-ASP/18/20 87.

374 ICC-ASP/18/Res.7 Review of the International Criminal Court and the Rome Statute System 2.

tions, investigations and prosecutions. For each cluster, the Assembly appointed three State Party nationals, in total nine experts, subsequently chaired by former Prosecutor Richard Goldstone.[375] The independent panel was given until 30 September 2020 to submit their report, in time for the 19th Assembly session.

Starting their mandate in late January 2020, the Bureau appealed to the expert panel to 'be as creative and inventive as possible and to not be paralysed by any taboo'.[376] After working for 8 months, receiving 130 written submissions, speaking to 246 current and former officials, leading 278 interviews including with Court principals, the Staff Union Council, 9 States Parties, 12 Assembly mandate holders, 54 civil society organizations and 6 academics,[377] the experts delivered their report to the Bureau by the 30 September 2020 deadline. The prowess of the panel was remarkable bearing in mind the Covid-19 pandemic context. Across the three clusters, the report contained 384 recommendations 'both short and long-term, with varying degrees of complexity, and urgency of implementation'.[378] The experts also suggested States Parties established a 'standing coordination or working group' to monitor and report on progress against the 384 recommendations.[379] A summary view of the recommendations shows the top three topics with most emphasis were on governance; investigations; and efficiency of the judicial process and fair trial rights.

Welcoming the report, the 19th session of the Assembly took the suggestion from the panel and established a Review Mechanism 'dedicated to planning, coordinating, keeping track and regularly reporting to the Assembly Presidency and the Bureau on the assessment of the recommendations'.[380] The Mechanism was not established formally as a subsidiary body under Article 112(4) but effectively functioned as such. It was to be led by two Bureau appointed State Party representatives and three additional ad country focal points to maintain regional balance, for a one-year period.[381] The Assembly was clear the Review Mechanism had to finely coordinate its work with existing Court and Assembly bodies already engaged in reviewing areas listed in

375 Ibid 10.

376 Bureau of the Assembly of States Parties, 1st Meeting, 24 January 2020 (2020) 2.

377 Report of the Independent Expert Review of the International Criminal Court and the Rome Statute System, ICC-ASP/19/16 234.

378 Ibid 9.

379 Ibid 10.

380 ICC-ASP/19/Res.7 Review of the International Criminal Court and the Rome Statute System 3.

381 Ibid.

TABLE 9.6 Independent Expert Review terms of reference (2019)[a]

Clusters	Topics
Governance	1. Management and governance culture
	2. Administrative role of the Registrar
	3. Unified governance and leadership
	4. Staff Engagement
	5. Adequate qualitative and quantitative human resources
	6. Flexibility and scalability in staffing levels
	7. Establishment of ombudsman/internal grievance procedures
	8. Strengthening performance appraisal framework
	9. ASP oversight and audit bodies
	10. Mandate and functioning of the Trust Fund for Victims
	11. The budget process of the Court
	12. Fair trial, defence and Legal Aid
	13. Strengthening public awareness and image of the Court
Judiciary and the judicial process	1. Election of the President and the Vice-Presidents of the Court
	2. Efficiency of the judicial process
	3. Development of process and procedures to promote coherent and accessible jurisprudence and decision-making
	4. Working methods of the judiciary
	5. Victims (participation)
	6. Reparations
Preliminary examinations, Investigations and Prosecutions	1. Number and function of Deputy Prosecutors
	2. Preliminary examinations
	3. Prosecutorial strategies
	4. Investigations and case-preparations
	5. Structure of the OTP
	6. Completion strategies

a Ibid 8–9.

the expert's report. The main objective was to 'avoid duplication and benefit from synergies'[382] but also to recognize ongoing efforts at reform previous to the independent expert report. The Assembly allocated two time-bound objectives to the Review Mechanism. First, it was tasked with submitting to the Bureau by April 2021 a document categorizing the recommendations assigned to the Assembly, the Court or both.[383] Subsequently, by June 2021, the Mechanism had to propose a 'comprehensive action plan for the assessment of the recommendations'.[384] In addition, and based on the action plan prepared by the Review Mechanism, the Assembly required mandate holders to submit a progress report on the implementation of assigned recommendations by 1 November 2021.[385]

To assist the Review Mechanism, the Assembly invited the Court to appoint focal points in each organ in order to 'engage and interface with the Review Mechanism in planning, coordinating, monitoring and reporting on the assessment of the recommendations'.[386] Unlike any other body under the auspices of the Assembly, the Review Mechanism had a wide mandate to guarantee the results from the expert review produced some level of impact. A rigid interpretation of the powers in Article 112 opens up the question whether the Bureau should have taken the role described in Resolution 7. If the Assembly's executive body was to provide management oversight to the Court, it surely could also perform the tasks assigned to the Review Mechanism.

Like the independent experts, the Bureau worked at speed to appoint in January 2021 Ambassador Paul van den IJssel (the Netherlands) and Ambassador Michael Imran Kanu (Sierra Leone) as leaders of the Review Mechanism.[387] In February, Bangladesh, Chile and Poland were endorsed as ad country focal points.[388] During the inaugural Bureau meeting for Assembly President Silvia de Gurmendi in February 2021, the fully constituted Review Mechanism began its work.[389] As per Resolution 7 from 2020, the categorization of recommendations by entity and subsequent implementation plan were due in April and June 2021. In both cases, the Review Mechanism consulted widely with States Parties, civil society, the Court focal points

382 Ibid 2.
383 Ibid 3.
384 Ibid.
385 Ibid.
386 Ibid.
387 Bureau of the Assembly of States Parties, 19th Meeting, 28 January 2021 (2021) 2.
388 Bureau of the Assembly of States Parties, 20th Meeting, 5 February 2021 1.
389 Bureau of the Assembly of States Parties, 1st Meeting, 18 February 2021 3.

TABLE 9.7 Independent Expert Review Report (2020)[a]

Topic	IER recommendations
Total	**384**
I. Governance	86
II. Human Resources	19
III. Ethics and Prevention of Conflicts of Interest	9
IV. Internal Grievance Procedures	17
V. Budget Process	12
VI. Performance Indicators and Strategic Planning	5
VII. External Relations	22
VIII. Election of the Presidency	3
IX. Working Methods	15
X. Efficiency of the Judicial Process and Fair Trial Rights	27
XI. Development of Processes and Procedures to Promote Coherent And accessible Jurisprudence and Decision-Making	10
XII. OTP Situations and Cases: Prosecutorial Strategies of Selection, Prioritization, Hibernation and Closure	25
XIII. Preliminary Examinations	17
XIV. Investigations	37
XV. OTP Internal Quality Control Mechanisms	15
XVI. Defence and Legal Aid	16
XVII. Victim Participation	6
XVIII. Victims: Reparations and Assistance	19
XIX. Oversight Bodies	10
XX. Improvement of the System of Nomination of Judges	10
XXI. Development of the Rules of Procedure and Evidence	4

a Ibid.

and relevant Assembly mandate holders before submitting each report to the Bureau.[390]

390 Proposal for Categorization of the Independent Experts Review Recommendations and Remaining Review Issues, Introductory Note, available at: <https://asp.icc-cpi.int/Review-Court/Review-Mechanism> (2021) 1; Proposal for a Comprehensive Action Plan

The categorization report was submitted by the April deadline and approved by silent procedure in the Bureau in May.[391] While warning the categorization exercise was not a 'scientific endeavour',[392] the Review Mechanism clarified nothing prevented interested entities to engage in consultations to collaborate across their areas of responsibility.[393] In this context, the Review Mechanism assigned 72% of recommendations to the Court, 8% to the Assembly and 20% to both bodies. The Assembly retained the exclusive responsibility to implement the experts' recommendation in relation to the improvement of the system of nomination of judges. On the other hand, the Court was solely responsible to act on recommendations about the budget process, internal quality control mechanisms in the Office of the Prosecutor and victims' participation. These individual responsibilities assigned to the Court and the Assembly aligned with the statutory powers required for changes. For example, it is proper for States Parties to reform the process to nominate judges as per Article 36 while it is for the Prosecutor to refine internal quality controls in his or her office. The link between assigned responsibility and ability to act under statutory powers was important to protect the independence of the Court from undue intervention from States Parties during the review process.

The second deliverable to the Bureau by June 2021 was a comprehensive action plan to implement the assigned recommendations to the Assembly, the Court and both bodies. The plan included 'the allocation of the recommendations, the prioritization of recommendations … and timelines for their consideration'.[394] In practical terms, it offered a visual map to stagger waves of implementation by the Court, Assembly mandate holders and, in the case there was no apparent mandate holder, by the Mechanism itself.[395] To agree on which recommendations to prioritize, the Review Mechanism took the already existing suggestion by the independent experts in an annex to their

for the Assessment of the Recommendations of the Group of Independent Experts, Including Requirements for Possible Further Action, Introductory Note, available at: < https://asp.icc-cpi.int/Review-Court/Review-Mechanism> (2021) 1.

391 Bureau of the Assembly of States Parties, 3rd Meeting, 12 May (2021) 2.

392 Proposal for Categorization of the Independent Experts Review Recommendations and Remaining Review Issues, Introductory Note, available at: <https://asp.icc-cpi.int/Review-Court/Review-Mechanism> 2.

393 Ibid.

394 Proposal for a Comprehensive Action Plan for the Assessment of the Recommendations of the Group of Independent Experts, Including Requirements for Possible Further Action, Introductory Note, available at: <https://asp.icc-cpi.int/Review-Court/Review-Mechanism> 1.

395 Bureau of the Assembly of States Parties, 5th Meeting, 7 July 2021.

report.[396] In doing so, the Mechanism elevated recommendations 'identified by a great number of stakeholders'[397] or whether their implementation impacted other areas in the action plan. Using this methodology, 162 out of 384 recommendations were prioritized in the action plan. By entity, 64% of assigned recommendations to the Assembly retained their priority for implementation compared to 38% for the Court. These results were in line with the prioritization methodology which elevated proposals from the expert review report with the effect of disproportionally impacting other parts of the plan once implemented.[398] For example, the proposals on 'unified governance' had an outsized impact on other areas like the role of the Registrar and internal governance in the Office of the Prosecutor.[399]

With the action plan in place, the progress report from Assembly mandate holders and the Court submitted to the Bureau in November 2021 showed early signs of impact. Notably, Prosecutor Khan negatively assessed recommendation 48 from the report whereas the experts suggested moving to a structure of one Deputy Prosecutor in order to gain efficiencies in management and internal governance of the Office.[400] As an example of the independence of the Prosecutor under the Statute, the Review Mechanism had no legitimate authority to disagree or propose an alternative implementation suggestion. By the same token, the Registry reported progress on the Court's working culture, zero tolerance of bullying, harassment and sexual harassment[401] and the appointment of a focal point for gender equality.[402] Assembly President de Gurmendi reported progress on recommendation 169 calling for a strategy to respond to political attacks on the Court.[403]

By the time States Parties gathered in December 2021 for the 20th Assembly session in The Hague, the Review Mechanism had productively delivered on its mandate submitting the categorization proposal, the action plan and a

---

396 Report of the Independent Expert Review of the International Criminal Court and the Rome Statute System, ICC-ASP/19/16 223.

397 Proposal for a Comprehensive Action Plan for the Assessment of the Recommendations of the Group of Independent Experts, Including Requirements for Possible Further Action, Introductory Note, available at: <https://asp.icc-cpi.int/Review-Court/Review-Mechanism> 2.

398 Bureau of the Assembly of States Parties, 6th Meeting, 8 September 2021 (2021) 1–2.

399 Report of the Independent Expert Review of the International Criminal Court and the Rome Statute System, ICC-ASP/19/16 223.

400 Report of the Review Mechanism as the Platform for Discussion of IER Recommendations, available at: <https://asp.icc-cpi.int/Review-Court/Review-Mechanism> (2021) 1.

401 Ibid 2.

402 Ibid.

403 Ibid 3.

TABLE 9.8 Review Mechanism categorization proposal (2021)[a]

Topic / totals by entity	Assembly	Court	Both
	31 (8%)	278 (72%)	75 (20%)
I. Governance	2	70	14
II. Human Resources	–	12	7
III. Ethics and Prevention of Conflicts of Interest	–	3	6
IV. Internal Grievance Procedures	3	7	7
V. Budget Process	–	15	–
VI. Performance Indicators and Strategic Planning	7	2	3
VII. External Relations	–	1	4
VIII. Election of the Presidency	1	18	3
IX. Working Methods	1	2	
X. Efficiency of the Judicial Process and Fair Trial Rights	–	21	6
XI. Development of Processes and Procedures to Promote Coherent and accessible Jurisprudence and Decision-Making	–	9	1
XII. OTP Situations and Cases: Prosecutorial Strategies of Selection, Prioritization, Hibernation and Closure	–	24	1
XIII. Preliminary Examinations	–	13	4
XIV. Investigations	1	30	6
XV. OTP Internal Quality Control Mechanisms	–	15	
XVI. Defence and Legal Aid	1	13	2
XVII. Victim Participation	–	6	–
XVIII. Victims: Reparations and Assistance	2	15	2
XIX. Oversight Bodies	2	2	6
XX. Improvement of the System of Nomination of Judges	10	–	–
XXI. Development of the Rules of Procedure and Evidence	1	–	3

a Proposal for Categorization of the Independent Experts Review Recommendations and Remaining Review Issues, available at: <https://asp.icc-cpi.int/Review-Court/Review-Mechanism> (2021).

TABLE 9.9 Review Mechanism plan of action (2021)[a]

Entity	Recommendations assigned	Recommendations prioritized
Total	**384**	**162 (42%)**
Assembly of States Parties	31	20 (64%)
Court	278	106 (38%)
Both	75	36 (48%)

a Proposal for a Comprehensive Action Plan for the Assessment of the Recommendations of the Group of Independent Experts, Including Requirements for Possible Further Action, available at:< https://asp.icc-cpi.int/Review-Court/Review-Mechanism> (2021).

progress report. In addition, the Assembly received a summary report outlining the work of the Review Mechanism, including an updated matrix document with implementation status of the prioritized recommendations. The matrix document was 'based on the reports of the different facilitations and the Mechanism'[404] and served as a vehicle to assess progress over time. In this regard, by the 20th session, 41 recommendations were reported as fully implemented. Considered a 'living document'[405] the matrix was a useful instrument to monitor the degree of implementation by thematic area. In this sense, the Assembly of States Parties welcomed the progress achieved by the Review Mechanism and decided to extend its mandate, albeit without specifying a temporal end.[406] At the 23rd session in 2024, the Assembly discontinued the Review Mechanism.

As the Review Mechanism continued to offer a coordinating role for the reform process, Goldstone has affirmed the 'future existence of the ICC as an institution is assured'.[407] Perhaps too soon, Goldstone's assessment will require time for the structures, policies and practice of the Court and the Assembly to effectively evolve. Even if the review process becomes a 'turning

404 Report of the Review Mechanism Submitted Pursuant to ICC-ASP/19/Res.7, paragraph 9, ICC-ASP/20/36* (2021) 3.

405 Ibid.

406 ICC-ASP/20/Res.3 Review of the International Criminal Court and the Rome Statute System 2.

407 Goldstone, 2024 386.

point'[408] for the Court, it is worth recalling the Rome Statute does not operate in isolation from significant political forces like the United Nations Security Council and non-party States' influence like those of the United States, Russia and China.[409] In fact, a sign of progress against the backlash experienced before the review process will be the ability of the Court to become a trusted actor in the fight against impunity by conducting thorough investigations, securing convictions and influencing cooperation from States. For this, the role of the Assembly becomes crucial to support the Court, by for example, giving an adequate financial backing and electing judges fit for

TABLE 9.10 Review Mechanism matrix of progress (2021)[a]

Topic	Recommendation implemented
Total	**41**
IX. Working Methods	12
XV. OTP Internal Quality Control Mechanisms	7
XVIII. Victims: Reparations and Assistance	4
I. Governance	3
XIV. Investigations	3
II. Human Resources	2
VII. External Relations	2
VIII. Election of the Presidency	2
X. Efficiency of the Judicial Process and Fair Trial Rights	2
XI. Development of Processes and Procedures to Promote Coherent AND accessible Jurisprudence and Decision-Making	2
XII. OTP Situations and Cases: Prosecutorial Strategies of Selection, Prioritization, Hibernation and Closure	2

a Report of the Review Mechanism Submitted Pursuant to ICC-ASP/19/Res.7, paragraph 9, ICC-ASP/20/36* 6.

408 Powderly, 'International Criminal Justice in an Age of Perpetual Crisis' 9.

409 Peake, Jessica, 'Interdependence at the International Criminal Court: Reconceptualizing our Understanding of the Court and its Failures' (2022) 26 UCLA Journal of International Law and Foreign Affairs 82.

service.[410] More so, to guarantee the review process started in 2019 renders the intended results to assure the International Criminal Court is fit for purpose.

4 Conclusion

This chapter examined the practice of the Assembly's oversight of auxiliary judicial instruments and, given their close legal relationship, the amendments and review of the Rome Statute between 2002 and 2021. This analysis revealed the challenge States Parties faced to respect the independence of the Court while legislating on key legal texts like the Rules of Procedure and Evidence. In particular, this section showed how the tumultuous relationship of the Assembly with the African Union unfolded as the legal situations of Sudan and Kenya progressed through the Court. In this context, the chapter explained the inability of the Study Group on Governance and the Working Group on Amendments to prevent the politicization of changes to Rules 134bis, 134ter and 134quarter in the Rules of Procedure and Evidence during the 12th session of the Assembly in 2013. The second part of chapter 8 outlined the political process the Assembly underwent to agree the five amendments to the Statute between 2010 and 2021. In this context, the chapter described how the crime of aggression and starvation amendments put a disproportionate premium to decision-making by consensus in the Assembly even when only a small but powerful minority of States rejected a majority proposal. In this regard, the chapter questioned the value of lengthy and complex debates at the Working Group on Amendments and the Assembly when the uptake of ratifications to Statute amendments by members reached, in the best case scenario, 35% of States Parties in 2021.

Finally, the last part of the chapter covering the practice of the Assembly between 2002 and 2021 concluded with a discussion of the Independent Expert Review report and emerging outcomes of the State-led Review Mechanism established by the Assembly to implement the experts' recommendations. In doing so, the chapter showed that in 2020 the Review Mechanism assigned 72% of recommendations to the Court, 8% to the Assembly and 20% to both bodies. By the end of the first year of the Review Mechanism in 2021, 41

410 Hale, Christopher, 'The Way Forward for the International Criminal Court and Its Stakeholders: Focus Inward' in Heinze, Alexander and Dittrich, Viviane E. (eds), The Past, Present and Future of the International Criminal Court (Torkel Opsahl Academic EPublisher 2021) 168.

recommendations were reported as fully implemented. However, the chapter argued that even as the Review Mechanism continued to offer a coordinating role for the reform process, there were no guarantees the structures, policies and practice of the Court and the Assembly would evolve to tackle the deficits covered in this book. Even if the review process became a turning point for the Court, the political nature of its operating environment will challenge the degree and speed of reforms. Thus, the chapter concluded that a sign of progress against the backlash experienced before the review process would be the ability of the Court to become a trusted actor in the fight against impunity by conducting thorough investigations, securing convictions and influencing cooperation from States.

CHAPTER 10

Conclusion: Towards Unity in Governance?

The book has revealed that the Assembly of States Parties, as the injugovin of the International Criminal Court, has affected in tangible ways the system designed in the Rome Statute. Acknowledging the historical precedent and negotiations leading up to the Rome Conference, the impact of States Parties' practice over 20 years was noticeable in two main areas: institutional governance and judicial capabilities. In particular, on the institutional governance side, this book found the Assembly underwent a period of maturity where States Parties seized their governance role to enhance structures and processes to oversee the Court. In doing so, States Parties created a governance system led by the Bureau and highly dependent on subsidiary bodies and State Party–led topic coordinators. In particular, the role of the Committee on Budget and Finance, the Working Group on Amendments, the Study Group on Governance and the Independent Oversight Mechanism served as a vehicle to perfect the oversight capacity of the Assembly. However, the quality of institutional governance faced setbacks as the Assembly's adherence to its own rules and procedures was not always consistent with key statutory responsibilities. For example, the Assembly faced challenges to provide the Court with adequate elected officials and oversee their performance when confronted with allegations of misconduct or mismanagement.

This book also found the Assembly of States Parties had a disproportionate impact on some elementary judicial functions led by the Court. Notably, the intricate issue of adequate financial investment severely limited the capability of the organs of the Court. More so when the chronic issue of budget arrears by States Parties was left unresolved by the Assembly and no specific strategy to secure funding from the United Nations General Assembly for referrals by the Security Council was sought. In a similar way, States Parties' amendments to the Rules of Procedure and Evidence raised serious concerns about the line between oversight and encroachment on judicial independence. Politization of what should have been a rather technical exercise meant a deviation from consensus driven processes within the Study Group on Governance. Finally, the alarming inability of the Assembly of States Parties to enforce Court-mandated orders for cooperation, in particular for arrests, was another notable issue disproportionally affecting the judicial mandate. Compounded by tensions among States Parties, including those part of the African Union, the Assembly was unable to fully comply with its role under Article 112(2)(f). Only

© EZEQUIEL JIMÉNEZ MARTINEZ, 2026 | DOI:10.1163/9789004749979_011

mild diplomatic solutions were achieved, but without a demonstrable effect on States Parties refusing to surrender suspects.

Through an analysis of relevant governance provisions in 1937, 1943 and 1981, the second chapter found a precedent to Article 112 in the Rome Statute as part of the long history of multilateral judicial institutions. The legacy of the 1937 Convention for the Creation of an International Criminal Court, the 1943 draft Convention for the Creation of an International Criminal Court and the 1981 draft Convention on the Establishment of an International Penal Tribunal delineated a specific role for States Parties to enable the mandate of an international criminal court to fight impunity within each historical context. These three key moments also developed State Party responsibilities for governance and management, financial oversight, election of judges and prosecutors and enforcement of cooperation, which can now be found in the Rome Statute. By studying these three key moments in the history of governance choices for multilateral judicial institutions, the chapter revealed the politics, opportunities and constraints faced by all relevant actors to creatively forge the State-led governance structures that later influenced the ink and letter of Article 112 in Rome.

The third chapter explored the Rome Conference preparatory process between 1990 and 1998 finding the governance and oversight role by States Parties to the Court was only addressed during the last session of the 1998 Preparatory Committee. In doing so, the chapter concluded the strategy to create silos to tackle complex judicial and non-judicial issues in the negotiations achieved the final objective to adopt a draft text but at the expense of a comprehensive and detailed provision setting out the role and responsibility of the Assembly of States Parties. Given neither the process at the International Law Commission, the Ad Hoc Committee or the Preparatory Committee had resolved these questions fully, a host of layered unresolved issues were left to the Diplomatic Conference, including the membership, funding, arrears and non-cooperation enforcement by the Assembly of States Parties.

Consequently, Chapter 4 found that providing the International Criminal Court with an effective governing body was isolated to specific moments during the Rome Conference, without considering the function of such body in the larger institution and effort to create a system of international justice. Nested within the 173-page Draft Statute, States participating in the Rome Conference did not invest the same level of time or political focus on provisions dealing with the governance and oversight functions of the Assembly. In fact, while the Rome Conference succeeded in finding policy and legal compromises among key issues such as the jurisdictional regime, the proprio motu power of the Prosecutor, the role of the Security Council and the definition of war crimes, the governance provisions in Article 112 were uncontroversial and resolved in a matter of days. The drafting managed to balance views about membership, decision-making, voting rights, resolving non-cooperation issues and financial oversight responsibilities. However, the political role of the Assembly was not discussed jointly with other parts of the Statute that would have benefitted from a stronger correlation. This is the case with Article 112(2)(f) and Part 9 on the cooperation regime. While Part 9 assigned a role to the Assembly, Article 112 did not capture the exact procedural steps States Parties could take to foster adequate cooperation with the Court. This issue would become a source of disagreement as the Assembly of States Parties developed over time. The second part of chapter 4 focused on the 10 sessions of the Preparatory Commission. The examination of this period showed States tried to rectify the lack of focus on the Assembly albeit only advancing procedural steps for its creation. Thus, their attention went to drafting the Rules of Procedure of the Assembly, the Financial Rules and Regulations, the first budget of the Court and resolutions creating subsidiary bodies. As the Rome Statute came into force on 1 July 2002, the Assembly's first meeting in September was consequential to centre the effort of States Parties in their governance and management statutory role towards the Court.

The fifth chapter examined the practice of the Assembly's governance and management oversight statutory responsibility between 2002 and 2021. The Assembly's membership, leadership, procedure, and decision-making evolved considerably over time. The chapter found that, between 2002 and 2021, the Assembly of States Parties considered 517 agenda items and adopted by consensus 154 resolutions, 7 decisions, 4 recommendations and 2 declarations, these exclusively at the Review Conference in 2010. Led by 7 Bureau compositions, the Assembly held 32 meetings in total: 20 regular sessions plus 11 resumed sessions and 1 Review Conference. In the 20 sessions studied, the pinnacle of membership occurred in 2016 during the fifteenth session with 124 members. Even as membership changed, however, States Parties faced challenges to adhere to the principle of regional rotation agreed in 2002, greatly affecting the quota of power entitled to the African Group of States. In addition, the chapter argued that structural changes to the Assembly corresponded with specific challenges facing States Parties in their governance and management responsibility towards the Court. The Independent Oversight Mechanism and the Study Group on Governance were notable examples how States Parties devolved to these bodies key responsibilities to oversee elected officials and examine the performance of the Court. In this context, the chapter found the Bureau struggled to manage the proliferation of mandates assigned to States Parties, the level of engagement from topic coordinators, quality of reports and unexpected vacancies as diplomats were reassigned to other duties by their respective States. In addition, Chapter 5 found the Assembly of States Parties benefitted from its relationship agreement with the United Nations and the host State. Although the Court led the operational details of these agreements, the Assembly's use of United Nations services and advice as well as financial support from the host State, facilitated respectively the organization of meetings and establishment of the permanent premises of the Court. The Assembly, however, did struggle to further negotiate with the United Nations the cost recovery of referrals by the Security Council to Court totalling €75 million in 2021.

The sixth chapter examined the statutory practice of the Assembly on election, disciplinary measures and removal of Court officials between 2002 and 2021. The chapter found States Parties elected 54 judges (34 in List A and 20 in List B), 3 Prosecutors, 5 Deputy Prosecutors, 4 Registrars and one Deputy Registrar over 20 sessions. The Assembly did not impose disciplinary measures or removed any elected official between 2002 and 2021. The weight of the statutory election role, however, meant the Assembly dedicated 16 sessions to this item. Bearing in mind that each cycle represented a substantial amount of time and consensus building for nominations, assessment and elections, it is notable that criticism persists about the Assembly's ability to elect the most competent and skilled officials for the Court. Specifically to the election of judges, the chapter found that even after establishing the Advisory Committee on Nomination of judges in 2010, the Assembly still favoured candidates without the full backing of the Committee. The election of the Prosecutor followed a similar pattern whereas the Assembly instituted a bespoke mechanism each time, albeit with grave difficulty to follow its own procedure. Most notable, the 2020 Committee on the Election of the Prosecutor faced severe criticism by States and civil society for their search, assessment and recommendation procedure to the Assembly. Thus, the chapter argued the inability of the Assembly of States Parties to manage a depoliticized and merit-based election for judges and the Prosecutor risked the legitimacy and operational capability of the Court. In this sense, the chapter also noted the Assembly's effort to set up a permanent vetting system for elected officials. Next, when covering the election of the Registrar, the chapter explored the indirect, yet important, role of the Assembly of States Parties. It argued a more directive approach was required to guide the judges' election bearing in mind the integral role the Registry played in servicing the Assembly and enabling its governance role. Finally, while no elected official was reprimanded or removed by the Assembly, States Parties were confronted with public exposes criticizing the conduct of elected officials. Notable examples involved two judges, the first Prosecutor and the third Registrar. Despite the establishment of the Independent Oversight Mechanism, the available public record did not indicate any corrective action by the Assembly of States Parties. In fact, the chapter revealed that while the annual reports by the Head of the Independent Oversight Mechanism between 2015 and 2021 contained 6 out of 137 matters in relation to misconduct by elected officials, no action was necessary by States Parties. Overall, the chapter concluded the dual role of States Parties to elect and oversee the performance of senior officials has suffered from weak institutional oversight tools prone to political manoeuvres.

The seventh chapter examined the practice of the Assembly's financial oversight statutory role. The chapter found that between 2002 and 2021, States Parties approved 20 budgets totalling €2,22 billion. Of this allocation, the portion assigned for expenses of the Assembly of States Parties was €67 million. Overall, the budget approved by the Assembly grew every year except between 2010 and 2011 even if sightly (€103,623,300 versus €103,607,900). However, as a negotiated process between the Court and States Parties, the gap between what Court organs requested and the Assembly finally approved stood at €79,9 million (3.6%) in 2021. The chapter argued that this gap corresponded to three interrelated arguments. First, States Parties' willingness to fund the budget was affected by Court underspends during the first 10 years coupled with challenging external political and macroeconomic conditions. Noticeably, after the 2008 financial crisis, the premise of efficiencies and savings became the primary narrative for budget discussions at the Assembly. Even as Court organs, specially the Office of the Prosecutor, explained the impact of flat budgets and an increasing workload, States Parties pursued austere finances with minimal growth in real terms. In this regard, the chapter showed the outsized power of the Committee on Budget and Finance in determining the budget even as the Registry prepared substantive analysis to support funding increases. The other two reasons pointed at the chronic inability of the Assembly to recoup budget arrears from States Parties and funding from the United Nations for the Sudan and Libya referrals. By November 2021, the total amount of pending States Parties' contributions to the regular budget, the Host State Loan for the permanent premises and other fund was to €49.9 million. For Security Council referrals it stood at €75 million. Thus, the chapter argued that even as the Assembly's tightened its financial oversight grip over time, risking judicial independence, it did not engage effectively with cost recovery strategies aimed at States Parties in arrears as well as further negotiating a settlement with the United Nations.

The eighth chapter examined the statutory practice of the Assembly on enforcement of cooperation with the Court between 2002 and 2021. The chapter found that, despite receiving 11 referrals of non-cooperation from the Court, the Assembly did not succeeded in changing recalcitrant behaviour from non-compliant States. This was particularly problematic in the Sudan situation where the Court issued two arrest warrants against Omar Al Bashir. Despite referring 10 instances of a failure to arrest Al Bashir in the territory of a State Party, the Assembly did not take remedial action to motivate a change of behaviour. For example, even as the Assembly passed 13 resolutions and made one declaration during the Review Conference in Kampala in 2010 on the overall importance of cooperation with the Court, the situation did not improve between 2010 and 2021. Instead, States Parties focused on developing a range of diplomatic measures to influence cooperation with the Court, including a detailed procedure to respond to Court findings and a flexible toolkit of optional measures to encourage compliance. These measures were not effective. The chapter argued that while the Assembly procedures and toolkit on non-cooperation certainly had a role, without tangible and concrete actions to penalize non-compliant State Party behaviour, their utility was severely limited. In this context, alternatives have emerged to address this issue, including the creation of a dedicated subsidiary body, the imposition of penalties and fines and baring candidates for judicial elections from non-compliant States. In conclusion, the chapter insisted the severe issues with cooperation compliance should become a top priority of the Assembly of States Parties in order to avoid the paralyzing effect fighting impunity experienced between 2010 and 2017.

The ninth chapter examined the practice of the Assembly's oversight of auxiliary judicial instruments and, given their close legal relationship, the amendments and review of the Rome Statute between 2002 and 2021. This analysis revealed the challenge States Parties faced to respect the independence of the Court while legislating on key legal texts like the Rules of Procedure and Evidence. In particular, this section showed how the tumultuous relationship of the Assembly with the African Union unfolded as the legal situations of Sudan and Kenya progressed through the Court. In this context, the chapter explained the inability of the Study Group on Governance and the Working Group on Amendments to prevent the politicization of changes to Rules 134bis, 134ter and 134quarter in the Rules of Procedure and Evidence during the twelfth session of the Assembly in 2013. The second part of chapter 8 outlined the political process the Assembly underwent to agree the five amendments to the Statute between 2010 and 2021. In this context, the chapter described how the crime of aggression and starvation amendments put a disproportionate premium to decision-making by consensus in the Assembly even when only a small but powerful minority of States rejected a majority proposal. In this regard, the chapter questioned the value of lengthy and complex debates at the Working Group on Amendments and the Assembly when the uptake of ratifications to Statute amendments by members reached, in the best case scenario, 35% of States Parties in 2021.

Finally, the last part of the chapter covering the practice of the Assembly between 2002 and 2021 concluded with a discussion of the Independent Expert Review report and emerging outcomes of the State-led Review Mechanism established by the Assembly to implement the experts' recommendations. In doing so, the chapter showed that in 2020 the Review Mechanism assigned 72% of recommendations to the Court, 8% to the Assembly and 20% to both bodies. By the end of the first year of the Review Mechanism in 2021, 41 recommendations were reported as fully implemented. However, the chapter argued that even as the Review Mechanism continued to offer a coordinating role for the reform process, there were no guarantees the structures, policies and practice of the Court and the Assembly would evolve to tackle the deficits covered in this book. Even if the review process became a turning point for the Court, the political nature of its operating environment will challenge the degree and speed of reforms. Thus, the chapter concluded that a sign of progress against the backlash experienced before the review process would be the ability of the Court to become a trusted actor in the fight against impunity by conducting thorough investigations, securing convictions and influencing cooperation from States.

In conclusion, the International Criminal Court can only be fully appraised when it takes into consideration the responsibilities, choices and governance of its States Parties. Tracing 20 sessions of the Assembly of States Parties delivered a complex but rich understanding of the governance dynamics of the Court. Taking the findings of this book together, it is possible to notice the unrealized potential of States Parties to actively partner with the Court in finding a common vision to achieve the ideas embedded in the Rome Statute. In this sense, the book also found early signs of course correction within the Review Mechanism, which require further research. As such, this ongoing process to review and agree on implementation plans has the potential to address the intermittent trust and coordination deficit that has characterized the relationship between the Assembly and the Court between 2002 and 2021. As the International Criminal Court continues to play a role in the overall architecture to fight impunity, States Parties have an opportunity to strengthen the Rome Statute system as it enters its third decade. At a time, international law is defied by powerful States, the Assembly of States Parties to the Rome Statute have the responsibility to govern the International Criminal Court bearing in mind the long history of its creation and innate desire to end impunity for the gravest crimes shocking the conscience of humankind.

Bibliography

Primary Sources

Treaties

Convention for the Pacific Settlement of International Disputes (signed at The Hague 18 October 1907) 36 Stat. 2199.

Convention for the Creation of an International Criminal Court (16 November 1937) LoN Doc. C.547.M384.1937.V.

Charter of the United Nations (adopted 26 June 1945, entered into force 24 October 1945) 1 UNTS XVI.

International Convention on the Suppression and Punishment of the Crime of Apartheid (adopted 30 November 1973, entered into force 18 July 1976) 1015 UNTS 243.

Study on Ways and Means of Insuring the Implementation of International Instruments such as the International Convention on the Suppression and Punishment of the Crime of Apartheid, including the establishment of the International Jurisdiction Envisaged by the Convention, UN Doc. E/CN.4/1426 (1981).

Rome Statute of the International Criminal Court (adopted 17 July 1998, entered into force 1 July 2002) 2187 UNTS 3.

Case Law

International Criminal Court

The Prosecutor v Omar Hassan Ahmad Al Bashir (Warrant of Arrest for Omar Hassan Ahmad Al Bashir) ICC-02/05–01/09–1 (4 March 2009).

The Prosecutor v Omar Hassan Ahmad Al Bashir (Decision Informing the United Nations Security Council and the Assembly of the States Parties to the Rome Statute About Omar Al-Bashir's Presence in the Territory of the Republic of Kenya) ICC-02/05–01/09 (27 August 2010).

The Prosecutor v Omar Hassan Ahmad Al Bashir (Decision Informing the United Nations Security Council and the Assembly of the States Parties to the Rome Statute About Omar Al-Bashir's Presence in the Territory of the Republic of Chad) ICC-02/05–01/09 (27 August 2010).

The Prosecutor v Omar Hassan Ahmad Al Bashir (Decision Informing the United Nations Security Council and the Assembly of the States Parties to the Rome Statute About Omar Al-Bashir's Recent Visit to Djibouti) ICC-02/05–01/09 (12 May 2011).

The Prosecutor v Omar Hassan Ahmad Al Bashir (Corrigendum to the Decision Pursuant to Article 87(7) of the Rome Statute on the Failure by the Republic of Malawi to Comply with the Cooperation Requests Issued by the Court with Respect to the Arrest and Surrender of Omar Hassan Ahmad Al Bashir) ICC-02/05–01/09 (13 December 2011).

The Prosecutor v Omar Hassan Ahmad Al Bashir (Decision Pursuant to article 87(7) of the Rome Statute on the Refusal of the Republic of Chad to Comply with the Cooperation Requests Issued by the Court with Respect to the Arrest and Surrender of Omar Hassan Ahmad Al Bashir) ICC-02/05–01/09 (13 December 2011).

The Prosecutor v Omar Hassan Ahmad Al Bashir (Decision on the non-compliance of the Republic of Chad with the Cooperation Requests Issued by the Court Regarding the Arrest and Surrender of Omar Hassan Ahmad Al-Bashir) ICC-02/05–01/09 (26 March 2013).

The Prosecutor v Omar Hassan Ahmad Al Bashir (Decision on the Cooperation of the Democratic Republic of the Congo Regarding Omar Al Bashir's Arrest and Surrender to the Court) ICC-02/05–01/09 (9 April 2014).

The Prosecutor v Omar Hassan Ahmad Al Bashir (Decision on the non-Compliance by the Republic of Djibouti with the Request to Arrest and Surrender Omar Al-Bashir to the Court and Referring the Matter to the United Nations Security Council and the Assembly of the State Parties to the Rome Statute) ICC-02/05–01/09 (11 July 2016).

The Prosecutor v Omar Hassan Ahmad Al Bashir (Decision on the non-Compliance by the Republic of Uganda with the Request to Arrest and Surrender Omar Al-Bashir to the Court and Referring the Matter to the United Nations Security Council and the Assembly of the State Parties to the Rome Statute) ICC-02/05–01/09 (11 July 2016).

The Prosecutor v Omar Hassan Ahmad Al Bashir (Decision Under Article 87(7) of the Rome Statute on the non-Compliance by Jordan with the Request by the Court for the Arrest and Surrender of Omar Al-Bashir) ICC-02/05–01/09 (11 December 2017).

The Prosecutor v Omar Hassan Ahmad Al Bashir (Judgment in the Jordan Referral re Al-Bashir Appeal) ICC-02/05–01/09 OA2 (6 May 2019).

The Prosecutor v Paul Gicheru (Decision Terminating the Proceedings against Paul Gicheru) ICC-01/09–01/20 (14 October 2022).

The Prosecutor v Uhuru Muigai Kenyatta (Second Decision on Prosecution's Application for a Finding of non-Compliance under Article 87(7) of the Statute) ICC-01/09–02/11 (19 September 2016).

The Prosecutor v Uhuru Muigai Kenyatta (Second Decision on Prosecution's Application for a Finding of non-Compliance Under Article 87(7) of the Statute) ICC-01/09–02/11 (19 September 2016).

The Prosecutor v Uhuru Muigai Kenyatta and Mohammed Hussein Ali (Annex I to Decision Replacing a Judge in Trial Chamber V(b)) ICC-01/09–02/11–890-AnxI (30 January 2014).

The Prosecutor v Bosco Ntaganda (Notification Concerning Judge Kuniko Ozaki) ICC-01/04–02/06 (1 May 2019).

The Prosecutor v Bosco Ntaganda (Annex I to the Notification of the Decision of the Plenary of Judges on the Defence Request for the Disqualification of Judge Kuniko Ozaki from the Case) ICC-01/04–02/06–2355-AnxI-Red (20 June 2019).

The Prosecutor v William Samoei Ruto and Joshua Arap Sang (Judgment on the appeals of Mr William Samoei Ruto and Mr Joshua Arap Sang against the decision of Trial Chamber V(A) of 19 August 2015 entitled "Decision on Prosecution Request for Admission of Prior Recorded Testimony) ICC-01/09–01/11 (12 February 2016).

Situation in the State of Palestine (Decision on the 'Prosecution Request Pursuant to Article 19(3) for a Ruling on the Court's Territorial Jurisdiction in Palestine) ICC-01/18–143 (5 February 2021).

International Labour Organization Administrative Tribunal

Palme v ICC (Judgment) No. 2757 (9 July 2008)

Secondary Sources

Books

Ambos, Kai, Treatise on International Criminal Law, vol 1 (Oxford University Press 2013).

Barriga, Stefan and Kreß, Claus, The Travaux Préparatoires of the Crime of Aggression (Cambridge University Press 2012).

Bassiouni, M Cherif, A Draft International Criminal Code and Draft Statute for an International Criminal Tribunal (Martinus Nijhoff Publishers 1987).

Bassiouni, M Cherif, International Terrorism: Multilateral Conventions (1937–2001) (Brill Nijhoff 2001).

Bassiouni, M Cherif and Schabas, William A, The Legislative History of the International Criminal Court, vol 1 (2 edn, Brill | Nijhoff 2016).

Benedetti, Fanny, Bonneau, Karine and Washburn, John, Negotiating the International Criminal Court: New York to Rome, 1994–1998 (Martinus Nijhoff Publishers 2014).

Bosco, David, Rough Justice: The International Criminal Court in a World of Power Politics (Oxford University Press 2013).

Çakmak, Cenap, A Brief History of International Criminal Law and International Criminal Court (Palgrave Macmillan 2017).

Crane, David M, Sadat, Leila N and Scharf, Michael P, The Founders: Four Pioneering Individuals Who Launched the First Modern-Era International Criminal Tribunals (Cambridge University Press 2018).

deGuzman, Margaret and Oosterveld, Valerie (eds), The Elgar Companion to the International Criminal Court (Edward Elgar Publishing 2020).

Glasius, Marlies, The International Criminal Court: A Global Civil Society Achievement (Routledge 2006).

Heinze, Alexander and Dittrich, Viviane E (eds), The Past, Present and Future of the International Criminal Court (Torkel Opsahl Academic EPublisher 2021).

Hillebrecht, Courtney, Saving the International Justice Regime (Cambridge University Press 2021).

Klamberg, Mark, Nilsson, Jonas and Angotti, Antonio (eds), Commentary on the Law of the International Criminal Court: The Statute, vol 2 (Torkel Opsahl Academic EPublisher 2023).

Kim, Young Sok, The Law of the International Criminal Court (2nd edn, William S Hein & Co., Inc. 2019).

Kofi Annan and Mousavizadeh, Nader, Interventions: A Life in War and Peace (Penguin 2013).

Kreß, Claus and Barriga, Stefan, The Crime of Aggression: A Commentary (Cambridge University Press 2016).

Lee, Roy S, The International Criminal Court: The Making of the Rome Statute: Issues, Negotiations and Results (Martinus Nijhoff Publishers 1999).

Lee, Roy S, The International Criminal Court: Elements of Crimes and Rules of Procedure and Evidence (Transnational Publishers 2001).

Llewellyn, Huw, An Institutional Perspective on the United Nations Criminal Tribunals: Governance, Independence and Impartiality (Brill | Nijhoff 2021).

Mackenzie, Ruth, Malleson, Kate, Martin, Penny and Sands QC, Philippe, Selecting International Judges: Principle, Process, and Politics (Oxford University Press 2010).

McDougall, Carrie, The Crime of Aggression Under the Rome Statute of the International Criminal Court (2 edn, Cambridge University Press 2021).

Moreno Ocampo, Luis, War and Justice in the 21st Century: A Case Study on the International Criminal Court and its Interaction with the War on Terror (Oxford University Press 2022).

Plesch, Dan, Human Rights After Hitler: The Lost History of Prosecuting Axis War Crimes (Georgetown University Press 2017).

Powderly, Joseph, Judges and the Making of International Criminal Law (Brill | Nijhoff 2020).

Ruffert, Matthias and Walter, Christian, Institutionalised International Law (Bloomsbury 2015).

Sadat, Leila Nadya, The International Criminal Court and the Transformation of International Law: Justice for the New Millennium (Transnational Publishers 2002).

Schabas, William A, The International Criminal Court: A Commentary on the Rome Statute (2nd edn, Oxford University Press 2017).

Scheffer, David, All the Missing Souls (Princeton University Press 2012).

Schermers, Henry G and Blokker, Niels, International Institutional Law: Unity Within Diversity (5 edn, Martinus Nijhoff Publishers 2011).

Schiff, Benjamin, Building the International Criminal Court (Cambridge University Press 2008).

Scott, James Brown, The Proceedings Of The Hague Peace Conferences (Oxford University Press 1920).

Stahn, Carsten and Braga da Silva, Rafael, The International Criminal Court in Its Third Decade: Reflecting on Law and Practices (Brill | Nijhoff 2023).

Steinberg, Richard H (ed), The International Criminal Court: Contemporary Challenges and Reform Proposals (Brill | Nijhoff 2020).

von Hebel, Herman, Lammers, Johan G and Schukking, Jolien, Reflections on the International Criminal Court: Essays in Honour of Adriaan Bos (TMC Asser Press 1999).

Werle, Gerhard and Zimmermann, Andreas, The International Criminal Court in Turbulent Times (T.M.C Asser Press 2019).

Journal Articles

Abtahi, Hirad and Charania, Shehzad, 'Expediting the ICC Criminal Process: Striking the Right Balance between the ICC and States Parties' (2018) 18 International Criminal Law Review 383–425.

Albers, Martin, 'Between the crisis of democracy and world parliament: the development of the Inter-Parliamentary Union in the 1920s' (2012) 7 Journal of Global History 189–209.

Ambach, Philipp, 'The "Lessons Learnt" Process at the International Criminal Court – a Suitable Vehicle for Procedural Improvements' (2016) 12 Zeitschrift für Internationale Strafrechtsdogmatik 854–867.

Ambach, Philipp and Rackwitz, Klaus U, 'A Model of International Judicial Administration? The Evolution of Managerial Practices at the International Criminal Court' (2013) 76 Law and Contemporary Problems 119–161.

Armstead, J Holmes, Jr., 'The International Criminal Court: History, Development and Status' (1997) 38 Santa Clara Law Review 745–836.

Arsanjani, Mahnoush, 'The Rome Statute of the International Criminal Court' (1999) 93 The American Journal of International Law 22–43.

Bassiouni, M Cherif, 'The History of the Draft Code of Crimes Against the Peace and Security of Mankind' (1993) 27 Israel Law Review 247–267.

Bassiouni, M Cherif, 'Enforcing Human Rights Through International Criminal Law and Through an International Criminal Tribunal' (1994) 26 Studies in Transnational Legal Policy 347–382.

Bassiouni, M Cherif, 'Observations Concerning the 1997–98 Preparatory Committee's Work' (1996) 25 Denver Journal of International Law & Policy 397.

Bassiouni, M Cherif, 'Negotiating the Treaty of Rome on the Establishment of an International Criminal Court' (1999) 32 Cornell International Law Journal 443–469.

Bassiouni, M Cherif, 'A Glimpse of the Association's History and Some of the Contributions of Its Members' (2015) 86 Revue internationale de droit pénal 817–825.

Bassiouni, M Cherif, 'Chronology of Efforts to Establish an International Criminal Court' (2015) 86 Revue internationale de droit pénal 1163–1194.

Bassiouni, M Cherif, 'Codification of International Criminal Law' (2016) 45 Denver Journal of International Law and Policy 333–364.

Bassiouni, M Cherif and Derby, Daniel H, 'Final Report on the Establishment of an International Criminal Court for the Implementation of the Apartheid Convention and Other Relevant International Instruments' (1981) 9 Hofstra Law Review 523–592.

Bauer, Steffen, 'Does Bureaucracy Really Matter? The Authority of Intergovernmental Treaty Secretariats in Global Environmental Politics' (2006) 6 Global Environmental Politics 23–49.

Bekou, Olympia, 'Dealing with Non-cooperation at the ICC: Towards a More Holistic Approach' (2019) 19 International Criminal Law Review 911–937.

Bekou, Olympia, 'The Independent Expert Review of the ICC: What Next for Cooperation?' (2022) 21 Washington University Global Studies Law Review 15–32.

Benedetti, Fanny and Washburn, John L, 'Drafting the International Criminal Court Treaty: Two Years to Rome and an Afterword on the Rome Diplomatic Conference' (1999) 5 Global Governance 1–37.

Berg, Bradley E, 'The 1994 ILC Draft Statute for an International Criminal Court: A Principled Appraisal of Jurisdictional Structure' (1996) 28 Case Western Reserve Journal of International Law 221–264.

Bergsmo, Morten, Bekou, Olympia and Jones, Annika, 'Complementarity After Kampala: Capacity Building and the ICC's Legal Tools' (2010) 2 Goettingen Journal of International Law 791–811.

Bergsmo, Morten, Buis, Emiliano J, Gordon, Gregory S, Inder, Brigid, Kaleck, Wolfgang, Ekeløve-Slydal, Gunnar M and Tianying, Song, 'ICC State-Party Governance in Times of Disunity' (2023) Policy Brief Series No. 146 Torkel Opsahl Academic EPublisher 1–4.

Bergsmo, Morten, Kaleck, Wolfgang, Muller, Sam and Wiley, William H, 'A Prosecutor Falls, Time for the Court to Rise' (2017) 86 FICHL Policy Brief Series 1–4.

Bevers, Hans, Blokker, Niels and Roording, Jaap, 'The Netherlands and the International Criminal Court: On Statute Obligations and Hospitality' (2003) 16 Leiden Journal of International Law 135–156.

Blokker, Niels and Kreß, Claus, 'A Consensus Agreement on the Crime of Aggression: Impressions from Kampala' (2010) 23 Leiden Journal of International Law 889–895.

Blokker, Niels and Muller, Sam, 'International Criminal Court' (2004) 16 Hague Yearbook of International Law/Annuaire de La Haye de Droit International 179–184.

Byron, Christine and Turns, David, 'The Preparatory Commission for the International Criminal Court' (2001) 50 International & Comparative Law Quarterly 420–435.

Caloyanni, Mégalos, 'The Proposals of M Laval to the League of Nations for the Establishment of an International Permanent Tribunal in Criminal Matters' (1935) 21 Transactions of the Grotius Society 77–107.

Carcano, Andrea, 'On the Governance of International Judicial Institutions: The Development of Performance Indicators for the International Criminal Court' (2019) 22 Max Planck Yearbook of United Nations Law Online 83–113.

Caron, David D, 'War And International Adjudication: Reflections on the 1899 Peace Conference' (2000) 94 American Journal of International Law 4–30.

Casey, Lee A, 'The Case Against the International Criminal Court' (2001) 25 Fordham International Law Journal 840–872.

Cassese, Antonio, 'On the Current Trends Towards Criminal Prosecution and Punishment of Breaches of International Humanitarian Law' (1998) 9 European Journal of International Law 2–17.

Cassese, Antonio, 'The Statute of the International Criminal Court: Some Preliminary Reflections' (1999) 10 European Journal of International Law 144–171.

Ciucă, Aurora, 'Romanian contributions to the codification of international law: Vespasian V Pella' (2018) 5 European Journal of Law and Public Administration 142–152.

Clark, Roger S, 'Amendments to the Rome Statute of the International Criminal Court Considered at the First Review Conference on the Court, Kampala, 31 May-11 June 2010' (2010) 2 Goettingen Journal of International Law 689–711.

Clements, Richard, 'From Bureaucracy to Management: The International Criminal Court's Internal Progress Narrative' (2019) 32 Leiden Journal of International Law 149–167.

Clements, Richard, 'ReVisiting the ICC Registry's ReVision Project' (2019) 17 Journal of International Criminal Justice 259–284.

Clements, Richard, '"Efficiency Is Paramount in This Regard": The Managerial Role of the ICC Presidency from Kirsch to Fernández' (2022) 21 The Law & Practice of International Courts and Tribunals 342–368.

Crawford, James, 'The ILC's Draft Statute for an International Criminal Tribunal' (1994) 88 American Journal of International Law 140–152.

Crawford, James, 'The ILC Adopts a Statute for an International Criminal Court' (1995) 89 American Journal of International Law 404–416.

Crawford, James, 'A Conversation with Emeritus Professor Judge James Richard Crawford Part 1: Early Life and Career' (2018) Eminent Scholars Archive, the Squire Law Library and the Faculty of Law.

de La Cuesta, José Luis and Ottenhof, Reynald, 'The Association Internationale de Droit Pénal and the Establishment of the International Criminal Court' (2015) 86 Revue internationale de droit pénal 1237–1250.

Deitelhoff, Nicole and Wallbott, Linda, 'Beyond Soft Balancing: Small States and Coalition-Building in the ICC and Climate Negotiations' (2012) 25 Cambridge Review of International Affairs 345–366.

du Plessis, Max, 'Reflections on a Storm: the International Criminal Court and its Work in Africa' (2012) 18 Australian Journal of Human Rights 161–186.

Dutton, Yvonne, 'Political Will to Amend the International Criminal Court's Aggression Regime After Russia's Invasion of Ukraine' (2023) 38 Maryland Journal of International Law 41–56.

Eikel, Markus, "Germany's Global Responsibility 'and the Creation of the International Criminal Court, 1993–1998' (2018) 16 Journal of International Criminal Justice 543–570.

Eldar, Ofer, 'Vote-trading in International Institutions' (2008) 19 European Journal of International Law 3–41.

Evenson, Elizabeth, 'Too Few Trials, Too Many Tribulations: The ICC's Terrible Year and Where to Go from Here' (2020) 52 Case Western Reserve Journal of International Law 433–449.

Ferencz, Benjamin B, 'The International Criminal Court: the First Year and Future Prospects' (2003) 97 American Society of International Law Proceedings 259–264.

Ferencz, Donald M 'Aggression Is No Longer a Crime in Limbo' (2018) 88 FICHL Policy Brief Series 1–4.

Fernández de Gurmendi, Silvia, 'Enhancing the Court's Efficiency: From the Drafting of the Procedural Provisions by States to their Revision by Judges' (2018) 16 Journal of International Criminal Justice 341–361.

Fernández de Gurmendi, 'Judges: Selection, Competence, Collegiality' (2018) 112 American Journal of International Law 163–167.

Fernández de Gurmendi, 'A Path to Global Justice: My Insider's View' (2022) 9 The International Journal of Ethical Leadership 3–12.

Fernández de Gurmendi, Silvia and Friman, Håkan, 'The Rules of Procedure and Evidence of the International Criminal Court' (2000) 3 Yearbook of International Humanitarian Law 289–336.

Fife, Rolf Einar, 'The Draft Budget for the First Financial Period of the Court' (2001) 25 Fordham International Law Journal 606–624.

Galand, Alexandre Skander, 'The Nature of the Rome Statute of the International Criminal Court (and its Amended Jurisdictional Scheme)' (2020) 17 Journal of International Criminal Justice 933–956.

Gallant, Kenneth S, 'The International Criminal Court in the System of States and International Organizations' (2003) 16 Leiden Journal of International Law 553–591.

Gissel, Line Engbo, 'A Different Kind of Court: Africa's Support for the International Criminal Court, 1993–2003' (2018) 29 European Journal of International Law 725–748.

Gissel, Line Engbo, 'Nomos and Narrative in International Criminal Justice: Creating the International Criminal Court' (2022) 20 Journal of International Criminal Justice 117–138.

Grossman, Nienke, 'Achieving Sex-Representative International Court Benches' (2016) 110 American Journal of International Law 82–95.

Guilfoyle, Douglas, 'Lacking Conviction: Is the International Criminal Court Broken? An Organisational Failure Analysis' (2020) 20 Melbourne Journal of International Law 1–52.

Hall, Christopher Keith, 'The First Two Sessions of the UN Preparatory Committee on the Establishment of an International Criminal Court' (1997) 91 American Journal of International Law 177–187.

Hall, Christopher Keith, 'The First Proposal for a Permanent International Criminal Court' (1998) 38 International Review of the Red Cross Archive 57–74.

Hall, Christopher Keith, 'The Fifth Session of the UN Preparatory Committee on the Establishment of an International Criminal Court' (1998) 92 American Journal of International Law 331–339.

Hall, Christopher Keith, 'The Third and Fourth Sessions of the UN Preparatory Committee on the Establishment of an International Criminal Court' (1998) 92 American Journal of International Law 124–133.

Hall, Christopher Keith, 'The Sixth Session of the UN Preparatory Committee on the Establishment of an International Criminal Court' (1998) 92 The American Journal of International Law 548–556.

Hall, Christopher Keith, 'The First Five Sessions of the UN Preparatory Commission for the International Criminal Court' (2000) 94 American Journal of International Law 773–789.

Heller, Kevin Jon, 'Options for Prosecuting Russian Aggression Against Ukraine: A Critical Analysis' (2022) Journal of Genocide Research 1–24.

Holthuis, Hans, 'Operational Aspects of Setting Up the International Criminal Court: Building on the Experience of the International Criminal Tribunal for the Former Yugoslavia' (2001) 25 Fordham International Law Journal 708–716.

Hudson, Manley O, 'The Proposed International Criminal Court' (1938) 32 American Journal of International Law 549–554.

Imseis, Ardi, 'State of Exception: Critical Reflections on the Amici Curiae Observations and Other Communications of States Parties to the Rome Statute in the Palestine Situation' (2020) Journal of International Criminal Justice 1–21.

Intelmann, Tiina, 'Keynote Address Lectures' (2014) 47 Studies in Transnational Legal Policy 7–12.

Jalloh, Charles Chernor, Akande, Dapo and Plessis, Max Du, 'Assessing the African Union Concerns about Article 16 of the Rome State of the International Criminal Court' (2011) 4 African Journal of Legal Studies 5–50.

Jarasch, Frank, 'Establishment, Organization and Financing of the International Criminal Court (Parts I, IV, XI–XIII)' (1998) 6 European Journal of Crime Criminal Law and Criminal Justice 325–344.

Kaul, Hans-Peter and Kreß, Claus, 'Jurisdiction and Cooperation in the Statute of the International Criminal Court: Principles and Compromises' (1999) 2 Yearbook of International Humanitarian Law 143–175.

Kirsch, Philippe and Holmes, John T, 'The Rome Conference on an International Criminal Court: The Negotiating Process' (1999) 93 The American Journal of International Law 2–12.

Kirsch, Philippe and Holmes, John T, 'The Birth of the International Criminal Court: The 1998 Rome Conference' (1999) 36 Canadian Yearbook of International Law/ Annuaire Canadien de Droit International 3–39.

Kirsch, Philippe and Oosterveld, Valerie, 'Negotiating an Institution For The Twenty-First Century: Multilateral Diplomacy and The International Criminal Court' (2001) 46 McGill Law Journal 1141–1160.

Kirsch, Philippe and Oosterveld, Valerie, 'The Preparatory Commission for the International Criminal Court' (2001) 25 Fordham International Law Journal 563–588.

Knottnerus, Abel, 'The International Criminal Court on Presence at Trial: The (in) validity of Rule 134quater' (2014) 5 International Crimes Database.

Kotecha, Birju, 'The ICC's Office of the Prosecutor and the Limits of Performance Indicators' (2017) 15 Journal of International Criminal Justice 543–565.

Kreß, Claus, 'The Procedural Texts of the International Criminal Court' (2007) 5 Journal of International Criminal Justice 537–543.

Kreß, Claus, 'Preliminary Observations on the ICC Appeals Chamber's Judgment of 6 May 2019 in the Jordan Referral re Al-Bashir Appeal' (2019) Torkel Opsahl Academic EPublisher.

Leigh, Monroe, 'Evaluating Present Options for an International Criminal Court' (1995) 149 Military Law Review 113–128.

Mahaseth, Harsh and Bansal, Ayushi, 'Asia and the ICC: The Development of International Criminal Law in a World Changing Order' (2021) 21 International and Comparative Law Review 162–186.

Mburu, Daniel M, 'The Lost Kenyan Duel: The Role of Politics in the Collapse of the International Criminal Court Cases Against Ruto and Kenyatta' (2018) 18 International Criminal Law Review 1015–1047.

McCormack, Timothy LH and Simpson, Gerry J, 'A New International Criminal Law Regime?' (1995) 42 Netherlands International Law Review 177–206.

Medina, Romina and Opinion, Ann Clarice, 'Interview with Judge O-Gon Kwon' (2021) 2 Asia-Pacific Journal of International Humanitarian Law 1–7.

Mills, Kurt, '"Bashir is Dividing Us": Africa and the International Criminal Court' (2012) 34 Human Rights Quarterly 404–447.

Mochochoko, Phakiso, 'The Agreement on Privileges and Immunities of the International Criminal Court' (2001) 25 Fordham International Law Journal 638–664.

Moynier, Gustave, 'Note sur la création d'une institution judiciaire internationale propre a prévenir et a réprimer les infractions a la convention de Genève' (1872) 3 Bulletin International des Societes de Secours aux Militaires Blesses 122–131.

Mudukuti, Angela, 'The Procedure for Appointing the International Criminal Court Prosecutor: High Moral Character and the Need for Comprehensive Vetting' (2021) 19 Journal of International Criminal Justice 747–757.

Muller, Sam, 'Setting up the International Criminal Court: Not One Moment but a Series of Moments' (2004) 1 International Organization Law Review 189–196.

Mumford, Marcus R, 'Building Upon a Foundation of Sand: A Commentary on the International Criminal Court Treaty Conference' (1999) 8 Journalof International Law and Practice 151–225.

Mundis, Daryl A, 'The Assembly of States Parties and the Institutional Framework of the International Criminal Court' (2003) 97 American Journal of International Law 132–147.

Newton, Michael A, 'The International Criminal Court Preparatory Commission: The Way It Is & The Way Ahead' (2001) Virginia Journal of International Law 204–216.

Nilsson, Cecilia, 'Contextualizing the agreement on the privileges and immunities of the International Criminal Court' (2004) 17 Leiden Journal of International Law 559–578.

Nimigan, Sarah, 'Electoral Success at the ICC: A State-Level Analysis' (2022) 3 European Journal of International Law 1–28.

O'Donohue, Jonathan, 'The 2005 Budget of the International Criminal Court: Contingency, Insufficient Funding in Key Areas and the Recurring Question of the Independence of the Prosecutor' (2005) 18 Leiden Journal of International Law 591–603.

O'Donohue, Jonathan, 'Financing the International Criminal Court' (2013) 13 International Criminal Law Review 269–296.

Ochoa, Juan Carlos S, 'Settlement of Disputes Concerning States Arising from the Application of the Statute of the International Criminal Court: Balancing Sovereignty and the Need for an Effective and Independent ICC' (2007) 7 International Criminal Law Review 1–43.

Peake, Jessica, 'Interdependence at the International Criminal Court: Reconceptualizing our Understanding of the Court and its Failures' (2022) 26 UCLA Journal of International Law and Foreign Affairs 79–130.

Pella, Vespasian 'Towards an International Criminal Court' (1950) 44 American Journal of International Law 37–68.

Plesch, Dan and Sattler, Shanti, 'Changing the Paradigm of International Criminal Law: Considering the Work of the United Nations War Crimes Commission of 1943–1948' (2013) 15 International Ccommunity Law Review 203–223.

Plesch, Dan and Sattler, Shanti, 'A New Paradigm of Customary International Criminal Law: The UN War Crimes Commission of 1943–1948 and its Associated Courts and Tribunals' (2014) 25 Criminal Law Forum 17–43.

Polli, Maura, 'What Can 92 Countries Agree On' (2003) 12 International Law Students Association Quarterly 6–9.

Powderly, Joseph, 'International Criminal Justice in an Age of Perpetual Crisis' (2019) 32 Leiden Journal of International Law 1–11.

Rauxloh, Regina E, 'Good Intentions and Bad Consequences: The General Assistance Mandate of the Trust Fund for Victims of the ICC' (2021) 34 Leiden Journal of International Law 203–222.

Romano, Cesare, 'The Price of International Justice' (2005) 4 The Law and Practice of International Courts and Tribunals 281–328.

Rosenne, Shabtai, 'Antecedents of the Rome Statute of the International Criminal Court Revisited' (2000) 75 International Law Studies 387–420.

Rosenne, Shabtai, 'Poor Drafting and Imperfect Organization: Flaws to Overcome in the Rome Statute' (2000) 41 Virginia Journal of International Law 164–185.

Sadat, Leila Nadya, 'Reforming the International Criminal Court:" Lean In" or" Leave"' (2020) 62 Washington University Journal of Law & Policy 51–76.

Sadat, Leila Nadya and Carden, S Richard, 'The New International Criminal Court: An Uneasy Revolution' (2000) 88 Georgetown Law Journal 381–474.

Sarkin, Jeremy Julian, 'Will the International Criminal Court Be Able to Secure the Arrest of Vladimir Putin When He Travels?: Understanding State Cooperation Through Other ICC Non-Arrest Cases Against Malawi, Chad, Nigeria, the Democratic Republic of Congo, South Africa, Djibouti, Uganda, and Jordan' (2023) 12 International Human Rights Law Review 26–68.

Saul, Ben, 'Attempts to Define 'Terrorism' in International Law' (2005) 52 Netherlands International Law Review 57–83.

Schabas, William A, 'International Criminal Court: The Secret of Its Success' (2001) 12 Criminal Law Forum 415–428.

Schabas, William A, 'Documents of the Review Conference of the International Criminal Court; Introductory Note' (2010) 49 International Legal Materials 1325–1340.

Schabas, William A, 'The International Criminal Court at Ten' (2011) 22 Criminal Law Forum 493–509.

Schabas, William A, 'International War Crimes Tribunals and the United States' (2011) 35 Diplomatic History 769–786.

Schabas, William A, 'The United Nations War Crimes Commission's Proposal for an International Criminal Court' (2014) 25 Criminal Law Forum 171–189.

Schabas, William A, 'La Cour Pénale Internationale à Vingt Ans. Un Bilan Géopolitique' (2023) Annuaire Français de Relations Internationales 911–925.

Scheffer, David, 'The United States and the International Criminal Court' (1999) 93 American Journal of International Law 12–22.

Schabas, William A, 'A Negotiator's Perspective on the International Criminal Court' (2001) 167 Military Law Review 1–19.

Schense, Jennifer, 'Necessary Steps for the Creation of the International Criminal Court' (2001) 25 Fordham International Law Journal 717–736.

Segesser, Daniel Marc and Gessler, Myriam, 'Raphael Lemkin and the international debate on the punishment of war crimes (1919–1948)' (2005) 7 Journal of Genocide Research 453–468.

Sharma, Kritika, 'The Curious Case of Rule 165 of the Rules of Procedure and Evidence: The Effect of Control Exercised by the Assembly of States Parties over the International Criminal Court' (2020) 20 International Criminal Law Review 285–317.

Sluiter, Göran, 'Appendix II:'An International Criminal Court is Hereby Established'' (1998) 16 Netherlands Quarterly of Human Rights 413–420.

Sluiter, Göran, 'Enforcing Cooperation: Did the Drafters Approach It the Wrong Way?' (2018) 16 Journal of International Criminal Justice 383–402.

Smeulers, Alette, Hola, Barbora and van den Berg, Tom, 'Sixty-Five Years of International Criminal Justice: The Facts and Figures' (2013) 13 International Criminal Law Review 7–41.

Smith, Stephen Eliot, 'Is the International Criminal Court Dying? An Examination of Symptoms' (2022) 23 Oregon Review of International Law 73–96.

Ssenyonjo, Manisuli, 'State Withdrawal Notifications from the Rome Statute of the International Criminal Court: South Africa, Burundi and the Gambia' (2018) 29 Criminal Law Forum 63–119.

Stahn, Carsten, 'Modification of the Legal Characterization of Facts in the ICC System: A Portrayal of Regulation 55' (2005) 16 Criminal Law Forum 1–32.

Sterio, Milena, 'The Trump Administration and the International Criminal Court: A Misguided New Policy' (2019) 51 Case Western Reserve Journal of International Law 201–210.

Strijards, Gerard, 'The Institution of the International Criminal Court' (1999) 12 Leiden Journal of International Law 671–682.

Suikkari, Satu, 'Debate in the United Nations on the International Law Commission's Draft Statute for an International Criminal Court' (1995) 64 Nordic Journal of International Law 205–222.

Symonides, Janusz, 'Towards the Launch of the International Criminal Court' (2002) 11 The Polish Quarterly of International Affairs 59–76.

Tallgren, Immi, 'We did it? The Vertigo of Law and Everyday Life at the Diplomatic Conference on the Establishment of an International Criminal Court' (1999) 12 Leiden Journal of International Law 683–707.

Trahan, Jennifer, 'The Need for an International Tribunal on the Crime of Aggression Regarding the Situation in Ukraine' (2023) 46 Fordham International Law Journal 629–648.

Václav, Vlček, 'How Many and Why? Size Variation of National Delegations to Plenary Meetings of International Organizations' (2021) 56 Czech Journal of International Relations 8–33.

Van Schaack, Beth, 'Negotiating at the Interface of Power and Law: the Crime of Aggression' (2010) 49 Columbia Journal of Transnational Law 505–600.

Verweij, Harry, 'The International Criminal Court: Alive, Soon Kicking' (2001) 25 Fordham International Law Journal 737–749.

Villacis, Renan, 'Working Methods of the Assembly of States Parties to the Rome Statute' (2018) 18 International Criminal Law Review 563–575.

Voeten, Erik, 'The Politics of International Judicial Appointments' (2009) 9 Chicago Journal of International Law 387–405.

von Lingen, Kerstin, 'Setting the Path for the UNWCC: The Representation of European Exile Governments on the London International Assembly and the Commission for Penal Reconstruction and Development, 1941–1944' (2014) 25 Criminal Law Forum 45–76.

Wang, Chen, 'Issues on Consensus and Quorum at International Conferences' (2010) 9 Chinese Journal of International Law 717–739.

Warrick, Thomas S and Bassiouni, M Cherif, 'Organization of the International Criminal Court: Administrative and Financial Issues' (1997) 25 Denver Journal of International Law and Policy 333–395.

Washburn, John, 'The Negotiation of the Rome Statute for the International Criminal Court and International Lawmaking in the 21st Century' (1999) 11 Pace International Law Review 361–377.

Washburn, John, 'The Formation and Nature of the International Criminal Court' (2006) 14 Michigan State Journal of International Law 11–17.

Welch, Claude E and Watkins, Ashley F, 'Extending Enforcement: The Coalition for the International Criminal Court' (2011) 33 Human Rights Quarterly 927–1031.

Wenaweser, Christian, 'Reaching the Kampala Compromise on Aggression: The Chair's Perspective' (2010) 23 Leiden Journal of International Law 883–887.

Wiebelhaus-Brahm, Eric and Ainley, Kirsten, 'The Evolution of Funding for the International Criminal Court: Budgets, Donors and Gender Justice' (2023) 22 Journal of Human Rights 31–46.

Witschel, Georg, 'Financial Regulation and Rules of the Court' (2001) 25 Fordham International Law Journal 665–673.

Yengejeh, Saeid Mirzaee, 'Rules of Procedure of the Assembly of States Parties to the Rome Statute of the International Criminal Court' (2002) 25 Fordham International Law Journal 674–687.

Zacklin, Ralph, 'The Failings of Ad Hoc International Tribunals Symposium: The ICTY 10 Years On: The View from Inside – A Tentative Appraisal' (2004) 2 Journal of International Criminal Justice 541–545.

Zavala, Osvaldo, 'The Budgetary Efficiency of the International Criminal Court' (2018) 18 International Criminal Law Review 461–488.

Zimmermann, Andreas, 'A Victory for International Rule of Law? Or: All's Well that Ends Well? The 2017 ASP Decision to Amend the Kampala Amendment on the Crime of Aggression' (2018) 16 Journal of International Criminal Justice 19–29.

Book Chapters

Ambach, Philipp, 'A Look towards the Future – The ICC and 'Lessons Learnt'' in Carsten, Stahn (ed), The Law and Practice of the International Criminal Court (Oxford University Press 2015).

Ambach, Philipp, 'Article 2 Relationship of the Court with the United Nations' in Ambos, Kai and Triffterer, Otto (eds), The Rome Statute of the International Criminal Court: A Commentary (3 edn, Beck/Hart 2016).

Ambach, Philipp, 'Article 112 Assembly of States Parties' in Ambos, Kai (ed), The Rome Statute of the International Criminal Court: A Commentary (4 edn, Beck/Hart 2022).

Arsanjani, Mahnoush, 'Financing' in Cassese, Antonio, Gaeta, Paola and Jones, John RWD (eds), The Rome Statute of the International Criminal Court: a Commentary, vol 1 (Oxford University Press 2002).

Baetens, Freya, 'Identity and Diversity on the International Bench: Implications for the Legitimacy of International Adjudication' in Baetens, Freya (ed), Identity and Diversity on the International Bench: Who is the Judge? (Oxford University Press 2020).

Barberini, Roberta, 'Assemblea Degli Stati Parte' in Lattanzi, Giorgio and Monetti, Vito (eds), La Corte Penale Internazionale: Organi, Competenza, Reati, Processo (Giuffrè Editore 2006).

Barriga, Stefan and Blokker, Niels, 'Entry into Force and Conditions for the Exercise of Jurisdiction: Cross-Cutting Issues' in Kreß, Claus and Barriga, Stefan (eds), The Crime of Aggression: A Commentary (Cambridge University Press 2016).

Bassiouni, M Cherif, Ferencz, B Benjamin, 'The Crime against Peace and Aggression: From its Origins to the ICC' in Bassiouni, M Cherif (ed), International Criminal Law: Sources, Subjects and Contents, vol 1 (Brill Nijhoff 2008).

Bellelli, Roberto, 'Obligation to Cooperate and Duty to Implement' in Bellelli, Roberto (ed), International Criminal Justice: Law and Practice from the Rome Statute to its Review (Ashgate 2010).

Bellelli, Roberto, 'The Law of the Statute and its Practice Under Review' in Bellelli, Roberto (ed), International Criminal Justice: Law and Practice from the Rome Statute to its Review (Ashgate 2010).

Belliard, Edwige 'France' in Kreß, Claus and Barriga, Stefan (eds), The Crime of Aggression: A Commentary (2016).

Bergsmo, Morten, 'Institutional History, Behaviour and Development' in Bergsmo, Morten, Rackwitz, Klaus and Tianying, Song (eds), Historical Origins of International Criminal Law, vol 5 (Torkel Opsahl Academic EPublisher 2017).

Bergsmo, Morten, 'Unmasking Power in International Criminal Justice: Invisible College v. Visible Colleagues' in Bergsmo, Morten, Klamberg, Mark, Lohne, Kjersti and Mahony, Christopher B (eds), Power in International Criminal Justice (Torkel Opsahl Academic EPublisher 2020).

Bergsmo, Morten and Dittrich, Viviane E, 'Integrity as Safeguard Against the Vicissitudes of International Justice Institutions' in Bergsmo, Morten and Dittrich, Viviane E (eds), Integrity in International Justice (Torkel Opsahl Academic EPublisher 2020).

Bergsmo, Morten and Rackwitz, Klaus, 'The First Budget of the Office of the Prosecutor' in Bergsmo, Morten, Rackwitz, Klaus and Tianying, Song (eds), Historical Origins of International Criminal Law, vol 5 (Torkel Opsahl Academic EPublisher 2017).

Birdsall, Andrea and Lang Jr, Anthony F, 'The International Criminal Court and Global Constitutionalism' in Lang Jr, Anthony F and Wiener, Antje (eds), Handbook on Global Constitutionalism (Edward Elgar 2017).

Blokker, Niels, 'International Organizations or Institutions, Secretariats' in Wolfrum, Rüdiger (ed), Max Planck Encyclopedia of Public International Law, vol v (Oxford University Press 2008).

Blokker, Niels, 'Constituent Instruments – Creating a Genie that May Escape From the Bottle?' in Cogan, Jacob Katz, Hurd, Ian and Johnstone, Ian (eds), The Oxford Handbook of International Organizations (Oxford University Press 2016).

Blokker, Niels, 'The Governance of International Courts and Tribunals' in Follesdal, Andreas and Ulfstein, Geir (eds), The Judicialization of International Law: A Mixed Blessing? (Oxford University Press 2018).

Blokker, Niels, 'Governance of the International Tribunal of the Law of the Sea: The Role of the Meeting of States Parties to the Law of the Sea Convention' in Del Vecchio, Angela and Virzo, Roberto (eds), Interpretations of the United Nations Convention on the Law of the Sea by International Courts and Tribunals (Springer International Publishing 2019).

Bohlander, Michael, 'Article 36 Qualifications, Nomination and Election of Judges' in Triffterer, Otto and Ambos, Kai (eds), Rome Statute of the International Criminal Court: a Commentary (3rd edn, Beck/Hart 2016).

Bos, Adriaan, 'The Experience of the Preparatory Committee' in Mauro Politi and Nesi, Giuseppe (eds), The Rome Statute of the International Criminal Court: a Challenge to Impunity (Routledge 2001).

Bos, Adriaan, 'Assembly of States Parties' in Cassese, Antonio, Gaeta, Paola, Jones, John RWD and Eser, Albin (eds), The Rome Statute of the International Criminal Court: A commentary (Oxford University Press 2002).

Bos, Adriaan, 'From the International Law Commission to the Rome Conference (1994–1998)' in Cassese, Antonio, Gaeta, Paola, Jones, John RWD and Eser, Albin (eds), The Rome Statute of the International Criminal Court: A Commentary, vol 1 (Oxford University Press 2002).

Broomhall, Bruce, 'Article 51 Rules of Procedure and Evidence' in Triffterer, Otto and Ambos, Kai (eds), Rome Statute of the International Criminal Court: A Commentary (3rd edn, Beck/Hart 2016).

Ciampi, Annalisa, 'The Obligation to Cooperate' in Antonio, Cassese, Paola, Gaeta and John, RWD Jones (eds), The Rome Statute of the International Criminal Court: a Commentary (Oxford University Press 2002).

Ciampi, Annalisa, 'Legal Rules, Policy Choices and Political Realities in the Functioning of the Cooperation Regime of the International Criminal Court' in Bekou, Olympia and Birkett, Daley (eds), Cooperation and the International Criminal Court: Perspectives from Theory and Practice (Brill 2016).

Clark, Roger S, 'Article 119 Settlement of Disputes' in Triffterer, Otto and Ambos, Kai (eds), Rome Statute of the International Criminal Court: a Commentary (3 edn, Beck/Hart 2016).

Clark, Roger S, 'Article 121 Amendments' in Triffterer, Otto and Ambos, Kai (eds), Rome Statute of the International Criminal Court: a Commentary (3 edn, Beck/Hart 2016).

Clark, Roger S, 'Article 123 Review of the Statute' in Triffterer, Otto and Ambos, Kai (eds), Rome Statute of the International Criminal Court: a Commentary (3 edn, Beck/Hart 2016).

Cogan, Jacob Katz, 'Financing and Budgets' in Cogan, Jacob Katz, Hurd, Ian and Johnstone, Ian (eds), The Oxford Handbook of International Organizations (Oxford University Press 2016).

Conso, Giovanni, 'Some Reflections on the Rome Conference' in Politi, Mauro and Nesi, Guiseppe (eds), The Rome Statute of the International Criminal Court: a Challenge to Impunity (Routledge 2001).

Crawford, James, 'The Work of the International Law Commission' in Cassese, Antonio, Gaeta, Paola and Jones, John RWD (eds), The Rome Statute of the International Criminal Court: A Commentary, vol 1 (2002).

Crawford, James, 'The Drafting of the Rome Statute' in Sands, Philippe (ed), From Nuremberg to The Hague: The Future of International Criminal Justice (Cambridge University Press 2003).

de Gabriel, Eulalia, 'La Propuesta del Tribunal Penal Internacional de Gustave Moynier, un Proyecto Antiguo Recientemente Rescatado (1872–1998)' in Carrillo Salcedo, Juan Antonio (ed), La Criminalización de la Barbarie: la Corte Penal Internacional (Consejo General del Poder Judicial 2000).

de Gabriel, Eulalia, 'Érase Una Vez… La Responsabilidad Penal Internacional: Del Impacto De La Primera Guerra Mundial En Su Evolución Conceptual Y Pre-Normativa' in Gamarra Chopo, Yolanda and Fernández Liesa, Carlos R (eds), Los Orígenes del Derecho Internacional Contemporáneo Estudios Conmemorativos del Centenario de la Primera Guerra Mundial (Institución Fernando El Católico 2015).

de Hoon, Marieke, 'Negotiating the Crime of Aggression: Between Legal Autonomy and State Power' in Bergsmo, Morten, Klamberg, Mark, Lohne, Kjersti and Mahony, Christopher B (eds), Power in International Criminal Justice (Torkel Opsahl Academic EPublisher 2020).

de Hoon, Marieke and Lohne, Kjersti, "All the World's a Stage': Constituting International Justice at the ICC's Assembly of States' in Boer, Lianne JM and Stolk, Sofia (eds), Backstage Practices of Transnational Law (Routledge 2019).

Donat Cattin, David, 'Decision-Making in the International Criminal Court: Functions of the Assembly of States Parties and Independence of the Court's Judicial Organs' in Lattanzi, Flavia and Schabas, William (eds), Essays on the Rome Statute of the International Criminal Court, vol 2 (Editrice il Sirente 1999).

Donat Cattin, David and Verpile, Melissa, 'Integrity and the Preservation of Independence in International Criminal Justice' in Bergsmo, Morten and Dittrich, Viviane E (eds), Integrity in International Justice (Torkel Opsahl Academic EPublisher 2020).

du Plessis, Max and Grevers, Christopher, 'The Role of the Assembly of States Parties for the ICC' in Steinberg, Richard H (ed), Contemporary Issues Facing the International Criminal Court (Brill Nijhoff 2016).

Ferencz, Benjamin B 'Epilogue The Long Journey to Kampala: A Personal Memoir' in Kreß, Claus and Barriga, Stefan (eds), The Crime of Aggression: A Commentary (2016).

Fife, Rolf Einar, 'Generating Incentives to Appoint Women to the International Bench: Experiences with State Practice' in Baetens, Freya (ed), Identity and Diversity on the International Bench: Who is the Judge? (Oxford University Press 2020).

Ford, Stuart, 'How Much Money Does the ICC Need?' in Carsten, Stahn (ed), The Law and Practice of the International Criminal Court (Oxford University Press 2015).

Ford, Stuart, 'Funding the ICC for Its Third Decade' in Stahn, Carsten and Braga da Silva, Rafael (eds), The International Criminal Court in Its Third Decade: Reflecting on Law and Practices (Brill | Nijhoff 2023).

Gadirov, Erkin and Clark, Roger S, 'Article 9 Elements of Crimes' in Triffterer, Otto and Ambos, Kai (eds), Rome Statute of the International Criminal Court: a Commentary (3 edn, Beck/Hart 2016).

Goldstone, Richard J, 'The International Criminal Court: Origins, Challenges and Desirable Reforms to Strengthen It' in Falk, Richard and Lopez-Claros, Augusto (eds), Global Governance and International Cooperation (Routledge 2024).

Gradoni, Lorenzo, 'Article 112 Assemblée Des Etats Parties' in Fernandez, Julian, Pacreau, Xavier, Maze, Lola and Decaux, Emmanuel (eds), Statut de Rome de la Cour Pénale Internationale: Commentaire Article par article (Pedone 2012).

Hale, Christopher, 'The Way Forward for the International Criminal Court and Its Stakeholders: Focus Inward' in Heinze, Alexander and Dittrich, Viviane E (eds), The Past, Present and Future of the International Criminal Court (Torkel Opsahl Academic EPublisher 2021).

Halff, Maarten, Tolbert, David and Villacis, Renan, 'Article 115 Funds of the Court and of the Assembly of States Parties' in Ambos, Kai and Triffterer, Otto (eds), The Rome Statute of the International Criminal Court: A Commentary (3 edn, Beck/Hart 2016).

Harmsen, Robert O and Strijards, Gerard AM, 'Article 3 Seat of the Court' in Ambos, Kai and Triffterer, Otto (eds), Rome Statute of the International Criminal Court: A Commentary (3rd edn, Beck/Hart 2016).

Heller, Kevin Jon, "A Stick to Hit the Accused With' The Legal Recharacterization of Facts under Regulation 55' in Carsten, Stahn (ed), The Law and Practice of the International Criminal Court (Oxford University Press 2015).

Inder, Brigid, 'Conformity, Leadership and the Culture of Integrity at the International Criminal Court' in Bergsmo, Morten and Dittrich, Viviane E (eds), Integrity in International Justice (Torkel Opsahl Academic EPublisher 2020).

Jacobs, Dov and Staker, Christopher, 'Article 52 Regulations of the Court' in Ambos, Kai and Triffterer, Otto (eds), The Rome Statute of the International Criminal Court: A Commentary (3 edn, Beck/Hart 2016).

Jenia Iontcheva, Turner, 'Accountability of International Prosecutors' in Carsten, Stahn (ed), The Law and Practice of the International Criminal Court (Oxford University Press 2015).

Jones, John RWD, 'Composition of the Court' in Cassese, Antonio, Gaeta, Paola and Jones, John RWD (eds), The Rome Statute of the International Criminal Court: a Commentary, vol 1 (Oxford University Press 2002).

Karagiannakis, Magda, 'Article 43 The Reigstry' in Ambos, Kai and Triffterer, Otto (eds), The Rome Statute of the International Criminal Court: A Commentary (3 edn, Beck/Hart 2016).

Karagiannakis, Magda, 'Article 44 Staff' in Ambos, Kai and Triffterer, Otto (eds), The Rome Statute of the International Criminal Court: A Commentary (3 edn, Beck/Hart 2016).

Karns, Margaret P, 'General Assemblies and Assemblies of States Parties' in Cogan, Jacob Katz, Hurd, Ian and Johnstone, Ian (eds), The Oxford Handbook of International Organizations (Oxford University Press 2016).

Khan, Karim AA, 'Article 34 Organs of the Court' in Ambos, Kai and Triffterer, Otto (eds), The Rome Statute of the International Criminal Court: A Commentary (3 edn, Beck/Hart 2016).

Khan, Karim AA, 'Article 79 Trust Fund' in Ambos, Kai and Triffterer, Otto (eds), The Rome Statute of the International Criminal Court: A Commentary (3 edn, Beck/Hart 2016).

Kirsch, Philippe, 'Reflections on the 20th Anniversary of the International Criminal Court' in Stahn, Carsten and Braga Da Silva, Rafael (eds), The International Criminal Court in Its Third Decade: Reflecting on Law and Practices (Brill | Nijhoff 2023).

Kirsch, Philippe and Oosterveld, Valerie, 'The Post-Rome Conference Preparatory Commission' in Cassese, Antonio, Gaeta, Paola and Jones, John RWD (eds), The Rome Statute of the International Criminal Court: A Commentary, vol 1 (Oxford University Press Oxford 2002).

Kirsch, Philippe and Robinson, Darryl, 'Reaching Agreement at the Rome Conference' in Cassese, Antonio, Gaeta, Paola and Jones, John RWD (eds), The Rome Statute of the International Criminal Court: a Commentary, vol 1 (Oxford University Press Oxford 2002).

Klabbers, Jan, 'Treaties and Their Preambles' in Kritsiotis, Dino and Bowman, Michael J (eds), Conceptual and Contextual Perspectives on the Modern Law of Treaties (Cambridge University Press 2018).

Klamberg, Mark, 'Article 112 – Assembly of States Parties' in Klamberg, Mark (ed), Commentary on the Law of the International Criminal Court (Torkel Opsahl Academic EPublisher 2017).

Klamberg, Mark, 'Article 112 – Assembly of States Parties' in Klamberg, Mark, Nilsson, Jonas and Angotti, Antonio (eds), Commentary on the Law of the International Criminal Court: The Statute, vol 2 (Torkel Opsahl Academic EPublisher 2023).

Klamberg, Mark, 'Article 121 Amendments' in Klamberg, Mark, Nilsson, Jonas and Angotti, Antonio (eds), Commentary on the Law of the International Criminal Court: The Statute, vol 2 (Torkel Opsahl Academic EPublisher 2023).

Koskenniemi, Martti, "A Trap for the Innocent ..." in Kreß, Claus and Barriga, Stefan (eds), The Crime of Aggression: A Commentary (Cambridge University Press 2016).

Kowalski, Mateus, 'Article 87: Requests for Cooperation' in Klamberg, Mark, Nilsson, Jonas and Angotti, Antonio (eds), Commentary on the Law of the International Criminal Court: The Statute, vol 2 (Torkel Opsahl Academic EPublisher 2023).

Kreß, Claus, 'On the Activation of ICC Jurisdiction over the Crime of Aggression' in Šturma, Pavel (ed), The Rome Statute of the ICC at Its Twentieth Anniversary (Brill Nijhoff 2018).

Kreß, Claus and Prost, Kimberly, 'Article 87 Requests for Cooperation: General Provisions' in Ambos, Kai and Triffterer, Otto (eds), The Rome Statute of the International Criminal Court: A Commentary (3 edn, Beck/Hart 2016).

Kreß, Claus, 'Article 87 Requests for Cooperation: General Provisions' in Ambos, Kai (ed), The Rome Statute of the International Criminal Court: A Commentary (4 edn, Beck/Hart 2022).

Lachowska, Anna, 'The Support Work of the Courts Registry' in Doria, José, Hans-Peter Gasser and M Cherif Bassiouni (eds), The Legal Regime of the International Criminal Court: Essays in Honour of Professor Igor Blishchenko (Brill Nijhoff 2009).

Laucci, Cyril, 'The Wider Policy Framework of Ethical Behaviour: Outspoken Observations from a True Friend of the International Criminal Court' in Bergsmo, Morten and Dittrich, Viviane E (eds), Integrity in International Justice (Torkel Opsahl Academic EPublisher 2020).

Lee, Roy S, 'Creating an International Criminal Court: Of Procedures and Compromises' in Hebel, Herman AM von, Lammers, JG and Schukking, Jolien (eds), Reflections on the International Criminal Court: Essays in Honour of Adriaan Bos (TMC Asser Press 1999).

Leslie, Vinjamuri, 'The ICC and the Politics of Peace and Justice' in Carsten, Stahn (ed), The Law and Practice of the International Criminal Court (Oxford University Press 2015).

Lovat, Henry, 'International Criminal Tribunal Backlash' in Heller, Kevin Jon, Ohlin, Jens, Nouwen, Sarah, Megret, Fred and Robinson, Darryl (eds), The Oxford Handbook of International Criminal Law (2 edn, Oxford University Press 2020).

Mamolea, Andrei,'Vespasian V Pella: International Criminal Justice as a Safeguard of Peace, 1919–1952' in Mégret, Frédéric and Tallgren, Immi (eds), The Dawn of a Discipline: International Criminal Justice and Its Early Exponents (Cambridge University Press 2020).

Maunganidze, Ottilia Anna, du Plessis, Anton and Stahn, Carsten, 'The ICC and the AU' in Stahn, Carsten (ed), The Law and Practice of the International Criminal Court (Oxford University Press 2015).

Mégret, Frédéric, 'The Rome Conference: Institutional Design and the Constraints of Diplomacy' in deGuzman, Margaret and Oosterveld, Valerie (eds), The Elgar Companion to the International Criminal Court (Edward Elgar Publishing 2020).

Mégret, Frédéric, 'Rethinking the International Criminal Court as the Court of its State Parties' in Palmer, Emma, Harris Rimmer, Susan, Bikundo, Edwin and Clark, Martin (eds), Futures of International Criminal Justice (Routledge 2021).

Mochochoko, Phakiso, 'International Cooperation and Judicial Assistance' in Lee, Roy S (ed), The International Criminal Court: the Making of the Rome Statute: Issues, Negotiations and Results (Martinus Nijhoff Publishers 1999).

Mudukuti, Angela, 'The Gap: Gender and Geographical Imbalance at the ICC, 20 Years On' in Stahn, Carsten and Braga da Silva, Rafael (eds), The International

Criminal Court in Its Third Decade: Reflecting on Law and Practices (Brill | Nijhoff 2023).

Nesi, Giuseppe, 'The Organs of the International Criminal Court and their Functions in the Rome Statute: the Assembly of States Parties' in Lattanzi, Flavia and Schabas, William (eds), Essays on the Rome Statute of the International Criminal Court, vol 1 (Editrice il Sirente 1999).

O'Donohue, Jonathan, 'The ICC and the ASP' in Stahn, Carsten (ed), The Law and Practice of the International Criminal Court (Oxford University Press 2015).

Ogwuma, Odo Annette, 'Article 37 Judicial Vacancies' in Ambos, Kai and Triffterer, Otto (eds), The Rome Statute of the International Criminal Court: A Commentary (3 edn, Beck/Hart 2016).

Pace, William R and Schense, Jennifer, 'The Role of Non-Governmental Organizations' in Cassese, Antonio, Gaeta, Paola and Jones, John RWD (eds), The Rome Statute of the International Criminal Court: A Commentary, vol 1 (Oxford University Press 2002).

Pellet, Alain, 'Settlement of Disputes' in Cassese, Antonio, Gaeta, Paola and Jones, John RWD (eds), The Rome Statute of the International Criminal Court A Commentary, vol 2 (Oxford University Press 2002).

Piiparinen, Touko, 'Secretariats' in Cogan, Jacob Katz, Hurd, Ian and Johnstone, Ian (eds), The Oxford Handbook of International Organizations (Oxford University Press 2016).

Ramberg Krutnes, Anniken 'Reflections of the Facilitator for Cooperation in the Hague Working Group, 2012–2015' in Bekou, Olympia and Birkett, Daley (eds), Cooperation and the International Criminal Court: Perspectives from Theory and Practice (Brill 2016).

Rao, S Rama, 'Financing of the Court, Assembly of States Parties and the Preparatory Commission' in Lee, Roy S (ed), The International Criminal Court: the Making of the Rome Statute: Issues, Negotiations and Results (Martinus Nijhoff Publishers 1999).

Rao, S Rama, 'Article 113 Financial Regulations' in Ambos, Kai and Triffterer, Otto (eds), The Rome Statute of the International Criminal Court: A Commentary (3 edn, Beck/Hart 2016).

Rao, S Rama and Ambach, Philipp, 'Article 112 Assembly of States Parties' in Ambos, Kai and Triffterer, Otto (eds), The Rome Statute of the International Criminal Court: A Commentary (3 edn, Beck/Hart 2016).

Rastan, Rod, 'Can the ICC Function Without State Compliance?' in deGuzman, Margaret and Oosterveld, Valerie (eds), The Elgar Companion to the International Criminal Court (Edward Elgar Publishing 2020).

Roberts, Geoff, 'Part 11 Assembly of States Parties' in de Hert, Paul, Flamme, Jean, Holvoet, Mathias and Struyven, Olivia (eds), Code of International Criminal Law and Procedure, Annotated (Larcier 2013).

Rwelamira, Medard R, 'Composition and Administration of the Court' in Lee, Roy S (ed), The International Criminal Court: the Making of the Rome Statute: Issues, Negotiations and Results (Martinus Nijhoff Publishers 1999).

Sadat, Leila Nadya, 'The International Criminal Court and the Transformation of International Law' in Scharf, Michael and Sadat, Leila Nadya (eds), The Theory and Practice of International Criminal Law (Brill Nijhoff 2008).

Schabas, William A, 'Follow up to Rome: Preparing for Entry into Force of the Statute of the International Criminal Court' in Politi, Mauro and Nesi, Guiseppe (eds), The Rome Statute of the International Criminal Court: a Challenge to Impunity (Routledge 2001).

Schabas, William A, 'Interacting with Academic Institutions' in Bergsmo, Morten, Rackwitz, Klaus and Tianying, Song (eds), Historical Origins of International Criminal Law, vol 5 (Torkel Opsahl Academic EPublisher 2017).

Schabas, William A, 'The Dynamics of the Rome Conference' in deGuzman, Margaret and Oosterveld, Valerie (eds), The Elgar Companion to the International Criminal Court (Edward Elgar Publishing 2020).

Segesser, Daniel Marc, 'Hugh HL Bellot: A Life in the Service of the Prevention and Punishment of War Crimes and Crimes Against Humanity' in Mégret, Frédéric and Tallgren, Immi (eds), The Dawn of a Discipline: International Criminal Justice and Its Early Exponents (Cambridge University Press 2020).

Sluiter, Göran and Talontsi, Stanislas, 'Credible and Authoritative Enforcement of State Cooperation with the International Criminal Court' in Bekou, Olympia and Birkett, Daley (eds), Cooperation and the International Criminal Court: Perspectives from Theory and Practice (Brill 2016).

Smith-van Lin, Lorraine, 'Non-Compliance and the Law and Politics of State Cooperation: Lessons from the Al Bashir and Kenyatta Cases' in Bekou, Olympia and Birkett, Daley (eds), Cooperation and the International Criminal Court: Perspectives from Theory and Practice (Brill 2016).

Swart, Bert and Sluiter, Goran, 'The ICC and International Criminal Cooperation' in von Hebel, Herman, Lammers, Johan G and Schukking, Jolien (eds), Reflections on the International Criminal Court: Essays in Honour of Adriaan Bos (TMC Asser Press 1999).

Trahan, Jennifer, 'The Assembly of States Parties' in deGuzman, Margaret and Oosterveld, Valerie (eds), The Elgar Companion to the International Criminal Court (Edward Elgar Publishing 2020).

Triffterer, Otto, 'Can the "Elements of Crimes" Narrow or Broaden Responsibility for Criminal Behaviour Defined in the Rome Statute?' in Stahn, Carsten and Sluiter, Göran (eds), The Emerging Practice of the International Criminal Court (Brill 2008).

Triffterer, Otto, 'The Object of Review Mechanisms: Statutes' Provisions, Elements of Crimes and Rules of Procedure and Evidence' in Bellelli, Roberto (ed), International Criminal Justice: Law and Practice from the Rome Statute to its Review (Ashgate 2010).

Vasiliev, Sergey, 'Victim Participation Revisited – What the ICC Is Learning About Itself' in Carsten, Stahn (ed), The Law and Practice of the International Criminal Court (Oxford University Press 2015).

Vasiliev, Sergey, 'The Crises and Critiques of International Criminal Justice' in Heller, Kevin Jon, Ohlin, Jens, Nouwen, Sarah, Megret, Fred and Robinson, Darryl (eds), The Oxford Handbook of International Criminal Law (2nd edn, Oxford University Press 2020).

Vasiliev, Sergey, 'Judicial Governance Entities as Power-Holders in International Criminal Justice: A Plea for a Socio-Legal Enquiry' in Bergsmo, Morten, Klamberg, Mark, Lohne, Kjersti and Mahony, Christopher B (eds), Power in International Criminal Justice (Torkel Opsahl Academic EPublisher 2020).

Wiley, William H, 'Effective Leadership, Management and Integrity in International Criminal Investigations' in Bergsmo, Morten and Dittrich, Viviane E (eds), Integrity in International Justice (Torkel Opsahl Academic EPublisher 2020).

Woolaver, Hannah, 'Withdrawal from the International Criminal Court: International and Domestic Implications' in Gerhard Werle and Zimmermann, Andreas (eds), The International Criminal Court in Turbulent Times (T.M.C Asser Press 2019).

Yáñez-Barnuevo, Juan Antonio and Escobar Hernández, Concepción, 'The International Criminal Court and the United Nations: a Complex and Vital Relationship' in Lattanzi, Flavia and Schabas, William A (eds), Essays on the Rome Statute of the International Criminal Court, vol 2 (Editrice il Sirente 2003).

Zimmermann, Andreas, 'Article 124 Transitional Provision' in Triffterer, Otto and Ambos, Kai (eds), Rome Statute of the International Criminal Court: a Commentary (3 edn, Beck/Hart 2016).

Reports

Global Institute for the Prevention of Aggression, Proposal for the Amendment of the Conditions Under which the International Criminal Court Exercises Jurisdiction Over the Crime of Aggression (2023).

Human Rights Watch, Commentary for the March-April 1998 Preparatory Committee Meeting on a Permanent International Criminal Court (1998).

International Commission of Jurists, The International Criminal Court: Third ICJ Position Paper (1995).

Mettraux, Guénaël, Fisher, Shireen, Groome, Dermot, Whiting, Alex, McIntyre, Gabrielle, de Hemptinne, Jérôme and Sluiter, Goran, Expert Initiative on Promoting Effectiveness at the International Criminal Court (2014).

Sands, Phillipe and Sow, Dior Fall, Independent Expert Panel for the Legal Definition of Ecocide, Commentary and Core Text (2021).

Scheffer, David, Developments at the Rome Treaty Conference (Department of State Dispatch, 1998).

United Nations War Crimes Commission, History of the United Nations War Crimes Commission and the Development of the Laws of War (1948).

Women's Initiatives for Gender Justice, Gender Report Card on the International Criminal Court (2013).

World Federalist Movement/Institute for Global Policy, Center for the Development of International Law, Center for UN Reform Education, Rome Report of the Coalition for an International Criminal Court (2018).

Web Pages

Ambos, Kai, 'Interests of Justice? The ICC Urgently Needs Reforms' (EJIL Talk!, 2019) <https://www.ejiltalk.org/interests-of-justice-the-icc-urgently-needs-reforms/> accessed 6 September 2020.

Cannock, Matt and O'Donohue, Jonathan, 'Don't Ask and You Won't Receive – Will the ICC Request the Resources it Needs in 2019?' (Amnesty International, Human Rights in International Justice, 2019) <https://hrij.amnesty.nl/icc-zero-growth-dont-ask-and-you-wont-receive/> accessed 10 May 2018.

Carcano, Andrea, 'On the Exercise of the Judicial Function at the International Criminal Court: Issues of Credibility and Structural Design' (Questions of International Law, 2020) <http://www.qil-qdi.org/on-the-exercise-of-the-judicial-function-at-the-international-criminal-court-issues-of-credibility-and-structural-design/> accessed March 31 2020.

Charania, Shehzad, 'A Test of Our Resilience – An Interview with the ICC Deputy Prosecutor' (Justice in Conflict, 2016) <https://justiceinconflict.org/2016/08/10/a-test-of-our-resilience-an-interview-with-the-icc-deputy-prosecutor/> accessed 3 June 2021.

European Investigative Collaborations, 'Court Secrets' (European Investigative Collaborations, 2017) <https://eic.network/projects/court-secrets.html> accessed 10 May 2017.

Gordon, Gregory S, 'Selecting the ICC's Next ASP President: High Scrutiny for High Stakes' (Opinio Juris, 2020) <http://opiniojuris.org/2020/11/16/selecting-the-iccs-next-asp-president-high-scrutiny-for-high-stakes/> accessed 20 November 2020.

Heller, Kevin Jon, 'Judge Ozaki Must Resign – Or Be Removed' (Opinio Juris, 2019) <http://opiniojuris.org/2019/03/29/judge-ozaki-must-resign-or-be-removed/> accessed 29 March 2019.

Heller, Kevin Jon, 'The Coming Kerfuffle Over the Next ICC Prosecutor' (Opinio Juris, 2020) <http://opiniojuris.org/2020/07/17/the-coming-kerfuffle-over-the-next-icc-prosecutor/> accessed 8 September 2020.

Kersten, Mark, 'The Next ICC Prosecutor, a Symposium' (Justice in Conflict, 2020) <https://justiceinconflict.org/2020/04/08/the-next-icc-prosecutor-a-symposium/> accessed 10 April 2020.

Prince Zeid Raíad Zeid Al-Hussein, Stagno Ugarte, Bruno, Wenaweser, Christian and Intelman, Tiina, 'The International Criminal Court Needs Fixing' (Atlantic Council, 2019) <https://www.atlanticcouncil.org/blogs/new-atlanticist/the-international-criminal-court-needs-fixing> accessed 24 April 2019.

Trahan, Jennifer, 'Amending the Kampala Amendments: A Proposal to Harmonize the ICC's Jurisdiction' (Opinio Juris, 2023) <https://opiniojuris.org/2023/10/02/amending-the-kampala-amendments-a-proposal-to-harmonize-the-iccs-jurisdiction/> accessed 3 November 2023.

Wilmshurst, Elizabeth 'Strengthen the International Criminal Court' (Royal Institute of International Affairs, 2019) <https://www.chathamhouse.org/expert/comment/strengthen-international-criminal-court> accessed 12 June 2019.

Index